Breakthrough Strategies of Wall Street Traders

17 Remarkable Traders Reveal Their Top Performing Investment Strategies

Bill Bodri

Top Shape Publishing, LLC
1135 Terminal Way Suite 209
Reno, NV 89502

ISBN-10: 0972190763
ISBN-13: 978-0-972190763

DISCLAIMER

TABLE OF CONTENTS

BILL BODRI

ACKNOWLEDGMENTS

First and foremost I would like to thank the remarkable traders and investors who agreed to be interviewed on their actual trading-investing systems and for revealing the trading rules and breakthroughs that led to their extraordinary success. Per his usual kindness, Martial Adair lent me great assistance by editing these interview drafts to make them much better. A pleasant debt also goes to the many people who provided introductions for interviews including John Newtson, Jami Stout, Gerard de Condappa, Charles Mizrahi, and Raymond Barros.

Introduction

How do I become a better trader? How do I become a better investor? Basically I'm interested in trading and investing so how do I improve my game? How do I start making more money?

When I became chief editor of the *Income and Assets* newsletter it was divided into two parts. The first part involved an interview with a highly successful trader or investor (several of whom made over a million dollars in trading profits starting out out with less than $10,000) designed to help active trader-investors improve their skills and make more money. The idea was, "Here is someone who succeeded doing what you love and I hope you can learn from their methods to become much more profitable." Many of those track records or techniques are simply remarkable.

The second half of the newsletter was oriented to those who were more interested in passive income rather than active income gained through trading. The topics in this section revolved around high-yield investing (rather than trading for profits), hard assets and asset protection strategies.

The interviews with these remarkable traders and investors became the basis of this book, while the special reports and analysis from the second half are contained in the forthcoming title, *High-Yield Investments, Hard Assets and Asset Protection Strategies.*

Why the trader-investor focus and thus this new book? Who needs another book that interviews people who have become successful at making money in the markets? As an ex-Wall Streeter who spent years creating all sorts of trading systems, analysis rules, prediction methods and investment models for large firms and individuals, I have collected a substantial investment library on all sorts of topics. You might have done so as well. Much of the trading or investing information in those books fascinates, entertains and informs, but more often than not, for one reason or another you usually cannot *really* use the strategies discussed to make any money.

What I therefore wanted was the explicit how-to rules from traders and investors who figured out to succeed in the market, "success" information from individuals who carved out profitable niches using strategies you might also use at home in your study or basement. Although I come from the fund management field, I wasn't looking for methods that required lots of money, time, and resources due to the competitive advantages they entailed. Rather, I sought out successful traders and investors who used simple methods that a common man might also learn how to master.

Therefore these interviews are unlike most others because they are packed with how-to materials, which often include the *exact* rules for profitable trading and investing systems you can immediately apply. This type of information is not only hard to find, but priceless to possess.

That is how this book differs from many others in this genre. Naturally you will learn the life stories of seventeen individuals who made trading or investing into their living. That is remarkable in itself because many want to do just that by quitting their jobs and making trading or investing their living, but not so many succeed at it. You will therefore learn how they became involved in the markets, what they tried that did and didn't work, how they mastered the inner emotional demons that interfered with trading, how they triumphed over different challenges, and how each seemed to make some unique breakthrough in systems, learning, philosophy or style that finally enabled them to *exceptionally* succeed to an extent that separated them from their peers.

Inside you won't just find generic general ideas. Here you will usually find the exact rules they follow to make money, which is the information everyone seeks but the very stuff that most people ordinarily don't want to share. In other words, *this book is designed to help you profit in trading and investing*. If you are losing in the markets it might help you become a winner, and if you are already making money I am hoping it helps you become even more successful. That's its goal. All the books I write have the aim of helping you improve your life.

At the end of each interview I also asked each of our seventeen remarkable trader-investors to look back on their lives and the struggle they went through to get to where they are today. "Can you offer any advice to others so that they can avoid the pain?" I asked. Most successful trader-investors have gone down a long road of false starts, winding trails and gut wrenching losses until they finally found a technique that worked and learned the lessons they needed to know that helped them stick with that winning methodology. They were kind enough to share these stories and words of wisdom to others along the path of Wall Street and life in general.

Your own story might be in some ways similar to one or more of these experts, or a lesson learned might strike you as the one you particularly need, and therefore in the reading you might find yourself some surrogate trading mentors. Whether a newbie at the markets or experienced trader-investor, I especially wanted you to receive some trader-investor or life lessons that will help you going forward.

That summarizes the gist of what you are about to encounter. If you want yet more of the investing lessons that I feel should be passed on to the next generation to ease its way, including possibly your own children or grandchildren before they start upon the road of investing, then you should probably investigate my earlier book, *Super Investing*, which was designed to transmit just that sort of content. It contains information you just cannot find elsewhere. However, this book is partly a how-to manual designed to propel you ahead with some new trading or investing techniques as well as insights that have led others to profits. Following the wisdom of Ralph Waldo Emerson who said, "As to methods, there may be a million and then some, but principles are few. The man who grasps principles can successfully select his own methods," it contains both methods and principles to help you with your trading and investing.

Chapter 1
Mike Ser and Andy Man
The Benefits of a Trading Coach

In a book on profitable trading and investing methods I want to start out by emphasizing the importance of engaging a trading coach if you are a beginner. I can almost guarantee that the money you spend on learning from a coach will be far, far less than the amount you are likely to lose by simply delving into trading and investing without knowing what you are doing. In short, trading coaches will help you learn how to cut your losses to save you money and help you make more money via the disciplined trading rules they teach. A good coach will introduce you to profitable trading techniques and help you dramatically reduce the inevitable losses you will suffer as you go up the learning curve. A great coach will not only introduce you to profitable trading methods and strategies, but help you find the one that fits you best, help guide you in your training to master that profitable technique, and teach you how deal with losses, manage your emotions and treat trading like a business.

For this first interview we will turn to two Canadian coaches who have been very successful at teaching ordinary people how to trade the markets, several of whom have become millionaires through their tutelage. Successful trader Mike Ser was running just such a coaching firm in Canada when he met Andy Man, who made his first million dollars in trading due to Mike's lessons. Andy eventually became Mike's partner and the two joined me in this interview to discuss the basics of how ordinary people can use charts and simple methods to trade. In our conversation you will learn a philosophy as well as a set of trading rules of entries, exits, targets and stops that may help you jump to the next level of trading achievement. Both Mike and Andy achieved personal trading success only after endless hours of market study and personal introspection of their own trading styles, and they generously share their breakthrough insights and strategies for others.

Mike, let's talk about you first. How did you get started in trading and how did you end up with this special niche of teaching newcomers how to trade and teaching experienced traders how to trade better?

Mike: I've always been very entrepreneurial. Before I did training I started three businesses because I wanted to be my own boss and to be able to call my own shots. I discovered trading in 1999. I started during the whole dot-com boom. I was working for a technology company at that time which was publicly trading on the Toronto Stock Exchange. I joined the company when its stock was $1.20 and within six months it went all the way to $15. This was my first opportunity to see the amount of wealth that was created through trading by knowing which company to invest in. I therefore quit my job and became a full-time trader because the amount of money that I was earning from trading at that time was more than my salary.

When I became a full-time day trader everything was initially great. What I didn't account for was the market crashing because I then found out that I didn't actually know what I was doing. I was at the right place but at the wrong time. Without giving up on my dream of becoming a full-time trader I spent the next three years trying to figure out the ways that I could get back to the same success I was having previously.

That was a very excruciating time with a lot of tests to see whether I had the mental capacity to become a trader, whether I had the persistence to become a trader, and whether I had the proper skills to make a very good living through it.

At the time I was day trading both Canadian and American stocks, but the majority were U.S. stocks. I was using a regular Canadian bank trading platform.

After those three years, did you get back to the level of success you had attained previously?

Mike: When you don't have any consistency in trading you doubt yourself – you doubt your ability, you doubt your level of knowledge, and you doubt whether you are trading the right instrument or strategy. During that period of time I underwent a lot of soul searching in terms of trying to figure out what trading style fits my personality, how much I should be trading, what time period I should be trading, what instruments I should be trading … a lot of those questions. When I went through this process I came to some conclusions. If you go through this process, too, you will figure out what it is that you are good at and what your personality is suited for in terms of a trading style.

During those three years I discovered what I wanted to focus and specialize on in the trading field. After those three years I found that my area of expertise and focus should be on technology stocks and ETFs. That was my key to getting successful again.

That's a major problem many traders have. They don't know what their strengths and weaknesses are and they don't know what they should focus on. Therefore they try absolutely everything, jumping from this to that and mastering nothing – with inevitable losses. They usually end up going through many losing methods that don't suit them. Do you have a series of questions people should ponder or a methodology they should run through to find their niche or trading style?

Mike: The most important thing that I discovered is that what you decide to do should really start from the big picture and focus on the question, "What is it that I want to achieve?" What is your financial objective, what is the lifestyle that you want to have in terms of when you want to be in front of the computer? What are the specific strategies you feel more comfortable with?

Once you have done a top-down analysis like this then all you really have to do is put together a plan that will help you get there.

Let's just say, for example, that I felt that I was a more aggressive trader, a trader that enjoys researching and looking at technology stocks in the U.S., that I liked to trade in the morning, and that my goal that I wanted to achieve was to develop a consistency through day trading. That's me.

After I understood what I previously had done successfully and found out a certain style or strategy that fit me then all I really needed to do was to keep doing the same things that previously brought me success. I could also then measure the success I was generating on a daily or weekly basis and determine how those results could ultimately help me to achieve the financial goals I set for myself.

This sounds like an interesting process. Do you have a formal list of questions people can use to help them determine these things?

Mike: We have a questionnaire that we always give our students to help them personalize their individual trading plan. For example, are you a morning person, evening person or night person? What is your risk tolerance on a scale of 1-10 where 1 is being risk adverse and 10 is being a big risk taker? What are some of the sectors or areas you have a genuine interest in learning more about? What is the amount of capital that you are initially starting off with? How much do you want to achieve through trading? What are your financial goals?

From people answering those types of questions we will have a pretty good idea what they should focus on, what area they should specialize in and how they should approach their trading.

What are the trading styles you would normally end up recommending to someone? From your experience in reviewing multiple successes and failures, what is the short list of strategies you normally recommend to aspiring traders?

Mike: It all starts in terms of someone's objective and lifestyle. We ask people if they have a full-time job. If so then during market hours there is no way that the person should be day trading or intraday swing trading.

For those people who have a full-time job we tend to get them to focus more on swing trading. We want them to become a trend trader or momentum trader. We want them to learn how to identify trends in the market, whether up or down, and want them to learn how to stay in the trend until it's over.

Another example is the following. When I first taught Andy, who you will meet in a moment, we were initially focused on day trading strategies looking for breakouts and breakdowns. We were also looking for catalysts for technology stocks that would move them in the direction of the trend. What Andy realized, because he had a full-time job at that time, was that he couldn't be in front of the computer when the markets were up and running because he was working in the field. Therefore we personalized his trading towards swing trading so he didn't necessarily have to be in front of the computer.

Additionally, Andy wasn't a morning person. He didn't want to get up early in the morning. He preferred trading in the evening so we had to find instruments that were more active in the evening. What we found for him that was a great fit was trading in the gold and silver precious metals.

Is it your general strategy to recommend trend trading to most people with full-time day jobs? In other words, with all the types of trading available is this the style you most often recommend?

Mike: For myself I tried many different types of trading including scalping, intra-swing day trading, swing trading, position trading, investing, etcetera. I tried many different styles. In general because the markets these days are a little more volatile compared to the 1990s, but because there are always up and down trends in the market lasting days, weeks and months, that's the type of time period we want to focus on. Particularly in those types of time frames you will see trends you can capture that are some very good percentage moves up or down.

With swing trading you don't have to be in front of the computer every single day or spend lots of hours in front of the computer on a day-to-day basis. We don't feel that this is very conducive for a lot of people. So what we do is try to help people identify certain trends and teach them how to enter orders for when the trend changes. Once they are in a position they don't need to be in front of a computer. All they need to do is put their stop in place, move their stop to breakeven at the relevant time, and have a certain idea when to add to existing profitable positions or look to exit a profitable position.

We think that there are trends in the markets that last for days, weeks or months and we feel that it would be easier for people to capture larger daily trends rather than small intraday swings. People always ask us what type of traders we are. We are momentum trend traders.

Mike, you went through this difficult three-year period after doing quite well trading the markets. What happened to your track record?

Mike: When I was trading through the whole dot-com boom I achieved a lot of success in a very short period of time and I was expecting that same type of result to continue. I was easily having $10,000 and $20,000 days during that time period. However, when the markets didn't go in my direction I still had that type of mentality so it was very difficult for me throughout those three years to achieve the same level of success.

I took a step back and said, "I only want to make a very realistic $200 per day." This was on a $25,000 account. When I achieved that I said, "Okay, I want to make $500 a day."

Throughout that time period the area I focused on was trading technology stocks. They weren't going up, but I didn't know how to short the market at the time. I tried put options, forex trading, trading futures, but all that type of thing just didn't give me the comfort level that I previously had so I went back to what I was comfortable with, which was trading technology stocks. When technology stocks weren't going up then I started looking into trading gold stocks. In 2002 it was the start of the gold bull market and that's where I was able to still trade an asset instrument that I was comfortable with. It was something where I was able to use the skills I had developed earlier.

In 2004-2005, after having achieved some consistent profitable success throughout my years of trading, I then worked with a broker, CMC Markets. They had seen the type of results that I was generating in my accounts and they offered me the opportunity of working with them to train their existing clients. That's how in 2005 I started teaching other traders how I traded.

What did they notice you were doing differently from their other clients that they flagged you?

Mike: I cannot say what the other traders were doing, but I was basically following the trend. I was utilizing technicals whereas a lot of their clients didn't even know how to read charts. Technical analysis wasn't prevalent yet and most people still looked at trading as just buying and holding. What I had done differently is that most people are usually long in the markets instead of looking to also profit on the downside through shorting. I was looking at technicals to determine my entries and exits and I was also profiting when the markets went down, too.

It's pretty amazing today to realize that just a few years back people didn't know about basic chart patterns or even recognize the phrase "technical analysis." The general knowledge level about trading has gone up dramatically over time, but I think that human psychology has remained

relatively the same. Along those lines, how would you tend to characterize the typical person who comes to you to learn trading or improve their trading in terms of a before and after scenario?

Mike: There are many aspects to this. When they open up a trading account most people can only think about one thing: "How much money can I make?" Our philosophy is totally different. Our first thought for everything is, "How much risk am I taking and how much risk am I comfortable with?"

Our whole objective in how we teach students to approach trading is to focus on risk. The only thing that you can control in the markets and in your trading is the amount of risk you are taking. That's what we emphasize. If you are comfortable with that risk then once that risk has been minimized or once a trade goes to a breakeven status we would tell students to move their stop-loss.

Our whole objective, the number one concern before any trade is taken is determining how much risk you are taking. Second, once you have that risk taken care of, the next question is, "When can I get to breakeven on my trade?" Once you are at breakeven on a trade, the next question is, "Now how can I maximize this profit?" Only after they take care of the risk component do we get our students to focus on how much they can win.

What are the general rules for money management that you apply to this type of philosophy? Do you have a general rule for stop-losses and trading sizes?

Mike: We always tell people to only trade with risk capital that they can lose without affecting their day-to-day or month-to-month lifestyle. We do have some guidelines on how much risk you can take. For people who are generally conservative we say to look to risking ½-1% of your capital per trade. Typically, average-wise it is generally 2% per trade.

Our approach is to be as conservative as possible in the beginning and build some house money, which means profits. Try to build that profit pool and once you have that pool you can then take more aggressive risks. That's because at the end of the day you are then only risking your profits and not your principal.

In any case, you must first determine the risk you want to take percentage-wise per trade. People who are more conservative use 1% but generally we can say 2%. We developed a risk calculator where once you determine what your risk amount is, which is what you are willing to risk if the trade doesn't go well, then depending on the type of trading instrument you trade you can determine where the stop-loss level should be.

What we try to do in terms of entry points is we want to buy as close to a certain support level as possible so we use a lot of trend lines to determine where our support and resistance levels are. For example, if we were to buy on pullbacks we would set our entry a little bit above our resistance level and set our stop-loss right below that support level.

Generally speaking, depending on the type of instrument that we would focus on and trade we have general guidelines for traders as to where to put their stop-loss levels. Once they enter in their stop-loss level and know what their percentage risk is they then know exactly how much they are risking. If they are comfortable with that then they can go and enter that order into their brokerage trading platform. If they are not comfortable with that then they can reduce the amount they want to risk on the trade.

Okay, so let's now turn to your partner Andy, who made a million dollars in the markets after you taught him how to trade. How did you two meet?

Mike: Andy was an individual who came to one of the seminars that I had hosted and he liked the philosophy I told him, which included the fact I mentioned that the standard of living costs in Vancouver were quite high. He knew that his current salary as a civil engineer wasn't a way to build financial security. He was looking for ways to build wealth and wanted to put together a side project to accumulate wealth. He went through my trading program and I'll pass it over to Andy so he can tell the rest of the story.

Andy: My family moved to Canada in May of 1997. I was around sixteen to seventeen years old at that time and after that I went to school in Vancouver and then I went to university. Because my father is a civil engineer I took it as my university major, basically following what my father did.

Now throughout my university time I was looking around for alternatives. I was actively looking to build something else rather than just be a civil engineer. I could see that civil engineering could give me a stable job but not let me achieve financial freedom. I liked the idea of building financial freedom but with the resources and network that I had there was no way I could do it at that point when I was in my twenties.

Stop there. Are you actually staying you were attracted to trading because you wanted financial freedom or wanted to build an extra source of income? I'm not asking about what you thought after the fact, but rather what was your real initial motivation?

Andy: I think at the beginning I was actually looking for financial freedom in the future and I needed to plan ahead. Trading was not the only method that I was looking at back then. I was actually looking to build my own business, build a real estate portfolio or do trading. At that particular stage I had no money to build my real estate portfolio and no network to build my business, but trading sounded like something I could do myself, which attracted me to it.

So you were thinking, "I'm a civil engineer. I'm going to make a living but I'm not going to become wealthy through this route so let me look around. What else can I do? I can start a business on the side, do real estate on the side or I can do trading on the side." Next you ruled some of these things out and finally said, "Okay, let me try trading to help build financial freedom."

Andy: That's right.

That's a common story with people who aren't interested in their jobs and who turn to trading, but the problem is that if you just jump into trading without any preparation you can and will lose a lot of money. Most people who jump in without training don't succeed. You can lose everything and in fact, that's probably the most common story for people who start trading without first taking courses from mentors, experts, or whatever. Many just end up losing all their money because they had no one to teach them the right habits. In any case, let's delve deeper into this decision process that set you on the course of learning how to trade the markets.

Andy: I basically went through my abilities and said, "What can I do?" Back then you needed certain money to invest in real estate and I didn't have the money. For business you needed a good business partner and a good network. I didn't have any of those back then either. But trading is something that you could do by clicking on a button and making money. At least that was what I thought. My thinking was as simple as that. It's more complicated than that, of course, but back then I thought that maybe I could start small with a few thousand dollars and grow it big.

Did you ever do trading before you met Mike?

Andy: No, I knew absolutely nothing about trading when I met Mike. I found him by using Google to search for "trading training online."

Wow, you were one of the few who decided to spend some time and money learning from others about how to trade before jumping in.

Andy: I heard a lot of horrible stories of people losing money to the markets. Back then when I started, taking a course cost me $3,000. It sounds like a lot of money but before I started trading I knew that I could easily have lost that $3,000 - everything – in trading because I didn't know what I was doing, so spending the money on training was a wise decision.

Another key thing is that I liked the idea of using leverage because without using leverage you cannot make money at a fast pace. It makes things a lot easier. It makes achieving financial goals faster. You see, I did not want to settle for some type of investing. I was not looking for learning about investments and investing. Specifically, I was looking for leveraged trading.

Because you realized real estate investing was actually leveraged, too, so you realized that some form of leveraged trading would make you the most money?

Andy: Yes, I decided that leverage would be one of the things that could lead me to financial freedom much faster if I learned how to master it. I realized that without using leverage it would take a much longer time.

"Get rich slowly" is an equally fine path and sometimes the absolute correct path for people. Some advisors think it might even be the proper path for most people since most people will not spend the time studying either the markets or trading. Most people also won't work on controlling their emotions so that they don't sabotage their own trading. In any case, if I understand you correctly you are saying that you thought deeply about all the dimensions of this and then decided to learn leveraged trading to build financial freedom partly because it was a fast road if you mastered it and were successful at it.

Andy: No – you are missing something. I was aware of how to get rich quick, but I also wanted to be safe. I was interested in how to get rich quickly but safely. That's why I was looking for someone who already did it to teach me how to do the same thing. I was looking for a shortcut.

Ok, so you go to this seminar and meet Mike. What did you initially learn from Mike before you started trading?

Andy: When I went to Mike's training course he taught me great materials on the basics of trading because I knew nothing about trading or the financial markets. I didn't even know who Ben Bernanke is. Seriously, that's how I got started as a trader. Back then when Mike was teaching me he was more of a day trader who was trading the tech stocks, but that strategy did not work for me. The reason is because back then I was a full-time civil engineer and the hours that the market was open exactly overlapped with my job. I had bills to pay and could not risk getting fired if I was trading when I was working.

Mike and I figured out that we should find something that fit me at least timing-wise, that worked on my schedule. There are lots of things that trade twenty-four hours, but with my limited knowledge back then I chose to trade gold and silver. First of all because "gold and silver" sounds simple; they are shiny metals and I could visualize them. As to the currencies and FX markets that also traded twenty-four hours, I didn't know anything about currencies or economic data and how it could affect the currencies. I didn't even know how to read a Euro versus U.S. dollar relative chart where I could figure out which currency was going up and which one was going down. I didn't even know that. That's why I chose to trade gold and silver since they had a twenty-four hour market and I could actually trade after I got off work.

Were you trading a futures account?

Andy: I was using CFDs. They are a market derivative contract on differences that mimic the market. In other words, they are derivatives contracts that mirror an actual underlying instrument. In this case I was basically trading the equivalent of gold and silver futures.

Mike: The CFDs are only available on the Canadian market. They are not tradable by U.S. residents but they are freely traded in Canada. The CFD is a derivatives contract that mirrors the underlying asset. There are CFDs on stocks, spot gold, and spot indexes.

Andy: For gold and silver they are equivalent to futures contracts but the contract size can represent much smaller quantities because you can break it down. For instance, instead of having to trade 100 ounces of gold on a futures contract you could break it down to trading just 10 ounces of gold with a CFD. They represent a much smaller fractional part of the underlying assets so you can better control your risk.

With CFDs you also cannot take delivery. Trading-wise it's pretty much the same as futures contracts, but operational-wise you cannot take delivery. They had the advantage that by using them I could start with a very small trading account. Back then a full contract of silver or gold required $6,000 in margin but I could cut it down in size using CFDs, so they were a lot easier for people to trade. For U.S. traders you would have to trade futures as the equivalent.

You decided that gold and silver were the two markets you were going to trade?

Andy: Yes, I actually started paper demo trading in 2007 and started actual live trading in 2008. My first experience in actual trading was of losing money. My first trade was a loser. I lost $30 when I thought gold was going up and got stopped out at a loss. I got scared. It might not sound like a lot but back then $30 was a lot of money to me.

What happened next is that I tried to figure out what was wrong, what was missing. I tried to learn from my mistakes. I tried to figure out more about the gold market and what affected it. For example, one of the figures that impacts the gold price is the non-farm employment change which is released every single month. It is definitely something that impacts how gold does.

Back in 2008 the gold market crashed because of the financial crisis and went down to as low as $750. I missed the entire opportunity but I reminded myself that if this is going to happen to me next time I need to be ready to take advantage of it. Back then I was still too new. I had all the concepts of what I needed to do but when you actually have to trade you may have the right concept, but there is so much emotion on top of it, like greed, that it goes against you. That's what I experienced in the entire year of 2008.

Back then I was trading $3,000. I was doing 1% trades back then like Mike taught. A problem was that I was not thinking like a trader but like a consumer. Thirty dollars was a pretty nice steak back then so when I lost $30 I lost the chance of having a great meal, so that's what I thought. I still did not have the mindset of being a trader. I still had the mindset of being a consumer instead, which was a fault interfering with my trading.

It was the amount of money that I was losing that bothered me. You never feel great when you are losing money, especially in the very beginning of your trading career, but I took that as a lesson to improve my trading later on. Later on I was able to turn a small amount of money into a larger amount by riding gold back from $700 to $1,000. I was able to make some money off it and turned $5,000 into $100,000. However, a problem was that I was too greedy and this was causing me to give almost half my money back.

I experienced a lot of ups and downs before 2011. I looked back at my trades and realized that I was falling in love with my position, especially when a particular position had already made me so much money. I fell in love with my positions and kept holding onto them. I wasn't really following what the market was doing.

What rules for exiting a trade were you violating? What are the rules for getting out that you were violating?

Andy: I was really good at defending my trade. At the end I was still making money but not as much as I wanted. Say the market went up $1,000. I might end up hoping it would still go up and then not realize that the technical pattern had hit a major resistance level, or the MACD or RSI might be showing that the market would be going down. Emotionally I would still be hoping that the market would continue to go up and that's the mistake that I made. That's basically what happened between 2009 and 2011.

Even so, those trades actually made me a better trader because I learned from my mistakes. I knew what my mistake was. I needed to know when to exit and needed to tell myself to do it. After learning this about myself I actually photocopied the trades I did and put this on my desk in front of me to remind myself, when similar situations happened, not to make the same mistakes again.

That's great. Did you have photocopies of just good trades or both good and bad trades?

Andy: Mostly bad trades. I didn't look at the good trades too much. I focused on the bad trades because I tried to figure out why I made those mistakes and wanted to improve on them. That process actually produced my big trading success in 2011. I was trading silver back then and I recognized a setup that ended up as a big trade because I had studied the charts of my past trading mistakes.

You have been saying that you were using the same trading strategy those years but improving on your execution and discipline to eliminate mistakes. Can you tell me the exact entry and exit rules that Mike taught you to use in your trading? In particular, can you tell me the exact exit rules you had been violating?

Andy: For exit rules I'm using technical analysis to figure out where my exit is. For instance, using a daily chart there might be a multi-year resistance. You should draw it on the price chart. The longer that particular resistance has held over time the more solid it is and the more likely it won't be broken. Once you see a major resistance level, and when the MACD starts to go back down and RSI is in the 70s and volume is high, we can say that technically the market is going down.

Second, we want to look at the fundamental basis. Back then we wanted to see how the U.S. dollar was doing because it had an inverse relationship with gold and silver. If you actually saw that the U.S. dollar was going up you probably needed to be aware of its effect on gold and silver. When the dollar is going up, then very likely gold and silver will go down. I was also looking at that. Everything on paper was telling me I should be exiting my position, but back then I wasn't disciplined enough to follow the rules.

Most people are frequent short-term traders doing several trades a month. Therefore they usually don't look at these big multi-year support and resistance levels for entries or stops. What are you using as an exit rule for shorter trades?

Andy: I don't do quick trades. The reason why is because I'm always looking for a big trade. For longs I am looking for one to three-month trades. That's the period I'm willing to hold in the right trend.

What I was actually referencing was the long-term cash gold price chart so that I had a pretty good actual picture of how the overall market was doing. I was using the cash gold chart to draw the major support and resistance levels.

With the long-term cash charts you can go back far enough to find resistance. You couldn't do this with futures charts because of the premium between cash and futures. If you used futures charts you would have to do some adjustments so I was utilizing the cash gold and silver charts from Kitco.com. They had a lot of cash data related to gold and silver so I used those charts because I was focused on those two markets back then.

Remember, what I was doing was not trading every day. I only traded when there was a good setup. Let's say I was looking for a long trade. Specifically I would look for a double bottom or flag or ascending triangle or other things like that. To go long I am looking for a chart pattern hitting a major support.

To exit a trade, the key would be whether the price broke a trend line. That's the signal that I should exit the trade. When prices would break trend lines that were hitting support or resistance levels, that was always a warning to me that I had to exit a trade.

There are hundreds of chart patterns that people can study. What are the chart patterns that you focused on learning for your buying and selling? Let's put them into two categories.

Andy: For buying I will be looking primarily for these three patterns: a (1) double bottom, (2) ascending triangle and (3) bullish flag.

For selling and short-selling I will be looking primarily for these three patterns: a (1) double top, (2) descending triangle and (3) bearish flag.

Those are the biggest, highest probability patterns. There are a lot of chart patterns out there, but those are the highest probability ones. To be honest, the head and shoulders pattern is actually an ascending triangle as well. This makes it simple.

To get out of a bullish trade I look for the price to be breaking an ascending trend line. For getting out of a short I look for the opposite, namely that the market is breaking resistance with prices going back up.

Those trading rules for entries and exits are pretty simple, which is great since it means that you can make a lot of money by learning just a few patterns instead of having to learn one hundred patterns. The next thing is that you must be extremely disciplined in following your trading rules. Now we have already mentioned your trade size as well as stops, exits and entries. Do you have any other trading rules you can share?

Andy: Yes, I have a list of trading DON'Ts: (1) Don't trade during consolidation. (2) Do not trade during holiday hours like the Christmas holiday, New Years, or things like that. (3) Do not chase a missed opportunity. Let's say that if the market is going up and you missed a setup that the market had, such as an ascending triangle. If the market already went up, do not chase the market and try to buy it. Just skip the trade. If you missed the trade then just miss it. If you chase the trade then very likely you will get stopped out which is something you don't want to happen.

Some traders watch dozens of markets or even more. Are you still only watching one or two markets to trade?

Andy: Back then when I was working I only watched two markets, which were the gold and silver markets. Now I am looking to expand my expertise in the index markets and the oil market as well. It's still just a few markets. For indexes I mean things like the Dow Jones, S&P 500 and NASDAQ.

For identifying chart patterns in these markets I don't like to use pattern identification software because if I use the program or some other computer generated system I will subsequently be relying on it. Trading is a skill or activity where you are supposed to learn to be 100% responsible for everything you do. I don't want to have an excuse for myself by relying on the computer identification of charting patterns. I want to make myself responsible for whatever I do so I don't use these things.

Now we have your short list of recommended chart patterns that people should learn without relying on computer software to find them. How do you suggest that people should learn these

patterns?

Andy: There are a lot of information sources out there, especially online. These chart patterns can be found on Google and so you can study them on the web.

The key is that people should learn to recognize these patterns. They might learn them, but learning how to also trade them or recognize when they are happening in real time is hard. Everyone can tell the market has already moved up. Many people can even identify that what they are seeing is a double bottom or bearish triangle, for instance. What makes it difficult is watching these patterns set up and patiently waiting for it.

I know a lot of people who have won trading contests would take past winning chart patterns and study them over and over again until they were burned into their subconscious mind and they could instinctively recognize them immediately.

Andy: I have an encyclopedia of technical analysis. It's good to read, but when you apply the information to trading you should try to keep things as simple as possible. A lot of the technical analysis books are over-complicated. There is a lot of information, but they actually information-overload me. When you try to cut out the unnecessary information then those are the three patterns I like and that's pretty much it. A lot of the patterns are an expansion of these basic three that I mention. A triple bottom, for instance, is an expansion of a double bottom and could even turn into a quadruple bottom. Anyway, those are the key highlights of what I am using.

What's interesting is that you mentioned you kept charts of what you did wrong in trading and flipped through them all the time to remind yourself of errors you should not repeat.

Andy: When I was looking at my losing trades I was not particularly looking at the chart patterns. This was key, but part of this was that I was also working on my psychological mindset. I was actually working on it back then as well.

Many people are like Mike and you in that they only buy or short sell stocks after they break through support or resistance levels. That's a common strategy for trading with penny stocks as well.

Andy: I do a similar thing. For longs I look for an instrument I'm trading to make some type of bottom pattern and if it shows confirmation by breaking through resistance then I buy. If it breaks through support then I will start to sell.

Once in a trade you then draw an upwards or downwards sloping trend line, and then if the market breaks through the relevant trend line you get out. You don't care how much profit percentage the trade has made when it breaks the trend line, or how much you hope it will make but you just get out as soon as it breaks the appropriate trend line. Is that correct?

Andy: Yes.

All right, now we have your basic strategy and the history of your psychological development in learning to follow trading rules, especially exiting a trade. What I want to hear about now is the story of how you turned $1,600 into over one million dollars, and the key factor which was previously missing that - once supplied - enabled you to do that.

Andy: Back then silver was actually sitting at $50 in May of 2011. That particular setup was almost exactly the same thing I saw in 2008 when I started trading, but was an opportunity I missed. Because I actually kept this pattern on my desk, like I explained previously, I was able to compare the two patterns and saw they were almost exactly the same. When it was happening I didn't know it, but after some study it looked almost exactly the same to me so I started to trade this particular trend.

I started off with $1,600 in my account. I didn't actually short the market betting it would go down from $50. I actually started trading the market when it broke support at around $45 and that's where I started shorting. In about a week the market went all the way down from $50 to about $33. That's when I actually saw the market hitting a major support and that's when I told myself that I have to exit my trade. That particular decision to exit my trade was from recognizing the mistake I learned from the previous case scenario. And during when I was actually reviewing my mistake I was actually thinking, sitting with cash in my hand, "Hey the market can be going back up. Maybe I can actually reverse my trade from short to long."

So that's what I did. When the market went down from $50 to $33 I was turning $1,600 to approximately $30K. I then made a decision to go back from short to long and I turned $30K to approximately $100K. When the price of silver reached $39, the setup was similar to what was seen in 2008. I expected just a short-term rebound where the market would likely go back down. I told myself that when it broke support I needed to exit my order and turn my trade back to a short. I was actually shorting the market at around $39 back down to $33 where it formed a double bottom, and I said that's it and turned my approximately $150K into approximately $300K in just eight business days.

That was the first big trade that I made. Later on I was a little overwhelmed after that, but not during the trade because I was actually following the trend and my rules rather than looking at the numbers I was making. Later on in September, I looked and saw that the market was setting up a descending triangle on a daily chart. It was exactly the same as what happened in 2008 again so I was betting for the market to go down. I had already withdrawn some money, so I actually started with a $240K account, and in three days I turned it into $1.1 million. Overall in that particular year I made around $1.67 million.

This is a great story with lots of lessons: study your past mistakes, study the chart's history, follow the trend and don't look at the money being made during the trade so that your emotions don't get in the way and so on. How have you been doing since then? What is your track record now and what has it been percentage-wise for the last couple of years?

Andy: Right now I am getting an average return of around 80% per year, but I am not trading as big an account as I used to. I stopped trading accounts over one million dollars because there is a policy in Canada that once you make over one million dollars a broker will not pay you back if they get into trouble. You can make $2 million, $3 million, $4 million or $5 million, but if they get in trouble you will only get $1 million back. I don't want to take that risk so I don't trade as large an account as previously.

The second reason I'm not trading as large an account as before is that I took out most of my money to start building up my real estate portfolio. From the very beginning before I even started trading that was one of my goals, and now in 2011 I finally had the capital to do that. I started using that money to build my real estate portfolio in order to generate some passive cash flow. At the end, the objective of making a lot of money was not my goal. Building financial freedom was my goal and that's why I did this.

That's what I tell people. Trading can make you a lot of money if you learn how to do it successfully, which is why I like helping traders become better at it, but you also want to turn some of that cash into more solid wealth. Everyone who trades should strive to improve their trading skills, but an over-reaching goal should also be to accumulate wealth that is not dependent on the ups and downs of trading since trading returns can suffer tremendous swings. Real estate is one of the options that can help transform trading profits into a more passive stream of dependable income. Have you switched a lot of your money to the field of real estate investing?

Andy: Yes, after taxes probably about half of my money is in real estate now. Most of what I have are rental properties like houses and condos. Back in 2011, I saw an opportunity in the U.S. real estate market when it was not so hot back then. For example, I bought a condo with a $128K market price, but got it for $83K because it was a foreclosure. Now I rent it out for $1,120 per month. After everything, including taxes, the yield is roughly 10%. It's not bad for real estate and you have the capital gains, too.

Okay, so you started with $1,600 and took it to $1.6 million by the end of that particular year. Next you took out a big portion of it and put it into real estate, about half of your trading capital, and now it is throwing off cash for you.

Andy: Yes, it is throwing off cash flow for me so that I have the choice to quit my job and do whatever I want. At the end I just need something to pay off my bills.

In other words, there is trading as a way to make money just as there are other ways to make money, but only if you learn how to do it successfully. If you make some substantial money through trading then you will have the option of turning that cash into other assets that will throw off yet more cash such as rental real estate properties, farmland, oil wells or businesses. You can even invest in hard assets like physical gold and silver that can serve as a form of insurance to protect some of your money.

Andy: Yes, you have to diversify, but you need to know your goal before you plan everything. I actually planned out the real estate portion a year ahead of its execution. I didn't do it because I saw it. I planned it out ahead and when the opportunity arose I had all the tools to actually execute the plan.

You are the perfect example of someone who became successful in trading and then put some of his

winnings into something more passive that didn't rely on the constant volatility of the markets. When you see all the students who come to you and Mike, do any of them have any of this mindset? Do many believe they will become millionaires through trading? Do you think people can actually repeat your personal success? You don't want to promise anyone that they will become a millionaire by trading, so being extremely realistic - as if you were talking to your very own son - what would you tell him about what he could realistically expect with trading?

Andy: One of the most commonly asked questions I get is, "When can I quit my job and become a full-time trader?" I tell people that I am not a full-time trader. I only trade part-time. I made my million dollars when I was working a full-time job as an engineer working 8-8:00 and 8-12:00 while actually trading at night. I finally quit my job in 2012 when I started the trading coaching business with Mike. This is my first goal I mentioned in the very beginning. Besides real estate I wanted a business as a source of income.

I also tell my students that success in trading can give you freedom of choice for what you want to do. You don't need to be a full-time trader and you can still make a lot of money. But this is all dependent upon becoming successful at it. The good thing about the trading strategy I am using is that you don't need to trade full-time but you can still make a lot of money.

But can people repeat what I did? We don't know. The key is that at least we want people to be able to make money first. If you cannot make money then you cannot talk about making a million dollars. At least make a few hundred dollars a day such as $1,000 a day or even $100,000 in a day. Aim for that first.

You have this list of trading don'ts such as "don't trade during consolidation, holidays or chase missed opportunities." Do you have a list of trading do's?

Andy: Do wait for opportunities because one of the biggest mistakes is that people overtrade. Patiently waiting for a setup is a MUST.

Second, learn from your mistakes. A lot of people who lose money blame the market and say it didn't go in their favor, but to be honest you are always responsible for what you did. Everything that you do you have control over. Do not blame the markets for everything, but blame yourself instead.

When you take responsibility that is the time that you can become a better trader. Mistakes and failure will make you a better trader if you review your mistakes and keep them in mind so that you try not to repeat them. You have to keep this in mind. This is one of the lessons that I always try to keep in mind.

Another thing you must do is identify your goal. Focus on one thing at a time. At least that is what I do. I am a very focused person. When I do see something happening I just focus on trading one or two things. If you spread yourself too much then you need a lot more knowledge to know what is happening in those other sectors. One single person alone cannot manage trading four, five, six or seven different instruments. It will wear you out so just focus on one or two things and do not trade five or ten things at a time, especially using leverage. You can invest in five or ten things but we are talking about trading using leverage.

You also recommend people to trade using chart patterns, correct?

Andy: Yes, technical analysis is the key like chart patterns, trend lines, RSI, and so on. Second, fundamental analysis is also important such as whether we are in a recession or low interest rate environment and so on because that's how we determine the long-term trend. Technicals give the entry of where to enter the market while fundamentals give you a longer-term view. They also help tell you when is the best time to trade the markets as well.

What is the smallest toolbox of indicators you want traders to have ... the minimum set of tools they need to understand?

Andy: Trend lines, support, resistance, RSI, MACD, and volume.

For understanding volume, people need to know that it often warns you about the trend. For instance, on a day when the market is actually starting to go down and hitting resistance, watch out if there is heavy selling. The stock market is just a buyers and sellers market, and you can tell if the majority of people are selling from the volume. If there is high volume on selling activity then the market is likely to go down more. Watch out - the market can be going down when you see heavy volume on selling.

What are your general rules for stop-losses?

Andy: When you want to be more conservative the stops should be around 1-5% when initially entering the trade. What you use in this 1-5% range depends on how many of these tools are pointing to the market going up or down. For instance, if three out of five of the tools show the market is going up then that is not a high probability play. You therefore want a low risk if you want to enter a trade like that and around 1-2% is considered a small risk stop.

On the other hand, if you see five out of five tools confirming the same picture, like I did when I saw the double top in silver hitting $50, then you can get more aggressive and risk about 5%. Of course the 5% I'm talking about all depends on whether you feel comfortable risking that money. If you have a $10K account and you are facing a high probability play and you are still not comfortable losing $500 then you have to scale it down. You have to feel comfortable to make the decision to risk $500 or 5% of your account.

Now I understand your initial stops. When do you move your stops to breakeven?

Mike: We try to move the stop-loss to breakeven once it moves one times your stop-loss amount.

Our goal is that once risk is minimized we then try to maximize profits. We are looking for big trades, mega trades and bigger trends. We do have some targets in mind in case things don't go according to where we think they should go, and then we look to exit. We do have targets in mind but we prefer to focus on adding to positions rather than exiting positions.

A lot of professional traders say they won't get into the trade unless there is a 3:1 reward to risk ratio or some number like that. Do you guys teach anything like that?

Andy: We do look at that. For us it is at least a 2:1 ratio. If I am risking $5 then at the minimum I am looking to make $10. Most of the time when we go over a trade and it doesn't fulfill the requirement of the 2:1 ratio then we either don't do the trade or see what we can do to improve the trade such as tighten the stop-loss or widen the target. If those things aren't feasible then we just don't trade.

You also said you liked to add to profitable positions. Can you explain your process for doing that?

Mike: Adding to ongoing positions is a concept called "pyramiding." When pyramiding you use a portion of your position's profit to be able to buy more positions. Most people have the philosophy to buy low and sell high, but what lots of losing traders do is buy low and then buy lower, averaging down. We don't do that or recommend that.

We buy low and then buy higher and higher because the higher price validates that our position is working in our favor. Typically when we enter a position and it goes in our favor we like to see the trend consolidate. After an initial move up we like to see the trend consolidate and form some type of support level or consolidation level. Once it breaks out of that consolidation level we will look to add another position. If it goes in our favor we look for consolidation or look for levels where there is some defined resistance level and when it breaks above that level we also add to positions.

Andy: When you have lots of shares or contracts the scale of positions are added in the ratio of 4:3:2:1. Your bottom position would be 40% and the next addition would be 30% and so on.

The key thing regarding pyramiding is that it is a doubled-edge sword just like leverage. You really need to know how to identify a trend to use it because if you use this particular strategy in a tight consolidation you will end up losing a lot of money. You only apply pyramiding when you see a big uptrend or downtrend but not during a consolidation.

Risk management is the key to this because every single position will require its own stop-loss. You need to manage your risk well by moving your stops to breakeven when necessary to protect yourself in case the market goes against you. If you add to a position then you are adding exposure to the risk as well. If you don't manage your risk well then it can be really dangerous.

Can you give me an example of the stop-losses being changed? I want to make sure the idea is clear.

Andy: Let's say that silver is at $50 and I short the market at $50. My first stop-loss will be at $50.30 and as the market goes down to $48 I will put on another short position. My first position will by then have a stop that has already been moved to breakeven. The initial stop-loss for that new additional position will be $48.30. As the market keeps going down you will then keep moving your stops down. So my second position will have a stop-loss at $48.30 while the first position I entered is already making money and I changed its stop to breakeven. As the market moves I'll keep changing stops.

You will have multiple stops. Don't ever, ever put in just one big stop order. Don't do that. Very likely people will have an average price for when to exit, but if that particular point gets triggered as a stop and the market keeps moving in your favor then you will get stopped out making very little money while the market keeps continuing as you expected.

The good thing about separating your entries is the following. Let's say you shorted the market at two different prices, a higher and lower one. Let's say that you got stopped out with the lower entry price.

Since you separated your stops for the two separate entries you will still have an entry at the top of the market, so your trade will still be running. If the market keeps going down you will then still be making money on at least one trade because you separated your stop-losses rather than lumped them altogether into just one.

Let me summarize this interview so far starting with the motivation for trading. If you succeed at trading then you can start using some of the capital it generates to enter upon a different road of wealth such as by investing in income producing assets. But let's leave that aside even though it is something I personally encourage and a road that Andy himself chose from the very beginning and has started to achieve because of trading.

What you two are saying is that to be successful at trading you must first find the unique style of trading and the markets which match your personality and interests and which fit the restrictions put upon you by your job and lifestyle. You are also saying not to try to trade too many things but to concentrate on just one or two markets when getting started. You have also found that most people aren't suited for day trading because they have day jobs, so you most often end up recommending that people should try to master momentum trend trading.

    Andy: Correct.

To do all this you suggest they learn some technical analysis charting patterns in order to learn the highest probability exits and entries. You also have to learn how to manage stops and there are other trading do's and don'ts people should generally follow. That all being said, I want to know what you think is the minimum toolbox in technical analysis that aspiring traders, and even old timers, need to learn.

    Mike: All we are ever doing in terms of using patterns, trend following or technical indicators is basically trying to identify what is the lowest risk opportunity to get into a trade where if it doesn't go in our favor we would take a small loss. To do that traders, for their minimum toolbox, need to obtain a basic understanding of technical analysis indicators, trend lines, and chart patterns to help identify entry levels and exit levels for trades.

    They also need to know potential catalysts for their market because we do not believe in being purely technical traders. We hold positions for weeks or months if they are working in our favor, so we do look at the fundamental catalysts of economic data that could move the markets. We are looking to see the overall news that could trigger trends. In terms of our fundamental research, we are also looking to see what's going on in a specific market sector or the general U.S. economy because of those effects on the U.S. indexes.

    The question is what are some of the factors or catalysts that we need to be aware of as drivers that might push the technicals, meaning that they might get us into entering a position based on the technical level.

Are there any specific websites or TV shows you might recommend to traders?

Mike: There is a website called ForexFactory.com where we get our global economic data calendar to see what is coming up.

Actually what you should watch or look at all depends on what you trade. For instance Andy mentioned gold and silver so he looks at Kitco.com. If we are waiting for certain economic data to come in then we sometimes tune to CNBC for general market sentiment during the day, but we generally try not to be swayed by what is going on now. Rather we want to look at the bigger picture and not be swayed by fluctuations on a day-to-day basis.

Mike, to wrap things up please give me a run down of the money management rules you recommend to students because this is often the key to winning and losing in trading.

Mike: There are quite a number of general rules.

The #1 rule is risk. The rule is to always minimize risk. Once it has been minimized then we look to play with house money, meaning profits. That's rule #1.

Rule #2 is that we look for big trends. We like to look for opportunities where there is an ability to make a lot of money. We look for bigger trends in the market.

Rule #3 is that once an opportunity has moved in your favor then you should look to maximize the profits, so instead of looking to exit positions you should look to add to winning positions.

Another rule is to know what your plan is, know what your objective is. The market is a marketplace. It is a marketplace for you to be able to generate profits, a marketplace for you to spot opportunity so have a plan, know what you are looking for, and get what you are looking for in the market. Once the market says it is over then exit your position.

Another rule is to utilize leverage as a tool. Leverage is a double-edged sword. Use leverage when you are playing with house money, meaning when you are playing with profits.

People are formulaic. Just to be clear, what are the general percentages for stops once again? Countless traders lose money because of their stops so I want your risk management lessons to be heard over and over again.

Andy: Typical stop sizes depend on the type of instrument you trade. The usual risk amount we take on trades is between 1% and 5%, which is the size of the stops. If the trade went wrong then you would probably lose 1-5%. If the trade went in your favor then you should move the stop to breakeven when it makes the same size profit as your stop-loss and then your risk is usually breakeven at that particular stage. As time goes on, if the trade moves more in your favor then you can lock in some profit.

Locking in profits all depends on the trend. Let's say the market still has room to go down because it isn't even near where our profit target is. In that case then just let it ride and only lock in 1% or ½% profit because you need to give the market some room to move but without getting your trade stopped out.

The problem is that each market is different and reacts differently. Crude oil and silver, for instance, are very volatile and move differently. If you want to hold onto those particular trades, for instance, I would probably tell you to move your stops to breakeven because those markets are very volatile. For markets that are less volatile, such as gold and the Dow Jones and things like that, you have a luxury to move down your stop-loss a bit. The theory behind all this is that every instrument has its own personality.

We are just trend followers so once we are in a position where our risk has been taken care of we then look to ride the trend.

Let's move on now to some success stories of other students besides Andy who made his million dollars trading.

Andy: I'm just one of three millionaire students who Mike has trained. We also have a lot of case studies where students didn't make a million dollars, but had full-time jobs and were able to generate a second income through the trading methods we taught.

We had one student, for instance, working at a port. He started trading earlier this year. Half a year later he got the hang of it so that he could start making good trades on a demo account. He transitioned to a live account a few months ago. One of my jobs is to give ideas that students can take advantage of. He was able to take an idea that I mentioned, tried to ride a trend involved with this idea and turned $1,600 into $7,000 in just a week.

Another student was a civil engineer in Australia who was frustrated with his job and who had been trading for quite a bit of time. He was not a new trader. He came to us and tried to learn what I did. In the beginning he was still making his old mistakes. The key thing was that he listened to our advice and found he could finally profit from the market as well. Previously he was never disciplined enough to move his stops or even put in his stop-losses. That's why every single month he was putting more money into his account. I emphasized to him that putting in stops was very important. That particular advice turned him around to at least make $1,000 in the same trade as well.

In other words, you had a trader who lost money for years, taught him to use stops, and this turned him into a winning trader.

Andy: Yes. We also have a lady who didn't know anything about trading a year ago. She started from scratch because she didn't even know how to use the computer very well. She didn't know how to use an Excel spreadsheet. It took her a little longer, almost nine months to get used to it, but she was able to start from scratch not even knowing how to use the computer and then started to make some real money off of trading. There were some challenges for her because of the technical difficulty in learning to use software but because she had the will to do it we were able to help her achieve her goal as well.

Mike: Another case is a gentlemen we call "the most improved trader." This was a trader who was trading for two years. He had a lot of emotional challenges. He sold commercial real estate and was very good at his job. He was looking at trading as a potential second income for himself and something where he didn't have to deal with clients. His biggest challenge - and we had to work with him over a year on it - was getting him to be patient. We tried to not get him to do exactly what we do in trading but to find something that fit his personality.

He wanted to trade something a bit more volatile. Even though he practiced swing trading he felt that his comfort level was with day trading, so we worked with him to advance his skills on day trading. That's where everything turned around for him because he was very, very good with being very aggressive with risk but not good at managing risk. We helped him turn around and he has been able to build a consistent day trading income between $500 and $1,000 per day.

There are two types of traders who come to us. One type are complete newbies who know nothing. For instance, we had a dental hygienist who had no formal type of training. She didn't know what she was doing yet sometimes she made money trading and at other times she lost money because she didn't have any set rules or system. We were able to help her structure a program where she learned how to focus on risk. We helped her with the strengths that she had and focused on helping her learn how to minimize risk.

Everyone has his own strengths. We help people minimize the risks of trading and help them leverage the strengths they have in a specific instrument or strategy. What we found, and this is what we discovered from the training approach we developed years ago and have further refined, is that we should not try to teach people exactly what we do in trading. We don't want them to copy us exactly. We try to help people understand what their own goals and objectives are because those are the guidelines of what they should focus on in trading. To us trading is a tool.

What we found in looking at the three millionaire success stories is that they achieved their success through three different areas of specialty, through three different types of trading instruments and three different backgrounds.

You know Andy's story. The second millionaire success is a gentleman who focused on trading penny stocks. He understood the fundamental side. He was an IT guy who was struggling financially. He was looking for ways to generate wealth – a situation very similar to Andy's. In his spare time at work he took our program and applied what he learned to the resource sector. What we found for him is that he wanted to focus on that particular area, specifically on penny stocks. We helped him leverage the strengths he had and the focus he wanted to accomplish. He was eventually able to turn $5,000 into a million dollars trading the Canadian resource market.

The third gentlemen is an American in New York whose 401(k) got decimated during the financial crisis and he looked to me to help him build back the 401(k) that he lost through the financial crisis. It was perfect timing because he was able to utilize the tools that we had. He was an entrepreneur who had his own business. He was not really looking to make a lot of money. He was in his mid-fifties just looking for a steady type of retirement return for when he was about to retire. He was able to take advantage and utilize the tools we had to leverage his focus on U.S. equities, specifically financial institutions and ETFs, to be able to turn to the amount he lost in his 401(k) into $1.1 million dollars.

Great. Now the last question. How can people get in contact with you guys?

Mike: They can go to our website: sermantraders.com. We also have a Youtube channel where Andy gives a market update several times per week. Or they can send us an email at contact@sermantraders.com.

Thank you for revealing the trading rules you two typically teach traders. I hope that people who want to improve their trading skills have learned a lot from our conversation and contact you if they want help themselves. Best of luck to both of you.

Chapter 2
Raymond Barros
From Failure to Success in Trading

Raymond Barros – successful trader, professional fund manager, author and trading educator – initially failed miserably at the beginning of his trading career by losing his entire trading account several times in a row. He suffered through seven consecutive years of gut wrenching losses before he finally made the breakthrough in learning how to become a successful trader. When he finally turned the corner, he went into the fund management field where he achieved a 20+% CAGR track record in returns.

After finally hanging up his fund management shoes, Ray became a professional trading coach in Asia who teaches the tools and thinking skills that help traders improve their returns and avoid the most common trading mistakes. In this interview you will find new and refreshing ideas on how to develop a winning attitude, rules for money management, and how to wait for a trend to confirm itself in order to achieve lower risk entries. A particular highlight is Ray's statistical method for determining when he should raise or lower his position size.

Ray is widely recognized for having developed a new and unique theory of market structure that simplifies Elliott Waves and provides a clearer road map of how a market structure is likely to unfold. He uses his simplified "Ray Wave" and "Barros Swing" to trade the markets along with Peter Steidlmayer's Market Profile zones that we will introduce in detail during a later interview.

In his early unprofitable days Ray was searching for the Holy Grail or perfect trading system that would never err, but he now teaches that the best or most profitable strategy is to think of the market in terms of probabilities. Rather than assuming certainty, he emphasizes that you should organize your trading to recognize the forces of probability that govern the markets. In other words, you should wait for confirmations rather than proactively trading in anticipation of what you think the market will do. Furthermore, he seconded the opinion of Mike Ser and Andy Man that you should adopt a trading system and style which matches your personality in order to maximize your chances of winning in the markets. This is an interview with many takeaways on what to study to become a more profitable trader.

Ray, you started as a lawyer. Can you give us your background on how this turned into a career in trading?

Well, I probably started trading about a year or two before I sold my legal practice. No, that's actually not true. Going back a little bit here, it was in the first year of University that I got involved in trading. In those days we had a mining boom in Australia and there was a stock called Peerless. That thing was about a 4¢ or 5¢ stock and it rallied up to $2 or $3. We had bought it quite near the lows and I'd love to say we held on to it and then sold it at the highs, but we actually saw it go all the way up and go all the way down and ended up losing money on the bloody thing. That was my first experience with trading. I wiped out my account in that little thing called Peerless.

I started my first year of University, which would have been in 1966, and I remember that that was my first trade. Later in 1980, which was a year or two before I sold my legal practice, I was going to Hong Kong from Sydney where I was living at the time. My wife's parents were in Hong Kong and my father-in-law said, "Do you do trade?" I said, "What's trading?" He was trading the Hong Kong gold market and I said, "That looks easy" because it was just trading a sideways range. I was watching him trade and he was buying the highs and selling the lows. He was looking for a breakout and I thought, "Oh, just sell the highs and buy the lows. How hard can that be, right?"

We started with one contract and traded that way for about a month. I made enough money to buy my wife a beautiful fur coat, kept whatever I had left and kept on trading when I came back to Australia where I subsequently succeeded in losing all that I had. If I hadn't bought her the fur coat then I would have lost it all, but I didn't tell her that. Sometime later - six or nine months later - I said I wanted to give up the law. I was thinking that I'm such a great trader but I sort of dismissed the fact that I had blown my trading account. I started trading anyway and that's how I got into it.

Then eventually you just quit your law business, your law practice?

Yes, I basically sold the law practice in order to become a full-time trader. I gave my wife a fur coat but I put aside the fact, I *denied* the fact that I actually had lost money. Had I not sold the fur coat I probably would have lost my shirt, but I just put that to the side and I sold the legal practice.

In about eighteen months after selling the legal practice I had lost every single penny that I had gotten from the legal, which was quite substantial in those days, and then my wife Chrisy basically supported me for the next seven years. A couple of million dollars in today's language went down the chute and my first successful trading year was finally in 1987.

What happened that finally turned you around? What had you studied that didn't work and what did you come up with that finally worked for you?

You have to remember in those days - this is in Australia - what we had were mainly get rich quick schemes. Now for trading I read everything I could - Gann, Elliott, Wyckoff. Whatever you had I read it, but it just didn't click for me. I was looking for this idea that somehow I was going to find a magic system that would not be wrong. I tried putting in stops and they would get knocked off and if I didn't put in a stop I would lose a ton of money.

I remembered there was some sort of congestion system - I think the Nofri Phase Congestion system - where basically if you had the market going two days in one direction then you would enter a position in the opposite direction. Let's say your market went up two days in a row on a closing basis. You would short sell on the second day's close and you would look to get out at the first pullback. If you went up another day then you sold again and you would exit it on the first pullback.

They would claim a 90% win rate with this system. Well they would probably be right provided that you only looked at the last trade that you did! What about all the days where you entered the short sell lower down, if you know what I mean? It was that sort of thing that I was trying to play with at the time looking for a way of not losing. Of course there is no such thing. It just didn't work.

So what finally clicked?

You know I'm often asked that question. My wife Christine (Chrisy) was supporting me and she hates me telling the story, but I owe so much to her. I had blown the account umpteen times. I had blown it again and again. Basically I went to her one night and said, "Look, darling please, please, please just give me another chance and just give me some more money. I only need to have twenty-five grand and it'll be fine." I don't know where she got it from, but she gave it to me on a Friday morning. She gave it to me and I was day trading in those days. I was trading the S&P. Those days the S&P was $500 a big point. It had about a four-point range that night and I bought every high and I sold every low and by the time that night was over I had blundered $25,000 in one night.

I remember sobbing. It was deep wrenching sobs. I was trading in my office. We had a two-bedroom apartment and many years later she said she heard me sobbing and she didn't know whether to comfort me, because she knew what had happened, or come and take my head off because I had blown it again.

That was the last time I ever blew an account. That started the bounce in about '85. Then I went and did a course by Pete Steidlmayer on the Market Profile. We were really running very tight on money and I said to her I really have to go because I think this is it. It was announced in a little ad in *Futures* magazine and I said I have to give this a go.

That started at least putting me on the right track in realizing that the market was a probability game. At least that's what I got from Peter's lectures. I kept going back and about two years later I had my first win. To be honest I think I was just lucky that year. I happened to get short the Friday before Black Monday and that sustained me for the year, but it gave me the confidence or belief that I actually could make money.

I think '88 was more or less a scratch year, '89 I made real good money and then in '90 I remember my broker suggested that I become a fund manager.

I didn't like the way that we had to basically sell ourselves in those days. If you didn't have a sustained track record you had to go on all these shows. I didn't like that. Chrisy comes from a fairly wealthy family and through her we put a bunch of people together. We managed to start with 20 million Aussie dollars in 1990 and that was it. I never looked back after that. We closed that in 2010. We ended up with AUD 943 million, so that was a good result.

What was the rate of return?

About 23% compounded. I had a peculiar way of doing things. I didn't charge a management fee because I didn't know any better in those days about management fees. I basically charged a fairly high incentive fee and I would only charge it at the end of the period. They were locked in for three years unless I lost 30%.

Basically I kept the same people except for losing one guy when I had a very bad run for two years where I didn't make any money. It was in '99 or '95 … something like that. I can't remember exactly unless I look at the track record. There was a slab of period where I just didn't make any money and luckily these guys had become friends so even at the end of the period they stayed with me except for one guy. Then in 2007 I lost two people because they asked to be pulled out because of the crash. They lost money elsewhere and they needed the money so I let them out of it. So I only lost three people. We started with twenty and we lost three, but I managed to retain the others.

I never realized until much later how much of a rarity that is in the fund management game because most people pull out fairly quickly. They don't stay with you. The whole fund structure was very different and I was just lucky with the people that I chose.

From my experience of that time period usually you would lose at least 10% of your clients per year just because of divorces, taxes, itchy fingers and so on, but you did better than that with your client retention rate.

I am so grateful now - looking back and knowing more about the industry - and I was lucky that I had just found the right people and we clicked. We became really good friends and they just stuck with me even through that bad period. I couldn't imagine that happening if I hadn't been so lucky.

What has your personal track record been since then? How are you usually doing in your trading?

I have my ups and downs so let's have a look. The best year ever was 2010. On the top of my head I think I made 137%. I've never ever had that sort of return in my entire period. At that point I resigned. I said to Chrisy that if she didn't mind then I was giving it up because one of the things I have seen over the years is that people take the highest rate of return and treat that as the norm. I always promised myself I was going to get out at the top.

I remember reading about the basketball player who used to play for the Bulls, Michael Jordan. He retired at the top and then he couldn't help himself. He had to come back into the game and it just wasn't the same. I promised myself that I would quit at the top, which was just as well because in 2011 I just didn't realize that QE had caused the markets to lose diversification and so I got hurt badly in the early part of 2011. It took me a whole year to recover. It was a scratch year and it was very hard to recover. As to 2012 and 2013 they had been reasonably good, but this 2015 I think is going to be my best year.

One of the things that I always have trouble with is that I make a lot of money and then I … well, let me put it this way. I firmly believe that as far as methodologies are concerned there is an ebb and a flow. There are times when everything you do will be right and you have to push that and take advantage of it. There will also be times that everything you do is wrong and totally confused. At that time my advice is to pull back and reduce the amount of trading you do and wait for that to depart. Otherwise you'll give a lot back.

From 2013 to 2014 my performance was quite similar to what happened in 2014-15. I had a good run until January and then February and March. In April of 2014 I lost 15%, and it took me all that time to recover until about August of 2014. January 2014 was a good month. Then February, March, and April were really bad months because I lost 15%. This is 2014 going to the end of August before I recovered what I had lost, and then September, October, November, and December were really good months. January this year was fantastic at almost a 60% return, and then I started going into what I call "ebb phase."

I was giving a talk about this in Shanghai or Sydney about how you have to be careful about ebb phases and I was talking about my personal problems. One of the guys in the audience said, "Well have you ever thought about just exiting more quickly rather than holding on and waiting to be stopped out?"

What happens when I trade is that I will exit my first third, which means I will take profits at twice my stop so that after that I can't lose money. What happens when I'm in ebb phase is that the market price doesn't get there. It just doesn't get to that first third so I take the full 2% losses and I won't make any money. This guy said, "Why don't you just get out more quickly" and I thought, "Well, I never thought of that." This guy had been telling me that he had just lost an arm and a leg in the market but offered me this great idea.

I started applying it this year when I noticed I was getting into ebb state. I was always able to recognize that state, at least in the recent past, but I just haven't been able to do anything about it so I did that. In 2014 I did maybe twenty trades during February, March, and April. This year I've done forty-seven trades but my end result is that I'm still in ebb state yet I'm up about 1%. I've done forty-seven trades with equal profits and losses and a 50-50 win rate, but I'm exiting very quickly. If the market doesn't do what I want it to do, and I'm very clear about what I want it to do, I'm out.

Every now and then you learn something new. I've just turned seventy. I've been in the market over thirty years and I've learned something new. One of the reasons I love to teach is because somebody will say something like that and you think, "Yeah, I never thought of that. Let's give it a go."

Can you explain the ebb state in more detail?

Okay, ebb and flow. I see that there are three states of trading: flow, normal and ebb.

Ebb is when everything you do is wrong. Everything. You choose your best quality setups - your things that work for you - and they just don't even get to that first third.

Usually when I get into a trade it will do something. It will move a little bit in my direction as a general rule. It doesn't normally stop me out, but I just would hang in there because I was looking for that first third and it wouldn't get there so then I would take 2% losses. I would save a lot of the situations because I reduce the amount of trading I would do.

As I said, if you look at February, March and April of 2014 I only did twenty trades as compared to forty-seven trades for the same period this year. The difference is that I'm not letting the market stop me out. I'm just saying, "Well, it's not behaving so I'm out." So you win a bit, you lose a bit and it's been a great difference for my results. My view is that if I go into flow state at some point or even normal state then I don't have to chase my ass.

So "ebb state" is when everything is going wrong and "flow state" is when everything is going right?

That's right.

And "normal" is what?

If I could put it this way, in flow state I did ten trades in January this year and when I made that 60% every one was a winner. Last February, March, and April of 2014 we did twenty-seven trades and every single one of those trades was a loser except one because that actually got to its first target. It didn't make any money, but it got to its first target so it stopped out. It didn't cost me anything, but twenty-six out of twenty-seven trades lost money. That's the ebb state.

Right, but average or normal is …

There is a normal win rate. For my normal state I'll make money around 47% to 53% of the time. That is my normal state. Even if I get stopped out on those trades then because of that half my trades at least go to the first target so I can't lose. I don't lose on them.

I understand what you are doing now. The problem for most people is that they don't know when they are in ebb state because they keep thinking the next trade will turn it around, and they don't know when they are in normal rather than in flow.

It's always that way. It's always going to be a step behind so what I've done is calculate the statistics so I know what my expectancy of return ought to be when I'm in a normal state. I put a lower and upper limit around my average trading results and when it gets above that I'm in flow and below that is ebb. Around the average is normal.

If I'm trading I keep an eye on it using my monthly results. Since I'm trading a lot now I'm looking at it on a weekly basis. If my results are showing an expectancy return that falls outside the norm then I'm in either ebb or flow state. It's just hindsight trading knowledge, but at least it's an objective way of looking at where you are.

After a while you get a feeling, you get that confidence to say, "Okay, I know what this market is going to do" and the market actually does it, but when you're in an ebb state and think you know what the market is going to do it then it does the exact opposite.

Are you looking at the profits or are you looking at the win rate for this statistical calculation that tells you whether you are in ebb, flow or normal state?

I'm actually looking at the expectancy of return. My expectancy of return formula is my average dollar win multiplied by the win rate minus average total loss multiplied by the loss rate. I subtract those two numbers to get a dollar figure and that allows me to say, "Okay, my return is falling within the normal parameters so I'm in normal state" or, "Oops, my return has fallen two standard deviations (or more than one standard deviation) below the normal rate. I'm now in ebb state." It's always going to be slightly behind but that's okay.

Are you doing that monthly?

I used to do that on a month-to-month basis. Nowadays, because I'm doing a lot more trading I'm doing it on a fortnightly basis every two weeks. The trades I use in the calculation are the ones since I last did it. If I don't have enough trades I will take the whole period but generally now because I'm doing forty-seven trades - which is double the normal size - I'll just take whatever the full blast of fortnightly trades was. If I'm doing it today then I'll include the number of trades I did since a fortnight ago. Now I've got about fifteen trades, for example, that's enough for me to get a general feeling.

This is really good. Most traders don't have any objective rule that tells them when to increase or decrease their trading position size and this can help them a lot. This is a mechanical rule that tells you when to increase or decrease your bet size or even trading frequency.

If you want to get a little bit technical, Pete Steidlmayer and I like the following much better than the excel spreadsheet but it involves a little bit more work. There is a firm called Market Delta in the States (MarketDelta.com) which makes available on their website what's called a calculation of the "value area." Pete didn't use the mean in this trading result evaluation. Instead he used the mode as the mean of the first and second standard deviation ranges. He did this because trading results are skewed as you are probably aware. It's not a bell curve normally, especially over the short term, so if you use Pete's approach to calculate the value area with this idea then it works very, very well.

It sounds like what turned you into a winner was that you were looking for a perfect system and finally turned to a probability view of the markets that allowed for losses. Your mindset changed all of a sudden because of learning Peter Steidlmayer's Market Profile. You are still a subjective trader, so now how do you look at the markets and determine whether you should be long or short? What are your setups and your general rules?

Essentially I developed a thing called the "Barros Swing," which was a take-off on Gann's swing chart. Basically Gann had this three-period swing chart, which is price-based only, and I developed a thing called the Barros Swing chart, which is basically a swing chart that uses both price and time to draw the swings. It's very difficult to explain. It's freely available on my website so people can go in there and see what I did.

Joseph Hart developed a similar sort of swing. We calculate it very differently, but it's a similar sort of concept. I'll use the 13-week swing on a weekly chart to give me my quarterly trend and it's just that simple.

Have you ever seen a swing chart? If you take out the bars, if you hide the bars, the trend will be whatever those swings can be drawn on. What this does is it allows you to distinguish trends and time frames, which to me is the critical thing.

You asked me what is the first thing I would do? The first thing I would do is to identify the trend of the time frame I'm trading. The good thing about swing charts is that it's very easy to calculate statistically whether or not a swing is overbought or oversold. One of the problems I have with indicators - whether you use RSI or Stochastics or whatever – is that you are using a fixed period, but if you are looking at an 18-period swing, for example, an impulse move can go a long way. It can go much further or be much shorter and you can use statistics to work out what is normal. You can work out what is a normal swing, impulse swing, what is a normal corrective swing and you can do that in time and price.

If I have to say one thing that has made the difference for me now it is that I've got a solid base for identifying what is the trend of that time frame I'm trading and whether that trend is likely to continue or change. That helps me in terms of my position sizing because I do get aggressive when I think the market is just starting to break out. Take 30-year bonds for example. I think it's just starting to break out. I will start to take some relatively heavy positions at the start of the trend and less so as the trend matures.

There was a trader who put together a book of the probabilities showing the frequency of the size of the swings …

Arthur Merrill. He did percentages though. His were percentage swings.

Yes, that's right! So you use something like that to determine swings?

No, it's nothing like it at all. As I said, the website will actually explain it. It really is quite difficult to explain. I don't want to bore you with the details.

I just want the general picture or procedure such as you first do this and then that. What exactly do you do?

Well, think of it this way. I generally trade the 18-day swing as a general rule, which is a monthly trend, and reference the 13-week swings. Those define the quarterly trend. If you think about it there can only be three trends: up, down and sideways. That up, down or sideways is within the context of the larger time frames so that's the first thing I would determine.

Let's say, for example, that the trend in the larger time frame is up and then the 18-day gives you a sell signal - what I call a "Wyckoff up-thrust change in trend" pattern on the 18-day. I now have to decide whether the 13-week trend is really going to correct and if it is, will there be enough in it if I take this trade. That's because of the following.

Let's say it's trading at 2300 and that the correction is only going to go to 2200 and I want to get in at 2260. Well, there may not be enough in it for me to take the trade, but if the correction is likely to end at 1800 then that's a whole different ballgame. By putting the 18-day within the context of larger time frames and then answering the question, "Is this thing likely to continue or change?" I get my strategy. I then know if I want to be long, short, or occasionally I don't know what's happening so I'll stay out of the market.

Now once I've got that then I'm going to look for a place to take the trade, which is what I call the "zone." Usually I'm a responsive trader unless I'm looking for a change in trend pattern. If it's a continuation pattern then I'm looking for a pullback. I buy dips and sell rallies, and then I look for some setup patterns that will tell me support or resistance will hold. Then I look for some evidence that the selling (if I'm looking to sell) or buying (if I'm looking to buy) has actually come in. So I'm looking for a bullish bar and I'll buy at the close of that bullish bar. Last January that's what actually happened.

All right, so you've worked out this system, it works for you and it's got a great track record. Is this what you teach people or do you recommend people study something else?

I actually filter a lot of my audience as much as I can. Whenever I'm doing a gig I ask the organizers to put out a survey and usually what I'm looking for is someone who is a bit like me when I first started. I had a lot of experience losing money. I'm looking for people who aren't newbies because it's very hard to break the mental mindset of a newbie, especially in the Far East. They all want to spend no money, have no capital and want to get rich yesterday. I don't want that. I'm not there to help these guys.

Interesting. You're finding that the newbies are hard to teach rather than the guys who are trading and losing money?

Yes, I actually find that the guys who are trading and losing money have at least a realistic appreciation of the market. And then there is something that's happened only in the last eighteen months or two years that I picked up. There is a thing called "acceptance commitment" in the commercial world of training. In the psychological world it's called "acceptance commitment therapy" and this particular branch of psychology has had great results for wife beaters, drug addicts, alcoholics you name it ... stuff where you have to spend twenty years on a therapist's coach to get some very, very good therapeutic results.

What's it called again?

Acceptance and commitment training or therapy. As I said this is really good stuff.

Basically, ACT has two principles. The first principle is that we accept those things - the bad things - that are not under our control. If my wife dies I'm going to feel sad. There is nothing you can do about it, but how do you respond to that sadness? If you deny it, if you try to suppress it then it can come back in a really bad way.

Just think about it in terms of trading. If you just had a bad run or you are losing money and you try and suppress the fact that you are losing money - "I can't afford to get out of this trade because if I get out I lose too much money" - that's the worst thing that can happen to you. So ACT has a series of four tools that deal with accepting the things you can't control.

It also has a thing called "value committed action," which means the things you can control so you can take positive steps to achieve whatever your goals are. These are a function of the values that we hold. I found that to be exceptionally good for people in trading who have had a bad run and they are now ready to change.

I've never heard of this for traders.

Well, there is only one other chap, and I've got a lot of time for him, named Dr. Gary Dayton who works with this. He actually recently wrote a book called *Trading Mindfully* and in it he mentions ACT. He doesn't go into the theory of ACT in the book, but all of the things he suggests the trader do to help improve their trading are ACT based. If you want to get an idea of how to apply it for trading then that's the book I would get.

The easiest book to get on ACT is *The Happiness Trap* by Russ Harris. It's written in layman's language and so is very easy to read.

If you google "ACT acceptance and commitment therapy" you will get a whole bunch of books from a lot of psychiatrists, but they are hard to read. I like reading and I do a lot of reading, but I did find a lot of those books heavy going. However there is one book called *ACT Made Simple* that is better than most.

I want to put this out there for people because I think there are a lot of traders and investors who want to change to become more profitable and more successful, especially with emotional control, but they've never even heard of this.

Yeah. This stuff is the best thing that has come out for change behavior. It is really, really good.

Okay, that's excellent. That information will help a lot of people who want to improve their trading and investing results and will therefore pursue it. Let's turn to your trading rules now. When you are personally getting into a trade you said you use the Ray Wave and you look for a zone and low risk entries. What type of setups are you looking for? Can you describe your initial entry points and initial stop placements?

Let me just take a step back and show how this all fits together. I'm basically a Wyckoff and Market Profile user. I see Pete Steidlmayer's Market Profile as an extension of Wyckoff. They both look at the relationship between range and volume to give people an idea of trends. Most of the Wyckoff stuff is "change in trend" patterns and how to identify when a market is likely to be changing its trend. Then after a breakout I'll use the Market Profile.

I'm not sure if your readers are very familiar with Market Profile. It has actually evolved over time. When I first looked at the Market Profile, it was looking at a daily bar in 30-minute segments. That's how the profile was created and then we looked at long-term activity charts and all sorts of things to determine what the longer term was likely to bring.

Then Peter came out with what was called the Steidlmayer distribution. Basically, a profile begins when it begins and ends when it ends and in the Steidlmayer distribution you could combine several days or several months of profile depending upon what time frame you were looking at. Eventually that became the Market Profile.

Then he developed software called Capital Flow and I stopped calling Peter after that because I couldn't understand it. The only people who understood how to use Capital Flow were Peter and his programmer. He never really wrote a manual about it so I gave up continuing my education on it at that point.

I use the Market Profile once the market has broken out of congestion, which is when there has been a change in trend pattern, we've had the retest on Wyckoff terms and now the market is trading markup days - what Wyckoff called the markup phase.

The Ray Wave for me is an objective Elliott Wave, if I can put it that way. I actually got the idea from Tony Plummer and his book, *Forecasting Financial Markets*. He put me on the idea that Elliott waves are actually three-wave structures and a five-wave structure is actually an exception to the rule.

What I did is make it objective. In my process we look at the corrections and I tweak corrections that are within 20% of one another to be part of the same structure. Together with the Barros Swing statistics this helps me identify when a wave structure is coming to an end.

If you think of it in terms of objectivity, the most objective stuff is the Wyckoff Market Profile. You are reacting to the price action rather than anticipating it. The Ray Wave seeks to anticipate price action and you've got to be real careful with that because you can see whatever you want to see. If you are not very objective in your analysis you will have three or four different scenarios until the market tells you which one is coming out, but if you force it you'll be like a normal Elliott Wave user and you will see whatever you want to see and that's not the whole idea of the Ray Wave.

I know a lot of people have been burned by using Elliott Wave expectations so this simplified Elliott might be of interest to them. Are there any books that you would recommend to learn the Wyckoff method and this three-wave structure?

Well, I can't recommend anything on the Ray Wave because nothing is in print. I've done one seminar on it and I stopped teaching it because what I found was that you need to be at a certain stage in your trading to use it best. Even with the guys that I like to teach I think that they are better off letting the market tell them what it has done and then reacting to it rather than trying to anticipate it. That's because they started going from intuition to intuition, if I could put it that way. I didn't want them to do that so I found it wasn't helping them at all. That's why I had second thoughts about it, so there is nothing on the Ray Wave.

In terms of Wyckoff there is the Stock Market Institute in Arizona. That's a very, very good thing. It is mainly for stock traders. I think the guy's partner was either a student or a friend of Wyckoff. He has put a couple of indicators in the course that he teaches so if you are a stock index guy or stock trader it's great for you. Dr. Gary Dayton is also a Wyckoff man who doesn't go into it quite as deeply. He's trading futures and a number of instruments and he is also a good source for Wyckoff. They are the two best sources for Wyckoff.

Wyckoff is great. If someone wants to learn about market structure I do believe they should study him a bit. In any case, the general thing is that you have developed your own way of analyzing the market and after you know the direction of the market you look for a buying zone.

Yes, well basically if you look at setups you've got two types of setups. Let's say I'm looking to buy around the 1500 to 1470 area for argument's sake. I want to buy on dips and sell on rallies. I've only got two types of what I call setups.

As the market comes into the zone, the usual one is that the correction sellers will start to go away. The selling is finished so you get contraction in volume and range. That's one kind of setup.

The other kind of setup was taken from Market Profile and is called "negative development." For example, the market makes a low, rallies and then makes a new low but there is nothing there and you get this huge bar up. It should have kept on going because we've taken out the previous low so as a breakout trader you would expect the market to keep on going in the direction of the breakout, but instead it reverses and goes in the direction of the original trend. That's what I call negative development. The market does something unexpected and resumes the original trend.

That's the other kind of setup so basically there are two types of setups.

What are you usually doing for your stops and profit targets?

Well, my stop is a function of four things. The volatility of the market and the tick size are obviously what I call "market conditions." If the market is very volatile then the number of contracts you are trading is going to be reduced. On the other side are your win rate and your average total win amount.

These are the four components of how I determine my size.

Finally I ask whether I'm in the flow, normal or ebb state. If I'm in flow then I will increase the position size. My maximum trade size in flow is double the normal position size. In the ebb state the minimum is about a third of the normal position size. When I'm in normal state it's whatever it is.

The amount that you are risking is going to be the final arbiter. For example, let's assume that I've decided I'm in normal state and am prepared to risk 2%. Assume my volatility says I can do thirty contracts but when I put in my stop I find I can only do twenty contracts. Well, then I'll only do twenty. The reverse is also true. If my stop allows me to do thirty contracts but the volatility only allows me to do twenty then I'll only do twenty contracts. So those two things together depend upon position sizing, which is just really important in my view. I think one of the reasons people lose a lot of money is because (A) they don't maximize their position size if they are doing well and (B) they are too big when they're going badly.

The second thing is I have this thing I call the "rule of three."

Usually I will exit the first third of my contracts at twice the original stop amount and then leave my stop where it is. I'll exit my first third as soon as the realized profit covers the stop of the two remaining thirds. If I enter a trade at $100 and have a $2 stop then as soon as the market moves to $104 I will liquidate a third of the position. That's because now I won't lose on the trade even if the market stops me out on the remaining positions that are controlled by the original $2 stop. This therefore means that if I get stopped out then I don't lose on the trade.

Then I will take out the next third of my contracts at a logical objective.

For example, if the market is trading in a sideways range I have what I call a "primary buy, primary sell zone." I'm buying at the bottom of a range and selling at the top so my logical objective will be to sell at the top end of the range where I would exit the second third of my position. When I do that I bring my stop to break-even on the last third, and then after that it's just a trailing stop function for when I get out of my last third.

Now the good thing about that is that I can keep going by pyramiding the position. I can keep pyramiding the last third until such time as I think that it's now too risky to be adding positions. This allows me to accumulate in very strongly trending markets. I can keep accumulating positions until that particular trend comes to an end.

Is there a particular market that you like to trade and some markets you stay away from?

I don't trade commodities. I don't trade sugar, coffee, soybeans or commodities like that. I occasionally trade crude but you could say that I stay away from the commodity markets as a rule. I will trade gold. I have not traded gold for a long time, but I think it is just trading in a very narrow congestion range.

The other thing I might mention, which hasn't come up, is that I really use fundamentals as a backdrop to my trading. For example, I won't be trading gold until I see the inflation rate really start to rise. I think that is when we'll see gold go back into a bull run, but until that happens it is trading a sideways condition market so I'll leave that alone.

I like foreign exchange. There is a thing called a "relative strength meter" on the internet that is worth it because it's free. What the currency strength meter does is this. As you are probably aware, in foreign exchange you are always looking at pairs. This currency strength meter – and there are a couple of free variations of it - will show you whether a single currency is trending up or trending down or going sideways.

The first thing I do when I'm trading currencies is look at this. I'm looking to buy a strong currency and I'm looking to sell a weak one. Right away you can get rid of a lot of currencies. For example, at one point just very recently the weak currency was the Aussie dollar and the strong currency was the U.S. dollar. They are the currency pair that I would trade. Six months from now it might be that the Euro will be the weakest currency and Sterling is the strongest or whatever, but that's where I start from.

I love to trade the stock indexes. Maybe now I'll go back into them. I think QE (quantitative easing) for me did a lot of damage. With QE you either have to be long the U.S. stock markets or the European stock markets but not the Chinese markets - just the European FTSE or DAX and the U.S. stock markets. You either had to be long or you had to be out simply because the QE (quantitative easing) had distorted the price mechanism. It drove the sellers out of the market so we didn't want to be short. I think that's starting to change for the U.S. market. I'm not sure about the European markets because they have only just started their own QE.

I think for a lot of things you can't just assume that what happened in the U.S. is going to happen in Europe. However, that is the assumption being made: "Okay, we'll just transfer. We were making a lot of money in the U.S., QE was there, now that's going away so we're going to go to Europe because they've only just started." I don't think it is quite that easy and as we can see the DAX has actually been going in reverse even though the European ECB has said we are just going to keep pumping money into the economy. But it hasn't done what the U.S. did so we need to be really careful about those lessons.

When we see this bear market start - and I think it's only question of time probably sometime this year - then I'll probably go back into it or at least if the distortion of QE goes away or reduces somewhat then I will go back into trading the stock indexes. Right now I am basically trading foreign exchange.

That's quite a long answer to your question.

Now I know your basic type of trading analysis and the parameters of a typical trade so let's switch gears. You've had a lot of students through coaching as well as through your training seminars. I want to talk about what you consider "generic success." You've seen all sorts of people come into trading and have seen both successes and failures. Looking at all these people, what do you think it takes to succeed and how should people pick the strategy they should use? How do they find the best fit and what should be their qualifications for trading? There even some people who definitely shouldn't be trading so what do you tell people?

Okay, first and foremost when it comes to trading I want to look at their expectations of what it takes to be successful. What do they think it is going to take to be successful? Often a guy comes to me and he says, "I have a couple hundred thousand dollars, but I don't want to do too much work as far as studies are concerned because I've got the money and I'll just buy myself a system and some software. All I have to do is just follow signals and that will be it. I don't need to know anything about risk management. I don't need to know anything about the market. I don't need to know anything about myself. I'm just going to become successful because I am successful now."

You know, the ones I'm talking about here are people doing very well in the business world. They are professional doctors, surgeons, and so on. They have done very well outside the market. They are the worst kind simply because whatever happens in the outside world and what happens in the markets are two different things. The markets are designed in a way to bring out the very worst in human beings and you have to actually turn the paradigm on its head. You have to turn human nature around in order to be successful in them. If you define losses as painful then you have got to actually embrace them. You have got to accept losses as being an actual part of the game. You actually have to take more losses in order to be successful.

Therefore when someone comes to me with what I call a "closed mind" where he *know*s what it is going to take to be successful, and when you talk to him you find that's coming from experiences outside the market, then he's the kind of guy where you can say, "You're not going to succeed."

Do you find certain occupations have that more than others?

Yes. I think that's a good question and I think the short answer is "yes." I think the people who are looking for certainty in the market - architects, engineers, people who believe there is a magic formula that will translate into profits simply because human beings look for certainty – don't do well. Certain professions like engineering and architecture are the kind that bring out the worst in you when it comes to trading.

I find women are better traders on the whole as a group than men. Their ego gets less in the way. They are more willing to admit, "Well, I'm wrong about this. How do I solve it as the problem?" whereas a man will tend to say, "I'm not wrong." That's a general comment because not everyone is like that.

Surprisingly the people who are more likely to succeed are probably the artists, the ones that are more right-brained. They are more open to being wrong. And generally I found over the years that the ones who have succeeded extremely well were people with that sort of artsy-fartsy background. They came in with reasonable, realistic expectations: they're going to have to work hard, they're going to have to turn things upside down, they are going to have to put years of effort into it and it's not going to happen overnight but whatever it takes they are going to do it.

You need an edge to succeed at trading and your personality plays a role in success. What do you tell these students who come to you about how they should pick the strategy or method they should master because it suits them?

There are actually some objective tests that you can do. Larry William's son, Jason Williams MD, wrote a good book on this subject called *The Mental Edge in Trading*. There are actually certain qualities that you can use. I think it is the NEO Personality Inventory test that you can do which shows openness, agreeableness and so on. Certain qualities show up in good traders.

I know about that book. One of the conclusions was that in stressful situations successful traders feel less anxiety and vulnerability to failure than most people feel. Good traders also had low anxiety and vulnerability scores on personality tests. People who tested for high orderliness ratings were inclined to systematic trading styles so the test helps you figure out what style of trading you

might follow. Also, people with high excitement scores tended to overtrade, especially if they also tended to be overconfident. If the test showed that you had these qualities then you should make it a personal rule to avoid leveraging, pyramiding and overtrading.

There are also a couple of other different types of personality test. If you search on the net for "winning personalities for traders" then a couple of these tests will come up and they are all much and much the same. You will get a certain cross-section of personalities that make better traders and others that don't.

The thing for me is that I think you need to suit your personality to the methodology you are going to use. For example, if you are an architect or an engineer with a need for certainty then you might be better off with a mechanical system simply because at least under certain conditions it is going to give you the same trade. The important thing you have to be careful with is the assumption that the technical conditions upon which the system was founded are actually still valid, right? That's the first thing I would say.

Secondly, the retail trader tends to want to use the system for every type of trend. However, the professionals that I know who trade mechanically will first define the trend and then apply the system to it so they are not actually using the system to enter, exit and manage the trade or whatever. They are first defining the trend and then saying, "Okay, this system is good for an uptrend so I'm going to use it there. This other system is good for a sideways trend so I'm going to use it there." They are not trying to use one system to trade all types of trends. That's if you are someone who needs a lot of certainty in mechanical systems as support.

Other people are probably a cross-section who can normally follow rules. However, in certain situations, like the crash of 1987, when the market is crashing down and the rules say you should buy, this guy is not going to do it because as far as he's concerned it just doesn't make sense. He is a cross between the mechanical systems trader and subjective methodology trader.

Then of course you have the people who are in the pits and just pure gut feel traders. They tend to be disappearing now. So you've got those three types of traders. You've got to find what your personality is and try to find an approach that suits.

And there I think that you might go into the "deliberate practice" of Anders Ericsson to achieve trading excellence. He taught this model of learning how to acquire new information and how to turn that information into skill. One of his pre-conditions is that you really need a coach because a coach gives you the needed feedback that is so essential to his model of learning.

I tend to agree that even if you don't get a professional coach you need to learn off one another so what I do to my students is put them into groups after a course. Some of them keep going with it and some of them don't, but the ones that have stayed in a group will come back with really good stories.

I'm going back to Singapore and I'm going to visit some of the groups. The last time I was there, which was about three months ago, the groups were coming back with really good stories about how just talking about their trades within the group made so much difference to them. They use the group as a coach, but not professional coach. I think you can put it that way.

In general you have seen many stories of ordinary traders. How much money do people usually need to start trading and how much should they risk? What are the general rules that they always

mess up and what rules should they always follow in general? I'm looking for some general principles we can give to people.

First off I need to say that the traders of today, except for the Americans, have this great advantage called contracts for difference or CFDs. I know they had them in London, but I'm not sure if that's still going. However, certainly in the Far East the contracts for difference allow you to trade almost with any amount.

For example, if you are trading $1 million in foreign exchange then 100 pips is $10,000. If you are trading $100,000 then 100 pips is $1,000. We can go down to micro where 100 pips is $10 so with CFDs you are now able to adjust the size of the contract to allow you to meet your capital base. This is unlike when I first started trading futures. We had no choice … the S&P was $500 a point and that was it.

I know CFDs are illegal in the United States. I think it's because they don't want to compete with the exchanges, but I assume that there is no rule preventing the Americans from opening an account with a foreign CFD house. I know that you are not allowed to trade them within the United States because they banned the license and they're illegal.

CFDs mean you can start with a very small account.

A very small amount so let's go back to what is required. Again, it's a question of the volatility of the market, the tick size, and then with what you've got in terms of your track record. Let's assume you've never traded before, absolutely never traded before, and you have no history so you can't look at your win rate or average win so you're going to have to look at the market conditions.

One of the best things that I found for that is the old turtles formula, which basically said to take a percentage of the capital you are prepared to lose and divide it by the dollar value. They use a 14-day ATR but you can substitute other measures according to the same concept. For instance, you have 2% you are prepared to lose divided by the 14-day ATR dollar value and that will tell you the maximum number of contracts you can trade. Then you look at your stop that you put in, and whatever is the smaller of the two is what you are going to use for position sizing.

If you adhere to that, which is a pretty conservative approach to position sizing, then you won't ever blow the account assuming that your account has an edge, your trading plan has an edge. That's the other thing, but as far as the money management is concerned the position sizing is really critical.

The other thing you have got to be careful with is that when you are trading a wide range of instruments you need to set a total portfolio risk amount. I always say that you probably don't want any more than half of your average return per annum as a portfolio risk, so if you're making 15% per annum then you don't want a portfolio risk that is more than 6% or 7%. If you've never traded before then about 6% would be good if you're using a 2% risk on each trade. Three times your normal size is what I would put as portfolio risk.

The other thing that people don't think about is when to add the profits to and when to subtract the losses from your capital base used in the calculation. The reason I say that is because if you just risk 2% of your capital you are always going to risk the maximum amount at the peak of your capital base and the reverse is true at the low by definition.

I think you should stagger the amount when you add your capital. You don't add it straight away and similarly you don't deduct it straight away from the losses. You have to reach a certain level. Those are the sorts of things that I would consider in terms of money management.

I read someplace where you said that about 90% of traders are going to lose money because they are not committed to trading. They are just caught up in the glamour or excitement of it so if they don't try to improve themselves and their method then they'll eventually run into losses.

That's certainly true and unfortunately that was true when I was trading. In the trading educational field we also pander to this, especially in Singapore. You need to be committed to the idea that trading can make you wealthy, but it's going to take time. You're going to have to use the compounding of profits over time to generate the wealth. You're not going to get wealthy overnight and you're going to need a capital base to start. The larger the capital base when you start the better the chances of turning that into a large number of dollars over time.

I think they need to do those two things. It's going to take time to become wealthy and it's going to take effort. It's not going to just happen. As I said, trading is the most difficult occupation in the world so newbies have to come in with that expectation. When I do coaching and look at the questionnaire I like to give, if they don't pass that understanding requirement that they must be prepared and committed to putting in a fair bit of time then I'll knock them back. I won't take them as students.

The other thing that might be surprising is that I won't take an individual on as a student if they don't have any pain about not making it. They have to *hate* not getting to where they want to go. For me it's not just wanting to get there, not just having to commit to get there, but what about failure?

When it comes to motivation, what people don't realize is that motivation is comprised of four parts, not two. You've got the pleasure of success and the pain of not getting there, but there is also the other side of that. There is the pleasure of not achieving it. If I don't take any action then there are things I am not going to have to give up whereas if I'm going to become successful I'm going to have to put in time, effort, and money. Well, if I don't take any action then all of that time can be used for something that I might really enjoy. That's one thing.

Then there is the pain of taking action as well. There's usually fear. To get from point A to point B you usually have three or four fears that are going to block you from doing it. If we don't do it then we won't have to confront these fears. So you need to look at the pain-pleasure equation from four angles and that is what is really critical.

Going back to what I was saying, if someone doesn't hate not getting to where they want to go - where failure is not an option - then usually trading knocks them out. The path is just too difficult.

They need that and motivation as well?

Yes, they need both sides. They need to want to be successful and they need to hate to fail.

You know an exceptional trader is regularly making over 25% a year. Warren Buffett has a fifty-year rate of return that is better than 20%. Do people ever come to you with an idea that is just outrageous for what they think that number should be?

Absolutely, and let's be fair to Warren. He's trading billion of dollars. I'm nowhere near that. I'm not in that league. I always believe that it's easier to make a return on your capital when it's smaller in size. Once you get to a certain amount it's hard to generate a decent return because of the size and so on.

But going back to your question, yes, too many. As I said I'm speaking to about five hundred people and I will swear to you at least half of them are going there thinking they are going to make a lot more than what is realistic.

I'll give you an example. I was in Sydney not long ago giving a talk to newbies and I said, "What do you think is a reasonable return?" I was speaking with a whole bunch of newbies. One guy said, "I only want to make 10%." I said, "That's just amazing. Well, 10% over what time frame?" He then told me that he meant 10% a day. I said, "10% a day? How many days are you going to trade?" He said, "I'm going to trade only 100 days per year because I don't want to work any more than that." Okay, all right. They do come with some very unrealistic expectations.

What return percentage is it that you think most people believe they are going to achieve through trading?

Well, it really varies. I've got people who think they're going to double their money over twelve months and 100% is quite common. I've had as much as 100% a quarter. They think it's quite reasonable.

Why don't they realize that no mutual funds or big traders can make that much? Is that because they're just ignorant of the field?

I really can't answer that question. I wish I could say it is just ignorance but it's like, "Yeah, I know that happens for other people because sometimes their size is too big." Generally it is as if it doesn't exist for them. They're living in a world of their own, that's what they are going to do and no rules apply for them because they know that they can do it.

From your experience is it true that most people in general want to get rich too quickly from trading?

Yes, too quickly irrespective of how much they start with, irrespective of the size of their capital base. About four years ago I was talking to a group of very wealthy traders that a broker had brought me in to see because he was concerned that these guys were losing so much money that they were going to blow their accounts. They were very, very good clients. One particular man that I was talking to had lost around two and a half million Aussie dollars in about six weeks and when we talked about changing he said, "Well, I'm not going to change. I can afford to lose and it's just going to be a question of time. At least I know that if I don't change then this is the path that's going to be there, but if I change I'm going to face uncertainty."

I said, "But look at your results. If you keep trading like this then next month you'll be out another two and a half million dollars." "No, It's just going to change," he said.

That's the mindset they come with and this includes people with big dollars. They weren't small $10,000, $5,000, or $2,000 accounts so the dollar amount doesn't come into it. You think people with large amounts of money would have more sense, but they don't.

That's the type of person who wants to succeed, but there's no pain for failing by losing money?

Exactly.

Well, do these people have the wrong methodology, lack emotional control or are they jumping from one method to another without giving methods a chance to work? What are you finding are the big problems with traders?

Well the biggest problem is to me the expectation. They want you to talk about emotional management because they don't seem to come into it. They are looking for a methodology that promises them they will make money without any effort and capital. When they learn that the market can bite by then it's too late. They lost all their capital.

I told you my story early on because I was in that boat. I just didn't know any better and in my day the people weren't telling me. Nowadays there are some really good people yelling it from the rooftops, but people don't want to hear this. They come into the markets and they are looking for this Holy Grail that other people are selling to them. Then they say, "Okay that didn't work," but they still have capital so they'll go somewhere else. However, they didn't really change because they are still looking for that easy win.

Yet people are saying, "Look, that's not the way to go. This is what you have to do. It's going to take effort. Don't trade big relative to your capital size, and get down to micro levels to make sure that you can actually make money before you start putting real hard dollars at risk."

Well, what's the point of trading a micro account where if I lose 200 pips it's only $20? Well, it's not the money. It's showing what you can do. If you can make consistent money on twenty bucks at $10 a hundred pips then once you show me you can make that money you can put in your hard-earned. But they don't want to do that. They want to start making money from day one.

Is there a course to take, methodology to use or book people should read to help learn or achieve that emotional balance? I'm really curious because you really have been through this and I haven't heard this type of information from other traders or investing professionals.

The educators out there - at least the ones that I know - will tend to say the same thing. They are telling newbies that you need to put in the time and you need to put in the effort to master trading. It's something that won't just come naturally. I don't know that it's not being told.

Yes, but for instance you mentioned some things like ACT and so forth. It's shining through everything you've said that you have really done a lot of work on how you should manage fear, stress and the emotional aspects of trading. You've really worked hard on yourself in those areas. You've found several specific psychological or therapeutic models to help you personally conquer things and most people aren't usually mentioning those.

The short answer to that is that this is just my nature. I don't know of anybody who is actually doing this even in my area of the world, right? I've always gone outside my sphere to pursue this.

I'm just reading a book called *The Mental Disciplines of Forex Trading*, and the author is going through the traits you need. He says you need confidence, you need emotional stability and he goes with a general description, but my mind immediately says, "Okay, that's all very well but how do I get there? What specifically do I have to do in order to get from point A to point B?"

Exactly, that's what I want to know. You sound like you worked that through on how to get confidence, as an example, whereas most coaches usually just say you need confidence. I'm looking for hints I can pass on to traders and investors about the roots of that emotional mastery process.

Okay, the only roots that I can give you are that (A) I love to read and (B) I will pursue that. For me the internet is a godsend because if I think of a question I can go on the net and it will come up with an answer. Whether that's the answer I want I don't know until I try, but I have tried a lot of stuff.

ACT came up because someone said something about fusion. I've never heard of the word "fusion." It's one of the concepts of ACT where we become one with our thoughts. It becomes our reality. Our thoughts become our reality, if I can put it that way.

An example is that you're watching a horror movie and you get really scared. *You're in there*. You're the person to whom that horror is applying. That's when you fuse with your thoughts.

If you're talking about trading there's a very funny video you can find on the web. A day trader went long on a Friday and it was the time that a Softgems trader found that he was illegally trading so they were dumping S&P futures on the market because they were just getting rid of the position. This guy refused to get out of his day trade the night before with a one-point loss or whatever it was, and then the market just kept falling in the night session. This guy had televised himself and he's swearing and saying, "F this and F that" and throwing the chair. He's televised all of this and he's refusing to get out of the position. I'm thinking to myself, "Why don't you just hit the exit button? Just get out of the trade."

From the video I recognized the platform he was using. He was trading with Interactive Brokers and you could see his account deteriorating as the market was going down and instead of hitting the exit button he's just swearing and jumping up and down. That's what I call "fusion with his loss." He just wasn't going to be able to take any action.

That's how I came across ACT. One of its major principles is that you should look at thoughts as thoughts, not as reality. You notice the thoughts but you don't get caught up in them. That's the way my mind works.

Have you found any other big psychological bodies of knowledge or research that can help traders?

Yes. ACT is unique in where it stands, but when it comes to the kind of mental state and the practices you need to apply then certainly deliberate practice is in getting the knowledge. When you are trading then Mihaly Csikszentmihalyi's book, *Flow,* has some pertinent information, but there's a guy Steven Kotler who wrote the book, *The Rise of Superman*. That's quite a new one. He's actually taken this a lot further.

Kotler is suggesting that what we need is to have certain brainwaves - binaural brainwaves - operating at the time before, during, and after a trade and I do use that a bit. You can download these free binaural things. You could prepare for your trading with these things in your ears, while you're trading it keeps you focused, and after the trading where I'm reviewing my trades it helps me make my analysis.

That's something else I would recommend. Kolter's book is called *The Rise of Superman*. It's very, very well written and if you take a little bit of trouble to try and implement his suggestions you will actually be very, very well rewarded for it.

He's listening to binaural beats before and after the trade?

Before, during, and after the trade … especially for day traders.

I'm familiar with the technology but I've never heard of anybody doing that. That's cool. Let me now ask you one of my favorite questions. If you were a genie and you could wave your magic wand to go back in your life and change something about just trading, how would you change things?

Well, just for the trading I would want to have – not so much for me - what traders have today, which are what I call "genuine educators." There was just too much "get rich quick" when I first started trading. It cost me too much money. I'm not denying my responsibility for it, but there was just nothing available. I had to fly to the States and it was just luck that I caught Pete Steidlmayer's little thing on Market Profile.

If you were a genie and you could wave your wand and eliminate the bad habits of traders or improve really good habits, what would you do for them?

If we could I would say to come into the markets with very, very clear expectations of what is possible and what is not possible. People talk about "you have to have big goals." One of the things about New Age goal setting is that you have to have big goals. If you don't have big goals then you are never going to reach the stars.

The problem for that sort of approach is that the big goals may be well beyond your skill level. It's all right to have big goals if you realize that you don't have that skill and you are going to have to work towards it. Too many people, when it comes to trading, had big goals without looking at where they actually are.

You know the next step to setting goals is, "Where am I relative to where I want to go and what do I need to do to get there?" People don't ask that question. They're being sold on ideas like in *The Secret* where you just visualize what you want to do and God will deliver it to you. Life doesn't work that way so if I had a magic wand the thing I would do is give them reasonably realistic expectations.

Let's look at this another way, and then I want to get to your life lessons in general. A lot of people are failing at trading but you're not failing at it anymore. Why is it that you are succeeding and what do you do differently that they don't do? What are you doing since it's not necessarily the system you use.

No, it's definitely not the system though to me the system is important. I say that mind, method and money are important where there is multiplication between each of these factors. You are only as strong as your weakest link, and systems methodology is important because without it you don't have an edge and then you are not going to make money no matter how well your money management or how well your psychology is, but for me the system is the easiest part of trading success.

I think the hardest part is this. I've always been someone who hates to lose. Let me answer it in this way. When I was a kid I used to play badminton a lot. I played a lot of badminton from a very early age. From around ten or twelve years old I was playing against the adults. I was playing the junior championships in Hong Kong and of course I would initially get thrashed. I thought I was pretty good, but you're playing an adult and you're a ten-year-old child. I used to absolutely hate losing and my dad said to me that it's okay to hate losing but you need to learn from it. You just can't keep doing the same thing over and over again and not learn from your losses. I eventually became the youngest junior badminton champion in Hong Kong. I think I was about sixteen, fourteen, or fifteen at the time.

I was lucky I had a role model that taught me the right lessons. The reason I think I succeeded was because of that. My mind can be very slow at learning when it comes to trading. It took me seven years but eventually I did learn. I had the good fortune to find someone who would give me the time and the means to learn what I needed to learn, but I had to contribute to it. I contributed with commitment and with the continuing effort to change whatever was not working so that to me is the story. I persist, I'm committed, and if something is not working then I will change. I may not find it straight away but I will continue changing until I find what I need.

What about for other people? If they don't have trading coaches, which is what I recommend, what fewest books would you tell them to turn to if they're newbies or even if they have been trading for a while but want to improve their skills? What are the fewest great ones or useful ones or whatever?

Unfortunately there are no good books out on Steidlmayer's new Market Profile. Pete is not an author. If you wanted a really good book on traditional Market Profile, which uses the 30-minute bars that are still useful for day trading, there is Jim Dalton's *Mind Over Markets*. That's a wonderful book.

For me Wyckoff was a lifesaver, certainly, so anything on Wyckoff. There is a book by Hank Pruden on Wyckoff. That is an excellent book.

There is a recent book I mentioned by Dr. Gary Dayton, *Trade Mindfully*, which I would recommend for psychology. He's a good author, he writes well and I love the material that's in there.

In terms of risk management there is not a lot out there. I can't say I could recommend a book on money management. None of the books that I've read cover what I would consider the essential aspects of it so I would have to leave it with those three books.

There are a lot of good books and a lot of great books but those are the three books that I think will give students the best bang for their dollar.

What about in terms of finding the trend of the market or a system? Are there any books you would recommend for that?

The Wyckoff method is really a complete methodology, but the main disadvantage of Wyckoff is that he doesn't define the timeframes. He talks about short-term, long-term, intermediate-term and that's all very well but what does it actually mean, right? So that's his weakness, but take that away and it's a complete system.

It will show you what is a trend - how to define a trend - and shows when that trend has come to an end through his change in trend patterns. You'll define the zones, define the setups and you'll define what I called triggers, entry bars, and targets. All that is in the Wyckoff methodology so it's probably one of the most complete methodologies around.

You had also mentioned Joseph Hart when you were talking about how you developed the Barros Swing.

Yes, Joseph Hart. "Trend Dynamics" is the name of the course so it's not actually a book. He is also very good. It was very good. I got a lot of ideas from there as well when it came out.

Okay, let's wrap it up. What do you do with the money you make from trading? Do you recommend traders keep pouring it back into the markets or that they should take it out and use it for life, or once again invest it in stocks or real estate or something else? What are your life lessons on this?

I'm laughing at this because you might think that my life lesson is funny. When I first started trading one of my biggest fears was that I'd go bankrupt when I started to make money. So essentially the way I have it organized is that Chrisy gets 85% of the income and I get 15%. Out of that 85% she gives me back 20% to replenish my capital base and she keeps the rest. She is the one that does all the other investments. She and her sister recently brought a property. I think it's the wrong time, but I have nothing to do with real estate. She basically takes care of the portfolio other than trading.

I would definitely recommend you take money out of your capital base. You don't want to keep pouring it in. I had a friend of mine who did that and it's a sad story because recently he got caught in that U.S.-Swiss thing. I don't know if you know that the U.S. dollar-Swiss rate collapsed big time and he actually committed suicide because of that so you don't want to go into that boat. You want to pull money out and then you want to live with it. You want to make sure that you enjoy life a little bit. You never know what life is going to bring. And then look after your wife. That's my model at the moment.

Lastly, when you give seminars and see all these people they probably ask you some common questions again and again. There has got to be something that irks you that you really wish you could get them to accept, but which never seems to click in their minds despite saying it hundreds of times. Now is your chance to bring this up.

Okay, well, let me just say this in public if I can and I've said it in private many times. You have seen speakers who get on stage, they finish their talk, and immediately are surrounded by a million people, right? This happens every time I speak and I guarantee you that the first twenty questions will be "I am in XYZ" or "I'm long the U.S. dollar" or "I'm short the U.S. dollar. I sold it at against the Aussie at 87¢ and it's now trading at $1.15. What do I do with the position?"

That is my pet hate because you know what I'm going to say. I've just been talking about it for over ninety minutes - how to cut your losses, don't let it go over to a certain amount, blah, blah, blah. But immediately after you've just spent ninety minutes talking about this they ask you this question that is begging for the answer, "Cut the loss."

But they'll then say, "I won't do it because I don't want to lose too much money." That's my pet hate. It's always the case. I'm not the only one who hates this. I talked with Joe DiNapoli after we had done a couple of gigs together and everybody has these things happen to them. People don't really want advice. They just want for you to tell them what they want to hear and when you don't they get pretty shirty about it.

I'm laughing because I've seen what you are describing dozens of times. Last question Ray is where can people find you and your trader education materials?

Sure. I'm on the web at www.TradingSuccess.com. The website has some articles and free materials such as the MIDAS method of technical analysis by Paul Levine, how to draw Barros Swings, information on the Wolfe Wave and market commentaries as well as other topics. The blog would be interesting to traders because it has explanations of some of the things we talked about.

You can also contact me at ramonbarros@tradingsuccess.com. My website has lots of articles, but you can also find my book, *The Nature of Trends: Strategies and Concepts for Successful Investing and Trading*, on amazon.com.

Thank you and best of luck. I hope I'm as sharp, successful and active as you when I also reach my seventies.

Thanks, Bill. It was fun.

Chapter 3
Eric Hadik
High Probability Trading

Eric Hadik, trader and expert market analyst at InsiideTrack.com, is the author of several trading newsletters that combine cycles, Elliott Wave, and Gann projections with historically proven technical indicators to come up with winning trades. Known for his ability to systematically combine both subjective and objective analysis, Eric has created a sequential hierarchy of indicators that trigger low risk, high probability trades. For those who like to combine various types of subjective analysis (such as cycles and Elliott Waves) together with objective tested market indicators, Eric offers a great model for how this can be done.

In this interview Eric reveals how he creates his unique trading plans and projections and provides valuable forecasts on his expectations for gold, the dollar and inflation for the 2016-2021 period. As reported in the press and as discussed in this interview, he points out that cycles suggest this period will be filled with financial turmoil.

Eric, let's start with how you got started in trading and investing. Also, what trading methods have you tried that got you to where you are today?

In getting started I took an interesting route. I guess a lot of people come across trading and investing from different angles. I was actually still in high school and my first big job was working at a grocery store, a meat-cutting store. After a couple years there I was a full-on meat cutter or butcher, and the owner of the store as well as a friend of his had both been dabbling in the silver market. This was very late '70s, early '80s and he had been trading in some Ginnie Maes, which you never even hear of anymore. They are long gone.

He knew that I had a head for numbers and really didn't know what direction I wanted to go after high school. He used to tell me to come in early, he'd grab *The Wall Street Journal* and he tried to share with me his very limited knowledge on futures. It didn't take long until I was hooked. I'd say that my first introduction to technical analysis was through the *Elliott Wave Principle* and other writings of Bob Prechter. I still greatly respect that approach to the market and I do have it as a backdrop for some of what I use. It has definitely been an influence all along.

Then I encountered an organization in Houston, Texas that was doing seminars on technical analysis. They had an approach that was termed a "cybernetic approach," but I guess you could use the term "synergy" or "synergistic approach." There was this idea of having multiple indicators that were already proven to have stood the test of time and therefore had some credibility and reliability. When they were converging - whenever there was a confluence of those indicators - that theoretically increased your percentage or probability of winning on a trade. That's where I really took a leap forward with technical analysis and many different aspects of it.

It's just been an evolution since then being introduced to many different technical tools. When it all comes down to it, it's also one of those things of really sticking with what works and pushing to the side what doesn't or at least what doesn't *for you* because there are some very valid technical tools out there which I found just did not work for the time frame I was approaching, for my own risk tolerance and because of other more personal aspects to my trading.

For some of those I just learned what I could learn from them and then pushed them to the side. Throughout this time there was a growing interest in cycles and that has probably continued to grow more than anything to get me to the point that I'm at.

Now I understand how you got started in cycles for which you are famous. You went through an Elliott Wave introduction to the markets and regular technical analysis using indicators and then you finally bumped into cycles analysis. Then you got into the cycles deeper and that's your major way of trading now, wouldn't you say?

I'd have to say even starting from my Elliott Waves introduction that cycles were at least in the backdrop of several of the tools and indicators I was studying. In fact, I also got introduced to the works of W.D. Gann a couple of years after my introduction to Elliott Wave, and Gann would be the one that really got me hooked on cycles.

I'd say my first couple years of studying half a dozen of his books - plus I also had his huge trading manual - those first couple of years I was more or less coming to the conclusion that I couldn't use any of it. It was either too general or too esoteric or too subjective in some respect, but I think it took coming back to Gann's work a second time after studying a lot of very specific technical indicators – ones that were very objective and very consistent – that I then began to see more of the things that he was trying to convey or he was conveying that I just wasn't quite getting. A lot of his work I think should be used as a backdrop or the foundation upon which to build a particular trading campaign. That's even how I use cycles. They set the stage for me. They are the foundation or underpinning, but I have to have very specific technical indicators corroborating those cycles before I'll do anything with the markets.

You have several newsletters that offer market forecasts based on your special way of combining everything together. Traders want to become like you, so can you speak a little bit about what you offer in those newsletters and how you do it so people can understand whether you are a short-term or long-term trader, and how you're putting together all the things you have studied in the trading sphere?

Sure. Actually, I'm not trying to be all things to all people, but we do offer basically three different publications. Each is tailored to a little bit different time horizon as far as the analysis and trends. The flagship publication is a monthly newsletter *InsiideTrack*, which addresses broader stroke, longer-term cycles. That publication, in addition to getting very specific with the markets, will also discuss a lot of other external cycles such as natural cycles and geophysical cycles. By that I'm referring to anything from earthquakes and volcanoes to other things that occur on a repetitive pattern but where it's hard to identify what that pattern is.

I will deal with cycles on a socio-economic perspective, and discuss geopolitical risings and fallings and bring that altogether into a practical "what can we do with this, how might this impact the coming months or years?" That's half the newsletter and the other half is taking it specifically to different markets that I follow. That publication covers a much wider swath of cycle analysis.

Then we offer a supplement to that if someone wants intra-month updates. There are at least three and sometimes as many as six or seven of those intra-month updates. They have a little bit more of an intermediate time horizon. Then the more frequently updated and more numbers-intensive publication, really the one that's the most popular, is the *Weekly Re-Lay*. That is published each weekend and then there is at least one intra-week alert, sometimes more depending on if much has changed in the analysis or if anything needs updating.

As I said, that is really just focused on the specific markets that we cover. Once in a while I may mention some of those broader cycles that are coming into play, but for the most part this is just addressing the technical indicators that are at work, what they're showing, and where they may be triggering a trading strategy or trading opportunity. Then there are many numbers listed for certain support-resistance levels and trends or points that I follow. It's very technical analysis in nature.

Is that for the futures markets or for stocks? What are the markets you cover?

Primarily it's the futures markets, but as you probably realize that covers so many arenas. Based on feedback we've gotten, I know that at least half of our subscribers are using the cycles and the signals in many other vehicles from just your basic stocks to ETFs to all different types of funds and interest rates and precious metals.

One of the primary futures arenas covered are the stock indexes and within that I'll give an analysis on the Dow Industrials, the S&P 500, and the NASDAQ 100. Then there is a page on interest rates that hits the 30-year bond, 10-year notes and also Eurodollars. There's one on currencies, another on precious metals and then on commodities. It's a pretty wide swath of the markets and as I said, we know that it is utilized far beyond just the futures signals that are given in there.

The *InsiideTrack* newsletter, the big one, is long-term oriented. You can use it for strategy because you are talking about geopolitics so a strategic person or position trader could use that, but if you're a more active trader you're probably more likely to use the *Weekly Re-Lay*. Does that sound accurate?

Exactly. That's a good synopsis of it.

You started with technical analysis and you studied Elliott Wave Theory, you studied Gann and you went into cycles. What are you doing now to arrive at trading or investing rules for recommendations? Your newsletter is very popular, so what exactly are you doing where people can say, "I understand that. I want to have somebody's information on that so I can use it."

Right. It is a multi-step process from my perspective. I have certain indicators and certain tools that I view as the big picture, the setting of the stage and the getting of the trend change points identified. Under that categorization I would include the cycles and a bit of Elliott Wave analysis I do. With Elliott Wave I repeatedly tell my readers that even when I mention a particular wave count or wave structure I'm not going to debate or even get into the intricacies of a whole wave. I want to know more about wave characteristics as opposed to wave counts.

That is something that I found very valuable in Elliott Wave analysis, which is knowing what each of those waves is going to do differently from the other. My goal, what I'm trying to get the subscribers to do is catch a third wave, which is recognized as typically the dynamic, accelerated wave that usually covers the greatest magnitude in price. I want to get into that early and try to ride it as long as possible. Once that is complete I am more content to save my ammunition and wait for all that noise to filter out in the consolidation where people often get burned if they are trying to trend trade. I'm looking to capitalize on that.

Again, that's one of those "set the stage" type of indicators, and some of Gann's work is the same. Once I have that then I've got different levels of technical indicators. There are some that show me, first off, overbought or oversold leading into that turning point. If I'm looking for a bottom I've got other corroborating indicators that say, "Yes, we've gotten oversold. We're starting to show some divergence at the lows." It's reinforcing from a little more objective standpoint what the more subjective analyses are showing.

Then I have a group of reversal technical indicators. Really just two primary ones but they are the ones that give me my initial trigger. That's where I've now seen the signs that a bottom is taking place in this example. It probably held some key support levels, which is another thing I didn't mention. This is the fact that there are also support and resistant zones that are applicable to the different time frames and the different parts of the trend so it all works together in synergy. I get that reversal signal and so that's the first entry point or first signal of looking for an entry point, but very quickly after that I've got a second level of triggers that are a little bit larger degree so that they can quickly confirm that this wasn't just a quick counter-trend signal. Then there is a third level of all-out trend reversal confirmation signals.

Once we get into a trade there are specific expectations, especially since in a lot of cases you are going against the major trend even though the minor and intermediate trends already started to show signs of reversing. Risk management is really one of the keys within that whole structure because a lot of people - when they think about something like cycles or even Elliott Wave to some degree – believe there is too much ambiguity as far as, "Okay, I think that the structure is this so I want to buy the market here, but where exactly do I identify if I'm wrong and it's time to get out?"

That's where I really see the value in a lot of the technical indicators that I use. It's this sequence of a multi-stepped process of getting a trend to change and also capitalizing on the moves in there. First, I'm looking for a short-term third wave thrust and then an intermediate-term third wave thrust on an accelerating or escalating level of trend and degree until I've got that move where I believe it's going to be something that lasts at least a few months and is the larger degree third wave from a trader's perspective.

You can have massive first and third and fifth wave impulses on a multi-year basis, but that gets very impractical from a trading perspective. I'm just looking for those things on the daily and weekly basis, and sometimes as a multi-month move that I want to capitalize on.

Let me try to summarize this so people can paint a picture in their mind. You use cycles, Elliott Wave analysis and Gann to come up with trends and change in trend points. Those are your three primary tools and you're using those to figure out major tops and bottoms so that you can come to a conclusion like, "Here's a safe entry" or "Here's a safe exit for this market." Is that right so far?

Yes.

In other words, we can say you do a lot of technical analysis work and you come to a conclusion like that. For instance, there might be a lot of cycles bottoming right now and an Elliott Wave analysis shows the price structure is a fifth wave down and the Gann shows us the proper timing for a trend change. Then you'll say, "Okay, this looks like we're going to have a trend change. It might be time to start buying." Then you actually get into the trade. For that decision you are going to switch to using proven technical indicators that must trigger in a sequential manner to confirm your conclusions. That being the case, what technical indicators have you found most valuable for the actual trade entry, such as at a low for longs or at a high where you want to short? What have you found are the most valuable ones that people should be following?

I've got a few reversal patterns that I rely on for the reversals that I have a higher confidence level in and I describe them in my work and in a technical trading manual that we offer for subscribers. One of those is actually a very simple price pattern called a "two-close reversal." It's a form of a key reversal, but the market has to take out the two previous closes in that reversal. That's very simplistic and that is only one kind of trigger point that I use. However, I use some price patterns like that and in particular ones that I have seen occur more often at tops and bottoms, which gets into a couple of the other ones like what I call a "double key reversal." I give some samples of these on my website so anyone can learn those.

They are some of the real preliminary signals that I'm using. However the thing that I rely on most to convince me a trend has changed - but also for trying to be in on the early facet of that trend change - is a proprietary indicator whose calculation I don't reveal. I simply call it my "daily trend indicator" and "weekly trend indicator." There are even specific characteristics of that which I explain.

I'll give the levels where it's going to be triggered and it's something where it has to go from down to neutral to neutral again and then to up. It can't go straight from down to up. That's all explained, too, in the technical manual that we offer and in some of my other work, but it is essentially a process of getting those initial reversal signals. I guess that really was your question there so I should stay focused on that.

Do you have a list of these tools or indicators like the two-close reversal, double key reversal and so on? Are there any others that you could add to the list?

At the initial preliminary signals I was referring to, those three sum up what I'm looking for right out of the gate in a trend reversal. This is where these technical indicators, combined with wave characteristics, really help me when the two work together. The synergy there is so valuable to me. What I mean by that can be understood by my trend indicator that I just described and how it has to go from down to neutral on at least two daily signals. It has to go to neutral before it can even reverse to up. What I have seen and I explain in different ways is that if the wave structure has turned - if you're going into a new impulse wave structure – you will get that full reversal pattern where the trend is down and then it goes neutral, it stays neutral again and finally turns to up, but that is not a signal to pile in. That's because often when it finally gives that confirming trend reversal signal that is the top of the first wave.

It's a real good honing element for Elliott Wave analysis, and then you are quick to enter the second wave correction. It's almost like you have gone as far as you should and now the markets want to test and see just how strong this trend reversal is. Often with that daily trend, once that indicator has turned positive the market will quickly go into a reaction. Often that trend will go neutral twice, but it will not reverse down.

When I get that whole formation, and then get one of these reversal signals off that first pullback (the most reliable is if I get a daily two-close reversal after the two neutral signals), that is one of the more reliable sequences that confirms to me, "Okay, we've just signaled that a second wave correction has taken place. Now it's time to enter a more accelerated third wave advance."

The same thing applies on a weekly basis with the weekly trend signal, but obviously it takes longer for that sequence to unfold. The same things holds even on a monthly basis. It is a sequence, which is really the best term I can use, of these signals that is important.

That point is also often a time when you get certain moving average techniques ready to roll over. That's because any moving average includes several past days in its calculation so it takes time for it to both flatten and to be in a position to turn up. Often this one and two wave sequence gives enough time for the primary moving average channel that I use to flatten out. That's another corroborating factor.

So you see this whole pattern and the synergy of it is what really keys me in to "Okay, I've now had multiple things telling me this is a second wave bottom. This is not the start of a new decline. This is where I really want to get a bit more selective about getting into the market, committing to it a little heavier than off of the initial low."

Eric, do you have any statistics on how successful this approach is? Is it usually 70% or 80% right when you have the confluence of all these things? Do you have any percentage numbers on anything in terms of how well it does?

Early on I had produced numbers on different indicators and how they worked - their success rates - but it was more when I started combining them that I saw you start to hone down. I do not have the exact statistics on the overall combination. That's what I will also say upfront with my work. It is about 75% technical and objective and about 25% subjective with some discretion.

It's that combination of all of them that works where each of the indicators had a strong enough reliability rate on its own to be factored into the whole trading plan, but I do not have the exact statistics on each one over the last few years.

I know you are looking for a confluence of factors setting the stage for a trade and you are using indicators to look for a confirmation. You also said you have a second and third level of indicators. What are they?

Really, the moving averages and a couple other lagging indicators are it. If I just identified the first and second waves on a daily chart along with the daily indicators then shortly after that the weekly trend indicator should then also reverse to up.

Part of it is also escalating the timeframe one degree and that's where I get an added level of confirmation, which is because I recognize where those indicators usually reverse within the structure of a trend.

Now when you are taking a trade are you putting everything on at the very beginning of the trade or are you scaling in slowly such as by putting one contract on initially and then others after further confirmations? How are you scaling the volume on your trades?

Right. I definitely advocate the approach of multiple contracts or multiple shares, whatever you may be using, for both entry and exit. When I'm entering I'm looking at a range of entry so I get the signal and I will look to put on roughly a third of the position very quickly or right away at those price levels. However, I also accept that in many cases there is a certain level of retracement after that because an even smaller first and second wave may be on the hourly chart.

I'm looking to enter at a range that is at and below the trigger point and roughly in thirds. I'll identify where that range is so I'm looking to enter a third of it near the top, a third near the middle, and a third near the bottom.

On the opposite side of exiting it is much different than that. I will look to exit a third of my position when the minimum objective - based on some of these indicators - is reached. At that point I don't have to have an actual sell signal there. Exiting is where I want to cover a quarter to a third of the position depending on how much it is, and if there is as much money management and risk control factored into that as there are technicals and trends. Essentially I would be looking to exit a third of the contracts or shares to where now the risk point on the remaining two-thirds, even if they weren't yet into where they should trigger profits, has now taken enough out of this trade that barring any unforeseen things in the market the overall trade should be profitable even if the trend stops at that point and just retraces or you realize that you're wrong on the bigger expectations. That's where the first third is exited.

Then the second third needs to hit and give an initial reversal signal - a short-term reversal signal - and there are trailing stops coming up the whole way, too, so sometimes that is what triggers the remaining exit.

As long as most of the indicators are still valid - still showing what they were showing at the onset - the final third will be held as long as possible with trailing stops narrowing as the market accelerates higher. That narrowing is based on specific indicators and price levels of previous or trailing lows and supports.

When most people are doing this type of analysis that combines subjective and objective factors it's easier for them to understand getting in at bottoms rather than shorting at tops even though shorts and longs are opposites. Granted that in most markets the declines can look and act entirely different than the run-ups, do you approach tops in the same way as bottoms? Does your cycles, Gann and Elliott Wave approach with technical indicators lead you to treat shorts differently than longs?

I approach tops and bottoms pretty similarly, but addressing your question the thing that I am looking at with extreme tops and bottoms is this - I'm looking to try and still be in a short position and covering that short at the bottom, not necessarily initiating longs. Same thing with a top, meaning that if I'm really trying to hone in and get a precise top picking mentality - which can be a very dangerous approach – it is to exit longs and then wait for more of that first and second wave sequence to unfold.

For the most part, I'm so much more comfortable buying the second low or selling the second top than the first one. One of the key things is that you have also got a very clearly defined risk level where you are going to be wrong. If you have seen a bottom form and you have seen an initial rally and a pullback then if that is a two-wave low by Elliott standards it shouldn't take out the previous low. Maybe it will give a quick spike.

Sometimes you have some kind of divergence rules there so you want to give yourself a little bit of room, but if it gives a close below that previous low then something is wrong in your interpretation or in the signals. Even the technical indicators are not right all the time, not even close. It's a numbers game. You have to accept that. That's why I would much rather be buying a secondary low.

In addition to that, in most cases if you are looking for the dynamic move, if you're looking for your money to do the most efficient work in the shortest amount of time then you want to be close to that third wave acceleration point. If you bought the exact bottom – and I've seen people who do really get lucky and buy really close to that exact bottom - then you get that first wave rally. Things then look great. Then all of a sudden you get the second wave pullback, which sometimes can be 75-80% of the first wave advance. Often with that approach the trading gets stopped out and maybe with some small profits right near the secondary low, which is where I want to be entering.

It also means that you have had a lot of extra time to be sitting in this market. Most people have a limited amount of capital so it's devoted in different areas at different times based on what the markets are showing. I want to utilize that capital efficiently and buy those secondary lows where I feel the acceleration point is much closer in time. I've got the more clearly defined risk points and there are a lot of factors going in my favor at that point.

Buying bottoms and selling tops - I think they are both dangerous. Like you said, the selling top can be a more precarious thing. I guess in theory you could say with buying a bottom that a market can only go to zero but with selling a top there is infinite upside risk theoretically speaking. It is also that markets do act more violent at parabolic tops which is why you get things like a saucer bottom that takes much longer to unfold whereas with a top like that it may take a while before a full-blown downtrend kicks in after that. However, you are going to have really big sharp moves coming off of a parabolic top.

In summation to your question, I'm looking to be exiting existing positions at those precise tops and bottoms, not entering shorts at precise tops and buying entering longs at precise bottoms.

I got you. Let's try to make this more concrete for people. Suppose there is a market that you are not trading - like bananas - and that there is a bananas futures contract available. Let's then say somebody gives you twenty years of banana price data and they want you to come up with a forecast or trading strategy on this using your subjective-objective technical analysis combination approach. What would be your steps? Walk me through what you would actually do with that price series.

It would be first distinguishing between monthly, weekly and daily trends and seeing what each of those are showing. Really the first thing I look at when I pull up a chart that I'm not familiar with is this trend indicator I use. That's because I want to see in particular whether the daily and weekly charts are in up, down or neutral trends. That is going to really determine what I'm trying to do over the coming days or weeks and that is also a little different than a big long-term forecast.

I want to start to set up this sequence of the hierarchy of indicators that I use. If I've got a weekly trend that has turned up and is pulling back and the daily trend is down right now, the first thing I'm still doing is looking for these indicators to give me the go-ahead to start formulating a trade. Therefore that daily trend would have to reverse back up before the weekly trend could turn down. Then once I get that then now I'm starting to take it to the next lower degree.

Distilling it down, the simplest thing is looking for a sequence of one and two waves and preparing for a third wave, but the key is that I've got several technical indicators that have taken the guesswork out of that for me. Again, it doesn't mean they are always right, but they are objective. They tell me, "This is where it has now signaled that a two-wave bottom is forming. This is where it is signaling to get into the market. This is where it's telling you that you would be wrong if this is not a valid signal."

I would start by looking at the trends and also any noticeable cycles. To explain the cycles I use a couple of approaches to cycles as well. One is using some very established time-tested cycles and another is by observation and analysis to see what particular daily cycles have really impacted that particular market over the last two, three or six months. By just running some quick analysis on a market like that you will often see a particular cycle that is governing the market during the current time frame. By combining the cycle work with the technical work - by looking for the trend indicator to turn - that kind of puts things into the category of, "Okay, this is a market where now we are looking for the next level of signals to actually trigger a trade."

Again, it's that multi-step process where I'd be first and foremost looking at the trend indicator, and then once that gives me the go-ahead I'd be starting to look for the sequence of indicators to kick in.

Do you have any numbers on how successful your method of trading is?

I don't have any that I publish. Actually, another key thing concerns what you were mentioning early on about what I learned from trading. One of my first exposures to trading was a man who was trading just the bond market at the time. I watched his system and saw how he was approaching it. When he spit out the numbers his trades were right about a third of the time.

That's a typical statistic for trend following from my own experience creating systems and futures funds on Wall Street. If you have a 5-to-1 or 7-to-1 profit/loss ratio then that low percentage doesn't matter. You will still make a lot of money.

That is exactly it. On the bonds, his average winner was either 31 or 32 ticks and his average loser was about 6 ticks. From an emotional standpoint a lot of traders couldn't handle taking losses that frequently or that many. Just looking at it most would be saying, "Why do I want a system that is accurate or has winners only 30% or 40% of the time?"

Then I also was exposed to some systems and indicators that claimed 80% reliability or accuracy. I'd start to really peel back the onion there and saw that the accuracy came from the following. There may have been certain lines from a grid that was on the chart and the system rules were that if it crosses this line there was an 80% accuracy rate that prices would cross the next line. Crossing the line meant the price is supposed to reach the next one, but then when you determine what crossing that line meant it means the price has to close above the line. Sometimes when it closes above the line it is already 75% of the way to the next line or next trigger point.

Therefore, when you would take that "80% accurate system" down into realistic trading and theory into practicality, it blew up. The 20% of the time when it was wrong - because there was this very broad "keep holding on" until the thing shows that you are convinced you're wrong - often those trades would wipe out a dozen or so previous trades.

That's the problem with "high reliability trading." You can get a system with 95% accuracy but just one of those "5% of the time it is wrong" moves could be so big that it absolutely wipes out all of your profits. The reason I was asking the question was a lead-in for the following question. You are using thinking to combine subjective and objective trading styles, which is something many traders and investors aspire towards. What they would want to know is why you think you are succeeding at this while others are failing? What are you doing that is different? What are the lessons for others concerning absolute do's and don'ts for this style of trading and investing?

I think that there are a couple of answers to that. These answers would come under the heading of principles or philosophy as opposed to a specific "buy at that point" or "sell it at that point."

One of the principles is to definitely know your own strengths and weaknesses. One of the analogies I've used in some of my writing is that it is like having two people in real estate where one is doing small residential homes and getting nice little commissions on a consistent basis while the other does commercial real estate and really focuses on building stadiums or something. Even if he's sitting there and hasn't been able to build a stadium for six months and the other guy has been doing really well, the guy building stadiums doesn't have to worry about what the residential guy is doing who is taking consistent little bites out of the real estate market.

I've seen the parallel to that in trading where you'll get someone who starts to trade one approach, perhaps an approach that's more effective during consolidation like swing trading. The market breaks out into a big trend and they see someone who just made a killing on a particular trend trade. All of a sudden they are questioning their own approach.

The trend trade involves a lot more patience. It usually involves higher risk. When you are swing trading it's kind of smaller bites and smaller risks if you are proportionally setting up your risk and potential reward like it should be done.

In trading you really have to stick with what you have found to be not only effective but also within your mentality, your structure, even your available time. Someone who is only available to look at the market for an hour or half-hour per day shouldn't be worried about the day trading successes that they are reading about somewhere. They should be focusing on something that is more conducive to their available time, their risk tolerance and even the size of their account.

That's one key thing and within that what I have really become comfortable with is the fact that there are going to be some big trades I miss. If I miss them because my indicators did not line up like they should have or this one just was triggered without the perfect scenario lining up, then okay. That's part of what I accept with my trading discipline, which is that old adage, "I'd rather be on the outside looking in than on the inside looking out." This is better than jumping into trades impulsively because you see something over there but it didn't set up your whole systems scenario like it should. More often than not you are going to get to a point where you're in that trade and wishing you had never taken it.

You have to be comfortable with one or the other. There are some people who say, "I don't want to miss a big trade no matter what." That's one entirely different approach to trading. I personally want to be keeping my risk at a reasonable level. I have a more conservative risk approach so I want to be keeping that clearly defined and at a reasonable level and still setting myself up for the most possibly successful trades. However, when a big trade goes by and I'm not in it then I'll try to see if there is anything that maybe should be tweaked for the next time around, but it would take many of those instances to even consider tweaking it.

I'll see if there is anything that can be learned from that and then just dismiss it because there is another winner around the corner every day. I'm not chasing the hot money. Often you'll have traders hearing, "Okay, just in the last couple of months gold and silver have been really hot. They've had some big swings while the grain markets have been just consolidating near their lows." If you're focused on grains or if your indicators are telling you grains are building a base and getting closer to that point where they are going to be entering a more accelerated move then don't worry if gold and silver are swinging and that didn't adhere to your plan. You must stick with your game plan and not worry about anything outside of that.

It goes back to that Jesse Livermore approach of being deaf, dumb and blind, which is really just being in the zone and blocking out the distractions. Really, that feeds into my overall approach of looking for these third waves.

By definition, if an Elliott Wave structure has really eight overall waves - five up and three down to be a complete structure - two of them have the characteristic of a third wave, namely the third wave on the way up and the C-wave on the way down. That's two out of eight waves. That's about 25% of the waves and they are often more accelerated so when you are talking about time there might only be 15% to 20% of the time spent in an overall trend. That's when I want to be focused on the markets and that's when I want to be trying to capitalize on them. When that market has shown that it has reached fruition I still monitor it looking for anything I didn't expect or for an extension that's being signaled. I'm starting to focus my attention on other markets that are in the formulation stage of getting ready to enter that third wave.

Let's go into your personal lifestyle. What are you doing everyday for analysis and trading? What services are you monitoring? What websites, platforms and subscriptions are you using?

The majority of what I'm assessing and analyzing in terms of data is just in-house. I wish I had the exact quote of Jesse Livermore, but I'm trying to block out all distractions and be deaf, dumb and blind to them as he said. I don't want to be influenced by a lot of the white noise out there. It's just very basic charts throughout the day and doing my analysis throughout the day. When there is a day or a point of the day where it is clear that nothing could be triggered then I'm turning my focus to some of the bigger picture research that I'm doing.

Are you using platforms like Thinkorswim or TradeStation to be monitoring all this stuff?

No. I just have my own system set up as far as data and analysis and charts. Then I will also utilize some online charting and data for comparative purposes just to make sure that it's all in sync. No, I'm not using TradeStation or Thinkorswim. By honing it down to some very specific and for the most part pretty simple technical tools I have done away with a lot of that. For years going back to the early days, whether it was the CQG terminal with dozens of available indicators and moving forward into TradeStation and some of your other choices, it was too much white noise for my approach.

One thing I have also tried to stress with my readers is that I am so much more interested in what the numbers are revealing. The charts give you an illustration of it, but if you don't know the actual numbers of what you are looking at on a chart then it becomes so subjective like with Elliott Wave or with other patterns: "Well okay, I see this flag pattern" or "I see this pennant pattern." It's almost a 50-50 shot whether that thing is going to resolve itself by accelerating back up into the uptrend it came from or whether it's a topping formation that is then going to break down. If you don't know the numbers going into it - and really my trend indicator is the first number that I'm referring to - then the charts become almost some distraction.

The very first thing I want to see is what the numbers are showing before I even pull up a chart. Has this particular indicator been triggered? Has this one been triggered? Then I will look at a chart as opposed to vice versa. I know that the majority of traders pull up the charts first and then start assessing things.

Yes, your approach is unusual.

That's not necessarily how the evolution went, but it's where I've gotten to at this point. Having seen enough charts for thirty plus years and knowing what they are reflecting it is by understanding the numbers.

You are going to compare this sometimes to a doctor looking at a read-out of any sort of chart. To most people it's a bunch of lines or blips, highs and lows or some numbers. The doctor knows first and foremost what they represent and what it means before looking at that chart. That is what is really key to me. I think a lot of people jump into the charting and start putting all these lines, channels, waves, fan lines and speed lines on it and so on. All of a sudden you can hardly even see the ticks on there because there are so many other lines.

Okay, so what if you're even right? What is it showing you? Is it just going to go to the next line that is two ticks higher? What is this telling you? I think that you need to put the charts in the proper perspective and know the proper sequence of when to rely on them.

A lot of people look at the charts and then they make their predictions based on the pattern of the chart or the cycles they find or Elliott Waves and so on. Can you make predictions on the future trend of a market from just the numbers? In other words, by looking at your numbers without the chart can you give a prediction of what a market is going to do?

You definitely have to use them hand-in-hand. I'm not by any stretch of imagination discouraging the use of charts or advocating not using them, but to me the first stage is confirming what that trend is. For instance, with Elliott Wave Theory what really started to veer me away from it was the subjectivity of a lot of the minor waves within a wave and what that means. When you are talking about projecting waves it is much simpler once I have the numbers assessed.

Let's say that I am in a trade and the daily, weekly and monthly trend have reversed up so that I've got very high confidence that this is an impulse wave. Let's also say that some other indicators confirm this which work hand-in-hand with that. Now the charts will certainly make it easier to see those turning points so you can then measure the distance of the waves and then project accordingly.

Again, it's an illustration of what the numbers are already saying. If the numbers identified what each swing point was and you could see the timeframe of them then yes, you could just as easily make those projections based on the numbers because really once you look at the chart you need to figure out what the corresponding numbers are anyway. If you are measuring a certain wave and you say the third wave is typically at least 1.618 times the magnitude of the first wave then you need to know the numbers of the low and high of the first wave, and the low of the third wave, to now project out what your first target is on the upside. You definitely have to use them hand-in-hand, but I choose to start with the numbers whereas I think that the majority of traders start with the chart.

In terms of predictions or projections I know that you believe 2016 will be a big year for gold. This is a good time to ask you for your predictions for the larger macro trends for commodities like gold.

That whole scenario with gold - and with actually a lot of things I am discussing at this point - was definitely starting from a really big picture scenario. Over the last six to eight years I have been increasing my focus and intensity on this time frame that we are in. The initial range I have always identified as 2013 through 2017, but within that time frame there were more specific times.

There is a consistent 40-year cycle that has been uncanny through the entire history of our country since 1770s. It even dates back well before that when you look at basically a struggle between currency, gold, silver and economic panics and crises in the last couple hundred of years. As to this consistent 40-year cycle, I was looking for a major transition point and a repetition of that cycle in 2013 to 2017 and then the big first phase stretching into 2021.

Within that, all of my work on some yearly cycles and some monthly cycles for gold was showing that we should be negative from 2011 down into the second half of 2015. During that time, since 2012 and 2013 I've been talking about 2016 being the "golden year," but to clarify that I'm not saying that gold is going to the moon in 2016. I was saying that I thought 2016 would be the first year that gold would start to see some sustained rallies and successive rallies instead of just rebounds. When you look back on it later then it would be what they identified as the turning point in gold.

With what you are asking as far as the longer-term projections, currently those projections are more cyclic in that I thought 2016 would be this big transition year. I thought we would see an initial pretty big advance and a decent pullback within that, and then 2017-2018 would be more when that third wave starts to take hold and you see an accelerated move up. I've only begun discussing in publishing some of the longer-term targets and objectives so right now I'm not comfortable discussing them until I've laid them all out for my readers, but from a timing standpoint I'm looking for gold to be really going through a wide bottoming phase in 2016 and then starting to accelerate up in 2017-2018.

I'm looking for the dollar to be peaking in this timeframe and entering a bit more of a crisis stage in the years to come. There are a lot of other things that correlate to that as well from financial panics.

There is even a 40-year cycle of food crises where you see sharp spikes up in price of at least a couple of food commodities. I'm not trying to put forth a sensational chicken little "head for the hills" type of thing, but there definitely is a consistent sequence of these types of events that I want my readers to be aware of.

We've seen that general prognosis in forecasts from other analysts. You were saying you'd expect the up move until about 2021?

Yes.

Did you say that the dollar is peaking now, or in 2017-2018, and afterwards is supposed to drop? Do you have any dates on the dollar trends that you could give?

The majority of my work looks for a final peak in the second half of 2016. There are a couple of technical signals that have been triggered recently that give me a little pause with that expectation such as it could be a secondary high later in the year as opposed to a final high. The majority of my longer term is still showing that the dollar has got another wave up and ideally the peak will be during the second half of this year. It may take some time to roll over to the downside before a real serious downtrend takes hold, but starting in 2017 you're looking more to the downside for the dollar.

Here again, to me it's uncanny how accurate this 40-year cycle has been as far as pinpointing these major seismic shifts in the dollar and in gold. If you even just take the most recent sequence of that 40-year cycle and look at the '70s, it started out with the gold shock in 1971 where Nixon shut the gold window for convertibility. It was exactly forty years after that event that gold peaked in 2011 right to the month basically - August 2011 is forty years from the August 1971 gold shock. In 1973 we had the collapse of Bretton Woods and by 1975 you had the dollar effectively being backed by oil. The year 1975 was when the whole of OPEC agreed to price oil in dollars. To me 1976, even though it's a subtler lesser-known event, was the real defining one which was the Jamaica Accord that basically decoupled gold from any of the fiat currencies.

That 40-year cycle helped pinpoint 2016 for me as a major turning point and really from July of '76 into early '80 is when gold saw the majority of its move. So here we are forty years later with gold showing signs of getting ready for another strong advance. As to the dollar, when you really look at the dollar compared to gold (pricing it in gold) that period from '76 to '80 was an all-out collapse in the dollar even though when it is just compared to other currencies that doesn't look nearly as serious.

So if gold goes up it would do so from now through to your 2020-2021 period, which is obtained by adding forty years to the 1976 to 1980 period? And it might come from individual cycles analysis as well?

When you go back to that sequence there are very consistent things that happened at specific years, and in most cases the whole shift stretched into the year one of the next decade. Even back in 1775, that was when we basically had our first experiment with fiat currency and the Continentals were issued. Almost out of the gate those Continentals started deteriorating in value and by 1781 (which is year "one" of the next decade) they were worthless and removed from circulation.

Then you went forward into the 1800s and you had the whole battle for the re-chartering of the second U.S. Bank. That came to its first culmination in 1816 when Jefferson, who was fighting against it, lost his battle. They re-chartered the bank and immediately you went into some financial and economic malaise and you had a panic in 1819. By 1821 that cycle was finally bottomed out.

Forty years later in the 1850s, you had the government reducing the silver content in coins so it was basically devaluing the currency. By the mid-1850s you had silver being suspended and then by 1861 gold was suspended. Forty years later in 1896 you have probably one of the biggest political battles over gold, the gold standard and the silver standard. Williams Jennings Brian was supporting the silver standard and giving his speech about, "You shall not crucify mankind upon a cross of gold." There was that whole battle.

Then there were two panics in the 1890s that led to 1901 when the gold standard was re-established. Again, you go forward to the 1930s and have gold confiscation, silver confiscation, a second panic and second recession in 1937 which, if it weren't for the events of 1929 and 1932, that recession is identified as the worst of the 1900s aside from the initial stock market crash and Great Depression. By 1941 was when the whole sequence was ending.

There is actually, if you look at it, also an overriding 80-year war cycle to be aware of going all the way back to 1781, which was the culmination and end of the Revolutionary War. The Civil War started eighty years later in 1861, and then we have our entrance into World War II at 1941, and next we have 2021.

There are multiple things that occur along with this 40-year cycle and just this very narrow window of time that is maybe seven or eight years each forty years. It has many of the same consistent characteristics from a dollar or currency, gold and silver battle to panics, economic crashes and crises. I could also rattle off each of the droughts, famines, and food crises that occurred in that same timeframe. I'm not saying necessarily that one is causing the other, but there is something very consistent that is creating this period of great turmoil.

Funny enough, I was reading more recently about even a 40-year cycle they have identified in the sun called the Great Conveyor Belt that influences the oscillations within the sun, sunspots, geomagnetic storms and the polarity of those storms. It's on a very consistent 40-year cycle, which would give you some rationale for the fact that these periods of upheaval are occurring on a very consistent 40-year basis and like I said, they go back well before the 1770s. I've listed and documented some of them as well.

I'm with you here on gold going up and the dollar going down just because of the fundamentals of the excessive debt situation, deteriorating debt quality, side-effects of QE finally hitting the street, and the push by China and Russia to replace the dollar and dollar based systems in world trade, particularly in oil trading. Do you see a hyperinflationary event coming with these trend forecasts or just a dollar debasement? Also, you mentioned that there you saw inflation cycles peaking. What's your synopsis for the general picture and timing of inflation in general?

I do expect to see some severe price inflation in specific commodities and probably in some natural resources. I think that it could be due to a combination of dollar issues as well as natural shortages, disruptions, or whatever that may be. Often even with those food shortages and food crises sometimes that is only a period of a few years. Many times it's only a couple of years period. However, depending on who you are and where you are a couple of years of that can either be deadly and dire, or can be a serious condition that you have to adapt to and make it through and out the other side by becoming wiser and stronger.

I think it's going to be both. I don't like to go too far in speculating on it because it does become that alarmist, sensationalist type of thing, but there certainly is a pattern and a synergy of events just over the last few years, which is really since the beginning of the 2013-2017 time frame I mentioned. That's when these events started kicking in, and they have a very similar theme. It's really about battling the global supremacy of the dollar.

When you look at 2013 and 2014 you have the BRICS Bank or the BRICS nations announcing and starting their new development bank. Then at the same time you have China getting together with many of the Asian powers and starting the Asian Infrastructure Bank. At the same time Russia started the Eurasian Economic Union. For each of these institutions, one of the stated goals was to offer alternatives to a lot of other countries, alternatives to the IMF and the World Bank that basically is the U.S. and Europe and a few other industrialized countries. That's where the influence and the power come from.

You've got this steadily intensifying battle that is still far from its tipping point. It doesn't really appear on a lot of people's radar, but there is also a momentum there and a trend there. It's like a saucer bottom where it's slowly developing this bottom and you want to be ready for it if and when it enters that parabolic stage because if there comes this point where there is enough synergy among competing nations then you will have trouble.

You can even look at the topics coming up in the election debate right now. At least one primary candidate is talking about how we are going to restructure every deal. We're going to tell China to go do this and that with their deals. Well, it's a two-sided affair there and when these nations, whom you think you're going to just tell to go stuff it, hold a lot of your debts and there is a symbiotic relationship there then you better be careful about the unintended consequences.

A lot of these nations have at least set the foundation for their own attempts to level out the economic and currency power around the world. If you ever got to the time where there was just even the inkling that they could be somewhat successful and that even if it were just a basket of currencies that started to replace the dollar as the global reserve currency then trouble is around the corner. That is one of those tipping points where the day before you are still thinking everything is okay even though there are some struggles and then all of a sudden the masses accept that, "Oh, wait a minute. There is a shift that has been going on. Now we realize it." Then everyone tries to head for the exit doors at the same time. That's the type of thing that I am certainly staying attuned to. I'm trying to keep aware of all the signs both on the charts in all the markets combined, and also in the fundamentals and in whatever developments and announcements are coming out around the globe.

Great. I was trying to get the dates for when you thought price inflation was big within that 2021 period. Is that within there as well?

I think that inflation is going to be steadily increasing. I think in 2017 to 2018 we'll see a second level of inflation starting to take hold where 2016 was your initial rise. You'll see some things start to show that. The years 2017-2018 are strong candidates for a pretty serious move up in price inflation for a lot of commodities and then there is another phase getting out closer to 2021.

A lot of that certainly becomes more specific and honed as time progresses and as other data is available both on the charts and just in fundamentals. That will certainly become more specific, but that's the general road map of what I'm looking at specifically speaking.

It's good that we got a chance to talk about fundamentals and forecasts because I rarely discuss these topics with most traders and investors. I wanted to seize this opportunity because you have an expertise in putting these all together. Now if somebody wanted to start mastering your way of looking at all these subjective methods as well as the technical way of using indicators then what books or resources would you recommend that they read to start developing the ability to do this?

One, that I still hold in the highest regard is the *Elliott Wave Principle.* That's not just because of its explanation of the Elliott Wave but because it also really deals with that whole process of the global economic structure and what is going on behind the scenes. Right now you are in the first and second wave where the bottom is slowly being built, but that dynamic third wave hasn't taken hold. There's a lot of that. When you really dig down into it and start to understand the Elliott Wave it gives you a very good identification and classification system of those different phases of economic activity.

That is one of the books that I recommend. There have been so many books that I've read over the last thirty years and types of seminars that I've either viewed or attended and …

I know it's difficult but just off the top of your head there must be some really good books you would recommend for people so that they can become better traders and investors. Can you just name a few which pop into your mind?

The thing is that in many of those cases I may have gone through a two-hundred page book and found one useful nugget. In most cases, in the early going of the first ten or fifteen years I was trying a lot of these systems and approaches and having some successes and getting burned by some of the things that weren't maybe described as well as they should have been. That evolution has helped me hone that all down. Again, they might not get my one nugget out of a two-hundred page book so would I recommend that book for someone to read if they might miss what I ended up ultimately getting from it? I would be very reluctant to do that because people tend to just say, "Okay, let me find this Holy Grail and follow it all."

Beyond the *Elliott Wave Principle* there were a couple of the Gann books early on that gave me some of that same overall mentality, but again that's more big picture type of stuff. A lot of it has been trial and error in the twenty to thirty years since first starting with the Elliott Wave. I think at this point I'd say that the *Elliott Wave Principle* would be the primary book. I'd have to think about and even go through my bookcases to see which ones I think could still offer some value.

Let's start to round this up. Are there any life lessons you wish you knew when you got started in investing years ago that you would really like to pass on to people so you could bootstrap them far ahead if they were to consistently follow the advice?

I think there is one thing that ties into some of those trading philosophies we were talking about earlier. It's the idea of treating trading like a business. I even had some people say this to me early on and I didn't listen at first because so often you get into it with the lottery or roulette wheel type of mentality of, "Okay, I'm going to hit this big trade and then be able to retire and go sailing." It starts you on a very dangerous path and it is very hard to come back from that.

When you treat trading like a business it goes into that idea where I was talking about comparing the residential realtor and the stadium builder or seller type of real estate investor. You know every business – I'm thinking of retail businesses in particular – has its niche and certain products that it is manufacturing and selling. It is not worried about some other business that is having a great quarter off of selling a certain type of food when they are in the business of some sort of technology that might be in the doldrums. I think that you really have to take that mentality with trading that you are going to stick to what you have determined to be your product or product line and not worry about all the other things available. Also you must be prepared for the downtimes or the lolls and even during those times should not be looking at someone else who is successful if it is for completely different reasons.

There are a lot of other principles that go along with that mentality of treating trading like a business. For instance, most businesses don't make their entire annual income in a few weeks or something, aside from some of your retailers between Thanksgiving and Christmas, but other than that it is more of a consistent thing. You have your ups and downs. You just want to make sure that on balance the ups outweigh or exceed the downs. You are learning and you are often having to adapt along the way, but stay consistent with what works for you and what is within your overall mentality and risk comfort level.

Any other lessons or something you would change in people's approach to investing that would make them more successful, or perhaps something that irks you so that if you were a genie you would wave your wand to eliminate that fault in people?

Really, what I was describing about the interplay between charts and data is that really understanding the numbers behind the charts is important. I'll try to give an illustration here. If a market went rapidly from 50 to 100 and did it in two days time, and another market went from 50 to 100 in ten days time and then both of them saw a 50% retracement, the wave structure would look almost identical when you're looking at a chart.

However, there are time-price indicators that are very important to me. They incorporate both price and time. The fact that that initial thrust took two days or ten days begins to assign different levels of significance to different price points on the way back down. All I'm trying to say is that a very similar looking wave structure on a chart - when you break it down into the numbers - may have completely different significance or distinctions within it. That's so even when we were talking a little earlier about certain moving average channels and not being able to roll over to the upside or the downside. If this wave structure has taken fifteen or twenty days, as opposed to five or ten days to have its initial thrust and then its pullback, then you are going to get a much different structure of some key moving averages because of that time-price relationship.

I don't know if I'm adding more confusion or more clarity, but I'd want people to recognize that knowing the numbers is equally or more important than the charts. Knowing them inside and out is equally important because the numbers and the chart are really the same thing. One is just a line drawn between those numbers, but you should know what they mean and their significance before just looking at patterns. Yes, a picture is worth a thousand words but looks can be deceiving. You have to factor both of those into the mix.

To wrap it up, where can people find you? What websites do you run and services do you offer? You mentioned the newsletters you write but where can people find you and your services?

The flagship website is InsiideTrack.com. A few years ago we also started some secondary sites to handle all the analysis on the specific 40-year cycle and so I have 40yearcycle.com. There was another cycle that I have seen very uncanny in the markets and that's at 17yearcycle.com. That's a third website - 17yearcycle.com.

Really, the InsiideTrack.com site is going to give the explanation of publications, give you a lot of the indicators that I mentioned as well as some explanation of them so that at least you can get a taste for it. Then we have a trading manual that goes more in-depth with those indicators, but that's going to give you all of that type of administrative information. The 40-year cycle site is loaded with articles and reports that I've written over the last five to ten years leading up to this period.

That sounds great. I appreciate your time and insights and how you put this all together. I'm pretty sure traders and investors will find quite useful your methodology for welding together cycles, Elliott Waves and Gann with proven indicators, trading patterns and even fundamentals to come up with your trading plans. Best of luck to you, Eric.

Chapter 4
Gareth Soloway
The Price, Pattern and Time (PPT) Trading Technique

Many traders go through an arduous and painful process of learning before they finally arrive at a profitable trading style that suits them. For instance, many fundamental investors pass through the roads of fundamental analysis, value investing, dividend investing or contrarian investing before they learn how to become a great long-term investor. Many technical traders often pass through day trading, swing trading, momentum trading, systems trading, indicator trading and yet more methods before they, too, finally arrive at a methodology which produces consistent profits.

On the road of technical analysis, studious individuals will commonly study all sorts of things such as chart patterns (flags, pennants, head and shoulders, etc.), timing methods (cycles, Gann, Elliott waves, planetary configurations, Daniel numbers, price bands, etc.) and indicators (MACD, RSI, ADX, stochastics, etc.). Information overload definitely affects traders in this field.

How can you simplify things so that your charts aren't cluttered up with useless information? How can you weld it all together, but make it so simple that you derive a systemic means of highly profitable trading decisions?

One such solution comes from Gareth Soloway and Nicholas Santiago, founders of IntheMoneyStocks.com, who developed a simple but highly reliable method of trading called PPT – "Price, Pattern and Time" trading. Stumped by trades that didn't make money, Gareth and Nicholas finally made their trading breakthrough when they discovered that a good trade always had three components. By enforcing the rule that three components must always be there before you pull the trigger on a trade, they have developed a highly reliable and profitable trading methodology that works for day trading, swing trading and even for other fields such as real estate investing.

How good is the method of combining price, pattern and time? Regular PPT trading results for 2012, 2013, 2014 and 2015 are, respectively: 709%, 497%, 647%, and 350%. Here are the PPT options trading results for 2014 and 2015, respectively: 1,012% and 1,669%.

In this interview I talk with Gareth Soloway about the PPT methodology so that you can clearly understand how it works and incorporate all or parts of these ideas into your own trading style. Because so many traders insist on a confirmation of several factors, as explained by Eric Hadik, it might be a great idea to create your own trading checklist of PPT for each trade.

Gareth, let's first go over how you got started in trading and the stages of learning you went through in order to develop your current trading methodology. I want to understand what trading styles you previously tried as well as how and why you ended up with the particular form of trading you now use.

Okay. Going back a ways, when I was in high school I had never been previously exposed to the stock market. My parents were teachers, we didn't have a lot of money and it was just a struggle. What ended up happening was that there was an investment club offered in high school and I said, "Ah, what the heck. This is kind of interesting."

I started to mess around with it a little bit and this was in the mid to late '90s when the tech bubble started to build. I started to play the Yahoo Finance Investment Challenge back then. Some people who were trading back in the late to mid-'90s might remember that challenge. During the tech bubble, it was amazing to me that even though it was a fake account with fake money (they gave you a fake hundred thousand dollars) I was able to make twenty or thirty thousand dollars, fifty thousand, a hundred thousand dollars. I could double my money in a month during that period and that's what hooked me into the whole idea of investing and trading. That's really where I got my start.

At this point in time in high school I wasn't really using any of my real money. To be honest, at that point in time I didn't have much. I ended up going to college and early on in college I was already obsessed with trading while seeing these small-caps and these micro-caps going nuts in the tech bubble. I basically came to my parents and I said, "Listen, I know you guys are not big investors but I really want to take a just little bit of money and try an account here." That's what I did and they said, "Okay."

I put just a thousand bucks into what I think was an E*TRADE account back then. They charged you $20-$25 a trade in the mid to late-'90s so it wasn't exactly low-cost trading, but I started playing around with it. I still remember in those late '90s that some of these micro-caps would just go nuts and I could make a little bit of money off them, so I started to get a taste of real money being made.

Now don't get me wrong because I made plenty of mistakes back then. I remember buying into PPDI, which is a funny story. PPDI is the NASDAQ ticker for Pharmaceutical Product Development Inc. I think it got bought out for ten times what I was buying it for back then a few years ago, but what happened is that I got into this stock. At that time I would put most of my money in a stock and it just went down. I think it went from $12 or $13 to $9 or $8 and I was getting frustrated so I did what an investor does when they are frustrated. I didn't have much money, it was all tucked in this one stock and so I basically wrote an email to the company. I wrote an email to the CEO. I think I found the email on Yahoo Finance at the time. Sure enough, I wrote, "Oh, I'm very disappointed in your stock's performance" and all this nonsense.

One morning, I woke up in my dorm room half-asleep. I went into the bathroom to brush my teeth and my roommate came in. He said, "You have a phone call." My mouth was full of toothpaste at the time, but I picked up the phone and said, "Hello? This is Gareth." On the other end I heard, "Hi, this is the CEO of Pharmaceutical Product Development. I got your email and I just wanted to call you and be very reassuring to our investors."

Little did he know that I only had a hundred shares of his stock. I was probably one of his smallest investors out there, but this incident just connected me more to Wall Street. Not that the CEOs these days would ever answer these emails personally or give calls to investors, but that was just another cool little situation that developed in my early years of trading.

The stock actually started to go up after that. I made most of my money back and I moved out of that company. I just continued to try to trade and this took me to the post-college period.

For my first job out of college I worked for MetLife doing insurance and financial consulting. I had to get my Series 7 and all that stuff. Honestly, I didn't like it. I didn't like having to cold call people. I wasn't great in that respect and I started to say to myself, "Listen, I'm going to put in a year here. I'm going to give it a full shot, but I really want to be a trader. I want to go out and do this for myself and I'll do whatever I have to do to do it."

I ended up quitting after a year and I literally had accumulated maybe about $10,000. I went to a prop firm and I gave them the $10,000. I said, "Hey, listen. I want to trade for myself. Can I do it out of your office?" They said, "Yes, you can. We're going to give you 5-to-1 or 10-to-1 leverage on this." Then I just started to trade.

Now I was paying commissions and I was really living by myself. I actually moved into my friend's basement at that time because I didn't have much other means to get by so I was paying only a couple hundred dollars a month in rent. I was just trying to trade over and over again and I was still struggling. I was trying to learn the ropes and I didn't really have much guidance.

A few of the traders in the office were trying to get me to short Taser (TASR) and I still remember shorting Taser when it was on a rip. I lost so much money because they kept on teaching me the wrong methods of trading. They would tell me, "Oh, it's going up against you, let's short more, let's short more" and I was on a limited account. Ultimately, I would lose money and I would have to take money out to pay my rent and bills and I had to go find another job. I literally started working three jobs. I was a bartender, a bartending instructor, and I had a couple other little side gigs that I was working. My whole purpose was just to continually put more money into that trading account and live as frugally as possible so I could just focus on learning how to trade.

How were you learning? Were you reading any trading books or were you just picking up things from people at this time?

To be honest, at this stage of the game what I was really doing was just following charts, watching them and listening to people in the office. I was at the time in my low 20s. It was really in my early years so I was looking at everyone around me thinking things like, "This guy is forty-five years old," or "This guy's got to know what he's doing. He's here and he seems like he's a millionaire. He's got tons of money. He just sits here and he is fifty years old and he's trading so I have to listen to him."

So there were no books or courses? You were just ...

To be honest, I didn't do any of that stuff. I literally tried to just follow people who seemed successful around me. For the most part I picked up little tidbits, but it wasn't anything that I found in the long term to be a successful thing. A lot of them were making the common mistakes that 99% of all traders and investors make: buying highs instead of shorting highs, going and doing the wrong thing and buying more if you are out-of-the-money (losing money) and just keep loading up. Then you would see these traders blow up. They would lose half their account in one day because of that.

In the beginning I got swept into some of these bad things, but I was just so diligent so I started saying, "Listen, there has got to be a way to do this where you have to be disciplined and you have to look at certain things in the charts and find out really what goes on."

The bottom line is that as I progressed I slowly started to get better. I started to avoid the bad trades, the trades that weren't good chart setups, and I started to find the little better ones. My business partner, Nicholas Santiago, ended up trading in the same prop firm office as me. He was a broker for years before and he had decided to just start trading on his own as well.

We would have lunch everyday. I still remember going to Baja Fresh in Long Island every day and we would just discuss the charts nonstop. We actually got together at one point and said, "Listen, we have to figure out a way to work these charts. We have to study them and find out what price, pattern and time factors basically equate to a profitable trade." So again it was price, pattern and time. That's what we came up with as the three keys to making a good investment or good trade in any chart.

So that's the key of your methodology?

That is the key exactly. That's the key of the methodology - price, pattern, and time. We call it "PPT" for short.

If you look at price on a stock, we all want to buy at a certain price. If you look at a pattern, you'll notice that throughout history - and it doesn't matter what period in history - there are certain chart patterns that when they form then the prices will go in a certain direction let's say seven to eight times out of every ten.

If you combine that with price and you get an accurate price - let's say it's a 200-bar moving average or prices are going into a double bottom - and you have the right pattern then what you are doing is you are adding those two together. Let's say that one has a 70% success rate and the other has a 70% success rate. If you add them together you get about an 85% success rate or 80% success rate.

Then we also came up with what we call "time counts." Time counts are a series. If you look at the earth - and this is getting a little bit more out there, but this is extremely important for those of us who are true technicians - if you look at the world, if you look at anything then you are going to notice that there are key numbers that repeat and that are very important. If you look at the Bible, certain numbers appear unbelievably often in the Bible. If you look at any religious book you will find the same thing so it doesn't even have to be the Bible. If you look at Fibonacci, for instance, Fibonacci numbers and proportions occur naturally in nature continuously. What we were finding is that certain numbers are very key.

Now add that portion into the methodology of price and pattern. So now we're adding a time factor into that. By adding in that time factor we were able to find out that if you have those three methods in a chart then you are actually upping your percentage win rate to between 80% and 90%. That's really what we found out.

Now it takes some time to really study and learn it but once you're able to find these three keys then trading becomes much easier and investing becomes so much easier.

Is that your approximate win rate right now? Is it in the 70-80% range?

Yes, exactly. Exactly.

Are you using this trading method with stocks, options, futures, small-caps or large-caps or whatever? And how long are those trades that you are usually taking? Is this swing trading or is this day trading?

This actually goes through everything. What we do is this. During the day I'm a day trader and so is my partner. We help people learn how to day trade. I call out of all my day trades live: "I'm entering X,

Y, Z at $20," for instance, and people can all follow me.

On a side note, we also do swing trading, which is for those people who aren't really able to day trade because they have a nine to five job or because it's just not something that they are interested in. We will give out our swing trades like, "I bought Microsoft at $25." I put it up live for people to see and they can follow me as well in that respect.

So people are able to follow me on all sides and again the win rate is around between 70-80%. It's an amazing win rate, but you have to follow the methodology to get it. We have a lot of people come to us and I teach them, but then their emotions will let them be swayed and they will see just one PPT factor instead of two or three. Then they will take that trade and all of a sudden they lose on that trade. Well, you didn't have the other factors there!

Let's go into the exact PPT methodology. Can you give us the exact methodology for trading with price, pattern and time? What are you using for price? What are the patterns that you use to confirm that? And then, what timing triggers are you using such as cycles, time counts, Fibonacci day counts, Daniel numbers, lunar cycles, eclipses, equinoxes or whatever?

Let's start out with just a trade. Let's imagine you have a stock chart. It could be Apple or it could be anything. We will look at the daily chart because we'll use swing trading as our example, but the beauty of the methodology - and I just want to make this statement because I think it is important - is that it's relevant to anything you trade. Whether you are day trading, whether you are swing trading, whether it is commodities, stocks or forex, these rules apply to all of those charts on all time frames. You can really apply it to any sort of thing you want.

Now if you look at the types of daily charts we use then you are going to see that we don't put a lot of nonsense on the chart. We have our 20-bar moving average, our 50-bar moving average and our 200-bar moving average. We use the simple ones. I always say, "Keep things simple so use the simple moving averages."

Aside from that, that's all we have on our charts. We don't use a lot of Gann or MACD or all that other stuff and the reason is because you are just really trying to find pinpoint levels for your price. To give an example of how to get into the price point, when I look at a chart I'm looking for key pivots on the chart. That could be a double top, a double bottom, a gap fill, a gap window, a hit at the 200-day moving average, 20-day moving average, 50-day average … anything that is a key point on the chart that price is coming straight into.

I'm not a big fan of zigzags. If you're chopping sideways it's like white noise on the TV. It basically just skews everything. What you are looking for is a direct move in one direction, up or down, of a stock into one of those factors.

Now once you get that factor it doesn't mean take the trade. A lot of amateurs will say, "Oh, we just hit a gap fill so I have to take this trade." No, you have to find one of the other PPT factors along with it because you are trying to bump your winning percentage up to a point where the odds are so much in your favor that you are going to win.

If you just take a gap fill then you probably have a 60% chance of making money on that trade, but in all fairness 60% is only a little bit better than gambling at a casino. At least at the casino I get free drinks and I get to look at pretty girls. There are some benefits with that 60% win rate, but I really want to get it upwards from that.

That's why we get to the pattern factor. What pattern is it making into that key level? Do we have a bull flag? Do we have a bear flag? Do we have a straight shot on a three-bar surge?

Three-bar surges, if you didn't know, are direct moves that end moves. If you are going in a downward move - let's say it's a three-bar surge so there are one, two, three big candles on the daily chart - into a double bottom, that's going to signal the likelihood of a bounce with a very high success rate.

Lastly, it just gets into the time factor. The time factor is a little harder for me to go into because it gets into cycles and things like that. But as to the time factors, when you have key time factors going into (converging at) these same levels then it's going to up that percentage even more.

What are you using for time factors? Are you using cycles?

Yes, it comes into cycles. It basically is based off cycles into certain … well, this is one of our proprietary secrets, which makes it really hard for me to divulge, but ultimately yes. You are dealing with cycles, you are dealing with eclipse type stuff. For instance, we just had an eclipse last night or into this morning somewhere in the world. That was a key signal that we look for. There are certain things like that that come into relevance when you're looking at the time component of the trade.

It doesn't sound like you are using any risk/reward ratio to evaluate your trades. You are just looking to see if it follows this price, pattern and time combination.

Yes, but I think a key is that you always have to be aware of risk versus reward. For instance, let's say a stock is up 300% during the course of the year. I have to look at that and I have to make a judgment call and say, "Okay, I have a bull flag at the absolute highs. The chart is ridiculously extended. Do I really want to go long here?" The answer is probably "no" because again it's at all-time highs and I'm not a big fan of taking that amount of risk. But again, that risk assessment should always be done. You always want to do a little bit of risk assessment.

It sounds like your style is not like the traders who say, "I won't take the trade unless there is a 3-to-1 or 5-to-1 reward to risk ratio." It sounds like you are primarily looking at these other things when setting up the trade to say whether it will probably be successful or not and that the risk/reward ratio is not the defining criteria.

Right, right. Exactly, exactly. Basically, what you want to do is you want to find the PPT within the chart – the price, pattern and time factors - and then ultimately the last thing you want to do is take a note about whether this pattern will work out.

Let's say we have a bull flag that is cupping the 200-day moving average support with a time count. Okay, great setup. If the upside on that trade is 10¢ and the downside if it fails is $10 – because even if you are winning 80% of your trades you can still expect that two out of every ten will still fail – I want to make the assumption that this is not going to be a very profitable plan. I mean, okay, so I can get 10¢. What's that going to make me? One hundred, two hundred, three hundred bucks versus losing thousands, right? So you do want to make a little bit of a case on the risk/reward as well.

Do you have stop-losses on these trades?

Yes. I think one of the most important things is to always have a stop. To be honest, it's one of the biggest things I struggle with even as a current trader because just naturally as humans we never want to admit we are wrong, but you have got to have it. You have to be able to say at a certain point, "This is my maximum loss."

Let's say I enter a trade and I'm looking to make $2,000. You have to say to yourself, "Okay, well what's the maximum I'm going to lose?" Now, you generally say the same amount of $2,000 to the downside so that's where I'm going to cut it.

Every trader, every investor is going to have a different risk tolerance and we all have to figure that out for ourselves. I know traders who are with us that are okay losing $25,000 to $50,000 on a trade or making that. On the same side or on the other side there are other investors that have a smaller trading account. They have a smaller investing account. They might only be okay with losing $500.

Everyone has to be individually aware of what his max loss is and you just have to abide by it. No one wants to take a loss but honestly, looking back, I wish I had taken more losses in my history when I was younger because I'd have a lot more money if I cut those losses for a smaller loss.

Gareth, it doesn't sound like you have a percentage rule for taking a loss or a chart pattern rule that if it hits the bottom of this bar or something similar then you are out. It sounds like you are doing it by figuring out in your head how much money you can risk. Is that correct?

Well, let me just explain this. With every trade I put out to our members there is always going to be a stop-loss I give them. So let's say we are buying at a double bottom based on a three-bar surge into that double bottom. Let's use that as an example. What I'm going to tell our members is that if you confirm the trade - and I'll go into confirmation even though it's one of our proprietary things - if you confirm below the double bottom then that is a breakdown in which case you want to stop out.

Now I still may have a max dollar amount listed based on that factor. For instance, I may buy a certain amount of shares where if that happens then that is my max loss. But basically it is going to be a technical factor that is going to trigger the stop out.

Just to explain "confirmation," it is one of the proprietary factors we have got here, but I will divulge this to you. All right, so if we close below a double bottom let's say we have a low pivot from a month ago at $20 on a stock. If you come into that double bottom then you are going to expect a bounce. Okay, so we buy at $20 because it gets down to a double bottom.

Now if it goes below $20 then the average person is going to say, "Oh well, it broke down." That's actually not true. Institutions will play games with double bottoms where they will actually push it through the double bottom and even close it at the end of the day below that low to try to get the amateurs to throw in the towel.

What we have developed is something called the "confirmation signal," which is actually the true indicator of a breakdown. Let's talk about what we are calling this true indicator of a breakdown. The way you are going to use it is when on a daily chart the price closes below that double bottom - you need to look for a secondary close below that low.

For instance, let's say we close at $19.80. Okay, you got your first close below at $19.80 and the low is, let's say $19.80 as well on that candle that day. The next day is the caveat, right? This is the day where the institutions flush out the small investors by closing the stock price below that low where the small investors threw in the towel and stopped themselves out, and where they are just trying to get those shares so they can push it back up.

Well, if that happens you are still in the trade. You haven't stopped out yet. However, if the next day the market closed below that $19.80 then that tells you it is a true breakdown and that is what we call "confirmation," which is that it's confirming below that double bottom.

How did you find this particular confirmation signal and these proprietary rules? Is that from personally looking at thousands of charts or did you use TradeStation or some other computer program to do backtesting?

After years of trading it was something that I just kept on wondering about. A lot of people would say, "Oh, it just broke the low of the day. Should we stop out?" I would continue to see that this pattern was happening where a lot of times they would just bring it below that low and then the next day the price would pop up and then start to rally from that point on. At other times it would close below that low and it would start to go lower and continue to break down even days and days after that.

I started to just see this pattern develop and so I started to do backtesting. I would go to charts and backtest, backtest, backtest and I started to see that the high success rate on that confirmation signal made it an extremely accurate way of telling if it's a true breakdown or a fake breakdown. I noticed that my confirmation signal would work with a winning ratio of eight out of ten times, which is north of an 80% correct rate on that signal.

Your backtesting was just from observation to confirm it?

That's right. I literally sit behind these charts probably eight hours, nine hours, ten hours a day and have been doing that for day after day and year after year. Eventually you start to see these things repeating and I'd note that. Once I started to note that then I started looking back at charts historically to see if that was pointing out.

I always like people to hear the benefits of reviewing historical charts over and over again if they want to become a trader as well as the importance of marking their own trades on charts and constantly reviewing those, too. You mentioned looking at historical charts and that you yourself started your entire trading career with paper trading. Do you recommend people should start with paper trading if they want to get into this field?

I think with day trading and even swing trading that it is important to get into paper trading, but not because you can trust your returns when it's not real money. Your emotions are going to be 100% different when you are dealing with fake money versus real money. The reason paper trading is important is because you need to become familiar with the charts, how to read them and learn how to make the right decisions to either get in or get out.

In addition, you have to get familiar with your trading platform, especially if you are going to become a day trader. You have to act very, very quickly as a day trader. I've seen so many people new to the game double-click the button and then they bought two times the amount of shares they meant to buy. And then, "Oh, no!" it went against them and they lost a lot of money.

You really want to become very familiar with all these things and paper trading is a great way to do that. Once you start actually trading - and this is what I say to our traders as well - start out with just a hundred shares because of your emotions. You want to build up your emotional tolerance and you don't want to go from zero to a hundred miles an hour right away, so start out with just a hundred shares. It doesn't matter if the commission is equal to what you make on the trade. What you need to do is prove to yourself that you have the methodology down, that you have the ability to even make a couple of dollars, and then slowly up your share size.

You know a lot of people come to me and they have a $30,000 account and they try to throw it all in the trade right away on their first trade. Emotion over-captures them, they start going nuts and then they make the wrong decision because of that. That is something that is a big pitfall for a lot of traders.

You have a set of chart patterns that you are looking for to find potential trades, and you know from standard technical analysis that this one usually leads to a bull run, this one is a bearish pattern, etcetera. How are you using the moving averages on top of that? Can you give us an example of the 20-bar, 50-bar and 200-bar moving average? How is that matching with the pattern?

I'll give you a good example of it and hopefully just by talking about it you can envision it in your mind. Let's just say we have a bull flag, right? A bull flag is a sharp move up followed by the flag pattern, which is just a sideways right angle or slightly right angle that is slightly lower.

The first thing is that you get that flag pattern to start to form. The way I would incorporate the moving averages is as follows. What you want to see is that the moving average is working like a floor underneath the price pattern being formed, like a cup. Imagine you take your hand and you are holding a ball in your hand and just cupping it. You want the moving averages to act as a gentle hand underneath that stock because basically it is going to be security, or what we call "support," for your flag pattern, okay?

Again, imagine you have a bullish pattern. You already know that it is a pattern that generally plays out to the upside, and now if you can add a 50-day moving average or a 200-moving average that is just coming up underneath prices then it is going to just lift it gently higher. All you need is a little bit of a push up on that stock off that bullish pattern and you will start to breakout. Once the breakout begins you are going to get more momentum traders jumping on-board and it will start to take off faster and faster.

In other words, you are looking for the price pattern to be just sort of lying on top of or below the moving average line, which is then the support or resistance.

Exactly. Those are the ones I love the most when talking about bullish patterns or bearish patterns and when you have the moving averages. For bullish patterns, obviously the moving averages need to be underneath prices and the opposite thing for bearish patterns. If it's just above the bearish chart pattern then it is going to act like a ceiling and push it down.

What is your short list of chart patterns that people need to learn for this?

The basic patterns you are going to look for and which I think are important to know are a head and shoulders pattern, a M pattern, W pattern and a cup-and-handles. A "cup" is a basing pattern and a "handle" is what we call a bullish consolidation or bull flag pattern. That's an important one. So bull flags, bear flags, and that's about it. When it comes to patterns it is very simple. As crazy as it is the methodology doesn't reinvent the wheel at all. It just takes what historically has worked and simplifies it to the point where every average investor, even newbies, can learn it if they just put a little time into it.

And then if we add time into the equation, correct me if I'm wrong but what you'll do is you will determine it's a cycle high or a cycle low and then all of a sudden you'll say, "Okay, take the trade."

Exactly, exactly. The timing will often be the signal to actually jump in. So you start to get a flag pattern, we start to get a bullish pattern sideways, and the moving averages are gently underneath. As to the time factor, once the time hits then it is just like it has turned noon or it's midnight and BOOM! That's when you jump in the trade and then it's off to the races.

If I summarize it, basically we have a moving average that serves as your support or resistance. It's creating a base or a roof to the price pattern that you want to form above or below it and then the cycle or time count comes in.

Yeah, really as soon as that time factor hits then you buy. It's just very simple. For instance, say we have five or six candles running sideways and we know the cycle is going to hit on this next candle. Bam! We buy right there when you have those other factors right there, too. Again it's a beautiful trade and the only time you will use that confirmation signal that I talked about earlier is that it will be how you stop out. If you can confirm below the key level you just stop right out.

So you just buy on the day when all the PPT factors come together and there is nothing to wait for. Is that just it? Can a person just put on their trade and then walk away for the day?

Exactly, exactly. I would suggest knowing your stop, or at least checking back and making sure in case the stock starts to fall that you have a stop of sorts in there and then have your target in as well. We have seen a lot of these chart patterns will play out literally within a day or two, which is amazing. You can get 5-10% gains on swing trades in a day or two.

How do you exit a trade? How long do your trades usually last and what do you use to exit them?

A lot of times what I'll do is that in my mind I will have an amount that I'm looking to make percentage-wise, which might be 10% on a swing trade or more. However, what I'll try to do is coordinate it with a key technical point. Let's say the bullish pattern is breaking to the upside and we have a gap fill coming up. I'll try to coordinate that exit right around that gap fill as well.

In other words it's really, "Let's see if there is a chart pattern to go for" or a percentage that you

usually make on a trade and you just sort of combine the two artistically. Would you say it that way?

Yeah, exactly. I use both to my advantage. Just one other little side note here, too.

It's always important to be aware of the market. You might be focusing on just one stock, like Apple or Microsoft, but be aware of what the markets are doing because, for instance, let's say we bought Apple on a bullish pattern breakout on a time count and it's moving up towards gap fill. If it is not quite at gap fill yet, which means it could go a little bit more, but then the market starts to show a really ugly pattern, then play it smart.

We always say, "No one went broke taking a profit." There is no sense in squabbling over a 10¢ move in Apple when the markets are starting to break down because you could lose the $5 in profits you already have.

Let me ask one thing to be clear. In all these trades you are not looking at fundamental analysis at all?

No. The only thing related to that is that we stay aware of when earnings are going to be reported because earnings bring a new level of risk into the game. Let's say I'm in-the-money on a Google investment. I'm swing trading Google and we are coming into earnings.

Often times we'll move out ahead of earnings. A lot of people are like, "Oh, let me roll the dice. Let me take that because maybe I can make 10%." Sure you can always make 10%, but remember it goes both ways. You could lose 10% so I'd much rather safely pocket - and this is goes into being a very safe and conservative investor which I think is important - I'd rather pocket a small gain and not go into earnings because I don't know what I'm going to get. Occasionally I'll hold into earnings, but honestly a couple of times I've been burned.

I think traders can now understand the pieces of the PPT methodology and how you put it all together. Looking at my own track record I can see that many of my losing trades were missing one of the PPT factors and now know that you should not take a trade based on having just one factor alone. Does the PPT system work on all markets and is there a special type of market or sector where this really outperforms?

The PPT will work on any chart, but the one caveat is when you have a very thin chart, which means a stock trading on thin volume. We are talking about stocks that trade only 10,000 shares a day and situations like that. The only negative is that I don't use PPT on stocks that trade that thin because let's just say it's a $2 stock and it only trades 10,000 shares a day. That's $20,000 in money that went into that stock in one day. I could literally do that amount of shares myself and if I did that I could crush the stock by 5-10%. It puts you at a little bit of a disadvantage on those really thin ones because one person can affect the price so much and stop you out on those stocks. So with the micro-thin stocks I would not use it.

I use it on everything else whether you are talking about a mid-cap stock, large-caps, an ETF, forex, commodities and even options. You can use the method with options, too, but you don't look at the options chart. I always suggest when you are doing options to look at the actual stock chart and use the same methodology. For instance, my partner put out a WYNN call option just two days ago and yesterday it already hit his targets, but he was looking at the WYNN chart on the daily and then utilized that PPT information to play the calls on WYNN.

Why don't you tell us a little bit about your expertise in picking really high momentum stocks with PPT? Can you tell us how that came about?

Believe it or not, we are not huge on following momentum. What we like to do is refer to ourselves as "the first one in the trade." What we will do is basically utilize the methodology to find the stock that is just about to break out or just about to reverse off a key level. And again, utilizing the PPT system allows you to do it.

I'm always cautionary to our members who are followers of momentum mainly because when you are in a momentum trade and you already see that it's moving up sharply it means that you are buying and you are paying a higher price for that stock than you could have had yesterday or the day before.

The way I talk to people is that if you go to the store you want to find a gallon of milk on sale for $1.99. Now, if you go to the store and you find milk selling for $5 or $10 a gallon we don't all rush in and say, "Oh my goodness, we have to buy the milk at $10 a gallon." We say, "You know what? Let's wait until it's on sale next week at $1.99 and I'll come get it at that point."

That's the same way I view trading and I think that is one of the biggest problems with the average investor. CNBC and others hype all this nonsense out there, which gets people hyped up to buy stocks when they are at their highs or short them when they are at their lows. You have to use that same criteria. The same thing applies when you go to the mall because you need a new pair of jeans. I'm not going to buy the ones where the price just went up to $500 for that pair of jeans. I'm going to look for the jeans that are a great pair, but they are on sale.

That's the same thinking we have to use in trading and that's been one of the most successful things. I can't tell you how many times a stock is breaking up and trust me, my gut is like, "Oh man, I'm missing the trade," but you've got to use discipline to say, "You know what? There is always another trade out there. You don't need to chase that trade. Find the chart that is setting up perfectly and then jump in on that perfect situation." So again, we are not really momentum traders in that respect.

What are the best qualifications for people to learn PPT trading? What are the qualifications in terms of their personality or strengths and weaknesses and what's the emotional discipline that they most need to learn? What I'm looking for is an aspiring trader to say, "I can do this type of trading because it matches me." I also want to know what are the caveats that they have to know about. Can you discuss this a little?

I think one of the main things that is super important is that you can give me anyone and I can teach them what we do. Now some will learn faster than others. What we found is that if you have a very open mind and you are willing to absorb the ideas then those are going to be the people that will make money quickest. Now if you are very stubborn and if you have discipline issues then you are going to take a little bit longer. You are going to get burned a little bit more on trades that you might do on your own that will ultimately cause you to have a couple of losses.

What we found is that people who have been in the market and really followed the hype and the CNBCs of the world, those people are the hardest to teach because they have this predisposed notion of, "Well, the Cramers of the world are correct" or "We should just follow what the media is saying." You really want to start to think for yourself independently.

For instance, a great example of this was about three years ago when Apple put in a top and was above $700 at the time. I still remember the media was talking about it nonstop. Literally everyday when you flipped on CNBC and any of the other channels it was, "Apple is at new highs! Apple is at new highs! This is amazing. It's going to go to a trillion dollar market cap!"

Think about this logically. What you had to keep in mind is that when every word is bullish, when the media is spewing that bullishness to the average person then they are all going to be buyers. Now by the time the average investor is a buyer then who is already in the trade?

The institutions are *already* in that trade. The average intelligent investors are in that trade. The pros, the money managers, they are all in the trade already. So once you get a small investor to buy into Apple because the media is pushing it then the question is who buys next?

For a stock to go up you have to have more buyers. The key is that once the average investor is all in that trade, it's done. It's going to reverse and we saw that with Apple with the upgrades. I still remember the upgrades to like $1,000 a share on Apple back when it was just above $700.

The bottom line is this: don't worry about what the media says. If anything use it as a contrary indicator. We actually tell our members to make sure to shut off the news and do not look at that because it is going to sway you emotionally to do the wrong thing. If anything use it as a contrarian view.

If you had a magic wand and you could wipe out the bad characteristics of most of the people who fail in trading, what would you would wave your wand to wipe out and what would be the thing that you would wave your wand to amplify so that you could turn someone into a successful trader?

Here is what we find is the most problematic thing for investors, whether you are a day trader or a swing trader. It is honestly the discipline. If I could have a magic wand and make everyone super disciplined and get them to just follow the rules then you would have everyone being a successful investor.

It might sound crazy but the PPT methodology is not hard to grasp. It is just rules and you just look for price, pattern and time. Three things … if they appear in a chart then you buy or you short. It's very simple. The only reason people ever fail doing what we do is because when a setup does happen to go against you they sit there for days and days and weeks and weeks hoping it turns around instead of stopping themselves out and that's a major, major issue.

As crazy as it sounds the biggest battle any investor will ever fight in terms of being a profitable Warren Buffett-type making billions for the rest of their life is their own discipline. That's the biggest thing. If you can have discipline then you can learn anything in the charts and make money consistently, and a ton of it, too.

Is there any scanning software or special websites that you have found that are most valuable for people who want to trade PPT after they learn it?

Well, we have had members actually program algorithms based off of the PPT. We have never done it ourselves, but you can take the rules and just plug them into a lot of these software programs and they will scan for them in the charts.

To be honest, because I'm behind the charts 24/7 I just go through charts all day long and I'll find these setups myself. We also have a chat room so a lot of the members in there - we literally have hundreds of people in there - will be scanning with me so it is almost like our own scanning body.

This is probably one of the biggest benefits for me myself because imagine this. I'm in a chat room and I only have two eyes to look at charts. But when you have a hundred or two hundred other people looking at those same charts and scanning then they are posting to me, "Hey Gareth, look at XYZ chart. Look at that bullish consolidation." That's the beauty of what we have done here. It has created this group of like-minded investors and traders who are all going to work together to help us all become more profitable. They do it for me, too, to be honest.

Since you are looking at hundred of stocks in a day are you looking at the most actives or something else? What is the group that you usually concentrate on?

I would agree one hundred percent that it is the most actives. One of the keys is that you need stocks of a volatile nature to do trading so if a stock is in a ten cent range and it just goes up five cents, down five cents, up ten cents, down ten cents all day long then there is really not a good risk-reward trade there. You are not going to get a good setup. But if you have a stock that just reported earnings for the day and it is getting crushed by 25%, chances are it is going to come in with a certain time count to a key level - and we label them as gap plays in the chat room - and we can play that for a significant bounce.

Always think of it like a ball, right? If I roll the ball on the ground then it's really not going up and down much. It is just rolling. But if I were to drop that ball from ten feet in the air then it is going to have a big bounce, right? Think of the chart this way and that's how you want to play it. When prices fall from ten feet in the air into a key support then when you have PPT you are going to get a significant retracement just like a ball bouncing off of the ground.

What about books? Are there any books that you would recommend people to read to help learn the necessary chart patterns you want them to recognize or trading skills? Books they can get from Amazon.com?

If you are a pure beginner just go to Amazon.com, type in "technical analysis" and see what books pop up. Any basic investor book is probably okay. I don't have a specific favorite myself, but again any sort of technical analysis book is fine.

Basically what you want to do is you just want to get the basics down. You want to know what a moving average is. You want to know what gap fill is. There are probably a lot of people that might read this interview and say, "Well I'm not really sure what a gap fill is." These are basic terms on the technical side that you just need a definition for and you need to see a picture of and then you'll remember it from here on out and that's just your basics. You get those basics down and you can just learn the PPT from there and go on your way.

You don't really have any special useful book that you recommend to people like Murphy's or anybody else's?

To be honest, I don't have a favorite. There is *Technical Analysis of Financial Markets* by John Murphy. It's a pretty comprehensive guide to trading methods and applications. *Charting and Technical Analysis* by Fred McAllen is an okay one, too.

There are a few different ones, but again I stress for investors and traders to really be pure and this is the way I want most of them. If people come to me and say, "Hey, I learned ten different ways to trade based on this," I honestly will tell them, "Forget it, like literally wipe that out. I want a clean slate. Now let me teach you this method because you will never use that other stuff again."

Again, you need to know moving averages, you need to know gap fills, double bottoms, double tops, … things like that. But you don't want a lot of stuff clouded because it will make you start to question, "Do you have a great PPT setup here?" Based on the PPT methodology you might know that you should go long, but now you remember this thing you learned from some other book and you're now thinking, "Wait a minute, maybe this pattern is 'eh~'" and then you don't take the trade. Then you miss out on the trade or something like that.

I would honestly say you need to learn some basic technical analysis, but as an average trader or a beginner you don't need a lot. You just need patience and discipline and to know the basics and then the PPT methodology.

Can you give us any stories of successful students with PPT trading or any track records? That always helps people understand the power of the trading method that is being explained.

We just had someone yesterday brand new to us and they just said that they made $20,000 on what I think was a $100,000 account. They made $20,000 in one day as well as $16,000 the day after. It was really an amazing story from someone new that just came to us. Funny thing is that it was a woman and we've always found, believe it or not, that women make great traders because I'll tell you this - and this is one of those funny things but it comes back to discipline. Women don't have the ego of men and the ego is the one thing that will get people in trouble. That stubbornness of not admitting when they're wrong kills people and so women make very, very good traders.

I know that they make good traders but have you found that women, in general, make better traders?

I would say that the success rate of a woman who tries to be a trader is better than a man. If you took a hundred men and a hundred women then I would say a higher ratio of women than men would become successful traders.

I want to take your style of trading and try to create the profile of successful people using it by cutting it in a couple of different ways. How can you partition successful PPT traders into different types and say that Type A personalities are a little bit more successful than Type B? I don't care whether the partitioning is done by gender, previous trading experience, education, discipline, etcetera. How can you partition success and non-success, or success and super-success, into two

categories for the PPT style of trading?

So you're saying which ones will become successful and what are the characteristics or personality traits of successful PPT winners?

Yes.

I think the first characteristic is what we already mentioned, which is just the simple ability to admit when you are wrong. The second characteristic is having a very analytical mind in terms of seeing the charts and just saying, "Okay, well X is at the correct level, Y is there and Z is right there."

Honestly, I can sit down and I can teach a ten-year-old how to trade in and he would probably be the most successful trader in the world because he would be starting so young. But it's very much just looking at that chart and saying, "Well, what factors are there or not?" What I always tell our traders and investors is to have a checklist in front of them. You write down "pattern" and then you have "price" and then you have "time."

Every chart you bring up you just ask yourself three simple questions. Is there a pattern here? Yes. Is there a time factor? Yes. Is there a price point? Boom! And if it does check out, if the checklist works, buy the trade or short the trade depending on what it is telling you to do.

Have you ever tried taking a boot camp of kids and then teaching them how to trade?

My partner actually has started to teach his son and we actually have members who have started to teach their kids. In fact a couple of members in the chat room have their sons or daughters trading with them now.

It's really amazing. Honestly, it makes me feel wonderful to see some of the comments these people leave on how I changed their lives or how my partner and the methodology changed their lives. I love seeing them pass it on generationally to the younger ones and start to teach them because again, you are talking about people here who might be retirees, they might be college kids, they might be middle aged with family, but they are literally getting to the point where they are able to be financially independent for the rest of their lives.

Think about that dream, that dream of us sitting down at a computer and making money. As long as my fingers work to click the mouse when I'm eighty to ninety years old I can sit down and I can make a thousand dollars in ten minutes in the market in the morning. Then I can go play golf for the rest of the day if I want. It is a dream. There is nothing better than being a trader or a small investor.

I always try to put a big emphasis on teaching the next generation the very best methods out there for whatever it is they should learn. You have to take the best techniques and teach them to kids or teenagers or twenty-somethings when they are still open to learning and the world is still in front of them. This is a great thing that you are doing. Aside from that, do you have any stories of traders who have turned around their lives or trading careers from learning the PPT system? Can you give me any of those stories?

Well, we did have someone who I think worked at a convenience store. I don't know if it was a

7/11 or anything like that, but it was an amazing story how he came to us. It is a sad situation but one of his parents or both of his parents had passed away and he had come to us. Basically he had a little bit of inheritance money - probably $30,000 or $40,000. He was thinking to himself, "Listen. I haven't gone to college. Do I really want to be in this environment for the rest of my life just working at a convenience store making minimum wage or a little bit above?" In the beginning he came to us and you could tell he was very nervous.

I talked to him and I said, "Listen. If you are going to be successful here you have to just first of all relax because scared money is not going to make money. What I need you to do is start out trading with very, very small lots - literally a hundred shares of a $20 stock. If you are trading Apple then trade twenty shares of Apple. Just show me that you can do this and make it work."

He started to study the methodology and I gave him a little extra helping hand as well, which I do with quite a few members that show such interest. Literally within two to three months he was at the point where he was making literally $5,000+ a month on that $30,000-$40,000 account. You are talking about a 10% return month-over-month and exponentially growing it, therefore making more and more.

I think by the end of the first year he had turned that $30,000-$40,000 account into $100,000 so it was amazing. Honestly it was amazing, but it just shows you. He was a disciplined young student of ours and the young are really the ones that don't have the predisposed knowledge of what's been pushed on the investor from Wall Street for years and years, which is totally false. Those are the ones that have the best shot at really becoming lifelong traders and super profitable.

Just a couple of other really, really wonderful stories. I actually just received three bottles of wine that were made by a member of ours. He literally makes his own wine and it was such a kind gesture because he basically said to me, "Listen, I came to you, I'm a retiree on a fixed income and I just make wine." It isn't anything professional that is sold out there to the masses or to tons of stores. It was just something that he does on his own. He makes it for his family and friends and so forth and he literally said to me, "Based on what you guys have done for me you have changed my life. You have moved me from being just stuck on an income going forward to the point where now I can actually enjoy going on vacations and go on trips. I can trade from anywhere in the world, too. I log in from Australia or wherever it is at that period of time and trade with you. I can make the money to pay for my vacations."

We have countless stories about people just like a woman named Rhonda in the chat room. She is one of the very best, probably one of the top traders in our chat room. She came to us literally years ago, probably five to six years ago. She's been a member that long. She has been with us straight through and you could see her progress. She slowly came from being an unsure trader and unsure investor to one where she is the one calling out a lot of the setups in the chat room now.

I love seeing that turn where I now feel confident in her abilities when she tells me, "Gareth, take a look at Apple's chart pattern right here. Look's like a great setup." I'll look at it right away, but even before I look at it I'll say, "I know it's going to be a good trade setup." She's got it down. She is one of the ones that has her son trading with her at home now, too. They trade together and I think that's a wonderful thing when parents do that with their kids. It's good family time and at the same time it is something that will stay with them for the rest of their lives.

Let's switch hats once again because we are coming near to the end of this interview. You mentioned previously that when you first started out in your career you were helping people get

their financial house in order. Now that the PPT basics are covered I want to understand what financial advice you would give people now so that people receive the benefits of your wisdom after so many years of trading, dealing with so many people and seeing so many different financial situations.

One of the big things that everyone needs to really be aware of is their full financial situation. Not everyone can be a day trader and not everyone can be a swing trader. I'm a big believer that everyone can learn how to trade the markets, but the important thing is that when you learn how to trade the markets accurately you are going to be able to apply that same thought process and that same discipline elsewhere. Discipline is one of the most important things in investing and in trading. You can apply it to anything else.

When you want to get your financial house in order you need to obviously be aware of your investments like your stocks and stuff like that, but you also want to be aware of your other financial factors like real estate.

This is actually a cool story related to that. My partner and I, by using the charts and the cycles and the time factors, were able to predict exactly when to buy real estate. Everyone needs a well-diversified portfolio, which might include real estate. You just cannot put all your money in stocks and hope the market doesn't crash like in 2007, 2008, and 2009, right?

What we ended up doing is that he ended up buying his house in 2011 and I picked mine up in 2012. I have a beachfront condo literally overlooking the beach. It's a beautiful place and I was able to get it as the first one in the building. I knew the real estate market was going to turn and I literally jumped in. I think I paid $865,000 for it and it's now worth $1.1 million just a few years after that. Again, that gives you a sense of how important it is to learn how to read charts and understand the cycles because you can apply it to so many different things.

I also think it is very, very important to be diversified all the way around. Just going back to getting yourself in a financially successful position, make sure you have a well-diversified portfolio of real estate, stocks as well as gold. I'm honestly a big fan of having a little bit of gold on hand. I think gold is a very important commodity to have. I have gold, literally physical gold that I hold. I have some GLD right now as a swing trade.

I also have a stock portfolio, I have my short-term trading which is day trading, and I have my swing trading. I also have longer-term investments.

I also have some Bitcoin. It might sound a little crazy or out there but I don't think it's a bad thing to be diversified even in things that. It may turn out to be nothing but I like to hedge my bets. It's all about hedging yourself.

If something happens – and I do honestly worry about the future based on what the Federal Reserve and the global central banks have done - I do really worry that five to ten years down the line there could be a major issue with currencies across the board because let's be honest, all these central banks are printing ridiculous amounts of money. Sure you are not seeing inflation right now, but once you start to see inflation I worry that it will really start to take off.

As to something like Bitcoin, even if you only have $100,000 in total don't put a lot in Bitcoin. Put maybe $1,000 into that, just a small amount because with Bitcoin if something ever did go crazy you would see it double, triple, or quadruple in price. The same thing could happen with gold. Bitcoin could easily go back to $1,000-2,000 per Bitcoin and that can be a huge opportunity to hedge yourself against risks in the future. So always be diversified. Always be aware of the potential risks out there.

You mentioned real estate is one way to diversify. Other than investments are there any other ways that you recommend? Since we already talked about short-term trading this gets into your long-term investing ideas.

I started my own business. Obviously the company I have now is IntheMoneyStocks.com. I would always encourage people to start their own company. I think it is one of the only ways you can ever really be financially independent and enjoy yourself. Sure we can all work fifty years in a job we hate and maybe make good money, but there is nothing like having your own business. There is nothing like being able to control your own destiny.

Absolutely, if you can then try to own your own business. There are so many ideas out there still to be thought of. Look at *Shark Tank*. *Shark Tank* is a great example of that. I would definitely strongly encourage people on that front. For real estate, as I've said, it is just an amazing opportunity for long-term investors.

I do think the key is to be a little of everything. What I always tell people is that I want to be the long-term investor, I want to be the short-term investor, I want to be the day trader.

With long-term investing I don't hold a lot of stocks long term but I do hold real estate. I do have other investments that are longer-term plays that are just going to sit there. With property they don't make more land and at this stage of the game with the climate changes probably the amount of land available in the future is going to be less. You want to have a little of that, but at the same time you should diversify out to shorter-term investments as well.

Let's turn to your thoughts on the future financial risks facing us because many individuals are worried about some of the very same things you are worried about and which I'm concerned about as well. If we have some type of financial catastrophe, such as the collapse of the dollar or anything such as hyperinflation or deflation or what not, how are you preparing for that? What are you expecting might happen and what should people do? Do you expect trading to still survive or what?

I think trading will always be around. We have previously seen bubbles burst in the late '90s into 2000 and then we saw 2007. The Federal Reserve is absolutely the catalyst for these bubbles occurring more and more often. If you look at history, we have had bubbles in the past but they have been much more spaced out. However, because the Fed has meddled so much in the financial system, whether it's printing trillions of dollars per QE or what, it has basically created a quicker and quicker boom-bust cycle. Even lately you wouldn't say that the economy is in a boom whatsoever, but essentially we are building up into another collapse in the market.

The beauty of it is that as a short-term trader - and this touches upon what I said earlier about long-term investments such as gold and maybe a little Bitcoin and some other things like real estate - my short-term investments are stocks because I do not trust the market at these highs right here. That is not to say we cannot go up another 10-20% in the market. If the Fed continues to print money then sure, we are going to go up a little bit more and a little bit more. But there will be a reckoning day, no doubt about it, and again we will see a massive collapse. My fear is *that* because the Fed is meddling more and more.

Greenspan essentially created the real estate bubble when he started to meddle after the tech bubble collapse in 2000. That is what actually created it. Now the Fed has meddled again even more so and my worry is that every collapse is going to be a bigger and bigger one until the ultimate catastrophe. So I can't stress enough and think it's very important that you don't want to put a ton of money in stocks.

Don't let what I'm saying freak you out too much because you have to be conscious about other things, but be diversified and have some gold in your portfolio. Silver is good, too. Also think about diversifying out of currencies into other things like a little bit of Bitcoin here and there, which is not a bad thing. Again, if you put a few thousand dollars into Bitcoin, what is the worst that is going to happen? It can go to zero, but at least you are hedging yourself in case there is a massive collapse of currencies. I think that is so important so I can't stress that enough.

Here is the last question. I always tell people that if you want to go up the learning curve for anything - for instance starting your practice as an architect, doctor, lawyer, trader, etcetera - then find somebody who has been doing it for thirty years and ask them what lessons they have learned and then immediately insert them into your life for that field. They are going to tell you, "Here is your 'To Do' list and here is your 'Don't Do' list." With that in mind, you have seen so much pain and suffering and so much success in trading that I'm sure you have got a short list of pithy advice for people that might be burning inside you. You might have a list of things you really want to instill into people, so what is it that you would tell people that is going to improve their trading skills and eliminate their errors or pains? If you wanted to pass on the keys to success what would you tell people?

That's a great question. Number one, just to make it clear to everyone I think it's important to understand that I wasn't born a genius at trading. I came up from grass roots having never traded at all and I never even heard about the stock market until I was in high school. I basically went from there and slowly learned and I had plenty of lumps along the road.

I always say to people who are IntheMoneyStocks.com members in the chat room and the research center here that if I could have cut my losses in half when I was younger then I literally would have millions more in my bank account right now because of exponentially trading and making money.

The number one thing every trader or every investor needs to know is that as you are learning *go light*. Go light because you will make mistakes and that's okay, but the key is *lose small*. Lose small. Don't risk a lot early on until you prove to yourself.

If I had control over everyone that I trained I would literally restrict their account to only be able to trade one hundred shares or fifty shares or twenty shares and then I would look at their track record. This is probably a great thing to do for everyone at home. Look at your track record of every trade you have ever taken. Analyze why each trade was right or why it was wrong and also say to yourself, "What was my overall percentage win rate?"

Once you can prove to yourself that you get to about a 70-80% success rate in trading then start upping your share size. Then do it again because as you raise the money that you are putting in your emotions will come back into play. They are going to test your discipline again and you are going to ultimately see if your track record stays the same or drops. Generally as most people up their money their track record will drop because of fear and emotion. Once that track record gets back up to 70-80% then raise the investment capital you are putting in again and again.

Again the beauty of it is that traders such as myself, or swing traders or day traders, don't care if the market goes up or down. That's what I love. You never want to wish the market down. I don't wish the market down, but remember if the market goes down then you can trade it that way, too. Just be a short-term trader and short it or buy the dips and wait for the bounce. It can all be done so beautifully like that. Really again, I don't care if the market collapses in the future. There will still be lots of money to be made for everyone.

That's fantastic advice. Thank you for the interview Gareth and for revealing the PPT method of IntheMoneyStocks.com.

It was honestly a pleasure. It was fun.

Chapter 5
Dr. Adrian Manz
Day Trading Proven Market Tendencies

Dr. Adrian Manz of TraderInsight.com employed an intensive statistical study of stock market data to develop a variety of unique day trading systems that have an outstanding track record of success. In his interview you will learn about several highly successful trading systems he developed by understanding trader psychology and the statistical behavior of market movements.

In particular, Adrian will share the actual rules for an intraday position system, a scalping system, an opening gap system and a "sub-$10" system that trades stocks under $10 in price. Using these and other proven systems, Adrian is able to pull money out of the markets on a consistent basis and has become a popular teacher willing to transmit his unique techniques to others.

The breakthrough nature of Adrian's techniques comes from having done extensive data analysis on the statistical nature of order flow momentum so that he could hop on the high volume price activity of institutions in the markets and also make use of the propensities of high frequency trading. The consistent returns of the many systems you can create this way enable you to treat trading like a business.

Adrian, can you give us a story of how you got started in trading and how you ended up with the trading styles that you are using now?

It's kind of a convoluted story, but we started in graduate school. When I say "we," I mean my wife Julie and I. We met at the Claremont Graduate University and we were both working on our MBAs and PhDs at that time.

I'm going to say probably the reason that we got into the trading field was that we were doing a bunch of quantifiable evaluations of market data. We were really focused on behavioral finance at that time. That was the bent that we were taking on organizational psychology and social psychology. We were trying to figure out if there was a way that you could go through and figure out how and why markets work, and then figure out if you could help organizations like investment banks and trading operations get their traders more profitable.

You were both going for PhDs in Psychology?

Right. We both hold doctorates in Psychology. Mine is straight up Organizational Psychology. Julie's is Social Psychology and then Consumer Psychology. Also we both have MBAs.

It's a weird way to get started in trading but we met late and we decided, "Okay, we are getting married and we're thirty years old." We thought, "Do we really want to be traveling all the time?" You know, it was a brand new marriage and everything. So then we started trading. We said we are going to put our ideas to work and we wanted to see if maybe we had something here.

This was in 1999 and I'm going to say that what saved us and kept us from collapsing with everything else that was going on at that time was our particular bent on the market. Our view at that time was that the New York Stock Exchange is made up of specialists who are the guys who handle the orders. Now they call them "market makers."

We were in a unique position because the research we were doing was to get to know a bunch of specialists and to get to know how the floor operated so we got very, very comfortable with what was happening down there. We focused entirely on New York Stock Exchange stocks. The thinking behind that at that time was that there is one guy (the specialist) who handles the same stock every single day. If we got to know the personality of a bunch of stocks then you were going to get a good feeling for what that one guy (the specialist) is going to do every time the stock does a certain thing. So we developed this system that was really based on a bunch of statistics and a bunch of number crunching to answer questions like, "Here is what's going to happen if you get an expansion of range in volume today. Here is what's going to happen if you get a ratio pullback today. Here is what's going to happen …"

We went through this and there are nine patterns that I identified. This became the basis of systems we later developed.

Were these like Steidlmayer patterns or something else?

Well, the only thing I look at is price and volume because I wanted the stuff to be portable across markets. When you start using indicators things become very specific to the instrument that you are using in trading. I created them based on a bunch of quant stuff. I created them based on a bunch of statistics and in the end I wrote a book about it that was entirely based on a baseball analogy. The book was *Around the Horn: A Trader's Guide to Consistently Scoring in the Markets*. It contained all the statistics, but was always taking you back to the fact that you are going to identify patterns.

One is an expansion of range in volume, which I call a "fast ball setup." One is a gap and go setup called a "line drive." One is a reversal setup I call an "infield fly." There are also patterns I call a "3-2 pitch," "backdoor slider," "switch-hitter," and "double header."

I went through all this data and came up with these patterns and we have been trading them ever since. For us, we got lucky. We got into the markets and it was easy to be profitable right away because it was all momentum driven. However, we felt like we didn't know what we were doing so we wanted to find some way to focus our energy and have something that was sustainable because you knew momentum wasn't going to go on forever.

Once we started trading these patterns it wasn't easy at first. There was a bunch of refining we had to do and we spent a lot of money figuring out how to get a system to work. But really what it came down to was that you've got these patterns.

The "around the horn" pattern is really a metaphor also for the fact that markets move cyclically. Markets are sort of moving around in these circles or "around the horn." What you want to do is you want to be active in stocks that are currently being marked up or marked down and you want to completely stay away from stocks that are grinding sideways or in those accumulation or distribution ranges that they get into.

That's pretty much it for the core trading strategy. You are just going through it every day. I flip a thousand charts every day and I still to this day look for the NYSE stocks with those setups. The markets have changed a little bit. The markets are a little bit more focused on electronic trading on NASDAQ, but we still do enough size on the NYSE that it goes down to the floor for the most part and it is traded in the booth. What else can I say about it? It pounds! It has had one losing month since 2006 and the rest of them have been gainers. I'm going to say its performance has been slow and steady. You know, it's not 1,000% gains that you're about. This is definitely trading for income.

What are the usual returns per month?

You're doing roughly 6% a month, which sounds like a whole lot of money but when you think about it you are working a trading system every single day and you're sitting in front of your machine every day. If you have a trading account of any kind of size then you are making a nice living from just that part of the trading plan.

But you have to sit in front of the computer to trade these systems? You can't automate it?

I do automate it. We used to sit here pretty much for 6½ hours a day doing trading. Now everything is to the point where you can automate lots of things. I use RealTick.com for example. What I do is either use a conditional order before the open, which allows me to just tell the machine every single thing that I want to have happen over the course of the trading session for those stocks, or I'll use a bracket order.

The difference between the two order types is that a bracket order is going to tie up your money and executes faster than a conditional order. Bracket orders are going to be more efficient than conditional orders. Bracket orders tie up your money the minute you place them, but conditional orders only tie up your money if the order actually triggers.

You're looking at one thousand charts every day? Are you screening them?

They just sort of pop out at you all the time. We do this income trading boot camp with small groups of guys and they will sit there and ask whether they should buy a stock scanner to help them go through the charts and find opportunities. There is a scanner put out by just about everybody who is licensed in one form or another. For instance, you have TradeStation scanners, MetaStock scanners and RealTick scanners.

I actually don't use any of that stuff so I'm a terrible sales person for all these plug-ins because what I do is I put together a list. The list of New York Stock Exchange stocks that I'll scan is a group of stocks that trade more than 350,000 shares a day all the way up to about six million to seven million shares a day. They have to be trading above $35 and not more than $110 a share.

This gives me a list of 1,000 stocks and I load that up in a minder in RealTick. If you sit me down and you're running the TradeStation scanner on a computer right next to me and I'm flipping through the charts, I can pretty much be done in roughly the same time as TradeStation that is scanning for the same setups. It's just a function. I've been doing it for so long that I'm sure it's some kind of muscle memory or something at this point.

Are you looking at the daily bars for finding setups?

Yes, right. I look at the daily bar for the setup and then what I do is I set my profit target on the daily bar where I'm looking for support and resistance. My trading is super nuts and bolts looking for things that happened in the market, looking for where the bodies are buried, so to speak, as far as previous price behavior goes. Then I'll set a support or a resistance stop.

If it's a long trade it is going to be a resistance stop target. If I set up a short trade then I'm going to be focused on the support. Then I go to the intraday chart - the five-minute chart - and again I look for support and resistance and that's where I'm setting up a stop-loss.

What I then do on those is go through and pop them into a spreadsheet, and then I have a look to make sure that my reward-risk ratio is better than one-to-one for each one of the trades. If they are then they go into my core list of trades. Those are the ones that we monitor. Those are the ones that give you the returns per month that people can go through and use to sort of validate everything.

Every trade that we have done back since 2006 is documented on the site. Everything is published today for tomorrow and that section of the trading plan is completely replicable. There is an entry, a target, a stop and money management rules.

For instance, you get into a trade, a trade goes to stop-loss and you are out. If the trade goes 50% of the distance to the target then you move your stop-loss to breakeven. When the trade goes 10¢ to the target then you move your stop to the 50% level. And then when you hit the target, if you have size then when you have a big position on you will take off half of it and use a trailing stop. As long as your broker has a trailing stop server, which most of them do, you can set a trailing stop up, and if you are trading five hundred or one thousand shares then you just take the whole thing off at the target. That's part one of my trading plan.

Part two of my trading plan is the section of stuff called "Stocks to Watch." Those are trades where I couldn't find a one-to-one or better reward-to-risk ratio. For those I use a mechanical stop of 1½ to 1 and I just bracket those orders up. People are most comfortable with the around the horn portion, but the stocks to watch portion really knocks it out of the park. I don't book those trades. I don't keep records of those on the site or anything because it's a harder trade to do during the day. That makes them harder to replicate and I'm not going to frustrate everybody.

Let's get to that in a bit. A big question I've always wanted answered concerns your day trading experience. With the markets having changed so much due to high frequency trading are you having any interference with the trading robots out there?

What it's done is dramatically change the nature of the profit target. Really, what we were trying to do – let's say from 1999 to 2006 or even in 2007 or 2008 - was trying to hop on the price activity that was going to be driven by the institutions so we were always looking for opportunities. This has evolved over the years. We used to sit here and watch the tape. We used to look for size orders on the tape and we would take those size orders as targets or entries. It was based on the fact that we know that the specialist on the floor or $2 broker, when he sees an order for 100,000 shares, is going there because he wants to transact that thing.

Those were really wide profit targets then. If you look through the results on the site - even those of 2006 and 2007 - your profit targets were 90¢ on the trading plan. What has happened now is that we have shifted focus from "we want to do what the institutions are doing" to "we want to do what the institutional HFTs (high frequency traders) are doing," so our profit targets have become 40¢ or 50¢. They have really narrowed over the years.

You have to do more trades in order to get in front of these opportunities because what you are really doing is trying to pick up on the expansion of range in volume. I know the HFT guys. I know what they are looking for. They are looking for the order flow to return in the morning and they are going to pop in and they are going to pop out and I want to make sure I'm out before they are.

So you can actually beat the high frequency traders at their own game?

Yes. Well, even though they are fast (they are using co-located machines or whatever) an entry triggered is going to be an entry. They are going to look for validation of a setup just like you are and they are going to target the same thing you are. Everybody thinks they are in it for a penny or two and they're not really. They are in it for … you basically want to go to the next pool of liquidity. You want to run a price right through all the illiquid places that it trades and you want to get out when it's not a big pocket of illiquidity that is going to turn the price trend around.

That's the gist of the first part of the plan. It has always been about following … well, the elephants are going to move through the market and they are going to leave footprints. You are just looking for those footprints and saying, "I want to follow along and I want to profit because of their actions," and not because I'm some genius or something and I know where prices are going to go. It's more like, "I'm smart and know how to get in front of opportunity and that's all I need."

Adrian, you've got an intraday position system, scalping system, opening gap and sub-$10 stock system. Are they all day trading systems or do any of them last longer than a day? Are they all just very short-term trading methods?

It's all short-term trading. We used to swing trade this because the same patterns work in any timeframe. Actually, we used to swing trade quite a bit. Julie would handle the swing trades and then we just got to the point where we were looking at the two things and really the swing trades weren't putting up numbers that were much better than the intraday trades. It made more sense to have access to the leverage offered by day trading and to just stay focused on what we do best. So this is what we do best.

We are not very comfortable taking stock home overnight. I don't have one share of stock in any kind of retirement portfolio. We buy real estate instead. That's our retirement plan just by virtue of what we do so we do this intraday and the way that we stay focused and profitable intraday is because we focus on the business as traders, not as investors.

Incidentally, that's what I've found a lot of the best traders and investors are also doing. They put their trading profits into other assets that are not related to trading or investing at all such as real estate, a business or something else. Now before I get into some of the actual patterns you trade it sounds like you found some consistent price patterns by doing a lot of statistical research. You turned those behavioral tendencies into trading rules which eliminated the emotional side of trading. Is that a correct explanation?

Right.

What's made you successful in doing this when most people who are day trading or pattern trading usually fail? What do you think you are doing right that other people are not doing and which causes them to fail?

I think that when you run across somebody who is unable to do this the very first thing that usually pops out for us is that they are shooting from the hip all day. They will use an intraday scanner, let's say for momentum, and they try to hop on the momentum every time they find it, or they'll find something going on in the news and they will try to hop on it. When you are trying to jump on a moving train it is not a recipe for success usually.

I'm going to say that 60% of the guys who we have trained at these boot camps - it's a small number because there are only twenty people at a boot camp and we have only held three over the years – but my biggest success stories with them are people who came in after having lost a lot of money because they are convinced they're doing something wrong. The guys who are hard to get through to are the guys who make a little, lose a little and think they might be on to something. It is hard to identify why they are not making money because sometimes they are making money and sometimes they aren't.

I'm going to say that the majority of guys who fail, (1) are trying to hop on board after a stock takes off, and (2) they are hopping from one strategy to another without really getting to know it. They will come, look at a strategy on a site and they will say, "Well, looks like this guy is making money. I'm going to try what he is doing." Then they try what he is doing. They are only three or four days into it and then conclude, "Well, it doesn't seem to be making money so I'm going to try something else." They hop around from one thing to the next and they never really land in a place that is a good fit for them.

The good fit, from our bias on this, is that if it's not psychologically a really good match for you then you can take the best trader in the world, have him train you and you are not going to be able to replicate what he does so we give people four different strategies that we are doing. I'm going to say a quarter of the people inevitably gravitate toward one or the other.

Some people like the really, really structured around the horn stuff that is a trading plan. It's got exact rules: You are going to get in here and you are going to get out here. This is what you are going to do along the way.

Other people like my scalper setups. The scalper trade stuff that I do starts right off the open. It's always in super liquid NASDAQ stocks. It's almost always Apple, almost always Alibaba and Gilead is on there a lot. There are always three stocks and a bunch of different volatility bands that you are looking to scalp through. You make your money right on the open. They like it because it's fast, they are done, they are out. It's a first hour kind of a trade or they also gravitate to the gap trade.

For the gap trade, a lot of people like opening gaps and so we've got a statistical system that handicaps the opening gaps. It gets out with a 95% confidence interval. Once that gap hits you've got a very high probability that the price is going to reverse and move back. Not that it is going to close the gap, but it's going to reverse and trade back in.

These things appeal to people for different reasons and the people who are unable to make them work are the ones usually who go and say, "Well, that one got a big return so I'm going to give it a shot."

It sounds like you have discovered what everybody else says, which is that the trading system or

style you use has to match your personality.

Right, right.

You also mentioned a common story that most people who just jump from system to system or method to method usually fail. As another instance, those who chase after momentum trades by following the crowd are probably entering a little too late to make money. Is that what you were saying before?

Yes. I mean I have watched some of these guys. They are taking these trades late because they are watching it and they say, "Okay, I'm going to wait for a pullback." And then, it's going and it's going and it's going and then they just can't take it anymore so they just fire off a trade. Sure enough you are always going to pick the wrong time. Right when you can't take it anymore is usually when the thing reverses and comes back and clobbers you.

For the psychology I know it's more complicated than this, but let's make it simple. Two groups of people come to your boot camp. You are saying that you've found that the ones who turn around their trading so that it becomes profitable are the ones who aren't egotistical but say, "I'm doing something wrong?"

Right. It's definitely the case of the few.

Why are the other guys coming to you if they are not going to use your system?

Well, the guys who come usually wind up using the system, but they are paying a lot of money to be there. There was also a very high bar for entry. We turn away a lot of people. For a typical boot camp, the process is that we get about four hundred applicants for these things. They go through a very unique screening process. A former boot camp attendee will talk to an applicant first about the boot camp and try to get a feel for whether this is somebody who is a good fit based on their own experience. That boot camp attendee sends the list over to Julie, "Here are fifty people I think are worth talking to." Julie gets on the phone with them and talks to them and tries to see if it is a good psychological fit. Is this likely going to be something that they are going to excel at? If they are then we actually have a little psychological inventory that we have used over the years that they quickly fill out so we can figure out how risk diverse are they, how detail oriented are they, how likely are they to follow the trade.

By the time they get in the door of that thing you really have twenty people who seem to be qualified for our style of trading. I would be willing to put you on a phone with a random sample of boot camp attendees. They are all trading and they are all making money. It's a great testimony to what we are doing, but then here is the bias. They were hand-selected. They are not twenty random people off the street. They are people who we thought were a very good fit for what we are doing so they wound up being very successful doing what we are doing.

We did this vetting process a different way previously and it was a nightmare. A giant list of people came in and then the problem was hell on earth to get through this list and get it narrowed down to twenty people. Right now it's a very different process. I'll go around the country to these meetup groups that TradeStation or eSignal has - the big groups. I give the attendees a very honest look at what we are doing.

I don't get up there and make it look easy. I get up there and show them that trading is a business and trading is hard. This is the hardest thing you are ever going to do in your life and this is how I do it. Then we just let them self-select. I give everybody one of my books and I say, "Read the book. Take what you learn today." They also get a little response card that says if they are interested in the boot camp then please get it back to us.

Now you have finally got a guy who has already seen that we are not offering some miracle get rich quick thing. We are not offering some, "Here are some easy ways to make a $100 a day" thing. We are offering, "If you want to make a living trading then here it is. This is what you are going to do."

You know, the self-selection part of it has been working really well. Talking to the people from the previous boot camps has been working exceptionally well because it really does separate out people who are window shopping from people who want to make their living with trading. And then at the boot camps we found out that the easiest way to get these guys on board is to do a first hour trading room thing that is also run by previous boot camp attendees. They don't get paid for it. They are just in there doing their trades that they learned in the boot camp. It's three days of intense learning, but the first hour of the day I'm going to be trading strategies live because I want you to see that you can earn money doing this.

At the last one we did in Miami, in the first hour trading 1,000 shares each of the days we booked $4,800 in profits. That gets these people focused on, "Okay, I see it now. I see it. Not only was I interested in this thing, but it's a good match for me. I better pay attention to what's going on here and really learn what we are doing."

You know, I have one guy who just sent us his blotter and a write-up thanking us for it. He is doing better than we do. He books thousands of dollars every day. He says that everywhere he looks he sees opportunity.

I'll introduce that later because it will help traders to understand what you are doing and determine if there is a fit with their mentality or style, but let's first go into what you can reveal in terms of some of these trading systems and trading rules. You have an intraday position system, scalping system, opening gap, and sub-$10 stock system. What's the most popular one?

The most popular is going to be the sub-$10 because that brings a lot of people in off the sidelines. That's sort of an older system of mine that we repurposed to sub-$10 stocks and it works really well for those issues. You are looking for the same kind of gap that you are looking for on the high dollar stocks. In the case of the sub-$10 stocks we had originally thrown them away because they are just as likely to move up as they are to move down. There is a two standard deviation gap with volatility, a two standard deviation gap of the typical volatility that you would expect on the stocks, but isn't enough that catches the attention of the people who are looking to fade them usually. But, what it does is that gap is typically news driven and it's usually enough that it really sets the sub-$10s in motion.

Then, really all these guys are doing with them is you take the first five minutes of trading and you bracket off the top and the bottom of the bar. You are just looking for a break either above or below that bar and you are going to take a 10¢ profit or you are going to take a 3¢ loss. It sounds crazy but I would say that if you want to prove it to yourself then log into the trading room for the next week or so and you will see these guys. I don't fool with them too much because you are making $100 and it's not really our game. They are doing 1,000 shares and those things are so liquid. We screen them so that half of the stocks trade more than 750,000 shares a day. They also have to have a tight spread. They must also have a range on a typical day of at least 75¢. So you're getting a big move on a low dollar stock, typically on these stocks. These are not pink sheets. These are the AMDs of the world's stocks that used to be high-flyers but are now just trading at a low price.

How many stocks meet those criteria in a single day?

I'm going to say there are usually five or six that are lined up on that scanner.

Oh, so there are only about five or so. A day trader only has to watch five or six of those stocks and you can take that trade for all of them?

Yeah, most of these guys bracket them all up. This involves two bracket orders. After the first five minutes are over with them you say, "Okay, we're going to take a high of the first bar of trading or low of the first bar of trading and whichever one of those hits first, that's the bracket that's going to trigger." The trade is going to have a 10¢ target and 3¢ stop-loss.

I really do focus them on it. I say, "Do not eyeball this thing and decide whether or not you are going to get out. Just put the order in and get the order out there. Your size is not large enough trading this that you are going to affect the order flow. You are going to able to get out but if you decide, 'Oh, I am going to hop on this one. I am going to try to squeeze some more out of it,' those stocks almost always reverse on you and get you out at zero."

Everything we do is based on statistical number crunching that we have done. Ten and three (10¢ and 3¢) are really good parameters for the sub-$10s.

Have you done this testing with TradeStation using the five-minute bars? What do you use for backtesting all the stuff?

The backtesting is done through statistical programs. TradeStation doesn't really give you statistics, but TradeStation will give you an idea whether something is working or not. TradeStation backtesting is kind of quirky.

It sounds really crazy but we will go and just run the numbers through SPSS and do a statistical work up on things just to see whether we are on to something. Nothing that we put out in front of you is ever sold on the basis of a backtest. It's always sold based on a walk forward (after testing) and were we able to make money out of it.

Rick is in there every day. Rick is trading through a vehicle called SureTrader or something. He has a lot of accounts. He's got accounts with TradeStation and he has an account with the RealTick broker but this whole thing came about because we have people who said that the biggest impediment to using these strategies is because they didn't have enough money for the PDT ("pattern day trader") requirement. Then Rick said, "Well, there is this place in the Bahamas or wherever they are that will let you trade it today with $5,000. You can have $30,000 of trading capital and they'll let you trade without meeting the PDT requirement." So he opened an account there and this guy on the sub-$10 stocks is booking three to five thousand dollars a month. It's like a 10% return.

That's a lot.

It's crazy. You know it is always easy to get a big return on a small account. It's really impressive.

I like the fact that you reduced it to only five or six stocks you have to watch. This is really a strategy for people who don't have a lot of money.

Yes. There are three strategies in there focused on the first hour. That's one of them. You could easily do 2,000 shares or 3,000 shares on it. They don't move very fast. They hit that trigger price and they kind of sit there for a while. I'll watch them. I'm watching the tape and you'll see 5,000, 10,000, 15,000 shares go off and then it starts moving.

So there are a total of three strategies for that based on the first five-minute bar. Okay got that. What is the second most popular strategy of the four you teach?

The opening gaps, namely the two standard deviation gap methods. There are some articles written on this.

What I am trying to do is give people an idea of what the system is and what the exact rules are so they can determine in their mind, "I can do that," and they learn something from our conversation.

If they are using TradeStation then this one is very easy to program. If they are using RealTick then it's just the matter of putting it into an Excel spreadsheet and then RealTick will bounce the data out to Excel and Excel will produce out the gap for you.

We developed this as a part of number crunching we did back at grad school. As far as the statistics making their way into our trading, this is the one where that bleed-over happened, but it's super simple. All you really have to know is, "What is the standard deviation?" It's how far on average can we expect things to move from the average before we can expect them to start moving back towards the average.

How are you measuring that? Are you measuring from close-to-close or are you using the bar heights or true ranges?

Well, it's interesting that whenever you are measuring something statistically what you want to do is measure something that is close as you can possibly be to the actual phenomena you are interested in. We used to toy around with the implied volatility on the front month contract to develop the gap based on that. We also looked at all sorts of volatility measures and then what we came around to using is the true range.

We use true range as a proxy for volatility, not average true range but just true range and we look back ten periods of that. Then we say – this is programmed up in RadarScreen - "What is two standard deviations of true range?" We add that to the average. So you take the average, you add two standard deviations of true range to the average true range, and that's the gap then that TradeStation is looking for - or RealTick or whatever scanner we happen to have running on that day - and it just sorts them to the top.

So here is your list of stocks that met the two standard deviation opening gap for the morning, and then we just look at the charts as if it is a pullback so we look at the opening gaps for the day. Let's say it gapped higher. Now we are looking to fade the gap, looking to short it. If the first bar is the bar that makes the lowest low on that gap higher and the second bar moves through it then we are going to enter on that second bar when it violates the low of the first bar. If those lows are moving higher so that it looks like a deeper and deeper pullback then we just ratchet our entry to the next bar. Each and every time we just move it up, move it up, move it up and then finally when we get the violation we are in.

If it's a deep enough of a pullback, or it is deep enough of a pull into that opening gap so that we've got room for a target from the lowest high to the open of the first bar of trading, then that's the first target that we use. If it goes right off the first bar of trading or we don't have a deep enough move to really make a dent in that opening move then we will either target a floor trader pivot - just a standard pivot line that the RealTicks of the world or TradeStations of the world have built in - or we will target a Fibonacci expansion. So if the first bar was a real big bar I'm going to snap a Fibonnaci study on it and look at the 382, 50% and the 618 extensions as targets. Not because I am a big believer in the spiraling sea shell Fibonacci proportions and all that stuff. I simply know that lots of people watch that stuff and when they don't know where else to look then that is one of the places they look so we essentially try to front run those guys.

Makes perfect sense. I would come to the same conclusion. If people use these things for some reason then your knowledge that they use those targets is what you should try to take advantage of. Now how is the performance of this type of system and who is usually attracted to this? This sounds like you have to be there in front of the machine and execute this in real time.

Yes, you have to have eyeballs on these. You need to know what's going on. You definitely don't want to take every gap.

The guys who go to the boot camps are universally in love with this strategy because this is definitely the biggest bank. You are going to make money with this just about every day, but you could lose your shirt with this every day.

I think today there were eight or nine gaps and the key is you have to very, very quickly access what each one of those gaps is doing. I help them in that first hour of the trading room. I still go through and tell them, "Okay guys, here are the four stocks on this list that I am actually interested in." It's based on things like, first off, how tight is the spread because some of these guys will get murdered in these things. The best looking setup is one like a $120 stock and the spread on the thing is 45¢. They don't think but they go and hit the bid to get into it, and then as soon as the Ask price prints once they are already looking at the fact that they have hit their risk and they are looking to get out of their trade.

I look for the gap on the first bar. What I want to see is that I have a nice narrow range on the first bar and ask is it having a hard time pushing further in the direction of the gap and is the spread tight? Then I'll look to fade it on the next bar. If it's a gap that is moving higher and it looks like it's just picking up steam as it goes then I tell them, "Let's just avoid this one, this one and this one are out."

If it's a gap that is moving a little bit higher and we are looking to short it then the next thing I do is I look at the indexes. What is the market doing? How is the sector doing that the stock is correlated with? Is it a consumer discretionary stock? Is IXY (the S&P Consumer Discretionary Index) taking off to the upside? If it is then maybe that is what is pulling it higher and then let's wait and see if the index comes in a little.

That is a skill-based trade, but it's definitely a skill you can learn and it's just a matter of you should *not be anxious* to take that trade. You have to be doing a real objective evaluation in your mind: "Am I trying to get into this today just because this is my favorite trade and I think I can make some money and be done? I want to go swimming (or go to the beach or play golf or whatever I do)." That's a bad reason to take a trade. Did everything line up exactly the way we wanted it to? If that's the case we are going to go and we are going to fade it.

The other thing I do is use TradetheNews.com quite a bit in my trading. I'll use TheFlyontheWall.com and TradetheNews.com. I just use them quickly to see what generated the gap. Let's say it's just some earnings news. You know the stock, you know the company beat earnings estimates by a penny or by two cents or something, and then I like the gap. If it's a deal breaker like "CEO of the company went to Tijuana and killed a hooker" then that's a bad setup. That stock gapped for a reason. That distribution just shifted on you.

So how are you tracing this out? Do you find the gaps the night before?

They pop up in the morning. It sounds like a frantic show here in the morning but it's not. You have enough time. These gaps appear right on the bell. The thing is populated with one to three. Today it was heavy with six or seven. I just copy those symbols and I paste them in TradetheNews.com or paste them into TheFlyontheWall.com - usually TradetheNews.

TradetheNews.com gives you a lot of corporate data. I don't read it all because you can very quickly glance at it to see why the stock gapped. It might be an analyst upgrade or the company had better than expected earnings or the projections are better and so the stock gapped. Those gaps tend to be like a specialist or market maker taking it up to where he is willing to sell or taking it down to where he is willing to buy. All you are looking to do is catch some of the reversal. You are not looking for this giant move. We are usually looking to make forty or fifty cents on this thing. Sometimes you get lucky and get a couple of bucks out of it, but for the most part you are in that same sweet spot again of forty, fifty or sixty cents where we used to get one dollar, two dollars or three dollars.

Is that making it tougher for you? What do you do to handle it? Are you increasing your leverage or trading more?

We have added a lot of strategies. Over the years we have gone from just trading the very replicable part of the trading plan. I'm very honest with people and publish the plan.

Mark Patel is my broker for years and he worked at Terra Nova. He called me in 2003 and said, "Listen, you are making money and if you are making money you are leaving money on the table. You have either got to get your head wrapped around whether you want to manage money or you have got to go into doing some trader education. One way or another you have a real asset you are sitting on here and you aren't doing anything with it."

The end game was that we published our results because what we wanted was to run a fund and we have done that in various iterations over the years. My problem is that the stuff I do is not super scalable. I run into these guys and what they want is that 6% a month, but I cannot deliver 6% a month when I am trading 20,000 shares. It tails off.

Well maybe you could if you had a hundred different positions each day. It sounds like it's only a few positions for each strategy.

For the money that we are running … actually two of the boot camp guys and I are doing a trading authorization essentially for … let's just call it one of the banana republics. This particular government is looking to make a decent return on their money. They are happy with like 15% a year and 15% a year is something we can deliver just doing basket trades.

We take the core stock on the trading plan - that is actually just a trigger event for us since we don't even trade the one that is the core on the plan - but there is a basket that goes around it. If you had Beazer Homes (BZH) on the trading plan you would be looking at Toll Brothers (TOL), looking at Horton (DHI), looking at PulteGroup (PHM), looking at the whole basket of home builders. They tend to perform pretty well in terms of correlation to that underlier. So you just keep your fingers crossed, it's been working all right.

This sounds like it is very popular with traders simply because the traders have to use their brain to think. Most traders like that.

I am hoping that is why this is popular. I am always very discouraged when somebody who went to the boot camp tells me that they are just trading the plan because really that whole thing is focused on teaching them how to put together their own plan, how to find opportunity and get in front of this stuff. I always use the analogy that I can get hit by a bus tomorrow and then you are out of business. The whole purpose of doing this is to use your noodle. You have to start thinking about what's happening and make something happen.

The opening gaps are things they can very easily find themselves. It's just that they prefer to have me give my thumbs up or thumbs down. There are a lot of cases.

I've become very good friends with all these boot camp guys. There is a very small number of them. I see everybody who has been to a boot camp at least twice a year. I try to tell them, "Look, I am forty-eight years old and things happen to people. You need to go and look for the gaps yourselves and figure out why they are likely to go or not. It's not about me telling you what to do or you should just subscribe to the trading service," although I never found that was a particularly good way for people to do this stuff.

What do you teach people for creating a trading plan? I always want traders to learn how to create them and follow them to the letter.

You will understand when you look at it. Here is our reasoning for doing it the way that I'm going to tell you. I live on the West Coast. I am a very, very bad decision maker at 6:00 a.m. in the morning, but I am very good at decision making during the mid-afternoon when I am setting these up. I try to set up everything so that it could be executed in my absence by somebody who doesn't know what they are doing. That's my criteria for how a trading plan should be structured.

When I teach these guys to set up the trading plan I say, "Look, you have got to find stocks that are doing something that has a predictable outcome. When you find something that has a predictable outcome then you need to go through and see if you can structure it in a way that makes sense in terms of what the markets are saying."

A lot of the problem that I see traders have is that they will base a profit target or a stop-loss on something arbitrary like, "I want to make $1,000 a day and I don't want to lose more than $300 on any given day" or "I don't want to lose more than 1% of my account on any given trade" and then that's how they set the stop.

I tell people all the time that the market does not care how much you are willing to lose or how much you want to make. All the market cares about is where is the liquidity. You are trying to get in where something is about to happen and liquidity is thin. You are looking to get out where something is going to stop happening because liquidity is high.

I have them go through and I say, "For your trading plan, you have to have a logical place to enter the position." That's usually on a validation of whatever we saw happening yesterday. We saw an expansion of range in volume for instance. That's my core trade. Now you look at the chart and you see we've got the widest range of the past ten sessions and we got the widest and biggest volume of the past ten sessions. So the first thing you do is you open up today's ticker tape and what I want you to do is look at what happened going into the close.

First up, how many trades were lock trades? How many trades were going off in hundreds? If you are using RealTick then how many of those trades were iceberg orders, right? How much activity was going off where people were hiding the size that they were actually trading? How many of the trades were irregulars? How many of the trades were coming in after the market or during the market from another time of day and showing a very large print?

You are going to try and figure out whether the institutions are pushing the price or it's just a stock that is being run by retail. You really want to be on the institutional side. With all the stuff that I am doing you want to be focused on institutional trades.

Now you have a trade that makes sense from the vantage point of whether a lot of activity was happening going into the close. If so you have a very high probability that over the course of the session somebody was focused on the volume weighted average price (VWAP) and trying to pick up that stock relative to the VWAP and they couldn't get it done, so at the end of the day they came in and they started hitting the Ask price. The fact that it went out with big size says to me that I have a high likelihood this is going to continue in the morning. The next morning, if I do see that it is getting hit again and I see that price pushes up - usually I use 10¢ as a threshold - about 10¢ above for a long above the previous day's high, then that's going to be my entry trigger. Today I put that on the trading plan for tomorrow.

Then I say that you have to find a logical place to put a proper target, and what I do is just have these guys learn how to really, clearly, visually identify support and resistance. I've got them drawing lines so by the time they leave boot camp they can go through and really identify where the significant support and resistance is on a chart and now they have a target.

Then I go back down and that's done from the longer time frame. I tell them you want to find your stop-loss in the time frame you are actually going to trade. Now go and look at the five-minute chart and go through there and see where is the support and resistance.

I have a look at the big move of the day and do a volume weighted average price for the big directional move of the day. I have them ask whether those two things are in proper order. Is the natural support and resistance that you have going to be after the VWAP if price moves through it? If so price would have to get back down through today's volume weighted average price in order to hit our stop-loss.

When all those pieces are in place then now you have your entry, you have your target, you have your stop, and you have your money management rules. It's just those rules that I told you about before. You want the trade to get to risk free as fast as possible. Obviously you don't want to ratchet in too fast so we wait until 50% of the distance to the target. It just so happens that 50% of the distance to the target tends to be one of those fib numbers. It's just coincidence and when it hits that number they move it to breakeven.

You know when you look at my results you are going to see lot of zeros. That is because a lot of these things turned around and stopped you out for nothing. But we always take the second entry and what you will also see is that a lot of those zeros never generated a second entry, which means they would have gone to the whole stop out and therefore your money management saved you from taking a pretty big adverse move. You managed to get out of the thing and you were done with it. It never retriggered. In order to retrigger we have an 8¢ threshold, so it has to move 8¢ beyond the entry price in the other direction and then the machine resets the entry criteria.

Have you ever looked at your statistics to determine the number of times it stopped out at the breakeven point and you would have made money if you had held on?

It tends to be the case that the second entries are the best entries, so if you look through the results you will see that there are a lot of zeros and then there is a re-trigger the same day. A lot of times that happens within five minutes or ten minutes of being taken into breakeven. I am going to say the second entry might be best, but you rarely get a second entry. It's probably that six or seven out of ten trades which stop you out of breakeven wind up going in completely the opposite direction.

Toll Brothers (TOL) today was on the trading plan as a short. It went down, it got to "50% to the target" and I am just looking at it right now. It is trading up at $36.90 and the stop was going to be $36.82. That means you got taken out at your $36.51 entry price because it had moved down to $36.32, reversed, it took you out, and then went all the way to the stop-loss so you got a zero.

But you know, what that does is that it leaves you with a real good ratio on the day because as regards the other stocks on the trading plan we have that Burlington (BURL) hit the profit target, RHI hit the profit target, OC actually stopped you out for a loss and Toll Brothers stopped you out at breakeven. You wound up making money, but if you had taken a full stop on Toll Brothers then the two losers would have wiped out the two winners. Not wipe them out because the ratio is better than one-to-one, but it would have significantly dented profits and here you are out of the way.

So it really pays to raise the stop to breakeven eventually.

You have got to be disciplined. If you don't have money management you are never going to make money. That probably goes back to your earlier question of why people lose money. It's because they don't have a clue how to manage these positions once they are in them.

Do you think that is the biggest thing for money management? If you had to rank things, what do you think is the biggest rule people have got to follow or the biggest thing that they are not doing that is killing them?

I am going to say that number one is the psychology. You have to pick something that is a good match for you and most people don't. Most people are attracted to these bullshit emails that tell them you are going to make 1,000% doing something and they actually believe it and they get burned. It's a gambler's mentality. This is the worst cause for failure. Then the second thing is that there is no money management. Risk free is not a consideration in their trading.

Trading is all about managing risk. I have worked with guys who put my stuff out for prop traders. They want to have their proprietary trading firms trade the stuff I create. I say, "All right, what's my function here? I appreciate that you are buying some plans from me. What do you want me to do with this?" They say, "We want you to manage the risk at least for a couple of weeks here. We want you to be the risk manager and set these parameters up so that our guys understand how to risk these guys."

And they can't do it?

You can do it if you are dedicated to doing it, but if you are just sticking your toe into the water and you are trying this because you got the notion that it's easy or something then I find that is the place people fall down. They might have a stop-loss, they might actually take the stop, but they don't have money management rules in-between.

I've done a lot of these Traders Expos and things over the years. I speak at the Expo pretty regularly. You get to know people because you get to talk to people at these things. I get a lot of people in those rooms and I'll do a show of hands. Let's say I've got five hundred people in the room. I'll say, "Okay, how many people here have had an intraday trade that turned into a losing trade and they wound up holding onto that position because they thought it was going to come back?"

It's befuddling, it is absolutely startling how many hands will go up. As they've got their hands up I will say, "Because you think it's a good stock, it's going to come back, right? Let's keep those hands up if that's the reason." And I will tell them, "So on Wall Street, what I want you to know is that we call those 'portfoolios.' You have all been sucked into the worst habit that you can possibly get into and nothing will put you out of business quicker because you didn't have a disciplined money management approach in place. You are going to run out of money."

If you were a genie and could wave your wand and eliminate some bad habits in traders or improve some really good habits, what would you do for the day traders?

I would immediately apply structure to all of their lives and say that this is a business and you have got to treat it like a business. There is no business in the world that you would ever run just by the seat of your pants and expect to be successful with it. All that holds true here more than anywhere else. In trading you have got to know what you are going to do before you do it and when it's time to do it, you have to follow your plan exactly by the letter.

I would also say you have got to stop evaluating whether you had a good day or a bad day based on whether or not you made money. For us, nothing will get me a kick in the hindquarters quicker than if I made money on a day where the plan wasn't supposed to make money. It's like I went and took a trade sort of by something I thought I saw. Julie will always be like, "The measure of success is what?" For us the measure of success is, "Did we follow our plan?"

When I worked for Wall Street I used to invent mechanical systems and we used to follow them to the letter. We found out that over the course of the annual year the portfolio lost money when we didn't follow the system exactly, and when we broke the accounting down to quarterly results we also found the same thing. People don't realize that following the trading plan is really important and I just wanted to bring this up to emphasize that fact. Other than that, are there any other systems that people might be interested in that you might be able to describe rules for?

I touched on the scalper system and that one is very simple to set up as well. I teach this quite a bit. You take a stock, but you must find one that is super liquid. That's a stock trading ten million shares per day or better. Today you go through and you try to find ranges that have traded in areas where you can identify support and resistance. What I do there is identify three ranges for each one of the stocks on the plan and usually they are adjacent ranges.

Like today for Apple, it was based on the after-market yesterday. I was long from 129.96 up to 130.14 and then again from 130.14 to 130.35, and then again from 130.35 to 130.52. I just set those ranges up. I'm only looking for stocks that have about a 20¢ travel range - a 20¢ to 30¢ travel range. I set those up around the open so what I'll do is watch before the opening bell and I say, "Where is Apple trading prior to the open?" Let's say it was trading at 130.20 or something. I'll say, "All right, if it hits 130.35 get me in and then just get me out." I just bracket the order up and I'm ready to go.

Over the course of the day I'll always bias it based on those ranges. Again, I only take it in the direction that the thing was biased from yesterday. So today after the earnings it came in and everything. Actually the first trade of the day on this one I lost money, but I only lost 15¢ a share. That shows it's not going to kill you because you have the bracket in place.

You weren't sitting there, you weren't saying, "Oh it's going to come back, it always comes back." You didn't endure what wound up being this $4.00 move to the downside. It really works. It was a very fast market on the open and I got out of Apple with exactly the stop that I had pre-programmed because it's very liquid. Even though the Level 2 screen or whatever was jumping all over the place I had a limit order in, I wasn't going to take the slippage, it wasn't some market order in order to get me out of the trade and it got me out right where I wanted to get out.

They are good trades. They are real solid. We've got tons of free videos on the site showing these. On the homepage I would say there has got to be a hundred videos of these strategies that we talked about today, but not the around the horn stuff because that's boring and you can't show somebody a video of a 6½ hour trade. But for the opening hour trades we've got real money trades on the home page there and just about every day there are two new videos for these guys to look at.

Okay, so we have an idea of the systems that you are using. We know you are making around 6% per month and some traders can make even 10% a month, which is outstanding. What personally

are you doing every day to achieve this? Are you setting this up the night before and then you get up in the morning, set up the trades and then walk away?

What I do is set everything up the night before. In the morning I come in and I trade the first hour. I do that religiously. I'm here for the whole first hour. I've got everything pre-programmed that can be pre-programmed. The first hour trades are the only time that there is really any kind of discretion in what we are doing, so after the first hour usually I either go for a walk on the beach or I go for a walk up the canyon. I like to hike the canyon for an hour. During that time Julie will stay here. She's keeping an eye on things and doing money management and moving stops around and stuff. When I come back I'll sit in front of the machines for another half-hour or something, but by this time of day this stuff is pretty much on autopilot.

Sounds like a great lifestyle! Are there any special websites you suggest people to peruse if they wanted to get into this type of trading? Are there any books you suggest that they read, and any services you use or websites or subscriptions or books to recommend?

As far as my books go, the two books that I wrote include *Around the Horn: A Trader's Guide to Consistently Scoring in the Market* that is from 2003. It's just all the patterns. It's definitely all the patterns that I look for every day. They are all in there.

And that's good enough for people if they wanted to learn how to do it?

I always tell people you are not going to learn how to trade from a book, but it's good enough for them to get the setups, the parameters on how to put it together and examples of a trading plan. I've had people over the years that buy the book and buy the scanning software from TradeStation or MetaStock and they just work it into their routine and they do all right with it.

It'll give them a chance to see "does this match my personality?"

Exactly. Then the other book is *Trade Secrets: Powerful Strategies for Volatile Markets*. That takes one of the trades, which is the core trade that the whole "around the horn" thing is built on - which is an expansion of range in volume - and it takes an expansion of range in volume and shows people how it would really apply to every one of my strategies. You could do this with every one of the strategies that I trade, but I took that one and I showed them, "Here's how you trade this in the core form doing it as a planned trade for the next day. Here's how you trade this as an intra-day trade based on news chatter. Here's how you do this as a swing trade. Here's how you do this as a reversal pattern."

I'm just trying to show people in that book how robust something can be that works for you. There is always something right inside what you are already doing. If what you're already doing is profitable then there are probably other things that you can mine out of that data. Those are my books.

As far other books that I have found useful, I'm going to say I probably have read just about everything out there so it is hard to say one thing is really better than the next, but I like some of the old things. I like *Reminiscences of a Stock Operator*. I like the Bernard Baruch stuff from way back. I like things that add color to the fact that nothing has really changed since people were trading this stuff under a Buttonwood tree. Not all that much is different. It's about human psychology and it's about what happens when people see opportunity. It's what happens when people think they are missing an opportunity.

I did like the *Disciplined Trader* quite a bit, by Mark Douglas. I haven't read it in years but I liked it. I thought the Jack Schwager stuff was good - the *Market Wizards* stuff. I also really happen to like a book by Art Collins that was called *When Supertraders Meet Kryptonite*, which was sort of the other side of the Jack Schwager kind of tale.

Really, I read everything I can get my hands on and I would just kind of suggest people do the same thing. You can never be too smart and you can never learn too much so if you've got time to sit in the Jacuzzi then take a book with you.

Any website recommendations that people should take note of?

For websites I don't really look too much anymore in terms of strategy sites. I do use TradeTheNews.com. I use TradeTheNews pretty extensively.

And TheFlyontheWall.com, right?

Yeah, I use TheFlyontheWall.com too. As news sources go I like those quite a bit. TradeTheNews.com is much more expensive but TradeTheNews gives you a lot deeper look into what's going on and gives you a lot of actual stuff. It tells you how funds are re-balancing. You get all sorts of information from TradeTheNews.com that you are not going to get anywhere else. We have been at this for seventeen years and when we started I had a bunch of websites that I really liked, but I don't do a lot of surfing anymore.

Adrian, you are not a long-term position trader like a Warren Buffett value investor. You just go into the market on a daily basis and day trade to make money. Everybody has a different philosophy about their style of trading so I hope you can talk about why you prefer this to longer term position trading and how you use some of the trading profits you've generated to get into real estate. I want people to get the idea that, "Oh, so that's how to do it. I shouldn't be trading for excitement. I can make this into a business and use the profits for something else." I want to hear what you and Julie had considered before coming up with these sorts of strategies.

A lot of this is timing. It's great to be smart, but it's even greater to be in the right place at the right time. A lot of these things happened by function of coincidence. We got into the markets when the markets were really booming. At that time when you held positions overnight - because we held them over in 1999 and 1998 when we started trading - we thought that if you held these over then surprises were really going to happen in your favor and you were going to walk away with a ton of money. Then, of course, you find out that surprises very frequently *don't* happen in your favor and you wind up not sleeping very well because you are wondering what's going to happen in the morning.

We looked at this and we said, "Okay, we've got a predictable revenue stream based on what we are doing during the day and you can leverage that so much, but you can leverage that much more in the real estate market." Therefore we bought a beach house down on Balboa Island. The idea was that you are taking your trading money, you are putting down some money and all of a sudden you are sitting on this giant asset. We bought our place in the Palisades in 1998, which was the same thing where you are just putting a little bit of money into it and then you've got this asset. Then we bought a place up in the mountains.

Everything we bought we bought where we wanted to be. We bought a place on the island because we like it there and we thought we wanted to move there. That's a whole other tale since Balboa Island is not necessarily a place you go to live, but it's a nice vacation place and my kid likes to go there for a few days. As long as he can bring friends with him we are okay. For a lot of the rest of the year we rent that place out so we picked a place that has vacation rental potential and we rent it out over the course of the summers. It's paid for itself over the years.

The place in the Palisades is another one. It's in a location that we love. We thought we were going to be here for five years. We've got these beautiful sprawling views of the mountains and we are right at the beach.

It just became evident to us that if you levered into the right things when they were cheap then it's just like stocks. It's a recipe for making a lot of money. If you bought real estate out here at the top of the market you obviously got hurt, but everything that we got into is fine so far. This place in the Palisades we paid $400K for and we are sitting on millions of dollars worth of real estate here. The place on the island we bought at $1.2 mil and it's worth $3.2 million. You could just as easily have bought it at $3.8 mil and be sitting at $3.2 mil now and saying, "Adrian gave us some terrible advice here."

You're saying that rather than putting money into stocks you wanted something else that similarly had leverage, and real estate not only fit that requirement but seemed better to you from a risk-reward perspective?

The motivation was to have real estate that would drive income. For instance, the place in the mountains is big and you could rent it out for the ski season if you wanted. We actually go skiing quite a bit so we use it for that. The place on the island you could rent out over the summer and it pays for itself. The place in the Palisades is a place that we live in primarily.

Each one of the properties that we bought was something where we said, (1) we know it can generate a lot of income, (2) we know that if we needed to, if we wanted to, we can have these places pay for themselves, and (3) they are all places that are very desirable and where we want to be. They are where we would be happy living. They met our criteria.

I was not interested in being a slumlord. I was not interested in picking up some 8-plex somewhere and trying to beat the rent out of people every month. I was interested in high quality real estate that was most likely going to appreciate in price, and if the absolute worst happens and it goes down in value then it is not like sitting on a stock that went down in value where you look at this thing and it's an abstract thing that you own. It is something real, it's something tangible, and it's something that you actually want to go to and have in your life. Julie at one point just said to me that it's not just about sitting here all day pushing money around. We want to feel like we are doing something real and that still holds true today.

Okay, great. Before we get to your website, are there any success stories of students that just really

strike you and tell a story you would love people to hear?

We've got one guy who was extremely realistic. He's a smart guy, a very bright guy and when you talk to him you can tell he's just as bright as sunshine. He called us about the boot camp and he said, "Look, I'm only looking for the possibility of making $300 a day at this. If I can do that, I would consider this a success story." He works for the TSA at the airport. We said, "Rick, absolutely you can." That's the most realistic thing we've ever heard in our life.

How large an account size does he need to make that?

With a $30,000 trading account, he was levered up and he was doing all the trades. Slowly but surely he's added money to what he's trading. I think now he's trading about a $50,000 account but this guy is pulling $4,000 or $5,000 a month out of the markets and he says if he can add just a little bit more to what he's doing then he feels like he's set. He's got the rest of his life planned.

There's another guy, Wayne, who is a real disciplined guy. He was a special ops guy in Iraq and he came into the boot camp and he said, "I'm trading forex currently and I'm making some money, but I can see that you guys are really managing to clean up with the markets. I think I want to do this. Do you think I can do this?" Julie was like, "Well first off, if you're making money in forex then something is upside down here. You are probably going to be able to make money doing a lot of things."

He came to the boot camp and he sent us this glowing testimonial last week. He said, "Before I went to this thing, I didn't see anything on the charts that told me what to do. Now I pull up a chart during the day and all I see is opportunity and opportunity and opportunity." If this guy keeps going the way he's going then he's on par to pull down $200K to $250K dollars on a $50,000 trading account. It's crazy.

Okay, let me show his letter so people can get a better understanding of how you are trading and what you can achieve based on his own personal experience and feedback:

I just wanted to give you an update following the Miami Bootcamp. Once I got home and really started plowing thru the manual and a lot of the online course videos and thinking hard about my approach I had a powerful and profound shift in perspective.

I have been trading stocks as swings and using daily charts to plan my entries using patterns and then managing them, sometimes for weeks. Some stocks go and make good gains, but in the past couple of years many of the breakouts and moves have failed, or the stocks just reach a point and selloff quickly and relentlessly during sector rotation and whatever. I saw time after time where weeks' worth of gains were erased in a single day's selloff. It was hard to keep profits and frustrating to say the least. Or I would give the stocks plenty of room to allow for deep pullbacks and retracements, only to get stopped out because the norm has been for the pullbacks to take out prior swing lows where my stops were and then get bought back up.

The Bootcamp and my subsequent study with your approach caused me to make a dramatic shift in thinking. Hey, I can now trade the same setups, plus many new setups, but trade with sufficient SIZE and focus on smaller, more probable intraday targets and achieve much bigger gains. Wow, what a concept! Lol! Not only that, but by day trading only I can take full advantage of margin in the sizing as my targets are hit during the day and I move to the next trade or call it a day early if I want.

These realizations and applying them to my trading has made an epic improvement in my trading execution, my profits, and my overall outlook. Whereas I used to fret day in and day out trying to manage a handful of stocks with all my buying power tied up in them, see gains wiped out in overnight gap downs on news and what-not, now I focus on making successful trade after trade during each day and bank steady gains almost every day. I sleep well at night and focus on my plan for the next day, which you so graciously line out for us. I cannot begin to express how powerful this is for me and how grateful I am for your efforts and teaching. This is just awesome.

And I haven't even scratched the surface of using all the tools and insights you have made me aware of, from market insights, to new setups and targets, to trade and platform tools.

Your teaching and offering of services, from the War Room where we bank solid daily income to your online courses, and especially the Bootcamp, will enable newer traders to get a massive start into trading and shave years off their learning curve. For traders like me with some experience, you have enabled me to make a monumental shift in profitability with far less stress in the trading process in a very short time. The whole package is just extraordinary, from your high-quality, concise videos done with superb professionalism, to the quality of care and support you and your team provide us. I am truly grateful and proud to be a member of your family.

What trading method is he using and what is Rick using?

Rick and Ken Olson run the group for the previous attendees of the boot camp. It's like a mastermind group. They all stay together after the events. Rick runs the room with Ken, and Rick does the sub-$10s, the opening gap trades and he does the plan trades. He does all three. Actually, Wayne also does all three.

Ken Olson is an interesting guy. He was on my trading plan for five years making money trading it and then came to a boot camp and I said, "Well it's interesting that you're on the trading plan and you came to the boot camp." He said, "Yeah, I'm making money but I'm not making as much money as you are so I've come to see what else you are doing." He is an interesting guy. I think he was a cop. Ken Olson was the cop who went in and shot those guys at that Luby's massacre in Texas so he is a real interesting character. He trades mostly the discretionary, the opening trades, the gap trades, and then he focuses entirely on the core portion of the trading plan. For most of the guys who go to boot camp I must say that 60% of them just do the whole megillah and 40% of them sort of pick and choose what they are after.

Please give us an introduction to your website where people can get more information on all these trading methods.

It's TraderInsight.com. It's been around since 1999. Originally it was just kind of a blog with my thoughts like how every other thing starts. It's gone through a bunch of iterations over the years. Today the site is a portal primarily to what I'm doing. We've got some options guys on there as well, but really 90% of what the site is about is just an avenue for people to try what I'm doing or to have a look at what I'm doing. There is a ton of videos at the home page. All you need to do is go to the site. If you go to "Video" you can see there are probably fifty or one hundred videos in there.

It's great if people want to come in and try the trading plans and everything. That's fantastic, but the videos are there as much to weed people out as they are to bring them in. I really don't want to spend a ton of time going through these trading plans with people and trying to convince them that it's something that they are going to like. I prefer they convince themselves and then they come in actually ready to do it. That's the purpose of the videos. The videos are definitely not "trading is easy." The videos are definitely, "Here is how this strategy is working, this is what you have to do, and these are the kind of orders you have to be prepared to enter." It gives people a level of skill. It gives them an idea of what the baseline is.

I'm laughing because that is the right way to do it, which is to give people the information so they can de-select themselves. That's why I ask master traders and investors about their exact system rules so that people can decide whether or not they can adopt that style. I don't want people to be wasting their time or your time either.

Yeah, I really don't want a thousand new customers. I want a few customers who this makes sense for.

Last question for you is whether you are ever going to do the statistical analysis of the markets again to see if you find some new anomalies that you can create trading systems out of?

We are always looking for new ideas, but it winds up being the case that they are largely derivatives of a lot of this stuff. I feel like not all that much has changed over time in the market in terms of how you as an individual can really approach it. I'd love to be running some algorithms that pick up on this stuff and sort of take care of business for you while you are at the beach, but I've just never been particularly good at putting those algorithms together.

The reason I was asking is because the core of what you are doing now was discovered in grad school and I was just wondering if you are itching to repeat that initial type of investigation to update numbers or find something new.

I like doing it. I use RealTick, Julie uses TradeStation. So we have it and I'll sit down and write code or sort of pick apart someone else's code and see what's going on. But the reality is that every time I write something that's too complicated, it tends to work for a little while and then it sort of fizzles out.

Every time I go back to this core stuff and then just focus on where the order flow is. I tell people all the time that I'm an order flow trader and I'm just looking for where the money is moving, and if I could figure out a way to automate that then I'd be stoked. But in the meantime, I'm just doing what I'm doing.

That wraps it up Adrian. Thank you for the interview and especially for revealing the rules to your systems. I think a trader can now know whether or not he can follow your work, which he can see in your books or on your website, and he can get in contact with you at TraderInsight.com. Best of luck to you.

Thanks. It was fun.

Chapter 6
Steve Hawkins
Trading With The New Market Profile

Many traders and investors are familiar with the statistical charting methodology of Market Profile created by Peter Steidlmayer in the 1980s, but few can truly say that they became experts at using it. Peter's longtime partner, Steve Hawkins, wrote one of the best books available on the Market Profile and agreed to discuss some actual trading rules that you can use, based on Profile patterns, as well as the evolutionary changes that have developed in the Profile since its early origins.

Previously, Raymond Barros explained how his entire trading style changed because he started incorporating Profile thinking into his trading plans while Adrian Manz also explained the importance of taking advantage of statistical market patterns by turning them into tradable systems. In this interview Steve discusses what the Profile can reveal about the market's statistical structure and as a publishing first reveals several systems that actually take advantage of various Profile patterns.

Steve, why don't you tell me about your personal trading history? How did you get started in the trading field and how did you get to where you are now including the various paths you went through?

My background is that I'm from the Midwest. I'm from Chicago. I actually went to school at the University of Illinois down in Champaign, and I majored in finance and economics. I really didn't have a lot of background in trading, per say, borrowing my father's and mother's investments and stocks and things like that so I didn't have a real thorough understanding of it.

When I did graduate from university in the early to mid '80s, the job market wasn't the best and I really wanted to get involved in something that would have some upside. I felt sales would be something that would offer that opportunity. One thing that actually did interest me, even though I wasn't knowledgeable in the topic or had a lot of experience in it, was equities.

I took a job with a boutique firm here in Chicago that had traded over the counter as well as exchange traded stock instruments. Essentially I was a salesman doing a lot of cold calling like everyone else who started in the field who initially got all of their friends and family involved in stocks. That experience wasn't good because what they were pushing and what I was selling to them just to generate income were stocks that were marginal at best, and eventually most of the investors lost money in those trades. At that point I realized that if I wanted to stay in this field at all it was probably wise for me to try to learn a bit more about it and understand the approaches that I should use to try to generate my own ideas.

At that same time, I coincidentally came in contact with a friend of mine. My offices were kitty-corner from the Board of Trade, as were his, and we happened to be in the same building. He actually had partnered up with Pete Steidlmayer to start up a company that was pushing the Market Profile and had produced newsletters and helped institutional traders understand the methodology. This friend of mine was from high school where we were relatively close. In high school I was a good athlete so he felt that good athletes could become good traders and he asked me if I wanted to get exposed to the methodology.

While I was working at the stock brokerage house I was initially going between floors and trying to understand the approach when Pete would give classes. I would sit in on them so I gained a decent understanding and then from that point forward I started working with the school. It was called "Market Logic School" and on a monthly basis they would offer week long classes on the methodology. They would probably have thirty to fifty people every month going though these sessions and I started out just really trying to help the individuals understand the methodology a little bit. If they had questions they might call in or sit next to me and gain some understanding. After I got more proficient at it I started working with institutions helping them understand it. Then we got involved on the brokerage side of things, the institutional side.

I started giving recommendations across all markets using the methodology and that's essentially how I got involved from the trading side of things. My focus has been on the Market Profile and I do think it's a wonderful tool. To this day, as I said, I'm working with Peter Steidlmayer developing software. I've been doing that with him since 1991. We've had two iterations of the program and our most recent one is called "Capital Flow 32." We've been building that out since 1998 and we continue to make it better. That's essentially how I got involved in the business and is what my focus has been.

Primarily you are using the Market Profile to do most of your trading?

Yes, I use the Market Profile. I have access to the standard charting, the CQG that a lot of future traders have access to, and I would say I have a decent understanding of lots of the technicals. There are some technicals that I see merit in and others that I do not, but I do overlay other things with the Profile to help me generate something that is hopefully a more reliable signal, but the core of what I do is within the Profile methodology.

As I said, we have done a lot of things within the software that we've been developing that moves it away from the legacy of the traditional Market Profile. I believe it has a lot of other information that it generates that really helps the trader see things more clearly.

Okay, can you give me any track records of your own numbers or those of clients showing how successful a trader you can become using the Market Profile?

I think it is difficult to talk about success from that standpoint, at least for me. I'm at the Board of Trade and so we have a lot of customers, a lot of exposure to people on the floor and how the locals trade on the floor. They have a smaller capital base but with more leverage so it's really hard to statistically say that it is a 30%, 50%, or 80% return.

However with Pete, my partner, we have been developing one program where he says this - and I'm not going to misquote him at all and you might not believe it - but he feels that you can make a million dollars with all this volatility we see in the markets today. One should be able to make a million dollars a day assuming you have the capital base that allows for you to trade a hundred, two hundred, three hundred contracts. The approach would be essentially to try to understand the volume overlay within the context of the price structure and find situations where one can utilize the program to add to one's position.

Pete is adamant about that fact that one should be able to make that kind of money. I've never made that kind of money in a day, but that's what he feels. I guess we'll see if it proves itself out over time, but that's what we are trying to work towards.

Before we actually get into the Market Profile and how it works, a lot of people have said that the high frequency robot trading has really skewed the market so that there isn't a real price discovery mechanism anymore since the prices are all being manipulated. Since the Profile gives us a microscopic view of price behavior, have you noticed anything from the Market Profile charts and analysis that would lend you to be able to confirm statements like this about high frequency trading?

With some of the ways that one looks at the Profile and then general trading, I'll say that there is a lot of noise in the marketplace and I equate high frequency trading to noise to some degree. Way back when we were on the floor there were situations where big traders would be able to move the market just because they had the deepest pockets. They had the biggest capital base. To some degree I think you are seeing the same thing within the high frequency world whereas a lot of them are more momentum-based. I think it's almost like they are all trading the same strategy or derivative of that strategy, which is more momentum-based.

Once the market does start moving it does have some degree of follow through, but what I'm always trying to look for in my trading is just the opposite. I'm trying to find those situations in which the participants, whether they are high frequency or whatever type of time frame they might be trading, are offsides on their trades. That's because I feel that the quickest vertical move is going to happen when the person who is on the wrong side of the market is forced to cover. They just want out whether it's a long or a short. They want out, they want to take their loss and they want to move on to the next trade. If I can find those inflection points, so to speak, that is going to offer an opportunity. You see those in high frequency trading. You also see those in the longer-term or swing trading setups.

I think really you can get run over to some degree with these high frequency tradings. It's just so momentum-based so I think that one thing that I would advocate is that traders trade with less leverage initially. Otherwise there are some people who have come up here into the office at the Board of Trade and they are trying understand how they can approach the market. They want to put on trades where they can risk two or three ticks and to me that two or three ticks risk is just noise. I'll take the other side of all of those trades because I'm sure that net over time I would come out ahead of that because that's an unobtainable objective as far as I'm concerned.

Right, but what I'm trying to get at is whether you can, through the Market Profile, guess what the program traders are going to do. Basically, by looking at the structure of the market that is revealed by Market Profile can you guess what the strategy is going to be?

In addition to the Profile that is obviously overlaying bars with letters we also have a volume component so you can actually see the volume footprint of what is going on in the marketplace. I

BREAKTHROUGH STRATEGIES OF WALL STREET TRADERS

definitely think that you can see areas in which you can anticipate that something is going to happen based upon the volume.

We talk about markets going from balanced to imbalanced. From a volume standpoint we are still looking at that volume perspective and seeing some type of what we call the "minimum trend" where we get a little push away from that volume reference, up or down, that could be the impetus for those high frequency guys to start to come in. It's something that one can do. The difficult thing about it is when I trade I try to trade a portfolio. If you want to try to understand what they are doing then you are forced to just watch one market or two and I think the best trades or the best approach to trading is trading opportunities and not markets. I might be looking for something to happen in the corn or the gold and instead things are happening in the Australian dollar and the copper. You can see little footprints or indications of what's going to happen, but I think that is a difficult way to try to trade the markets actually.

All right, instead of the theory let's get into some specifics because a lot of people don't know what the Market Profile is thus making our discussion too nebulous. We want to tell them that this is what it does and this is how you use it.

Okay.

Are most of the people who use Market Profile day traders or are they momentum traders who are going to hold a position for a couple of days? Also, can you run us through some of the most perfect or most common ways to make money with it in terms of setups?

Okay, sure. Through our experience I would say a large percentage of people who use the Profile - because we've been involved with lots of different banks and funds and institutions and things like that just because of its perception of value - are day traders.

They are just looking for where there is a preponderance of letters, where would be the accepted areas of value that is a fair price area. Then they are going to look to see where are price extremes at the top or the bottom of the Profile shape. Are there extremes? Are there single prints?

I like to say that the Profile is a snapshot, a picture of the market. I think it allows for a person to gain that visual and it gives them some levels to lean against from a trading standpoint.

Okay, so let's explain the Market Profile a bit for our readers. As I understand it, we can segment the market into 15-minute segments or 5-minute or 1-minute segments or whatever you want as a time period. We can use an alphabetical letter to tag the price with a time segment with A being the first segment period of the day, B being the second period and so on. We can even adjust this by volume and build up a Profile shape showing the proportion of the time that the market traded at each price level. That usually builds up, let's say, into sort of a bell shaped curve or other shapes. Is that correct?

Correct, yes. I think way back when the liquidity was on the floor you would see more of a tendency for a bell curve. There wasn't as much money trading in the markets and so the locals would set up the range and the price would just oscillate back and forth, and then that range would become compressed and compressed and compressed and then the day would be finished. That was in the early eighties when Pete developed the idea of the Profile that was more of a balance. We would call it a "3-1-3" type of a structure whereas now it's much different. It's almost like a price fix. The way the market acts is like when you get an economic number announcement where you get some type of an imbalance and then you are just going to get the developments skewed more towards the top or the bottom of that vertical range. I would say that today you are seeing more skewed Profiles visually than what we used to see, which was more balanced.

How can people use this to make money? Give me a method such as, "If we see this type of structure then here is a rule to get in and get out of a trade." Can you give me three or four perfect setups using Market Profile that any type of trader might use? I don't care if they are an institutional trader or a day trader or whatever.

Sure, okay. It's talking about the skew. If you visualize a skew we would call it a "3-2-1 up" pattern. If the "1" is where the preponderance for the letters are then we would say a "3-2-1 up" would look like an uppercase "P."

Okay.

What typically happens or quite often happens is that the market is going to maintain its imbalance for the duration. If you are late to the party and you didn't get involved then the 3-2-1 would be a buying setup. Then what you want to be trying to do is getting involved with the market trading against the "2" or somewhere where you are in the belly of the Profile as far as a buy setup would go, and looking for the market to then vacillate between that belly and the top of the Profile. You are just essentially trying to put something on where if you missed the bigger vertical then you can still trade the balance. Seeing how you've got a skew to the upside you should be buying it first and then selling it.

In other words, if you get sort of the P-shape in terms of the distribution of the prices in the Profile pattern, and you have missed that whole run-up, what you are going to try to do is get in at the belly of that P-shape and get out near the upper part of the P?

Correct, yes.

Okay, and so people then can develop lots of trading rules on these possibilities. They can get in and out of trades several times during the day or whatever because this type of structure usually hangs there for most of they day. Is that what you're saying?

What we found with trading in general is that you want to trade early versus late. The earlier you see it and the earlier you recognize it then the more stable that structure is going to be. Obviously you are going to have to wait a number of hours for the market to develop but early on, when you see it, you are going to want to start putting your orders in the belly and try to get the trade. And you want to be more aggressive really also because that "3-2-1 up" as we call it might continue to trade higher.

If you want to err on the side of being aggressive early to enter the trade, and not so aggressive in getting out if it does start working for you, then later in the day you want to be less aggressive in buying it because that 3-2-1 visually could actually roll over and build a 3-1-3. That area, that belly that you bought against actually might end up being more middle of the range versus the bottom. So trade early and early on give it more room. Later on you are doing it a couple of times at best and then you are stepping away from it.

All right, if somebody has that sort of P structure and they get in at the belly and they are just doing day trading, from your statistical analysis where should they get out? At the fat part of the P or a little bit upper? What statistically is the best place to get out?

If you are getting it late then you just want to get out at the fat part because the tendency for markets is that once you set up some type of range then the ranges are going to start becoming contracted so you want to get out more towards the fat part. But if you get in early then you definitely want to try to give it the opportunity to actually see if it could expand the range higher.

Got it. All right, give me another pattern that people can sort of envision in their mind so they can then say, "Oh, I see what you are doing."

Okay. What we have seen is that markets go from balanced to imbalanced, so assume you can find a situation in which the market is balanced (where we get lots of letters across an area) and then it starts moving away from there. The moving away from there is because the buying overwhelms the selling or selling overwhelms the buying to create what we would call "single prints."

Then if you can allow for another period to develop - and we will just assume that we are starting to develop some form of a little sideways action - those single prints are an area of imbalance. They are an area in which the buyers overwhelm the sellers or vice versa. Those buyers or those sellers who created that imbalance or that minus development should try to defend that position, so when you see single prints within a Profile you want to try to lean against those single prints thinking that they cannot be taken out.

If it is my starting point, when I see single prints I'm going to tend to put an order halfway back through the single prints and then put a stop back through the other end. If the market can't achieve that halfway back point then there is more underlying strength or weakness in the market so you might have to adjust it. But that's a good approach to trying to trade a market that is just starting to move vertically. You want to get onboard and it's a good way to manage the risk as well.

Can you translate that to the words of a buy order here or a sell order here or an exit order here so people can visualize this a little easier? You're using specific Market Profile lingo that a lot of people don't know. They're seeing single prints where a market just went up from say 100 to a 101, to 102 to 103, 104 and it didn't repeat any prices. That Market Profile pattern is what you call "single prints." Where would you put a buy order or a sell order in after it's done all that?

If it goes up higher … like you said, 1, 2, 3, 4, 5, 6 … then it is pushing the higher prices so those single prints are below us. The market then starts trading sideways so we'll say it starts trading between 4 and 6 (104 and 106). So what I try to do - and we'll just say that the single prints are between 100 even and 104 - is I'm going to put my buy order halfway back. I'm going to put it at 102 or 103 or whatever is my best judgment. Then I am going to put a sell stop to take me out of the trade at 100 because at that price the single prints have been taken out and what I'm trading for is some degree of minus development or imbalance. That's been taken out (if it hits 100) so I have to reassess things and take my loss and move on to the next setup.

Okay, now people can visualize it. How about another type of trade? Is there any other favorite trade or most profitable or most common type of trade you can talk about?

I would say this for the way that we look at markets. If you have the ability to overlay volume at time versus volume at price, then if you are building your Profiles and you get a situation in which you are tracking the volume that's occurring within these fifteen-minute or half-hour segments then note the following. When you see the heaviest of the heavy volume at some type of a market extreme, or we'll say at the top or the bottom of a developing range (and that's a difficult part because what is a developing range - is that over the last month or week or whatever?), then if you can see some type of volume excess within the Profile so that just the heaviest of the heavy volume is at a price extreme …

Let me illustrate. For a fifteen-minute period we have an algorithm within the program that looks at three hundred bars. If I'm looking at three hundred fifteen-minute bars and I'm seeing the heaviest of the heavy volume at the top or the bottom of a range then I'm going to try to fade that. The idea is that when the heavy volume comes in and if they are trying to push new lows or push new highs and fail then there is going to be a good chance that it comes back and trades back through the range.

I have friends in New York who trade individual stocks with our program. They are big traders and they make millions of dollars a year just trading these simple setups. Within our software it's nothing more than you see it generate a red Profile when we get the heaviest volume. They just lean against these red Profiles at the tops or bottoms of a developing range. When it doesn't work they are taking small losses. When it does work they could round up a big profit on their trades.

In other words, let's say there is a trading range for a stock and at the bottom of the range or top of the range there is heavy volume so it's sort of bracketed. If you go to the bottom of the range you would be a buyer and if you go to the top of the range you would be a seller thinking that it's sort of stuck in those ranges.

Yes, and then the most conservative and I would probably say the best approach would actually be if it goes through the bottom and then comes back up. Let's say it's a stock trading between 110 and 125 so it breaks down to 109 and then back up to 111. I'm going to try to buy it at 110½ or 111 with the idea that it's not going to trade another buck lower than what I bought it at. The first level where I'm going to look is back towards the top of the trading range. You have to monitor your trades dynamically, but that would be my expectation on a trade like that.

Okay, great. Please give us some other examples of how to use the Profile. I read about the Market Profile when it first came out years ago, but nobody really gave any trading strategies like this.

Yeah, I think that is one of the shortcomings. I think that you have to understand that when Pete first came up with the approach or the theory the technology wasn't what it is today and we didn't have the abilities to create the charts we have today. Within the context of our program there have been lots of things done that now create a higher-level tool. I think that with these higher-level tools these things pop out at you a lot more than they would have way back then.

I think we have a better tool to work with so hopefully we are able to generate things that are more objective. The key to trading is generating objective output. If you can do that then I think the next step is automation, and then essentially you are able to create something that can be a revenue generator across all asset classes, which is what I try to do in my trading.

Do you know of anybody who has taken the Market Profile and actually turned it into a system that executes buy and sell orders automatically?

No, that's what people approach me to do actually because I think, just as you mentioned, that the strategies that we have conveyed to people really are very limited. It really forces one to use a term that we have of "self discovery." It forces one to generate his own ideas and that's a difficult thing to do. I don't really think that there is anyone out there doing that right now. As I said, that is one undertaking I'm trying to do and I probably have a better understanding of the methodology than most people. It's still a big nut that I haven't been able to crack yet, but that's what I'm working towards.

Fine, but are there any other strategies that people might think about if they get Market Profile or any of the versions of it? What is another strategy besides trying to trade the "P" and the volume values? What are some other strategies that a lot of your traders like to use?

There is another one that we call the "trapped money scenario." If you have a similar type of setup where you are getting some type of a trading range, whatever it might be, then this one isn't so much a function of volume. It's more a function of the price action.

If you've got a situation in which you are developing this trading range and then you start pushing below it or you start pushing above it and you try to spend some time up there (or down there) and it isn't able to expand the range by any degree, and then it comes back in the range, that's a scenario that is very, very good to try to fade as well. We call that a "trapped money scenario."

If you think about what is happening, people are trying to get involved with the market under the guise of the range being expanded as maybe the next leg up or down. They initiate their positions and it doesn't unfold that way so they are forced to liquidate their positions. They are essentially trapped with bad trade location within the bigger structure and that being the case then as it starts to go against them they are going to be more aggressive in trying to get out of their trade just because it's bad location relative to what has been occurring in the structure.

How do you take advantage of that when you see that?

The way that I take advantage of it is that you're able to just visualize this structure within the market, some type of a bigger balance area. Then you are seeing some prints developing above the top or the bottom of the structure and then failing back into the structure. That's the way that I, or we, try to trade it.

There are some simple ideas that we have within our program where you make these big composite Profiles. A composite Profile is just formed by aggregating a bunch of Profiles together. What we found is that there is a certain amount of time that you can expect the market to try to trade with a directional impetus and then once it gets to a certain amount of horizontal time it gets old and stale. Once it reaches that condition, it's going to be more likely to try to reverse the direction that got it to that point.

If you can try to do nothing more than understand what we call the "internal time clock of the market" or where the market is as far as development time goes then early on you want to be trying to go with it, and later in the development it is more of a fade (going against it). You have to visualize the bigger structure of a big, big bell curve with lots and lots of letters across horizontally, but placed more at a certain area and then a little bit of a skew at the top or the bottom. Then you would have another smaller Profile separated from the current one and it tries to push up through the top or down through the bottom. Once it gets out to twelve common letters across the Profile, the point of control, then that's stale. If it starts coming off then you want to be trying to fade that move thinking it is going to trade through that bigger structure.

Any other favorite strategies of your really successful traders who use Market Profile?

Yes, there are different things. If you try to visualize what the background is in the market then what we have is we are building these bigger composite Profiles. We are always referencing the third one back as far as what we call a "pivot" that is going to help you understand what is the bias for the trend. We use certain amounts of time within these units. If you can build or visualize Profiles that are about thirty hours or sixty half-hours of time and then try to visualize where those are in relation to each other then that is going to help you understand what is the trend.

You can use that as a backdrop. We are always trying to look at the market from the background or the foreground so if you can visualize it from that context then it is going to help you understand what is the bias. It eliminates one from just reacting such as "because the market is higher I'll buy it" or "it's lower so I'll sell it" or vice versa. You can understand that if you have some method that gives you a perspective of where the trend is then that is going to help you in your trading as well. That is a way one might be able to do that with just trying to visualize Profiles.

You came up with thirty hours. Is that because thirty-two is statistically large enough to let you compute the average of anything and you just rounded down to thirty, or because that number comes from some sort of testing, or is it because thirty hours is a certain number of days and that it actually gives you the best look at determining where the trend is in a market?

With our research we started at ninety-eight half-hours or forty-eight or forty-nine hours of trading. Markets have become more dynamic, but those forty-eight or forty-nine hours were coincidentally close to a week's worth of activity for the markets that trade more than just a short session. However, what we have seen in the last twenty years or ten years is that the markets have become much more dynamic, meaning much more vertical so we have started speeding up that process of generating this background picture. The next thing that we found that was reliable from our research was sixty half-hour periods.

We are more proponents of creating a general overlay as opposed to something really specific to one market because that creates too much customization. We really don't want to move ourselves towards something that is really too optimized or customized. We just really want to have something that is a good overlay and that based upon our research is a good starting point.

For a more vertical market, I would say that when the crude was moving a lot a year to six months ago then you would want to even speed that process up more. When markets slow down then you want to slow that process down also because you don't want to get all these false starts. You really want to have something that's credible. As far as the way that the program works, when an imbalance comes into something that is balanced then it is going to cause it to segment because it's not hard-coded actually.

It's something that is going to be minimum of sixty half-hour periods or ninety half-hour periods, but it could be more than that if there is no imbalance coming. We are really trying to focus on the situations of markets going from balanced to imbalanced and when that imbalance comes in then visually or conceptually it would be similar to the momentum guys coming in and is that going to have any type of follow through. That's what we are trying to look for.

Over the years you have tested lots of things through research and that's a little gem, which is to be using that time frame for analysis. Are there any other gems that you found through Market Profile studies that could help traders in general? Any other information like that?

Yes, there are things. We try to focus on the speed of the market. We always like to say that the "largest" move that you see in the market as far as vertical and the "fastest" move as far as time really is going to be the one that is going to set the tone. What I'm always looking for is that fast move.

If you are looking at a Profile like we alluded to with this P shape, you might actually create a Profile in which, using the old terminology, it is something along the lines of a "trend day" where you are building higher highs and higher lows or lower highs and lower lows. If you are building something like that throughout the day then that's going to set the tone for that day and the next. In fact, I shouldn't use the term "days" because we don't look at days anymore per say, but for that Profile it will set the tone for the next two or three Profiles.

When you get some type of vertical imbalance where you are getting what we would call a "skinny Profile" or the market trading through time then that is going to be something that you are going to want to be trying to lean with. Say that that is the dominant direction for the market for the next two or three Profiles. We look at these Profiles and they have to be at least six to seven hours in length so that would be the next fourteen hours of trade.

Okay. That is a good gem. Are there any other findings like that which you have discovered through research? I don't care what particular areas they cover, but am interested in any findings that you guys have discovered because of analyzing price structures, and that you wish regular traders knew. Anything along those lines …

There are a number of other things we have talked about and this one would equate more to your people who are trading more actively in two days. You look at the price array and you see all of the volume occurring within the price array. Back in the day, as you alluded to, the Profile was more symmetrical where you got the preponderance of the volume more towards the middle of the range, but now we are actually seeing more situations of what we would call a "dumbbell shape" as far as the structure goes.

Right.

That being the case, you are getting a lot of volume at the top, a lot of volume at the bottom, and then more volume void in the middle. We have found that you are going to get some degree of symmetry within the volume. When we see something moving away from what we would call a volume node then through our observations this evolves over time.

Say that the market is not moving a lot. We'll talk about the S&Ps. You might get 50,000 or 100,000 contracts traded at this volume node. We call it a "landing spot." Typically we are going to say there are just a couple of landing spots within a day. What we try to look for are situations in which you see this volume area coming in, it starts moving vertically, and we're going to be looking for some degree of symmetry or equal amount of volume at the next landing point.

If I'm selling the S&P at 2010 then it might have a couple prices above that level where there is a small amount of volume. Then you start building a big volume node right there and then it starts coming off. You can see some prices down below you where the market traded partially during the day where you have 30,000, 40,000 or 50,000 contracts. I'm going to be inclined to set my cover not on a price per say but on a volume. So say I'm selling the market at 2010 and I see 100,000 contracts at that price. Say I'm short and I've got two or three points in the trade, or four or five points. Who knows where it's going to unfold to? That's something to look at.

I remember one of the guys who uses our software. Pete told me that he called him and asked him what he thought about the S&P when it was a skinny Profile day. Pete noted that within the price array the highest volume at any price was only 25,000 contracts. Essentially the market was trading through time so he told the individual, whether he was long or short, to be long or be short until you see a symmetry relative to that volume.

I think that day the market traded twenty-five handles high or lower. We don't want to have any preconceived notions on where we are going to cover, but this is one where we are more dynamically monitoring this setup and it's utilizing volume. It is refreshing to try to trade something counter to what everyone else is doing, which is predominately trading off of price.

I think that this is a different way of viewing things and I think that based upon our experiences with it there is some good value in it. I think that is something, another little tidbit that we have observed that is a good way to trade.

Did you say that it traded twenty-five handles both higher and lower?

No, no just from when the individual put on the trade. You saw an area to be longish, you put the trade on and there was this landing point. We'll say the market worked higher. We'll say there was a landing level four or five, six, seven ticks higher so you trade until you see the market build a similar amount of volume at a price or if it goes back down and adds another small number of contracts, we'll say 500 contracts at the price, and then get out. Essentially, we are trading volume to volume.

Now why are some people successful at using Market Profile and others are not? How can you differentiate them? What do the most successful guys do and not do? What do the unsuccessful guys do and not do?

I would think that early on when the methodology first came out it was generating a daily Market Profile. Everyone saw the same picture, which you know couldn't be argued from that standpoint. I think whether someone gained understanding through talking to Pete Steidlmayer or Mr. Smith down the block or other people who are self-taught or other people who are promoting themselves as experts in the field, I think part of it has to do with how they generated their knowledge or understanding of the methodology. That would be the first thing, and I would say the most important thing I see.

I don't go out and try to see what's out there relative to the methodology or things like that, but I think that a lot of people take liberties with how they are promoting the Profile's usage, what they offer, or they made changes to the approach that I don't see a lot of merit to. You are putting something out there on the internet and selling it whether it's a system or a service or education. I don't think that some of the sources are credible and so that can obviously create a bad name for something or at least people won't be successful with it. That would be the first thing.

The second thing is that just like anything else things have to evolve. We have a program that we have been developing. One version is from '91 to '98 and one is from '98 to now so we continue to change it and hopefully improve it. I think a lot of people who are utilizing the old methodology are not staying current with how markets have evolved.

Additionally, I think using software that automates things and generates a database, different pieces of information, signals and things like that is being objective. I think for a lot of people who use the Profile that some of their ideas or trades that they are looking for are more subjective.

Why don't you characterize for us the most successful traders using this? Is there anything that strikes you about the guys using this who are most successful in terms of their track record or their performance? What are the common characteristics of the big successes?

I think the first and foremost characteristic is being objective and disciplined. We have different people at different funds and banks and what have you using the program. I think that they have good discipline. They understand risk. They stay within themselves as far as trading goes. They have realistic expectations on what something can provide for them as far as a methodology or an approach. I would say that those are some of the main things that I see that successful people use within the context of the Profile.

Is there anything else that you want to cover or you would say to people if given the chance? Anything you want to say about Market Profile in general, a message you want to pass along, or just any topic you want to tell traders?

I think that trading is a vocation, a profession. I think that one really needs to invest in themselves as far as trading goes. I think that you really need to become a student of the market to become successful. Using the analogy of a pyramid, you want to try to build a base and try to expand from that base.

I think that a lot of people today, whether they are going to go and buy a system or they are going to subscribe to a CQG and read some books on trading technicals, whatever their approach might be they have to realize that it is going to take some time to become professional or successful in their endeavor. You have to be realistic about that and also be realistic about what your potential is as far as making money goes.

Pete always likes to say, "It takes ten years for someone to prove that they can be successful in trading," that being primarily because he has to go through the economic cycles and interpersonal things and things like that. What we have seen here at the Board of Trade is that a lot of people are successful because they are at the right place at the right time. Maybe they buy their membership and go down to Florida in a drought. Maybe everyone is long the market and they make millions of dollars in six months or three months and they lose it all in the next four, five, or six years.

You have to just understand whether your success is based on ability or luck. I think you can differentiate some things like that and that is going to help you be successful. If you make some money and you think that you are the next Paul Tudor Jones then maybe there is a chance that you actually might be, but the probability is that you will not be. Just keep working hard and if you work hard and are disciplined and objective then I think that it is a wonderful business to be in from the perspective of mobility and flexibility as far as the hours that you can work and markets you can trade. It gives one lots of freedom, but it is very difficult to be successful in this field. If you do work hard at it then I think you can make a living and hopefully a good living.

Is there any small subset of books that you would recommend traders read to help them get oriented to the field or become better traders?

Yeah, I think it's always worthwhile to just really try to get a big global macro perspective on things as well as get exposure to things that are totally different than what one might be involved with from your day-to-day analysis and things like that. I like to read about demographics. I think that's important.

For cycles some friends subscribe to one guy who's pretty good as far as cycles go.

Who is that?

The newsletter is *The Weekly Re-Lay*. I forgot the guy's name, but he's from a suburb here in Chicago. It's nice because he gives these big longer-term cycles and dates. Not that I would trade off of those per say, but if something that you have within your approach lines up with something they have then it might give you a higher degree of confidence to do something. If you see their cycles are pretty accurate then that might even be a point where you would be trading a bigger position.

What we like to tell people is that you really want to be able to try to vary your volume and so the quality of the trade involves how you differentiate a ten lot trade from a fifty lot trade. If you can do that then you're going to be very, very successful in your vocation.

As to seasonals, being here at the Board there are all the grains and things like that and so I'm cognizant of the seasonal component of things. There is a service that a friend of mine looks at and he forwards me stuff from. It's called Investiquant.com and what they do is they have all the last one hundred years of history for a lot of different markets. They try to incorporate the seasonals with different other statistics and then try to give you some type of a probability of the market closing higher or lower. If you can factor that in a little bit then I think that is useful as well.

Those are really good references. Any other resources or books or anything else besides these services? Any others that come to mind?

I always like to read the books of Nassim Taleb, the author of *The Black Swan*. He is always interesting in what he has to say as far as his perspective on things. I read all of his books. I'm trying to think of some of the other books that I think are worthwhile but I can't think of anything off the top of my head right now.

It's time to wrap this up. Looking back on your trading career you have talked to a lot of people who are traders or institutions, fund managers and so forth. What strikes you from all these interactions in terms of things you wish you or they had known when first getting started in trading, or general life lessons that you keep hearing from all these people that you really just wish other people knew because it would make them more successful and eliminate a lot of hassles in their learning curve?

I think one thing is this. As I said before, now lots of locals are no longer on the floor here at The Board of Trade, but there were once lots of locals on the floor and lots of them did very, very well. I think the added benefits were having liquidity right there, the access to the information, or the ability to trade leverage and so a lot of them did extremely well in their trading. Then, even though they could see the writing on the wall as far as the trading moving to the screens, a lot of them never really re-factored their skills. You have got to recreate yourself and they were not willing to do that. I don't know if they were just thinking that their way of trading would come back into vogue or whether they thought the floor would come back into favor. I really don't know.

I think one thing that I would say is for a person always to try to improve themselves because things change, markets change, and your approach is going to probably change. If your approach doesn't change then you are going to probably be left behind. I think that is one of the things that I would tell a young person coming up.

No matter how successful you are I think you always have to try to look at what's going to be the next thing that is going to help me stay where I am or become more successful. I think it is going to be evolving your approach. I don't necessarily think you need to throw away what you are doing and start something over from scratch, but just try to evolve or tweak what you're doing and stay current. That is going to help you in your future.

Great. If people want to learn more about Market Profile and what it has to offer, how can they find out what you guys are doing? Is there a website or is there contact information?

I can give you two websites. Steidlmayersoftware.com would be one. Then Profiletrading.com would be another. The one site where I'm posting trades to really try to get people to understand some of the decent trades and objective trades that would be Slow2Fast.co. That's another site that I've started building out five or six months ago with the idea that it's going to be a good conduit to get people up to speed on the methodology and give them some objective trades real time. That way they can see how they unfold and things like that.

What is it called?

Slow2Fast.co is the site.

Okay, Slow2FAST.co ending in ".co" instead of ".com," which might throw some people off. Is that going to include videos of Market Profile charts and how you took the trades?

No, it's just actually utilizing the methodology. I'm utilizing the software program and taking screen captures and noting certain things on them. I'm generating it real time showing "This is the entry price, this is your stop and the initial exit," and then seeing how it unfolds.

That's sort of like what we were trying to discuss with the "P" and so forth right?

Yeah.

Bingo. Perfect. Now if somebody wants to learn more about Market Profile in terms of literature is there a short list of books?

Not to beat my own chest here, but I would say that the book that I wrote when we were first talking years ago is probably the best book. I wrote it in 2001-2002 and I think that's probably when I first talked to you. That's when it was published so even though it is twelve years old I think that it's the best book that really covers the current methodology. The name of that book would be *Steidlmayer on Markets*: *Trading with Market Profile,* the second edition. That's a good book. It goes over the old Profile and tries to segue into the new and how we use the new and gives some examples.

Yes, that's the standard book that I tell everybody to use. If I remember correctly there were nine different basic types of patterns. Correct me if I'm wrong, but is that correct and has it expanded over the years?

No. You're talking about when we would really try to visualize the market from a day perspective. What we have evolved to instead is that within the software program we use algorithms that segment the Profiles based upon a minimum amount of time, and then horizontal and vertical imbalances. So we are really just trying to create all these little data sets that tell us when a little bit of an imbalance comes in. We are not really looking at the market from that old standpoint which involved initial balances and range parameters and things like that.

The "initial balance" used to be the first hour of trade, but nowadays with 24-hour markets everyone always asks what is the first hour of trade? How do you look at things like that now? I don't really have a good answer for that. I can give you lots of different answers, but I think that from where we are sitting we really feel it's pretty necessary for a person to try to evolve their own approach.

It's almost like a high-definition television. If you have a low resolution television where you just look at daily Profiles or use high resolution where you are looking at lots of little Profiles then you are going to hopefully get a clear picture with lots of little Profiles.

That is what we have really tried to do, which is create a database, some type of an output that helps one understand what is the direction of the market. Are there levels where the market could fail for different reasons because you had failed buying or failed selling or there are volume things that one can work with to try to trade off of? As we talked about before, where are single prints within Profiles? If you combine lots of pieces of information that I've alluded to then hopefully it's going to give you a clearer picture to try to trade off of.

I know a lot of traders use the range of the first five minutes of the day, or the range of the first fifteen minutes to set their trading approach for the rest of the day. Have you guys done any studies on approaches like this?

What we have found is that you really have to optimize things like that because when markets are volatile there should be more interest in them. What we see in Chicago about the floor is … well, we'll say the bonds used to open at 7:20 but now because there is no floor anymore we are actually seeing lots of activity come in at six o'clock. The grains used to open at 9:30, but they have a re-opening at 8:30. You are seeing more volume coming in at 8:30 now than 9:30. We haven't done any studies per say on fifteen minutes or five minutes but we have done some research on when is the best time to open. It has really evolved from the fact that it used to be the floor but now is no longer the floor.

That's pretty much it Steve. Is there anything else that you really want people to know?

I think the more that one can create their own ideas versus trying to defer to others is great. I never watch any of those financial news TV shows. I don't have any of that stuff blaring in the background because I think that they are going to have some type of a bias. If you have friends and you talk amongst each other and one has a trading idea so that you put the trade on, what's the probability of him calling up when he gets out? I think the more independent you can be in the thought process is better.

We have tried to do it before working with some big energy companies trying to "trade by committee" so to speak. You always refer to the highest, most senior guy to take his ideas because if you go against him and you are wrong then you are in trouble. If you go with him and you are wrong then no problems. I just think you really should try your best to be as self-sufficient as you can. Generate your own ideas and your own methodology. It's going to allow you to be more successful.

Okay. Thanks a lot Steve. I really appreciate you doing the interview.

Okay, thank you.

Chapter 7
Mike Messier
Catalyst Trading The Biotech Stocks

Many investors and traders are familiar with big biotech firms like Gilead, Celgene and Amgen. However, few are familiar with names in the small-cap biotech stock arena, which is populated by little companies without income that are struggling to make ends meet. These smaller biotech companies raise capital in the hopes that their potential pharmaceutical will eventually be approved for sale by the FDA. Naturally they must update investors as to the status of their drugs in the FDA approval process.

As a result, small biotech firms periodically make announcements to update investors on how their potential drugs are faring in Phase 1, Phase 2, and Phase 3 clinical trials stipulated by the FDA. The news announcement of a drug's status within the FDA approval process is called a "catalyst" or trigger that can propel the price of a security dramatically. The date that an announcement happens is called the catalyst date and naturally this event affects the fortunes of the stock and the company.

As a short-term trading strategy you can buy these stocks if you expect a price upswing before a major positive news announcement, or you can short them after a news announcement is concluded. Learning how and when to do so are the essential ins and outs of becoming a profitable "catalyst trader," which is a type of trading that very few traders are familiar with.

In order to understand the how-tos of "binary event catalyst trading" I interviewed Mark Messier, founder of BioRunUp.com, about how to find the best biotech catalyst opportunities and how to safely trade these stocks ahead of these known catalyst dates. This is a different type of trading than that based on technical or fundamental analysis and it has its own particular rules of dos and don'ts.

Mark, why don't you tell us your background and how you got started in trading?

My background is actually in criminal justice. I got certified as an intelligence analyst for the Department of Justice in California and I was working for a local law enforcement agency doing criminal analysis and intelligence analysis. My family has a blue-collar history of law enforcement, but it wasn't really completely the angle that I wanted to go. I didn't want to be out there on the streets getting shot at. I was doing the criminal analysis type of thing, however, which was always interesting to me.

Can you give us an explanation of criminal analysis and intelligence analysis? Does that background have anything to do with your development of skills in trading the markets?

It is basically studying human patterns and that's kind of where I think the match to trading is. I believe that so much of being successful in trading depends on human psychology, such as understanding the emotions involved in trading and what people are thinking and doing before they do it.

I think this plays closely to criminal justice in terms of tracking crimes because part of what we would do was pattern analysis. It is part of crime analysis to basically try to predict what was going to happen before it happened, and this is very similar with the stock market as far as analysis is concerned. You are basically studying human patterns by using trading patterns and saying, "Okay, this worked in this particular sector or for these particular stocks," or "There were these particular ingredients that went along with the run-up and it was a very successful trade." You can even backtest these types of analyses to conclude, "Wow, that made a huge run, it was a very good position," and so then you can look forward to similar results for the same pre-conditions in the future.

What are the criteria for certain stocks that I want which will show me they are all set to make a good run? The biotech sector is a perfect area for that kind of analysis and that kind of trading because it is all catalyst based. You can see what worked in the past and then just look for those types of positions coming in the future as you are going forward. When you are looking to pick a buy for a certain type of stock you have to set out the right ingredients and make sure they are there before you buy the position.

This criminal analysis analogy sounds really interesting, but it's still a bit theoretical to me. Can you give me some examples of what criminal analysis is and what you would actually do?

Basically with investigative analysis we would read all the case details of a crime. Say it was a bank robbery and therefore I knew the patterns that the criminal used. Obviously they hadn't been caught yet, but we knew the time of the crime or day of the week that they went into the bank, the clothing they were wearing, the type of bank, where was it located and so on. That's kind of a basic scale. In other words, we basically tried to figure out some patterns of a serial case so that we knew where to move resources to possibly catch the criminal in the future. That's an example of the analysis done for somebody who is robbing banks in a serial fashion and how we would try to best determine where they most likely were going to hit next.

In other words you would say, "Here is an unsolved case so let's try to find any possible patterns within it." Then you would use your analysis to predict where it is possibly or probably going to happen next and then you would put the resources there?

My mind has always kind of worked in that way. I learned how to pick a direction and that's kind of of how my mind works. I didn't know it at the time, but it was a nice transition into the stock market.

When you initially went into the stock market would you say that you were a fundamental investor back then or a technical trader? For instance, were you looking for patterns of fundamental pre-conditions (such as the right P/E ratio) as per your criminal analysis career and then expecting stocks having those criteria to go up? Or were you looking for technical chart patterns that they had to satisfy before you expected a stock to rise?

It's kind of a mix, especially in how I started. What happened was that I had a little bit extra money when I was in college because I had worked for Bank of America for a short period of time. When I was working for Bank of America the stock was at $40 or $50 a share. I hadn't looked at the market in a long time and it was late 2008 and then the beginning of 2009. I was just listening to the radio while I was driving for work and I heard that Bank of America was down to like $3 a share. I couldn't believe it. I was like, "What the hell is this?"

I was basically ignorant as the market fell apart in 2008 because I wasn't trading the market. When I finally heard the share price of the one ticker that I was familiar with I was like "holy crap." I knew what a big company Bank of America was because I had worked for them and I thought - it was partly a little naive on my part - but I thought this company is too big to fail, I have a little bit of money and I know where it was trading before. I thought that maybe it was a good idea to take some of that money and start using it in the market and so I did.

That was basically my first foray into trading, which was that I bought Bank of America stock. That trade kind of gave me a taste of the market. Bank of America went up and I then doubled or tripled my money. It wasn't very much money at all. This is going back to my initial $2,480 that I started with in trading during March of 2009 so that was the start of my involvement with the stock market.

While I was researching Bank of America I got into really researching stocks and then I started noticing other tickers around. One of them was Cell Therapeutics, which is CTIC, and that was the first biotech stock that I ever bought. It was under a dollar at the time. I forget the exact pricing but I made a big gain on it. It was like an overnight thing. It started to get some momentum going into a catalyst date. I can't remember if it was a clinical trial or if it was a FDA decision, but there was some sort of catalyst and I watched what took a while for Bank of America to make a move happen much more quickly with CTIC, a biotech stock.

I thought, "Wait a minute here," and I started looking into different biotech stocks and started finding other ones that had similar catalysts whether it was a Phase 3 trial (that is basically where you get an outcome on a drug in a medical trial) or whether it was a FDA decision. I noticed something incredible with a FDA decision that because it is a government regulatory agency they actually gave a day where they were going to render the decision. I started to find those biotech stocks that were small-cap companies but which had progressed to the point where they were able to submit a drug to the FDA.

These stocks are at the point where the whole company is riding on this decision that the FDA is going to give them. They are not like Pfizer, which every couple of weeks has a drug coming up for a FDA decision and which has blockbusters in the pipeline. We are talking small-cap companies that have built their company around one drug. The FDA decision is a "make it or break it" type of event, but you have a date to trade around for that event.

In my research I started to notice that there is a price run-up pattern around those decisions and that's where the name of my website "BioRunUp" (for BioRunUp.com) came from. I started to notice a pattern with biotech stocks, namely that they would "run up" to these catalyst dates. The beautiful part about it was the following. When we are talking about a regulatory catalyst like a FDA drug approval decision, that date wasn't something nebulous like "sometime in the first quarter" or "sometime in the second quarter" for when the government was going to announce a decision on whether the drug was approved for public sale. You had a specific date like "March 16, 2015" for example.

You had the exact date?

Exactly. I consider myself to be pretty conservative and so it provided a date to trade around. I noticed something when I looked at the patterns of these dates. I started to pull up previous biotech stocks and they all made a similar move. Around three months before a FDA announcement there wasn't much volume in the stock and then as it got closer and closer to the catalyst date it just ramped up. This happened every time because everybody started talking about the upcoming decision. It was a big deal for the company and so the share price would go up and it happened every time.

I was like, "Why can't I locate these biotech companies that have catalysts that are definable?" The best ones are the FDA decisions because with those you have an exact date. However, companies at times will give pretty specific guidance even on clinical trials. They will say that they will announce results "maybe in late April" or "we will present at this conference on this date."

My goal and focus since that time has been locating biotech stocks that have defined catalysts where I can safely enter the trade when nobody is talking about them and then hold into the position while everybody starts to talk about them. Before the attention is focused on the stock every time you will be thinking, "When is this one going to start to move?" Then suddenly out of the blue everybody is talking about it and it runs up to that catalyst. Then you have a choice. You have a decision to make.

Personally, I don't like to hold through catalysts. I have seen them become positive and then there is a sell reaction on the news announcement (a "sell on the news" reaction). This is extremely common in biotech because there are a lot of retail traders that come in and when they don't see the stock immediately move in the direction they want on a positive catalyst then everybody sells at once and the share price drops.

There are just so many variables after the fact of an announcement, which can hurt the stock price whereas you can consistently be making gains up until that point. That is why I like to exit positions before a catalyst announcement date. There is no need to take the risk of holding the stock through the actual catalyst itself when you already have substantial gains and there are plenty of other biotechs to roll to the next catalyst.

It seems you are like a lot of professional traders who have weaned themselves off emotions to become successful. It sounds like you are just trying to make money with the trade and then go onto the next one rather than trying to hit one big home run. You just want to make some money with minimal risks and then move onto the next trade.

Absolutely. I found over time that there are so many catalysts and trades that you can be in without taking that risk of holding on through the actual event. This is one of the rules for this type of trading: you cannot fall in love with a biotech stock. I have seen people do that so many times. They fall in love with the story, they fall in love with the drug, they start dreaming of huge gains and sales and the stock going up ten times overnight. They fall in love with the stock and become blinded at anything that could be a negative sign about the company and they end up getting hurt.

Let me summarize everything so far. You got involved in trading because you were working at Bank of America and bought some stock after its price collapsed figuring that it would have to rebound. Afterwards you looked around at other low priced stocks and noticed that one of them, which was a biotech stock, started moving like crazy even faster than when Bank of America's stock rebounded. That's what steered you towards focusing on the biotech sector.

Exactly, and I noticed a trend. If this small-cap stock can move this quickly then I figured there has got to be more like them. What are the key ingredients, what is the trend that is the same with these fast movers? Number one was that they were biotech stocks and number two was that there were definable catalysts.

I don't do this for large-caps drug companies. For instance, you will have Pfizer get a FDA approval and the stock will only go up half a percent. There is no move. What really breaks it down is companies where they are really financially riding on this decision to come home. At BioRunUp.com we keep a database of mostly small company biotechs and there are over three hundred companies in there with potential catalysts coming up.

Does that mean there are three hundred potential trades in a year, or would it be six hundred potential trades a year because of two dates? Can you explain what those dates are and the difference between a FDA decision and clinical trial announcement? How many trades are potentially possible a year?

I would say that in the small-cap space there is probably up to a thousand trades potentially because companies have multiple catalysts. I will try to break it down, but I don't want to get too technical and overload people with information because it sounds much more difficult than it is. But basically, between getting a drug from testing to approval it goes through Phase 1, Phase 2, Phase 3 and then the company can submit the drug to the FDA for a decision on whether or not it can sell the drug.

Each clinical trial gets larger and larger and larger. In Phase 1 they might merely have ten people they test the drug on, and then in Phase 2 they may involve one hundred and fifty people, and in Phase 3 they may have one thousand five hundred people because they just move it along within the process. The higher the phase clinical trial usually the more the stock will react because it is just one step closer to getting to the point where they can submit it to the FDA for review of all the data. The FDA will assign them a date where they will issue them a decision and then once they get that positive decision they can market it and sell it and that's when everything happens.

One company from beginning to end can have multiple catalysts through the entire process for one drug. You have Phase 1, Phase 2 and Phase 3 and then the FDA's submission. For some companies like CTIC - I am still trading CTIC which was the first biotech I ever traded and I think this is the same drug as five years ago - it takes years to go through the whole process.

In other words, a Phase 1 catalyst would be a company's Phase 1 announced clinical trial results, a Phase 2 catalyst is the company's Phase 2 announced clinical trial, and a Phase 3 catalyst is the same thing whereas the "FDA decision" is the final decision where the FDA gives the biotech company a binary "yes" or "no" ruling on whether they can market the drug or not.

Yes. One word we use all the time is PDUFA, which stands for "Prescription Drug User Fee Act." It is the law that Congress passed allowing drug manufacturers to collect fees to help fund the drug approval process, but that is basically what the FDA calls the process of issuing approval for a drug. The FDA catalyst is the PDUFA date. The FDA decision, or FDA catalyst, is the PDUFA.

You mentioned that there is usually a substantial price run-up in a biotech stock before a

company's catalyst, which is what you trade on the bullish side. What is the best lead time ahead of the catalyst dates that is optimal for getting into a trade? Other than just the upcoming date alone is there also an accompanying volume pattern or chart pattern that is also necessary for a potential trade? In other words, what is the normal lead time before a catalyst and how do you actually decide whether to get into a particular trade when there are so many options available?

Usually it depends on the market. One part doesn't depend on the market, which is that with standard reviews we will know about ten months ahead of time when the FDA decision date is. That's part of the process. They submit to the FDA and then the FDA says, "Okay, we have accepted your submission and we will issue you an approval decision on this date in the future." For a standard review that is about ten months out. For a priority review where the FDA says this is a drug with an unmet need then that is six months out.

We have those dates that far in advance. Usually the biotech stock does not start to move until right before a catalyst. We are in a bull market right now and biotechs are really hot right now so anything with a catalyst date is going to really start to run. If it's a market like this then three to four months out you can buy the stock and just tuck it away.

Obviously there are other factors that I look at such as whether the company needs to raise cash, how much they are burning, etcetera because I may not want to buy a stock four months out if they are running out of cash and I know they are going to offer before the catalyst. Then I may hold off, but generally speaking in a bull market like we are in then three to four months out you can buy the thing and tuck it away.

You have three hundred of these potential dates. How do you tell which ones to trade? What are your specific criteria?

In order to get down to an actual FDA decision we have a database with over three hundred catalyst events in it. Within a year there are probably fifteen to twenty that actually come up for a PDUFA, meaning a FDA decision. Those hundreds of events then whittle themselves down to the ones that we are going to watch. Those fifteen to twenty are the best ones to trade. Those are the tightest catalysts and get the most attention because they are FDA decisions.

You mentioned that a Phase 1 trial might involve ten people while Phase 2 and Phase 3 trials involved more people, and that the stock price at those times usually shows larger volatility. I know there is no real number you can tag to what happens at each clinical trial phase announcement, such as "favorable Phase 1 trials can jump a stock 10%, Phase 2 trial results can typically cause 30% price increases, Phase 3 positive results usually lead to 50% gains" and so on, but are there any tendencies you have noticed along these lines? In particular, I'm very interested in finding out what usually happens pricewise with positive FDA announcements.

It's hard to give a number for these things because it is so dependent on the specifics such as what the drug is trying to treat and how good the data is. Phase 1's may not get a lot of price bump because the results are based on such a small sample size. Phase 2's generally tend to get more volatility and you get a better idea of the drug's future from a Phase 2 trial. If a drug is going to fail it usually does so in Phase 2 because in Phase 1 you can't get a statistical analysis. Basically you are making sure that it's safe and they think it's kind of working in Phase 1. In Phase 2 you get to the point where there are enough people involved in a trial where things can become statistically significant. Phase 3 is almost like, "We just want a larger sample size."

Phase 2 can be the most volatile although when you get Phase 3 data that is what they are going to be presenting to the FDA for approval. It is the most important date, but as far as the turning point is concerned then when it comes to what means the most and what can come out of the blue and surprise then a lot of times it is Phase 2.

What percentages are the stocks usually moving because of these catalysts?

It's so hard to give that kind of answer because we've seen ones that make 200% moves because the market was not expecting it and it surprised people. There is a lot of guesswork that goes into estimating a drug's potential and the potential price movement for a positive announcement.

The average volatility per year for stocks selling for less than a dollar is many times what it is for the S&P 500, so I am asking that question because I am trying to get some estimate of the potential price movements for different biotech catalyst dates. I want traders to get a feel for the size of moves involved with this type of trading and want them to understand what portion of that move you are trying to capture, such as a typical percentage profit you are trying to make out of a trade.

As far as the percentage to make out of the trade, usually when we are talking about a run-up we are talking anywhere between a 20% and 100% price increase just in the basic move up to the catalyst.

There are a million factors in that. A big factor is how defined the timeline is because a lot of people get excited when they know they can safely trade in and out of the position because of the defined catalyst date, which just brings more attention to the stock. Then it tends to run up more because people aren't in the dark. When somebody says "second quarter data" this can be any time within a three-month period, but if they say "end of April" then a lot of people are going to get in and play the stock because they know that if they get out of the stock in mid-April they should be okay.

In other words, when people feel that they have an exact date with a FDA catalyst they will then get into the stock three or four months ahead of that time. They will just play it knowing that it might go up 20% or 100% so they are just playing for a certain percentage of that.

Exactly.

Because there are no real fundamentals they can depend on are they using technical analysis to know when to *exactly* get in?

That's the thing - with biotechs it's nearly impossible to trade fundamentals because most of these small-cap biotech companies just lose money all the time and have zero sales. This is all so speculative. Fundamentals with these companies just don't really work.

Technical analysis can help in locating where the 50-day moving average is and seeing if it is kind of gliding along but holding support when it is two or three months out. If so it is probably a good time when you can enter a trade. One of the things I will do is that I will come in on those areas of support early, and if it wants to break down out of that support area then I can stop out and later get back in.

In other words, you are usually using support and resistance to trade?

Yes, very basically yes.

Okay, you know there is going to be an announcement about a drug and it's going to be on this exact date given by the FDA. You therefore have three or four months to trade the stock before this catalyst appears. You use some type of analysis to get in, namely some rudimentary charting support analysis, or you just get in blindly. You have got to get out before the catalyst date, which makes perfect sense. The question is when *exactly* do you get out of the trade? How do you decide to exit the trade and how many days do you usually get out before the catalyst?

With a FDA catalyst where you have the date you are relatively safe up to about a week before the catalyst. I generally recommend scaling out of a position. Maybe two weeks before the catalyst you should take a quarter off and then maybe start peeling back every few days.

It isn't a rush to the exit. You don't want it to be a rush to the exit, but at times it will really heat up during the actual catalyst week because then everybody is talking about it and expecting it. Most everyone is very thankful that the FDA generally sticks to the timeline it sets. They can come out early, they can delay it and be late, but they generally stick to the exact day that they say that they will issue a decision. Just so that I don't get caught a couple of days early I generally recommend exiting about a week before the catalyst.

Let's backtrack a bit. You basically started trading with roughly $2,480 and your site Profit.ly shows you have made over $500,000 by trading. Were the bulk of these profits due to actually trading biotech stocks?

The very beginning was just a small trade in Bank of America stock, but the vast majority of that amount was due to biotech stocks. That wasn't made in a few trades. I am not looking to get rich overnight or to swing a home run every time. I would like to get up there and make 20-30% in a trade and be able to roll to the next catalyst. You need a basket of stocks to do that with. It's hard for me to say how many trades that was in general, but I would imagine that was over several years. I wasn't over-trading or day trading ten stocks a day.

I am trying to figure out why you in particular are successful while other people are not successful in this niche. Before we get into your actual trading rules and style, what do you think it is that you absolutely must do to be successful in this niche?

This goes along closely with my trading rules and is just a different way of saying things. The reason why I think most people fail in biotech is because they fall in love with the stocks. They put too much of the portfolio in one position. They believe that a stock is going to make them rich, they put their blinders on to any risks or any problems and they get greedy. They think, "Wow, it's gone up this much, but if I hold it through the upcoming catalyst I can make even more. I'm reading the Yahoo message boards and they are saying it's going to go up ten times on a FDA approval. Man, imagine how much money that is."

I look at it more as an analyst in the sense of, "Okay, this has a catalyst. It's running up so let's take the risk off and let's move on to the next trade." I will just continually roll and roll and roll positions over while I see so many people falling in love with a company's story and end up blowing up their portfolio when the clinical trial later fails, the FDA gives a surprise decision, or some information comes out about the company that they didn't expect. They blow up their account and then say, "Biotech is too risky and I never want to trade it again."

How much of your portfolio will you usually risk on a trade?

I hope people have a retirement portfolio that they can trade with. I know that saying I will put 10-20% of my portfolio into a biotech stock may seem extremely risky for some people, but I will do that because I am going to trade it with what I feel is minimal risk in the sense that I know when to get in, I know what to expect, and I know when to get out. So let's say 15%.

Do you have a hard stop-loss or mental stop-loss for your trades or none at all?

Usually I will have a mental stop-loss. I don't hard stop anything because with biotech stock you can have misunderstood news come out and shake people out of their positions yet the stocks can still close green after a drop of 10%. There is definitely some volatility in biotech stocks. Therefore I don't use a hard stop.

Usually that ends up burning people with biotech because an initial reaction is panic, then people will figure out what's happening and then there is some bounce. I will put a mental stop at 10%, but I will definitely have to analyze why the trade isn't working before I will just write it off.

Are you looking for a general percentage gain when you exit a profitable trade or are you using a general heuristic like, "Wow, I just made 20% in two weeks time so let me take profits," or "I already made 50% so let me take profits because that's exceptional and I don't care about anything else that comes down the line"? Basically, are there any criteria that help you decide when to get out of a winning trade?

Usually it's a time frame. If I buy a stock and all of a sudden it makes a 30% move and we are still a long distance from the catalyst then I think it is smart to take your profits and wait for a pullback and then get back in. However, with catalyst trading overall it is based more on timelines than it is on actual percentages each time.

That's great. Let's now go back to why you think people are not successful with trading biotech catalysts. You said they might fall in love with the stock and might bet too heavily on one position as well. I'm looking for any other biotech trading "don'ts" to warn people. Are there any other

things that potential catalyst traders should be warned against doing?

One part of the "do not do" list - and something people tend to overlook - is ignoring a company's history. I know it's hard to do fundamental analysis with biotechs, but there are a lot of junk biotech stocks that just roll over and over again and they burn shareholders. Management is basically trying to just come up with crap to keep their jobs and to keep churning out a product, so it's very important that traders look at a biotech company's history, how long it's been around, how many drugs have failed and so on to really get an idea of the company.

Generally what happens is that the better the quality biotech out there then the better the run-up is going to be. That's why there are so many different factors with each run-up that have to be considered. You can have a company that has a long history of failure where they sometimes just acquire some other drug - some other no name drug - and also try to push it through the approval process. There are plenty of junk biotechs that play the same games over and over like this. Their run-ups tend to not exist and they just burn through shareholders.

That sounds like the behavior of penny stock pumpers and dumpers. Does anybody rate these companies so that you can avoid those in particular?

What's difficult about that is that small company biotechs in general just have a bad rap. A lot of people will just consider any small company biotech to be junk or to be a pump and dump stock. It's difficult to rate those. There are definitely certain stocks that I won't trade. Their history is the reason why certain ones are not moving very much.

There are key types of catalysts that will really get a stock moving. Not every FDA decision is equal. You can be talking about a FDA decision for a drug where there is already a good drug on the market and this is just like a "me, too" inferior product, or you can be talking about some new cancer immunotherapy that is the hottest thing around and it's just going to go gangbusters on a FDA decision. Not knowing the details or the science (because I am definitely not that kind of guy), but understanding what area of the market they are trying to penetrate and how *hot* that sector is will influence whether or not it is really going to get some momentum and make a difference on position size, etcetera.

In terms of the announcements, someone can grade these and say this is a "me, too" drug application or this is a "hot area" drug that will probably move higher because of the uniqueness. Are there any other categories that you can use to grade the companies, drugs or catalysts?

A pretty good example of that is, for example, when we had all this Ebola stuff going on a while ago. Every junk biotech came out of the blue and said, "We are working on a vaccine for Ebola" or "We are starting to investigate by putting together a clinical trial," and then the stocks would go through the roof like a pump and dump. Then they would drop and pull back down. I guess day traders were really making big money off the Ebola plays a while back but then that kind of disappeared.

As far as there being a general grading criteria for these biotech catalyst plays, we don't necessarily do that. The ones that we trade and put out to our subscribers are ones that we feel are going to move so we automatically filter those out.

People can now understand what they should *not do* if they want to delve into this type of trading. On the other hand, your success in this niche must be attributable to some positive factors, too. There are other people also trading catalysts in the biotech space, but since you guys are extremely successful at it the logical question is why?

Number one is discipline - just doing the opposite of what the people who are failing are doing, and that is not falling love with the stock.

If it is not working, if your thesis is not validated by the trading action around it then cut losses quickly and don't ride something. Do not double down, do not all of a sudden try to justify why it should be going up or in your own mind start thinking, "Oh no, no just double down, double down." You must have good risk management in that sense.

I think one thing we do really well is that we have a skill of identifying areas of the market or the companies that have catalysts of the right niche. They have the right key words, the hot words that are out there in the marketplace that will attract attention. We are good at locating those stocks before they have already made a big move.

The key is getting into these ones while nobody is talking about them but recognizing that the potential of that particular drug is huge, the potential market is huge and that similar companies have had similar run-ups of such-and-such an amount.

You also have to somewhat look at company fundamentals. I know I was kind of bashing fundamentals earlier because biotechs are so bad, but you are going to get hurt if you take a large position just based on the timeline for a biotech company that has no money and is running out of cash quickly. That is because they are going to raise more capital.

One of the best opportunities to enter into a run-up for biotechs is on a "raise" a few months before a catalyst, so hold off on taking some positions when you realize this company is going to need to raise money. Nobody is really talking about them right now, the share price is low, they are going to have to dip down, the share price is going to get hit and that could provide an excellent entry free and clear of any of that overhead going into the catalyst itself.

Some fundamental analysis about the company definitely comes into play. One of the first things that I look at is the company's cash position. When we have a few months, like six months or so, before a catalyst then I am always examining the company's cash position. I actually want these companies to raise cash because that clears out their overhead so I will be watching and have an alert set.

I want to be saying to myself, "Excellent. This company raised cash, they have a catalyst two months out so this is a good time to initiate the position" because now we are basically in a dead zone for news. That's what we want. I don't want any surprises between when I take a position and when I close out a position before the catalyst. When it comes to biotech stuff the hype will start to spin and create around itself. Everybody will want to get in.

In other words there are three hundred small-cap biotech companies of interest, you select the ones that are going to have a FDA decision or announce their Phase 2 or Phase 3 results or whatever, but in addition to selecting those that already have a predetermined special "catalyst" date you also sort of grade those stocks in terms of their drug's potential hotness. Out of a thousand potential trades in a year you are whittling it down to a smaller amount of trades based on all these filters.

Exactly. You say that a lot better than I do.

Another key criteria is when a company raises money. A "raise" is when they are raising cash by selling out shares. When they raise money it means that they did an offering, which is a public offering or a direct offering. This removes an overhead burden.

What can be really frustrating is if you take a position in a run-up, the stocks starts to act well and the company says, "Okay, we are running out of cash, we need to raise some money," and they do an offering. This is extremely common in biotech.

Remember these stocks are not generating any income. They make no money. The only way they make money is by selling shares. If they don't have a partner lined up, if they don't have any kind of cash flow - which most of them don't - the only way they actually can pay their electric bill is by selling shares.

This can happen often so it's very important to realize what the cash position is on a biotech before you take a position in it yourself. You don't want to buy it just before they raise because oftentimes with biotechs - because there is so much risk involved - they have to raise at a discount. So when a company is trading at $8 a share and then they have to raise at $6.50 you don't want to be the guy who just bought at $8 and watch that get hammered when it is something easy to see that it is going to happen. If their burn rate is ten million dollars and they have ten million in cash then guess what? They are going to raise money in the next three months.

Where do people find that information on their own? Do they look at an SEC filing?

Yes, that's where I find it. You have to look at SEC filings, which most people don't do. That is part of the due diligence process that we do before we buy a stock for subscribers. I would feel irresponsible if I didn't look at that kind of information before I took a position in a stock and that's where you find it. You have to dig through a SEC filing. You can get the information off Yahoo but usually they are just referencing the SEC filings so I would rather go there myself.

Let's now get into exact trading rules. How do you analyze a situation? How does a stock get on your watch list and what are the one by one steps of what you are actually doing? Please run me through the entire process with all the pieces so that people can really understand how catalyst trading works.

The number one most important thing that defines a trade for me is a *definable legitimate catalyst*. If the stock does not have a catalyst, if a biotech does not have a defined date for a binary event which means some type of "yes" or "no," then you should pass on it.

Was the clinical trial successful? Yes or no. Did the FDA give a decision? Was it positive? Yes or no. That's what biotech comes down to – binary events that are catalysts.

If a company does not have any definable catalyst - meaning it is a binary event, it is a yes or no, a clinical trial or a FDA decision and more importantly definable - then one of my rules is that if I don't know when on a calendar I am going to exit a position in a biotech stock then I won't buy it. That's because "definable" to me means I can measure my level of risk. It means, "Am I going to be able to know when to safely exit without putting my neck out there?" and if I don't have that then I am not going to take a position.

For example, there is a stock out there right now and the company has huge data coming up. They reiterated that it will happen in "late April." I listened to the CEO conference, I read the transcripts of the quarterly conference calls, I listened to the different conference presentations and she said, "end of April." This is for a clinical trial.

I want a huge catalyst followed by a definable date. If she said, "We'll announce results in the second quarter" then I wouldn't trade it because of the likelihood of me taking a position now and the data coming out in a month and a week getting into April, which is a risk just too high. I need to know exactly when I am going to exit before I enter into a catalyst position and that is the number one thing I look for when it comes to a trade.

Let's say today is February 25th. You've got a list in front of you of all these potential catalyst dates. How do you prioritize opportunities to decide which stocks you are going to trade? If you could only do one or two, which ones would they be?

The one that I would select to trade is the biotech that I feel would make the largest move based on the actual catalyst itself. You can have a $2 stock and sure it's got a FDA decision but that doesn't really mean much when a positive decision for the company will push the stock price to $2.50 a share. You will get a run up to $2.50, but big deal. That's a 25% move, which is nice but nothing outstanding.

Maybe you've got another biotech stock that is trading at $15 a share and if you just look at the options chain you can see that three months out they are pricing it to be near $30 or $40 a share. That sends off a lot off alarms that the volatility in this stock is huge.

Chances are that because of that huge volatility and a definable catalyst I am going to be able to safely enter and then exit the stock. Also, the likelihood of a high percentage price run-up increases based on the projected move seen in the options chain.

This is great. It's a gem. In other words, if someone wants to be a catalyst trader they don't have to become a medical expert to evaluate a drug's potential or anything like that. Smart people are already factoring all sorts of complicated information into the options price so you can just look at the options chain for various biotechs and see which stocks offer a bigger potential percentage gain than the others and then just focus on those.

Yes, exactly. That's kind of cheating, but that's a good secret you can give out because that's huge. I can give a specific example of that right now.

There is a company called Celladon. CLDN is the ticker and you can compare it to BLUE, which is a similar type of stock. BLUE just ran up from $20 to a $100 based on positive data over just like five patients. Basically they may cure sickle cell disease. These are both companies that are curing diseases. This is a huge area of the market.

CLDN is employing a similar method to what they use, but it's for heart disease and it's a make or break type of clinical trial, but it could be huge. If you look at the options chain for CLDN, it's a $15 stock and right now I guess it's closer to $18. The $30 calls in May, which is only 80 days out, are trading around $5.50 per call. You have $30 puts trading around $17 so basically it's showing that there is massive volatility surrounding this catalyst.

When you have massive volatility you are going to get a lot of hype so you are going to be able to safely predict that a run-up is going to occur. It is going to get hyped because it could be huge.

What is exciting about Celladon (CLDN) is that this is the stock I was referring to when mentioning the conference presentation where the CEO said "end of April." "Late April" is what they put out on the slides in one of their filings. The CEO said "end of April" so you know the stock is a pretty safe hold between now and mid-April and if you look at the trading action on the company recently you'll see that it is starting its run-up. We bought this company at $16 just a couple days ago and it's closing at $18. The reason is a huge catalyst, tight time frame, and potentially big move. If you put those together you get a good run.

You have all these dates and you can guess which stock is going to be a big mover just by looking at the options chain and seeing where the large volume is pricing the stock. With the options chain you can get an idea of what stocks have the biggest potential. If you have a way of grading the potential drugs as "hot market" or "me, too" or whatever then that helps as well. Either works but if you can match those two criteria then you have a better chance of saying, "Okay, of these dozens of dates coming up these are the top several stocks that I really want to trade because of the potential."

Yes, and you know that is actually kind of a way to cheat the system in the sense that you don't need to be a scientist to be able to know about the drug particulars. When you start digging into the medical research behind these drugs it becomes overwhelming. Fortunately my partner Mike is a pharmacist so he is great at doing that kind of stuff. I'm great at identifying and researching the stock, but looking at the options chains is a great way of cheating. Not all of the stocks are options tradable but most of them are, which is great.

From your descriptions I'm trying to find some way to filter down a list of many dates to just a few of the best opportunities so that people can test this style of trading with the utmost safety and minimal risk if they want. Let's say that you now have a catalyst date and you are interested in a stock, you've done some analysis, you know the options chain looks good, and it's three months ahead of the catalyst. Do you have any particular technical or fundamental rule for getting into the trade such as a support level or something like that, or is it just that you did all this other research first and then it's just a blind entry sort of thing?

With the timing, say you have three months out. When we are talking timing you are not in a rush to buy once a catalyst is identified so I like to watch a stock for a while. I like to see it go down. I like to see if it drips down on low volume and whether it holds an area of support, which is what you can look at the moving averages for. You can see, "Okay, it's going to hold there. This looks like a good entry."

I can get a good entry based on moving averages or based on levels of support and then hold the stock. If it decides it wants to break down a little bit - because it could break down for a month or so and then start a run a little bit later - I can stop out if it breaks key levels that it has basically been parked on for a while.

I'm not trading it as a momentum trade. I'm trying to get in while the volume is low. That's when I want to buy it and I don't want to influence the price just because generally I want to buy it when nobody cares about it. When volume comes in ahead of a catalyst then it's usually coming in to drive the price up because more people are talking about it.

For support levels, are you trying to buy at the support or when it goes down through the support level?

I don't like to buy when it's breaking through support. I want to see it hold support. My stop-losses are different the farther I am out from a catalyst. If it is three months out I want to take an initial position in the stock. If it is just not ready and it broke a key level of support and now there is an air space there of 10% where it could drop then I just want to cut my loss. I can get back in next week or in two weeks.

I almost never average down. I usually just cut the trade if it's not working, which sometimes happens because I'm in too early. If it drops maybe I'll let it settle out, find some support area, show me that it's got some support and then I'll take a position into it.

For support are you also using chart patterns or are you just using moving averages?

Generally I like to use a 50-day moving average. That's just my personal preference to see if the price will hold, but overall I like to look at just the chart pattern. The chart doesn't have to have the 50-day or the 200-day moving average. You just have to see on the chart what areas previously have acted as support in the past.

Usually with those areas, especially with biotech, it seems like you could find support, but when there is no catalyst then there is no reason to buy these companies. Generally they will bottom out in an area and that area kind of acts as support when really only the long-term holders are in. When the momentum traders come in then that is when you know you get the price moving up.

Let's say somebody gives me a list of fifty tickers. I'll go in and the first thing I'll do is see if there are any catalyst dates coming up for any of them and I'll make a calendar. I'll mark any catalyst dates as a Phase 1, Phase 2, or Phase 3 announcement or FDA decision. For those catalysts that are within a three to four month window then I'll see what the options chain shows because I don't know anything about pharmaceutical medicines and their potential. In general I'll assume that the larger the options chain volatility the larger the potential winner, so I'll rank them by the biggest potential winners, then drop the bottom ones and just concentrate on the top set of opportunities. Now I'll examine which stocks are riding near their support levels and generally look for safe entry points for the trades. Is that a reasonable description of how you might get into a biotech catalyst play?

Yes, that's reasonable if I'm just looking at a batch of stocks that are all almost equal. But as far as the best trades they usually come up when companies release some kind of information whether it's at a conference or whether it's a quarterly update and the key is that timeline. So a company will immediately move to the top of my list if they have a catalyst with a tight timeline.

What you said will work if I had fifty FDA decisions that were all basically created equal, but you know those ones are fewer and farther between than the clinical plays so somewhere in those criteria is how much we can narrow down this catalyst to safely trade it. I think that is part of the big reason why my account is growing or grew in the way that it did, which is because I didn't hit these big losses that a lot of traders suffer, especially biotech traders. A lot of their problem is that they took huge hits because they held too late or they held into an actual catalyst itself.

The criteria of being definable within a few weeks period – "Can I narrow down this catalyst to when it's actually going to happen?" - that immediately bumps things to the top of the list. It doesn't matter what kind of catalyst it is. If people have a date to trade around then so many catalyst traders out there are like, "I can hold up until this day (or the day before)," and generally that buying will start.

It seems you are taking almost all the trades with definable dates without any special selectivity to it. Just as long as you have that catalyst date you'll trade it?

Right. Obviously there are ones that I'll pounce on because they can be huge like this CLDN trade. You know if a company comes out and they say, "Hey, we've got Phase 3 data that nobody has seen yet and we are going to be presenting it at this conference in two weeks," then I'll buy it. I'll buy it because everybody else is going to be buying it whether or not it is going to be a huge mover or not. That depends on how hot the market is and right now it's really hot so anything with a date is going to move.

So you are just going to get in, but see if you can get it near a support level because that's the cheapest, lowest risk area?

Right, exactly. And there are different kinds of plays because some of the biotech stocks out there - like with a FDA decision where you get the date either six months or ten months in advance – will have news coming out and maybe the stock jumps 5% or 10%, especially when it has a FDA date. That's when you know the application was accepted to be reviewed for approval. You might get a move, but then you've got months and months of no news and it slides back down.

With other companies you'll be like, "Okay, they said they were going to have data in the second quarter, but now they just came out and said they are going to be presenting it in late April." So sometimes you can't sit back and wait to find support with a position. Sometimes you get the news when everybody else does and you have to recognize immediately when you see, "Oh man, they just moved this from a very broad catalyst to a very defined catalyst. It's going to start to move and the time period between now and then is short so we need to buy it now."

Since there are hundreds of these companies, where is the information pipeline that aggregates all these together so that you can follow hundreds of different announcements?

That's one of the things that we offer at BioRunUp.com, which is where we have our tracking database. We call it our "catalyst calendar." You can download it or you can view it within the site. Within the categories that are all sortable are the catalyst date, the market cap of the company, and all sorts of other criteria.

But what are you doing to update this information so that you are on top of things and it stays timely? Are you watching dozens of websites?

I'm watching that everyday as new things come out. I have a paid news service called NewsEdge (NewsEdge.com) that I use. News comes in every morning. I see as it happens every time a biotech firm puts out either a press release or an SEC filing. Then I pop it open and scan it real fast. I know what to look for and part of that is whether they are going to be presenting data at a certain time and if so then I start to dig a little bit more. That's step one. Every biotech press release that comes out will literally pop up on my screen. That's part of what subscribers like, which is that what we do is we are watching those. I know what to look for so they don't have to.

I think my partner, Mike, runs a Google news scan or something like that. Every morning he goes through reading all the news and then he hand enters everything into the database, but he filters out all the crap that isn't going to make a difference. He is not saying, "I'm only going to do things for what I'm going to trade." He will filter the news such as, "Okay, this is an actual catalyst." Maybe it is a one-month or maybe it's a six-month timeline, but if it's a catalyst then he'll input it into the database.

Now I understand how you are entering the trade but later you must exit the trade. Do you just exit one week or two weeks ahead of the catalyst? What are the exact rules?

For a FDA catalyst you can hold closer to the actual date because you have that date. It is very rare that they break it. It can happen, they have done it, but it's pretty rare so generally for those catalysts where it's a FDA decision then within a week you are safe.

You know when the stock makes a huge move. All of a sudden it's pushing up, all the momentum is there, it breaks out and it pushes up and it's two weeks ahead of time and it's made a huge gain. I've got no problems with taking my profit. I'm not set on a week. The momentum is there, the buyers are coming in instead of everybody going, "Oh crap, this is selling off, I need to take my profits now." You don't want to ever have to sell in a panic. You want to sell when it's advantageous for you.

Maybe you'll miss a continued run-up but if the gains are there and the momentum is there and the volume is there and you've got a good profits then take half off, take a quarter off, or take it all off. Pay yourself along the way.

I now understand how you find the firms, how you know when to get into the trades, and how you know when to get out. Do you ever do anything on the short side?

Not in this market. You get blown up if you go on the short side in biotech. It's insane right now but we have in the past and generally because we understand the news. The shorting has usually been news based. Shorting can come into play after post catalyst, and selling the news is a big deal.

We don't do long-term fundamental shorting in biotech. It's not worth wrapping ourselves up in that. However, if a company comes out and they have confused the retail market with the way they've worded their press release and the stock has made a big gain when it shouldn't have then we will short it. It really is market dependent so right now you will get blown up if you short biotech so we are not shorting at this moment, but we will at times. We have and we will. It's a good way to make money.

One of the trends that we didn't really talk about is on FDA decisions. For a small-cap biotech, when it gets a FDA approval one of the biggest moneymakers that we have had consistently is what we call the run-down. You know there is a biotech run-up in price. Well, there is also a run-down.

Basically you've got all these traders in for a catalyst - for a FDA decision. You have got this catalyst and it comes and the drug gets an approval. Well, the majority of the traders that are going to stick in the trade for an approval were obviously expecting it to get approved. What happens is, especially on retail driven trades (we're not talking Pfizer, we're not talking about the big boys, we're talking about just the small-cap biotech that's got all the traders cluttered in there), is that you have got a FDA decision and everybody is hyped up. These people think they are going to make 200% on their money, it's going to double, or it's going to triple. Then the stock doesn't even move and it starts to go down because there are no buyers coming in. Everybody is already in the stock that wanted in on it. You've got all these people who didn't take their profit before the FDA decision because they were thinking they were going to double their money and now all of a sudden … uh oh, it's not even going up. Then it starts to go down and then all of them start to sell it at once.

The vast majority of small-cap biotechs close red the day of their FDA approval, which sounds totally crazy but until you have experienced it you wouldn't believe it. You don't know how many people I know who have had that moment where it's like, "Oh my gosh. I took all this risk going into the decision. It was what I expected, what I hoped for and then I lost money," or the stock closed red on the day.

Generally you've got this run-up where all this retail trading is piling in and then you've got this run-down where traders are thinking, "Oh man, my money didn't double" and then the stock just bleeds for a period of time. We will make money with shorting it on an actual FDA approval. There is generally some kind of spike and then it sells off.

You can trade that with options. We have an options guy who has made a fortune selling out-of-the-money calls into FDA decisions. You are going to make all your money, you are going to make 100% on a rejection because the calls aren't going to hit. On an approval usually it doesn't go up to where people want and then it fades, and then he collects all the money anyway.

He is a smart guy. He is actually a chemist for a midcap biotech company. He knows, "Okay, here's the company and they have given us their projected sales, what they hope to make, and we can look at their fully diluted share count and what the market cap is." Most of the times these things run up to well over what fair value is on an actual approval with full what-the-company-expects-to-sell. That is how out of control these things get and when that reality hits they fade.

You also have this gap. You've got a FDA decision where they say, "Yes, you can sell your drug," and now that they have got the okay they are building up their sales force and marketing. They are going out to doctors, they are trying to sell the drug, and there is usually a good six months between a FDA decision and when we are going to start to see sales numbers coming in after the launch. Those six months of dead air in small-cap biotech are a lifetime. Nobody wants to wait that long. You've got this dead space. Well now, nothing is going to happen and people just sell the news and it fades. It's the most classic "sell the news" scenario that there is and it happens almost every single time. Shorting that is another way to make big money and I've done that a lot.

Does he or do you sell the options the day of the announcement?

Well, usually the volatility is in there before the announcement. He is better at this than I am, but

I have followed him in on a lot of these trades. He will sell some while the huge premium is there and then on the day of the announcement when his thesis is validated that this thing isn't going to the moon. And then quickly … say it's at $10 and it moves to $11. If he was selling $14 calls before then now he's like, "All right, I can safely sell $12 or $13 calls and they will safely expire within a couple of weeks."

We now know how you analyze a biotech situation, we know your basic trading rules, we know the general chart pattern of support you are looking for, we know the catalyst you are looking for. We sort of have a list of dos and don'ts for this type of trading. The don'ts are: don't fall in love with the stock and make sure the company doesn't need to raise money. We have the dos: focus on the definable dates and don't hold to the catalyst dates but get out ahead of time. The perfect opportunity is one of these grade A drugs with a great catalyst as well as options chain volatility and that puts the stock on the watch list. Then you just trade it for a chunk of the move. You are not trying ride it to the moon. You are basically doing a short-term trade and you just want a gain rather than super home run because you are looking at this as a business where there are many other trades afterwards and you don't make all your money with one super winner.

Exactly.

If that is the case then what type of personality succeeds the most for this type of trading? I mean there are a lot of guys who want to do momentum trading, day trading, long-term investing, contrarian trading and so on. I want people to see if they have a psychological fit with this type of trading, so have you noticed any common threads among the personalities of the traders who succeed with biotech?

The trend seems to be those who do well with swing trading and not necessarily momentum watching every tick because you can get overwhelmed with just watching it day-to-day, but the general pattern needs to be there of the run-up. We are talking about a month or two so we are talking about swing traders. It is definitely not day trader types.

In my opinion those who seem to do the best are the ones who can take emotion out of it, the ones who can analyze a stock and not get wrapped up in the story, not get wrapped up in the emotion of greed, but those who can step back and analyze it, trade it, and move on to the next one.

If somebody wanted to master catalyst trading, how much time would they have to spend at this? Is this a full-time job where they have to sit in front of the computer all day?

To be honest, the more time you put into something the better. That's not what people want to hear. They want to hear that someone else, like us, does all the work but the more time you put into it the better that you will get at it. However, if you can be selective and narrow it down just to the specific catalyst that you want then you don't have to sit in front of the computer all day. You can just have a watch list.

You can buy within general time frames like two to three months out. You don't need somebody telling you, "Okay, this is the moment so buy right now. You have to get in now." You have got a long period of time so if you are able to sit back and to process the information then you don't need to be in front of your computer all day.

A lot of these stocks have experienced run-ups already by the time a trader hears about them or finds them. What should traders do when they see that a biotech has already run up an appreciable amount but there is still three months to go before the catalyst? Should they be waiting for the stock to drop down and touch a support before they enter the trade?

That is why I like to use the 50-day moving average. There is nothing magical about it, but it is just a reference point. It is hard to not enter into a position after the stock has already made a move when there is plenty of time and you are three months out. Chances are that it has made a move for a reason and it is going to continue to make that kind of move.

I always like to look at near-term support. I'll pull up the one-hour chart and see how it's been trading for the last couple of weeks, what areas it has been holding and what it bounced off of ... those types of things.

The run-up generally accelerates close to the catalyst. I hate chasing stocks. If I see that it's gone up 50% in the last three months and it's three months to go before the catalyst then I hate that. But generally you don't want biotechs that are trading like crap going into a catalyst because those probably are not going to run up very much.

These are just momentum plays and CLDN is a perfect example. When that stock BLUE went from $30 to a $100 or whatever then because CLDN is in a similar space the stock went from $12 to $20. Then it dipped back down to $16. It has held that level of $16 and now it's starting to make its move as it gets into its catalyst.

You know you can't always pick the bottoms. You have to trust in the catalyst and the momentum that is going to come with it.

The biotech catalyst trader doesn't have to be a day trader?

No.

How do you think this sector will do during a bear market?

There is a lot of speculative money in biotech because this area is not like oil where oil is just down. Biotech as a sector may pull back, but you always have specific catalyst plays that are on the brink of becoming huge. Those are going to make money whether or not the market is hot. It is not immune to market swings. It is speculative, but you just have to be a more selective and tighter with your timeline. You cannot just throw money around and expect profits.

In other words you would expect this time of trading to do well in a bear market?

Yes, it would be tighter and instead of having that basket of like twenty stocks where you are thinking, "This one kind of has a catalyst and I can trade around it," you might have to be like, "I just need the ones that are a big deal." You may have to narrow your basket to five or three stocks by picking the best ones. The turds aren't going to float just because everything else is going up. You just have to be more selective, but they will still move. Obviously in a full market meltdown everything is going to get hit, but specifically related to catalysts they are going to move because it's a big deal.

You mentioned websites doing some hard work for you, for instance NewsEdge, Google News, etcetera. Are there any other information sources out there that potential biotech traders should know about if they really want to do this on their own?

I personally love looking at SEC filings. I think you can link to those from Yahoo but in reading the last quarterly filing, the annual 10K or any of the recent 8Ks then make sure to take note of the company's financial position, the disclaimers that come in on the 10K filings (because a lot of times they will talk about other companies that are coming with similar drugs), maybe lawsuits they have, etc. Those are the areas to pay attention to.

You need a news source to basically get the tickers for the overall sector. From there you need news you can trade off of, which is either in the form of press releases or going through conference calls and quarterly filings, etcetera.

That's where you would be if you started from scratch. You would have to come up with the list of every small-cap biotech and basically search for news on every single one of them and read their filings to try to find what the catalyst is. The only time you are going to hear it is when everybody else is talking about it and that's too late. That's what we provide.

What's the most common question people ask you all the time, and what is something that really itches you? I am talking about something you really want people to know that that they don't really get and it irks you or presses on your mind about this niche?

It always irks me when people say, "Tell me what to buy so I can double my money by tomorrow" or by next week, or in the next month, or within a certain time of period. There are risks and you can lose money. If it were absolutely that easy then everybody would be doing it.

It does take a little bit of work and one of the things that I always like to see people do is to learn paper trading. I always recommend that if people are new to trading that they do some kind of paper trading. When it's paper trading then in reality it's not real money so you are not going to psychologically trade the same way that you do with real money. But take into account what we have talked about and why we are talking about it in the sense that you can't trust emotion to take a hold of a trade, and greed especially.

Once you allow those things to creep in and you don't do your analytical work and you don't think about things - not necessarily scientifically but at least methodically – you are going to end up getting hurt and it's not going to be pretty with the market and with biotech in particular.

There are always variables and this is something I say all the time, but in small-cap biotech there is just no reason to expose yourself to the risk of holding into a catalyst. There are so many variables that come into play. A drug can be perfect but then the FDA can come back and say, "We inspected the facility where you were making the drug and the minimum wage worker there was not wearing their hairnet and that's a violation," and now you have to reapply for something. I mean there are just so many variables that are beyond your control. Never hold into a catalyst, ever.

That seems so simple but you would not believe how many people end up saying, "Oh man, I broke that rule, you know, and now I lost 50% (or whatever)." Just never hold into a catalyst.

For biotech trading or for trading in general, are there any books our members might want to read from Amazon.com that you think can help people?

It's hard to tag a particular book because a lot of the ones that deal with biotech specifically are way too scientific and you know the sector itself is changing every six months so it's hard to do that. That's why I tend to focus on fundamental stuff like trading psychology because even the fundamentals are different in biotech like we've said.

The biotech companies don't make any money so it's hard to trade on fundamentals. Usually charting will go along with where to maybe pick an entry when you've got time. We are not technical traders, but other than that technical analysis may help with selecting an entry and maybe seeing where it might break out, but the psychology behind it is what I think really drives it.

Anything else in terms of advice, words of wisdom, or do's and don'ts you want to pass onto people?

I think trading psychology is extremely interesting because it helps you understand yourself, make yourself a better trader, and really understand why stocks are moving the way that they are especially in a very emotional sector like biotech. I like learning about that kind of thing.

That is just a personal thing, but as far as rules are concerned another rule that I like is this: Don't come up with what you want to happen and then look for a million reasons from other people to support why you think that. For instance, people want a stock to go way up. This is part of falling in love with stock but a little bit different. They think, "This is going to get FDA approval, I know it" and then they go to the Yahoo message boards and all they do is read a bunch of other people who are saying the same thing. Then they start to believe it themselves and all they are doing is coming up with an idea that they want to happen, and then they try to validate it in their own mind from outside sources.

Yeah, they try to justify a trade rather than unemotionally evaluate the facts.

Exactly, and with biotech that is so huge. When people do that they get burned and I see it all the time.

Can you talk about how successful you have been at this in terms of a trading record?

I started with $2,480 in March of 2009, it dipped to $2,265 in April of 2009, and then grew to around $580,000 within five years. But a big move from $2,480 to nearly $285,000 was within a two-year period, so the number depends on how you want to stretch it out. Over five years there were 593 trades according to my Profit.ly record. That's about a hundred trades a year minimum.

Is your average trade holding period about a week or month?

I try to hold trades for two to six weeks generally and I'm usually going for a 20-30% move. Obviously, if something is going to catch momentum then I am going to hold it.

You don't need a lot of money to trade these because most of these stocks are under $10 a share, correct?

Right, under $10 and you know what? It's funny, but those are the ones historically that have made the biggest moves. People like buying those stocks under $10. The market cap can be the same for a stock priced at $25 a share and nobody wants to touch it. Everybody wants the $2.50 stock. It's just the way it is.

Have you found a broker who is really good for these? I'm asking because the biotech stocks are typically low price and low volume stocks. Also, are you using Thinkorswim or some other special trading platform for these trades?

I use Thinkorswim.com personally. I also use three brokers. I use TDAmeritrade.com to trade these longer swing positions out of my IRA so I don't pay taxes on all this. I use OptionsHouse.com for options generally because of their pricing. I'm not looking to do a lot of research, which is why some of the other options brokers are more expensive. I just want to execute an order. Then I use InteractiveBrokers.com for quick either day trade positions or usually for shorting. Basically you can say that I have Interactive Brokers for shorting, Options House for options and then Ameritrade for long-base trades.

If somebody wants to get into this type of trading can you describe how people can get in touch with you guys for more information, such as how to gain access to your catalyst database service?

We understand that it is a lot of work to narrow down the entire small-cap biotech sector to a list of the relatively few stocks we think are actually worth trading. There may be other gains or surprise gains with surprise news, etc. but identifying the ones that we can successfully and continually trade without risking profits is the goal of our BioRunUp.com service that we provide. We provide that database for people who want to download it, look for their own diamonds in the rough, hidden gems, or maybe somebody has got a special interest or experience with cancer medication or whatever. They want to narrow it down to trading certain areas.

We provide that with BioRunUp.com, but I think the guidance that we really provide and asset that we offer is not only the real time trading of the companies that we are buying with why and then posting that in real time for subscribers. It is also the watch list of what we are watching and the positions that we are considering taking along with the timing on those.

There are other services, plenty of other services that I know where they will just come up with a ticker out of the blue and then everybody is rushing to buy the stock. Generally what we try to do is not be like that. Some of these catalysts come up immediately with news, but a lot of these catalysts we know about months ahead of time. We talk about them in webinars and then in our watch list: "Okay, you know we are coming up on this FDA decision that is in May. Nobody is really talking about it right now but you might want to watch these areas on the chart, and start to take a position in it because it is going to heat up."

We try to provide a lot of that filtering down to the catalysts that are important and cut through a lot of the BS, the hype, and the greediness that a lot of retail traders seem to fall into in order to narrow down and clear the air for our subscribers as to what we think are the list of stocks that have the potential to make big moves into their catalyst.

In other words, you run a website called BioRunUp.com where you come up with a short list of biotech companies with their catalysts and dates and you also hold webinars on various biotech opportunities. Is that correct?

Yes, and also articles about specific stocks. You can also follow our trades. My partner Mike has more positions than me. He is generally more active than I am. He will trade in and out of positions quicker. I tend to hold them a little bit longer. People love to follow what I do because of that.

The people who get attracted to trading biotech the way that we do are not day traders. Some of the other guys I interact with who run day trading services don't even know what the ticker is. They are trading the ticker and have no idea of the catalyst that powers why it is moving. They are just looking at whatever. Unless you do that full-time it's hard to do that.

What attracts people to us is that there are companies that are making huge moves and traders don't have to watch it everyday. With these things you can buy a position today. Obviously it's better to watch it a lot, but you can close your eyes for a period of time and then have an idea of around the week when you want to close the position out. For people with full-time jobs and lives and families and stuff that tends to work better for them.

Thanks for talking with us Mark. For those who have never investigated the biotech field or heard of "catalyst trading" this has been wonderful information. As you have explained many times, it is a speculative type of momentum or swing trading, for a limited period, before a definable date event whose potential outcome is unknown. I'm sure many will check out your catalyst service that finds these catalyst dates and wish you the best.

Chapter 8
Dr. Gary Drayton
Trading Mindfully

Trading psychology has to do with the mental aspects of trading including how to control your mind and emotions in order to improve your trading results and skills. The topic has been addressed by quite a few authors including Dr. Gary Dayton, author of Trade Mindfully. With a background in sports psychology and optimal performance, Gary has developed specific mindfulness meditation and mental diffusion practices to help traders improve their trading skills and outcomes.

Starting out as a futures trader, Gary experienced the same emotional challenges as other traders and saw firsthand how they interfered with his trading outcomes. Drawing upon his professional training, his breakthrough came from developing an approach to trading psychology that has become extremely useful to individuals who want to confront emotional and performance issues to become better traders.

In this interview I asked Gary to reveal some of the techniques he uses to help traders deal with their emotions and become more profitable traders. You'll enjoy Gary's interview as we delve into the reasons traders should learn mindfulness practice, how it actually physically changes your brain to make you a better trader, and many other insights he has gleaned over the years as a trading psychologist and trading coach.

Gary, you are a trading psychologist. You are the author of _Trade Mindfully: Achieve Your Optimum Trading Performance with Mindfulness and Cutting Edge Psychology_. You are an expert at helping traders deal with the emotional and mental challenges involved with trading and we both know that the psychological aspect is sometimes the biggest obstacle to trading successfully. Can you recount your history on how you became a trader, how you're trading now and also how you became a psychologist and then started focusing on helping traders?

Sure. I got into trading in sort of an odd way, but probably a way that many retail traders follow to get into trading. I received a booklet in the mail one day about trading. This was probably a thirty-five or forty page booklet showing example after example of how you could buy low and sell high and how easy it was. Obviously it was a promotional material, not really trading material. It was promoting somebody's trading system, but I bought it.

When it came it was in a book format with a bunch of charts, and I remember staying up all night reading it and re-reading it and thinking that this was just the greatest thing that I'd ever seen. That's really how I got into trading.

At the time I was just finishing up my degree in psychology and writing my dissertation. I got into psychology as a clinical psychologist, meaning that I work with people with mental disorders such as depression, anxiety, schizophrenia and that sort of thing. I also had a specialty, actually, in addictions – alcohol and drug addictions. I was working as a psychologist and I realized very quickly that though I had a couple of successful trades to start off with it quickly turned unsuccessful and I started to lose money. That's when I began to realize indeed how important psychology was to trading.

Were you trading stocks, or options and were you going for short-term or long-term trades?

I was trading futures. I was trading cocoa, cotton, the currencies, the British pound, and the S&Ps. I was in the futures market at that point, and still am by the way. Today I trade mostly the S&Ps but I look at the 10-year notes, crude oil, and some of the currencies as well. Again, all futures markets. I have always liked the futures. I think they're very transparent and they have good leverage. Obviously that's a double-edged sword, but if you know what you are doing it can be very profitable. The exchanges are pretty good in terms of making sure it's a fair market. As fair as fair can be in these markets, the futures markets are pretty fair.

Anyway, I was a psychologist and I quickly realized that trading involved an awful lot of psychology, probably more so than most people would account for or would admit to. I began to focus in on the performance aspects of psychology because trading really is a performance activity.

I was fortunate that as I was finishing up my degree - or actually I finished it and shortly afterwards - one of the professors who was at the school I went to, which was Rutgers University, also was a very well-known sports psychologist in his own right. He was a sports psychologist for major league baseball and national football teams. I worked with him for about a year after I graduated in sport and human performance psychologies and I took that information and other psychology knowledge that I had and I started to craft, first for myself and later for others, an approach to trading psychology.

In your book, which you titled *Trade Mindfully*, you recommend mindfulness practice and you say there is cutting edge technology there. Let's talk about the book a little bit and then some of the exercises you give traders to help them improve their performance. The first question is what is "mindfulness" and then what are the cutting edge technologies or new approaches that can help traders? What are those two things?

Mindfulness isn't so cutting edge. It is here in the west, but it isn't in the Far East. It comes out of the Buddhist, Taoist, and the yoga traditions of East Asia, India, China, and Japan. I'm talking about Zen kind of stuff where mindfulness dates back 2,500 years or more and it's a way of observing the mental chatter and the emotional chatter that we have that goes on internally in the mind. Stepping back from it, rather than buying into everything that the mind tells us, we can step back from that by using techniques of mindfulness.

Let me just make one thing clear and that is that mindfulness certainly has religious and spiritual aspects to it. I'm not talking about those kinds of things here. I'm using it in a totally secular way. I am just using the technique and the methodology. You can go beyond and pursue spiritual practice if you like, but I'm not using it in that way. Although it is an ancient technique or method, science here in the 21st century in the west has sort of discovered mindfulness and recognized it as a very powerful technique.

Let me just give you a couple of examples related to trading where it is so powerful.

That's what I want to know. I want people to know how they can apply it to their trading to improve their trading results and get over some of their blocks or obstacles because for many discretionary traders who don't use a set system their primary trading battle is within their mind.

Right. In trading psychology and in western psychology the conventional wisdom is that you have got to get control over those emotions. You have got to grab hold of them, suppress them, beat them up, make them submit to your will and your demands.

That is really a crock of nonsense. That really is not possible to do. I have been in the game of psychology, or not the game but the profession of psychology for twenty years or more and I've never yet met a single person who can control their emotions consistently for any period of time.

That goes equally true for thoughts. We just don't have control over our mind. All kinds of research shows this, but one of the best studies comes out of Harvard University where a clever graduate student created a phone application and asked people, "What are you doing? Are you thinking about what you're doing as you're doing what you're doing?" He randomly checked in with people who signed up for this, and they have a substantial number of data points, and it's very robust research. They find that 47% of the time people are not thinking about what they are doing regardless of the activity, except for one activity, which happens to be sex.

Whether we are in a trade, whether we are talking to somebody, whether we are doing a hobby, or reading a book, or watching a television program it doesn't really matter. Half the time we are not thinking about what we are doing.

Is that not being aware, not being mindful? Is that the definition of not being aware or mindful?

Yes, it starts to approach that. Mindfulness is all about being able to catch yourself when you get off track, when you start thinking about other things randomly. It is bringing yourself back to the task at hand.

Let's then get back to some examples with traders and how this can be used to help them.

Sure. Obviously, if you are in a trade let me give you an example of how the mind works. This is very common with people. It was common with me when I was trading and trying to figure it out and it's certainly common with lots and lots of folks.

We get into a trade so let's say we go long in the S&Ps and we are looking for seven or eight points, a good run in the S&Ps, say on an intraday basis. The trade starts to go in our favor, it's ticking away at a point, point and a half, two points and we are feeling pretty good.

Then the market starts to pull back a little bit and starts to tick against us. Our minds will, for many of us, kick in and start to tell us, "Gary, you better take this trade off now. I know you were looking for seven or eight points. Well you got two, that would be good, so why don't you take it off? It's better to bank profit rather than to risk taking the loss. You don't want to have another loss, you know those are no good, blah blah blah." The mind will just go on and on and on cranking away on its own recognizance.

What do we do? Typically we take the trade off because we feel the pressure that the mind is giving us. We think it's coming from the market, and we certainly have had losses in the past and that's coming into play while also the market is ticking down against our position a little bit and starting to eat into our profits. There is something to the fact that the market is showing us that there is a potential for loss, but in reality we are crafting that idea that we are about to have a loss and we better get out now before we do have that loss.

That idea is entirely crafted by the mind. What we do is we buy into it. We believe it uncritically. We take the trade off because we feel very uncomfortable and we don't like that feeling of fear, of loss. What happens? We leave. The tension and the nervousness and the fear drain from us and we feel good about it, feel relieved and that feels good. It's also very reinforcing. We are going to do that again in the future.

The main point is this, we believe the mind, we get out of the trade, we feel the relief.

But then the trade continues on in the direction that we originally anticipated. It goes on up four points, five points, six, eight points. Even farther than that … ten, eleven, twelve points. What is our mind telling us now? We are sitting on the sidelines. We are not in this trade any longer. We have got a point and a half, maybe two points in this trade, and now it's gone off better than ten or twelve points. What is our mind telling us now? If it's like my mind it's telling me, "You idiot, what did you get out of that trade for? Are you never going to learn?"

Now it becomes toxic and what do we do? We buy into that as well and we feel bad about that. That is being *fused* or believing our mind and being mindless in the process, not being able to step back from it. No trader ever asks this question, but it's a really important question to ask, "Which mind was right?" Was it the mind telling you to get out of the trade because you were about to have a loss? That was moments ago or minutes ago. Or was it the mind telling you that you are an idiot for doing exactly what it told you to do just minutes ago?

That's the problem we face as traders, and really as human beings with this thing called the mind. It is really great in a lot of ways. It helps us create trading plans and trading strategies. It put people on the moon and we can fly across the globe in a matter of hours. You and I are talking on Skype, I don't even know how it works, and somehow we are talking over the internet and we are far away from one another. All that is from this mind that we have and that's done in a positive way.

Current psychology is this - that we probably overuse the mind in that way and we believe it because it is so helpful to us. We believe everything that it tells us or nearly everything that it tells us. That's what gets us in trouble.

Mindfulness is the one thing that is very powerful when we practice it. It begins to give us distance on what is going on in the mind versus what we really want to do as traders.

How do or should traders practice mindfulness? How do traders get over fear and greed and what you call mental blind spots? In your book you say there are thinking traps and mental shortcuts we succumb to, so how do you use mindfulness to get over these hurdles so that you can become a better trader? What exactly do you do?

In the book I give numerous examples of mindfulness techniques that traders can use, both formal and informal exercises. The basic formal exercise is to sit and watch your breath. That's an ancient practice where we try to focus the mind in on the sensations of the breath coming in and going out of our noses or coming in and filling and leaving our belly. It doesn't sound like much. It sounds like, "How could that ever be related to trading?"

In fact, it really is. If we can focus in on the breath and maintain our concentration there then we are building mental muscle. The brain isn't a muscle, but it kind of acts like one. The more we use it in a specific way the stronger it becomes in that way. What we are talking about is developing attention and focus. The mind will definitely wander. As I said, half the time we are not thinking about what we are doing so it will wander when we are practicing mindfulness.

That's the whole goal of mindfulness - to notice exactly when the mind wanders and then to bring it back to the task at hand. In the process of doing that, in the process of practicing mindfulness it begins to teach us that our thoughts are not always true. They are not reflections of reality all the time and they don't have to be believed or acted upon as if they are commands coming from some general of your internal army. That's what mindfulness teaches us.

We can apply that in trading if you think the analogy here is that we are going to focus on our trade and manage our trade just as we would learn to focus on the breath. We are not going to be able to stop the thoughts or the feelings that arise within us. We are going to have all kinds of thoughts and feelings arise when we are in trades. When we are mindful we can notice those as simply thoughts that come and go on their own, feelings that come and go on their own. You don't have to pay them all that much attention.

We notice them and we assess them, "Is this a valid thought or not? Okay, maybe I'm a little fearful of getting a loss, but when I re-evaluate the trade that I'm in I don't see any supply coming into the market, I don't see anything going contrary to my initial trade idea so I'm going to stay with this." That's how mindfulness would work, how we would practice it and how we would use it in trading.

This sounds like it is more important for the discretionary trader who's deciding things in the moment versus somebody who actually has a rules-based system.

Show me somebody who can stick to their rules.

Well that's what I want to get the conversation focused on. There are all these people who are systems-based, rules-based or computer-based traders. Do they have problems at the entry and exit or in the middle of the trade because if they were just following the rules with discipline they would always get in and out by order and otherwise leave the trade alone? How do you apply it to these guys?

Sometimes it's the entry or the exit. People will override their system and not take their trade.

Systems are based on the probability profile of historic trades, and in order to capture that probability profile you have to take every trade that shows up. You are going to find people who are going to look at a trade that comes up and say, "I can't take that trade, that's crazy." They will override the system, but then they are violating the probabilities of the system and they're not trading a system any longer. Now they are in the discretionary camp, but they are in a worse discretionary camp than most *good* discretionary traders because they are trading off of emotions, not off of discretion or what the chart is really telling them.

The old story is, and I've seen this over and over again, you take any two traders and give them the same system but they are going to have different results. It's because their psychology is going to come into play. Whether it's at the beginning, the end, or in the middle of the trade, psychology will come into play. Understanding trading psychology and developing some sort of a method - and I would recommend very strongly mindfulness - is really important whether you are a discretionary trader or you are a systems trader.

Because people are often defeated by their emotions, and I guess the two biggest ones that people cite are fear and greed, how do you suggest they handle them at the entry and exit and middle part of the trade? Should they try to eliminate them, just watch them, or use them? Should they test them and then say, "That's not really valid"? How should people handle their emotions in trading? Should they try to eliminate them?

No, because the more you try to eliminate them the more you are going to have them. Again, out of Harvard - different department up there - the cognitive psychology department has shown for the last thirty-five, forty years that the more we try to suppress and control either thoughts or feelings it is almost like we are telling the mind, "I don't want to have fear so don't let me have fear. I'm not going to respond to it, I'm not going to be a slave to it." The mind takes this almost as if it's a command, and says, "Okay, yes sir, I'm not going to have fear."

What will the mind do then? It's going to be monitoring for fear because you don't want fear, right? The mind is going to be monitoring for you any semblance of fear that arises on the horizon, any fear that comes up. If you start to have a little nervousness or a little bit of anxiety then your mind is immediately going to kick in and say, "Warning, warning, fear is on the horizon. Better gear up and start to deal with it." What happens then? Your focus is no longer on your trade. Your focus is now going inside into your internal state.

Where is that fear coming from? What fear is that? Suddenly what you didn't want you are getting. In fact, in the process you are most likely amplifying it because you are now placing your attention on it. Again, mindfulness comes into play here. Mindfulness teaches us that we are not going to get rid of fear. We are not going to get rid of thought. Try to have a day without having an emotion even if you are not trading. Just a regular day. Don't get upset, don't get bored, don't get frustrated, don't have any anxiety, don't become sad, don't become happy, don't become joyful, don't become excited. Just try to go through a 24-hour period like that.

I guarantee you will not be able to do it. It's impossible. Why? Because we are human beings and emotions, whether it's fear or happiness, they are all very helpful to us. We have them for a reason, and it's part of being a human being. This whole idea of trying to get rid of them and eliminate them is crazy. It's crazy in making.

I believe that you mentioned the emotions of fear and greed. Mark Douglas taught us that greed is really just the flip side of fear. It's the fear of not getting enough, or not making enough money, or leaving money on the table. Greed itself is a fear-based emotion, and trying to get rid of that you are just going to make it worse for yourself as a trader.

Let me tell you a story that Larry Williams, the great futures trader, once told a group I was in. I hope I'm remembering this correctly because it was years ago. He said he was always buffeted by fear and greed and realized he had to become indifferent to those emotions to successfully trade.

Now I don't remember what he did exactly but it was something along these lines. To get at this roller coaster of emotions he went to Las Vegas and sat down at a roulette table for hours. He took $1 chips and he just kept betting on black or red. I don't remember what the color was but it was so he didn't have to keep changing his mind about what to do. He had a little system of some type that was almost a 50:50 win sort of thing, which I know is impossible in roulette but I'm just trying to give you the idea of what I remember. Over several days he just sat there for six or eight hours a day playing the same color with a process of betting until he became indifferent as to whether he won or lost. He became indifferent as to losses and learned how to just follow his system without his emotions getting in the way. He trained himself how to take losses and not get tangled up in emotions that would stand in the way of him following his system.

It's a story I always remember because most traders are greatly affected by emotions. He wanted to learn how to become indifferent to the end result of the trade and just trade the tested system. That's different from mindfulness, but you can also say that this is training yourself to master your emotions. Are there any technologies out there that you know of that would actually help you to do that or would you just say mindfulness itself is a better sort of thing to do? How do you handle that when you know, for instance, you are being greedy or fearful on a trade?

It's a clever thing that Larry Williams did actually. If I had the opportunity to interview him then I would ask him a few questions. I bet that he did experience the ups and downs initially and as time went on he began to realize, "These ups and downs really don't matter. These emotional ups and downs really don't make a whole lot of difference as long as I follow my process of betting," whatever that process was. The outcomes sort of take care of themselves and he became mindful of the swings in his emotions by following his process.

That is not an unusual thing. Even traders who have twenty, twenty-five years or more experience and have been successful traders still have emotional swings. Tim Bourquin talks about this in his book *Traders at Work*, and he and I have discussed this quite a bit. Tim went around and interviewed a couple of hundred people who were highly successful traders, many of whom had been in the business for ten, fifteen, twenty years, and he was surprised to find that even folks with long histories in trading still were uncomfortable at times in their trading chair.

In other words, they get into a trade and they would feel fear. They would feel discomfort about the position that they had on. He said that they just basically learned to deal with it. They learned on their own how to handle it. The point being that even after twenty years, and I would bet dollars to donuts even though I've never talked to Larry Williams and I have a lot of admiration for him as a trader (I read pretty much all of his books) but I would bet that Larry still gets uncomfortable from time to time as well if he were honest.

I remember another story about some person who was afraid of graveyards so he went out and sat in them for hours to remove his fears. I have also read an opinion that policemen, because they are exposed to crime, become desensitized to it after a while and then it doesn't upset them so much. Some of them, however, cannot psychologically handle it well so they put on stomach weight (or muscles) as a buffer to insulate themselves from what they see on a daily basis. In other words, they

put on a large layer of fat or muscle to psychologically insulate or protect themselves from the negative environment as sort of buffer. I wonder if traders do similar things to insulate themselves and buffer their emotions rather than just practice mindfulness?

Sure, everybody does that. It's not just traders. We are not anybody special here. You can take any person and look at them and you will see people become overweight because they are eating to satisfy certain emotional drives. They might drink alcohol after work or take drugs to dull the tension or the anxiety that they feel. That happens all the time. It is not just in trading. It just happens here in trading as well.

Do you also find a lot of people sabotage themselves in trading because they can't handle success? I've heard from a lot of people in the trading field, who actually try to help others, that some people cannot actually handle trading success and try to sabotage themselves. Have you ever found this and if so how would you handle that with mindfulness?

That happens occasionally, but I think it is more reported than is really fact. I think people struggle more with fear being the number one emotional problem. I think people struggle more with that than anything else.

What can they do about fear? What are your techniques or technologies for dealing with fear or greed?

Give me a problem, and let's do an analysis on a case study basis. Give me a fear-based trading problem and I'll give you a way to deal with it.

I'm looking at a market that's been declining, and I really want to get into that market but I'm afraid this thing is going to keep crashing lower so I don't even get into the trade because of that.

Are you trading other markets and trading those?

No, let's just say I'm just trading this one particular market. There are a lot of people who are afraid to get into a stock like Apple because they think it is near a top and then they miss the trade and it keeps going up, or they are afraid to get in at what they think is a bottom. They think it's not the right time and that it will go lower and then they also miss the trade.

How would I answer that? That's not what I would consider to be a recurring problem. If we are at the top and maybe it's not a good time to get in then I'm not going to do it. If you were telling me for example, "This market is a great market and I'd really like to get in, but I'm just fearful of having a loss or getting into the market and then it goes against me. I've been trying to do it for the last three months and I haven't been able to do it," then that would be something a little bit different.

If that was the case then I would talk to people about a number of different things. First off, a lot of people don't even have a good process of making trades. They don't know what the right entry technique might be. There are dozens and dozens of different entry techniques and it really doesn't matter what your technique is, but you need to have one. Whether it's a key reversal bar in a pullback, or a break of a downtrend line to go long, or an uptrend line to go short vice versa, do a little research and figure out what your entry technique will be and know where your stop is going to be.

In other words, what I would encourage people to do is have everything associated with that entry and the protection of that entry figured out ahead of time … not when you are about to take the trade. I'm talking about what your entry technique is going to be, what your stop is going to be, where you are going to take the trade off and so on and so forth.

Then if they haven't done this before, I would have them simtrade this, paper trade it. I wouldn't sit in front of the markets day after day after day doing that, but I would get some historic data, I'd set them up with this and have them simulate their trading. Let's say that they are a day trader. I'd give them six months of historical data and we would go through and have them simtrade that and look at their results.

We would be practicing some mindfulness as we're doing this and understanding what the kinds of thoughts are that come into the person's head when they were about to take a trade. Usually it is associated with some sort of a loss. I would do some diffusion techniques around those thoughts and around those feelings. All of those methods are described in my book.

I'd be preparing them both on a technical and performance basis: technical in terms of knowing what their entry is and performance basis in terms of having done the simulation trading and getting a track record if they haven't done that before … and 90% of retail traders haven't done that. Then I would prep them mentally as well by developing some of the skills - diffusion and mindfulness skills - that I talk about in the book so that they can start to handle some of those thoughts.

Again, we are not trying to get rid of them. We are not trying to suppress them or control them, but just have a different relationship to them.

Are there more advanced mindfulness skills that traders and investors should know about? How can they be applied to trading?

Diffusion is a good one. Again, it is like mindfulness in that it teaches us to step back from our thoughts and certainly can be applied in trading. For example, let's take a trader who - you talked about greed before - jumps into the market. The market starts to take off and he's in there or she's in there without batting an eyelash, without even checking to see if there is a good trade there in terms of a setup and the situation meeting criteria that they have in their trading plan. They just jump right in.

One of the things that will go through a person's head, the head of a person like this, will be, "Oh, the market's going to take off. I'm going to miss out on some fantastic profits. I've got to get in and I've got to get in now." Believing that thought compels them to act and the action is pressing the button and entering the trade.

One way to step back from that is to teach them to say to themselves something different instead of, "Oh, the market is going to take off and I'm going to miss out on a lot of profit. I have to get into the trade." We teach them to step back a little bit by saying, "I'm having the thought that the market is about to take off. I'm having the thought that there is going to be a lot of profit to be made. I'm having the thought that I have to get in now."

Doing that changes the complexion of the thought patterns that the person has. It sounds simple, it sounds very basic and people may read it and think, "Why would I bother doing that?" But if you do it sincerely and earnestly then you begin to notice that there is a vast difference between, "The market is going to take off" and "I'm having the thought that the market is about to take off." "I'm having the thought that ..." puts it in the proper category of just having a thought.

It is not that the market is actually going to take off. The thought that the market is going to take off is not always actually reflecting reality and truth. It's just a thought. It is just a set of thoughts prompted by a little movement in the market.

When we acknowledge that view as just thoughts being prompted by a little movement in the market then it kind of cultivates for us a little mental space where we can check ourselves and say, "What's really important to me? Is it jumping into the market and again getting hammered because I was impulsive, or is it being a good trader, trading competently, assessing the market for good, quality, choice, trades and trading those rather than being whipsawed back and forth by my mind making me jump into the market?"

That's an example of a diffusion technique that is helpful for traders. We can combine formal mindfulness with diffusion techniques so that people begin to recognize that what is going on between the ears doesn't really reflect what is really happening in the chart. We don't have to act on those thoughts.

In your book and in your practice you recommend what you call "high value trading actions," or HVA's, which are specific actions that are under a trader's control. Why do you emphasize these? How do these help traders and investors?

We forget really about what the right moves are and what's important to us when we're under the throws of an emotional hijacking. When we start to be fearful and have fearful thoughts what we want to do is deal with those. We may be thinking that the right move is to not pull the trigger on the trade because we believe the thought that we are having that we are going to have a loss. However, what we are really doing there is not responding to the market. We are responding to our internal state. We are acting in the service of our internal state.

In other words, we are not taking the trade and therefore we don't have to have fear. We are not acting as a trader. We are doing everything *but* acting as a trader. Acting as a trader means doing the "high value action" that is important for the trade and that in the end is important for us as traders. Pulling the trigger is obviously the high value action in this instance of taking the trade. When we do that, when we know what the high value action is and when we take that high value action then we are acting in a way that is important to us. If we are a trader then it is taking trades in this instance rather than acting to assuage our emotions. That is the whole idea behind high value actions and high value mental skills.

I really believe people should work with trading coaches, but before we get into that I want to ask you about the psychological research that can be applied to trading. There is a lot of research from the neural cognitive sciences that has been done in terms of functional magnetic resonance scans of the brain where we can see all the active areas. If you had to pick one, two or three studies that traders really should know about then what would they be? I'm talking about a study where you would say, "Here is a study you need to know because this has impact on your trading. You should put this in the back of your mind because it will help you change the way you manage yourself."

What would those studies be from all the new science out there?

I will just cite one. Britta Holzel has done a lot of great work. She is a German psychologist, but also works here in the United States. She and her team did a study of highly stressed individuals who are otherwise healthy physically and mentally healthy with no mental disorders but very stressed. Sounds like a lot of traders I know, in fact. She split the study participants up into two groups, and she had taught one group mindfulness and the other group didn't do mindfulness.

She did it for two months - eight weeks - and took brain scans. You talked about FMRI's, functional magnetic resonance imagery, which allows us to see what brain areas get activated and the size of those brain areas when people are thinking or doing tasks.

She did this study for eight weeks and she had people practicing mindfulness during that period of time. She took brain scans at the beginning of the study and at the end of the study and what she found was absolutely remarkable. She found that the fear center of the brain - the amygdala and a couple of areas around the amygdala that trigger when we become anxious and fearful - the actual brain structure in that area shrank. It shrank. She also found that people reported much less stress when they were practicing mindfulness.

She had a control group. Half of the people did mindfulness and the other half didn't. Both groups got brain scans before and after the study and she found that the people who were not doing mindfulness continued to have high stress and did not see any shrinkage at all in the amygdala, the fear center of the brain.

She also found that the prefrontal cortex area grew in size. That's the part of our brain that houses logical thinking, rational thinking, our abilities to compare and contrast, and plan and evaluate. It also, by the way, modulates or regulates the information coming out of the fear center of the brain. Those brain areas are highly interconnected. That area grew in size and in connectivity.

Mindfulness does very positive things for us in terms of fear, which I believe is the number one trading problem, the psychological trading problem traders face. It actually changes the structure of our brain. We can go a little further with this, and you've heard I'm sure, Bill, of loss aversion?

Yes.

It's the tendency that we have to view losses on a psychological scale much more so than wins. In other words, if we had a winning trade of say $1,000 then that feels pretty good, but if we have a losing trade of $1,000 not only does it feel bad but it really feels like we have lost $2,000 or maybe $2,500. The order of magnitude on a psychological basis is much greater in loss.

That causes us to do all kinds of things like cut winning trades short, hesitate on pulling triggers or holding onto losers longer than we should trying to avoid the loss. Loss aversion is one of the big banes of traders. Good research shows that loss aversion is housed in the brain area of the amygdala. That makes sense. It is the fear center. We fear loss, it's a threat to us, and so this area of the amygdala is what gets triggered when we are under threat.

We know that mindfulness has a very dramatic effect on that area of the brain in a very positive way for traders. That's why I say that mindfulness is the number one mental skill that traders ought to learn not just because it's a cool thing to do but it's because there is some incredibly good research coming out on this.

How should they learn this? Is it best to go to a trading psychologist? Is that the proper type of coach or do they just pick up, for instance, your book and try to do it themselves? What do you recommend?

I would start with trying to do it myself. Pick up the book, *Trade Mindfully*, and try those exercises within it. I laid it out pretty much as a manual for trading psychology so first see if you can't do it yourself. A lot of people should be able to do that and if not then you can look towards a trading psychologist to help you out.

Trading is all about being able to stand on your own. A lot of self-reliance is required here. The best way to do things, I believe, is if you can develop these skills on your own. That would be a big plus for you.

It's pretty clearly written about in my book. The techniques and the approach are pretty straightforward. It's not a lot of mumbo jumbo. It was very sophisticated psychological material but it's not written in an academic way or anything like that. I tried to make it accessible to people.

I don't want to take anything away from the other trading psychologists. We've had big contributions to the field by Van Tharp, Howell, Williams, Mark Douglas and others. How do you think you have added to the field in terms of understanding or how do you think you are different from some of these other guys? What are you emphasizing that you don't think is stressed enough or how do you think you are differentiated from the others a little bit, or how have you pushed the field forward in a certain direction to further help traders?

Out of the folks that you mentioned I'm probably most like Mark Douglas in the idea that we really have to follow a process. Trading is a probabilistic endeavor and you really need to follow a process and be true to that process as much as you can. The biggest difficulties you are going to face are going to come in the form of fear. I think I expand it a little bit by showing people that trying to control and suppress emotions is really the wrong approach because it distracts you from your trading. You are now engaged in emotional struggle rather than trading.

You have to break free of that with mindfulness being the easiest and best way to break free from it. Although Mark talked about following the probabilistic model of your trading plan, I have amplified that a little bit more and talked about a process for not just following your plan but of developing yourself as a trader using that process both to create better performance attributes that you have as well as overcoming things like fear and other emotional issues that you might have.

Let me put it this way Gary. If somebody came to you and said, "I want to master the mental and psychological aspects of trading so that I can become a top, top performer," then what reading list would you have them go through and what skills would you have them work on? What would you tell them to read, learn and master in any particular order if they wanted to excel in the trading field? Please give me a short reading list or set of skills and courses or whatever.

I would probably encourage them to read Dan Kahneman's *Thinking Fast and Slow*. I would encourage them to take a look at Anders Ericsson's work on deliberate practice. I would refer them to Mark Douglas's *Trading in the Zone*. I'd refer them to my book, and I would suggest they take a look at a very new book written by Philip Tetlock called *Superforecasting: The Art and Science of Prediction*. It is a very impressive book. He's done some very good research.

That is a really great short list for people. There are a lot of good books out there, but people want to avoid wasting time or money looking for the best to start with. Most would ask, "You are the expert in the field so please give me just the diamonds out there that will be quickest in helping me become a better trader or investor." That's a really good list so now let me ask you this. If you were a genie who had a magic wand and you could wave it over a room full of traders to make them better performers, what would that magic wish be in order to help them become more profitable traders? What would you magically change in the aspiring traders who wanted to improve their skills and profit outcomes?

What I would do is I would have them focus on process rather than results. That would be my magic wand wish for all traders. If I had the magic wand - my father was an amateur magician so I have his old wands in fact - I'd wave the magic wand and encourage people to think about process rather than results.

Results are important. I'm not saying that they are not. We need to keep our metrics on our trades and on our performance and those metrics are very useful in helping us hone down our skills and our trades. But we need to focus on process.

Really, what's most important in trading is to understand that you have to have a process, a trading process and that you need to follow it. By doing so - this is one of the things that Douglas talked about - by doing so you will maximize the opportunity for the probabilities of your trading plan to occur. When we don't follow our process sometimes we get a good result from that and that will happen, but that's really just dumb luck. Most of the time when we don't follow a process we are going to lose and that's justified.

You shouldn't be winning if you don't have a process. Sometimes when we have a good process we will have a bad result and that's bad luck. That is unfortunate. Most of the time when we are following a good process and we get good results that is what we should be expecting. When we follow a good process then the results will be taking care of themselves. When we are just focused on results and not thinking about our process and not acting in concert with a good process, we are really putting ourselves at the vagaries of the market. Then it's good luck if we get a good trade and it's not really bad luck, but it is what we deserve if we don't get a good trade.

Do you have any success stories you can share of people who have used mindfulness to turn their trading around? We don't need names but I'm interested in case studies like, "I had a trader who did the following ..."

There are a lot. Let me think of a good trader. Well, one good trader was really hamstrung with the first trade that they took in the day. If it was a winning trade then the rest of the day generally went pretty well. This is a day trader ... most of my work is with day traders, by the way. Even if they had a losing trade, if they had a losing trade after that first win then that was okay because they could make it up and they generally came out of the day in positive profit territory and certainly with a good mindset.

On the other hand, if they had a losing trade then the following would happen. He would get in to kind of test himself and see what his response was to the market. He had this whole idea that he had to be sharp and quick and be in tune with the market right from the get go. If that trade turned into a loss then two things would happen. First, he wouldn't take the loss right off. He would let it run a bit until it got out of hand and then he would take it. Then he had a large loss and that affected him for the rest of the day.

To make a long story short, I worked with him for about five months. It usually does take somewhere between three and six months to get somebody out of their head and into their trading. We worked on a number of different things. Part of it was process and focus and honing in on better trades to take right off of the open in the morning.

The other aspects of it involved mindfulness and involved the diffusion techniques that I talked about in terms of how he viewed that loss both as it was happening - so that he wasn't taking such large losses - and then after that loss occurred so that it didn't affect him for the rest of the day. As I said, in about four or five months he turned his trading around quite a bit and became a much more profitable trader and much more even keeled emotionally speaking.

Can you give me another example?

Sure. One guy I worked with was a very good trader. He had a real good grasp of technical analysis, had no problem getting into trades and no problem managing the trades. What his problem was, many times, was getting out of a trade. He would set a profit target and take the trade off at that target. When the trade would continue to run that bothered him because he felt like he was leaving money on the table.

It bothered him so much that he would hold onto trades much longer than what he should have and so rather than taking the trade off at the profit objective he would hold it. It would oftentimes back up on him and he would continue to hold it, very frequently wiping out all the profits that he had. Occasionally he would take a loss from it. He would get despondent about this. He didn't have a clinical disorder, but you would consider it depression or sadness. He would get blue and that would affect his trading for the rest of the day and oftentimes carry over into the next day or two.

Again, we worked on mindfulness. Through that we worked on actually having him develop a system. It was an interesting challenge because what I asked him to do he didn't think he could do initially. I said, "I want you to take all the trades that you did over the last period of time and I want you to identify those that went farther than what you got out of the trade. Then I want you to figure out from your indicators what might have told you that the market was going to go farther." He didn't originally think that he could do that, but he did and he found one indication that was reasonably good. It wasn't perfect, but it was reasonably good at telling him that he would get more out of the trade than what his original profit target was.

He built a modified system around that to take some of the trade off at his profit objective yet hold a piece of the trade if this indication came up. We also used mindfulness and diffusion and the other kinds of things that we talked about. In this case, what I'm trying to explain is that we were using process to better develop his trading strategies. At the same time we were using process to better develop his mental skills so that he kind of worked on both ends towards the middle to become a better trader.

That's great. That's what you use a coach for. Can you give me a case study of someone who was terrible at trading when they came to you and you helped them turn it around? These were two success stories and you helped them get better, but I want to hear about someone who was losing money and you helped them become a profitable trader.

One woman came in. She was quite wealthy, had been very successful in business and was rather bored. She wanted to have some excitement in her life and took up trading to do that. She was pretty much a novice trader coming in and she wouldn't just put a contract on. She'd put a hundred contracts on. She had some technical skills, but she would see a trade setup occur that she had never traded before. Looking at the markets she would see something occur. She might have read something in a book and then saw it coming in on her charts so she'd lay a hundred contracts down on it.

It would take my breath away when I thought of all the money that she would risk, but she could do that because she had substantial amounts of money. In this case, the problem wasn't so much mental as it was not having good technical skills. It's one of the things that I want to be clear about. It's the reason why I'm giving you this example. All the good psychology in the world isn't going to mean a whole heck of a lot if you don't have good technical skills or you don't have a good fundamental system.

I don't know how you trade, but most of the traders I work with are trading off of technicals. I certainly work with hedge funds that are doing more fundamental analysis, but again it all relates back to process. You have to have a good, solid process in order to trade well. You have to have those good fundamental or those good technical skills plus good money management, a good understanding of risk and know how to try to control that risk.

There are really three parts to trading. One is method, the second is money management and the third is the mental side of the game, the psychological side of the game. Psychology supports and underpins all of that, but it can't replace it. It cannot replace either money management or good, solid knowledge skills and abilities in trading. You have to have those in order to have psychology work.

With this woman we really went to the basics of developing a trading plan and sticking to it along with all the good money management skills and all of that before she became successful in trading. I wanted to point that out because I think it's really important. People sometimes come in and say, "My problem is psychology," and many times it's not. Many times it is a lack of knowledge, skills and abilities on the trading side of the ledger and that needs to be developed first before you start focusing on the mental aspects.

Do you have any stories of people with very little money who were lousy traders but who turned it around?

Yes, too many of them. They all come to me when they are broke!

Yes, I know. They don't have money for the coaching, but can you give us an example of one of these guys? What is the most common archetype or template that you see?

The most common is that people do start off with a decent trading account and they blow through it because they haven't developed the skill set for it. I'm not talking about mental skills. I'm talking about technical skills. They come and they say, "Gee, now I can't take trades. I've scared myself so much in the market and I have had so many losses that I can barely pull the trigger." That's a common one.

I tell them, "Well we have got to work on this now for a little bit. It's going to take some time," and it's almost like they say to you, "You can't fix me in a couple of sessions? I don't really have money for this." That is the basic problem.

Let me just say something here about this in my own trading. One of the things I went through in my own personal training is that I tried every rocket science indicator that was out there - Fibonacci, pivot numbers, all kinds of fancy stuff - and I found that none of that stuff, for me personally, worked very well.

One day somebody said, "You really ought to take a look at the Wyckoff methodology." I thought it was a new indicator or a new trading system. I said, "How does that work?" They laughed at me and said, "No, Wyckoff was a person who came into the markets in the late 1800s and he died in the early 1930s, but he wrote a couple of courses that are really worthwhile taking a look at."

I thought at the time, "How could anybody who wrote about and traded in the early 1900s have any value at all in today's markets with computers and the internet and all of that sort of stuff?" In fact, I learned that it has a lot to do with the markets.

One of the things that Wyckoff said is that, "I say this to all new traders who want to get into the markets. Few listen to me, they go in with their savings and they are like lambs walking in to be sheared." I think about it more like standing in line for the guillotine. They want to jump right into the markets. I did this too. I understand this. They want to jump right into the markets and trade and make a million dollars by next week, but that's really not possible.

If you do get into the markets and you trade and you are doing it without having the requisite skills then success is really just dumb luck. That happens a lot, but you can't sustain it. That's what I would suggest, which is to understand this. Trading is a tough game, it's a set of both technical and mental skills that has to be developed. It takes time to develop those.

I want you to look back at your life lessons including things you wish you had known when you got started. If you have a room full of traders and you could basically get them to absorb anything then what would you tell them along the lines of, "This is my life lesson for trading or life in general. This is what you guys need to know"? Imagine that they are all twenty-year-olds or thirty-year-olds. What do you want to tell them?

Practice, practice, practice and then practice some more until you get good at the skills you need to have to trade. That is basically what I would tell them. You want to play on the Olympic level here because the markets are a professional level playing field and you have got to be skilled in this. Otherwise the market will take your money from you no questions asked.

An athlete who dreams of being an Olympic athlete doesn't just dream it. They go out and they do it. A tennis player who wants to be a professional level tennis player doesn't just hang around the neighborhood courts and hack around. They go and they really work at it. They wouldn't consider setting their foot on a tennis court in a professional game without having coaching, without in fact having practiced for years to get to that level by playing lots and lots of matches and having lots of losses and making lots of mistakes, but working hard to figure out how to correct those mistakes and how to have winning days and winning matches and such.

That is what is required in trading, too. It's no different. Sometimes in the industry we hear - and I was subject to this, too - all you have to do is buy long and sell high and that it's such an easy deal to do. It does seem easy in retrospect, but when you are sitting on the live edge of the chart it is not an easy task to do and you really do need to work at it and work at it hard.

Gary, people can find you through your book *Trade Mindfully*, which is sold on Amazon.com. You also have a website called Tradingpsychologyedge.com. Can you tell people how they can reach you if they want to learn more or perhaps get involved with you as a coach?

Sure. A couple of things … first of all, on my website Tradingpsychologyedge.com there are free resources and I would suggest you start there. I do teach the Wyckoff Method as well as mental skills and we have three or four offerings there that are free to download that you can avail yourself of. There are also plenty of articles and blog posts on the site. You can kind of get a sense of how I think and how I work from those.

My book is available from Amazon, you can also get to Amazon.com through my site. On my website there is a contact form that is fairly easy to find and you can get directly to me through that contact.

It has been great, Gary, with some incredibly useful information on how to start mastering the psychological aspects of trading and on the first steps of developing a system or style that has rules of process for stops, profit targets, entries and exits. I am super glad you mentioned Wyckoff. There are a lot of other traders who have also said they owe their trading skills to Wyckoff and you seem to have zeroed in on one of the best ways of analyzing the market with that recommendation. I appreciate the time you've spent with me teaching people how to become better traders and how to deal with the mental chatter in their minds that affects trading. I hope people consider contacting you if they need a trading coach to help them learn mindfulness meditation and these other techniques of deliberate practice and refining their method to reach the top level of performance that's possible. Thanks, Gary.

Thank you, Bill. It's been a pleasure.

Chapter 9
Tim Sykes
Profitable Penny Stock Trading

You would be hard pressed to find a more frightening stock market niche than the penny stock arena. Prone to frequent pump and dump schemes, most unwary individuals lose their shirts chasing the hyped promises of tremendous penny stock profits. It is hard to find profitable traders in this arena at all, and yet trader Tim Sykes has made millions in this extremely volatile field time and time again. What was his breakthrough?

In this interview Tim will reveal the trading rules he uses for consistently making profitable trades on both the long and short side of the penny stock market. Pump and dump scams run by the mafia (The Wolf of Wall Street boiler room type operators) don't scare him because he has learned how to entirely avoid or piggyback their scams for trading success. He currently has a 15-year track record of profitability as well as a list of successful students who have also mastered his techniques for low-price stock trading.

Many traders over the years have asked me how they can get started trading the markets with very little money. Their first thought often turns to penny stocks, but I have always avoiding discussing this particular niche because of its track record of nearly total ruin. From Tim's story, however, you will learn how some particular trading rules, many of which are similar to those promoted by Mike Ser and Andy Man, can help you successfully navigate these waters and beat the market manipulators by anticipating their manipulations. This is one of the most intelligent discussions of penny stock trading you are likely to encounter, and the insights on trading rules can be used for higher priced stock trading, too.

Tim, how did you get started with trading and in particular with penny stocks, which are stocks that generally sell for less than five dollars?

I got started trading in high school. My parents gave me control of my roughly $12,000 bar mitzah gift money and they said, "Have fun with it, put it to work in the stock market" and as a high schooler they thought I would lose everything. They thought it would be a good lesson for me.

Instead I turned the $12,000 into over $120,000 in one year of high school and then nearly one million dollars after my freshman year in college. It wasn't due to the normal stocks. At first I started to trade the big stocks, which at the time were Netscape and Yahoo, but the stocks just didn't move. I had such a small account that my account balance wasn't going up enough so I eventually found penny stocks because they were so volatile.

I know that the average volatility of S&P 500 stocks is much, much less than that of stocks trading for less than $1.

With penny stocks some of these companies can go up 50% or 100% in a day or two. I was like,

"Wow, that's what I need for my smaller account." I have become an expert at this unloved niche because I think it is ideal for where smaller accounts can really grow fast if they follow certain rules.

I think this niche is ideal for everybody with less than $100,000 to their name. I think it's ridiculous how CNBC, Bloomberg, and all these major financial channels focus on business news. That's great if you are trying to trade like a hedge fund or mutual fund. Making 20% per year for those guys is great because they are managing millions and billions.

If you make 20% on a $50,000 account this is $10,000 for the entire year. I always want to earn an extra $10,000 but that amount is not going to change my life. So the niche is really for people who have smaller accounts and they want to have the potential to really grow it.

Stocks like Google, GE and Bank of America get all the headlines but their stocks just don't move. You have to recognize the volatility of penny stocks and embrace it. If you utilize it correctly and know the right patterns and right trading rules then you can really grow your account fast.

When people hear the words "penny stocks" the first thing that immediately comes to their mind is the risk. How is what you do different from the typical penny stock trader who ends up losing everything?

Most people look at penny stocks like Lotto tickets and they are always trying to find the next Microsoft. They think that is how you make it big. That is just not reality. It's such a long shot. There have been a few penny stocks that have gone on to become multi-billion dollar companies, but that is like finding a needle in a haystack.

I prefer a much lower risk strategy and I tailor my approach to taking on lower risk. Because I know that penny stocks are so volatile I don't need to hit a huge homerun. I can hit singles so I try to find volatile penny stocks where they can double or triple in a few days and I try to take the meat out of that move. I try to take 50% gains here or 30% gains there. While stocks are tripling I don't try to capture everything. I just want to use that stock to grow my account and do that several times a week or several times a month.

Do you think that this is the key to your penny stock trading success, which is the fact that you are just going for a little bit of a big trend?

I try to be like Ichiro Suzuki. Ichiro is one of the biggest hitters of all time in baseball and he just goes for singles. It's not that he can't hit homeruns, but he knows that homeruns and grand slams are much lower odds so he has specialized his whole career in hitting singles and that is what I do. If you do enough of them (hitting singles) and stay in this niche and really get the hang of it then a good strategy can grow an account to millions of dollars.

Is your trading style something that works continuously without interruption in all types of different market environments or do you have to wait for some special fundamental market conditions to really do well?

That's the beauty of penny stocks. There is always something moving based on world events, promotions or some new technology. Usually there is anywhere from five to ten really hot penny stocks at any given time and they are all moving 10%, 20%, 50% or sometimes 100% per day. They are really not that difficult to spot. What is difficult is staying disciplined and that's why I use specific trading rules that are specifically designed to keep me safe.

For instance, driving can be very scary to someone who has never driven a car before. You have this huge machine that can go very fast and is very dangerous. You hear about accidents all the time. However, if you stay within the lanes, follow the red lights and stay within the speed limit then driving is very enjoyable.

That's very similar to trading penny stocks. You are safer if you learn the rules such as cutting losses quickly and focus only on companies that have good earnings as opposed to focusing on companies with pie in the sky technologies. You must pay attention to the road signs in the penny stock market.

Based on your past success it sounds like you have a very tested selection process for picking penny stock trades. I am always interested in ferreting out the secrets of trading success for some particular approach and so I have to ask what you are doing for trade selection and risk control that is different from most penny stock traders?

When you are dealing with smaller accounts the key is staying in the game. You cannot afford to risk blowing up and losing everything because then you are out of the game. It doesn't matter how good of a penny stock you find if you have no money to trade it with and then cannot profit so you need good risk management. It is so, so important. It is the most important thing.

Any time I am in a penny stock, whether it's a long position or I am shorting them (betting against a penny stock promotion scam that causes a temporary run-up in penny stock prices like you see in *The Wolf of Wall Street* movie) … whether I am long or short I always, always, always cut losses quickly and never risk disaster.

Disaster is the number one problem that traders have because they let their egos get into the trades, they don't cut losses, they add to their positions when they go against them and say, "Oh, maybe it's going to come back." Sometimes they do come back and they saved themselves, but they played with fire. Sometimes when you play with fire you are going to get burned. I don't ever want that to happen so no matter what my position is I never let a loss get more than 10%.

Do you use stop-losses to lock in that 10%?

With penny stocks the market makers can actually see all the stop-losses and because penny stocks are not actively traded you don't want the market makers to see where you are at. A lot of people have been taught to use hard stop-losses in other market sectors but with penny stocks the market makers just take the stops out and then put the stock price back up to where it was before. The market makers are just laughing to themselves.

Therefore with penny stocks I use mental stops so I am watching a stock more often. You cannot really just leave your computer for two weeks at a time and not look at the stock. I usually check in, even when I am traveling, once a day just to make sure there is no news and it is not really breaking my 10% rule.

Because penny stocks are so cheap, everyone wants to know how much they need for a small account and how many stocks they can be trading. How much money does somebody need as a minimum to start out trading penny stocks?

Some of the top students I have trained started out with $1,000 or $2,000. My top student Tim Grittani started with $1,500 of his own money and in four years he has now grown it to $2.1 million. I know that sounds crazy but I also started with $12,000 and grew it into $1.65 million in four years. When I started making money with penny stocks people said my results were crazy, luck or fraudulent but I've actually trained other people to do this and so people are now saying, "Wait a minute there might be something to this."

That's why we are having this interview, which is because this is an overlooked niche where some people with the right mindset, qualifications, system and discipline can finally succeed in this market without needing a lot of money to start.

If you have $1,000, $2,000, ideally $5,000 or $10,000 then you can trade these stocks. I usually only have one or two positions at a time. I like to have a lot of cash on hand just in case to stay very liquid for any potential technologies that pop up or any press releases I can react to. There are new technologies with the mobile internet all the time. I like to stay very liquid and just have one or two positions from these hot penny stocks that are moving.

Let's talk about your top student that you just mentioned. What did he do differently than the other people you have trained in order to have that big success? There has to be some differentiating factor.

He really wanted it. It comes down to how badly you want to be successful in this type of trading. Everyone wants to make millions but most people don't want to put in the time and effort to get there. I know that studying is not cool, it's not fun and lot of people stink at school but you have to do it. I stink at math and somehow I've made millions of dollars so I don't think it is about intelligence.

Tim Grittani is a great guy, a Midwestern kid just out of college. He deserves all his success, but I think the reason for his success was not based on intelligence. It was his dedication to studying. There are patterns you can learn, basic rules on how to protect yourself and how to find best stocks that are a basic roadmap or blueprint that he used to grow his account exponentially.

Let's follow up on that and go into some of the exact trading rules one should study and depend upon for success in this niche. I know you cannot teach everything, but people are always interested in examples of the exact buying and selling rules they can immediately use to understand how to trade a new instrument or niche. What are one or two exact trading rules people could use when trading penny stocks?

Rule #1 – you really need to focus on just *the most active penny stocks*. Do not listen to all of these companies that supposedly have all these amazing technologies but which only trade a few thousand shares a day. There are thousands of penny stock companies out there. Every one has big dreams and makes promises but almost none of them come true.

That said, there is a small group of stocks every single day you should follow. You can pretty much look at any financial website for just the *biggest percent gainers* and *most actively traded stocks*. Penny stocks are stocks trading under $5 per share, so you are looking for these actively traded penny stocks that are moving ideally due to some news.

I like buying some companies when they report good earnings, when the stock is up 20-30% and a lot of people are scared to buy it thinking, "Oh, it's up so much that I don't really want to chase it. Maybe it will come down." But if it is up 20% or 30% in a day based on good earnings news that is because the entire company is getting revalued at a higher valuation based on these new numbers.

Usually a small company trading at $2, $3 or $4 a share is viewed as a not so successful company. When one of these long shots really hits a home run in terms of revenues, growth, new users, sales, or sometimes the CEO is quoted in a press release saying business is looking great and stronger than ever, maybe margins are growing, … whatever the reason if the stock is up 20% or 30% on the day then I like to buy it that day because over that day, week or month the trend is usually up as more and more investors discover this new surprisingly strong company.

In other words, you are not simply chasing stories. Instead you are monitoring price action and only reacting to buy when the story behind the price action shows fundamental news behind it. You are often reacting to price increases based on earnings news and then getting in.

Correct. *Price action with a catalyst*. It's not just earnings. You might have a company that won't report earnings for another month or two but they might announce a big contract with a company like AT&T or Apple. When a small penny stock announces a contract with a Fortune 100 company you have to ask why this Fortune 100 company wants to work with this tiny little company. They must have something special. I'm looking for a positive catalyst and I'm looking for a good price reaction in the marketplace.

Sometimes you get a positive catalyst and no one looks twice at the penny stock. That's usually a tipoff to something very sketchy. Sometimes penny stocks announce contracts, but when you look down deeply into the SEC filings and legal filings they are not really that big.

For instance back in 2000 when I first started there used to be a penny stock that announced a big deal with FedEx. FedEx was going to work with this tiny company and the reaction was, "Wow, this is amazing." If you read the press release they were designating FedEx as their official shipper. They basically opened an account with FedEx and were putting out a press release about this. That's not a contract, okay? That kind of news should not be bought.

So you are first watching price action in this sector, finding a penny stock where the price action is very big - like a 20% move on the day - and then you are checking for fundamental news to confirm the move. If the news is something very significant then you consider buying.

Correct. If the news has legs.

Conversely I am often short selling on news because I like to bet against penny stock scams. Some penny stock scams can drive prices up 20% or 30% because of hyped up news. You have all these penny stock newsletters mailing and saying, "Wow, look at this. This penny stock is the next Microsoft or eBay or Google."

There is a lot of propaganda with penny stocks. When those stocks are moving up 20% or 30% in a day I look to short sell them because that hype usually fades since it is not based on reality.

How do you know that the news is hype versus real news with some significance? What are your criteria for determining that?

Penny stock pumping is very common and it is very easy to tell the difference between penny stock pumping and a real contract. A real contract usually has a press release where a big company who is using the smaller company's services is quoted. Something like "XYZ company has an amazing new product and we are excited to work with them."

When it is blatant penny stock promotion like in *The Wolf of Wall Street* boiler room type stuff the big company is not quoted in the press release. Sometimes there isn't even a big company. Down at the very bottom of the press release or email that you get is a disclaimer with very tiny print that says, "This company has been compensated five million shares (or five million dollars) to send out this press release." It is basically a very coordinated press campaign and most of it is lies. It is illegal, a very gray area.

I'm not a lawyer so I cannot say that what they are doing is fraudulent, but what I do know is that when someone is compensated to send out press releases and emails on a penny stock usually that means someone is paying them in order to dump the shares. They pump up the stock price in order to dump the shares. That is a "pump and dump" and those kinds of stocks can rise 20%, 30% or sometimes 50% in a day or two, but they usually come right back down the next day or next week or next month. They all inevitably end up at zero because those are the scams.

This is great information for how to identify scams, but how do you know you have the top for one of these scam promotions that you usually short? If a stock is being promoted it might keep going up for weeks so that you might lose your shirt if you short it. Are you looking for something else to confirm when you should short them?

This is the beauty of using trading rules. When you are down 10% on a stock you should cut your losses so that you don't risk disaster. If you are shorting a stock and it just keeps going, guess what? Some scams keep going for weeks or months. However, if you stick to the rules of cutting losses then you cannot get hurt that bad.

Also I don't usually look to short a stock on the first day that it spikes. I like to wait and see if it is up 50%, 75% or even 100% or 200% over the course of a few days or a few weeks. Penny stock pumping has a limited lifespan. Going back to my hypothetical example, somebody has paid five million shares or five million dollars for a series of emails or press releases to promote a stock. That money is spent and you have to think that every single press release or email that gets sent out means less money for what they want to do next time, but you don't know when the promotion will end. It is not an exact science. I lose sometimes doing this, but I win roughly three quarters of the time.

If you have a penny stock promotion campaign then depending on whether it is one million dollars, two million or even five million dollars they are spending, it usually only lasts one or two weeks. They don't have enough money to keep it going for several months, let alone years.

When I am *buying* penny stocks based on contract news or buying a company with good earnings I like to buy on the first day of that news because I am thinking that this good news has legs. When I am betting *against* a penny stock scam I prefer them to have already run up several days if not several weeks beforehand.

Are you usually more successful on your long or short penny stock trades?

It is a mix. I made my first million buying penny stocks. I made my second million shorting penny stocks. I made my third and fourth million kind of mixed. I just take the opportunities when they come up.

This is the beautiful thing about penny stocks. You have some companies that are good, some companies that are bad and then a whole lot of companies that are doing nothing. Sadly most people focus on the companies that are doing nothing because they believe in their stories.

If it is me, sometimes I might have two trades in my portfolio. One of them might be long and the other short. Because I believe I have a generally successful approach for both sides of the market I can profit on both of them. I therefore try not to be biased whether to go long or short. I just take the opportunities as they come in.

I know you have lots of different methods or rules for buying and selling penny stocks. Let's see if we can entice out of you another buy rule for low hanging fruit long trades. Is there any other situation that usually has a high probability of success for buying penny stocks? Also, are there any specific chart patterns for when you want to sell?

When I buy penny stocks I really like a specific volume. The volume is the number of shares that are traded in a day. If you see a penny stock that is trading one hundred million shares in a day - and many penny stocks do - then that is too much because everybody already knows about his company. You don't really have an edge because there is no real information inefficiency and so then we are basically just trading a lower priced version of Google. I don't want a stock which is being traded that much.

That being said, I also don't want a stock that is just trading a few thousand shares per day that nobody knows about. The problem is that it then won't have any legs because the word just hasn't gone out about the company. I like to buy companies that trade between 150,000 shares and 1,000,000 shares in a day. That gives me a very wide range of stocks that trade that much. They are kind of discovered but not really, and they are traded actively enough so that if I buy or short sell 1,000 or 5,000 shares I can get in and out quickly.

A lot of people make the mistake of getting very excited about a company and they buy 20,000 shares of a company that only trades 5,000 shares in a day. No matter how right you are it is going to take you at least four days to sell the stock based on the daily trading volume of the stock. Sometimes people take too big positions. You don't want to make that mistake. I like being less than 5-10% of the daily trading volume.

Do you usually use just one brokerage account to trade or several to break it up?

I usually use just one brokerage account. If I am short selling penny stocks there are very specific brokers I use. Interactive Brokers is great for short selling penny stocks and SureTrader is great. When you are buying penny stocks you can pretty much use anything. I have accounts at SpeedTrader, E-Trade, Scottrade and Fidelity.

Those are all big names so they are all within reach of most traders out there.

Correct. Almost anyone can trade penny stocks. You just have to open your mind. There is a lot of hate with penny stocks because people don't know the rules. A lot of people see a penny stock issue a positive press release and then they see it drop 50% in a day. Then their reaction is, "What's going on? Penny stocks are so crazy!"

If you actually took a second to look at that supposedly positive press release and you read the disclaimer at the bottom of it then you would see that it is not a press release but an advertisement and that the reason the stock is dropping is because it is a "pump and dump" scheme. You have to do a little more research than if you are reading a press release from a larger company like Cisco or Google, but if you look at it then it is not really that complicated. You just have to look a little bit closer.

It sounds like you are very much focused on press releases tied to price action. Is there anything that puts a stock on your watch list before there is a press release or price action?

I really love buying stocks that are about to hit 52-week highs. There are many technical traders out there who don't even care about press releases, news or catalysts but who are just looking at charts. One of the greatest technical indicators that is very popular and heavily used is a new 52-week high on a stock chart. This just means that the stock price is hitting a new high over the last year.

That is usually a good momentum indicator because it shows that people are willing to pay higher prices for the same company because theoretically that company is doing something right. When a penny stock hits a 52-week high, especially a penny stock, usually the trend continues based on the recent news, sector they are in, or anticipation over a new product that is coming out. The 52-week highs are great for buying penny stocks.

I really stay away from buying penny stocks that are on sale. You have a lot of penny stocks that are down 50%, 70% or 90% on the year. People love sales but you have to learn that sales on penny stocks are not the same as a Black Friday sale where you are going to buy a sweater that is 50% off for one day only and it is the same sweater whether you buy it on this special sale day or another day. If you buy a penny stock that is 50% off then you have to ask why it is 50% off. Why is the stock so low?

It is 50% down in price because there are so many sellers and there are so many sellers because the penny stock must have done something very bad whether they missed on their earnings guidance, whether their revenues didn't come through or maybe a new product bombed. Whatever the case may be penny stocks often issue negative news. That just makes them the average penny stock. That is why their stock price is traded so low. They are basically failures. They may be ready to go out of business.

I don't want to buy a penny stock that is going to be worthless in a year or worthless in a month or two and buy at 50% off *now* and think I am getting a deal. You are *not* getting a deal. You are buying something that is going to go to zero and you are paying a certain price that is way overpriced. By sticking to strong penny stocks that are uptrending - and I'm not saying you have to fall in love with them and hold them for years or decades because that's not a good way to trade penny stocks – but if you buy stocks that are hitting new highs and you ride the momentum then you can do very well.

Are there any indicators you use that tell you this is a stock I should be buying at the 52-week high rather than just blindly buying it when it crosses that barrier?

It all goes back to looking for big percentage gainers every single day. I use Finviz.com, which is a free website. I also use StockCharts.com. These websites have filters and scans that show you stocks making 52-week highs.

I keep it very simple. Having very simple indicators works best for me as long as I stick to the rules of buying good companies with good news with good price action and with good volume. When I stray from that then that's when I don't do too well.

What are the particular parameters of your typical scan? Is it a stock less than $5 making a 52-week high?

That's about it. I sometimes go up to $10 per share and ideally a volume between 100,000 and 1,000,000 shares per day. That's my basic screen.

How are you spending most of your time in prep work for tomorrow's trading? Also, are you spending all day in front of a computer when trading? In other words, how much time tomorrow will you actually spend trading and how much prep time do you need today?

There are a lot of traders who spend their entire lives in front of their computers looking for new news and always looking for an edge. Because my strategy is simple – and I have made it deceptively simple – if you embrace simplicity you don't have to be in front of your computer every single second. I want to go out and enjoy life.

I look every single night, no matter what, for at least twenty minutes at my screens to just find out what are the biggest percentage gainers today, which stocks are hitting new 52-week highs, and what are some traders talking about on twitter. I follow twitter now and then just to see some interesting stock ideas. By keeping it very simple I am not being strained. I am not saying to myself, "Oh, here's a new company with some potentially amazing new technology and it only trades 5,000 shares per day right now, but it could be good." You have to stay disciplined.

I have refined this over the past fifteen years. I didn't know this whole formula when I first began. I was all over the place spending every single second in front of the computer just looking at all sorts of different stocks. Over fifteen years I've refined what works best. I sometimes teach this to others who have basically confirmed what I'm thinking. I'm very proud of their success.

Is there any other chart pattern other than a 52-week high that they should be studying and focusing on?

The 52-week highs are nice but I also prefer a 52-week high that is just breaking out over past resistance from two or three years ago. I love looking back even longer than one year and trying to see where is the specific breakout point.

If you are just buying a stock based on its breaking a 52-week high then when you have companies hitting a new 52-week high five days in a row, on which day do you buy? Well, what if on the third day it breaks the 3-year high? So look back at multiple time frames if you want to add a little complexity that ups the rates of success just a little bit. In that way you can have yet another technical breakout indicator.

You have to think that there is a whole world of traders out there and they are using all kinds of software. Some traders use 52-week breakouts and some prefer 3-year breakouts. If you have a stock that is breaking out on a 1-year, 3-year and maybe even 5-year time frame then it shows up on even more traders' screens. When those traders like to buy it then it becomes a self-fulfilling prophecy.

Those are really good lessons. What about on the short side? On the short side is there anything else you are looking for other than the pattern that you already mentioned?

On the short side I am betting against scams and really bad companies. In those situations I am looking for support to be cracked. For instance, let's say there is a pump and dump that has been going on for two weeks and this pump has raised the stock's price from 10¢ to $3.00 a share. Let's also say that for the past two weeks it has held on to $2.50 per share. I'm talking about $2.50 because I don't necessarily try to pick the exact top.

Let's say it has tried to crack $2.50 once, twice, three times and failed every time. Every single time it tries to break that key level I am watching it. When it is a pump and dump and the stock is up for the wrong reasons and it is at a short-term top then when that crack happens at $2.50 I want to be there. That's because when it cracks just a penny or two to $2.49 or $2.48 a share that crack is enough to create a stop-loss tsunami. As a short seller I like to ride that stop-loss tsunami because we have all these automated computer orders that will get triggered in that wave down.

Let's say someone puts in an order and are long this pump and dump and they are thinking, "Okay, I'm going to protect myself and put my stop in at $2.50 a share." For two or three times in a row over a few days that $2.50 may be protected. On the one time it is not protected that stop-loss that they use is taken out, but because so many other people have their stop-losses right at $2.50 it doesn't just get executed at $2.49, $2.48 or $2.47. You have all these stop-losses piling up and it creates this tidal wave of sellers and no one can get executed.

I have seen penny stocks drop all the way from $2.50 to $1.00 a share inside of an hour. You can lose 50% on your long if you use those hard stops, which is why I don't use them. I use mental stops, but as a short seller I love the people who use those hard stops because I can make 30% in thirty minutes by taking advantage of knowing they are there. And as a short seller, when you know or have an idea where those hard stops are then if you can short just before they get taken out you can literally ride the wave of automated sell orders all the way down for an hour, a day or sometimes even a week and lock in very low-risk, high-reward profits.

That's the beauty of trading low priced stocks. With high priced stocks you have to be very right about the company and its business and products usually over the course of several months or years to make 30-50%. Down here in the gutter of the stock market you can make annual returns inside of a few hours or days.

That brings up the question of typical profit targets for trades like this. What percentage gain are you normally after for your trades and does it differ for longs and shorts? Also, how do you tell when you should wait for a larger profit than you normally would take?

I really like to take the meat of a move. If I am buying a company that is breaking out to a new high - ideally with good earnings or a press release about a new product - I'm trying to make 50% on the move.

Sometimes I don't get to 50% because that's kind of aggressive to try to make that in a few days or a few weeks. Most often I really only aim to make 30% so if I'm up near 30% it has to be something *amazing* for me not to take profits.

I'm pretty greedy so I don't like holding unrealized profits. I like realizing them and looking at the profit in my account. It helps me feel better and sleep better at night. In general, usually I am taking profits at 20-30%. That is my goal within a day or within a week.

A few years ago I bought this company called Liquid Metals. It was a classic penny stock. At 55¢ they had just announced an SEC filing with Apple Computers. Apple Computers was going to use their technology and they got $20+ million in a licensing deal. There was no press release. There was just an SEC filing.

The stock was already up and I said, "This is a special time and so I am going to hold it." I held it and made 50% as opposed to 30% and then I locked in my gains. Two days later the stock had tripled so I could have made 200%. I don't look to say, "What could I have made?" To me it is a question of whether I can lock in 20%, 30% or 50% gains. That's usually good on the way up for long trades.

On the way down when short selling penny stocks that are absolute scams that are worthless - and I've seen so many of these scams just get crushed 20%, 30%, and 50% inside an hour or two - I really try to do the same thing and make 20-30%. On the outside I make 50%.

A lot of my popular videos have shown live trades where you see me making 30% in thirty minutes. That's my most popular Youtube video. A lot of people try to make 30% over the course of the year. I prove that I can sometimes make 30% in thirty minutes using my trading system.

You've established that someone can start out trading penny stocks with a very small account. However, I always stress that traders should never enter a particular investment niche or attempt to master a particular trading technique or style when success in that arena doesn't really match their personality. Along those lines, what seems to be the common profile features of people who succeed with this type of trading? In other words, have you found any particular personality, psychology or behavioral traits that are predominant for the winners in penny stock trading?

There is definitely a type. I have several millionaire students now and they are all very similar. These millionaire students are big believers in justice. They really get a kick out of short selling scams. It's not just about the money that we make. It's really about exposing the scams and watching as the stocks drop. We don't really like scams but have to let the world know that they are scams, so justice is a big thing for those mastering the short selling strategies.

Also, people who like to think outside the box. To even trade penny stocks you are not going to be popular anywhere you go. Penny stocks are a very controversial topic and so people who are very independently minded, people who think outside the box and say, "This might be an interesting strategy to take up and I'm willing to try it," are found in this niche. People who are curious and those people who are willing to study and learn the rules are found here. Not people who think, "Oh, I can never trade penny stocks because people are talking badly about them."

People who are narrow-minded or set in their ways are not going to do well with penny stock strategies. Part of the reason for my success is that I'm pretty flexible and very adaptable. Sometimes I have to take a loss in trading, which a lot of people are not willing to do.

Many people are too rigid in their thinking and actions. For instance, if they are going to short sell a scam then some incorrectly reason, "Okay, this is a scam and I'm going to hold it until it goes to zero." If they think that way then they are not going to be able to cut losses quickly when they have to if the penny stock promotion scam keeps going higher. It's just not going to make sense to them. They are going to think, "Why am I taking a loss on this scam? Why don't I just give it a few months?" They don't realize the possibility that you can really lose a lot of money if you don't cut losses quickly.

You have to be disciplined. You have to think outside the box. There is not one specific type of people who trade penny stocks. It's good for men and women. I have some teenagers who have made $50,000 or $100,000. It doesn't matter if you are in the U.S. or international. It is just a question of whether you are willing to study, learn the rules and then trade.

This sounds like a success profile mostly for short sellers. Are you mostly focused on shorting penny stocks right now or are you usually doing 50:50 trading in terms of longs and shorts? Where do most of the profits lay?

It really comes down to just taking advantage of these opportunities when they come about and not having any expectations. I don't go into a month and say, "Okay, this month I'm going to try to make three longs and three shorts so I can be 50:50." Sometimes I see five earnings winners in a row and I have five long trades in a row.

In the past year we have seen a lot of marijuana stocks that have been just absolute scams so I did seven shorts in a row. I was shorting this whole police camera theme with the Ferguson shooting and NY police debate when a lot of these with police equipment stocks really spiked a lot. They didn't deserve to go up so I was shorting them.

Overall over the past fifteen years it's been 60% shorts and 40% longs, but in the past year of 2014 (which I should mention is a big time record year where I'm up nearly a million dollars in trading profits by trading small penny stocks off of an initial $500,000 account) it's been more 50:50 of longs and shorts. That is because we have been in a strong bull market and there have been so many penny stocks that have been breaking out to new highs so I have been taking advantage of that.

This is a very opportunistic strategy and it's ripe for anybody who really wants to try something different. You have all these people who are long-term buy and hold investors and people who are trading forex and options, but I've made my niche trading penny stocks successfully over the long term. I love this niche.

I start with $500,000 every year, which is what I did this year, but next year I'm going to start with $100,000 just to prove that I can really make a lot of money with a smaller account. But this year I'm up nearly 200% in 2014 so I'm crushing every major index.

That is an outstanding track record in this niche. Now recently a lot of people have been saying that algorithmic trading is interfering with the markets and the intervention is so massive and pervasive that it is destroying other styles of trading. Have you seen any indication that algorithmic trading is negatively affecting penny stock trading?

No. That's the beautiful thing about penny stocks. Mainstream Wall Street and most hedge funds don't care about these stocks. This is all low hanging fruit. I am competing against people with very small accounts and that's kind of nice. I love the fact that there is no competition and I don't have to compete against algorithms.

I always make the comparison that if you are going to play basketball then do you want to play basketball against Michael Jordan or do you want to play basketball against the midget actor Verne Troyer who played "mini-me" in the Austin Powers movies? Michael Jordon will be stuffing you non-stop because he is the greatest basketball player of all time versus Verne Troyer who doesn't have the height advantage that Michael Jordon has and so you can win.

The penny stock competition is very easy so it opens the door to so much opportunity for those of us who are willing to learn the rules, learn the subtleties and the patterns so that we can hop in and out of these stocks while ignorant people are just thinking, "This is the next Microsoft," and they don't understand the trading rules that work or differentiate between scams and earnings winners. They just look at a $2 stock and think this is going to $1,000. That's naive. This type of thinking is what you typically find in the penny stock field and is the reason why most people don't make money.

You are saying that, besides learning a particular style of trading penny stocks, one of the things that really differentiates the successful traders from the not so successful in this niche is how you look at things, namely your perspective.

Yes, it all comes down to perspective. You can look at penny stocks and say these are very unpredictable. That perspective comes from people who don't understand the rules of how this market usually works. They see a stock drops when it gets positive press that day and they don't get it. They don't understand the fact that the stock has been manipulated.

They look at companies that report good earnings and they think, "When a company like Google reports good earnings the stocks spike entirely all in one day." That's often the entire move because everyone is so excited about earnings whereas with a penny stock that reports good earnings the move takes weeks and sometimes even months because this is a much more inefficient field.

That's the beauty of this. These stocks have legs because not everybody is looking every single day. Those of us who do look every single day, those of us who take the time to look at the rules and look at the patterns have an inherent advantage over those who are lazy or narrow-minded traders.

This has been great information for active traders. If somebody really wanted to learn more about

mastering penny stock trading rather than just throw money at them and then lose it on these low priced stocks where would they go to learn more?

I think PennyStockConspiracy.com is the best website that has a ton of educational videos. I do use StockCharts.com for charting and Finviz.com. Yahoo Finance (finance.yahoo.com) is my go to website for just basic research. If you want to get into SEC filings and read these long, boring filings you can use OTCmarkets.com. These are all free tools and I use them regularly.

So someone doesn't really need a lot of money to get into this?

No. That is the gift and the curse of penny stocks. It is so easy to get in and a lot of people are attracted to the niche, but you do need to have some trading rules. You do need to have a plan. If you get into penny stocks and just throw money at them you are basically just throwing money away because you are not doing it correctly. You don't need a lot of money but you do need a plan.

Thanks Tim! This information will really help people get hold of some profitable ways to trade the penny stock niche, which isn't normally possible when traders treat it like a casino of low cost lottery tickets. Once again I see the reiteration of watching price action at support and resistance levels that must be confirmed by some other factor. Thank you for revealing some of your specific trading rules for which you credit your winning success and the best of luck for continued trading success.

Thanks Bill!

Chapter 10
Fred Carach
Penny Resource Stocks and High-Yield Investments

One of my favorite investing books of all time is Fred Carach's Forty Years a Speculator, which dramatically altered some of my investing viewpoints after it came out. In his book Fred explained how he slowly achieved financial independence, starting from very little income, by investing in Canadian resource stocks and high-yield investments. Basically he used fundamental analysis to invest in exciting penny mining shares, natural resource stocks and also high dividend investments whose returns would then be ploughed right back into more of the same. Relying on the laws of compounding, over time Fred was able to amass a bankroll that has made him financially independent.

Now seventy-three years old, it has been nearly a decade since Fred's book was first released. In this interview I asked him to update us on how his investment philosophy had changed over the last decade, what he was interested in buying now in light of the present ZIRP (zero interest rate) environment, and asked about any new strategies that he might have developed for the income side of his portfolio.

What you'll like in this interview is not only hearing how investing has changed over the past fifty years, but seeing how Fred uses his brain to analyze the various stock opportunities that he prefers. While some might call Fred a "speculator" because he often buys penny stocks, a more accurate description is that he is a savvy fundamental investor who takes well-considered positions in sometimes unpopular stocks that, because of their unpopularity (which is the way Fred likes it), probabilistically produce an aggregate return in spades.

Fred, let's start with your background and how you got into investing.

I was born and raised in Portland, New York, which is a small town about thirty miles from Syracuse with a population of about twenty thousand people. My father was a restaurant owner on the main street of the town and one of our big regulars was a stockbroker. He used to come into the restaurant with *The Wall Street Journal*.

In those days people did not subscribe to *The Wall Street Journal* because it was too expensive. At that time, in the fifties, every newspaper in the country cost a nickel and *The Wall Street Journal* cost around a buck. The saying was that only stockbrokers and rich playboys bought *The Wall Street Journal*. Paying a buck a day for any newspaper was regarded as outrageous, but this customer would come into our restaurant waving his *Wall Street Journal* around as if it was a status symbol, which it was. Everyone just stood there and gawked at him. I am sure that's where my interest in the stock market began because I was already very interested in it even as a kid.

Let me tell you the way people invested in those days because I remember it well. This goes back to the fifties. Nobody subscribed to *The Wall Street Journal* and no newspaper carried the stock tables except maybe *The Wall Street Journal* and the *New York Times*. There were no TV channels about financing or the market. There was no talk radio dedicated to money and finance.

Here is how people invested in those days and you want to know what? The typical investor at that time was far more successful than investors today because they had their heads screwed on straight. They would know nothing about the stock market but they knew about corporations. They bought the products. They bought General Motors products. They bought Ford. They bought Chrysler. They bought Coke. They bought Pepsi Cola. They bought Procter & Gamble items. The way people would invest in those days was this: if they liked the product or service they'd say, "Look, this is a great product or service. If the product or service is great then the corporation is going to make money for me." They would buy based upon that.

They were then married to their stocks. If they bought Coke they were fanatical about seeing to it that Coke was in their house at all times and nothing else and if they saw anyone else buying Pepsi Cola or a competitor they would have a fit. They would promote their stock at every opportunity and they were long-term owners. Five years was the minimum. They would hold these stocks ten or fifteen years because they believed in them. They knew they were owners of the corporation and they regarded that stock certificate not as a lottery ticket, but as a certificate of ownership and they regarded themselves as being faithful, long-term owners of the corporation.

If you stop and think about it, if you are a long-term holder of five years or more then buying corporations based on nothing more than the fact that you like the product or service is a great way to invest. That's the age in which Warren Buffett appeared. Everyone was a long-term buy and hold investor. There was none of this nonsense, "I hold a stock for five minutes and if it drops 5% then I sell it before it goes to zero."

Months would go by without these people knowing what the stock price is. They didn't care. They didn't care because they were married to this stock. Once every six months they would call up their broker - because they damn sure weren't going to spend the money on *The Wall Street Journal* - and they'd say, "Joe, what's my stock selling for?" Joe would tell him and then they would forget about it for another six months. In those days blue-chip companies would pay 4%, 5% and 6% dividends. People kept the dividends.

I'll tell you that the typical investor then - the retail investor - did fantastically more successful than an investor today even though the investor today knows twenty times more data, most of it which is worthless because they don't do fundamental analysis at all. That's the way it worked.

This sounds like Peter Lynch's *One Up on Wall Street*. His message was to just buy the companies you are familiar with that have great products.

That's right.

Do you think this is how people should be buying stocks today?

Well, today you've got a lot more access to data. I'm a firm believer in fundamental analysis. You should actually look at the company and analyze it. You need to know what the earnings per share number is, you need to know what the P/E ratio is and you need to know what the dividend is. There is more stuff that you can research depending upon the stock and situation.

Charles Schwab is my long-term broker. Tons of excellent free research is available through Charles Schwab. That's what I use to do my research. You get standard reports, you get inside sellers, you get all sorts of stuff and you can analyze the whole thing. It's really a tremendous asset. I'm firmly in the buy-and-sell camp.

You mean the buy and hold camp?

Yes. That doesn't mean that you never sell the stock. Every year at the end of the year there is tax loss selling time. At the end of the year you take a look at the stocks you have and if you find stocks that you no longer believe in then you get rid of them. In a typical year I'll sell ten or fifteen positions, something like that. However, I'll never sell a stock simply because it's down. I will only sell a stock because I no longer believe in it.

How many positions are you usually holding for your portfolio?

About eighty to a hundred positions.

Oh, wow!

I'm fanatical about diversification. Fanatical.

All right, let's go through your investment philosophy. I love your book, *Forty Years a Speculator*, which contains some of this, but let's update things. What did you go through to arrive at your philosophy in that book and what's your philosophy now? Let's go through your progression.

Well, basically I'm retired military from dual service. As soon as I got out of high school I joined the Marines. I spent four years in there. After that I got out, bummed around and could not find a job. I then put four years into the Navy so I had eight years in, and during that entire eight years I was earning essentially nothing. The first two years I was in the Marine Corps they paid me $79 a month. By the time I got out of the Navy eight years later I think my top pay was about $320 a month. Try getting rich on that.

I was always investing. I started investing as a nineteen year-old kid using what little I could get. With those few hundred dollars I would put it in the market, but it became clear to me very quickly that there is no way I could make it by buying blue-chip stocks. I could not afford to pay $40, $60, $80 for a blue-chip stock. I just couldn't but I could afford to buy the cheap stuff.

I think I recorded in the book when the big revelation occurred. When I was in the Navy I was serving aboard the USS Little Rock off Naples. We were cruising off the coast of Naples and I happened to pick up a magazine about somebody who had made a killing investing in Canadian penny mining stocks. The most important thing about the article was that they said, "You know what, if you're going to speculate in Canadian penny mining stocks then you need to subscribe to *The Northern Miner*, which is *The Wall Street Journal* of the mining industry." I've been a subscriber to it ever since. Through the articles of *The Northern Miner* I began to pick my stocks. If you are buying stocks that are selling for five cents a share, ten cents a share, twenty cents a share, or thirty cents a share then you can afford to buy a lot of stocks for chump change. That's what I had. I had chump change.

When these babies hit there is absolutely no resistance between a penny per share and a dollar per share. Zero resistance. In the stock market, if a stock goes to twenty to forty dollars a share you're going to get massive resistance because people are going to be pulling back. In the penny stock game if a stock goes for twenty cents a share to forty cents a share nobody pulls back. That's why they explode up to a dollar a share on any positive news.

So you got into doing penny mining shares simply because you didn't have any money?

That's right.

What was your final trading methodology for deciding which mining shares to buy and why did you stay in Canadian shares rather than go into U.S. shares? What became your exact trading rule that you developed which really worked?

Well, basically for many years I would rely almost exclusively on *The Northern Miner* for the data. *The Northern Miner* has an annual publication which I no longer buy because it sells at about a hundred bucks and you can get the data now right on the internet. Basically I relied heavily on that.

That explains the heavy Canadian focus although I remember from your book that you also only trust Canadian penny stocks because the Canadian listing requirements eliminate much of the potential pump and dump fraud that is found on the American exchanges. At this point I want to know what were the trading rules you developed for the penny mining shares? What became your trading rules for what would work?

Buying at the five year low.

Okay, so you would find a penny mining company and you would just say, "Buy at the five year low." That's it?

If I liked it. Obviously you research it and you have to like it based upon the mining claims, what it's in and its history. If you buy stuff that you like that is selling at or near the five year low then you'll do fine. This is not just in mining but in anything. The problem with today's investors is that they are hopeless trend chasers. The dominant thesis of the stock market today is not analysis, not belief, not stock picking. It is blindly following the trend. People mindlessly buy whatever is going up and they mindlessly sell whatever is going down. This is something I have no use for.

Okay, you found through research that you could buy penny mining stocks at five-year lows and these things would then be generally safe. If they wouldn't go bankrupt then how long would you hold a stock for? When would you get out of a penny stock? What return would you expect?

The classic rule is that you sell half of your position when a stock doubles. Since you are taking so much risk with the penny mining stocks, I would say when it goes up 300% then I'll probably sell half. You're dealing with a more risky beast by definition.

There is another thing. I'm massively diversified and my rule is that I never put more than 5% of my capital in anything. The riskier the investment the smaller the amount I put in. My typical placement in a penny mining stock to this day is from about one quarter of one percent to one percent (.25% to 1%). That's how much of my capital I will put into it. These are highly risky positions and if you put more than one percent in any of this stuff then you are pretty much on your own if it's selling for under a dollar.

That's also the great thing about it. You can afford to diversify massively. You can buy five thousand, ten thousand, fifteen thousand, twenty thousand shares for nothing. You then must hold onto it. You've got to be patient. Nothing works in this game, or as far as I'm concerned in the stock market, quickly. The minimum acceptable holding period is two years.

People today are just short-term fanatics. They'll hold a position for three months or six months and if it doesn't move they will say, "Sell this dog. It's not going anywhere." They are constantly chasing for something that will move. These short-time holdings just do not work. If you want to make the big bucks you must hold for two to five years.

There is a reason why Warren Buffett said his favorite holding period is forever. That's what truly works. You have got to get away from these three months, six months, or nine months short-term holding periods. Just recently I read an article that said as recently as ten or fifteen years ago the average term holding period was five years. It used to be ten years. People were married to the stock. They found something they believed in and they held onto it. Now it's about six months. Six months! People say they are long-term investors but they are not. What will happen to these alleged long-term holders is that a stock will drop five percent or ten percent and then they will immediately freak out and sell the stock. They say they are long-term holders but they are not.

There is another thing. The volatility of the stocks that you see today is simply enormous. Enormous. You would never see this type of volatility in the old days. Stocks go up and down enormously based on nothing. It's a common experience for me to see a stock that's had a big move, and I say, "Okay, let's find out why this big move occurred." You look at the reasoning behind the move and you'll see that it's nonsense. Simply nonsense. Six months from now no one will even remember why that move occurred.

Basically what you have today, in Wall Street lingo, is "trading the noise." I'm sure you're familiar with "trading the noise." That means you have got millions of people who are sitting there in front of their computer screens, who may call themselves "long-term investors" but are really day traders, and they simply trade the noise. Every positive news report is regarded as a buy and every negative news report is regarded as a sell. That's what they do.

What they are trying to do, and what is destabilizing the stock market, is that everyone is trying to be on the same side of the trade. You can't do that. You can't have a market where everyone is on the same side of the trade. What results is ridiculous volatility. The positive news report sends everything to the moon and the negative news report sends it into the gutter. It's insane, totally insane.

Let's take a look at the gold and silver mining stocks because there is a lot of interest in that right

now because of the low prices of the precious metals. What would you be buying in that sector right now, or how would you be looking at what companies to buy?

Can we start out with uranium first?

Sure, that would be great. I'd love to discuss your take on the natural resource sector in general.

All right. Let me tell you, there is a horrible truth about the natural resource market. I have been in this game for decades, and I have never seen anything like the catastrophe that's hit the natural resource market in the last two or three years. In fact, for the last four years. Actually, it's been four years because I track this stuff.

If you look at almost any natural resource stock you will find that around the spring of 2011 they all peaked right around April. Let's just pick a natural resource stock and see where it was selling at then. Since that time there has been one of the most incredible stock declines I have ever seen. It's across the board. It is affecting everything. It hit oil. It hit gas. It hit gold. It hit silver. It hit uranium. It hit lead, copper, zinc. You name it and it has crashed. I've never seen anything like it. Never!

All cycles reverse. Natural resources are not a luxury that can be dispensed with. If you think they are a luxury that can be dispensed with then take a look at the car in your driveway. You are looking at three thousand pounds of natural resources, not to mention the gas. This stuff is going to come back because it has to come back, but I just don't know when. I never would have believed that it could turn this negative so long.

Every day I see stocks in the natural resource sector that are down 60%, 70%, 80%, 85%, and they are selling stocks. They are selling stocks. Here is what has happened. Basically, one of the reasons why they are down is that with the prices today no one can survive. Let me give you an instance.

Gold production needs gold at $1,250 an ounce. It has got to have that in order for most producers to make a profit. They need $1,250 an ounce, but gold is stuck in the middle $1,100s. There just isn't enough money there. Silver needs at least $20 to $25 an ounce. It's at $15 an ounce. Almost nobody can make money at those prices. Oil needs $65 a barrel. The producers have to have $65 a barrel. It's not there. It's in the middle $40s.

It's insane. It is insane. Nobody can make money at these prices. If the prices continue they will put every company, every natural resource producer on earth out of business. They simply cannot survive. Like I said, natural resources are not a luxury that we can dispense with. You have got to have them.

I'm not a market timer so I have no idea when this is going to turn around, but I know it has to turn around. Basically I just hold on and wait for it. I do not sell. I mean, these things have been killed, killed, killed. I'm talking 80%, 90% declines. It's just incredible.

As to uranium, uranium needs $65 a pound. That's what they've got to have to be profitable. Uranium sells now at $35-36 a pound. Wherever you look the price that producers have got to have isn't there. It just isn't there. They are building today sixty-six nuclear reactors all over the world, but mostly in the third world because Western Europe and United States have more or less given up on them. Nevertheless uranium has a rich future because uranium gives you electrical energy 24/7, 365 days a year, no ands, ifs, or buts.

People think that renewables are the wave of the future. No, it's nuclear energy that is the wave of the future. Japan is what killed it because they shut down all their nuclear reactors, but they are starting to put some back online. I think there is going to be a tremendous shortage in the next couple years because people have just stopped mining it. They can't make money at it. Let me give you a few possible uranium plays before we go onto gold and silver.

Sure. Give me a few of your uranium plays. Also, there are all these opportunities so give us the rules for how you choose them.

All right. First one is Denison Mines. The symbol is DNN and it sells at 40¢ a share. Forty cents a share! It's the largest landholder in Canada's Athabasca Basin. The Athabasca Basin is critical. It's located in Saskatchewan, Alaska. It's the richest uranium ore body ever discovered. The basin has the richest uranium ores ever discovered.

This rinky-dink little stock - 40¢ a share - it controls 530,000 hectares within the basin. A hectare is about 2.4 or 2.5 acres. This is enormous. Enormous. It should be selling for two, three thousand dollars. It should be an incredible price based on the assets.

You know, the market only looks at income. If there's no income being generated then they couldn't care less what the assets are. That's the deal. Buy 5,000, 10,000, 15,000 shares of this sucker and just put it away with the idea that you are going to hold it for five years. You will be richly rewarded when uranium comes back. Like I said, you have got to have $65 a pound. Right now, it's about $36 a pound.

Nothing works today in the natural resource market. However it has got to turn around or else they are all going to go out of business. You need natural resources.

The next one I like is Fission Uranium at 50¢ a share. The symbol is FCUUF. It's also in the Athabasca Basin. It's in part of the Athabasca Basin known as the Patterson Lake South District, and just recently they made the richest uranium strike in the last thirty years. They hold 31,000 hectares in the basin selling for 50¢ a share. Do the same thing that you do with Denison.

One thing … I don't know if I told you this. For any penny stock, your maximum position is one percent of your play, one percent of your total capital. Typically, as I think I've said, I will put a quarter of one percent to one percent in any position. That's typical. If you put more than one percent into any of these babies then you're on your own. This is high-risk stuff, but the reward is stunning when they hit. You are talking about ten baggers, twenty baggers, thirty baggers. This stuff can happen in a red hot market.

Let's take another one. It's called UEX and the symbol is UEXCF. It's selling for pennies. Pennies! I think it's selling for around 9¢ or 10¢ a share or something like that. It owns 925,000 acres in the Athabasca Basin. Cameco, which is a major uranium play, owns 22% of it so they like it. It has a partnership with Areva, which is the French nuclear outfit that is big in nuclear energy and does the whole nine yards. It's got tremendous assets.

Everything that I'm talking about has been crushed, murdered, crushed. All right, so that takes care of the uranium plays that you investors might want to take a look at.

Let's talk about oil. What are your thoughts on the oil market as to whether it's going to rebound – if and when - and what you would be buying.

Sure. Like I told you, the oil market now is stuck in the mid-$40s. Nobody can make money there. It's got to be $65 a barrel, got to be at $65 a barrel. Everything in there has been killed. In fact, everything that I'm talking about today has been killed. You are at the bottom of the market. I just don't know when the upturn is going to occur. When the next turn of the wheel comes there is going to be enormous profits to be made in the whole field.

Let's take a look at Abraxas Petroleum. The symbol is AXAS and it is selling for about $1.50 a share. It was selling just a while back at about the $7, $8, $9 area but now it's down to $1.50. It owns 23,000 net acres in the Bakken in North Dakota. The Bakken is the greatest oil boom that this country has seen in generations, maybe since the 1920s. The Bakken, North Dakota has gone from nowhere to being the number two oil producer in the country based on the Bakken strike.

Anyhow this stock, selling for $1.50, owns 23,000 net acres in the Bakken and 7,300 acres in Eagle Ford (Texas), which is the most important Shell oil play in Texas. It's the Eagle Ford play. It owns an additional 17,000 acres in the Texas Powder River Basin plus 40,000 acres in the Permian Basin, which is an enormous oil and gas basin in West Texas and in New Mexico. As I said, Abraxas Petroleum sells for a $1.50 a share. It earned 43¢ last year selling at a P/E of 3.6. I don't think that includes the latest quarterly report, which may be negative now because they are simply struggling. Everybody is struggling. You can take a look at it, go on their website and do your own analysis.

The next one I like is Arsenal Energy. The symbol is AEYIF selling for $1.30 a share. This one here used to be $5, $6, $7 a share. It's selling at $1.30 now. The P/E is 1.43 and it pays a dividend of 4.7%. Like I said, I don't think that these numbers include the last quarterly statement. It is possible that last quarterly statement will be negative. I'm just giving you an indication. The values are just incredible.

Let's try another one - Bellatrix. The symbol is BXE selling for about $1.61 a share. Last year it earned 49¢ a share and it's selling at a P/E of about 6.8. Let me stress again that these numbers probably do not include the last quarterly statement, which may show a loss. Nonetheless, you can see there is tremendous value out there.

The last one in the oils would be Northern Oil and Gas, symbol NOG. The three-year high on this baby was $17.09, but it is selling now for $4.79. It is losing money, but I like it. You can check that one out. Those are the oil and gas plays that I like.

Let's now go to silver and gold. What is your whole theory on the precious metals and why you are picking those stocks and when you get out of those types of shares?

All right, here is the thing. On gold and silver I think that there has been a disaster for the last four years. What I think is going to ignite it and turn it around is the crushing level of indebtedness throughout the world. The level of indebtedness is so huge that the central banks of the world have got to be able to ignite inflation or they are going to kill everybody.

Japan has crushing debts. They can't grow anymore and one of the major reasons why they have stopped growing (they struggle to grow 1% a year) is that the level of indebtedness is killing them. Everyone has got zero interest rates now throughout the world, or near zero interest rates, because the debt level is so crushing that nobody can survive.

Western Europe has the same thing. Almost everyone has crushing levels of debts. They have zero interest rate policies, negative interest rate policies and there is a desperate attempt to ignite inflation because the debts are simply crushing the life out of them.

Same thing in the United States even though we are not as bad as Japan or Europe. We have crushing levels of debt. That's why the economy can't recover. It's because the debts are so huge that they are simply devouring everything. Sooner or later the central banks are going to figure out how to ignite the inflation they have got to have because with these huge debts you can't even pay the interest on the debts now, let alone bring it down.

That's what is going to ignite gold and silver and also natural resources, which are always an inflation hedge. I just don't know when, but they are going to find a way to ignite inflation. They've got to because the debts are simply unpayable. If the Fed raises the interest rates even a quarter percent I don't think this economy can handle it. I notice that every time the ten-year Treasury note just begins to approach 3% then the market crashes. I just don't think that they can do it. If they do then I think it's going to cause an enormous crisis. That's what I think is going to propel gold and silver. Silver is the poor man's gold. What will bring us out of this crisis, or out of these gold and silver doldrums is simply the desperate attempts of the central banks of the world to ignite inflation because the debt is simply crushing.

All right, enough of that. Let's take a look at Avino Silver, ASM, selling for $1 a share. It's a producer and it's breaking even, which is a miracle. It's located in the Mexican Silver Belt, which has some of the richest mining plains on Earth.

The next one I want to look at is Claude Resources. This is in Canada. The symbol is CLGRF and it sells for 60¢ a share. Last twelve months it earned 11¢ a share and is selling at a P/E of 7. Like I said on all of them, I'm not sure if they are still in the black based on their most recent quarterly report, but it's a tremendous value. It's a producer in Canada.

A favorite of mine, another penny mining stock that's in production is Comstock Mining. The symbol is LODE and it's at 60¢ a share. Are you familiar with Virginia City? Well, Virginia City is in northwest Nevada. In the middle years of the nineteenth century it was the richest silver strike ever made. By the time that the Civil War was being fought the Comstock mines were making enormous profits. In fact, the saying is that the Comstock mines financed the Civil War for the Union. They were making fantastic profits. By the 1920s the mines had all shut down because they more or less exhausted readily available ore. On top of that, they were simply a multitude of mining claims and they were always fighting each other and nobody could unite the package together.

Then this guy came along, a successful entrepreneur from San Francisco, he came in there and he said, "Look, I'm going to consolidate all these mining plains and we're going to see if we can't get back into business." He consolidated all the mining plains in the Comstock and they now own 8,300 acres of mining plains. They essentially own the entire Comstock. It's in production and it's on a break-even basis and it's getting better and better every year. It's selling for about 60¢ a share. Like I say, they are all struggling because they simply cannot make it on the prices right now, but they are at break-even and they are doing slightly better every year. I like it very much. I think it's coming back and I like it. That's the Comstock.

Let me give you some blue-chips in the gold and silver area. Hands down the favorite blue-chip is Franco-Nevada. The symbol is FNV and it's selling at $52 a share. This year it earned 48¢ a share. It's paying a dividend of $1.50. It's a gold royalty company. I love it. The best thing to do is just go on their website and they'll explain their royalty system to you. I love it. It's simply a superb place. I like it so much that on this play you can go as high as 3% or 4% of your investment capital. All the pennies, like I said, are between one quarter of one percent and one percent. You do not have more than one percent in any penny stock.

The next one I like is another blue-chip stock falling on hard times, which is Goldcorp, symbol GG. It's at $15 a share and losing money, but of all the classic gold producers I like it the best.

Another gold royalty company that I love is Royal Gold, symbol RGLD, selling at $50 a share. Earnings per share are 79¢ and it pays a dividend, but I can't tell you offhand what it is. It's the same type of royalty gold company that Franco-Nevada is. I just love these royalty companies.

The last one is another royalty company that is concentrated on silver, which is Silver Wheaton, symbol SLW, selling at $14 a share. Earned last year 42¢ a share. Really a great company that is still profitable and it has tremendous assets based on its royalties control.

Two more secondary gold companies and then we'll quit on this. Kirkland Lake Gold, which is a Canadian producer. The symbol is KGILF, it's selling at $4.38 a share and earned 24¢ a share last year. Really has a rich ore body. It is doing very well.

The last one is Klondex Mines, which is KLDX. Its earnings per share was about 37¢ last year. It's selling for $2.40 a share. It's a Nevada producer, a really a great little play.

That takes care of the gold and silver plays.

All right, so when you're looking at these gold and silver penny shares or higher priced mining plays, you might have a hundred in front of you. How do you determine which one you want to buy? Are you looking at the P/E? Are you looking at their profitability? Maybe they are all at five year lows so how do you pick the cream of the crop? Also, what is your holding period or profit target?

I'm very big on the history. Like I said, everyone has heard the saying, "Buy low, sell high." It's a smart way of doing things, but you know what? You give people a chance to buy low and sell high and they will turn you down flat. Try selling something that's in the gutter to people. You know what they will tell you? "What do you mean I should buy this stock? It's down 75% in a year. You must be nuts. Don't you know it's going to zero? You know what I'm going to buy? I'm going to buy Can't Lose Industry that's up 300% for the year."

They don't buy low and sell high. What they want to do is buy high and sell higher. They are convinced that there is always a greater fool that is going to take them out at a profit. When you give people a change to buy low sell high they turn you down flat.

What do you do when you have a hundred candidates? What do you actually look for besides the history? Are you looking at the P/E? Is there a rule that you would say, "Okay, of these hundred stocks ..."?

Most of the penny mining stocks don't earn anything. It's rare to see them in production. One of the things I am keen on is that you must look at the resource base so you should read *The Northern Miner*. It'll point out those that they think are decent. They don't make recommendations, but if you read it you will find out that you will automatically be pointed to a certain place.

The big thing I look for are ex-producers. There are tons of ex-producers out there. What will happen is that the price of the commodity will collapse and they will go out of production. Often they will be placed on a care and maintenance basis maybe for two years, three years or four years. I'm very big on ex-producers because you have got the infrastructure there so one of the things I look for is an ex-producer who has the infrastructure. The best way to find out is simply to go on their website and if the infrastructure is there you will see a photograph on the site showing you the infrastructure. You can make a pretty good judgment just by looking at the infrastructure picture. I'm very big on ex-producers who have the infrastructure there and who are maintaining the property on a care and maintenance basis.

You really have to consider subscribing to *The Northern Miner*. It is really a tremendous resource that will point you in the right direction. It's a weekly newspaper and it has been printed in Canada since about 1915. It's got a terrific track record. They'll take you on site, they'll show you the production, show you the reserves, show you the net acreage, etcetera, etcetera, etcetera. From there you can form an opinion. That would be what I would look for.

Look for ex-producers, look for stocks selling at or near their five-year lows that you really like when you research them and subscribe to *The Northern Miner*. It's really a great resource.

Okay. The ex-producers are the ones that will have the highest leverage when things rebound.

Exactly.

Then when do you get out? What is your rule for getting out of these things because you like to hold them several years? What is the rule for saying, "Okay, now I want to get out?"

I like to see a 300% profit and I sell half at that point.

What do you do with the other half? Do you hold on for another target?

I play it based on how they are doing. Traders like to talk about a sell discipline. I think that's nonsense. I'm old-school. You find a company that you really like and you just stick with it. What is going to be your big reward is the stuff you stick with for three years, five years, seven years, ten years. This is where the rewards are - not from buying and selling but holding onto the stock.

If you ever look at the stocks that made Warren Buffett his fantastic fortune there is nothing special about any of those stocks. Many people have owned those stocks and managed to sell them at a loss. Warren Buffett didn't. He says, "What is this thing worth?" He analyzes the stock using fundamental analysis and he says, "Look, if I believe in it then it's game over." If the stock falls then far from selling it he will buy more. He will add to his position. Why shouldn't he? He knows what the stock is worth.

The market is being driven by imbeciles who are mindlessly buying whatever goes up and mindlessly selling whatever is going down. The days are gone where the vast majority analyzed stocks and did fundamental analysis where they looked at the earnings per share, asked what is the P/E ratio, what's the book value, what's the net profit margin and what's the operating profit margin? Nobody does it now. Well, not nobody because I do. Some real professionals do, but most of them say, "Why should I do this? I might analyze this stock to death and it might not go anywhere. I will simply mindlessly buy what's going up and mindlessly sell what's going down." That's just what they do.

We live in a world today that because of the extreme volatility the most you can expect on the upside without a reaction is 15% to 20%. The stock will go up 15% to 20%, the clowns will find out some bad news report and they will sell it off, and as soon as it drops 5% or 10% it hits the fact that everyone has this sell discipline, which is either "5% down and I'm out," "7.5% down and I'm out," or if they're really courageous then "10% down and I'm out." They hit that stop-loss order, they're out of it, a landslide occurs and they brutalize the stock for no good reason and it becomes a bargain.

You've got a topside of maybe 10% or 15% without a correction, maybe 20% if you are lucky. As soon as it falls 5%, 7.5% or 10% they'll sell out and so their profits on their winning trades are minuscule. Every time they turn around they are getting hit with a 5%, 10% or 15% stop-loss order, which takes them out at a loss. This is just not a winning formula and yet this is hands down the most popular strategy going. Hands down. Everyone today is a trend chaser. I think they are nuts.

You have a lot of positions. You have eighty to one hundred positions. I remember from your book that you like about one-third to be penny shares and about two-thirds to be stocks that produce income. What is your portfolio's percentage composition in terms of penny shares, regular shares and income plays? What are you doing?

All right, I'm glad you asked. I'm up to 68% income and the rest is everything else. My goal is to be 75% income plays within two years. I've been in these up and down cycles one time too many. This is just a horrific cycle. It's time for me to start being a little more conservative.

You've built up a big portfolio. Are you able to give any percentage returns showing how well you have done over the years, how your portfolio has grown? Do you have those numbers?

No, I don't. I don't do it that way. Like I said, I buy and hold and take whatever the market gives me. I don't do that type of analysis. I think it's defeating because when you do the type of things I do then it's perfectly possible for me to have a stock that goes down 10% or 15%. Then I look at it again. Do I still like it? Yeah, so I'll buy it again and add to the position. If it still continues to fall I'll look at it again and I'll say, "Do I still believe in the stock?" If yes then I'll buy it again. As you well know, this is contrary to everything Wall Street tells you.

The famous Wall Street rule is that you never add to a losing position. You only add to a winning position because then all your buys are profitable. When I first broke into stock market investing that made tremendous sense to me and I would chase the trends like everybody else. You know what I found out? When you add to a winning position you just keep adding to it until finally it will have a violent price decline. Your average cost of the stock kept going up and you then have your head given to you on a platter.

I'm a conviction investor. I'm the old-school type since I'm holding this stuff for five years as a normal position. A lot of my stuff I'll be holding for five years, six years, or seven years. There is no profit to be gained until you actually sell the sucker. I'm in this for life. This is not a case of where I'm going out west, making my pile and then going home. This is it, baby.

Investors usually want to know whether you are trying to build up the portfolio or are you trying to generate income so that you can retire comfortably off the income that is generated by your income plays?

I retired in 2005. I probably take more risk than I ought to, but I love taking risks. My only concern is diversification. There was a famous speculator who said that diversification is the only freebie on Wall Street, and he's right. It is. I see people and then you ask them what their positions are and they have three or four positions and they've got 20% or 30% in a position. I mean this is insanity. Nobody can hold onto a stock if you own 30% in a single stock and it goes down 15% to 20%. I would bail out like everybody else. You must never allow yourself to be placed in that position. Never.

Let's talk about the income plays. There are MLPs and REITs, oil and gas trusts and income trusts just as you introduced in your book. What's your best recommendation for these areas and how do you pick them? Very few great stocks are now paying 6% and 8% in dividends.

Let me tell you what the story is on income. Let's get into it. I'm going to give you a whole list of plays that I like on income. They have been killed over the last two years and it is insane.

It's not so much that the dividends have dropped. I've got stocks that were paying a 6% dividend two or three years ago now paying 7% or 8%. Stocks that were paying 8% are now paying 10% or 12%. Stocks that were paying 12% are now paying 14%. It's because of the insanity of the stock market.

Let's digress a bit to how investing occurs today. In my day, everyone was a stock picker. Everyone picked stocks. Nobody cared what the market did. You picked stocks and you picked them based on fundamental analysis. What is the P/E ratio? What is the dividend? What is the book value? What is the operating expense ratio? What is the net profit margin? You did fundamental analysis on the stock.

Then they came in with the idea of indexing and they elevated the S&P 500 to the status of God. They're saying, "Look, you've got a single universe of five hundred stocks and that is what everyone should be in."

If you search the market you find out that there are about sixteen thousand stocks. If you count the penny shares and the pink sheet stuff then you have got about sixteen thousand shares, and everyone is concentrated on the same five hundred stocks in the S&P 500. Even that is an exaggeration. The so-called stock market experts, the gurus that you see on Bloomberg and CNBC, they will tell you that they are experts. These clowns have been on the street twenty years, thirty years or maybe more and have never owned a stock that was not a member of the Nifty Fifty.

I'm sure you know what the Nifty Fifty is. The Nifty Fifty are the most popular fifty stocks of the S&P 500. They are parading around as if they are experts and the only thing they have ever owned are Nifty Fifty stocks, which everyone and his brother owns. I love it.

Here is a typical question that an investor asks. They would say, "Oh great guru, what should I invest in?" "You're in luck, Screw. I just discovered three stocks. Let me tell you what they are. I just discovered IBM, Ford and Coca Cola."

How can you discover three stocks that have been in existence over a hundred years? All three of those stocks have been in existence over a century. They are family names that everybody in this universe knows and you just discovered them? What type of research is that?

If you see the plays that I invest in you will know that there has been some research here. I'm actually doing research. I mean you know what they say? "Oh, thank you great guru. Let me write down these three names before I forget them." But how could you forget IBM, Coca Cola, and Ford? How? That's my story on that.

You've got this market today in which the S&P 500 has been sanctified and everybody ignores that there is a market out there other than the S&P 500. Like I said, I turned my back on that forty years ago and I'm never going back to it. There are multiple problems to that.

Let's talk about the clone-ization of the stock market. The S&P 500 and the Nifty Fifty are dominated by institutional investors. You've seen yourself that it's all indexing. If you take a look at the enormous amount of money for the indexing funds - and then there are the closet index mutual funds and ETFs that pretend not to be indexes but are - when you look at them they dominate the market and their managers have stopped doing fundamental analysis. They have simply stopped doing fundamental analysis. The S&P 500 is what they invest in, case closed, and they feel that they have to invest in every stock.

What you have is this. In the market cycle everything goes up together in the S&P 500 - the good, the bad, and the ugly. They make no distinctions. You have got this ridiculous world, which is that stocks bleeding red ink and stocks that are fantastically profitable will all go up together when the stock market goes up and they all go down together when the stock market goes down. This is insane. This is insane and yet the market today is dominated by nothing more than this.

In my opinion there is no point in selecting a stock in the S&P 500 because of the clone-ization. If you want to invest in the blue-chips then what I recommend is the Vanguard Total Stock Market Index Fund or the Vanguard S&P 500 even though it's not much of the Vanguard Total Stock Market Index Fund. Just buy the whole market and forget it if you want to do blue-chips. Why mess around with this stuff? It's so clone-ized that they are all going to go up and down together because of the way the indexing works.

In fact, this is what I recommend newbies do. If someone new is coming into the stock market and they say, "What do you recommend, Fred?" then I tell them, "Look, buy the Vanguard Total Stock Market Index Fund, don't ever sell it and reinvest the dividends. Then, as you become more expert in the market, here is what you do - every time you find a target of opportunity you then decide whether you are going to sell 1%, 2%, 3%, 4% or 5% and put it in this market of opportunity. Over a period of years you can diversify out of the S&P 500 as you become more proficient and gradually build up some independent picks. Never put more than 5% in any single position, and of course the riskier the stock the smaller the percentage of your capital that goes into it."

Let's get into the income plays. People would definitely be interested in how they can build up income in their portfolio as you have done to become financially wealthy. What's your theory on income plays, your guiding principles and how you pick them?

Okay. Let's start with the rule of 72. Are you familiar with the rule of 72? That's the key. You simply divide the dividend yield you are receiving into 72 and that tells you how many years it will take to double. In fact, Einstein said that the eighth wonder of the universe is compound interest. He was thinking of a savings account that in those days paid 2.75%, but I will not touch a stock, an income play, that pays less than 6%.

At 6% you double your money in twelve years. That is the minimum acceptable dividend play that I will accept. People just don't know what they are doing there. Remember the rule of 72, right? If you invest your money at 1% compounded then it takes seventy-two years to double. At 2% it takes thirty-six years to double. At 7% it takes ten years to double. What are these people thinking of? At 8% it takes nine years to double. At 10% you double your money in seven years. At 12%, you double your money in six years. These are the types of interest rates you need, 6% plus.

Here is what has happened. There is another virtue that people don't realize. When you are holding these high income plays - 6% plus for five years or longer - you don't only get the compounding effect. You get an effect that nobody seems to understand today and why I don't know. That effect is dollar cost averaging.

Incidentally, you must always reinvest the dividends from a dividend play. You always reinvest the dividends - no excuses. Reinvesting the dividends is mandatory. Let me digress a little on this and complain.

Over the years, I've known dozens of people who invested in high-income stocks, high dividend plays. You know what they'll say? They'll say, "I'll never invest in another high income play again because I lost money on it." Here is what they'll say and I can't tell you how many times I've heard stories like this. "Oh yeah, I invested in a high dividend stock once. Paid $10 for the stock, it paid an 8% dividend, I held it for five years and I sold the stock for $8 a share and I lost money on it."

Well, if you owned the stock for five years and it paid an 8% dividend then you did not lose money on it. You made money on it. These people will go to their graves swearing that they lost money on it. This is the most common thing that will happen. They will insist that they lost money on it because they don't reinvest the dividends. The only way you know if you made money on an income paying stock is to keep track of the total return of the capital gains plus the dividends. You must also reinvest the dividends because that's the only way to do it. These people would all discover that they probably had made money if they had held it for five years and they just reinvested the dividends, but no they can't do that. It's stupid. You just talk to them and they'll tell you, "Oh, I lost money on it." Like I said, you will never convince them otherwise. Never.

Let me tell you what the story is on dividend paying stock. Wall Street does not believe in high dividend paying stocks. The highest dividend paying stocks that a Wall Streeter will accept pay 4%. There is a reason for this. If you invest in the S&P 500, which is where all the blue-chips are and which are the only thing that these people know even exist, a blue-chip stock will never get to pay much more than a 4% dividend. The dividend yield cannot rise much because investors are so desperate for high dividend paying stocks that they will not allow it to happen. They will simply plow into that stock and see to it that it's not paying more than 4%.

In the S&P 500, if the dividend becomes 5% or 6% then the Wall Streeters will draw back from it because they are suspicious of it. The only reason why a blue-chip stock pays 5% or 6% is because the dividend cannot be relied on. Because they think that the dividend cannot be relied on they won't buy it. You know what? They are right. If you are dealing with the S&P 500s then I would be suspicious of any dividend paying stock that pays much more than 4%. On the S&P 500 that's the way it works.

When you get in my universe - the universe of the small-cap, mid-cap and micro-cap - the rules are different. The institutional investors aren't there. What's there are retail investors, people like me, and that's the way I like it. I don't want to compete with institutional investors. In my world I don't compete with them. What happens is in this world you can get 5%, 6%, or 7% in sound stocks if you concentrate in REITs. I'm going to talk about REITs, mortgage REITs, and BDCs (business development corporations), which are my key criteria today for income paying stocks.

I've given up on master limited partnerships (MLPs) because I can't handle the tax problems. It just isn't worth it to me. They give you that 203K form and you can find out the profit that you thought you earned isn't there because of the way they handle the taxes. The taxes on the 203Ks on the master limited partnerships are just impossible. I simply quit on them because of that. It isn't worth it to me. It might be worth it to other people, but I just can't take the tax problems.

On my high-income investments I concentrate on three sectors. I concentrate on REITs, mortgage REITs - which are very risky - and also business development corporations or BDCs. Also there are a few royalty companies that I really like, but basically that's where I hang out for my income plays. These three categories, the REITs, mortgage REITs, and BDCs are all restricted by the rules that they pay no taxes if they pay out ninety percent of their income in dividends. All of them must pay ninety percent of their income in dividends to qualify.

What this means is that it is not unusual for these stocks to cut their dividends. Wall Street freaks out when this happens because in their world of the S&P 500 the typical dividend is about fifty percent of whatever the earnings are. Therefore they have this huge cushion. If you are paying out only fifty percent of your earnings in dividends then you have this huge cushion to fall on and if you cut the dividend that means that you are in deep, dark trouble. That's what Wall Street thinks. If you have to pay out ninety percent of your earnings in dividends then dividend cuts become always kind of probable because you have only got that ten percent margin there. A dividend cut in REITs, mortgage REITs, and BDCs (the business development corporations) does not have the implications that it has if you cut a dividend on the S&P 500 stocks.

Let's talk about one more thing that has happened that drives me crazy and which goes back to the clone-ization of the stock market. People don't do fundamental analysis now. What they do is they simply say, "We look at volume and we look at price and that's it, and we mindlessly buy the ten S&P 500 sectors." They might do sector analysis in which they put everyone in the same sector, and then they decide based on macroeconomics whether the sector is a buy or a sell. They will blindly sell everything in that sector or blindly buy everything in that sector based not on fundamental analysis but simply on the macroeconomic analysis. It is just crazy, man. Just crazy.

In fact, one of my pet peeves is the overwhelming dominance today of macroeconomic analysis over fundamental analysis where you are actually looking at the stock that you are buying and seeing if it's a good investment. What they want to do is they want to put everything in categories. They've got the ten S&P sectors and then they blindly buy and sell those whole sectors. It is insane. They are not doing fundamental analysis anymore. There is no fundamental analysis.

Here is what has happened in the last two or three years. Basically the stock market has reached the conclusion that all dividend paying stocks, especially that pay high dividends, are enormously at risk because the government is going to start raising the discount rate or fed bonds rate, etcetera, etcetera, etcetera, which then means that interest rates are going up. According to them, if interest rates are going up then all dividend-paying stocks are going to get crushed. Your average S&P 500 stock today pays a dividend I think of 2.3%, or 2.5%. That's what they pay. If you are assuming that interest rates are going to go up a quarter percent or half a percent or maybe even worse then it follows that the dividend paying stocks could indeed get killed so they mindlessly sell them off.

If you have got a stock that is paying 6%, 7%, 8%, 9%, 10% or 11% - and I'll show you stocks that pay this – then a dividend rate increase of a quarter or half a percent is not the end of the world, is it? But they don't know this. They simply put them in their categories and they blindly sell the entire category mindlessly. If you are in the sector you are hit.

What they have done is they say all REITs are a sell. Why? Because we think that the government is going to raise the interest rate a quarter of a percent or a half percent. All business development corporations, which are also high-yielding, all of them are at risk because the government may raise the rates a quarter or a half percent. All mortgage REITs - same thing. What has happened in the last two years is just the most incredible thing. I've got companies, sound REITs, that were paying 6% now paying 7% or 8%. They were paying 9% and are now paying 10% or 11%. The whole high-income category across the board has been going up.

Let me give you one that cracks me up here, which I'm going to talk about - Pennant Park. This is a stock that has been paying the same dividend for the last three years. Its quarterly dividend has been 28¢ a quarter and for the last three years it hasn't cut its dividend at all. During that time the stock has fallen from $12.24 a share to $6.31 a share. The dividend has not been cut and because of this price collapse the dividend yield is now 16%. It's at 16% and it's selling at below book value. It's selling at below book value!

This is what is more or less happening across the entire industry. They have mindlessly sold everything and as a result when you look at the stock patterns, when you look at a three-year chart of any of the REITs and the mortgage REITs and the business development corporations then it's insane. They are paying enormous dividends. While they may have cut their dividend once in the last three years for the ones I invest in the dividend cuts are minor and I'll show you how I play that game. But this is monumental, insane selling across the board - the good, the bad, and the ugly. The market no longer makes distinctions like I keep harping on. People simply mindlessly buy the entire category or mindlessly sell the entire category.

How do you pick what to buy in the BDCs and royalty companies and the ...?

All right, let me tell you what I invest in now. Let me give you a few of my picks on the income plays. Basically I insist on a 6% yield and I won't put more than 5% in any position. You just research them. Let me give you a few REITs that I really like.

The first would be Agree Realty. The symbol is ADC, sells for 32¢ a share and the price has been going up so that the dividend has dropped down to about a 5.8% yield. It's at about 5.8-5.9%. Even though it's slightly under my 6% rule I still like the stock and will hold onto it.

The next one is CBL and Associates. This is a huge owner of shopping centers all over the country and secondary markets. Sells for $15 a share and it pays a dividend of 7.1%. Fantastic. The dividend is as sound as the Rock of Gibraltar. In fact, I expect them to raise the dividend.

In the REIT world, P/E ratios are not appropriate. You have to look at the funds from operations, FFO funds from operations, because the income is always much greater than you would assume when you are looking at earnings per share. In fact, that is one of the reasons why REITs have been avoided the way they are, which is because Joe Blow investor takes a look at a REIT that pays a 6% or 7% dividend and the first thing that his eagle eye spots is the fact that the dividend is higher than the earnings per share. The genius says, "Well if the dividends are higher than the earnings per share then this thing is a scam because they are going to have to cut their dividends."

In REITs, because of their accounting rules all the depreciation and amortization is deducted from the income. Depreciation is simply an enormous factor when you are a commercial real estate owner and you own tens of millions of dollars of commercial real estate or hundreds of millions of dollars in some cases. The depreciation is enormous. What they do is, for earnings per share, is take the gross potential income and then also subtract the depreciation and the amortization which is a bookkeeping item that doesn't hurt the income.

The income on all these REITs is much higher than people would think when they look at the earnings per share. It's the funds from operations that is the key criteria - your earnings plus the depreciation added back in - because that is what you actually have in the till. That's cash in the till. That is one of the big errors that people make and that's why the high dividend payers have never enjoyed the fame that they deserve. Everyone looks at the dividends and they say, "Wait a minute, the earnings don't cover the dividends." Yes, it does if you use funds from operations, which is the real cash on hand that includes adding back in the depreciation and the amortization. That's the way that works.

I gave you Agree Realty and CBL and Associates, which pays 7.1%. There is another one called Core Energy. The symbol is CORR and it's selling at about $5 a share. It pays a 10% dividend. I think it's very sound and I like it. That's a 10% dividend payer.

Then there's Omega Healthcare, which is a healthcare industry company. The symbol is OHI. The stock is at $36 a share and pays 6%. Very sound, keeps raising the dividend.

There is another one I like, new kid on the block, Physicians' Realty Trust. The symbol is DOC. Sells for about $16 a share and it's got a dividend of about 5.7-5.8%. It's dropped slightly because the share price keeps going up and I like that even though it's slightly under a 6% yield. It's paying about 5.7-5.8%, which is slightly under my guidelines.

Then another one I like also in the medical professional field is Medical Properties Trust. It's MPW, sells at $11 a share and pays a hefty 7.6% dividend.

Those are the ones I like. You just do traditional analysis, but you've got to realize that you have got to look at funds from operations and that's the P/E ratio on these babies. Funds from operations, you just do traditional analysis, look at these suckers, do the fundamental analysis and that's how you get to them.

That more or less takes my favorite REITs away. Now we are going to get into the real risky stuff. Oh, with all these REITs you can go up to a 5% portfolio weighting. They are very sound. You can set 5% positions in all of them, up to 5%. Very sound.

Now I'm going to go get into the high-risk area. The high-risk area is mortgage REITs. You don't own equity. You simply own the mortgage and your profits are the leveraged spread between your cost of capital and the rate at which you lend out. Essentially they are really shadow banks. They perform the banking function without bank branches. They borrow cheap and they lend high. They are far more risky than the equity REITs and for these babies risk 2% of your capital tops. The top weighting is 2%.

Let me give you the first one that I like, which is New York Mortgage. The symbol is NYMT at

$6 a share and it pays a whopping 16% dividend. The P/E ratio, based on the latest, is 4.7. It pays 16% like I said.

Here is something we need to understand when we start getting into this area of dividend cuts. My rule is that when you are looking at a dividend payer that is paying 10% plus you assume that a dividend cut is at least a fifty-fifty percent probability. Okay? A fifty-fifty percent probability. You analyze it from that perspective.

You are supposed to do the research before you buy the stock and not afterwards. When you are researching the stock you look at it and say, "Look, do I think that the maximum potential risk for the stock is a dividend cut of 10% or 15%?" If the answer is yes and I like the stock then I will buy it even if I think that there is a high probability that the dividend will be cut.

Let me give you an example here, okay? New York Markets Trust at 16% has a 4.5 year payback before you consider the dollar cost averaging. Let me repeat. When you get these compounding babies it isn't just the yield or compounding that produces your net return. All the dividends that you accumulate during the holding period will also give you dollar cost averaging possibilities. If the dividends are reinvested in the play then by mathematical law you'll buy less shares when the price is high and more shares when the price is low if the dividends are reinvested. This is an automatic process. The dividends acquired during that four or five-year holding period – assuming you're buying them because the yield is the same or better - will be acquired at a price below the average trading price for that time period.

This is an enormous tip. You have now got two forces working for you. You've got the compounding and you've got the dollar cost averaging possibility. This only works if you are holding this stuff for four or five years. Give this stuff a chance to work for you.

Let me give you an example of what happened using New York Mortgage Trust. This stock now sells at about $6 a share. It was selling at $7.50 a share, okay? It paid 27¢ a quarter for a $1.08 annual income. That produces a 14.4% yield, okay? All right. The world came to an end. They dropped the dividend from 27¢ a quarter to 24¢ a quarter, which means the dividend dropped from $1.08 to 96¢ a share, okay?

Let me give you a trick of the trade that I use and which I'm very big on. People go nuts every time a dividend is cut. They go into absolute hysterics. As you know, after the trading day ends they will make the reports and you will get the analysis of whether or not the dividend is going to be cut. This happens after the trading ends. Not everybody but most of the market then knows that the dividend has been cut and the standard operating procedure when the dividend is cut is hysterics like, "Sell this dog before it goes to zero." Well, I've got a question for you. Why did you buy this dog if you thought it was going to zero? You're supposed to research this stock before you buy it.

Like I said, when I'm looking at the high-income stocks, when you are buying something that pays 10% or more then you always make the assumption that it could be cut 10-15%. If in your opinion it's going to be cut more than 10-15% then you probably shouldn't buy it. If it's only going to be cut 10-15% then you analyze the whole thing and say, "Is this worth it to me?" So let's take a look at what happens.

Here is the trick of the trade. It was selling at $7.50, right? Then they announced the dividend cut from 27¢ a quarter to 24¢ a quarter. Everybody thinks they are a genius. They think, "Oh, I'm going to beat the crowd" so everyone puts in a sell order. You've got this huge mass of sell orders, okay? A huge mass of sell orders, and they all hit the market between 9:30 and 10:00. All of them. During that first half-hour of trading, or the first hour of trading, that stock New York Mortgage drops from $7.50 to a low of $5.31.

You want to know what I would do? Let me tell you what I did. Instead of hysterically selling my position at $5.31 I added to my position at $5.31. What you do is you put a stop order in for the next morning's trade at a price that will guarantee that if you buy the stock your dividend yield will exceed the dividend yield that you were paid prior to the discount. For instance, at $7.50 you had a 14.4% yield. Here is what happened. They announced that they were cutting the dividend from 27¢ to 24¢. That first half-hour the stock fell to $5.31 a share. I acquired a bundle at $5.31.

Let's take a look at what happened to the stock I acquired. You multiply the quarterly dividend of 24¢ times four quarters and you get 96¢. You divide that by the dividend price of $5.31. I acquired that stock at an 18% dividend. An 18% dividend! Like I said, I did the research. I think it's a sound stock. I did my analysis.

When you are doing this stuff, man, give allowance for this stuff. You can make a fortune just doing this strategy. Wait for the dividend cut, have your order in there for 9:30 that morning when the jerks unload this huge mass of stock because they think they are getting out ahead of the crowd. They are not getting out ahead of the crowd. That first half-hour to hour of trading will be the low for the day and probably the low for the next two weeks.

In fact, if you want to sell the stock then don't even sell it the morning after they announce that they are going to have a dividend cut. That first half-hour the morons will crash that stock and drive that stock down. If you decide that you want to sell a stock because of a dividend cut or because it had a bad earnings report then wait two weeks. You will never regret it. For that two-week period after that crash decline that stock will continue to go up. It's cooler heads that prevail. You can see that this is just a fantastic strategy to employ when you get these high-yielders.

Another strategy that you can employ when you get the high-yielders is this. Suppose you have a thousand share position in New York Mortgage, right? They report that they are dropping the dividend from 27¢ to 24¢. You know what a brilliant strategy might be? Let me give you a few.

At 9:30 in the morning you have your buy order in. For what? Here is one strategy. You can find a deep-in-the-money call and simply make sure that you have got your buy price in way under - maybe 10%, 15% or 20% - the last option price. That call will probably crash along with the stock. You'll pick it up and because it's a deep-in-the-money call when the stock recovers during the next two weeks you are going to see a substantial increase over a two or three week period. You can then sell it off at a quick profit if you want to. That's another strategy you can use.

Another strategy on these high dividend payers is this. Say I have a thousand shares of stock, right? This is a pretty gutsy play here, but consider it. You can put in an order to buy another thousand shares even though you don't want them. At that first half hour put the order in at a price that will yield you around 18% or 20%, whatever you decide. You've got that yield, right? At 18%.

Why? Look, it's going to go up. You can bet that during the next two weeks that stock price will continue to go up because it's going to be crashed into that bottom. The first hour of the first morning is going to be the low. After that, it will trend back up. Bargain hunters will look at this thing and say, "Look, the stock price is insane. The dividend has been cut. It's just simply a screaming bargain."

Those are some dividend strategies that you can employ. Let me even give a few more obvious strategies.

The first thing is that you can build a fortress concept. All right, you have got the stock New York Mortgage. You write a call on the stock. You are getting the damn dividend at 16%, so then you write a call. Let me explain this. You always, always, always use the farthest out call that exists. This is another contrarian strategy. I'm a contrarian by heart. Everyone will tell you, "You always sell the ninety-day call. That's the shortest call and that's where the time decay is best and the smart money play is to sell these ninety-day calls and keep rolling them over." Bunk. It's mathematically correct and intellectually stupid.

I always sell the longest-term option. You'll never regret it once you get into it. You sell the longest-term call because that gives you the greatest amount of bucks up front. You would sell a call that is either at-the-money or slightly under the money. For instance, if the stock is at $6 you would sell the $6 call or even a $5 or $4 call if that is what is available. Don't worry about it. Get the longest maturity out there.

You get that money up front. Not only are you getting the whopping dividends from the stock, but then you are getting the call income from writing the call, which is going to be considerable. You are going to get that dividend up front, plus if the stock declines you can roll over the call and take cash out because you are going to be getting cash out of the call.

Then there are puts. The dividend is so high so why don't you buy puts to protect the downside? On New York Mortgage I would probably put the put in at $5 or $4. You don't need complete protection but probably only 50% or 25% of whatever the stock holding is. You don't need complete protection because not only do you have the dividend but you've also got the call that's going to be paid plus you've bought the put.

The put is highly leveraged. Say you buy two hundred dollars of puts. If you've got a two hundred dollar investment in the puts and the puts go into the money then you are going to have maybe six, seven, eight hundred dollars in those puts. When you put the whole package together it's a money machine. People just look at that dividend and they say, "No, it's going to be cut." When it is cut they freak out and sell. They're nuts.

Let me give you some more examples. All right, let's take a look at an 18% dividend payer, okay? You double your money in four years. Okay, let's say that the world comes to an end. They drop the dividend to 16%, okay? Guess what your payback period is? Your payback period is now 4.5 years. They dropped the dividend from 18% to 16% and your 4-year payback becomes 4.5 years. Is that the end of the world?

Let's take a look at 12%. All right, having a 12% dividend translates into a 6-year payback. They drop the dividend to 10%. You know what your payback is? It's 7.2 years. Is that the end of the world? I don't think so. Plus there are writing the call strategies, right? Then you get additional protection by being long with the puts. It's a gold mine. People ignore all of it. They say, "No, the dividend is too high. They are going to cut the dividend. It's a sucker play. I won't touch it." Then when they do cut the dividend it's automatic freak out. They sell. Naturally they sell at 9:30 and they get crucified.

All right, let's take a look at another one of my champions. I told you about New York Mortgage. This is another champion mortgage equity play, which is Western Asset Mortgage. The symbol is WMC. It sells at $12 a share and pays a 20% dividend, a 20% dividend if you can handle that. It is true that they cut the dividend twice in the last year. They were small cuts so it doesn't bother me. I'm protected because I've got the calls written out of it and I got a put on it. I got this fortress position and I'm taking the 20%.

Now like I told you the puts are highly leveraged. If you have a thousand shares you would only need to have puts to cover five hundred shares or maybe four hundred shares. Since they would be out-of-the-money, maybe one strike price or two strike prices below the current value of the stock, then you've got a lot of protection if there's a big crash, which is what you need protection on. You don't need protection for the small stuff because that enormous dividend will just grind away working for you. Let it work for you. Take a look at that play.

Anyway, Western Asset Mortgage cut the dividend twice but pays a 20% dividend. The P/E ratio on Western Asset Mortgage is 9. It's a great, great company. I like it. Risk no more than 2% of your portfolio and you should protect yourself. Protect yourself by using calls and some of the strategies that I've outlined, you know? Think about it.

Getting away from mortgage REITs, what's your philosophy on BDCs and royalty companies?

Okay. Let's talk about business development companies or BDCs. Basically they are shadow banks. They are banks really without a bank branch. What they do is they borrow at low rates and lend at higher rates just like the mortgage companies do, but they don't lend out for single-family homes. They essentially lend to businesses. They lend to private businesses that don't have stock issues or that can't qualify for bonds. Generally, they lend to private companies and businesses that are not corporations, that do not have listed stocks, or when they do have listed stocks the companies don't have the credentials for a bond but they can be very sound holdings.

Let's take a look at one I really like. You've got to look at funds from operations rather than earnings on these suckers. Prospect Capital, symbol PSEC. It's a $7.40 a share stock. Pays a 13.48% dividend. It cut its dividend slightly in the last year. This is the most hated stock I've ever seen. They cut the dividend, but I think the dividend is safe now.

Like I said, when you buy these mortgage REITs and the BDCs (business development corporations) and they are paying more than 10% then you automatically conclude that there is a possibility of a dividend cut. If you like the damn stock then even if it cuts the dividend by 10% or 15% you buy it, okay? You should have your strategy lined up on what you are going to do if there is a dividend cut.

One strategy is that you might buy a 25% position of what you want or a 50% position and say, "Look, I'm going to hold this one and I'm going to treat these ultra high dividends like gravy. I'm going to wait until I get word that they cut the dividend and then I will have that buy order in for 9:30 the next morning at a price that will guarantee that the dividend yield I get is higher than the old yield," like in the situation I told you about with New York Mortgage.

During that first half an hour then almost universally if they cut the dividend at that first half-hour of trading (9:30 to 10:00) they will drive that stock down to a price where the new dividend yield will be higher than it was based on the old dividend before the cut. You could build a strategy around that taking 25% or 50% positions and hoping that they would do that.

Once you got the stock you can get that additional position by writing those long-term options, by writing that call. When you write that long-term call you get that money out of there immediately. It's in your hands and if the stock drops you can roll over the call and take more money out. I'm very big on long-term calls because you can just keep rolling them over. You can buy additional protection if you want to simply by being long a put.

Now if the stock price goes up then the call price goes up, but you don't mind that you lose money on the call? You just deliver the stock?

Right. Here's what you do. You simply let them call it away. You let them call it away. You've got the dividends plus you've got the call premium, which is going to be considerable on a long-term call and if you are slightly under the strike price. You know what you do? You say, "I like it" and you just initiate the position again. So what?

How do you pick which BDCs to invest in? Do you like those better than the mortgage REITs? There are only few of them so most people know nothing about the BDCs.

Right, that's why I like them. I hope I made it clear to you that I'm a contrarian and I don't stampede with the herd. If you stampede with the herd your returns are lousy. Think about what happens when you stampede with the herd. You know what happens? Tom, Dick, and Harry are always ahead of you if you stampede with the herd. That's not what I do. I'm ahead of Tom, Dick, and Harry, never behind.

Let me give you another BDC that I really like. In fact, this is the high quality one. Prospect Capital was the first one selling for about $7.40, pays a 13.48% dividend, and has a P/E of 7. It is the most hated stock I've ever seen. Everybody hates this stock, and I can't figure out why. It had one small dividend cut in the last three years and they went berserk. In my opinion, this is a quality stock in the business development corporation field even though other people will argue otherwise.

Another I like is Ares Capital. The symbol is ARCC. Sells at about $15 a share, pays a 9.7% dividend and has a P/E ratio of 8. It's selling below book value. Both Prospect and Ares Capital are both selling below book value.

In fact, this is one of the shockers. Almost every business development corporation is selling below book value - all of them. Almost all of them are selling below book value. You see them selling at 70% of book value, 65% of book value, 60% of book value and tangible book value. It doesn't matter because book value is different in financial companies because they don't own depreciating assets.

It's all cash. They take depreciation from their earnings, but it doesn't depreciate. Book value really means something. They are screaming bargains. These people don't know how to analyze this stuff. I think Ares Capital is the jewel of the business development corporations. Like I said it has 9.7% dividends and a P/E of 8.

I'm going to give you a highlight, a risky one that's kind of risky. If you buy this one then definitely do not buy more than a 2% position. It's Pennant Park and the symbol is PFLT. All right, Pennant Park selling for about $6.80 a share sells at 70% of book value and has a 16% dividend. They made the incredible error of cutting their dividend slightly twice. The market just killed them.

Employ the strategies that I'm recommending on these plays. If you use the right strategies these plays are doable even if you can't depend on the dividend. They're doable.

So Pennant Park has a 16% dividend and is selling at 70% of book value, which is $6.80 a share. Let me tell you about them by announcing the incredibly stupid insanity that has crushed all high dividend paying stocks due to the stock market's obsession that the Fed is going to be raising interest rates. Take a look at what happened to Pennant Park.

Pennant Park three years ago sold at $12.24. Now it sells for $6.80, okay? At the crash bottom it sold for $6.31 a share. The quarterly dividend is 28¢ a share and it has not been cut in the last three years. No cuts in the last three years and during that time period the stock has fallen from $12.24 to $6.31 and the dividend has relentlessly increased to a 16% dividend. Go tell me the logic on that, tell me the logic on that. No dividend cuts in three years and the stock price has fallen from $12.24 to $6.31 and now pays a 16% dividend. It's insane.

Okay. Oh, I just remembered something I forgot to mention earlier. I'd like to go back to natural resources and talk about lithium.

That would be fine …

Lithium is about the only metal that hasn't been killed in the last four years. It's because lithium has a bright future. Lithium is a very unique product. It is the lightest metal known to man. If you threw a pound of lithium in the water it would float. If you put a match to it then it would burst into flame.

Most people predict this wonderful future for the pure electric cars, lithium-powered, and they simply assume that the lithium is going to be there to support these millions of cars that they want to produce. Somehow, according to their logic, the price of lithium is not going to go up. I beg to differ. The fact of the matter is that lithium does not grow on trees. If you take a look you have got about sixty to seventy nations that produce some oil and gas. You can count the nations that are producing lithium on the fingers of one hand.

There are three areas that produce lithium on this planet currently and the news is not good. The first is the Lithium Triangle in South America, which is where Chile, Bolivia, and Argentina intersect. That area is called the Lithium Triangle. This is probably the most efficient deposit on Earth. It's not mined. It's like they pump it out of the ground in the form of a brine like an oil well. Instead of pumping oil they are pumping out this liquid brine. Up to now it's the most efficient method of extracting lithium, which is out of this brine.

Unfortunately, there are only two known brine resources districts of any consequence. One is this Lithium Triangle in South America and I guarantee you they're not going to give the lithium away. As a matter of fact, a huge percentage of that resource is in Bolivia and their president is Evo Morales. He's a violent socialist and his attitude is, "If they are going to extract lithium from our properties then they are going to pay through the nose."

The other one is in Tibet. It's the same type of deposit. It's up in the high desert. In fact, both the South American Triangle and the Tibetan angle are in the high mountain deserts. Both of them extract as brine.

The only real third producer is Australia and they're producing this from a hard rock mine. In other words, it's not a brine. It's not regarded as being as efficient, but I'm telling you that if you think you are going to depend on these brine deposits for any substantial electric car production then you are living in a dream world. That's the attitude I'm at.

I've got two North American plays. Neither one of them is in the production because quite frankly up to now they can't compete with the Lithium Triangle in South American and the Tibetan Triangle. I'm telling you I think those brine deposits are very limited. They are going to find enormous difficulties in increasing production to any marked extent. They are going to have to go to the hard rock miners which are not as efficient and are going to cost you more. They are not going to really be able to ramp up production.

There are two I like in North America. The first one is Nemaska Lithium and the symbol is NMKEF. It sells for 21¢ a share, it's a Canadian play and it's a hard rock miner. It's not in production. Like I said, if you believe in lithium they are going to have to go to these hard rock plays.

The other one I like is Western Lithium, which is located in Nevada. It's about a hundred or two hundred miles from the Elon Musk Gigafactory. I frankly don't know why Elon Musk just didn't buy Western Lithium. He could have bought it up for a song. He still can. In fact it's a possible buyout by Elon Musk because it's only about a hundred or two hundred miles from his plant. Western Lithium, WLCDF, is selling at 23¢ a share.

On these babies buy five, ten, fifteen thousand shares, or twenty thousand shares. Put it away and forget about it. Tell yourself you are going to hold this stock for five years. You could have a five or ten bagger. These could be ten bagger plays if they hit. If they don't then what do you have into it? You've got chump change invested in it. Those are two lithium plays.

Let's get into oil and gas and trusts and whatever other trusts or just royalty companies.

All right. Currently, you know my rule about 6% dividend plays, right? Okay. What happened is that the oil royalty companies got murdered as you can probably imagine. They got murdered like everything else. I bailed out on most of them because I insist on the dividend return.

My two favorites that look like they are coming back, and the two that I would own right now you would hold them for a turnaround. They are paying a pretty hefty dividend. Oil is in the mid-forties, I mean $40 a gallon. You've got to have $65 oil and at $65 a gallon these royalty companies will go to the moon. Their income will just skyrocket. The first that I like is Sabine Royalties, an old favorite of mine. The symbol is SBR. It's selling for somewhere around 35¢ a share. It's paying in the 4% to 6% range. Like I said, if oil just goes back to $65 then it will explode.

The other I like is Cross Timbers Royalty, whose symbol is CRT. I guess it's selling somewhere around $15 a share. It is also selling for around that 6% to 7% area. The dividend deviates enormously from month-to-month because of the price decline. Those are the only two I currently own.

Permian Basin Trust was an old favorite of mine, but I bailed out on it. I just won't accept the dividend. Permian Basin Trust, symbol PBT, you could definitely look at it. When the dividend gets back to 6% you can jump on it. You can jump on it when the dividend hits 6%. That takes care of the only oil royalty companies I would consider right now.

Let's just summarize this because I want to understand this whole thing. It sounds like your overall strategy is that you want around 70-75% of your portfolio in income plays and the other 25% you want in regular stocks or more speculative plays.

Yes, for my age. If you are twenty years younger you would want maybe 50% in income plays. The older you get the more you want in income.

You just don't want to put more than 1% of your portfolio in a penny stock. If it's a safer stock you want no more than a 5% portfolio weighting. For the income plays you want the stock to be paying 6% in yield and then of course you are selling calls and buying puts using special strategies to try to increase that.

Yes. The standard REITs, all the ones that I gave you, they are all 5% plays but as to the mortgage REITs they are no more than a 2-3% investment. They are riskier. The same thing with the business development corporations. They are riskier. I would only give them maybe 2-3% positions in any portfolio.

If someone structures their portfolio this way do you think they are going to be more successful than somebody who is just buying and selling shares?

Absolutely.

Okay. You have put your investment philosophy in your book *Forty Years a Speculator* and developed it some more since then. Along those lines you have definitely achieved financial independence in a way others want to duplicate so why do you think you have you succeeded at this skill of investing whereas other people have not? What are you doing right and what are other people doing wrong in terms of investing? What is your recommendation to people?

All right. Basically, I owe my success to the fact that I'm an old-timer. I do it the old-time way, which is that you analyze the stock using fundamental analysis and you don't freak out and sell every time you get a 5% or 10% decline. You know, today the average holding position is six months. In fact, it's six months or a 5% decline, whichever happens first. This is no way to invest.

You have to be a conviction investor. I'm a conviction investor. I believe in all this stuff. I don't buy stuff that I haven't researched and believed in. That is what you've got to do. If you are just a conviction investor, hold on to your stocks, hold on to your positions, know why you bought them and don't freak out when you get a decline.

The quarterly earnings reports are a disaster. The reason why is because the only thing they do is they mislead people. Ninety days is not enough time in an operating business to make coherent decisions as to the profitability of the business. Ninety days is not enough. People say, "This is the most modern report. It's just coming out and this ninety days thing is what I'm going to rely upon. It's more accurate that the last twelve months." Bunk. If you have a choice between looking at the last twelve months and the last ninety days then use the last twelve months.

There is another thing people don't understand. Almost every business has a strong quarter of the year and a weak quarter of the year. Take a look at retail stores after the Christmas season. In their strong quarter of the year they are going to present dynamite results and buyers will look at that quarter and say, "Well, I've discovered the next Apple." Then in the worst quarter of the year, their weak quarter of the year, they are going to present horrific results and these clowns will bail out of the stock because they think the world is coming to an end.

If you realize that every corporation has a strong quarter in the year and a weak quarter in the year then you realize that these quarterly reports are nonsense. Plus, ninety days is too short a period. In fact, in Europe they don't have quarterly statements. They regard them as misleading and boy can I agree with that. They use six month statements and I think either Britain or Canada just decided that they were right and they stopped quarterly reports. I can't remember whether it is Britain or Canada, but they are going to six month earning reports. Believe me, it would be a great move forward because these quarterly reports just do nothing but deceive people. That is all they do.

What do you personally do everyday? What services do you monitor, websites do you use, or subscriptions do you have? Let's also get to books that you recommend people read to become better investors.

All right. Are you familiar with Seeking Alpha? I use that. I like that a lot. It's got a lot of good information on it. I'm on SeekingAlpha.com everyday checking things out.

If you are looking for a brokerage firm then I recommend Charles Schwab. They have tremendous analysis things there. There is just a tremendous suite of services that they offer for stock market research. Basically I use that.

I use *The Northern Miner* for my mining plays.

That is more or less the sources.

What books would you recommend people read? A lot of investors have read a hundred books so people always want to know what helped you create your style.

An old favorite of mine is *Contrarian Investment Strategies* by somebody who actually knows what he is doing, David Dreman. He's a contrarian like me, you know? I like that. It's an outstanding book. It's *Contrarian Investment Strategies*.

A next one that I really like goes into depth all the way back a hundred years and shows you cycles and returns. It contains excellent stock market cycles and that sort of stuff. It's called *Unexpected Returns* by Ed Easterling. Excellent book, it's totally different and it gives you the long-term perspective on stock market cycles that I think it is excellent.

The third one I would recommend is called *Using Options to Buy Stocks* by Dennis Eisen. That's Dennis Eisen and underneath that it says, "Investing using long-term equity options," which is something I do. Like I said, stay away from the short-term options stuff. It's a disaster. Everyone thinks it's brilliant. They keep talking about the time decay but forget about time decay. If you go to the longest option out there you will always prosper, you will always do better, and one of the things that happens when you deal with the farthest option out is that it never blows up in your face. Well almost never. Obviously sometimes it does.

When you are dealing with these short-term options you are constantly having your head handed to you because you are getting the stock put to you when you didn't want it or you are getting it called from you when you don't want it called from you. When you are dealing with the longest-term option out there it is rare for the stock to be called from you or put from you. You can have an intelligent strategy and not have the strategy blow up in your face by constantly having the stocks either put to you or called away from you.

I always sell the longest maturity options I can find. Always. You know this is not the Wall Street consensus. The Wall Street consensus is that the smart money always sells the ninety-day option because of time decay, blah, blah, blah, blah. Well, that may be true, but their assumptions are nonsense. My way is just more profitable. They are assuming that you would actually hold the option for two years. That never happens. I usually hold the options six months. Well, it depends upon market action but the only thing I can tell you is read the book and do long-term options if you've been messing around with short-term options. I think you are going to be a lot more successful.

Okay. You usually buy two years out, but do you buy in-the-money or a little bit out-of-the-money options?

It depends, it depends on the strategy. Suppose that I'm using the option and I have no intention of buying the stock. For whatever reason it's not a stock that I want to own, but I like it. One my favorite strategies - if there is a stock that I do not want to own but I have a positive assumption on it - is that I will sell the two-year put option. I will sell an out-of-the-money, maybe two or three strikes out-of-the-money option. You get the cash up front. People don't realize that. You get the cash up front.

I am talking about being short the put. You get the cash up front and you've got two years of that free money. If you are right about the stock because it's a stock that you have a favorable opinion of, but don't want to buy, then it can be very profitable. A lot of times you can just keep rolling over. You've got the money free for two years and if you are right about the stock then you will be able to roll it over for another two years, pick up more money, and every time you roll it over because there is more time value there you sell it at a profit. It can be a tremendous asset builder.

Okay, that's another great strategy. Let's go back to the books. Any other books?

No, those three I think are it.

Do you recommend people take money out of the stock money and then buy real estate or other assets that aren't in the trading arena?

I think everyone should own the roof over their heads. It's perfectly all right to own a vacation property. I own a vacation property out in Reno. I like that idea. I'm there a couple months out of the year in Reno because I want to avoid the summer heat. Reno is up in the mountains so I like that. I'm a fan of owning the roof over your own head and maybe a second property and maybe some raw real estate.

I'm a retired state certified general real estate appraiser, which means before I retired I was licensed to appraise everything from a chicken coop to the Empire State Building. The problem with real estate is this. It is a genuine asset category, but as an investment it's an overrated investment. The reason why is that people adore real estate, which means that consequently they always pay top dollar for real estate. In every nation on Earth the real estate prices are always at top dollar unless there are rent controls so that that society can afford to live. Because they are always selling at top dollar, basically increasing the prices is not easy. It's not as easy as people think.

During the last crisis that we just went through nine million people were foreclosed on. There were nine million foreclosures in this country since 2007. Nine million. These people didn't lose 10% or 15% or 20%. They lost 100% of their investment. The problem with real estate is that everyone thinks that they understand real estate. Everyone thinks they can't lose money on it. As a consequence, real estate is always overvalued.

I really like the REITs because there you see professional management. They get an appraisal on everything that they buy because of the fact that real estate is still pretty much an odd duck even though unfortunately that is changing. If it was up to me it would be an odd duck that nobody knew about forever because then I would maximize out on the dividends, but I don't think that is going to last much longer. Thirty-one nations now have approved REITs. Thirty-one nations have all followed our example and REITs are becoming more and more popular, which I'm not happy about. I would prefer it if nobody even knew they existed.

Now you can even do crowdfunding for real estate so you can even pick your own projects that you might want to invest in. This way you can avoid REITs but still have investment properties.

Yes, but that would be my attitude on real estate. If you want to own real estate then try the REITs for Pete's sake. You don't have the headaches and you know what the dividend is going to be in there. They own enormous commercial real estate. You can get enormous diversification. I just don't want the headaches of owning rental properties.

The equity REITs rather than the mortgage ones?

Well, the equity REITs are 5% plays on all of them. The mortgage REITs are far more risky and I would put no more than 2% in any of them.

We have talked for well over two hours, which is a very long interview. You're seventy-two now?

I'm seventy-three years old. Unfortunately, I've become very lazy. I no longer have the ambition that I used to have. I don't have to do anything because I'm financially independent. The only thing I've got to do is go to Europe every year, which is what I do. As a consequence I'm just not pumping out the work that I used to.

I'm trying to write another book. It's fifty percent completed. I've been trying for two years to finish it. If they threw me in prison I could finish it in two weeks, but I just can't come up with the ambition to finish the book. My working title is "Super Profits and Under Ten Dollar Stocks," "Super Profits and Below Ten Dollar Stocks," or "Super Profits: Investing in Under Ten Dollar Stocks."

I also have a website, which I haven't been updating. Like I said, I don't have to do anything. When you don't have to do anything it's awfully hard to motivate yourself, especially when you are my age. I haven't written any articles in the last year. I've got about forty articles on the website that you might want to take a look at which is at "forty years a speculator," which is written out in words.

That's FortyYearsaSpcculator.blogspot.com. Take a look at the articles and see if there is anything there that interests you. I also have articles on E-zine Articles. That's about it. By all means take a look at my website and you can actually see what I look like because I've got a few things on there.

Here is the last question for you. Do you have any life lessons or philosophy you'd like to pass along to the twenty, thirty, forty, fifty year-olds such as something you wish you had known when you got started in investing years ago or for life in general? Some advice you would like to give people? For instance, anything you want to pass on to people as investors who still have time to invest?

Well, I've more or less already stated it. Research the investment before you buy it. Research the investment before you buy it, be a buy and hold investor and don't freak out if the price declines or they cut the dividends.

You are supposed to do your research before you buy the stock. As long as you obey my rules as to how much you can put into it and you are diversified like I am then it doesn't matter. You are going to be right sixty to eighty percent of the time if you hold for five years. That's the big thing. By the time you hold an asset for the fourth or fifth year then unless you made a horrendous choice you will almost always be in the profit column just by holding the stock for five years. You will almost always be in the profit unless you made a horrendous pick. So hold for five years, research before you invest and for God's sake don't freak out if there is a bad earnings report or they cut the dividend.

There is also a time for selling. At the end of the year, you take a look at all of your stocks and if you decide "I was wrong about this" then sell the damn thing then but not before then. Every year I will sell maybe ten or fifteen positions that I decided I was flat-out wrong on. You don't sell because the stock is down. You don't sell because they cut the dividend. The only reason for selling is that you no longer believe in the stock. That's why you sell.

Is there anything that you know now that you wish you knew forty years ago that you want people to know?

No, I think that's it.

You talked about this before, but I always try to get at it a different way. If you were a genie and you could wave your magic wand and change something in people so they were more successful investors, what would that be?

Be a contrarian. You've got to buy low and sell high, but people do not buy low and sell high. Like I said, when they are in the gutter people won't touch that stock with a ten-foot pole. They want to buy stocks that ...

Like I told you, I've done this many times. I'll show some people a screaming bargain down 60% or 70% and they look at me with a look of total horror. They think I've lost my mind and then they will go out and buy something, some hot high-flyer that is up 300% on the year, and then they can't figure out why they get their head handed to them on a platter.

There is one more thing. I've touched on this, but let's do a little bit more. I'm repeating myself but I need to say that I hate macroeconomic analysis. Just a couple weeks ago a friend of mine who I've known for many years decided to buy oil stocks. He didn't own any oils, but he decided to buy oils. He was watching CNBC and they said that there was a prospect for a war and they were afraid that the war in the Persian Gulf would result in blocking the Straits of Hormuz and he said, "This is it, and I'll buy the stock." He blindly bought a couple of oil stocks based not on fundamental analysis but on this macroeconomic crap.

That's what you see today. I see people who have been in the stock market for years never analyze a stock. They do all their buying and selling based on macroeconomic nonsense. Alternating waves of optimism, of pessimism, they chase things up and they chase things down based on nothing more than the macroeconomic news of the day. They don't know the fundamentals of the stock. It's a lost art, a lost art.

So be a long-term holder, do the fundamental analysis and stop doing macroeconomic evaluations. What they do is that they look at what happened in Greece, look at what is happening in Europe, they make some grand sweeping statements about what they think the economy is going to do and based on that they buy and sell. No, you buy and sell based on the fundamental analysis of the stock.

Like I said for a newbie, just buy the S&P total stock market, the Vanguard Total Stock Market. It's a great way to get in and then keep reinvesting the dividends. As you find a target of opportunity after you've become acclimatized to the market then you can take 1%, 2%, 3%, 4% or 5% out of the Vanguard Total Stock Market Index Fund and put it into this target of opportunity you found. Remember, there is very little to be gained by investing in the S&P 500 because all those stocks are correlated. They are an institutionally dominated market. They are correlated. They all go up and down together. Why pick? Just buy the entire thing and be done with it.

Fred, I want to thank you a lot. First for writing *Forty Years a Speculator*, which opened up a new world of investing for me personally, and secondly for this interview that I think is probably one of the most comprehensive you have given over the years. It updates a lot of the things that you put in the book.

Okay. All right, thank you. It was nice talking to you.

Thank you Fred.

Chapter 11
Preston James
Winning with Weekly Options

Options have attracted countless people into the trading arena, but the honest truth is that most people lose money trading options. The same goes with futures trading. Over the years I've read the stories of nearly a dozen or so brokers who investigated their client records and found that 95%, 98% or some such proportion of options (or futures) traders lost money. If you asked me to find an options system that consistently made money I would be hard pressed to recommend any although I do like the dynamically managed spread trading systems taught by David Vallieres.

Seeking a successful options trader with systems to share I contacted Preston James, who was first introduced to options trading back in the 1990s while working at Fidelity investments. Preston eventually started his own options financial letter featuring directional trades, but when weekly options entered the scene he totally changed his trading methodology to become far more profitable by selling the weekly options for their premiums. If you are seeking consistent options profits then the way to go is to find systematic methods for safely selling and then collecting option premiums, which is a topic we discussed with Fred Carach as well. If you can combine this idea with the adaptive seasonal price projections that I described in my book Super Investing then you are on the way to creating a consistent options moneymaker.

This new breakthrough strategy of selling weekly options in a risk-protected manner, rather than buying them for directional trades, enabled Preston to achieve track record returns that were impossible via the standard method of betting on undependable uptrends or downtrends. If you want to get into the options field, rather than betting on longs and shorts I would encourage you to think carefully about Preston's systems and how he created them and consider a focus on selling premium rather than betting on stock price directions.

Preston, the first question is how did you get started in trading? How did you get started in this field?

The short answer is I graduated from University of Utah with a B.S. degree in finance, business/finance, and didn't feel like I learned anything. We learned about widgets and there were boring accounting classes and all this stuff. At that time Fidelity Investments - this was pre-internet - had four big call centers. One of them was in Salt Lake City and it became my employer. It's embarrassing what my starting salary was.

Basically I went to work for Fidelity Investments and ended up getting my Series 63 and my 7 so I could be licensed to take a phone call from a customer and actually execute a stock or an option trade over the phone. That's how we did it. That was right before touch-tone phone ordering came on the scene, but it was all done over the phone.

I was absolutely floored and fascinated by the whole world of stocks. I would wake up every day to do trading and had all these charts, had to figure out where stocks were and where they are now, had to follow dividends and it all just blew me away. I didn't learn one thing about it in my four-year degree from college.

How did you then go from that into actually trading for yourself and then developing your options specialty?

This was in the early '90s and it's funny because I still remember my first option trade. I almost had to take people aside and say, "Now what is a call again?" This option trade went for a three-for-two split, which is the most confusing thing in the world and I don't think I made money or broke even on it. However once you do that first option trade and you're not doing stock then a whole other world opens up for you.

I did my first option trade while I was an employee there and I really couldn't see any other way. Plus, I didn't have a big bankroll. All it takes is getting an option trade with the right kind of octane or the right leverage and you don't see things the same way you did before. So what I started thinking was, "What do you buy and how long do you buy?" because you have to be right inside the expiration term of that option.

I was just trying to read up on the next technologies and became what you could consider a swing trader looking for momentum: "Oh, everyone seems to be hopping on that over there." Of course inevitably, if you don't get your timing right they could all hop off. I had some pretty frustrating years trying lots of different things including fundamental analysis: "Hey, this company's got a good P/E ratio. It should go up." I quickly realized that it doesn't really matter what I want a stock to do, but this is all getting ahead of myself. This is all what I eventually tried, but initially I was just starting back in the '90s.

What did I do back in the '90s? I read the Peter Lynch books. I was real excited about fundamental analysis thinking, "Doesn't a stock have to go up because the P/E ratio is right?" and all these things.

What you quickly discover, of course, is that there are mad crowds out there and a moody market and the underlying value of what something should be worth really doesn't matter. It matters where the crowd decides to take the price. That job only lasted a couple years.

Now there was a gentleman in the later '90s who had commercials on the radio, had New York Times best-selling books and hailed out of the Seattle area. He started the whole stock-market seminar education. It was Wade Cook. He was a real estate guy and then apparently he started talking about stocks on the radio one day. He said the phone just lit up.

Anyway, he had his whole shtick about being a cab driver with his meter drop and all these things. It took off like wildfire. It just seemed like that was the first stock-market education and I was very intrigued. I was like, "Maybe this guy has got the answers," and we ended up moving to Seattle because my wife had some family up there. I spent a couple of years in the Wade Cook Seminar Organization until that went kaput.

You were in his organization. Did that teach you how to be a trader?

Supposedly. He had some very clever things, things that sounded really good on paper. He was a big advocate of getting in and then getting out really quick. He was an advocate of hitting base hits, "And that's how you're going to get ahead," and "Don't go for the home run," and all this stuff.

That experience led into 1999 and I had gone out on my own. I thought I had a couple of things under my belt and I had a website back in the day called "Bull by the Horns." It was pretty nicely named given what unfurled in 1999 where a gardener and a pool contractor and the person down the street, basically everyone was in the market enjoying these big, huge momentum swings. My website grew like leaps and bounds for about nine months and then everything went south after that due to the dot-com implosion and then ultimately 911.

There's a funny little thing in there, Bill, and I'll never do this again. I'll never make a prediction in public again. All these stocks had gone up and they were all charging back down and I thought, "There is no way stocks could go down anymore. There is no way." I had a couple of hundred people in a room and I said, "Hey, the market is going to recover. It has gone down too much. There is no way it could go down anymore." In fact, I pegged out a level and I said, "The market is going to be here by the end of the year. If not, I'm prepared to ski down a mountain in a pink thong," and guess what the market did, Bill?

It went south.

It did nothing but go south more than anyone could have imagined and 911 was a part of that, a completely unforeseen thing, so the next Spring I was on a Utah mountain in March and I paid my debt to society. We called it the "Wrong in the Thong Bare Market Descent" and bare was spelled B-A-R-E of course (instead of "bear"). What we'll do to keep subscribers!

It was experiences like that shaped things, I mean to start a service where people are listening to you and what you are doing is trading options. We made a fortune on the way up, but I just did not have my downside skills at that time. I guess I'm trying to paint this picture of how everything has evolved, so those are some formative things there. The crucial thing is that I used to be just a purely directional options trader, and with the advent of these weekly options that came out in the spring of 2010 I am a non-directional trader now and I've made more money in the last five years than any other time combined, hands down.

My best student right now is a lady in Oregon, and she's been with me for a little bit more than three years. She started with a $25,000 account and now it's a $3,000,000 account. It's that powerful, and I think women are better traders than men by the way. That's another thing I've learned.

You found that to be consistent?

In a roundabout way. There are always going to be exceptions, and I don't know how their minds work but they are organized. I think the organized trader is the winner, especially in today's day and age, and I think women have that better than men. Just that thing right there is huge, and actually following rules is one of their good points, too.

That's the big thing, which is following the rules. Let me ask you a question. You weren't really prepared for the first bear market of your life, but have you learned how to trade them since that

time? If you weren't a non-directional trader right now and we entered a bear market then what would you do?

I say all bear markets aren't created equal. There was a time, and I think it was like 2002 at some point when I actually interviewed Dan Zanger, who actually made $15,000,000 on the upside of 1999 and he made $15,000,000 on the downside. He was a pool contractor in Southern California and I think he's behind Chartpattern.com.

We were on the phone. I was so down and out. Again, this is 2002 so the market was correcting. It was horrible. In 2001 I'm skiing down a mountain in a pink thong and there was 911. In 2002, things had just not turned around and I remember asking Dan some things. He made this statement to me and I've never forgotten it. He said, "Preston, bear markets end." I just thought that bear markets were the new normal. Was he right? Yes, he was. Along came 2003 and from 2003 to 2007 it was just a wonderful time to be a call options buyer and an options trader. You just had a lot of wind to your back.

I met another mentor during this time in 2003 from Park City. They call it the Little Manhattan because there are so many New Yorkers that have second homes out there and there are tons of red eye flights between Salt Lake and JFK. It's really kind of weird. They will red eye it out here and they've got places all over Park City.

This gentleman was from New York and really liked one of the things I was teaching at that time and I'll tell you what it was. It's my pre-announcement setup. I was in *Investor Business Daily* quite often. I had an ad in a nutshell that said, "Hey, you need to discover this almost magic, little-known piece of news that makes a stock go up 86% of the time three to six months down the road, and it is not an earnings announcement."

You need to know about this and what it is. I'll just tell you, Bill, that this is a pre-announcement of better than expected earnings.

Those aren't all created equal either, but once I hone that in then it's fantastic. Why I'm even on the phone with you now is that I found that whatever little thing I've been able to discover and share with the world to people who are interested ends up bringing ideas back, stuff you've never thought of before. I've never, ever sat there and thought, "I've got all this figured out. This market stuff is nothing." I've always tried to remain curious, always tried to remain open, teachable and it just seems inevitable that when you share things then things come back and this gentleman came into my life.

He loved this pre-announcement setup and he taught me some things about the market cycle and some other strategies. It's because of this gentleman that when we were in 2007 and the market cycle started coming apart - but you didn't really see things on the surface - I was able to sail through 2008 as mostly a bystander because that market cycle went away. The market looked just fine, but there was lots of selling going on behind the scenes and that got me super cautious. Shortly after that in 2009, and then into the spring of 2010 when the weekly options came out, I changed a lot of the stuff that I did because of that.

Let's cover the pre-announcement trade because it's a bedrock setup. Today I will, with weeklys, do a slightly different application to this, but I think this is one of the things that is completely timeless, meaning you could learn this in 1995 or you could learn this in 2030 and it's still going to work for you. As a side note Zack's Research, which you are probably already familiar with, has been out there for thirty plus years. Their big thing they hang their hat on - and they've done four times better than the S&P

500 - Zack's "reason for the season" is tracking earnings revisions and what difference that makes in the stock price.

I have a podcast, by the way, where I go over this pre-announcement thing in depth, but I'm going to share it with you here, too. The most important thing to it is an eight-letter word. To make money with this and nothing else that eight-letter word is the word "surprise."

There are positive surprises and there are negative surprises just like in life. The right surprise can change a two-year downtrend in a stock and pivot it and make it go higher. It can make an uptrend continue. It can wake up a sleeping giant stock and make it start covering ground. That's all possible with the word "surprise."

There is no other thing as important to stocks as their earnings, earnings power, earnings momentum and where earnings are going. There are four things so let me tell you where I find them. I like going to Briefing.com and getting this information for free. Does it take a little bit of time and a little bit of digging? It does, but once you incorporate this as a habit then to me this is where you start. You will be introduced to all kinds of companies you have never heard of before and it's just really an awesome thing. It's under "Calendars" if you go to Briefing.com and you just go to "Earnings Guidance."

If it's your first time in Briefing.com then they may ask you for an email, but I believe you can get the earnings guidance for free. There was a study that I came across that I believe was on Briefing and it was done in early 2002, but it was about the year 2001. It said, "When a company has a positive earning surprise, 86% of the time the stock is trading higher three to six months down the road." I thought, "In 2001, that's the year all the internet companies went kaput and in 911 if it worked then could it work in a normal year? And does it ever." There are four criteria to make use of this, and I'm looking at some companies now in Briefing. I'm seeing four companies this morning that pre-announced something about their upcoming earnings.

Number one, is the stock trading higher right now this morning? These either come out before the open or after the close, so if I'm looking at their action in the market today then what they announce before the open today is being reflected in the share price. I need to see the stock trading higher. I like to see an entire day's average volume happen in the first hour. That tells me that people closer to it in the crowd who know way more than me are on board this stock, meaning I don't want to sit here and argue.

If the stock is trading lower, how many times have you seen earnings that look like they are higher - that they have reported higher - but the stock is trading down? I don't like to scratch my head about that. The crowd has to be in it.

The stock has to be (1) trading higher, (2) there must be a whole day's volume in the first hour, and (3) the stock must be above $15 a share, and (4) the stock must have options traded on it.

What I'll do, and there is a little more involved after this because then I want to look at the stock and see what trend it's been having. My favorite thing is to see a stock that has been uptrending that has been in a pause for two, three, four or five months and then a new earnings revision comes in and the stock is actually taking out a new high. That's what I call my "ideal setup." What will I do on that? I'll go three, four months out and buy a slightly in-the-money call option, so if that stock is $92 a share I'll go out three or four months and I'll buy an $85 call. That's the plain vanilla way to make money with the right pre-announcement.

When will you get out of the trade?

Now that depends on the overall health of the market. If we're in a bull market then that is going to help me stay in the trade longer. As we're recording this interview the market has been super volatile, super wishy-washy. A lot of people say we are in a bear market and it's harder to make money on the call side (on a bullish trade) when the rest of the market is dragging it down so I'll set tighter stops in a crazier market like this and just watch it. It's not for you and I to determine how high a stock is going to go. If the right surprise factor is in it, if a stock's been hanging out sideways for six months and finally the earnings surprise comes in then boy they can really gallop. There is a lot of lost ground a stock can make up for.

What is your typical stop size in percentage terms and when do you usually get out? Do you exit at a profit target or resistance line? Basically, what are your general rules for exiting the trade?

One date that I have firmly in mind is I always hunt down the next earnings announcement date. Everyone should know when that date is coming up because you don't want to be hanging out in a trade unaware that earnings are coming. I like looking back at the last two earnings announcements. I'm not just interested in how the stock reacted after the earnings. I like to see what the crowd did in the three to four weeks leading up to the last two earnings announcements. That's a real edge there, meaning that if you see an average move of 10% to the upside prior to the last two earnings announcements and I find myself a month away from earnings then I would sure like to get that.

Now it doesn't mean it's going to move 10% again, but these stocks do have momentum like that where there is not just one good earnings announcement but several in a row. I call it the cockroach theory. If you see one then there are more. There are usually more.

The earnings announcement is a big thing, but I'm not buying a call option for $14 to turn around and sell it at $15. I also don't want to lose more than 50% of my capital for an options trade. If I'm laying down $14 for a call option then if it doesn't work out I'm out at $7. I'm not going to ride that thing down to 50¢ of value.

Is that your general rule for most strategies?

For this strategy, those are two of my bedrock rules: Know what the earnings date is and don't lose more than half of your options capital.

You get out before the earnings date, but you try to ride it as far as possible based on the history, especially if it usually shows a pop.

Yes, and depending on how much of a ride I have. Say my call options tripled and we are at the day before earnings. If I am long a ten call contract trade then I might go buy ten puts. That's just in case that the worst-case scenario happens so I still keep most of the capital that I've made.

How successful have you been doing this in options? Is there a track record that you can give?

Like I said, since weeklys have come out in 2010 I have really gathered a really large following of people doing really well, and what is really well? You can get into the right option buying it for $11 and selling it at $111. The upside returns can just be insane. You can also get in big time trouble with options where you are constantly buying them and constantly doing directional stuff and then have a market that is not conducive for you doing that.

Since the spring of 2010 when weeklys came out it has really dramatically affected my results. I've got a video online that shows a $50,000 account going to $140,000 in a six-month period of time, so that is almost triple in six months. It's been conservatively between 200-300% a year since the spring of 2010 and I have video to back that up of my own trades and my own account.

In other words you are saying that you used to trade options directionally. You were doing well, but really everything has become revolutionized when the weekly options came out.

Yes.

Can you explain to people what these weekly options are and how do you trade them with strategies that are successful? Let's go over some of those strategies so people can say, "Yes, I can do that." What are your exact strategies with these things and why are you being really successful at these to make such great returns?

It's the only way I'm going to be trading between now and when I have a tag on my toe. Look, 80% of the stock market volume today is from institutional investors. They are pushing around 80% of the trading volume. The Fed is an institutional investor, but we're talking about the insurance companies, all the hedge funds and all that. Twenty percent of the players are me and you and the people reading this. The big "aha!" discovery that I had was that these institutional traders, no matter how cool a strategy I'm going to share with you here, can't do it.

I picture the institutions as being the size of an oil tanker let loose inside San Francisco Bay that's in this circle going back and forth throwing up this wake, and you and I are wave runners. No matter how much we want we cannot be that oil tanker and that oil tanker can't be us. Meaning, if we imagine in our mind's eye that we are a wave runner jumping over the oil tanker's wake, can the oil tanker be nimble enough to go around and do anything with its own wake? It just can't. They are their own player and we are who we are.

In this zero-interest rate environment that we've had you have all these institutions looking to make money in any way that they can. The reasons for the current volatility is because they turn into activist investors and because they get board seats and they float rumors and there's this and that, but there is all this money moving around to find the bigger return and it just doesn't sit idle in cash because that doesn't earn them anything. Therefore it's going from sector to sector and it's just crazy. That produces volatility.

Given all of that, when the weeklys came out – which are simply 8-day options that come out every Thursday morning and expire the following Friday - I realized something that used to keep me up at night. I do not exaggerate that at all. I could not get any sleep during some nights. When I was looking at the quote of a one-week option I realized that for the same strike price I could go out one month and the one week premium, if you added it up and times-ed it by four, would equal double the one month premium.

There are all kinds of reasons for that. This held from stock to stock, industry to industry. It didn't matter whether you were looking at Apple or you were looking at a 3D computing stock or an oil stock. The big reason for that is that all the players out there tend to focus on and have the most volume on the next expiring option, and so when the weeklys came out then all that action went there and that just pumps up the price of the option.

Understand something. I'm not talking about turning around and buying weekly options all the time. I'm talking about turning into a seller and crafting a strategy where you are selling weekly options that add up to double of what you were able to do before. What kept me up at night is that if you are now taking in double the income compared to before, but you have protection that doesn't cost you double then you have got an incredible advantage. What happened overnight with the advent of these weeklys that only you and I can trade at the institutions (they are busy buying stock and taking on these big positions) is a doubling of your returns on the same amount of risk. I'm an ex-college linebacker and I had a hard time getting that through my head and that's why I was having sleepless nights.

Weekly options are available on about 10% of the optionable stock universe, and what that means is that there is about 3,000 or so stocks that have options. We're talking about 300 of those 3,000 that have weeklys. They are the bigger names. They are the Googles, they are the Apples, there's Chipotle Mexican Grill.

I will take this pre-announcement strategy that we talked about as an example. Let's say you have a company that meets all of my pre-announcement criteria. The stock is trading higher, the volume is there, and there is new interest in that name. Maybe it was kind of dormant.

By the way, new interest in a stock helps push up the price of those options, and so in a nutshell I have a strategy that I call the "Money Press," which is what it simply is. I go buy a three or four month out put option (underneath the stock price as protection), and what I do every week is I sell weekly puts against it. This type of trade makes money with flat to upside market action in the stock. Because of the longer-term put that I buy, people that follow the Money Press and do this very successfully have fun because they can sleep at night. There is built-in protection no matter how bad something gets because you have a situation carved out where you can only lose a minimal amount and that's the fact.

In other words, if you sell put options you collect the premium.

Right.

You're saying that because you are selling these you are getting double the premium that you normally would get and you also protect yourself by buying a regular put that is priced normally.

That's right.

There is a risk to it so you cap your risk by also buying a put at the same time, but the put that you buy is, let's say, for two or three months and then what you're going to be doing is selling a weekly for every week for two or three months or whatever and then that way you're fine. Is that what

you're saying?

That's exactly right, and without buying that long-term put you would have to have a ton of money in your account because you would be naked selling those weekly puts. By buying those puts out there in time it totally flips the computer.

Almost anyone can do this. You don't need a special options requirement or tons of margin or a big account to do this. What it really leads to also is that this is where the small investor can be aligned with a pricey Google or Priceline. These stocks are just out there in price, they just seem so expensive at several hundred dollars per share, but as soon as you get your risk detailed then the small investor - I'm talking an investor with under $10,000 in their account - can trade the biggest names in the land.

Let's do an example of this with a stock like Apple. Let's walk through an example with Apple and tell people how to do this, and then explain the stocks we would not do it on. I'm assuming you just want to do this on stocks where you have a better chance of making money than with others, but for educational purposes let's just explain how you would do it with Apple.

Your readers understand that this entire discussion of mine, including this and the other examples, is for educational purposes only. No advice is being given or implied. I'm not a stock broker nor registered investment advisor or anything like that.

Yes, there is a disclaimer. Everyone should understand this is just for educational purposes.

I know. I'm just being tongue-in-cheek on that with you. Right now Apple is at $109.40 as I look at it right now, $109.42. For a Money Press trade, given that it was all ready to go and all this stuff, I would go out and sell - we're doing this analysis on a Wednesday - I would sell not this coming Friday but I would sell the following Friday's, say, 110 puts, and I would go out three months or so, three or four months, and I would purchase perhaps the 100 or maybe the 102.50 puts. That would be a Money Press. You'd be in business.

Then every week you would keep selling the puts?

That's right, and we know with options and their beautiful math that when we are constantly selling a weekly put or a weekly option they have a rapid time-decay. This happens in calls and puts that we are constantly selling an option that is having a rapid time-decay curve. I think it was Tom Sosnoff who said, "The three certainties of life are death, taxes and time decay in options."

When we buy a three or four month out option, if I buy it today and I wake up tomorrow there is hardly any time decay that's gone off those three or four month options. On the other hand, every time I'm turning around I'm selling the weekly option that has a rapid time-decay element to it, not to mention that it's double a one-month option. When we add four weeklys up then that equals double a one-month, which is what you had to do before.

A Money Press is a calendar spread options strategy. That's all it is, but I kind of coined the term and what I love about it, just as an aside, is that we can craft these after a company announces earnings.

We can craft these to sell twelve weekly periods where you don't even have to deal with the earnings announcement ever again. You just do it right between an earnings announcement. That used to be the bugaboo to do a long-term calendar spread out there nine months or twelve months. You had four earnings jokers to deal with. That's a little side note there.

Walk me through the trade. What exactly do you do? It's at $109.42. You're going to be selling puts, and the first one you are going to be selling is the 110 strike. What do you do then next week, and how many weeks do you do it? How do you finally finish a trade?

Absolutely. These are alive. You create a little animal here. I have a webinar every Friday where I adjust this and do exactly this. The idea is we get to not this Friday but we get to the following Friday, so it's a little bit longer than a week. This first one would be at that time, and perhaps you sold these 110 puts on Apple for $2.50. If we're talking about ten contracts then that's $2,500, which is what $2.50 means on an options quote. We'll just say that. If you do this on ten contracts then a 10-contract Money Press trade on Apple, which is what I'm talking about here, would probably take about $5,000 or $6,000 to do.

What I'm saying here is in the first week and a half you can have $2,500 as a credit back into the kitty. The mechanics of it are this. If Apple happens to finish above $110 by a week and a half, that two and a half dollars ($2.50 meaning $250) that you sold those options for would be worth the following. Let's say an hour before the close on Friday that Apple was trading at $111. Let's then say that your 110 puts are going to be worth about a nickel because obviously they are not in-the-money.

You can let them expire and keep that whole thing and wake up on Monday and sell some more. Or, what I like to do is buy those back for a nickel and then turn around if Apple was $111, sell the 111s for the following week and then take in another $2. You're about a week and a half away from $2,500 and then another $2,000. I always say that getting about two weeks into these you hardly have any risk left in a Money Press trade, and I don't know how to explain that to any broker. This was not on any of those tests that I took to become a licensed stockbroker, not even close.

You keep doing this until the one put that you bought is expired, or what?

That's another thing. That's a great question. I try to address this in people's minds that just because you buy a four-month out put as your protection it doesn't mean that you are married to that. That's your insurance. That's your nice, comfy pillow you get to lay down on at night. It's your bona fide insurance. It might as well be etched in stone but it doesn't mean that you are married to that and have to run that trade into that expiration of your insurance.

In fact, what I do very often is the following even when a month or two into this Apple Money Press. Maybe we are two months away from expiration at that time. I will go out and push that insurance out further so you don't have to just ride this trade. Just because you bought that insurance doesn't dictate where this trade goes.

That's fluid, too, but you can't just sell your insurance and then decide to buy some a week later if you are doing the weeklys. You have to do that inside the same order. Your account has to see that insurance. For this to even work the computers are set up where you have to have that insurance in your options account. You can't just do this without it, so it's a nice protection. You've probably done orders before and it says you can't do that. Maybe your fat finger did and you were trying to do something naked. Your brokerage won't even let you do it anymore. You have to be protected so that's kind of a fun thing.

What brokerage are you using for this? Are you using Thinkorswim or OptionsXpress?

There are so many good ones. I'm with OptionsXpress, and I especially love their walk limit feature that is very unique to them. I think they have a video on their site. I get nothing out of OptionsXpress. I wish I did. That feature right there alone just saves me so much time on Fridays, the walk limit.

It sounds like you have created some way to basically collect weekly premium on certain stocks that you have carefully picked. It is also the reason that you are more successful at this than most because in using weeklys you'll make double the amount of money as most typical options writers.

It's double the amount of money and that's why I spent a little time talking about the oil tankers and stuff because we basically kind of have a rigged market where 80% of the participants have all the money. It's because of that reality today that this works, too. It's not only a slick strategy, but I've had people doing this that will not do any other thing, no matter what. It's this or bust.

Here you have three hundred stocks you could possibly do this on. It doesn't work all the time. What are the criteria for the stocks that you select for doing this?

That's a very good question. A pre-announcement setup like we spent a little time talking about is a great setup for a Money Press. You could just look at that. It doesn't mean that the stock is going to have weeklys though. If there is a stock that sets up really well with the pre-announcement and you go to look and there are no weeklys then you can't do a Money Press with that. I think there are worse things in the world, right? We are not talking about digging ditches here.

The reason you are doing that one is because you want that 86% chance that the stock is going to go up so you are going to write puts on the stock. What other methods would you use to preselect stocks out of these three hundred candidates, namely the stocks that this is likely to work on? What other strategies or filters would you use to say, "Okay, we're going to do it on this one, this one and this one?"

It's a good question. Green Mountain Coffee at the time we are doing this is a really good example. It's just been downtrending the whole year with no end in sight, and then they had what I call a "demise day." They had a catastrophic 52-week low where the volume looks like a redwood tree compared to all the other days of volume, which therefore look like weeds at the bottom of a chart. A big, redwood-tree sized volume, a 52-week low … it's fire in the theater and everyone's out. It seems to create a vacuum right there and I never buy on that day, but I wait for the stock to recover. This is hard to discuss without a chart, but I call it the "Sunrise Demise," so that's another favorite entry point of mine. It's perfect for a Money Press trade because we don't need the stock.

Oftentimes a stock does not just V right back up. I like to think of it as a sprinter who has broken his leg and it just takes time to heal, but there's a slow mend. If you have a stock that's kind of neutral to going higher then it's perfect for a Money Press. For someone like Apple, they go through times of the year when they are doing the Mac World, the Apple World or whatever they do and there are product announcements like we just went through. There are new phones, there are new iPads out. That's usually a good time for that specific stock. It kind of depends stock by stock.

Another thing I'll tell people, Bill, is if you have that protection out there and you're selling these plumpy weekly options and putting that in your pocket then you are done searching for the next Microsoft and the next Apple and the next Google. There is only one Google. They won the internet. They own the internet. Priceline won in the travel games. You start dealing with stocks that are the pinnacle ones. They are not going out of business and they probably come back if the stock goes through a dip, so there are some fun things like that to put in the back of your mind with some of these names. There is only one of them.

Let me get this straight. There are about three hundred stocks that this is useful for because they offer weekly options. You are looking for situations like a pre-announcement surprise or a catastrophic low that obviously is a price it starts to recover from. Or maybe there is a seasonal issue or maybe it's a situation like Apple that always has product announcements that bias the stock towards the bullish side during that period. What you are doing is looking for various particular setups and then you basically use this standard process of selling the weekly puts on that process but in a protected fashion.

That's right, and all of what you just recapped will keep you plenty busy. We only have so much capital and there are multiple edges built in this. The setup is an edge. The Money Press itself is an edge. The double the premium that you can now collect is an edge. That really makes a lot of your risk go away.

You don't have to get into these things for too many weeks before the absolute worst could happen. It would suck because if the absolute worst happened, let's say it's like Volkswagen recently where they were caught with the emissions thing and the stock dropped and just got thirded like in one day. You don't want to see that happen to anything, but it's hard to lose money with what I'm laying out with you here.

Do you have to watch this on a daily basis?

No, and that's one of my favorite things.

You don't have to watch it on a daily basis. How many of these trades are you doing per week or per month?

At any given time I'll have between seven to ten of these on. I found that more than that is just too much work on a Friday, so I'll tend to make those seven to ten bigger in size rather than have twenty of them that are small in size.

You'll just do seven or ten of them and you do them all on Friday.

Usually Friday is the busy day. When I say busy, it's about probably sixty to ninety minutes.

Then what are you doing on a daily basis? Are you looking for new trades?

I try not to open my screens, but my computer is always there. I like writing and there are other things I do, but once that laptop is open it's so easy to go to your web browser and say, "Let's just check in on things." Things on a Monday can be drastically different on a Wednesday and then go right back to where they were on a Monday, and if you never paid attention you'd never go through that mental rollercoaster.

I almost size some things up on a week-to-week basis, and that is such a relief to what people think they have to do. They think they have to have CNBC on, they have to understand what the federal budget is and forecast if this or that is going to happen, understand what that upgrade means and you just don't have to know all that. You can take some deep breaths and relax.

That's the basic strategy and that's pretty much what you are now doing with all your websites? That's all you are doing and that's all you want to be doing?

Yes. There is some stuff that I like doing. Look, when the getting is good I like to be as greedy as the next person, but that's not always the circumstances in the marketplace. Like I said, we are going through some real challenging, volatile times right now. It actually is great for a Money Press because you have your protections and all that stuff is great, but there is also a thing where I go long. I call it the "Crowbar," which refers to opening a rusty treasure chest after you find it in a shipwreck and then open it. You need a crowbar to leverage it up so you can see the shiny glow on your face.

It's an aggressive long strategy, and the wrinkle on that is that if the stock has weeklys then you can sell weekly options on top. This would be call options and you would sell weekly calls. That has been a really big money-maker, but if you can't find any then by definition it means that the market is more challenging. If you can find a lot then that means the market is really good. It's kind of self-selecting.

What is the basis of that strategy?

I'll tell you right now. It's a stock that I find that is at an all-time high, that is at a 52-week high and that has doubled in the last year. You are never going to find a Walmart in a Crowbar. You're not ever, ever, ever, ever, ever going to see Apple do a Crowbar. They are too mature. They have grown. The idea is to catch a stock that is hot, that's going white-hot, and I usually find these companies that are usually five years old or less.

These are the companies out there really kicking some butt and taking some names. I'm anticipating holding it for most of the year and these are call options that I've bought for $14, and $17 and

$19 that go to $120, $130, $140. These are big time capital appreciations that make a serious difference in your brokerage account. When the getting is good I've got some Crowbars going, I'm opportunely selling some weekly income, but I always have a full stable of Money Presses going. That's my life, Bill. Seriously, right there.

When do you buy the calls and what exactly …

You want a little more color on the Crowbar? You have to strictly go by these rules. You can't say it's almost there, so I'll repeat those three rules and then there are two more.

You need a 52-week high. It has to be an all-time high and that's easy to find. You just do "max" on whatever chart you are looking at. Just do the max history. All-time high, 52-week high, and it's doubled in the last year.

I'm strict on that. You're not going to find them perfect. You're not going to find a $100 stock that exactly had a $50 low so that it is exactly a double. It's always going to be a little bit wishy-washy in there, but I don't want to stray too far from that rule.

Let's say I found a low of $50 and this stock is at $102. That's a little bit more than a double. I have a window where it's a double up to 10% off that multiple, meaning if the stock is at $100 to $110 then I'm a buyer in there if it's at a 52-week high all-time high and the low has been at $50, but I don't want to buy it at $120 if the low was at $50. I feel like the train has left the station on that. So you're not going to find them perfectly as a double. I'm looking for doubles plus 10%.

Then what do you do? You find those and then you just buy what?

You have to find a relative strength and earnings per share rating for the stock at both 80 or more, and that's easy to find on *Investor's Business Daily*. If I find all of those then what I do is the following.

We are just getting off of the summer right now. It's odd to find next fall's options. You could find next summer's options and you could find next January's options, but my idea is about a year trade so if I can't find a perfect option that is a year out I'll just try to find the next best thing. If it means going out fifteen months then I'll buy a fifteen-month option but I'm buying a call option, plain vanilla, and I like to get a little better delta on these which means you have to buy somewhere in-the-money.

I don't like to buy deep in-the-money. I absolutely do not like to buy at-the-money. I'm usually buying two to three to four strike prices in-the-money, and if someone is familiar with options then whatever that option premium is for that longer-term option I like to have half of it intrinsic and half of it time value. That might lose some people who are new to options, but I don't want to spend a fortune on the option. I don't want to buy an out-of-the money or an at-the-money. It's usually two to three to four strike prices in-the-money.

As an example, take a $110 stock where everything qualifies and lines up for a Crowbar. It's likely I'm buying a one-year out 95 call option. That's the trade and it's not a swing trade. I have tried to forget about them, but I do use that rule that if I'm losing half of my call option value then I do not want to ride that call option all the way down to zero. So if I feel some heat, if the heat is coming in the kitchen because I bought the option for $15 and it's now trading for $7.50 then I'll just sell that thing out and not ask any questions.

When will you sell it out in terms of profit? What is the exit strategy for that?

I like to let these run. These are special animals.

What I'm looking for are any options trading systems from you that are easy and profitable where people can say, "Yes, I can do that one. Yes, I can do that one, too. Yes, I can do that," and they have a really good track record. Are there any other strategies you can share besides selling the weeklys and doing this? Is there another great strategy that would be of interest to people?

I have a lot of success with stock splits, but there are not a lot of them these days. I call my strategy my "Powder Keg Breakthrough." The really interesting thing that I want to find with stock splits is first of all the date that the CEO picks out for when the stock is going to split, and another date in the future which is known as the earnings date. I get very curious if I see a company is planning to announce earnings within a week of the stock splitting.

The big example that just happened was with Netflix, which did a very, very ballsy and aggressive seven-for-one stock split. That sort of split can really swing both ways if you are not careful. You can over-split your stock, but they, curiously enough, timed announcing earnings on the day of the stock split. I'm just playing detective here. I asked, "Why would they risk announcing anything bad related to earnings on the day of their stock splitting?" It could be their ruin.

You're saying that if they are going to do that then you know it's going to be bullish, right?

You are reading that it's going to be bullish, yes.

In other words, if you know they'll split it within a week before the earnings announcement then you can expect that it is going to be bullish and therefore a natural strategy is to just buy the stock?

I wouldn't touch the stock. I would buy call options. It's a lot cheaper and has a lot more leverage.

Do you buy in-the-money options for that strike? What do you do?

What is fun is you have the dates out there, so it's fun. If they are happening in the middle of the month the traditional option expires on the third Friday of every month. You can even buy the right option that contains those dates and that's all you need. If this was coming up in mid-October then I would buy the October call options, maybe slightly in-the-money.

You are really going for bust here. If you buy a $5 call option I want to go through those dates and I just want to see what the stock is going to do knowing that the most you could lose is $5. Really technically, probably the most you want to lose is $2.50. I don't like riding stuff that I buy all the way down to zero. Yes, you could buy out-of-the-money calls. Some of these can really hit and be the biggest difference maker of a year or two in your trading.

This is a great strategy. Do you have any other unusual strategies like that? You've given us the pre-announcement strategy. There are the weekly options which you could use with the pre-announcement. There is the Crowbar and then there's this. Is there another strategy you can give me?

There is some other stuff that is a little boring, but I think it would actually run too long. What I just laid down will keep you plenty busy.

This is a lot of strategies for people to make money with. Usually master traders don't like to give this much. Now let's switch tracks. There are a lot of people who follow you. From your experience is there a certain type of individual who would do best with the option strategies that you teach? Which type of individual would usually succeed doing this and who does poorly at this?

There is a gentleman who follows me who rides around on a bullet bike motorcycle. I don't know if that means he's a risk taker, but he just tends to be penduluming meaning there are big, big swings in what he is doing. He also is a super-smart petroleum engineer, but he has stopped doing that because he's going to do trading. It almost seems like trading is just all-too consuming for his life and I think it's a detriment for him.

I compare or contrast him to another gentleman who is busy, he's starting businesses and the trading is "over here" in his life. He follows all the rules just spot on. In fact, he has taught me a few things. He's a dad, he's got two daughters keeping him busy, and he's busy with a main line of work and I think this works for him. In fact, he's just kicking butt doing this and I tend to think that it's the people who are doing other things that are being successful at this.

I don't know how I can explain that it's almost like you can just be too engrossed in the market and I think that's a danger. I think some personalities just get too caught up with the day-to-day blowhards on these cable channels, "Well, they're saying this and all that." They are also revenge trading. In other words, when something doesn't work out they throw this much more at it because it has to. The rules just go out the window.

To be successful at this I almost think you have to be doing something you love and have this work for you over there on the side.

I think you would say you shouldn't overcomplicate this and then your chances to succeed will go up. It should not be all consuming. If you try to do this full-time you would just be busying yourself with useless things, overcomplicating matters and messing up.

Yes. It's not full-time stuff to begin with, so why turn it into that? You don't have to.

How much money do people need to start trading these strategies?

They could get three or four Money Presses going with an account that's $10,000 or less. Now saying that, if you need to start there then I'd say start there. Even if you have a much bigger portfolio, if you just want to start with that then that's fine. This is such a game changer in the sense that all people's lives they have been told that they have to have $2.45 million in a nest egg so then it can earn this paltry interest. Then they can just draw down X amount and then the actuary tables say blah, blah, blah, blah, blah. However, it's just not the case with this.

With a couple hundred thousand dollars, and I don't think we have time to get into portfolio margin and the game changer that has been, but they could get positioned along some compelling dividend-paying stocks, own protection on those (sleep-at-night protection) and be sellers of weekly calls on top of stocks and doing Money Presses and other stuff too, and have a couple hundred thousand dollars kick out $7,000, $8,000, $9,000, $10,000 a month easy.

In other words, you are saying people should take a look at putting dividend stocks into their portfolio and then selling the calls on them to collect premium. You can also put on your Money Press strategy, too, which is using weekly options to do a mini calendar spread.

You want to have sleep at night and the other little fun thing there, especially when portfolio margin kicks in, is the dividends get paid out, and mentally I chock those up. It goes right across and pays my margin interest. I have zero margin interest expense. There are all kinds of fun stuff, but people have to stop what they are doing and actually look up in the sky and say, "If this is even partially right, if I can just rake in a couple of hundred thousand dollars I could really be done. I could be done with the rat race," and I'm saying, "Absolutely."

If you were to write a book about weekly options trading using these strategies then what would you include in the book as dot points without a lot of dialogue?

I would say Money Press. No, I would say with weeklys it is now possible that you can double the income on the same risk. There is a newspaper headline right there.

Number two?

I would say stop trading and begin windfalling. I have a product called "Weekly Options Windfall." That's all I could think of, Bill. I mean, regular trading conjures up the following. You have the stress of what to buy and then there is the stress of the trade going on. What if you sell out? I've asked people about this, "Look, if you buy something and it goes up $2 and you sell it, and then you notice a week later it's gone up another $20 you just feel like crap. On the other side, if you are in a trade that is not working out and it goes down $2 and you sell out at a $2 loss, if a week later the trade is down $20 then you feel like a million bucks. Don't you?" What I just said is that you feel horrible when you win and feel great when you lose. It's all backwards, and so there is the stress of when to get out of your trades.

What is killer about these weeklys - selling them and collecting that premium so that you are windfalling - is that you got the selling decision out of the way first. You are buying back sometime later. It really turns things on its head and it's hard to get through the beginner person's head. They have a hard time saying, "How do I go into Home Depot and start selling stuff? Hey, I'll sell that weed eater, I'll sell that hammer, I'll sell that gallon of paint." We're not brought up like that. You go into Home Depot to buy stuff; you don't go into a store and start selling stuff. Well, that's exactly what we are doing right here.

In other words, turn it around and start selling options. Collect premium instead of trying to win a home run by directional plays. It will produce a more consistent return and you'll have a steady paycheck. You'll make more money.

Also sleep at night.

What else would be in the book?

The Crowbar to make more money than you ever thought possible. I'm thinking about the Crowbar strategy right now which involves unlimited upside potential with fixed limited risk.

Here is a totally different question. Why are you successful at options trading now versus so many other people who have options services or whatever who aren't profitable, or people who trade options at home and aren't successful? What are you doing that's different?

I think they're hung up on the high-octane emotions because trading for some people is a drug. I think people get into the options and they are addicted. They're a druggy and they don't have any rules because options are so sexy. You can make so much money with them, but then they end up not making money with them at all. I think they are too close to it and I think I've got some methodical rules that take advantage of what the real world is out there.

I can't stress enough about this 80/20 reality and that we have to operate differently today versus any other time that you have wanted to become a trader. If you read a book from the '80s or a book in the '90s it was a different market and a different time. We are in a different reality and I believe all of this embraces this 80/20 rigged market. That's probably it in a nutshell.

Looking back now, what do you wish you knew in your twenties about the whole investment field that would have made you far richer today? You've taken this whole journey. What do you wish you had known back then - having traveled the path that you've traveled – that you wish young people would know so that they avoid errors and climb the learning curve quicker?

I would say that you do not want to neglect the power of compounding. I'm saying this in all seriousness. With a stock like a Disney or a R.J. Reynolds and the power of compounding dividend reinvestment inside of a tax-sheltered thing, it is spooky what that does through good times and bad in the market, so I would not neglect that area if you're saying go back to when I was in my twenties. There's that aspect.

I hesitate with that because I feel like I'm super passionate with what I know now because I struggled in doing and trying lots of different things. I just feel that I'm the trader I am and the person I am today because of being open and curious to learn. I just don't know that this would hit me with that impact if someone handed it to me.

That being said, I was always a buy-the-dip person and what I've learned over time is just because there is an innocent looking dip doesn't mean that it is just going to come back and so now, without hesitating, I don't bat an eye at buying something at a high because it's buying into strength that gets stronger. It's just been proven over and over and over again.

The big thing I'd tell my twenty-year-old self is how important the market cycle is. We kind of brushed up on that, but I look for a two-grade letter change. William O'Neil did some extensive studies which discovered that three out of four stocks go the overall way of the market and he termed it the "market cycle." The market is going to cycle up and it's going to cycle down. If you're going to be a buyer of call options, why would you want to fight a down market cycle? Also, you might just be buying call options and have the dumb luck that we are in a positive or an uptrending market cycle.

Three out of four stocks go the way of the market cycle. Knowing where that is - and I don't try to anticipate it because I just try to trade the market that we have at hand - he grades it from A to an E, and I specifically look at the S&P 500 and the NASDAQ index.

Incidentally, at the time we are discussing this they are both at an E, the worst grade you can get. When that letter E gets to a letter C then I am all perked up in my chair because what we probably have is an ongoing market cycle going higher. Three out of four stocks go with that. It's a huge edge.

If it's going up you are going to be selling puts and if it's going down you are going to be selling calls?

If it's going up I'm going to have more bullish positions. Those positions are going to be bigger. I'm more confident adding to those positions and I'm looking for bigger winners. If it's going down then I'm way more selective about the stocks. I'm trading smaller. They have to prove themselves more to me before I add to them. Just those things right there.

You're still bullish if we are in a mega bear market so you are still going to be doing the buys, but the stocks have to prove themselves. You are going to be using the weekly strategy. Is there some way you are going to change your strategy in a bear market such as by selling calls?

I mean if you owned a bunch of stocks then you would want to be selling calls all through a bearish cycle, but we talked about the Sunrise Demise. That's a perfect strategy to hang your hat on no matter how bad things get out there because the stock has already gone through its own valley of the shadow of death and so it's been proven to be a real resilient one no matter what the market cycle's doing, specifically the Sunrise Demise.

Are there any books you recommend people read if they want to become investors or learn this particular method of investing or anything like that?

The book I try to reread every six months is *How I Made $2,000,000 in the Stock Market*, by Nicolas Darvas. That tends to refocus me and get my brain on what it needs to be on. He did his best trading the furthest away he was from the New York Stock Exchange. Every time he thought he was going to ramp it up and really do it right he'd move to New York and have the ticker tape right by him and that's how he blew up his account, among other things.

What about any websites? Are there any websites that you want people to follow besides perhaps using Briefing.com?

I go to Investors.com and Briefing.com. I really like Finviz. It's short for "financial visual" I guess, so Finviz.com. You could just dial up. It's a way of scanning and sifting and sorting through pretty much any parameter that you want to put on there.

Right, so what do you look for at Finviz? Most people know that site, but what do you look for at Finviz?

For example, say you are searching for a Crowbar trade. I can dial up, "Show me every stock that has doubled this last year" or "Show me a stock that's at a 52-week high." Just those right there are going to whip out many possibilities and get you going. I can put in that the relative strength should be 80 or above, or if I want to get a shorter list I'll do, "Show me the 90s or above" and start with maybe six or seven stocks.

What do you use Investors.com for?

Lots of different things. I like their new high and new low list. I follow the market cycle on Investors.com. I like having the physical paper in the driveway, too, so I follow the market cycle. I like their spotlight articles on companies. There are some other things that I do during some real raunchy times in the market that help me determine if we are getting close to a bottom and things like that. There are some really fun tools in there.

Okay, so weekly options have revolutionized everything for you, right?

According to me.

According to you. For those already options traders please describe the strategy in short form, namely why people should use it and why you love it or anything you want. Encapsulate it. You're at a cocktail party. Tell me in a few minutes exactly again what it is, why people should be looking at this, why it has revolutionized everything for you and why this is what you now want to be doing until you die?

There are not many cocktail parties out in Utah. That's one thing I'll just pass along, but getting to the meat here I would say it's kind of not trading. Yes, you have to know or have a good idea what stock to do it on and yes there is an options strategy, but the traditional white-hot stress of trading is absent. The stress of every single time turning around, getting in a trade and getting out, getting back in a trade and then deciding when to get out, all that white-hot stress of traditional trading doesn't exist. You are taking advantage of real forces out there - the real world - and these forces are the ones creating this options premium that you are able to put in your pocket.

You don't have to have a fancy options level approval, which used to be a big deal. You came from that industry, Bill. You had to have the right knowledge and pedigree to trade all these highfalutin options. You don't have to have it. You don't have to have a big account. You access into the biggest names if that's what you prefer.

I don't see this changing. It's just a baby and a lot of people that you try to explain these weeklys to can't even understand ordinary options. Options have been out almost forty years now. Weeklys have been out five years and they beat the pants off of the regular way to do it, but it's so new that no one even knows about it so I try not to get too hung up. Why doesn't everybody know about this? They don't know about options anyway, let alone the latest five-year way of doing things. Not to mention that all of this probably takes a backseat to the fact that you make and keep real money. It seems fake. It seems like Monopoly money sometimes, but it's real money that you can transfer to your bank account and spend and my adage is that for any business you should be able to take money out of your business, not keep putting it in or reaching out to family members and having them put it in. The real bottom line here is just that, being able to take money out of your business and spend it on real things.

I have a gentleman I hung out with from Asheville, North Carolina and one of his daughters is into softball. I don't know if you know about sports these days, but this is a ten-month out of the year thing. I said ten months because ten out of the twelve months they are traveling around the club.

He goes, "The bats cost $300." I had no idea any of this existed. He goes, "When she finds a bat then we have to buy three of them because you just have to have them." I'm like, "Good grief, right there in one spot is $1,000 for bats." We're not talking about the clothes and the under armor and all the pads and the travel costs. I mean, mitts and things cost money today. The other maybe big thing is that our middle class is just being completely squeezed out.

I think this is the glimmer in the window on where those top one percenters are dealing. They are the ones that buy Priceline for $1,300 a share. They are the ones that have Google in their account for $640 a share. This is the tap-in way to bring down dollars from that world in my humble opinion.

How can people find out more about you and your options strategies? What are your websites and services?

My company's name is Traders Edge Network and we have an internet website called Tradersedgenetwork.com. I have lots of different websites. I want to give them that one so they can see the video and can get their hands on the Money Press because I have some really cheap info that they could get to get started on this and do it themselves if they want.

I teach just the Money Press in a little kit so they can try that. I have them cover shipping. It's like $7. I also have what I call my Weekly Option Windfall Insiders, my WOW Insiders, and it's $97 a month. I send out all of my own trades via an email update so a lot of those come on Friday and I do a live webinar on Fridays where we do live trading. There are also all these video tutorials for all of my strategies and setups they get as a member.

It basically sounds like you've come to the conclusion that it's better to primarily sell options and

collect the premium than just buy options, but you needed a systematic way of doing it so that there is less risk. There are some benefits in the weeklys that the premium now lets you double the income for the risk, which gives you more money to be made to cover the losses, and you have a better selection criteria for which ones to do it on. You have other strategies, too, that traders will be interested and the returns have been excellent. This has been killer, Preston. Thank you.

You're more than welcome.

Chapter 12
Geoff Bysshe
Rotational ETF Sector Investing

While the most successful traders view the markets as a way to make money, some people trade the markets because they are seeking excitement rather than profits. This is a sure road to ruin. To become profitable at trading or investing you should approach it like a business and aim for profits rather than entertainment. To do so you first need to find a proven investing method or trading style that suits your personality. If a trading or investment technique doesn't match your personality then it will be difficult to rally the discipline necessary to stay with following it, even if it is a winning trading technique.

If you are not interested in doing short-term trading or long-term investing yourself then another option is establishing an automated ETF sector rotation portfolio that uses relative strength comparisons of various instruments for its investment decisions. Geoff Bysshe and his partner Keith Schneider of MarketGauge.com have developed profitable sector investment models that automatically capture the biggest or fastest trends in the marketplace. The beauty of sector investing systems is that they automatically put you in the hottest markets and take you out of those positions when they stop trending strongly.

The benefit to these automatic methods is that you never have to figure out when to get in and out of a trade, which thus relieves a lot of the emotional pressure involved with trading and investing. Like computerized trend following systems, you simply remove your emotions from trading and investing decisions by religiously following the rules that put money in the bank. If you are not cut out for short-term trading or long-term investing, such as being unwilling to put a lot of time into learning how to do them properly, this is yet another technique that can still control a portion of your portfolio and help you to accumulate generational wealth over the long-term.

Geoff, you and your partner have a business called MarketGauge.com that specializes in relative strength investing. Can you tell us how you guys developed your particular style of automated trading? I'm interested in the history of what you have tried and learned in trading and how you finally developed this idea of automated trading for the ETFs.

Depending on how far you want to go back it's a funny story because my partner, Keith Schneider, is a little bit older than me. He is probably five or ten years older than me. I met him through an ad in the newspaper that was for somebody to drive him to the Commodities Exchange and be his assistant on the floor. To make a long story short, I took the job and that's how I started trading on the floor of the commodities exchanges in New York.

Keith had been a trader there for years. This was in 1990. He had already had multiple careers in trading because he had made his fortune in the gold bull market being a floor trader in 1978-1979. Then he had gone off and done a technology company called MarketVision. That was then sold and he was back on the floor and I was fortunate enough to hook up with him.

The way this all relates is that he had a very specific and mechanical approach to the market. It was based on point and figure charts and opening ranges. Even back in 1990 while we were floor trading we were looking at the markets using a very mechanical rules-based approach *and* he had seats on every exchange on the floor. The reason he had seats on every exchange on the floor is because as an independent floor trader you couldn't just go into a pit and start trading unless you were a member. If you had a membership on every exchange we could go to the hottest market.

Did he buy these seats or was he renting the seats?

He bought the seats.

That's a lot of money.

He did well in the gold bull market and they were investments. Also his perspective was – and this certainly was ingrained into me as well – you are better off being a mediocre trader in a great market than being a great trader in a mediocre market. Spending the money or making the investment in being able to go to the hot market at the right time was invaluable.

What we are going to talk about now twenty-five years later really is in part an adaptation of the way he was trading on the floor. The way I learned to trade on the floor was to go to the hot market and then once you're in that hot market you follow the momentum of that hot market. That's kind of how we got started and technology has enabled us to be more focused on the markets that we are trading. For good reason we have the computer do all the calculations we need and follow the rules rather than have me do it with the point and figure chart.

When I was in Wall Street doing automated computer trading back in the '80s we were just trading *all the trending futures markets* in a risk-adjusted fashion rather than finding the hottest markets and restricting ourselves to just those markets. What exactly were you doing to find the "hot market" and were you trading multiple markets at the same time? What were your rules for getting into those markets and for getting out?

Right, right. First of all, there is a little secret here or at least we see it as a secret. Our approach to the markets is that you want to find a group of assets that by definition should either be non-correlated to each other or they should be negatively correlated and all have something in common. The best example of this that most people can grasp quickly is the concept of industry group and sector rotation.

Theoretically - without even doing any backtesting or data mining - if you would take all the major sectors of the U.S. market, put them all in a group and make the assumption that our economy goes through its different cycles (business cycles or the larger cycle called the "liquidity cycle") then the flow of money will move between different asset classes and drive the business cycle.

If you just make it really as simple as you can then you can say, "Look, the business cycle will move money from one sector to another as it goes from recession to growth to overexpansion to contraction and back to recession." If you take all the groups that that money could possibly flow into and put that in your basket of groups then what you have now done is identify the universe of places where money is going to flow.

Now all you have to do is find a way to measure where the money is going. The beautiful thing about markets and the history of markets is that it's been proven by others on Wall Street - by academics - that if you look at the relative strength of assets in the way that we have just described them then that's all you need to do to find out where the money is going.

Next, you look at a time frame that is anywhere from three months to a year. From an academic point of view those time frames have proven themselves to be very useful in determining which trends are going to continue.

So we have a momentum indicator that is a little more sophisticated than just looking at the percentage price change of the instrument. It gives us a read on the strength of the trend over the intermediate term and by doing that we know which assets, or in this case sectors, are the strongest in our universe.

Are you looking at the entire universe of ETFs or with NASDAQ just the top one hundred NASDAQ stocks?

No. That's the secret, if I can call it that, which is that if you were to go and just say, "You know, I've got to find the strongest ETFs out of the 1,700 or 2,000 ETFs that are out there and I'm going to follow them," honestly it might work but I doubt it.

The reason is this: what's the relationship between all those 1,700 ETFs that the top ten should really be the ones that you should be in? One step further is that they may all be the same type of assets. They may all be gold-related. They may all be U.S. stock-related so you're not really catching any kind of diversity as opposed to when you define your universe of instruments to be in separate or uncorrelated groups. In this case we define our universe as the industry groups of the U.S. economy.

Then, by selecting the top groups – in our case we select the top three – we've got diversity between the different industry group trends and we have also got concentration. We're doing this in what we refer to as a model where it makes sense that the money is going to flow to different places within this model.

By doing it this way it does a few things. It makes tracking of what you are doing much simpler. You don't have to be weeding through 2,000 ETFs to figure out which ones you should be focused on.

On top of that you will understand which ones you are focusing on because we are only focused on twenty-one now and not thousands. With twenty-one we pretty much cover wherever the money is going to flow plus, and we'll get into the plus part really easily.

Take the top three, have a good measure of momentum, and you are pretty much off and running. The results of that have been pretty outstanding.

In other words, you are just taking the whole stock market and you are looking at sector ETFs in terms of industry groups, but a very limited number of groups?

Correct.

And you rank all of them by some type of trend strength indicator - some momentum indicator or

relative strength indicator - and then you just put yourself in the top three?

At its core that's what we are doing.

You don't care about correlation between the groups? I mean, the oil industries group might be very closely related to the oil exploration group?

Well the groups that we use are such that we try not to have too many ETFs that overlap. It really would be more like that we are invested in healthcare and semi-conductors right now. Those are two unrelated groups that are doing well right now. They are not really that correlated.

Now there have been situations. We do have an ETF in there that is a triple ETF, which is CURE. We also have IDB, which is a biotech, so you could argue that you are really leveraged if two of your positions are in a healthcare-related, healthcare/drugs field since it would make you kind of lopsided if they were selected at the same time for the portfolio.

Sometimes that happens, but if those are the strongest trends then that is where the money is flowing. But it would be really hard for us to have all three of our positions in the exact same type of industry group simply because we have covered all our bases.

This would be easier to understand if we know the industry groups you used so we could see how uncorrelated they were. Can you tell us the twenty-one sector ETFs that you trade?

Certainly. CURE, which is a healthcare triple. TMF, which is the 20-year bond triple. DRN, which is the real estate triple. IBB, which is biotech. SOXL, which is the semiconductor triple. XLY, which is consumer discretionary. FAS, which is the financials triple. TECL, which is the technology triple. XLP, which is consumer staples. BND, which is a total bond ETF, so that is a blended bond fund but it's not a triple. XLI, which is the industrials. IYT, which is transportation. PBW, which is clean energy. XLB, which is materials. XLU, which is utilities. SDS, which is the short S&P 500. IGE, which is natural resources. GDX, which is gold miners. OIH, which is oil services. Oh, and one more - ERX, which is an energy triple.

Correct me if I'm wrong but you've taken the U.S. economy, you broke it into uncorrelated sectors, found ETFs to cover the sectors, and for each of those ETFs you determine the trend strength. Then you invest in the top three, which means you are always getting in and out of the top tier of relative strength movers. You also do that with the top NASDAQ stocks, which are likely to be correlated to each other, but you are pretty much doing the exact same thing. Would that be correct?

Yes. That's a good general description of what we are doing. We take it one step further and we apply the same thing not only to just sectors but we also apply it to global equity markets. We have a global country approach, too. That's an illustration of how we think it's really important to identify where you think the money is going to flow.

Is the international exposure a separate thing or do you mix that in with the U.S. sectors? In other

words, do you put all the country ETFs you follow together with the U.S. sector ETFs and then run the relative strength system on this bigger group?

We do a blend of what you are describing. We have our U.S. Sector model and that operates independently. Then we have our country model and that operates independently. Then we have a Global Macro model, which instead of having just stocks or just sectors has other assets including global stock markets and regional stock markets and includes the VIX, interest rates, currencies and commodities.

We try to again take different asset classes outside of sectors, outside of specific countries, put them into their own basket and now we have got three different baskets that track where money will flow kind of in their own little universe.

Each one of those operates independently as well as in a bigger model that we call the ETF Complete. And so, rather than having three positions in the ETF Complete portfolio, we have nine positions but those nine positions are really just the three positions from each of the three different models all rolled up into one.

That's great. We'll talk about the track record of this because I'm sure you have been able to backtest it for a number of years and everybody is always interested in knowing the historical returns for systems trading whether real or simulated. Can you go over the exact rules and how somebody would use this automated system? What are the exact rules for getting in and out of sectors and how does somebody actually trade this?

Okay. I'll use the sectors as the example because as I said before I think that is what most traders can really grasp most intuitively and quickest, but really all three models essentially do the same thing with some slight variations.

In the case of the sectors, we actually have two different models, two different approaches. One we call the "basic approach," which is pure rotation, and the other one we call "stops and targets." We came up with the stops and targets approach because we had customers who just didn't feel comfortable with the idea of holding a position without a traditional stop.

Let's start first with the model that doesn't have a traditional stop. We've got three positions and those three positions are in our mind fixed. The reason that that's important is because we look at our models as having three kinds of buckets and each bucket, each position is the strongest ETF in our model of twenty-one ETF sectors. Now, strongest is determined by our TSI trend strength indicator. I couldn't even give you the formula for that if I wanted to verbally, but it's essentially a momentum indicator that looks at multiple time frames going out as long as six months, so it's six months down.

You are saying it is sort of like some weighted average of relative strength measures over different time frames for the same instrument?

Correct, and in fact if you were just getting started on this I put together a free report at one point to prove this concept to people. If you just took the six-month percentage price change of the various sectors using the major sector ETFs that are sponsored by the SPDR organization, and you only bought the top one and held it until it was no longer the top one then you would outperform the market. Conceptually that basic system will work.

Now the problem you will have if you try to do that is that you'll get a lot of churn and it's hard to stomach the pain and the calculations. It takes a lot of dedication if you are going to do all the math yourself. We have improved on that by taking the top three, expanding the list of sectors and having a much-better momentum indicator. We've got this momentum indicator and at the end of every day it gives us what the top-rated ETFs are out of our twenty-one ETFs. That's step one.

Okay, so you are doing it on a daily basis then?

At the end of the day we know what the rank is for each of our twenty-one ETFs.

The only reason I ask is because I know that Mark Boucher, author of *The Hedge Fund Edge*, did something similar. Gerald Appel and Sam Stovall also did something similar. They all performed extensive backtesting to find the best relative strength combinations for trading market or sector momentum. You guys are computing it on a daily basis, which actually makes it a lot more sensitive.

It is more sensitive, however we actually started with the idea of only changing our positions twice a week. Part of the reason for that for us was that as traders it's really important to make sure that whatever you are doing is simple to execute because if it gets too complicated and you get carried away with the math - and the computers can make it really easy to become this way now - you can make things so complex that when it comes down to actually executing it you just don't do it because it's too complicated.

Therefore we want to keep it really simple, but what wound up happening is that we found that rather than limit the time frame in which we are going to change our position we don't automatically sell if an ETF falls out of the top three tier.

Now if we talk about the NASDAQ model, with that model we actually do only trade one day a month. We shift our positions only one day a month. I would agree if someone were to say, "I've found that if I do this only at the end of the week to improve it" or "I do it only at the end of the month to make it better," I wouldn't argue with that. You could make that work, too, and you could have certain reasons for wanting it.

However, with the sectors and with the countries we have found that rather than wait that entire week for a move to perhaps either go against us or not be able to get into it we'll switch. At the end of the day we figure out who the top three ETFs are, but the top three does not determine exactly which one you're going to be in.

If you're already in a position and you're in the top three then you have to fall out of the top three by a significant amount before you change it. For that amount again we have a formula, but I couldn't give it to you off the top of my head. However the basis behind the formula is that we want the instrument to fall far enough out of the top three that it's unlikely to come right back into the top three with a few days of volatility.

Does "falling out of the top three" mean you're falling out in terms of the momentum rankings of the ETFs, like "now it's at rank 7 versus it was at rank 3 just a week ago," or are you measuring a

percentage price change that the sector has dropped?

It's based on the ranking.

Okay.

Now, it essentially works out to be a similar way, a similar concept because our ranking is going to change every day and the ranking is based on the change in different instruments so we are basically looking at the reasonable volatility of the ranking. If you have dropped far enough out of the top three rankings then it's not likely you are going to come back really quickly. Then we want you "out," we want the next ETF of whoever replaced you "in," and we always have three.

This means that for the guy who is only doing this once a week he is going to have that volatility probably factored in or accounted for because he is going to wait until the end of the week before he makes a decision. We, on the other hand, are waiting based on the volatility.

Have you tested different numbers of ETFs to be invested in rather than just three?

Yes, and we found that we didn't get much of a boost by going to higher group sizes. In fact, we did get a little bit of a decline in performance when we took on more than three positions. When we took on less positions it didn't necessarily make a difference, but we felt that we would much prefer to have the diversification of three positions rather than just one.

That makes perfect sense. The diversification will help with safety and might also cut down on switching costs somewhat.

The thing that having only one position will do is definitely lead to a more volatile equity curve.

You know what's really cool about this whole process is that Keith and I have been trading together for twenty-five years and between the time that we were on the floor and when we started MarketGauge.com, which was in 1997, we spent time at a couple of hedge funds. One of them was a multi-billion dollar hedge fund out of New York that was really quant-based.

We saw this essentially being done in this fund, but they were doing it before ETFs were in existence so they had to buy the baskets of stocks and they were actually doing fundamentals as well as momentum. As you have already pointed out there are other people doing it so in terms of as much as you can know – whereas we never assume that we really know anything as traders - but as much as you can know we kind of knew this idea would work.

It's just that we didn't really have the time to really make it happen because we are busy with other methods of trading. Eventually we hired a guy who had the capability where we were able to say, "James, we've had this idea for years. Could you just go ahead and just see if this works? We want to look at these ETFs and this is why." We explained things to him much the same way I just explained the system to you. We said, "We want to make sure we cover all our bases with where the money is going to flow and please go test it."

After that, there wasn't a whole lot of tweaking to be done to figure things out. We could have added a couple more ETFs. We could have thrown a couple more out, but at the end of the day it wasn't really making any difference. The numbers were the numbers.

The big difference though was that we originally tested it on ETFs that did not include leveraged ETFs and it worked. It worked great. For anybody who spent any amount of time on Wall Street and appreciates a risk-adjusted return it worked great. We were beating the market with less drawdowns and were not even in the market the whole time. Then what we found was that we could *juice* our performance – for lack of a better word – by substituting some of our ETFs with the triple leveraged ETFs.

The best example of that for people to understand was that rather than have the SMH to represent semi-conductors we have the SOXL, which is triple leveraged. When we are making a bet on semi-conductors with SOXL we are *really* making a bet on semi-conductors through the triple leverage, and that has really had a bigger impact on how we went from being just a good system to a great system than trying to figure out what the exact ETFs should be.

Does your present system have leveraged ETFs in there and do you have the inverse ETFs in there or do you use just plain sector ETFs without leverage?

We have leverage. Of the twenty-one ETFs, six of them are leveraged and the six are there primarily because we can trade them and can get leverage. I actually think that if they could all be leveraged then we would probably do all of them leveraged.

That being said, we are also talking to IRAs about using our model and they may actually pull us back to create a model that doesn't have any leverage in there at all because they simply appreciate the value of the model outperforming the market without leverage. For them, it doesn't have to be up 800% since 2007. They are happy with an increase of 300%.

Just to be sure, in selecting your twenty-one U.S. industrial sectors did you perform correlations or just logically pick different sectors?

We did test the correlations, but it was really after the fact. We didn't go data mining. Our selection of ETFs wasn't based on correlation. The selection is really based on common sense. We did a kind of sanity check later to make sure that the correlation was okay.

I was just trying to make sure. You're only looking at twenty-one instruments and you have to decide the top three out of the twenty-one versus a thousand different ETF-type products or whatever?

Right. That is it exactly.

And for the NASDAQ, I assume you're only looking at the hundred stocks in the NASDAQ 100 while for country ETFs you are probably looking at several dozen of them?

Yeah. We actually reduced the country possibilities to twenty also to keep it simple, and it worked.

What twenty country ETFs are you then trading?

We try to get representation from all the different regions of the world. There's the Americas and there is the Middle East, which was hard. The only one in there I think we have is Egypt. As to the Far East, we've got a bunch. I don't have them organized by region but I'll read them off and you'll get the sense: Japan, Germany, China, India, Hong Kong, Switzerland, France, Taiwan, Australia, Singapore, South Korea, Thailand, United Kingdom, Spain, Malaysia and Mexico.

Now there are more that we could add to this for sure, and as countries get more ETFs that trade better we could certainly add more in here. But this gets back to what we are really trying to do. We are trying to identify where the money is flowing around the world. It's not necessarily a fair statement to say that just because the FXI – which is the China ETF – is going up that Taiwan is going to go up and Hong Kong is going to go up as well, but if you have enough representation in the region it has worked.

Yes, I understand that. Have you tried to do this for commodities?

That's our Global Macro portfolio. The Global Macro model includes a handful of commodities and a handful of currencies.

We don't have a portfolio that specifically has the commodities and try to do that. We just haven't done it. We might at some point but we actually branched from the ETFs to the stocks - the NASDAQ 100 - primarily because we wanted to be able to leverage the fact if it works in stocks then certain traders will like to use it to trade stocks and the options for stocks, which are much better.

There are a lot of people who invest according to the "Dogs of the Dow" strategy. Out of curiosity, have you ever tried to test this on the Dow 30 stocks to see whether it outperforms the Dogs of the Dow strategy?

We haven't done the Dow stocks yet. We have started with the NASDAQ stocks because we felt that those were going to be more dynamic stocks in general. With the NASDAQ we do the top five stocks instead of the top three although you could use the top three and you'd do pretty well there, too. But again, with the ability to be a little more diversified and also be able to perhaps manage more money with five stocks rather than just three we went for five.

There is one thing that we've left out here. I almost feel like I'm hiding this, but I knew we'd get to it and that is this. It actually came up as I was reading through these names. I left out a few because we haven't talked about it yet.

Going back to how we decide what to buy we want to be in the top three, but we don't want to be in the top three if the top three are going down, right? There is no point, at least from our perspective, in just being long the strongest instruments in your universe if everything is going down.

If the U.S. market is just going in the basement then it's time to not be in any sector, right? There are a couple of ways that we deal with bear markets. First of all, we have in almost every model – I think in every model except for the NASDAQ – a bond component. We have TLTs or the TMFs. The TMFs are a triple that represent the TLTs, which in turn represent the 20-year Treasuries.

And so if we go back to the sector example, if the stocks are going down because nobody wants to own stocks then typically that means that investors are going to run for cover in bonds. If the bonds now become one of our top three then it's either a hedge or it's just almost an outright short.

In 2008, it was pretty much that being short the market was the same thing as being long the bonds. And so, we have the bonds and we also have the reverse ETFs such as the SDS (which is twice the inverse of the SPY return) if that becomes the leader.

The last rule to keep ourselves out of trouble is that if our trend strength indicator is negative then we won't buy anything. Earlier in our conversation I said that we are very strict about looking at having three buckets and so one of those buckets could very well be cash. It could also very well be one of the short ETFs or the bonds so that when markets roll over and go down – they have to go into a pretty protracted bear market for this really to pay off – it has been an important way for the model to not get crushed in the bear markets.

In 2008 when the financial system cratered I think one of our sector models was down 5% or 6% and the other one was actually up 5% or 6%. That's not because the sectors were doing well. It's because we got short. So that provides a balance and that's really important with any model where you are going to follow relative strength.

Our experience has been - and even from looking at the research of others - that the investors who do really well over long periods of time are the ones who figured out how to not have huge drawdowns where either they are going to quit the system or they are going to create a situation where they just lose too much money to recover from.

Is this all automated, and can you give us a rundown of the simple rules that you follow?

It's all automated and we have the rules dictate what the trades are going to be.

Can you sort of give us a rundown of what the trading algorithm is? For instance, step one is to rate all twenty-one ETFs for trend strength. Step two is to put your money in the top three. Step three is that if one of them drops out … Step four is that if the market trend is negative … If you could run it all down in this simple fashion then people might understand it better.

Yeah, you've already got it.

Well, except for the negative part that if it drops out and then gets back in, like …

Okay, I'll fill in the details.

Okay.

So now you know that not only do we have the sectors, but we also have reverse ETFs. We have a couple - not a lot - and the kind of question you get is, "Why don't you have reverse ETFs for every sector?" That's not our objective. Our objective is not to try and catch the ups and the downs of any particular sector for the sake of trading the sector, right? Our objective is to find the trends that are going to persist that are driven by the business cycle or bigger picture trends.

We've got the bonds to protect us when the big picture trend for equities is negative. We've got the inverse of the S&P 500 (the SPY) for when the trend for equities is negative and then we have the

ETF sectors. Then we have the trend momentum indicator, which we call the TSI, the Trend Strength Index Indicator. It's nothing fancy but is what it is so that's what we call it.

At the end of every day we rate our twenty-one ETFs - longs, shorts, bonds and sectors - based on the TSI. The top three are the ones that we want to invest in as a position assuming that they are all positive. If there is negative momentum as measured by TSI then we will not buy it. It doesn't happen very often, but it does happen. The reason it doesn't happen very often is because if things are really bad then we usually have strong TSI ratings on the stuff that is a reverse ETF for bonds. So if it is negative then you don't get in. That protects you.

Once you got your three positions then in order to get kicked out of a position you need to fall by a certain amount of volatility below the ETF that is ranked number four or number five. Again the reason for that is because when you are dealing with momentum-based trends you want to give an ETF the opportunity to pull back a little bit, reset, and then keep going as opposed to getting chopped up getting in and getting out of a number three or four or five position that keeps flip-flopping back and forth. If you do that you'll just be frustrated and you will just churn the account. You may not lose a lot of money except for commissions, but it will cost you money and it's not worth the aggravation.

You've got your top three. If you only have two then you're in cash in your third position. If you only have one then you're in cash for your other positions. Those are the trading rules.

There is yet one other trading rule to make it even simpler. We get in and get out on the open. At the end of the day when we determine that we need to make a position change then the next morning we get in on the open.

It is really tempting for traders - and myself included as a trader - to try and outsmart that. Sometimes you can but we have found that from an automated perspective we haven't found a better way to get in or get out then just getting in on the open and getting out on the open.

That's your pure rotational model. Then the only thing you need to layer onto that - and I shouldn't say the only thing but this is an important thing - is your position sizing. We allocate equal dollar weighted positions to each of the three buckets.

The next question would be what happens when one particular bucket gets much bigger than another one? Let's say that position number one is the position that keeps winning and position number three is the one that never really goes anywhere. Pretty soon you've got position one that has made significantly more money than position three. In that situation then you would rebalance and even up all your positions.

We have done a lot of work on how important rebalancing is and how frequently you need to rebalance. I've actually read other people who have come to the same conclusion as us that you can rebalance twice a year and you'll be fine. You can rebalance more frequently and it may help your overall performance a little bit, but you have to weigh that against the commissions and the slippage and the aggravation of rebalancing – essentially buying some and selling some of your positions just to get them to be equal dollar weighted. If you rebalance twice a year then you're good to go.

That's one of the numbers I found when I was doing research on automated relative strength trading systems, but I'm confused about one thing. You said that when you're out of stocks then the money is in the bond ETF, but you just said that you're putting it into cash.

If there isn't one that is a positive then you are going to be in cash.

Okay.

You may have a situation in the market where the TSIs are just negative and even the bonds are negative so there is nothing to buy. If there's nothing to buy, well let's say you've only got one thing that's positive. You don't put all your money in that one positive thing. In that case you've also got two buckets of cash, two positions of cash. One position is whatever that ETF is and the other two positions are cash.

What's the track record of your system?

Before I do that, now you understand how the pure rotation works, right?

Right.

Here's what we found. A lot of traders don't feel comfortable with the position of, "Hey, you'll get out when some other ETF becomes the new leader." The question from the traders is, "How will I know when that is?" The answer is that you don't. To make it more dramatic it's like, "Trust me, a new leader will come in before you lose too much money." That didn't fly with a lot of traders so we developed a second way of trading this, which we call "stops and targets."

I bring this up now because you asked me about the performance and because now you also understand the buckets. Now imagine that rather than only getting out of a position when a new leader comes in and replaces it, you now get out of a position because you get stopped out and you get stopped out based on an initial risk level of 15%. We never want any position to lose more than 15%. As it turns out, the biggest loss we've ever had without stops per se, just rotating, was 20% and the average loss is more like 10%.

Even though it can sound a little scary to not have a traditional stop, you do tend to be out in very manageable risk levels. But with the stops and targets model we have stops and then we also have targets. They hit certain targets so we'll scale out over three different targets. In that environment we have situations where you easily have two positions that are sitting in cash because you have been stopped out and you trade the exact same three, so the basic rotation model is dictating which ETFs you'll be in.

It's just that if you want to be more conservative and have a stop - so you can sleep at night knowing that if everything falls apart in the morning you are going to be out at a certain level - we have those two different models. The interesting thing is that the stops and targets model does not do as well but the equity curve is smoother.

For the basic model, we started testing it going back as far as we could while still having decent ETFs, and this pretty much left us back at the beginning of 2007. We were able to be in this model during the financial crisis. If you had started in 2007 and followed the method I just described then right now you'd be up 750%. If you followed the method that included getting stopped out and taking profits and profit targets then you would be up 620%.

To put that in perspective, the S&P 500 over that same period is up 46%. There have been a lot of ups and downs during that time but the SPY was really only up 46% from that time frame versus over 700% and over 600% if you are following the relative momentum system.

Have you put your own money into this system?

We backtested it and we came up with this in 2013. We backtested it so from the end of 2013 until now we have been trading it in real time and the results have continued to perform just as they did historically.

So 2014 would be the first year of no backtesting, all real time, and the SPY was up 11% while our basic model was up 45% and the stops and targets model was up 17%.

Have the real time results matched exactly, within a percent or so, of the model results so far?

It's the same.

Okay, pretty much the same.

Except for maybe slippage, but I guess what I'm saying is that in 2014 we didn't have the benefit - if you could call it that - of saying, "What if we do this?" and "What if we change this? What would it look like?" That performance is what it was because we couldn't go back and make any changes.

If you as a person were following this and the model got 45%, did you get 45% exactly? Only if you literally followed everything to the T, bought it on the open, and then you have to take out some of your commissions because we haven't factored commissions into these numbers.

Basically it's working exactly according to plan is what I hear you saying. It's returning exactly what the model says it should return with a tolerance for slippage and commissions. Do you know the compound annual rate of return?

We have it, but not off the top of my head. I'm not sure exactly what it is right now but it's in the twenties. I want to say 24% but I'd have to check.

What about the NASDAQ?

That's the ETF one. For the NASDAQ we couldn't go back all the way to 2007 because of data issues, and here again this is an important point about the integrity of the model.

The NASDAQ right now represents well over a hundred stocks. Even though they called it the "NASDAQ 100" to represent one hundred companies, some of the companies have more than one type of share that's in it, but that's not important for this conversation. The NASDAQ 100 has one hundred stocks, but we started tracking it back in 2008 and only forty-eight of the stocks in 2008 when we started are still in it.

It's really important when you are testing something like this that you actually know which stocks were in the index during the period that you are testing. There have actually been over two hundred stocks in the index during the period in which we've been testing it or trading it. We couldn't go back much further than 2008 at this point simply because we didn't have enough reliable data to be able to do it right so this model starts beginning in 2008.

It's been up 475% versus the QQQ, which is the ETF for the NASDAQ 100 that is itself up 147%. The model is up a little bit more than triple the performance of the overall index itself. We only just finished backtesting this model a couple months ago so in terms of real time trading it is just beginning.

The countries ETF model started in the beginning of 2007 and is up 279% since 2007. In this case we compare the performance of the countries model to the MSCI world index because that's kind of the benchmark for global equity performance, and since 2007 the MSCI is up 21%.

Basically what we are saying here is that if you just bought a world index - the benchmark world index in 2007 – you would be up 21% as opposed to buying the leading relative strength country ETFs where you are up 280%.

It's about ten times higher for being in the leading three countries, right?

Yes, the leading three. Right.

Why doesn't the county model do better than the U.S. sectors model? I'm guessing the reason this doesn't do as well as the U.S. sectors is because, and correct me if I'm wrong, you have some S&P sectors that are leveraged.

Yes, that is a big part of it, but also the sectors in general are going to be more volatile than the overall market. If you just think about our own market it is a lot easier for the semiconductors or the drugs or any sector to be up 30%, 40%, and 50% for the year. You don't get that in the whole index.

With the countries you are buying the whole country index so you just don't get the same level of volatility. Now in some of these lesser-developed countries you do get some pretty wild moves, but you're just not dealing with the same level of volatility in each individual instrument.

If you were to take our Complete Model then the track record is as follows. In the Complete the ETF sectors are one third of the strategy, the countries are another third of the strategy, and our Global Macro is another third of the strategy. You use all those in the Complete Model and then you have got nine positions instead of three. That is up 420% since 2007, which again is relative to the S&P's 46%.

How often is each model doing a possible trade so we can get an idea of how long the trade usually lasts? I want people to understand how easy it is to do this.

For the Countries Model the average trade length is about 110 or 120 days. You are not getting very many trades in the Country Model at every 120 days. You're getting about seven to fifteen trades a year.

In the Sectors Model I think it is about 60 days. In the ETF Sectors Model it's more like 20 to 30 different trades a year.

In the Global Macro you're talking about 50-60 trades in a year.

And for the U.S. sectors you can trade any day?

Yes.

For the Country Model you can trade any day but for the NASDAQ you are only looking at it once a month?

Yes, at the end of the month.

And that still holds when you combine it all together in the big boy?

Well, the NASDAQ model doesn't go into the big Complete strategy. NASDAQ is its own strategy, and a cool thing about the NASDAQ strategy is that we did the ETF strategy first. We did the ETF sectors first and that worked. As I was explaining previously we kind of knew it would work because we didn't invent this. It just makes total sense. It is common sense if you can get the execution down, which is not easy. I don't want to mislead anybody to think it's easy to figure all this stuff out, but it is a lot easier when you know that it's being done and you have seen it done.

So we did the ETF sectors model and it worked great. We thought this is probably going to work on countries and it did. Then we put the system in the Global Macro portfolio so that we would have more exposure to non-equity related trends and that worked, too.

We then combined those into the big ETF Complete. The reason we did that was to see whether or not the reduced volatility of the countries would balance out the Sectors and the Global Macro model results and provide a smoother equity curve and as it turns out it did. The performance falls right in-between that of the ETF sectors and Countries models and the equity curve is smoother.

I think the max drawdown on the ETF Complete portfolio is somewhere in the area of 15%, which is outstanding. It hasn't had a losing year and when the markets melted down in 2008 the ETF Complete was actually up 20%. It's down marginally this year, but its worst year has been 8% up. That's why we put them all together and then after that we moved on to the stocks.

We think it's important to really understand the basket that you are measuring as opposed to just measuring everything you know. *Investor's Business Daily* and *Value Line* will give you relative strength measures for every stock in the index and it's relative to every other stock in the index. This is a great tool and I'm a big fan of both of those companies, but there is a big difference between just taking every stock in the index or every stock in the exchange and saying, "Whichever one has the strongest twelve-month percentage change is the one I want to be in."

That's a far cry from saying we are just going to focus on the NASDAQ 100 quality companies. The exchange has already vetted them. The highest market cap stocks are primarily tech stocks, but not entirely tech anymore and we are just going to buy the leaders there. This is a totally different approach and as I said numerous times if you are really going to do this then it's really important to have a good definition of your universe. We are absolutely not just casting out a huge net and saying, "Give me the strongest of everything." That would be a big mistake.

Now our members understand your basic trading methodology. Who can stick with executing this and who is going to be most successful with this trading methodology based on your experience?

That's a really good question and I feel like I spent a lot of time coaching members on this very subject. The person who does the best with this is the person who looks at their portfolio and views their assets as assets and not as trades. The value of doing a model like this is understanding that you are following it for tested performance reasons rather than just going out and buying a random ETF or random growth stock or just the market in general.

If you just want to put your money in stocks and see how your decision worked out after two, three, four or five years then you should just go out and buy the index. If you can do that and not worry about it then you should just do that. If you would like to outperform that and you want to be a little bit more active and you are willing to sit over time then this is something that would suit you.

The way I like to describe how to do this is to look at it as if you are the type of person who would go out and buy a growth stock because you like the story and you are going to sit with the stock even if it pulls back 20% on you. You are not trading it short-term and you have a long-term view of a couple of years. Then rather than go out and buy that growth stock - which you know may or may not go up 50% or 100% over three to five years - and rather than be subject to quarterly earnings reports or be subject to those little CEO slip-ups that crush the company stock because it's something stupid … rather than subject yourself to that environment then this is another alternative.

That's because it has similar volatility. It has demonstrated that it has had years where it has been up 8% or even down a few percent, but it had years where it was up 80%. So you have the volatility there and you have the diversification of buying an ETF. Hence, if there is an earnings miss or if there is a CEO blunder then you are not going to get clocked for 20% in one day because you happen to be in a wrong growth stock.

If that's your mentality then you might take a chunk of your assets to do this. We call it a "portfolio" but that doesn't mean this should be your entire portfolio. It means it should be one investment approach and it should be an investment approach where you are looking out over holding this trading style for a couple of years. The people who get in trouble are the ones who say - and I've had quite a few of these – "Well, if it makes money for me in the next thirty days then I'll keep it. If it doesn't then I'll dump it."

To that person I say, "don't even do it" because if it makes money in the first thirty days for you that is not a fair judge. If it loses money in the first thirty days it is not a fair judgment either. You really have to look at it over the period of at least a year.

Now I don't have these stats for all the models, but we just did these stats for the NASDAQ 100. The statistic was that if you were to just randomly pick a week to get started in the NASDAQ 100 system and you say, "This is where I'm starting. What are the chances that twelve months from now I'm going to be ahead?" then looking at 370 weeks the chances of you being ahead twelve months later are 95%, so that's pretty good. Seventy percent of those weeks you will have outperformed the overall market as well.

One of the reasons that we have really pushed towards the automated systems is because this is where we want our trading to be. I'd like to be able to personally just throw a dart at a list of stocks and know that the list of stocks that I'm throwing the dart at has some kind of a statistical edge. That's the mentality that I think represents the best person for this type of system. It's longer-term. It's looking for some kind of an edge. I could relate it to perhaps the way some more traditional people think in terms of investing in low P/E stocks or stocks that have strong growth. When you have that mentality you are not getting shaken out because the stock has a bad hair day or bad earnings announcement, right? You believe that you have an edge by buying a company that is growing.

The analogy here is that we have an edge and we are buying the ETFs or the companies whose price momentum is growing. Not necessarily the fundamentals but the psychology behind the movement of the stock - the price momentum - is growing. When we get into a NASDAQ 100 stock, statistically in the first thirty days if we were to just trade the first thirty days - we buy it on day one and sell it on day thirty - our average gain will be somewhere in the area of 1.6 times our average loss and our percentage of correct trades is somewhere in the area of 60%.

There again I can throw a dart at that list of stocks and if I throw enough darts I'm going to make money. I don't have to interpret a chart. I don't have to do anything other than figure out who is the strongest in the group that we've determined that we are going to watch.

That's what I think is the best mentality for following systems like this. It's really a belief in the reasons for why you are doing it that are going to keep you in when you have a 15% or even a 20% drawdown. Those drawdowns will happen. If you are a trader who is trying to time the market and avoid those drawdowns then it won't matter with existing systems or anything else. If you're not prepared for the max drawdown then you're not prepared to trade the system.

I agree with your philosophy one hundred percent and always tell people that one part of your portfolio might be devoted to trading, a portion might be devoted to long-term investments, and one section can be automated if the track record of that system or set of systems is excellent. If it's going to be automated you should only use robust systems that have been tested. Geoff, aside from this type of investing, what would do for other parts of your portfolio?

I can't speak for Keith but I can speak about what I do. Admittedly I'm perhaps a bit jaded because I came out of college and started as a commodities trader. I wouldn't recommend that as a normal course of action because as a commodities trader you quickly get a perspective on how leverage works and how quickly you can make or lose money and you also become extremely technical most likely. So it actually has taken me a long time to really embrace fundamental investing, which I enjoy as much as I enjoy the automated and day trading.

Personally I have part of my assets in this type of automated trading and we are building out these models so we have more options for ourselves and for our customers, but I still enjoy picking stocks for the long term which some people would call "buy and hold." I don't call this investing "buy and hold," but I have stuff that I've held for years just based on fundamental beliefs in the trends that have nothing to do with this.

I have an active part of my portfolio where I'll be in and out of trades within the course of a day or several days. I literally do thousands of trades a year and this system that I'm just describing to you isn't going to be more than a hundred if I do all of them.

For me, I like to have certain stocks that I think for my own reasons have good timing on them. When the financials, for example, were really beaten up I picked a couple stocks that I thought were in it for the long term, such as JP Morgan and Wells Fargo. I've been in those things for what feels like forever for me. They have dividends, they are financials and so that's part of my portfolio. I have kids' money that sits in a 529 saving for college plan. I have nothing to say about that one because that's just another way to make sure there is money sitting there.

Right now I think that energy is where the financials were years ago. Could they go lower, could oil go lower, and could this be an extended period of depressed prices for a lot of equities in the energy space? Yes, it could be, but this is also the time to buy if you are the type of a person who is looking to buy something when it's cheap and "the blood is running in the streets" as the Wall Street expression goes.

For me I look at that kind of a balance. I think everybody has to understand, like I was just saying, that you have to believe in this particular approach. This is just one approach and it can work with any other group of approaches to the market.

If I were to tell my parents, for example, that they should do this they would take it to their financial adviser. He would say, "Well you know if you want to do this with your play money then you could do it with your play money, but the rest of it is going to be in your dividends stocks."

Are you investing in those stocks because they are undervalued stocks and they will bounce back or because they will pay dividends and keep throwing of cash into the future?

At the time I bought them for both reasons. JP Morgan and Wells Fargo are really good examples and that's why I brought them up. In 2009, the market completely fell apart and the financials collapsed leading the way, right? Then everything kind of bounced back and the financials had a period where they kind of went sideways for a couple of years.

In October of 2011 they kind of came down to the bottom of a big range. The markets pulled back pretty substantially and there certainly was a feeling on the street like, "Oh, no! Oh, no! Here we go again like in 2008. It's all going to happen again."

My perspective on it was, "No, this is not going back to those levels." You know this is a time where you look around and you find companies that are getting beaten up unnecessarily if they don't have a good dividend, such as in the case of the financials. If they don't have a good dividend now then they will come back.

As for me I was not doing Graham and Dodd analysis by the book. I was just looking for companies - in this case in the financial space - because that was what was just being thrown out and likely to have a strong dividend going forward. That just gave me more of a reason to hold it. In the case of JP Morgan's Jamie Dimon I just believed in the guy so that's why I liked that stock.

As to Wells Fargo, if housing was going to come back then Wells Fargo was going to be there. I had to believe that was going to be one of the companies that would survive and thrive. You know the reason we are talking about this, I think, is because here I'm the same person who is saying, "You should be completely automated."

Even when day trading I have really specific rules even if a computer is not executing them although we have computers that will do that, too. Even if the computers are not executing them I have really specific rules as to when I get in and when I get out. But I also have a part of my portfolio devoted to thinking like, "You know what? Jamie Dimon, JP Morgan, the financials, … they all add up to now being a good time to hold your nose and buy some."

What are you doing for day trading given that you have done all this automated stuff?

I'm a trader. I like to play like everybody else who has the luxury of being able to sit in front of a screen and trade when they want or turn another direction and not trade on any given day. Ever since starting with Keith on the floor we have been focused on what we call the opening range. That's the first five minutes or the first thirty minutes of the trading day. Anybody who is an active trader should understand the statistical edge that exists around the first thirty minutes of the trading day.

What I mean by that is that if you watch how markets trade around that first thirty minutes - and then around the first five minutes when you get a little better at it - there are patterns that will help you determine which days are going to be trend days and which days are not going to be trend days.

For me day trading is a combination of hopefully getting into a swing trade at a great price. Sometimes you take it at the end of the day and sometimes I let it develop into a swing trade.

Can you give me any idea of what those rules are?

We are not looking at the charts today, but here is a perfect example of how everything comes together with what we were just talking about. Here is a perfect example that pulls everything together outside of the automated systems.

I tell our members that one of the things you are going to find when you start trading with an automated system, like the ETF sector model, is that there is a benefit to it that you would never have expected to have gotten. That benefit is that you no longer have to figure out when and why to get in or get out of a trade. You can no longer beat yourself up for second-guessing or for not doing what you should have done, or doing what you should have done because if you follow the model then all that goes away.

We have been looking at automated systems for years and years and years. We have also been executing them with very specific rules, but many have not been as backtested as we have been with the closed group of twenty-one ETFs. Every single possible market opportunity or market condition since 2007 is encompassed in that system. So that's it. You just have to follow it as opposed to day trading rules where there is no way we could possibly have tested the rules against all the stocks on the exchange. We just couldn't. We know it works because we have been doing it, but there is still judgment in it even though we have systems that will execute all the rules. Right? So that's the automated part.

Now here is an example of something I literally did today. Schlumberger (SLB) happens to be one of the stocks that I want to be in just like JP Morgan and Wells Fargo from four years ago. I'm trying to time my way into it and like most traders, this isn't one where I'm not ready to hold my nose and just buy it like I did with the financials. However, I don't think I have to do that with Schlumberger because I think once it gets going then I'll have it at a really tight stop, and if it runs then great and if it doesn't it'll stop me out.

So here is what happened today. I've been in this thing small since it had a reversal on the 18th of this month about two weeks ago. I bought a little there, I bought some more and sold some as it kind of ebbs and flows. Today it has gapped higher and so did the market. It pulled back in the first thirty minutes, so I look at the first 30-minute range and that 30-minute range should be the high and the low for the day. If it's not, which obviously is not always the case, if it's not and it breaks that range then that's telling you that breaking to the upside is a bullish mode and you want to follow it. If it breaks on the downside then it's in a bearish mode and you want to follow it.

Now I just told you I want to buy Schlumberger. I don't want to sell Schlumberger. So there are two patterns, two basic patterns. One is the breakout and one is the reversal. Today Schlumberger gapped higher, pulled back, and established a 30-minute opening range that was right above the prior day's high.

Now when you break your 30-minute opening range low and you come right back into the 30-minute opening range then that is a reversal pattern. There are more specific patterns you can look at on a 5-minute chart, but essentially that is the big picture. When it did that today and did so right on top of yesterday's high, which is key support, and it's also doing so right around the 50-day moving average then I bought it. I bought it and I put a stop in.

So now I'm adding to an existing position, I put a stop in below the low of the day, and for me that's exactly what I would do with the day trade while my target would be the high of the day. Quite frankly, had we not been having this conversation, and I'm looking at the chart, I probably would have sold some of it against the high of the day and taken out 70¢ of profits on a risk that was probably about 50¢ and then I would let the other half go until tomorrow. And so, there I have just added to a position with what would have been a day trade. If it didn't rally and close well then I would have just sold it out, kept what I have, and try again when I have another good opportunity like that.

That's what I mean by getting into a position with always having a really low risk with those day trading tactics of using the opening range and rules for where I am going to set my stop. It has to do with both the high and low of the day and a percentage of the stock's average true range (ATR). Those have to be in alignment otherwise I'm risking too much, and I'm going to have targets. Once it gets to half an ATR (average true range) and a full ATR then I get to start thinking, "I should probably take some profits here" if this is a day trade. If it's a swing trade then I'll let it run. If it's a huge position trade then I want to let it run even further.

I didn't have to go searching for SLB. It's just on my list because it's one of the big stocks I'm watching. Everything came together today. I didn't have to think about it. I know my pattern, took the trade and with any luck tomorrow it will be fully broken above its 50-day moving average. The probing I've been doing for the last week will now have resulted in a nice swing position that with any luck will turn out such that maybe I'm right and this is the low in oils and we'll be talking in two years where I'll be joking, "Yeah, you know I still have some of that SLB I picked up when we were talking on that interview."

That's how it all comes together, but just by virtue of the fact that it took me all that time to tell you what I did you can see that it's a lot of work, right? You have to like that to do this.

That's wonderful. You're trading the SLB because it was already on your targeted watch list?

Well, I gave you that one because it's an example of how everything we were just talking about - different parts of your portfolio - came together. Yes.

And for your day trading rules, I didn't get all of them but is that pretty much the major trading rule that you look at?

I start with the opening range and work out from there. We've got numerous free books on the concept of the opening range. If you keep it simple then it's really simple.

Start with the first thirty minutes of the day. That's your range. The bulls are in control if you go outside of it to the upside. The bears are in control if you go outside of it on the downside.

Now, if you are looking at a day trade you don't want to fight a bigger trend. Play the direction of the bigger trend with your opening range. So, in a different scenario, IBB, I did the same thing today.

Now this happens to be an ETF that also happens to be one of our holdings for the automated system. I know right there that I like the major trend, but it did the same thing. It gapped higher. It established the 30-minute opening range and then it broke its 30-minute opening range but came right back up to it.

When the bears are theoretically in control as I just described and it's below its 30-minute opening range then I don't want to be a buyer because it could be one of those days where it declines. Remember, even in bull markets stocks have to go down. That's the day I don't want to be a buyer, but when it comes back into the opening range and I can put a stop under the low of the day and now I'm trading with the trend then now that's my day trade to get into IBB. If the market continues to head higher then this thing should head higher, too.

I do this with the indexes all the time. Even if I don't have specific stocks that I'm looking at then I look at the indexes. When I say the indexes I mean the SPYs, the QQQs, the DIAs and you can do it with the futures like the E-minis.

If you look at the world, or if you look at markets through the lens of that first thirty minutes of the day it will keep you out of pretty much every day that gets you decimated as long as you just have a rule that under the 30-minute opening range you do not want to be long as a day trade. Then you won't get killed. And be careful about when you do breakouts because there are certain times in the market where you know markets don't follow through, but you will learn that if you watch the opening range.

Those are fantastic rules for day traders. Thank you. You mentioned that you have some ebooks about this on your website?

Yes. If people go to MarketGauge.com you can find some free ebooks that will rotate. Sometimes it's a swing book but there is a day trading ebook, too, which is the opening range book, the opening range handbook. Then I just put out a book on how to buy at the low of the day.

Are there any other books that you recommend for people to read or websites if they want to get into automated trading, day trading, value investing or any other field of investing? Other than these ebooks, what are the most valuable websites or books that you would direct people towards reading?

I'm always fond of telling people, and most traders will say the same thing, that if you want to be an active trader then *Reminiscences of a Stock Operator* by Jesse Livermore is a great book on psychology.

If you want to follow momentum in a systematic way then *The Way of the Turtle*, which is the book about Richard Dennis's experiment, is an incredible introduction to the power of a trading system that is really simple. It's a demonstration of how you could give a successful trading system - that two guys made hundreds of millions of dollars with - to thirty people and some people would go on to make incredible careers out of it and others will fail miserably with it. Why, right? If you are interested in trading systems then I think that is a book that doesn't get enough recognition.

If you are interested in fundamental longer-term patterns and earnings and stuff like that I've always been a huge fan of William O'Neil and *IBD (Investor's Business Daily)*. His book, *How to Make Money in Stocks,* is not for the trader necessarily but I guess it depends on your background. If you come from the buy and hold camp it certainly sounds like a trading book, but the way Bill O'Neil puts together earnings and price momentum is a good perspective on markets as well.

Have you ever tried to take the IBD ratings and try to come up with a system using those numbers?

Until we had the resources we currently have it was hard, but I have been following that and at various times for twenty years in my career tried to put something together. The thing that I found difficult with following *IBD* or really anything like that is the following.

Let's say you take *IBD's* ranking of the fifty stocks of the week. It just takes so much effort to track what those fifty stocks of the week are and it's impossible to go back and backtest it. You basically have to keep a record of what those stocks are for years in order to be able to go back and look at it and it just becomes too much work.

You don't know this but I collected *Barron's* from the time that I was in college until about fifteen years later. I had every single *Barron's* in print because I'm such a nut about all the data that was in there so I couldn't let it go. I had spreadsheets collecting it all. I got a lot of flack from my college roommates for holding onto stacks of *Barron's.* It's a good thing I've always worked for myself because otherwise I'm sure the boss would have thrown me and my *Barron's* right out on the street. It wasn't until I finally embraced the fact that maybe I'd be able to get it all on computer - I think that was in 2005 - that I threw them all away. It was a sad day.

Yes, to answer your question I have tried but found it too cumbersome to get the *IBD* data going back without doing something like that. I would save *Barron's* and that would actually be another publication. It's not a book but I would read *Barron's.* I've read *Barron's* since I was in high school and I've learned a ton.

And you would read *Barron's* for what?

Everything. You never know what you are going to learn in there. Financial journalist Alan Abelson isn't around anymore. I learned so much from his sarcasm and the way he put things together in the markets. If you want to hear about the economy then Gene Epstein's articles cover the economy. You never know what you are going to learn from him. They really have insightful writers.

They have really become mainstream in probably the last ten years now. If you look at their cover it reads more like a money magazine group of headlines where they are really focused on why is this particular stock going to go up and by how much? And you'll get their analysis.

You would prefer them over *IBD* or *The Wall Street Journal*?

IBD is great if you like data. *The Wall Street Journal* in my opinion is great if you like news. *Barron's* is really great if you want to learn insights into how to analyze markets and stocks. You'll find articles in there that deal with relative strength investing from time to time. They will also interview somebody who will talk about why he is looking at the markets in a certain way.

I had countless *Barron's* issues where I would have notes on the front cover like "come back to this indicator" or "come back to this way of looking at sizing up a financial stock." It contained things like how do you look at or how do you measure the value of a financial stock versus an energy stock versus a REIT?

If that kind of stuff interests a trader then read *Barron's*. The way that this becomes valuable to me is this. Here is another thing that we taught day traders, which is something that I learned from *Barron's*. Before you had the TV doing it for you a company would come out with earnings and they would miss by a penny and the stock would get absolutely hammered. It didn't make any sense to the novice that they missed by one penny and they got hammered.

Well, they are getting hammered because Wall Street's expectation was such that they pushed it as far as they could. The fact that they couldn't even get one more penny out of their earnings report when they pushed it means that this is all they have got guys. If they can't even get one more penny then if this is a momentum stock the game is probably turning.

Analysis like that is something you generally don't get from *The Wall Street Journal* and you would never hear that on a normal news channel. You might now but ten years ago you would never hear that, but in *Barron's* you would get an interview with someone and he would explain that.

Because you asked me what book would I read or what book would I recommend to learn then if somebody picks up *Barron's* every week and says, "This is my college course on how to navigate the markets" it could be that.

What about magazines? Would you recommend *Forbes* or *Fortune* or anything like that?

I don't read them frequently enough to say anything good or bad about them. I pick them up once in a while, but if you ask me what I go spend my money on the answer is *Barron's*. I get it every week.

As to *IBD* the only reason I don't get the subscription is because I don't have enough time to read it, but I will get it on the weekends because I like the data. I get *The Wall Street Journal* every day because it's got the news, but the thing that I would learn the most from is *Barron's*.

You have given us the automated method for trading the ETFs. Have you guys programmed it up such that you offer MarketGauge.com signals that people can trade on their own? Is there a fund or Portfolio Cafe (PortfolioCafe.com) portfolio that people could invest in so they don't have to do this themselves?

You know we are working on that but we are not really allowed to market it. We do have a subscription service where the service provides all the history and real time portfolio alerts when any of the positions change. It also provides monthly coaching on how to deal with some of issues that we talked about. For instance, what kind of a person are you? How do you trade this? How much do you allocate to it without being a financial advisor, which I can't be?

That is the way someone can currently use it. We don't currently take money to manage for them. Keith has a private fund, but we are not allowed to say, "Hey, we can market this." As for right now we have to be registered. So, people can subscribe to the service and get the signals and follow the model on their own very easily.

Do you have a lot of subscribers?

We do. We have several hundred.

That's a lot. Okay, now an important question for those just starting out. If you had somebody in front of you, maybe it's a young kid or someone in their twenties or thirties, what would you tell them for how they should grow their wealth with all the investments and investing or trading methods available in the world? You've done day trading, you've done dividend stocks, value stocks, position stocks, automated trading, and so forth so what's your big view and big advice?

I think that's a really good question. My advice would be that you need to invest your money in a way that is consistent with your personality. You should enjoy the way you do it but chances are that unless you really love doing it yourself you should find some way to make it happen without you getting in the way. If you like doing it then you should take a piece of whatever funds you have and do whatever is consistent with your personality.

What I mean by that is that if you like to trade short-term then trade short-term but figure out what suits your personality because a lot of people think, "Oh, this would be great. I'll just get in and get out doing short-term trading to make quick gains," but really they are not cut out for it and it takes a long time to learn how to do it.

They are much better off - unless that is really what they want to do – to just figure out how to do simple stuff like this rotational strategy that we are talking about. Like finding strong ETFs - because now we have them (ETFs) - that represent big trends and just follow them.

But more than that consider the following. If you are not really into doing it yourself then as much as people will beat up the financial community you are probably better off getting somebody else to do it for you because it's just so easy to lose money. Take it slow and have a long-term view. The short-term view is deadly. You have got to love doing it yourself otherwise I think it is just deadly.

Are you saying that if you are going to do short-term trading you have got to love it and really be on top of it for day trading, otherwise just stay away? Is that what you are saying?

Yes, or just stay away entirely. I'm a person who is helping people do this so I see the people who are successful at it and I see the people who are never going to be successful at it. The biggest difference between those two groups is the person's dedication to really enjoying it.

The guy who comes to short-term trading - thinking he is going to do it because his broker just lost a bunch of money for him and now he's going to do it himself - is just making the same mistake in a different way. He is no better than his broker. Chances are that if his broker lost his money then his broker didn't know any more than he does, but you know what? He doesn't know any more than his broker so he is just going to lose it himself anyway.

I think a success key is recognizing that short-term trading and swing trading is not the answer unless you really like to do it and then recognizing that you are doing it because you like to do it. You should also still have part if not the majority of your assets in something that is just taking advantage of much bigger, bigger trends over time and takes advantage of time.

I'm saying this because you said the person is young. If you come to me and you are seventy years old then I'm not sure that would be the advice I would give you, but the young person should take advantage of time.

Don't think you are going to figure it all out. There are good people out there to manage money, but if you like it then get help to learn how you can do it and it's fun. There are some simple ways like these rotational strategies that can beat the market and they work.

Yes, they absolutely do indeed work. Geoff, if you had a magic wand and you could wave it to eliminate the negative traits of unsuccessful traders and amplify the positive characteristics of successful traders, what would you wave it for?

I'm trying to figure out the right way to say that you have to know when to take your losses. You have got to know when to take your losses. That's what gets people in the most trouble. There isn't a magic wand that would enable anyone to know when to take your losses. It's experience, right?

There could be a magic wand that would just help people to *realize* that is what they have to do. That's the first step. You have got *to realize* that that's what you have got to do before you can do it. You are not going to do it until you understand that's what you have got to do.

I like this opening range method for day trading. Is there anybody else doing what you guys are doing along those lines?

There are definitely people who look at the opening range from our day trading perspective. We are not the only ones who do that.

It was really popular among floor traders because if you think about it, and certainly back in 1990 when you didn't have computers, you had to basically do the charts in your head or have someone do it for you on paper, which is what I did for Keith when I started with point and figure charts. The opening range is a really easy way to evaluate the day's trend and so it is popular among floor traders. There is a great book on the opening range by Mark Fisher. I think it's called *The Logical Trader*. He was big on the opening range.

There are also a lot of people who look at relative strength investing. Like I said, we didn't invent it. The concept works. The trick, the difference between making it work and it not working really is in the execution, and those are some of the things that I tried to cover for you here.

Have you had any of your subscribers call up or write you and say, "Thank you, you have turned my life around in terms of trading because of your methodology"?

We have. For the relative strength stuff, which is about a year old now, we have had plenty of people who are really in love with it. As to having people come up and say, "You've changed our life," I can't say that we have had that yet.

However, the thing about the relative strength stuff and the automated system that we have found is this. We still teach people how to trade. Even though we are all automated we teach how to look at the markets and trade with discretion. That is where you get people saying, "Oh my gosh, I never realized that this is the way the markets work. You have changed my life and I'm doing great."

With the automated stuff now it's so black and white. It is just a percentage return. On one hand you talk about it being not necessarily pie in sky, but like "the answer," right? However the answer is no longer, "I'm going to make a the zillion dollars overnight." You're not. You are not going to. It's going to earn you a great return, but it's not going to be 300% a year, which is what a lot of traders go into trading thinking they are going to make.

You can teach many people how to trade and they still think they are going to make the 300% a year. If you teach them the automated system then now all of a sudden reality sets in, but the great part is that it's a good reality at least. It's a consistent return and it gets rid of the emotional stuff. It has so many benefits that the people who deal with trading the automated systems are much more grounded so they are not going to come to you and saying, "Oh, my gosh, you have just changed my life," but we have plenty of people who are really happy with it.

Thanks, Geoff. This has been a great interview with not just information on automated trading systems that are stable and offer high returns over the long run, but valuable because of the profile of who would succeed at this. Not just that, but you've also given day traders some useful information that will help them improve their trading, too. I wish you and Keith the best of luck. I hope we can talk again for an update in the future.

Chapter 13
Marvin Appel
Technical Analysis and Fund Management

Marvin Appel, the current editor of the Systems and Forecasts investment newsletter (started by his father Gerald Appel), manages investment funds for individuals using a variety of historically tested systems and indicators. By factoring market price, breadth and other indicators into his systems he is able to confirm market trends and dynamically adjust his portfolios for stock market risks. Basically, he has come up with tested technical ways to adaptively modulate his clients' exposure to the markets.

One of the few investment managers left who actually manages money with technical indicators (at Signalert Asset Management), Marvin explains the investment lessons he has learned over the years and what it really takes to succeed in capturing stock market profits with limited risk. A strong proponent of tested systems, Marvin provides yet another ETF sector rotation system that is far more profitable than an index fund. His main objective is always to match or exceed the risk-adjusted performance of the stock market.

Marvin, we know your dad became famous in the trading field. Why don't you tell us a little bit about him as well as what he produced for investors as a legacy. Then let's get into how you personally got into trading and the style of investing that you are using now. I want to know what progressed you to the point where you are today and especially want to hear what you investigated that you found didn't work as well as what worked that you are using now. I'm hoping you can summarize these sorts of notions to bring us to where you are now with your firm, Signalert, and what your investment methodology is all about.

Oh, thank you. My father got interested in the stock market in the late 1960s. The way he told me the story is that he got a stock tip from somewhere. He bought it, it went up, he felt like a genius and so he started buying other stocks and then lost money. Then he said, "Hold on, I have to figure this out," so he basically went about educating himself about the stock market to recapture the positive experience of making money and not getting burned again.

Part of that education was that he would read financial newspapers including one called *The Capitalist Reporter*. At one point he didn't like what he was reading in *The Capitalist Reporter* so he sent a letter to the editor saying, "I could do better than this." They sent him back a response, "Okay, well write for us." He ended up writing for *The Capitalist Reporter* under a number of pseudonyms and I'm not sure on what basis, but he actually had predicted the 1973-74 bear market well in advance. That was in print, so now he basically had a public track record.

In those days, the early '70s, writing financial newsletters was a very lucrative business. He started his newsletter, *Systems and Forecasts,* which I now edit forty-two years later. That was his main goal: to write an investment newsletter.

One of his subscribers said, "I like what you're doing, but I don't want to do it myself. Can you manage my money?" That's how he got into money management, and now basically the business is about investment management for individuals. We still write the newsletter and his original marketing plan was all based on getting subscribers who liked what they saw and who would hire him to manage their money.

In those days up until about fifteen or sixteen years ago, it was all about short-term trading. The market had a very high tendency that once it started to go up then it would continue to go up for long enough that you could trade on that. Then once it started to go down it would continue to go down long enough for you to get out of the way of a market decline in an early stage. The ideal trading system in those days - the '70s, '80s and '90s - used frequent trading with sensitive triggers to get in and out.

There were a limited number of mutual funds that would allow you to trade that way and especially in the late '90s they started clamping down on that, but that was the Holy Grail. Now the irony is that we now have ETFs - which means we can trade as frequently as we want - but the market doesn't behave the same way anymore so we have had to change the time frame of our trading decisions to be more swing and intermediate term, which is to say weeks to months of holding rather than just a few days. We have done this because the market doesn't have the same short-term correlations from one day to the next that it used to have. That was how he started, with basically trading mutual funds as quickly as a prospectus would allow him to trade them.

He also developed, in the late 1970s, the MACD indicator for which I think he is most famous. That is actually not a short-term trading indicator. That is a more intermediate-term indicator. Obviously you can apply it to intraday charts if you like, but we find that for trading diversified U.S. stock market vehicles like mutual funds and ETFs that it is best to do it on daily or weekly charts and then you are looking for holding periods of days to weeks or maybe to months.

He developed that in 1979 and that's one of the tools that we continue to use. The nice thing about MACD is that it is both a trend follower and an oscillator. You can use it to identify market trends smoothed of the shortest-term noise to get at the underlying trend, but you can also use it to recognize potential areas when the market has gone to an extreme and is at a possible turning point. That is his original contribution. It's still something that we use.

Myself, I grew up with this. In fact, when I was in high school and college I used to help dad with the algebra involved in predicting when the timing models would give signals. Basically, what are the levels that the market would have to touch in order to generate the buy and sell signal? You don't want to have to wait until the end of the day to calculate what's going on. You want to know, "Okay, if the NASDAQ closes tomorrow at 2,000 then that is a buy signal or whatever." I helped him with that as he was developing a lot of his systems and so I was always interested. My father was never one to leave the office. He took the office with him all the time so we were always talking about business at dinner and such so I grew up with this.

I actually started my career not in investing but in medical school, in graduate school. Did that, trained as an anesthesiologist, got board certified and got a PhD in biomedical engineering. Then in 1996, when I was done with all of that I was looking for a permanent job in the New York City area. The job market back then for anesthesiologists was very poor like the current situation. I said, "You know what? I always was curious about the business. The job prospects available to me at this time, as an anesthesiologist, aren't that appealing to me," so I decided to give the business a try. That was more than nineteen years ago and I'm still here.

We had, as I said, a lot of evolution to do over the past nineteen years because when I started it was all about short-term trading and technology stocks.

Yes, everything was about the fast movers back then.

Yeah, see it was about fast moving mutual funds. It had nothing to do with mutual fund stocks but the mutual funds that held them. It wasn't about valuation or anything. I was re-reading your interview with Charles Mizrahi and it was the opposite of his approach to value investing. You wanted stuff with momentum because you were in and out fast and you were riding on the trends.

When I started in 1996 that was the best moneymaker. Of course after the tech bubble burst in 2000 not only did that stop being the moneymaker, but as I said the market's behavior changed and the more rapid trading stopped working. We had to fly by the seat of our pants, basically, until we could develop slower systems that still had the degree of risk control that we had become accustomed to.

The comfortable thing about fast trading is that your loss on any one trade is likely to be very limited because if it takes a day or two of market decline to trip you out or a day or two of market rise to get you in then you are never far away from any big trend that may be emerging. Now there is no guarantee that trading fast means you are going to make money. In those days it was a good moneymaker but there was no guarantee. However, there is a certain comfort level of knowing that even if you guess wrong you are never very far, in a time or percentage way, from cutting your losses and getting out.

Problem is, of course, if the market is random on a day-to-day basis or even worse if it is mean reverting then all that short-term trend following is not going to help. That's the situation in which we found ourselves and so we had to adapt our trading systems to rely more on weekly data, not entirely, but more on weekly data and for fewer trades per year.

My father always used to say, "You basically win by not losing." You can't make the market go up but you can protect the client's money when the market is poised to go down. I believe that's still true. The important thing is to know that small fraction of the time when you really have to have a reduced exposure to the market because it is the most dangerous time and most of the other times, when the conditions are more hospitable, that's when you wait to see if the market goes up.

What are you guys now doing after having developed so many approaches over the years? What's your exact methodology for managing money? Are you managing portfolios or are you managing individual accounts? What is the mix of things that you are doing?

Okay, we manage individual accounts and investment partnerships but it is still based on technical analysis and we use a number of different indicators. One indicator that we use that's based on price is the death cross of the 50-day and 200-day simple moving average on the S&P 500. That happens to be on a sell right now and that is one of the price indicators we use. It cannot be the only indicator you use because most death cross sells actually occur near the end of market corrections rather than at the beginning except for in the case of the really major bear markets (like 1973, 1974 or 2000 or 2008), in which case the death cross gave you a timely exit.

For most run of the mill market corrections, when you see that death cross it is actually closer to the end than to the beginning, but it is still part of our arsenal because we want to make sure that any tools we use are the sort that would get us out in 2008. In fact we did mitigate our losses significantly during that bear market and we want to make sure to continue to do that if such an event should occur again which is far from certain but it could happen.

Other indicators that we used are based on market breadth, and right now it's an interesting time because the indexes are flirting with all time highs (cap weighted indexes like the S&P 500 are flirting with all time highs), but market breadth hasn't been great. There is definitely divergence between strength in the mega-cap stocks and in the performance of the broad numbers of stocks. That doesn't mean that the market is fated for sure to have another correction although I expect we'll see one next year at some point. But it does mean that, unless market breadth improves, gains in the indexes are likely to be limited.

You asked how we manage money. We use a number of different indicators. Some are based on price, some are based on market breadth and we modulate the client's exposure depending on how many of our indicators are on buy signals versus not. Right now our assessment of the market climate is neutral so we have about half or maybe a little more, half to two-thirds, of our client's equity exposure. I don't think anything bad is going to happen to the market, but this is not like 2013 all over again either. We still have some money on the sidelines and we are going into quieter things.

Another thing that we do, and I keep investors abreast of this in the newsletter *Systems and Forecasts* that now I'm writing since I took over for my father, is that we select sector SPDR ETFs. Every month we select up to three different sectors that we think are likely to outperform the broad market and we update those selections every month.

Right now we are speaking on December 2, 2015. Right now our picks for this month are energy, industrials and technology. We have our clients over-weighted in those areas and we'll do so for the rest of the month of December. We have pretty much continuous exposure to sectors except during those periods of time when market conditions really appear riskier than we would like, in which case we move the sector program allocation into cash as well.

Marvin, how are you picking those three ETFs? Are you just basing the selection process on momentum or are you doing some sort of other evaluation as well to come up with that short list?

It is all based on recent momentum. There is a tendency that sectors which have been in the top half of performers for the previous month are going to continue to be in the top half for the coming month. That is basically it. It's based on the one-month momentum.

What is interesting is that, historically, you could have outperformed the S&P 500 by equally weighting your sectors. Just by equally weighting the sectors as we do (we equally weight whatever sectors we pick) if you had decided that you wanted to hold the whole S&P 500, but in an equal sector weighted way then you would have outperformed the broad index.

That's an interesting observation that just by equally weighting sectors you could have added value. The other thing that is important is that if you could stay out of the worst sectors, the worst one or two sectors, you could also add value that way. Looking for sectors that are in the top half of the momentum, historically, has gotten you out of the worst sectors and has added value compared to just buying and holding the S&P 500.

We were talking before the interview about Sy Harding having passed away, a great seasonal

expert, and you know there is the old adage that you sell in May and go away and you then come back in during the Autumn. That basic rule has been combined with the MACD by *The Stock Market Almanac* authors to create a winning system. Have you guys worked that into your timing system?

Actually yes. We don't sell in May and go away but we do raise the threshold for entering the market, for getting buy signals. We make it a little harder for the indicators to give you buy signals during that unfavorable period, which historically has been May 1st to November 1st. We do incorporate that and it has worked very well in recent years.

It actually kind of confounds me. I'm not sure why it should be but this is one of the very few things that has been observed historically that still works quite well.

That's interesting. I've never heard of anybody who automatically raised the threshold of a trigger indicator on a seasonal basis. Can you give an example of what you mean by raising the threshold?

Well, for example, let's say the we need a preponderance of advancing issues over declining issues to recognize a buy signal from one of our market breadth indicators. We would need a higher number during the seasonably unfavorable period than during the seasonably favorable period.

Okay, I got it. Easy to understand.

Yes. That is one of the things that we do. Another thing that we have done that has worked out pretty well (and we're not the only ones who have done this because I've seen other writings about it) is to determine that the period that just ended - the two years to one year before the presidential election - is a favorable period historically for stocks. We had a market correction during that period, but stocks recovered. From midterm, from congressional election day to the pre-presidential election day (that one year period) is a favorable seasonable period and it is probably worth maintaining some market exposure in there. Again, I can't guarantee that it's going to work in the future but it sure has worked in the past that the election cycle seasonality is something that we have found profitable to help inform our trading decision.

How do you layer all of these systems together? Let's say someone has a million dollar account. Are you taking 10% and putting it under one system and 20% under another and 30% under another? How are you layering all of these systems together?

Okay. We basically have seven indicators that we group into three. One of our major indicators might be good for maybe a third of the client's equity exposure. Then another of our major indicators might be good for another third. Then the final cluster of five I call "continuation signals" really because they are not stand-alone trading systems but a composite, which is our third group.

We basically layer the client's equity in. We have different parts of a client's equity holdings trading according to the different systems we have. Now obviously there is a lot of correlation between all of the systems. Almost all of the trading we do is trend following.

If you have a bunch of trend following indicators then there is going to be a correlation between them but that is basically how we layer it in. Listen, every indicator has its quirks. Sometimes they are going to trigger and you wish they hadn't or sometimes they will fail to trigger. Any one indicator might fail to trigger and you wish it had, but by diversifying our indicators we are not putting too many eggs in one basket and we are using indicators that have a history of being on the right side of the major market trends, which is really what you are after.

Can you give us an idea of what those three indicator categories would be and the names of the indicators so people can understand what are you doing for the weightings?

Well, I don't want to be too specific because it's proprietary, but I will say that the one major indicator is based on sector breadth, namely how many sectors are on promising trends out of the universe.

One indicator is a simple price trend. It is a ten-month moving average crossing. It's as simple as that moderated with some MACD, which I don't want to get into, but basically it's looking at the price trend and then looking to see whether it's confirmed by MACD trend.

The last group is a bunch of indicators that by themselves are not on buy signals a lot of the time, but when they are on buy signals it's below market risk. As I said, the death cross is one of those indicators. One is based on the number of new highs made, one is based on net advances minus declines averaged over seven weeks, one is based on ratios of up and down volume. We basically are using a lot of breadth and price indicators any one of which if in effect is positive, but any one indicator isn't positive that often so we have the composite of those indicators which gives you more invested time when something is good about the market.

That's a good explanation for something proprietary. Do you do backtesting with software like TradeStation to come up with what works or to determine the historical track record of the systems?

Oh, absolutely. Everything we do is extensively backtested. Then the question is, as I said, the market's character changed about fifteen years ago so this is where it gets to be art as well as science. You could always generate a system that is backtested to look good. You want to make sure your system has some sense about it, that it doesn't have too many adjustable parameters and you want to see how it did during different market climates.

I remember in the late '90s I met someone who said that he was running a hedge fund and it was all about emerging markets and they were looking at five-year track records. They had all these trading strategies based on emerging markets during a five-year period from '93 to '97 when they did nothing but go up. Then after the currency prices hit in '97 and '98 they got killed in emerging markets because their backtest period didn't have any bear market history in it.

It's important when you backtest a system that you have both bull and bear markets in your test. The challenge for backtesting systems is that a lot of things that would have done very well getting you out in 2008 didn't do so well from 2009 to 2014. In other words, if you're too defensive you missed the paying bull market. If you're too aggressive then you got caught in the big bear market.

You do have to make sure that both periods are there and when you are choosing which systems to use, or how much weight to put on this or that system, sometimes you have to start with a market outlook and then say, "Okay. Given my subjective big picture market outlook, what systems are likely to perform best in this and will still keep me out of trouble if my big picture outlook happens to be wrong?" There is definitely a lot of subjectivity but we do believe in backtesting and for better or for worse the last fifteen years really gives us a very rich period of market history to backtest.

If you have been looking at it for the last fifteen years can you give me some idea of the performance of the simulated track record and any actual numbers on managed account performance so people can see how this methodology performs? What can we expect as a rate of return for systems trading in general etcetera, etcetera?

Oh, let's see. I have to pull out the old database here to get the numbers. Okay, let me give you an example. Some of the indicators that we are using actually were developed by my father way back, even as far back as the 1970s. For example, during the thirty-five year period from 1980 till the end of 2014 the S&P 500 made 11% a year, total return, and had a worst drawdown of 55%.

Now if we use our continuation composite, where any one signal is bullish and then you're in, then during that thirty-five year period it would have given you 14% a year with the worst drawdown being 22%. That's an excellent historical track record, but a 22% drawdown is still more than we like so if we set a higher bar for entering the market, if we require at least two of our signals to be on a buy before we get in then you only made 8.5% a year. That's not quite as good as the 10.9% that the S&P made, but instead of a 55% drawdown you only have a 12% drawdown.

In investing there is always a trade-off between risk and return, but you can see here we get very dramatic reductions in risk while maintaining most of the S&P 500 return. Our sector program has outperformed the S&P 500 in real time. We started using this about five years ago and it's outperformed in real time by about 3% a year. Going back hypothetically to 1990 it's done even better than that, but of course all systems do better during their hypothetical period than during real time, and it's done so with about a third less risk than the S&P 500. We further reduce the risk by sometimes abandoning our sector exposure and just moving to cash.

My goal is for our equity exposure to match the S&P 500 with about half the risk. If we don't meet that goal then at the very least we should have a better capture of the profits than of the risk. If we are going to make 80% of what the S&P 500 did then we should at the very least have less than 80% of the risk. Depending on the period you look at, if you look at a full market cycle of up and down I think we've done a good job in terms of matching or exceeding the risk-adjusted performance of the stock market.

Marvin, it basically sounds like you have systems you have tested, they worked historically and in real time they also work well. The question is whether you are following them to the letter and how you decide to change the batch of systems you use? In other words, do you change it based on what you think the market environment is going to be like in the future or are you fixing your systems in stone for a set period of time? Are you sometimes saying, "Well, these systems have worked best in the past for the type of environment we are in so now we will switch to using these that we've already tested for this environment and we'll stay with this batch until we are out of it"?

Well, nothing is set in stone because you develop systems, they work and then they stop working. You always have to analyze and ask yourself what has changed and you don't want to necessarily always be fighting last year's war, but on the other hand you cannot set anything in stone because, as I've said, the systems that worked beautifully when I started nineteen years ago do not work at all right now. There is a constant evolution.

If the world looks really bad we will air on the side of raising cash. Even if the system says we're on a buy we may say, "You know what? I still think that there's market risk. It may take our system a while to give us a sell signal." Very often we have anticipated or we have just made a subjective judgment and that helped us a lot when the tech bubble burst because the systems had stopped working and rather than continuing just to follow them we just made a subjective decision that said, "Look, the market climate is clearly unfavorable. We are going to increase cash positions and reevaluate what we're doing." That was a big success doing that.

Conversely, this year we did get out in a timely way before the August-September market correction and our systems that had done a good job at getting us out were slow to get us back in, but for part of our portfolios we decided that it seemed to us that as to the market climate the worst is over for this correction and so we anticipated some buy signals. We are more invested now than we would be if we followed our system set in stone. There is always a subjective overlay usually in the service of reducing risk further than the systems themselves would have us do, but sometimes also in the service of bottom fishing.

Could you tell me some of the things that you guys tried or investigated that didn't work that you really want to warn traders and investors to stay away from?

Okay. One of the things that we tried to do was short-term countertrend trading. We were looking for short-term oversold exchange traded funds and we would try to buy them at the early stage of a rebound. We picked a few funds. We got the hypothetical trading histories. We were using something called a Commodity Channel Index. It seemed to trade well hypothetically so we tracked a whole bunch of ETFs and we tried to buy the ones that would give this Commodity Channel Index buy signals and it didn't work. I think part of the reason is that we were tracking too many ETFs.

I would say if you are tracking a hundred ETFs then let's say just by random chance that maybe five of them will give you a buy signal. That's just because there is a random chance. Even if your buy signals have false positive rates of 5% you could have a hundred ETFs and be in any of them, but just by random chance five of them will trigger a buy signal and we had that.

First of all we found that you couldn't have a client portfolio ranging from one to one hundred ETFs. If you have a strong market and everything is on a buy then you are not going to buy a hundred different ETFs. On the other hand, if you have a flat or a weak market and only one or two things are on a buy then you can say, "Okay, I can put 5% in one or two different ETFs." However, it turns out that those buy signals were not reliable because we took the one or two out of a hundred that just happened to (randomly) generate buy signals. Those signals weren't as reliable.

I guess in research they call that the "shotgun approach" and I would caution investors away from that. I wouldn't screen such large numbers of candidates, stocks, ETFs, mutual funds, or whatever because just by random chance you are almost certain to get some kind of buy signal that is not necessarily going to be a meaningful one.

I think from my own experience it has been better for us to work with a limited range of mutual funds and ETFs, get a really good idea of how those behave and just trade those. Yes, there may be a great opportunity in Albanian stocks that I'm going to miss, but that's okay because that opportunity in Albanian stocks might be a real thing or it may just be a statistical blimp. More than likely it is going to be a statistical blimp that is going to go away. That is definitely one thing we did that didn't work.

The other thing I can say is that I'm a big fan of covered call writing and the long-term history of that strategy. Using S&P 500 index calls or Dow Industrial index calls has outperformed the underlying indexes on a risk-adjusted basis. I think that's a good strategy but one thing I've learned is don't get tempted by high volatility stocks or ETFs. It may appear that you can make up to several percent a month selling covered calls on high volatility stocks and ETFs but at the end of the day the payoff isn't there. There are enough big declines to wipe out all that attractive premium and more.

Our experience with the higher volatility covered call writing has been unsuccessful. Our volatility with the average or below average volatility covered call writing candidates has been quite successful.

Most people cannot come up with a *consistently* successful system for covered call writing. What's your basic system that you would recommend people use?

Oh, actually I do a number of things for clients but I can give you a basic system that I think will serve your readers very well.

Yes, pretend someone owns IBM stock or Apple stock. What would you do to be able to determine that now is a time when it is safe to write the covered calls? What would be the strike price and what's the maturity? What's the exact system?

I don't have a rule that's applicable to any particular stock you name. I can say, "Okay, you want to write covered with Apple so do this and do that." You have to get a feel for how the stock is moving and then you have to also get a feel for what your goal is.

For example, I have one client who inherited a lot of shares of Teva Pharmaceuticals at a low cost basis so she didn't want to have the shares called under any circumstances if at all possible, but she did want a little extra income. My strategy for her was to write calls 10% out-of-the-money with a goal of getting .3% or .4% a month in option premiums. That has been a strategy that has allowed me to write covered calls. Only once has she had any shares called and the rest has been a net increase in available income from the shares.

That's just one stock but you have to get an idea by looking at each stock and determining its trading range and what your goals are. My own philosophy for writing covered calls, if you don't mind having the shares called, is to write the call after some kind of retracement. I look at the chart and I see what is the next lower support area. If it happened to retrace to that then that is the level at which to write the covered call and you can do it one month out or three months out depending on how much protection you want from the amount of premium you take in. In fact, in my newsletter I think what we recommend is to have hot positions based on covered call writing on retracements.

The system I wanted to share that I think your readers can use formulaically is to buy and hold let's say SPY or some S&P 500 index type thing. You can write monthly nearest the money covered calls any time that the VIX is 20 or above. If the VIX is not 20 or above then you just hold the shares and don't write the call. That is a strategy. You have one decision a month. Either write the covered call if VIX is at average or above average, or don't write the covered call if VIX is below average.

That is a strategy historically that would have beaten buying and holding the S&P 500 by itself and it only requires one decision a month. Of course when it comes to that strategy if your shares get called you have to buy the shares and write another covered call next month. That's a specific strategy that I would highly recommend and I think you will get at least as far doing that, plain vanilla, as looking for stocks on which to write covered calls. The search for individual stocks is very difficult.

One stock that I've had very good experience with for writing leaps, and again I'm not saying I'd recommend it right now, but AT&T has like a 5% dividend. You can get a few percent writing covered calls so if you write a leap and you're prepared to sit on the position for a year your possible return is 10% and that's from a stock with below average volatility. That has served us well over the years.

I'm looking at the chart for AT&T right now. It's at $33.89. I think $32.50 is a better buying level. If your readers keep an eye on that stock and it happens to pull back to $32.50 then that would be a great area either to buy the stock for long-term holding or buy the stock and look about writing a one-year covered call.

Marvin, do you use any systems like seasonals or moving averages to determine if a stock is bullish or bearish before you do this? You would just blindly do it every month?

The basic strategy would be to just do it every month. For our own clients we do use our timing models to raise cash. We are not always invested in covered calls. If we don't like the market then if we are concerned about market risk we are certainly not going to just forge ahead with full exposure to covered call writing. The simple strategy I gave you still has a quarter less risk than the market buy and hold, and again for our clients we would further reduce the risk using our indicators.

Okay. What about gold? Do you ever recommend precious metals to people? I remember in the pre-interview session that we were talking about the fact that Richard Russell just passed away and he was a big gold bug.

When I started we had a gold timing model. Again, it was very short-term trend following. We have not used that recently. That's no longer a big part of our arsenal. We're in an interesting situation. I'm looking at the GLD, the SPDR gold ETF, which is as we're talking trading below 101. That is its lowest level since 2009 so it is intriguing but I've gotten burned doing covered calls on the Market Vectors Gold Mining ETF. It looks like it's trying to form a bottom. As a tactical trade for aggressive investors it might be worth it but it's not a big part of our trading strategy.

We mentioned in our conversation before this interview that Nelson Freeburg, who was a big systems person, had also passed away. He backtested strategies by Mark Boucher who wrote *The Hedge Fund Edge*. Mark had a system which Nelson backtested back to 1929 based on timing

interest rates to determine when to buy or sell the stock market. Have you done anything like that?

We have, and it has not been as powerful as using the market data itself. I wrote a book *Investing With Exchange Traded Funds Made Easy* and in that book I presented two interest rate indicators that have excellent historical track records. One is just whether the yield curve is inverted or not, using ten-year versus three-month T-bill rates, and the other is whether ten-year yields are higher or lower than they were six months ago where traditionally higher interest rates are bearish.

And so there is definitely a venerable history using interest rate indicators to time the stock market, but certainly in the last fifteen years the normal relationship between interest rates and the stock market has either dissolved or even gone backwards. In a period where deflation is the scare, any rise in interest rates means that deflation risks are more remote and that is also good for stocks. So, investment-grade bond prices have been tending over the last fifteen years to move opposite stock prices whereas in the '70s, '80s, and '90s they tended to move together. Rising interest rates used to be a leading indicator for stock market decline, but I would not think that is the same itself.

You know, I've been talking about the stock market. A very big part of what we do is bond market timing, particularly high-yield bonds, but also some investment-grade bonds, and I think it's still possible that trend following indicators with interest rates could be good timing models. Right now long-term interest rates have been mired in the 2% range so there is not been much trading opportunity, but if we ever do get to a period of time like the '60s where there is going to be the start of a long-term takeoff in interest rates then keeping an eye on indicators of interest rates could be a good bond timing model. One that I recommend is the six to nineteen week MACD of the 10-year treasury yield. When that is above zero it's bearish for investment-grade bonds and when it is below zero it's bullish. That is one indicator that I follow to get a sense of the investment-grade bond market.

I know people like John Hussman have done a lot of econometric analysis of fundamentals to derive technical investment models, but those models in the current environment haven't been working as well as they have in the past. Perhaps this is due to the excessive manipulation of the Fed which is destroying the price discovery mechanism of the market. Paralleling what you were saying, do you think the market fundamentals have changed so that past fundamental relationships no longer hold as tightly and therefore you can't use that type of analysis?

I think the problem is that people react so much more quickly than they used to so by the time you are going to get whatever the fundamental news is - whether it's earnings, employment data, interest rates or whatever - the market, in terms of economic data that is released with a delay, has probably begun to react even before the data comes out.

You know there are millions of separate decisions by individual traders who see something going on in their neighborhood that is going to ultimately be reflected in some piece of economic data that is coming out a month from now. They are acting on it before the data is released so I think that that's the problem, which is that the time lag that used to make these things possible to trade has evaporated between the lower cost of trading and the faster dissemination of information on the internet. I think it's a problem.

Just as the S&P 500 is itself a leading economic indicator, I think the market telling its own story is probably the most timely data you can get. That isn't to say that other people in their heads are able to make better quantitative use of economic data, but we haven't found it to be as helpful as simply turning to the market itself.

Great. Let's get back to some systems. You gave us a system for covered calls and bond timing. Are there other systems that you can give people where you're thinking, "Hey, you really ought to know about this simple method of timing the markets that is technical and which you just mechanically apply?" Is there anything else along these lines that you can give?

Yes. We have not touched upon high-yield bond funds. Especially with interest rates as low as they are, looking ahead over the next year or two in my opinion I think that is potentially the most fruitful area of the bond market.

In one of my books I gave a simple system that an individual investor can follow, which is that you look at the total return of your high-yield bond mutual fund, assuming they allow you to trade this way, and any time there is a 3% reversal from the last high point (as of the end of the month counting total return) you move to cash. And then you wait for a 3% reversal from the last low point to get back in. This would have kept you out of the major bond market declines that occur every so often.

You can't buy and hold high-yield bond funds because every so often there is a major market correction that wipes out the advantage of holding them compared to just holding an investment-grade bond index fund. So if you want to take advantage of those high yields you do have to figure out a way to manage the risk.

You know that sounds a lot like the old Nelson Freeburg weekly *Value Line* up 4%, down 4% buy and sell system.

Exactly, except this is applied to high-yield bond fund prices.

And it works really well, you're saying?

Yes, I have to say that there have been problems in recent years because there have been a number of whipsaws, but in terms of the long-term track record this would have kept you out of trouble in 2008 and it would have kept you in during 2009, which is a great period for high-yield bonds. So it's a simple way of managing the risk and you have to do it. It's mandatory. You can't be a buy and hold investor in high-yield bond funds.

From your experience do you have a lot of institutional traders that follow systems like that to manage big slabs of money?

Probably not because you cannot trade individual bonds this way and you can't even trade high-yield bond ETFs this way. It has to be open-end, high-yield bond mutual funds that behave much more smoothly from day-to-day that are amenable to this kind of system and big institutional investors are probably not moving in and out of open-end mutual funds. They probably have direct portfolios of high-yield bonds, which you can't trade.

So this is something that is really good for smaller size money managers or individual investors. The real trick, of course in addition to having the discipline to watch the funds and do the calculations which is not that time consuming, the real trick is making sure you are in mutual funds that will allow you to trade that way.

Some funds have a three-month holding period, in which case you probably couldn't use this system, but there are plenty of mutual funds out there who are willing to settle for a thirty-day minimum holding period and a system that only generates three or four transactions a year at most.

Nelson Freeburg was also one of the few trying to manage money by using systems. Who do you admire who is using systems to manage money, such as large portfolios? Are there any names that come to mind?

To be honest with you, I am aware of only one other colleague who is still heavily systems-based in managing money. I should be aware of who the competition is but I'm just not. I don't get clients from other people where they are telling me, "Oh, this guy's systems weren't working well." I get clients and people who are invested with some buy and hold type discipline and they had to sit through a major bear market. Also I don't lose clients who say, "Well this other guy has a system that is working better than yours."

My sense of the industry is that most of the players, and I'm thinking here of people like Paul Merriman, have really abandoned the use of systems trading. Many of the traders have abandoned the use of systems trading and have gone in a different way. So this is a long-winded way of saying I really can't name too many other people in my space who are trying to do what we are doing.

That's a really good answer. Maybe you can talk a little bit about those issues. Why are they abandoning it and why are you successful at this where the others are not so they are leaving the approach? Are they abandoning it because it's not working for them or because they found something better? Also, why do you think you're being successful at this whereas regular traders aren't usually that good at systems trading?

I think part of it is that, from a salesman point of view, it is a lot easier to say, "Oh look, in the last six years the market has been rising 15% a year on average. Get in on it." I think that that's a very popular perspective right now. I think it's an easier sell.

Back in 2009 when a lot of people got burned, it was a very easy sell to say, "Look, we had a system that got you out. If this happens again don't you want to be prepared?" The answer in most cases was "Yes," so I think that's part of the reason. Part of the reason is that it only takes one screw up to discredit your system.

Between my father and me we have a very long experience in trading, and as the phrase you used before "nothing is set in stone." We always have to be alert to the possibility that the system that worked last time isn't going to perform as well this time, and maybe that is what distinguishes us because I've heard stories about people who stuck by their systems and had no idea that, "Well gee, maybe the system wasn't going to work this time." They weren't even open to the possibility.

As Pasteur said, "Chance favors the prepared mind" and so we are prepared. We have our systems that are researched, but we know from our own experience that nothing lasts forever so we are always prepared to step in to exercise some judgment and to see if things aren't working as they intended. Then at least we can do damage control and regroup. And perhaps, I think to the extent I've heard of other people's systems not serving them well it's because they stuck with them for too long.

Okay, now an educational question. If somebody wants to become a trader or investor what small set of books or courses would you recommend they read so that they are a better manager of their funds, have a higher probability of making money, understand the market better or anything along those lines?

I'll tell you that my father basically taught me to use technical analysis and he even wrote a book called *Technical Analysis.* His name is Gerald Appel and the book is *Technical Analysis: Power Tools for Active Investors.* That is kind of an overview of his outlook on trading. That would basically be a summary of everything I've learned at his knee over all these years. And then my own approach is in a book I wrote called *Higher Returns from Safe Investments* that was published in 2010 by Financial Times Prentice Hall. That contains my views on income investing and I still think those lessons are relevant.

In terms of other people's books that I've read I liked John Murphy's book *The Visual Investor: How to Spot Market Trends.* The lessons I drew from that are really about drawing trend lines and horizontal support and resistance levels. It was a good way to get started with the idea of technical analysis. I also like John Bollinger's book, *Bollinger on Bollinger Bands,* so I think if you started with that as a reading list you would get a feel for technical analysis as we practice it.

Now I have to say that another book that I read was James O'Shaughnessy's *What Works on Wall Street.* It has nothing to do with technical analysis at all. It's really about a systematic approach to value investing. It's a different perspective on the stock market, but it's very rich in historical data so I would recommend that book as well.

It's important if someone is new to the investing world that you have to figure out what works for you. You know, there is more than one way to skin a cat. When I'm buying and holding stocks I only want to buy value stocks. I want to feel I'm getting a bargain. Not everyone is like that. Some people want to buy the next Google. Good for them, but that's a different kind of mindset.

You have to figure out what sits well with you. I'm very risk-averse. I don't want to just sit there and watch the market fall like it did in 2008 and have nothing to do with it except to tell myself, "Well, it always comes back, it always comes back." I mean, sometimes if you're early in retirement and you get hit with a decline like that then sometimes it can't come back. Some people are genuinely indifferent to risk, or maybe their financial situation is such that even if they lose their whole nest egg in the stock market they have enough money coming in from Social Security and pensions that it's okay with them and so they want to take more of a fling.

The important thing is first you've got to figure out, philosophically, what kind of investment strategy fits your personality. Once you do that, then you delve in deeper and practice and try. So with me it's all about the fact that I want risk-aversion. I want damage control. I want to make a little something when times are good, but I want to protect myself when times aren't good.

What do you want to tell people in terms of life lessons for investing or philosophy or just in general

that you wish you knew when you got started that would have eliminated a lot of the pains and the slow learning curve? Things that you have seen, things you want people to know, things you wish you could correct with a magic wand, ... things like that.

Okay, one is that you do have to limit major losses. As we say in medicine, "first do no harm." You do have to limit major losses and I think that should apply no matter what your investment strategy is. You have to have some handle on the risk.

The other thing is that - and this is hard even after nineteen years - you have to maintain a longer-term perspective. Any investment decision can go for you or against you in the near term so sometimes you have to ride out the bad times. It doesn't mean that the decision is wrong. It just means that it may not have gone in your favor right away. I realize that is somewhat contradictory. I mean, you kind of have to weigh the balance between reacting too quickly to every blip in the market versus ignoring disaster as it's unfolding before you. It's a very stressful thing. It's important.

I guess the bottom line is that every decision you make should have a rationale and then you can weigh your next course of action based on the rationale for the decision. If your rationale for buying into the market now is that new indicators are positive and the indicators are still positive but the market hasn't taken off like you expected then maybe it's safe to give it a little more time as opposed to your rationale being that you got tired of seeing everyone else make money so you piled in and now you don't have any guidance on what to do at all. So it's important, in my opinion, to have a rational decision, a basis for the decisions you are making and then you can help use that to guide your future course of action.

Again, it's important to limit risk. One disaster can blow up many years of good trading so you really have to avoid those disasters.

I always ask people the following. If you were a genie and you could wave a wand over a room of wannabe new investors, what negative trait of theirs would you eliminate or amplify? Is there anything that comes to mind?

What magic would turn the average person into a good investor? Actually I think that one trait is given short shrift in the financial media and in most financial industry advertising but I think it's really important, and that is the concept of risk-adjusted performance. Obviously it is easier to say that such-and-such made 10% a year. It is a lot harder to say that such-and-such made 10% a year but did it with half the risk of the market. You have to understand how to measure risk and all this.

So if there were one trait I would instill in people that I think would keep them well-rounded it would be to get comfortable with risk-adjusted performance. Evaluate your strategies and your performance that way rather than, "Oh, the S&P made 8% in October and I only made 6%." Well if you made three-quarters what the S&P did but you did it with half the risk on the way down then you are a genius. A lot of that tends to get lost in the financial media. That would be my one incantation, which would be to instill an appreciation for risk-adjusted performance.

Nobody stresses that, but we should definitely change the mindset in that direction. The last question before we get to your books, websites and services is this. Looking back on your career, Marvin, what do you wish you had known years ago? Looking back, how would you finish this

sentence, **"I wish I had known ABC" or "I wish years ago that I had adopted the habit of doing XYZ and then I'd be so much further along"? There might be some information, advice or habit you just didn't know about until the hard knocks of experience taught you the lessons. Or maybe you had heard of advice that you didn't instill in yourself and then twenty years later you realized, "Yes, it took me too long to learn that." What are the one, two or three things that you wish you had known or adopted as a habit twenty years ago?**

I think it was the late Martin Zweig who said, "Don't fight the Fed." I think that if I had had a greater appreciation for that it would have been a much happier time, especially over the last six years. That I'd say is the one thing. Again, it's hard because it's not really a function of whether interest rates are rising or not, but like they say, "Don't fight the Fed." I think that's something that we should all remind ourselves of.

Now interestingly we are starting, presumably in December, we are going to start the first Fed rate hike in more than nine years and so this is going to be a brand new market climate and we'll see what that portends. But I think it's worth reminding, and I wish I had reminded myself more, "Don't fight the Fed."

Going forward, what do you think about the upcoming macro-economics? A lot of people are worried about world debt levels and central banks losing their ability to do something. Do you think we are going to have any problems along those lines in the future?

I'm going to preface my remarks by saying I'm almost always too pessimistic and that's good for risk-management, but I'll just give you this bias for what it is because we are starting now at a time when the U.S. stock market is right up against its all time high and I don't see the catalyst for the kind of returns in the next five years that we have seen over the past five years. I'm not predicting doom and despair, but I am predicting a much more muted performance for the stock market and for the bond market than most people expect.

This is where having a little sense of the fundamentals helps. You could look at a long-term track record for investment-grade bonds and say, "Oh, 6% a year," but interest rates right now are 2% so going forward seven years it's almost mathematically certain that your return from investment grade bonds is going to be 2%, not 6%, and I don't think most people realize that. The stock market is less governed by the laws of math, but right now we are in a situation where the stock market is at all time highs, where corporate profit margins are at all-time highs and where economic growth, despite record Fed stimulus and central bank stimulus elsewhere, is quite sluggish. I have to assume this is going to usher in a period of below-average market returns going forward.

So this might well be a trader's market climate that we're getting into. If we have another correction next year, it could well be even bigger than the one we had this year. I'm not predicting another 2008, but unlike the case in 2011 or 2005 or 1994 where the stock market kind of stalled and then went ahead to surge forward, I don't think we are in that situation now. I don't see, right now, the catalyst that is going to push stock market prices significantly higher. I think it might continue to be a good environment for preferred stocks next year and maybe covered call writing and things like that. I think we are going to be in sort of a sluggish, stable interest rate climate.

I guess the big thing is that whatever happens your systems are risk-adjusted so that if it's a dangerous period they will lower your exposure. That's the benefit of having systems versus somebody who is fully invested.

If there is going to be another correction next year I'm hoping our systems will get us out. This year we did avoid the damage so the market is not going to stay flat by never moving. It's going to correct and recover and correct and recover and hopefully those will be tradable moves.

Marvin, can you tell us the names of your books so people can buy them on Amazon.com. Also please mention your website, and the services you offer. Let's wrap it up that way.

Oh, thank you. Our website is Signalert.com. Our main business is managing money for individual clients, again with a focus on risk-adjusted performance and on protecting clients from major market declines. I can't guarantee any future results, of course, but I can say that our track record of protecting our clients during major market declines has been very successful going back to 1973.

I write a newsletter, *Systems and Forecasts,* and that comes out bi-weekly with twice-weekly hotlines. That's for people who want to do it themselves but who want market commentary. We have a specific portfolio so if people want a cook book they can follow our portfolio as it's presented and if they just want an opinion on what the market climate is, and some particular trading recommendations, they can use the newsletter that way as well.

My most recent book is *Higher Returns from Safe Investments* and I've written other books, too. My first book was *Investing With Exchange Traded Funds Made Easy* and my father's book, which I think is out of print but now available on Kindle is *Technical Analysis: Power Tools for Active Investors.*

Okay, so that pretty much wraps everything that they can find you with. Are there any other services you offer?

No, that's pretty much it.

All right, great. I really appreciate the interview, Marvin, and best of luck to you.

Thank you very much, Bill.

Chapter 14
Josh Hawes
Turtles Trading and Futures Fund Management

I don't find many people who go from the institutional side of Wall Street to the retail side and then eventually build their own hedge fund and next a trend following service for the public. Josh Hawes, founder of TheTrendgrabber.com, talks about the ins and outs of trend following in the footsteps of the turtle traders, and explains how to orient your thinking to the world of systems trading and trend following in general.

If you have ever dreamed about duplicating the success of the turtle traders, who focused on using trading systems to trade futures, the first thing you should do is start to read about them to learn the philosophy of managed futures trading. Josh apprenticed with a turtle, and readily explains how to create and test futures systems for those who are interested in the world of systematic futures and stock trading.

Josh, tell me about your background. How did you get started in trading and what types of trading have you tried? Tell me the story of what worked and what didn't along the way to where you are now today in the investing field.

I started on Wall Street on the institutional side. In my very first internship I worked for a firm that Wall Street liked to call the "dark side." There I was under the Asset Growth management team that ran about thirty billion dollars. That was my first foray into Wall Street. It was a very interesting time to be thrown in amongst truly the whales and the titans.

It was at my time there that oddly enough I was looking at the returns of this behemoth and these guys that are supposed to be essentially magicians at making money, and I started asking, "Where the heck is the return for you guys?" This was in 1992, so this is when you could throw something out the window and it would go up. It was one of those things where I was still looking and I was asking, "Where are the fabled guys that you hear about?" That sent me down an interesting road where I really wanted to learn who were the true titans who were getting real return. I didn't care how much money they were managing.

You later learn that there are two kinds of different worlds in investment management. One is focused on what you return and the other is "I couldn't give a crap if you're killing me on return because I'm running thirty billion dollars." There are two sticks that people like to measure things by and I went down the road of asking, "Who are the guys with the great returns?"

This was around the time that the internet started coming out … not from a collegiate perspective, but when it was really hitting in the '90s kind of thing, the "You've Got Mail," right? One of the things that I did was look up the successful firms and check out who were these guys. I was looking at their 13F filings and other stuff so I would find these guys and basically would just take a shot at emailing them. I was a young kid and so I would just cater to their ego and say, "Can we meet? Can we talk? Can we do anything? I've been watching you from afar."

It was interesting because at that time I had become friends with the author Michael Covel who wrote all the books about the turtles. He was going out to actually see a fund manager who is a buddy of mine now, one of the original turtles and one of the most famous. I got to go out to see him speak. I went up to him afterwards and I said, "Hey, would you mentor me?" He said, "Look, you'll understand this one day, but I just don't have the time." I said I completely understand, but he gave me the name of another guy who had made his money and was out of the game now. I went and I reached out to him.

Sure enough, he decided to take me on and show me the ropes. He said, "Look, the number one thing that you can't do is you can't tell anybody who I am and the fact that we're working together. I hate Wall Street. I want to be out of the limelight. I just don't want any of that anymore." I told him I had no problem with that.

That was where my tutelage began. In all my study I realized that the most consistent and top performers all had the same strategy. Everybody knows it as "trend following." Now incidentally one of the things that I became known for when on the Street was being able to reverse engineer people's strategies. Being able to reverse engineer things, the funny thing is that you can find some of these "fundamental guys" and the truth is that they are actually closet trend followers. They'll never admit it because there is no story behind it, but it's really what they are doing at the end of the day.

Anyway, I just wanted to learn the ropes and sure enough did. It was basically in 2008 and I was running private money and we ended up killing it. We were up about 80% that year in this private account so I basically said that I had to go out and do this on my own.

Going into 2009, I decided that I was going to start my first hedge fund. I was ready to stop running private client money and step into the big boy world and so sure enough I later did. With that first Wall Street job, however, my whole goal at that time was first understanding investment management from the top-down perspective of the really big money, the thirty billion dollars in money. Then I had an internship over at Morgan Stanley's Wealth Management division because I really wanted to understand essentially the retail side of Wall Street, which is a bottom-up kind of approach.

A lot of people think about the market in terms of fundamentals through top-down macro and bottom-up fundamentals on a stock. From a very early time I realized that markets move based upon human decision so I really wanted to understand the humans that were involved in the marketplace from a big boy perspective and then from the smaller perspective of a successful business owner who had two million dollars to his name. How is he looking at it? How is he viewing the market through his eyes? I did both so I could get a complete picture.

It was around the same time when I was running my fund that one of my head floor traders on the NYSE, who had been head of UBS's floor trading for twenty years, came to me. I'd been helping him out a lot and he came to me and said, "You've helped me so much. We have to work together." So then I stepped into my next foray where I really wanted to understand market structure, especially (or specifically) market micro-structure.

The two of us started our own high frequency fund that we ended up running for about two years. Things worked, things were great and it actually ended up that we weren't defined as high frequency trading because that game is volume sniffing. It's hide and slide. It's a lot of stuff that gets pretty complicated where most people say, "Oh my god, do markets even work like this?"

What we basically did was define our own acronym for what we were doing. This was AITS – an

Automated Intra-day Trading System. Basically what we did was like high frequency trading because we traded across over eight hundred names all at once. Essentially we were just following the big boy capital flow using a few of the things that we had that were unique with regards to the market's micro-structure.

From there my buddy had had enough of Wall Street. He had been on the floor for so many years so he decided to say that he was done. He hung up the cleats per se. Today we continue to run our fund and also run and manage accounts and our investment firm.

After all these twenty years of learning and applying, one of the things that we specialize in and that we tell people is that we aren't trend followers. A lot of people are usually surprised to hear that. We say we are "trend capturers." That's one of the big distinctions and if you can begin to understand that concept then you can begin to put into frame how markets really work.

There has been a boom in this knowledge of trend following and related methods over the years. It's led a lot of people down a pretty dangerous path. You have to give massive respect to guys like Richard Dennis and the turtles for a few things and then there are other things that, to be quite honest, they had wrong. You can test them out and see what they are. That's one of the things we pride ourselves on, which is that we run like a billion dollar firm in a boutique setting from the aspect that we do a lot of research on all sorts of different ideas that we have, but we're able to move very quickly.

A lot of people know who David Harding and Winton Capital are. If you don't, they are one of the best hedge funds ever. They have ninety-five PhDs on their staff. What's funny is that once you reach a certain point you have a lot of bureaucracy that you have to deal with. Most of the time they are trying to figure out how to execute their huge size a lot better. They are not really expounding upon what they are doing in terms of the traditional metrics of how you should properly invest. They have figured out that game. Nonetheless, even the little tweaks that they do take a lot of time compared to us. There is a process to testing and research and whenever you understand that and you apply that and you can move quickly then it makes you a lot more nimble.

When the Euro came about my partner was the one of the original programmers who handled that whole thing for Merrill. My own background is on the engineering side with wireless software. We are both programmers, we're both nerds to be quite honest. That's how we both really came together and got into the business.

You mentioned something that was really interesting there, which is that Richard Dennis and the turtles got some things wrong with their trend following approach. Can you speak a little more about this?

Whenever we talk about this I always want to show massive respect to those guys because truly it's Newton's quote that, "If I have seen further than others, it is by standing on the shoulders of giants." We don't contend to be really smart guys. We're not PhDs like a traditional guy such as Larry Hite, but we feel this actually helps us. It allows us to see things as they are and not get lost in a lot of the minutia that your traditional science aspect guys can get lost in.

One of the original turtle traders is literally one of my best friends. I have coffee with him every week and he would get into an argument with me and blast me for this, but one of the things that we find is a fallacy that can affect you in trading is the belief most trend followers have that you have to have a static universe. They believe that your trading universe can't change. From a trend follower's perspective that's absolutely true. From a trend capturer's perspective that is false. There is a good clear distinction in that.

One of the things that you find is that you get some good books like those written by Andreas Clenow which really chronicle that trend following works great in the futures market, but it doesn't really work well on stocks. Well, the truth is that it actually does work well on stocks, but there are a few things that you have got to figure out in order for that to happen.

One of those things that we like to harp on for trend following is that you don't have to have a fixed universe (of a limited number of instruments to trade). My buddy and I talk about this all the time and amidst all of our friends, too. When you get a bunch of guys who are running millions of dollars, hundreds of millions of dollars or billions of dollars … when you're around a bunch of guys who essentially have the basics down then after that it's a matter of selling point differentiation, marketing, and then "what's optimal."

That's one of the things that we talk about, which is that traditional trend following does work. Do we absolutely believe it is optimal? No, not necessarily if you take the view that you have to have a fixed universe.

What do you mean by a "fixed universe"? Do you mean a small set of instruments that you trade and only those?

Yes, exactly. If you look at most traditional CTA firms - trend followers - what do they do? They are usually in the exact same hundred futures markets. Some of them vary ever so slightly. The firms that really figured it out, such as Winton Capital, went and did a good job of it. They basically looked at it and they said, "Hey this whole concept of diversification is true. We've tested the living crud out of it."

Modern portfolio theory is so much more complicated than having more than thirty names in your portfolio, which is why I harp on Jim Kramer all the time. However, the concept of modern portfolio theory is true in terms of diversification. The problem that a lot of old school trend followers ran into was that they were way too heavy in a particular sector. They would trade futures contracts, but they would have fifty contracts that were in energy or in agriculture. Your smoothest equity curve, your most robust investing style really came about because Winton was pretty neutral across all of those. It was like "Hey, we're not going to have more financials than agriculturals. We're not going to have more agriculturals than metals. We're not going to have more metals than energy."

That fixed universe is essentially this. Let's say our fixed universe is four assets in that we only trade gold, the S&P 500, oil and wheat. What traditional trend followers will do is say, "I can never trade outside of that universe." Now in the long run it works out fine. Why? Because correlation fluctuates in the long run. In the short-term you can have these times where you should never underestimate the ability for a market to trend based upon hysteria, based upon momentum. The reason why I say that is because sometimes concepts and themes in investing can take hold in the marketplace. That's why you will have someone say, "The market is just locked in step with oil." Bull crap.

Look, correlation is a fluctuating, oscillating number. Just because for ten days the market is moving in step with oil doesn't mean that in the long run you should base your decisions off of that. Why? Well, because go back as far as 2008 and you can see a time that it was the exact opposite. You've been in the game long enough to know that oil went up and what did the market do? Crashed like no other. Why?

Because it was getting too expensive.

Even then people have to understand this concept that every asset is bought or sold by an individual. Whether it is an algorithm or an institution or whatever it might be, that individual is buying or selling that asset. That buying and selling is not just because something else is going up and down. Sure you have pairs algorithms and arbitrage guys. That's a little bit of a different game, but at the end of the day they are still buying one contract of oil and they are still selling one contract of the S&P 500 if they are doing traditional pairs.

Over the long run, you get this broad asset class diversification by the CTA. The truth is that there becomes a limiting factor. Most CTAs will tell you we want more and more contracts to be able to trade. The reason why is they just want more and more diversified assets in order to be able to able to add more and more non-correlation to their inner portfolio. You get these people who just get stuck in this mindset of, "If I'm a trend follower then I'm only going trade stocks on the S&P100."

Our view on investing has always been to ask, "What is the most robust way to invest and what is the most optimal way to invest?" We view those things as similar. The reason why I say that is because there is certain stuff that can sell to the public and then there is stuff that doesn't look very sexy but twenty years out you'll be saying you wish you had done that. That's a long-winded way of answering that question, but there are some key points in there and some key things that a few people need to understand from that.

The interesting point that came out is that it's typically difficult to trade stocks with trend followings systems, but you mentioned that you can successfully do this. What are the criteria for a stock so that you can use a trend following system to trade it?

For us the criteria for investing are all based upon price trend, volume and volatility. Really, your trading strategy should be so robust that it should work on a futures contract and it should work on a stock. For us, investing is all about liquidity so as long as it's liquid enough to be able to handle us investing then we know that over time it will have a positive expectancy of working.

The truth is that filtering your universe is really normally based upon liquidity. Then you get a little bit more finite by looking at the concept of efficiency where basically the thought is that if I'm going to trade in something then I want to trade in something that's moving, moving well, moving pure and giving me my most bang for my buck. Volatile things are great. We like volatility but at the same token, accounting for volatility usually means you are going to have to trade less of that asset so we basically look at liquidity and efficiency for that.

In other words if it's liquid, if it's efficient and the volatility fits then you could trade it using your trend following methods, and you have specific measures for determining this. Of course you also probably first test to determine if you have a positive return using your trading system for it on past historical data, right?

Yes, what we actually did is model what we would call a fake random data stream. This is actually something that's super important because you get these guys who sell crap online. They will say, "Look how well our stuff did." The problem is that they are implementing in their testing what is called "hindsight bias." More and more people are getting knowledgeable of this. For instance, somebody gives you a two-year backtest and it's on long-only stocks. It's on basically only the best performers out of the S&P 500. There is massive bias to that so we always laugh when we see that.

As a fund we have access to data that most people don't although it is becoming more readily available. Proper delisted stock data becomes very important in testing. Many strategies that work in today's market defined by the universe don't work over the long run whenever you try to apply that back to stocks that were trading in say, 1950. That's one of the big things that we like to harp on, which is that you have to do proper testing.

Whenever you take into account every stock that ever traded and you do the very, very laborious task of accounting for dividends and stock splits and everything else then we like to say that most investing classes are what are called "pseudo random." The concept of momentum exists. The concept of a trend exists, but over the long run there is this element of randomness. That's why we love that book *Fooled by Randomness* by Nassim Taleb.

Whenever you understand this stochastic approach to markets you can then actually model random data where you can create fake stocks. You basically say, "How does our strategy do on truly out-of-sample data?" You'll hear all these testers probably say, "Well, I'll test for two years and then I'll see how it did on a year of out-of-sample data." That's great but your sample size is way too low. At the same time, let me know how it tests on truly random, made-up synthetic data.

What do you do? Do you take the average return and volatility and just project a random sequence in the future?

Pretty much. Like I said, you want to create that stochastic function around it. What do you essentially know about all stocks over time? Well, normally they are pretty random about seventy percent of the time. Then about thirty percent of the time they are going to be trending in some type of direction. Then you do that same approach with volatility.

Personally, I love doing it. Whenever I talk in a presentation I'll say, "Here is the stock of Sun Microsystems." Then I'll pull up another picture and I'll say, "Can anybody tell me what this stock is?" Most people will say something like, "Oh, that was whenever what's her name got bought out" or "That's Enron." I'll say, "Nope, that's a fake piece of data that we created."

There are a few things that you do and incorporate with that. The end result is that when you understand how markets work from a micro-structure all the way up you can then begin to build out data in order to test whether or not your strategy is robust. To us robust is being able to stand the test of time. Time for us is a mathematical equation.

Okay, so what's a description of the methodology of trading rules that you guys have finally arrived at for trading?

We are not that different from most traditional trend followers. There are a few things that obviously we have tweaked on. One of the biggest things is that we have what we like to call multiple exit points. That's because we can show people that your money isn't made in the entry. Your money is made in the exits. This is really true across usually most forms of investing as well.

Even real estate, when you sign on the dotted line (aka an "entry") it is usually the back end of that deal that is the exit point … at least for really good real estate investors. For us, we subscribe to the concept of being able to have a democratic approach to entry, aka we have this view that we have multiple signals that give us an entry point and if six of them are raising their hand out of those ten then yes we'll go ahead and consider putting that into the portfolio. Once into the portfolio we then manage different positions by different types of exits that we have. Those exits can range from anything such as concepts of momentum to even very long-term channel breakdowns or if you're short then channel breakouts.

Are you monitoring let's say a hundred different markets and then waiting until multiple signals trigger on one … and then you evaluate whether you should get in? Also, how do you determine your position size? It sounds like you are scaling out using different systems.

Our basic typical morning is essentially that we turn on the computers and they run their scans. Actually it happens at night since all of our stuff is automated. Then the next morning we wake up and the output of the scans is there. Essentially what we are doing is we're looking at the current portfolio. We are saying, "Does anything need to get out? Do we have any short set of pops and we need to get out? Do we have any longs that have gone down and gone through an exit point that we need to get out of?" If we do then we make sure to get out of those.

We look at the portfolios because we want to see how we are doing on the longs and shorts. We implement what is called a "long/short global multi strategy." We have multiple different kinds of strategies. We do that from the standpoint that our stock investing program is separate from our futures program. We're looking at the signals across all the different strategies and programs that we have after we've looked at the portfolio to see if anything has gotten stopped out.

Let's say that we don't have anything to do in our futures portfolio so we are looking at the stock side. On the stock side, if we had a long that just got stopped out - whether for a profit or a loss - we then look to see if there are any signals in anything long or short that could replace that. That's when we'd go through and we'd look at the signals that are generating. For us, you always want multiple confirmations - either some form of price, some form of price and volume, some form of volatility, some combination. Once those are there, if a signal is valid then we'll end up putting that on in the portfolio as long as the portfolio can handle that amount of risk and as long as the portfolio can handle that kind of long/short exposure.

All right. Can you give us a track record for your approach or how well it does, whether it's exact numbers or in general?

Yes. We like to always talk about track record with our clients in terms of what's called the MAR ratio. This goes back to the fact that a lot of people just want to hear about the big returns. Everybody wants to hear that they can get a 100% return, which is usually on the retail side. On the institutional side it's, "I never want to have a drawdown." We always laugh at that because institutions usually look down at retail and retail views institutions as rich jerks. The truth is that they are all grail hopping.

One of the things that we harp on other than that the money is in the exits is that you can't have reward without risk. Once you understand that concept then you have to ask yourself what is good reward to risk in terms of performance? Whenever you look at the performance of say the turtles you will find that most of them have a MAR ratio (your compound annual growth rate divided by your maximum drawdown), your gain to your pain of about point three (.3). Okay, if we were to multiply by a hundred that's basically saying they get a 30% return and have a 100% drawdown.

Now I know that you're going "a hundred percent goes to zero" and I get that. That just gives you an idea. We have found as long as you are able to incorporate multiple systems that a good MAR ratio is point five (.5). A really good MAR ratio is point seven five (.75). Basically a great MAR ratio is one to one (1.0). To give you an idea of who the true legends in the space are, only Paul Tudor Jones and good old Steven Cowen over at SAC Capital Advisors have ever had a MAR ratio over their whole period greater than one (1.0). Now we all know that Steven Cowen got in trouble for insider trading. That gives you an idea that even for the great guys who are getting a 20% return a year you can still expect them to at least have a 40% drawdown in their lifetime and guess what, they're good. For us, so far, our MAR ratio has been around point seven five (.75).

The reason why we don't ever talk about specifics in terms of return and drawdown is because one of the cool, unique things that we do is that we model our return profile based upon our client's risk tolerance. Sometimes we have very large corporations that come to us and they say, "We want to be invested, but we don't want to have greater than a 10% drawdown." Well their risk profile is different from a high net individual who is saying, "If you don't have a 40% drawdown I'll fire you." I can tell you, those guys exist. For us on that account our goal is to get a 40% compound annual growth rate return a year with a 40% drawdown. That is going to be very, very good. Some years you are going to kill it. With that kind of risk profile, you can have a 100% or 120% return and then other years you are going to lag and fall down. Your recovery period is going to be a bit longer.

My personal feeling on all of it is this. I have found over the long run that institutions, retail, professional traders really don't do well with anything greater than a 20% to 25% drawdown threshold. If you can find somebody that's kicking out a 12% to 15% compound annual growth rate then to be quiet honest they are killing it. The reason that I tell people that they are killing it is because most people say that the market goes up on average 11% or 12% a year after 7% inflation, whatever the number may be.

The problem is that the market's MAR ratio is point one (.1). That's in a very good optimal state. Usually what that means is you are hitting a 10% return a year and then almost always every few years you are getting a 50% drawdown. That's peak-to-trough. It's not month-to-month. If you can do point five (.5) in a MAR ratio you are beating the market by 400%. That puts things into perspective for people. That's one of the things that we like to talk about with our clients.

To give you an idea, one of our clients is a corporation and they don't ever want more than a 10% drawdown. The largest drawdown we have ever had for them is 4.65% and they are averaging every year about a 7.65% compound annual growth rate so I'd say that we are doing pretty dang well. Since their alternative is putting things in treasuries they think that we rock.

Just so I'm clear on this, are you totally following systems for your trading or is there some judgmental aspect to it on a daily basis?

That's a great question. We like to call it a 90/10 or 95/5 system. All trading is going to have to have a discretionary component to it. I know a lot of guys say, "No, it doesn't" with other objections. I can tell you that even the most systematic, largest institutional investors in the world who are paid to be automatic will face situations at the end of the day where if markets move in a certain way it will force them to make some sort of discretionary decision.

A good example of that is most trend followers, even your famous turtles, talk about the fact that you have to be 100% systematic. The problem is that even the turtles made discretionary decisions in 2008 on re-sizing their portfolios because volatility was increasing to crazy levels. Some of these guys, truth be told, could have actually done even better in 2008 but they decided to pare back because the volatility was scaring the living crap out of them. They could make 10% in a day for their portfolio. Even though they weren't losing 10% in a day they could make 10% in a day and for most institutional guys that will scare the crud out of you. There is always going to be some level of discretionary intervention.

For us, the discretionary comes in play as to why we have multiple exit points. We know that each one of our exits by itself has positive expectancy. We can trade our regular entries and choose one of our exits and over time we're going to make money. Now whenever you combine them all together it's like a concept that little incremental changes can do a lot from an exponential respect.

For us the discretionary component comes into play as follows. For example, let's say that we were short Greece. We were short Greece for literally about four months before Greece finally had an absolute collapse off. We had some institutions that were going, "Why the hell are you guys short Greece? What are you thinking? You're short Greece, you're short Russia. Russia's got an amazing CAPE ratio. You guys are going to get annihilated." Even though we don't risk more than one percent per position we still had guys who were saying what the heck are you doing?

One of the things was that we had a signal that came up in another country and another ETF that could have replaced Greece because it had gone through one of our minimum momentum exit points. We decided to leave Greece on because it hadn't crossed through some major exit points. The trend was still down and it was still going down, but it was just a little bit sloppy. Finally you had the breakdown.

That's one of our things we like to talk about with trading. True systems, your best systems are still painting a picture for you of price action. They are alerting your eyes to what you should be looking for. I always tell our clients that at the end of the day if we lost all of our computers I can still trade directly from a chart. That's because there are common characteristics of price action that you want to be incorporating. Computers are just doing the little annoying things that take up a good amount of time. That's an important concept of where the discretionary component can come in.

Look, could we have made money with the other entry? Absolutely, but we ended up sticking with our rules, not breaking our rules, but decided to keep the Greek short in there.

In other words the "95/5" means you are a discretionary trader less than 5% of the time and 95% of the time you just follow your systems. Frankly a lot of people don't succeed at trend following so tell me why you think that you are succeeding at this while others are not. What do you think you're doing to be successful and what do you see other people doing who are not as successful at this as you are?

I think that's a great question. You can run what is called a Monte Carlo simulation on a system to see its variability of return. You can go back to the turtles for a lesson on this. Even the turtles - either the second or third generation - went to Richard Dennis after computers had improved. They went back because they realized they were over-sizing on risk. This is actually bad because these guys did really well three years ago because the market was suited for it, but it could have ended in disaster. I think it was the third generation guys who ended up having to change that risk profile.

One of the things that we really do harp on is portfolio creation and having multiple exits. This allows you to be robust in terms of trading multiple asset classes at the same time. Where people sometimes fall down on the trend following side is that they are usually a lot more short-term oriented. We are a lot more long-term. In fact it's good in the institution world that sometimes we get confused for long-term investors. If a trend is occurring you want to stay in it as long as possible. That usually means you have to be a lot more long-term.

What happens is that trend following at its core isn't sexy. Everybody wants to tell you, "I want to be invested with Paul Tudor Jones. Look at how my $10,000 would have turned into $2,000,000." He's had a great track record, great everything, but guess what? He's gone through periods where his recovery time from a previous high in the equity curve has been sixteen or eighteen months. For a lot of people that is a long time. Usually after three months people start system hopping.

In fact, I actually got a chance to meet another famous turtle. We had got done meeting with this guy and afterwards I went back and asked one of my friends, "Why did this guy shut down shop?" He said, "At the end of the day he actually would add in discretionary components. He would stop taking entries. He would stop taking exits or he would think he could turn around."

I think after meeting more and more people that the truth is this. At the end of the day they are not following exactly their system as they would have you believe. I've seen that on the retail level and I've seen that on the institutional level. I'm mean you are just shocked about situations like this guy who has an amazing eighteen year track record but who decided to shut down shop. When you ask why did he have such a bad year you then start looking at his track record. You end up going through his trades while knowing what his system is and thinking, "Well, why did you take this trade? Why did you take this trade?" "Oh, I just thought that would be a good trade." You're like, "Really? You guys are the systematic guys. Did you seriously just say that to me?"

I see that rampant on the retail side. It's very rampant. If you're going through a drawdown I personally think the toughest thing is to follow your stop. I think most people say that's the toughest thing. For anybody who's actually been a real money manager, my position is that the toughest thing is putting on the next trade in the middle of a drawdown.

In fact Jerry Parker who runs Chesapeake Capital, a good buddy of mine, always tries to be the antithesis of the institutional world. A lot of people say the same thing as us, which is that the money is made in the exit. He actually goes to the other side and says, "No, the money is in the entry." I looked at him one day and I said, "What are you talking about? You know this isn't true whenever you do your testing." He replied, "No, think about it. It's like Wayne Gretzky says: for every trade I don't put on because I'm scared that override is not following my system, so for me the most important thing is following my system, which is usually following my entries and my exits. I can't get to my exits unless I put on my entry." I was like, "You know what, that's a really good point."

It is a good example of how everything is intertwined. I would adamantly say that too many people just don't follow the proper rules. Even when they do it is usually a little too short-term and it's usually a little bit over-leveraged. We have found that no matter what system we test the optimal volatility position sizing for something ranges between one and two percent. You would be shocked at how many people either (a) use too short of a metric for their position sizing or (b) are like "I need to get a winner back and I really like this trade so I'm going to risk 5% instead of 2%." That's just a recipe for disaster.

We tell our clients all the time, "Look, one of the cool things about us is that we don't think that one trade is better than another. We give all stocks an equal chance of being an outsized return." That can get you into a lot of trouble as well because it adds random variability to the equity curve, which over time is the bad volatility that you don't want to have.

Can we go over the types of exits you use? For instance, do you have a stock set of different types of exits or is each system's exit uniquely different? What do you do for exits since that is a big problem for most people if they are scaling out of a large position?

There are two things that go along with what I just said. One of the things you find in the institutional world is that there is only one way to actually do scaling. As to the institutional world the firms like Winton Capital know how to do it. They do it properly. For retail people they think that they understand it but they do it wrong. We actually don't believe in scaling out. The reason why is simply this - unless you're literally trading Warren Buffett's size, and even then if you are trading thirty billion dollars and you're in liquid futures contracts, you aren't moving the market. You really aren't. I have sat on sell side desks and I have seen massive flow go through but the large orders don't necessarily move the market.

As a retail person, you really don't need to be scaling out of position. Here is the reason why. Mathematically, fundamentally, if it's a good time for you to be scaling out then it's a good time for you to technically be going short or to be out altogether.

That's one of the things I harp on with people. Whenever you scale out of something essentially what you are saying in the marketplace is either (a) I shouldn't be in it or (b) I should be shorting that. You shouldn't be scaling out of something. We've done test after test and we've had idea after idea, and it never works out optimally. It never delivers the best risk-adjusted return. It's a fallacy because it makes you feel good. If something goes up big you're thinking, "I just don't want to lose." Most errors in all investing whether long-term, short-term, fundamental, technical, trend following, all that jazz ... most errors are because of the human mental weakness of wanting to appease what we are afraid of.

In terms of answering specifically your question about the exits we do have a stock set - whether it's futures or stocks or currencies - we do have a boxed set of exits that we are always using. You already said it. Some are based upon price, some are based upon volatility, some are based upon momentum, but we do have a boxed set.

Now a few of our strategies are unique because they are built around either (a) fundamentals or (b) volatility. Yes, there are times where we have really unique exit points. For example, if we are short a stock and the short ratio gets way too high then statistically we have found that there are certain points where you should probably get out. Those are very unique situations. That's what I tell people, which is that at the end of the day a good trading strategy over the test of time is able to use these same components.

After you have reached that point most of your testing tells you that something still isn't better than what you are already doing. You then start to find unique points in history that still aren't over-optimization. You still have to go through the process of, "What's our sample size. What's this? What's that?" As long as you go through that and you understand that this is a normal occurrence, but it is a unique occurrence across a large enough sample size, then yes, you can create interesting rules on the short ratio and stuff.

We can't go into your exact rules that you want to remain confidential, but you are following proprietary systems. You are not really a discretionary trader, but even so let's talk about the human weakness or personality factors that affect this type of trading. From your experience, what type of individual would do best with systems trading and which type of individual would do worse in trying to become a systems trader? If you want to succeed doing your type of systems trading then what are the basic skills that you need to develop and master?

I think that is a good question where I can give the absolute credit to my good buddy Jerry Parker. He always said that there is not a mentality for investing. There is just a proper way to invest.

I can tell you that I actually agree with that. I'm not a big fan of these people who say, "I'm more of a gunslinger so I like to be a swing trader." Then you get other guys who say, "Well, I'm a nerd and I'm a programmer so I should be a systematic trader." No, there are just results, right? That's the cool part about the market, which is that you either have an edge or you don't. How you get there is just either more optimal or less optimal than another alternative that is out there.

I'm usually not that big of a fan of saying, "My style of how I invest suits who I am as a person." I think people are pretty dynamic. I think we all go through stages in life where we change. For example, I might be an extroverted person but there are times where I'm introverted. I've seen it with introverted people where they break out of their shell for a little bit. I think that in taking that from a broad strokes perspective there are times in our life where we are more disciplined and times when we are not.

A lot of people say, "Oh, he's super disciplined and that's why he can follow his system." I actually have a buddy who literally ran hundreds of millions of dollars but who was the wildest guy you'd ever meet. He just followed his rules. You could call him up at 9:30 and it was, "I'm putting on my trades." Once it was done it was, "I'm going skydiving." There was this massive dichotomy between the two. So I'm not a big fan of saying people are suited for one or the other. It is just that strategies are either more optimal or less optimal.

Now, I will say that if you know that you can't follow your rules then regardless of your personality you don't need to be in the game. I think it was Van Tharp who said that people get out of the markets what they want out of it. That might have been Ed Seykota. I love that guy and study as much of him as I can. He said, "Look, people don't trade the markets. They trade their opinions on the markets." I can confirm that without a shadow of a doubt.

For instance, we once ran money for a family office and they brought us in to do some consulting. They asked us to test out their "strategy" because they knew that we could test systems. It took a lot of prodding because they didn't realize how many variable, discretionary components it had to it, but eventually we got to the point where we could basically test out what they were doing. We showed that over the long run their system did not have any edge over the general market. They didn't want to hear it. They still decided, even with the facts straight in their face that, "No, we think this is the right way to invest." Okay, no problem. It's your call.

I tell others all the time that I love people's opinions because I make money off of their opinions. I make money off of people's mistakes. I make money off of people's fear. I make money off of people's greed. I make money off of all sorts of human interactions because at the end of the day you have to understand that market mechanics fit psychology.

Let's say I have a hundred shares of IBM at $100 and I want to sell a hundred shares of IBM. Let's also say you want to buy a hundred shares of IBM and let's say that you want to buy them at $100. Does IBM move? No. There is a trade that occurs, but you just see a transaction at $100. The market has paired the buyer to the seller. The only way that a market can go up or down is by having an outsized, imbalanced order. Either somebody says, "I want 100 shares of IBM at a $101 because I want it right now. I don't want to wait" or they say, "I want 101 shares of IBM at $100."

You begin to understand that this necessity of "I want it now" is built into the system itself. People always get worried that this market is run on algos now. The problem is that algorithms still have to adhere to the same concept of *now*, "I have to execute *now*," otherwise you are waiting for the order to occur.

Once again that is a very long-winded answer to just basically say that if you can't follow rules then don't be in the game. If you can follow rules then understand the psychology of the markets based upon market structure and then you can really start to understand how your own psychology needs to meet that.

I've talked to another great researcher and investor who is working with family offices, too, and who tests out systems. What do family offices usually call you in for and ask you to do? What are their typical concerns and what do you usually do for them?

Family offices are a unique game. They are definitely a growing game. The family office industry is just absolutely exploding. It's intriguing because the issues that they have are very similar to basic, large institutions.

Typically we have this family and they had a business. Maybe they took it public in an IPO and the family is worth like a hundred million dollars or fifty million dollars. It's a substantial amount of money. The objective for that family eventually changes. Your goal is preservation of capital, not growth of capital.

That goes back to my days where, as I said, I wanted to understand the way that the market worked from top-down to bottom-up. Your retail guy who is looking to make a million bucks wants a 100% return because he wants to get there now. He's honest with himself.

A family office is like, "Hey, we made our money. I just don't want to lose it anymore." Your offices that are large enough eventually get to the point where they say, either (a) "I want somebody to run my money that I trust" and they begin to outsource that or (b) they want to bring it in-house with a managed account. The ones that will consult out to us are usually along the lines of, "We like this whole trading game. We got into it, we love liquid markets." It could be a family that may have made its money in real estate and they never really messed with the stock market other than traditional mutual funds, but now they are really getting into the "stock market game."

What happens in that scenario is that normally they are smart enough that they know they don't know what they don't know. It scares them that they don't know what they don't know.

What happens is that they go, "Hey, we have this idea of something that works. Can you tell us if actually does?" Instead of money managers we become strategy testers for them. For a while there is a real need to that. I think that for a few years, especially as family offices grew exponentially, you saw that kind of shift in thinking pretty large. Now it's come back to, "This whole thing of running money and running it on our own is pretty dang hard. We are just going to actually go out and have money managers do it."

Let's switch topics. Do you have any macro comments on the economy and world trends that you might discuss such as the fate of the EU, death of the dollar, opinions on real estate or interest rates and things like that? Since you are systems traders this doesn't affect your executions at all, but you probably discuss such issues with your friends and might want to say something about what you folks are typically thinking.

When my foray started it was in the big boy world where you really had to understand and learn how the world thinks. Absolutely over the super long run stock markets are based upon how well an economy is doing, which is largely based on demographics more than anything. In addition, policy shifts over time can have drastic effects on that. There really is truly a lag in information, which is why you can have trends up and why you can have trends down.

We really have our own personal views on some of these matters because personally you are still looking at your own finances. You are saying, "If A, B and C happens then what am I going to do"? Being a student of history, we look at the point that we are at in the world and we basically say, "Yeah, it's about to happen again" with regards to the perspective that paper currency only lasts ever so long. I'm always hesitant to say that because people hearing that will go, "Oh, you're a gold bug." I respond, "No, I'm not a gold bug at all. The only bug I ever am is if I'm buying something because it's going up and it meets my rules. Outside of that, it is merely an opinion that I have."

Markets can stay irrational longer than you can stay solvent. That's why I can have the opinion that a fiat currency will basically implode on itself, and we are starting to see that now, right? Negative interest rates are now being floated in the news. Even our own Fed is going to consider a NIRP policy, which is asinine. It's really stupid. It's really sad that people would consider that, but we tell people that there is no such thing as the "Pope of Finance." The market truly is hooked on this drug called the Fed. People have used that analogy before but it really is true.

The market in terms of its participants is still made up of humans. People think linearly but they react emotionally. Most investing is a form of reaction. One of the things when you look at the broader picture is that you feel that investors no longer believe that they can take a hit. I equate this to what is going on with Fed policy and the fact that 5% moves can spook the Fed from making a decision. This is now confirmed. You look at the conversations at the Fed and can see that a 5% move in the stock market can spook the Fed from making a decision. That's a very, very dangerous state that we are in.

Enough really smart people, smarter than I, have been able to quantify how much the rest of the world has dependent factors upon what our Fed does. The world has become highly dependent upon whether or not the Fed uses the word "is" or "the" in their statements. That's a very, very dangerous spot. Fundamentals aside, it basically shows that people have gotten to the point where it is almost like they are searching for the Holy Grail that cannot have losses: "I can't have another 5% drawdown on my account.

Oh, crap I can't have another 3% drawdown on my account." With that mentality you start looking for the thing that is going to solve the problem and the Fed only does really have so many options under its disposal.

When we look at the broader situation, I'm actually more afraid for the American economy and for the American spirit with regards to capitalism than I am necessarily with the Fed itself. That's what scares me, which is that people look to the Fed now as if whoever is the chairman is somehow this all-seeing Pope of Finance. There are some great books out there that chronicle this. For instance, when he was Fed chairman Greenspan went to go talk to Tom DeMark, the technical analysis guy, to ask where he thought rates were going to go. This is an actual legitimate chronicled story now. Even for me, who can still look at it with pragmatic eyes and who says there is no Pope of Finance, I still look at it and go, "Seriously?" It's like the movie *Armageddon* where the character Harry Stemper goes off and says, "You're NASA for cryin' out loud. You put a man on the moon, you're geniuses! You've got guys in rooms in other rooms that are just thinking up stuff. How have you guys not figured this out?"

That's the way I view the Fed right now. You look at it and you go, "Really? You guys are supposed to be the smartest guys." It's like a doctor who is looking at the symptoms and treating the symptoms and not the cause, which is because in some aspects it is the cause itself. There are some good books on this.

Whenever the system changes to whatever it may become it is not going to go back to a gold standard. I firmly believe that. But you can go back to a basket of commodities. That's one of the main reasons why China has been doing what it is doing in relation to getting that national reserve status with regards to the IMF. Outside of that, it's one of those things where you have to take the environment that you are in and realize that the, for lack of a better term, the "oh shit" scenario is that everybody gets screwed anyway.

I love watching and seeing stuff for the preppers. The truth is that in a "oh shit" scenario you're never going to escape it. It hits everything. There is nobody who's okay. I can tell you right now that 2008 was not the "oh shit" scenario. Rather, 2008 was a financial crisis. It was not a Main Street crisis as much as they want to tell you otherwise. The problem was that you were in an election year cycle and so it got turned into a Main Street crisis.

Usually financial crises precede main, huge moving events. I absolutely believe that it will occur. If it occurs in my lifetime, I have no idea how long the resiliency of the U.S. dollar will last. We'll definitely see. We will be there to capture the trend whenever it occurs.

Thanks for that. For somebody who wants to be a trader or an investor, with all the stuff you've tested and learned what would you then tell them to read? What books would you recommend them to read or things you would recommend them do to start going up the learning curve quicker?

This is my favorite question. The reason why is because I love testing people. I get people, especially young guys who come to me and say, "I want to learn how to trade. I want to learn how to invest." I was there. I was that guy who literally went to every big fund manager that I could get my hands on and go meet. I was asking them to teach me, mentor me. My ultimate test for everybody is always this: "Read this book, here's my email, tell me what you think." I could tell you that out of a hundred people that I will do that to I've only had two that ever sent me a reply.

What was the book that you sent them to read?

One of the best ones that I like people to start with is Curtis Faith's book on trading like a turtle. I also like Covel's book because I think it's good to chronicle those guys, but Curtis Faith's *Way of the Turtle* does a good job of usually helping people think in terms of multiples of R, namely risk. That's an important concept. If you want to last in the game then you have to understand risk management. Now from an investing perspective and from a "how to do this properly" type thing that is a great book. Obviously there are some good things in it. There are some trading issues that are in there that we wouldn't say are optimal, but they still work.

One of the other things I love people to read is Taleb's book, *Fooled By Randomness*. That's because after all my years in the industry the biggest thing I found is that the more money that you have in the industry and the sector the more that people are able to make money by basically spreading half truths. It's not that they do it to be malicious. It's not that they do it any other way. They just don't know better. The same bull crap has been passed down to them through four generations.

I love Taleb's book, *Fooled By Randomness,* because you really get to understand the sense that yes, there is what looked like random components to the markets. If you are not accounting for that, if you're not adjusting for that volatility, if you're not being more longer term than what you think you should be then you are going to run into trouble. I absolutely love Taleb's book on that. It's a great book.

From a psych perspective I love the book *Invisible Gorilla* just from the perspective that our mind plays tricks on us. When you look or stare at a chart your mind will play tricks on you. It's a pretty cool book but it's not a trading book. However, for an experienced guy like myself I can peel back every example, every psychological test they do in there and I can say, "Here's how that happens in the markets. Here's how this happens in the markets." From a psych perspective I absolutely love that book.

For understanding trends and the fact that people are crazy, it's an extremely old book but *Popular Delusions and the Madness of Crowds* is a really good book. Mandelbrot's *The Misbehavior of Markets* is good for its fractal view. It's good to understand the concept of fractals, but that's pretty tough though.

I talked about Ed Seykota. I absolutely love his book, *Govopoly in the 39th Day*. Now that's a little bit less on the trading side and more on the political side. It basically explains why we're screwed. That's another great book that I really like.

Those are probably key. If you work for our firm we actually do have our own curriculum that we require everybody to read. I am big on reading. I still will read any new trend following book that comes out. I still read everything that comes out. I'm huge on it. Who is it, Buffett said it best, right? "I've made money because I've read more than most." It really is true.

Whenever I was a kid, I'd meet money managers and they would look at me and they'd say, "How do you know this?" They would be shocked by my knowledge. I'd say, "I read every paper that you wrote or every interview you have ever given." I'd go find the transcript for it. People were just shocked. I was like, "Look, I love this stuff. I live it. I breath it."

We live in a day and age where there is a lot of information. I will say that I think I was very blessed in that I read the good stuff and the right stuff and didn't go down the road of crap. There is a lot of crap out there. I do count myself pretty lucky, pretty blessed for reading what I did read.

It's already been twenty years in this field for you. I'm sure that there are some life lessons or philosophies or things you wish you knew when you got started years ago that would have put you ahead. Are there any things you'd like to tell people who are just getting started or who are in the middle of it and you really want to help them?

It's funny because it is the age-old question of, "Do you want a million dollars or do you want to learn how to make a million dollars?" To be quite honest, I think most people at the end of the day would say they just want a million dollars. I always had the view that I want to learn how to make a million dollars. In the markets, it was that I wanted to learn not just what works but what's right, what's best. In my very first internship I had a chance to go down a road that would have made me a lot of money, but it wouldn't necessarily have made my clients the best amount of money. It wouldn't have been best. It would have been highly dependent upon only a certain type of market regime.

Therefore I would say to never stop searching for the truth. If there is really one weird thing that I've found amongst the guys that are really successful it is that they never stop hunting for the truth. They will test anything and everything. They'll grab the phone and they will call their other buddy who is running a billion dollars and say, "Have you tested this?" "Yeah, we absolutely did and we actually implemented something in it." Those guys will go back to their team and say, "We have got to look at this." If there is one characteristic that I've noticed across the David Hardings of the world, your Jerry Parkers, your James Simonses, all those guys, it is that they never stop hunting for the truth. I have massive, massive respect for that.

If I could go back in time and wave my magic wand then I would probably hurt myself and destroy the industry because I am such an avid opponent of buy and hold. It doesn't work. We statistically show this all the time. Take the traditional advice that you put 60% in stocks because you take your age (50 in this example) and subtract it from 110 and that's how much should go into stocks while the rest should go into bonds. Lives have been ruined because of this kind of advice. I'm a firm believer that this recent bond rally will absolutely end and it is going to decimate people. It's not going to be real estate this time. It's going to be bonds or it will be healthcare that cracks it.

If there is one thing that I could change then it would just be going back and cleaning people's minds. All the time I ask them, "What is the purpose of the stock market?" Most people give the normal reply that you're used to: "Well it's for a company to go public and to raise assets." If you talk with a common guy, however, a lot of them think that the purpose of the stock market is to go up for your 401(k) so you can retire. They don't say it explicitly like that, but at the end of the day the decision that they are making is based upon that view.

I always, always tell people that the purpose of the stock market is merely to facilitate the seamless transfer of risk between two parties. If you can understand that then it will completely change your eyes as to why you should be investing. That's my big thing, which is that the industry has done an absolutely great job of taking these really simple axioms, "Oh the market goes up 10% every year," and contaminating people's judgment. People are like, "Sweet, in eleven years I'll be able to retire" and this, that and the other. They never take into account the fact that if the market goes down 50% and their account goes down 50% then on average they will have to stay in the game for another twenty years. Can they afford that? Just that whole concept of reward and risk is something people must learn to understand.

I'll be honest. I got through it quicker than most people, but I went down that road of buy and hold and your traditional advice and related issues. It's just extremely dangerous. For somebody starting out I think buy and hold has an allure merely from the aspect that it doesn't require work.

I will tell you that the Holy Grail of investing has drawdown. I wish somebody had told me that because I hunted for the Holy Grail for a really long time. It also has work involved in it. Think about it logically … is there anything in life where you have been able to just stuff your money in it, not do anything with it, and it magically just grows for you? Life doesn't work out that way. It never does.

I can't sit on my butt and say I will get six pack abs in six months or eleven years. However, that's the kind of approach and mentality that people have. That's why people will say, "Why do you have so many exits?" This is because it is what is required to have an extra edge in the market. Having an extra edge requires work. The guy who buys thirty names and then goes out and tells the fundamental stories about why he likes them is making a massive bet that the market is always going up, which is something that we just don't like nor do we believe is optimal.

Any other words of wisdom, life lessons or anything else you want to leave people with? Anything else you want to discuss, recommend or comment upon?

You know I think that's a good question. One of the things that I will say is that people need to have their financial house in order before they invest. It really is true. I've seen so many people who say, "I have a thousand bucks to my name and I want to go buy a penny stock. I want that to turn into a million dollars." The market is not a casino. Its purpose is to facilitate a seamless transfer of risk between two parties. Too many people treat it like a casino. It's really not that.

The interesting thing I will say is this. There is an interesting proverb in the Bible that basically says that you never know when it's going to rain so the optimal time to plant is now.

You meet with anybody who is successful and normally they are usually these huge action takers. The market is dangerous because you never want to take action via the attitude, "Hey, I bought a hundred shares. Sweet, I'm in the game." No, take action by reading one of those books that I recommended. That's the kind of action that you want to take. Take action towards getting to the point where you can say, "I'm confident that I have a robust strategy that will stand the test of time" or "I found a guy and he'll teach me how to invest at the same time he's running my money."

Literally, two of our best clients are like that. A funny story is that most of our accounts were up last year when the market was down. Everybody was happy, but one of our accounts had a unique bond program in it and we were flat for the year. We were down like 1% or something, but he was ecstatic. I was just surprised. I'm a competitive guy, I've played a lot of sports and I was like, "We wanted your performance to be better than this." He said, "I know that you will, but you killed everybody else that I have out there. More importantly, I got to learn from you this year."

That's one of the things we like to do a little bit differently with our clients. If a client comes to me and he has a question on why we do something, I love answering because God forbid something happens where I get hit by a bus or whatever it may be, and if so I want my clients to be able to go and find somebody like us elsewhere if anything were to ever happen. Most people would say that it's insanely crazy that you might give business away to competition. I say, "No, we're not giving it away. I just want people to understand those things because the alternative is that they lose money." The world runs off of money. If you have too little of it then life sucks.

I just absolutely love that proverb that you never know when it's going to rain so now is always the time to plant. Always be working on it. You never finish. I think that goes back to the guys that basically always are seeking for that truth. It goes back to the fact that we have systems that work by taking random entries. We can literally get into something random, long or short and over time we will make money. Not a lot but that's how well our exits work.

That's just that whole point. You never know what's going to happen in the future. Just be constantly taking action.

Thanks, Josh. Best of luck to you with your website service, your fund and your research.

Thanks, Bill.

Chapter 15
Bill Spetrino
Creating a Buffett-Like Dividend Compounding Machine

Bill Spetrino, editor of The Dividend Machine newsletter at Newsmax.com, has over 80,000 subscribers following his dividend stock picking methodology. Primarily a long-term dividend investor, Bill has achieved a very successful 20+% CAGR track record as recorded by The Hulbert Financial Digest. Through his investing he has achieved the investor's dream of retiring early. If you have ever wanted to learn how to combine value investing (aka Warren Buffett) with dividend investing and long-term dividend reinvestment strategies, this is a man whose methods you should study.

Starting with just $8,000, Bill attempted to learn the principles of Warren Buffett's style of investing and ended up creating a perennial compounding machine comprised of strong dividend stocks that throws off so much cash that he could walk away from his 9-5 job and retire at the age of forty-two. He now lives comfortably just on the income from his investments alone. A less risky and slower investing technique than day trading, options trading, growth stocks or high flyer momentum trading it achieves its profits by acquiring valuable assets at bargain prices if and only if the company is deemed a long-term winner able to continually throw off cash.

Bill firmly believes that if you are just getting started with investing then you should start with a basic technique like buy and hold, and the best stocks to buy and hold are strong consumer goods stocks, purchased at bargain prices, that throw off dividends. Even if you want to become a trader, he advises that you learn how to be an investor first and that you especially learn how to value companies and buy bargains where there are situations of "imaginary fear."

Bill, let's start with how you got started in stock market trading and how that moved into dividend stock investing.

I graduated from John Carroll University with a degree in accounting. I was an accountant and then I started buying and selling sports memorabilia. Then I started buying and selling tickets. All my life I wanted to build something where I didn't work and I got paid. I thought to myself, "There has to be a better way." From the start I was always focused on how to become financially independent so that I could retire.

I wanted to get into real estate but the problem with real estate was that you needed a lot of money to start. Interest rates were 10-12% at the time and I didn't understand it so I didn't get into it.

With my accounting background I bought a stock, Phillip Morris, and I started to receive dividends from it. I remember my first dividend check was for $44 back then. My dad said, "What are you going to do, buy a Happy Meal with this?" But things have now progressed to where my last dividend check is now three to four times what I made as my annual salary at my first job.

Getting into dividend investing was a gradual progression. Most people look at investing as they are buying something so that they can flip it real fast. I thought of it as, "I'm going to be buying a business that is spitting me out money and I just want the money coming. I want that check coming every quarter."

I looked at the cigarette business - at the time Philip Morris owned Miller Beer and Kraft - and I thought, "Geez, this is a great business." My investing mentor told me before he died, "If people can't eat it, drink it, smoke it, fuck it, watch it, wear it or bet on it then forget it."

So I was in a position with Kraft. They had brands like Kool-Aid, Oreos, Philadelphia Cream Cheese. They had the brands. They had Miller Beer, Marlboro and all the big brands that controlled 50% of the tobacco market in the United States and 10-12% in the world. I just thought, "This was a good safe place to put my money," and I just kept buying more shares and kept reinvesting.

Every dollar that I saved I just kept putting into that stock. It was funny because in 1996-1998 everybody was buying a stock for $20 and it would go to $50 by the end of the day. My stock kept going down but I wasn't focused on that. I was focused on a goal. I knew that my goal was to be able to get $26,000 or $27,000 a year and then my house would be paid off. I thought, "Okay, when I get to that point I can retire."

You ended up only investing in one stock?

At the time I was invested in that one stock and later I was buying other ones, but in 1998-1999 there weren't a lot of good bargains. When I started there was a whole bunch of good bargains and then there were none. I stayed in a couple of big stocks like Abbott Labs, Budweiser, McDonald's – things I could understand. Those are easy stocks to understand. When anybody is starting out in investing they should start out with stocks they understand.

You're saying that you started out as a buy and hold investor? You weren't a trader?

Absolutely, absolutely. Buy and hold was the way I went. I started trading as I got older and learned more. Investing is kind of like learning how to ride a bike and trading is like learning how to do wheelies or stunts on your bike.

I'll tell you that most people who trade lose. They are just like gamblers. You are going to lose. I started investing with three people and they all faded out. I'll tell you why.

I was gambling since I was three years old. When you are out of money then you cannot play anymore. When you are wrong they take your money. When you bet for the short term you can have many losers. I know some of the best poker players in the world, including some of the famous ones like Doyle Brunson. They have all gone broke at one time or another in their career because they got a bad run of cards whereas if you are investing in buy and hold the story can be different.

I had a tobacco stock that dropped 50%, but I sat there and just kept buying more of it at a lower price. People were worried that tobacco was going to become illegal but the government got too much money from taxes. If you go to a state like Kentucky, Tennessee or even Virginia, you will see that there are people who grow tobacco. Tobacco cannot be illegal. The government needs the revenue from it. It was Napoleon who once said, "If I could figure out a better way to raise tax revenue then I would make smoking and drinking illegal," but he wasn't $17 trillion in debt like we are now.

Okay, so you started out in investing rather than in trading. You made that decision from the very start. However, was this dividend investing from the very start or were you originally using some other form of investing model to guide your decisions?

Yeah, it was dividend investing from the beginning. There weren't a lot of books that explained things back in pre-internet days. Today, there are tons of investing and trading articles. You couldn't really trade until the internet came.

I bought my first stock when I was in college. I made a $2,000 investment and was charged a $75 commission to buy it and $75 to sell it. That's an 8% commission. It was too expensive. You couldn't trade with those costs. Today, you can buy a million dollars worth of stock with a market order costing $5. You couldn't do that back in those days. When trading did pick up in the late '90s a lot of people got into it, but I was building my dividend machine.

I switched to doing some trading because I can do it now. Once you learn the basics of investing then it's much easier to trade. Warren Buffett can trade and Carl Icahn can trade. The reason they don't is because they have billions of dollars. They can't quickly get in and out of large stock positions but if you want to just trade with a hundred thousand dollars you can do that.

I have an account at StockTwits and I put two trades on yesterday that each made 1½% within a couple of hours. Now I didn't actually do the trades myself because I'm in a higher tax bracket now. I have what I want right now. I don't need to do it, but I know how to do it.

When you started out it was too expensive to actually do in-and-out trading so you ended up investing instead. Did you focus on a special investment style like Warren Buffett's or John Templeton's?

I was a Buffett clone. I followed Buffett. I bought some Coke a little bit after he did. I followed him into silver. I followed him into quite a few investments because at the time he knew more than I did and I wanted to know why. I needed to understand how he was thinking. There wasn't all the information there is now.

Investing is like anything else. It's a learning process. I remember Templeton saying to buy at maximum pain and being a gambler all my life I knew that you couldn't do anything obvious. If you bet football, if the outcome was obvious then everybody would make money. However, with a computer that finds things if you factor in enough data then you can make money.

I often combine long-term investing with trading. I'll put on a trade but if I have to keep it on a long time then I will because no one can predict what is going to happen in the short term. They can predict what is going to happen in the long term. It's easier.

Each person has their own skill set. My job as a dividend investor is to find imaginary fear. Like yesterday, for instance, I went long USO and long an energy stock named RIG, which is Trans-ocean. The reason I went long is because Prince Alwaleed came out and said, "Oil will never be a hundred dollars."

Well, first of all, Prince Alwaleed is one of the worst investors in the world. He was born rich. He bought Citigroup when it was way overpriced and then he bought it again right before the crisis telling everybody, "Yeah, I'm getting a bargain." He's not Warren Buffett. He didn't earn his money. He was born on third base and thinks he hit a triple. He was a pinch runner in the game. I put the trade on knowing that and then Boone Pickens came on the air and basically said, "I've made a billion dollars investing. Oil is my business and oil will be higher by the end of the year," and then the price of oil went back up.

I anticipated that would happen. I didn't anticipate Boone Pickens would come on TV. I just knew that because of Prince Alwaleed dummies were sitting at their TVs going, "Oh, I got to short this," while smart people are sitting there going, "I have to go long."

It's like when you are playing cards - if you're at the table for half an hour and you don't know who the sucker is then that means it's you. I try to combine street smarts and book smarts. I have an instinct I've developed. I've been gambling since I was five or six years old buying and selling things and if you're wrong then like I said they will take your money. That's what happened to my friends.

People ask me all the time, "My kid wants to be an investor, where do I send him?" I say, "Teach them how to gamble" because if you don't know how to get the odds in your favor then you aren't going to make money.

How do you teach them to gamble?

Well, what you would do is this. Let's say the kid likes baseball. You can get the odds off the computer and tell him, "Okay, I'm going to give you $3,000. I want you to pick what baseball team is going to win today." For instance, let's say the Yankees are playing the Red Socks and the odds are that the Yankees are 7-5 favorites, meaning if you like the Yankees you lay 7 to win 5. If you like the Red Socks you lay 5 to win 6. The difference in there is for the bookie.

When you do this for the kid he will start learning how to figure the odds. He'll start thinking, "Well gosh, if this guy pitches then ..." or he'll figure out various scenarios that affect the odds. For instance, when a team loses three in a row and they come back from a long road trip to play at home the kid will come up with scenarios like this to start figuring the odds. He will start thinking.

The trick is that you are now thinking and that you are developing a system that works for you. If I had a system, which I don't (though I have parameters that I use), but if I had a system I would never publish it because then everybody would be using it. I would destroy my advantage.

For instance, there was a theory in the old days in the NFL that if you bet against a team that played on Monday Night Football then you would win so many percent of your bets because (1) they had a shorter week and (2) they were on TV so people would overestimate them because they saw them on TV. That theory worked for a while until the bookies figured it out and then they started changing the line around. Something will work until it doesn't work.

John Templeton will tell you and Warren Buffett will also say to be greedy when others are fearful. Templeton will say to buy when there is maximum pain. You have to be able to spot imaginary fear and real fear to do that.

When the J.P. Morgan Whale incident happened I bought J.P. Morgan immediately because the fact that a trader lost money isn't a surprise. When you make big bets you are going to make mistakes the same way Michael Jordan is going to have a game where he doesn't make all his baskets. Those are the odds.

Were Warren Buffett and John Templeton your two gurus?

They were my two key gurus. I followed Buffett and I followed Templeton.

I'll tell you a funny story about Buffett's Berkshire Hathaway. I phoned them back in the old days because I wanted to buy Berkshire Hathaway stock. I called because you could get the annual report by phoning. Well, they didn't send it to me so I called them and I said, "Hey, I called previously. Please send me the report." A man answered the phone, which I now realize is Warren Buffett because he only had eight or nine people in his office. I had never heard his voice back in the old days but I've heard it now so I recognize it. He said, "I'll take care of that" real fast and before I could say thank you he hung up the phone.

I would read his annual report and my gambling background helped me because of what he said, "Be greedy when others are fearful and fearful when others are greedy," which was very helpful. He told everybody to read *The Intelligent Investor* by Benjamin Graham. To be honest, I hated that book. I'm an accountant and I couldn't follow it. It was very dry. But there were two chapters - chapters 8 and 20 - that were great.

In the book Graham talks about "Mr. Market." Mr. Market is here to serve you, not guide you, meaning that if you know what the price of something should be and everyone else doesn't know then you have a big advantage.

Just like right now to be long on oil stocks. If you believe oil is going to remain at this price for two or three years then you shouldn't be long oil. But I think that it's just not realistic that the price of gas is not going to stay this low. I just don't believe it. A gallon of gas should not sell for three times less than a gallon of milk. Something is not right about that. My instinct is contrary to the people going out onto the air saying there will be $13 oil. I don't listen to that stuff. If they really knew they wouldn't be telling anybody or they'd have billions of dollars like Carl Icahn or Warren Buffett.

Right now Buffett's down big on IBM. If you buy IBM at $150 you are going to be fine. You're getting it cheap. You are being his partner but you're getting in cheaper than him.

What I'm trying to get at is the origin of your investment philosophy. How exactly did you get into dividend stocks as your primary investment methodology? You said you were following Warren Buffett. Are you talking about in the '80s or the '90s?

Oh, no. When I started investing in the late '80s and early '90s I started following Warren Buffett by reading his annual reports because back then the famous investors would write a book only occasionally. I couldn't get information any other way than by reading his annual report. Peter Lynch wrote *One Up on Wall Street,* but Buffett never wrote any book. As a matter of fact, the first book that I read about him - and it is the best book - was called *The Making of an American Capitalist,* by Roger Lowenstein. It exposed his relationship with Kate Graham and talks more about his personal life.

What I got from him were the principles of what you need to do. As time went on it was trial and error that produced my investing style. For example, some people talk about book value. Book value in a bank is very important. However, for a regular company or consumer goods company, it isn't important. Each company is different, just like women. There is no set way to deal with women. You could say one thing to a particular woman and it would make her upset while saying the same thing to another woman would make her happy. It's the same thing with stock investing so what you have to do is stick to what you know best.

What I know is imaginary fear and real fear. I also know what the price of something should be and I can feel when it's wrong. I'll think, "It's just a wrong number," and I can feel it. I'm not always right, nobody is always right but in investing you have to consider the odds.

When you trade you are considering something in the short term and then the probabilities are "maybe it will and maybe it won't." However, long term is different. Over time a stock like Apple will do more business five years from now than it will now because the company has money in it already that they are going to invest. If your cash coming in is a billion dollars more than your cash going out every week and you already have two hundred billion dollars of cash sitting in your company then you probably will be worth more in the future. If I ask you personally, "Are you worth more now than you were five years ago?" you probably are worth more now. If you go back another five years, you are still probably worth more now than at that time because you've had the power of compounding working for you.

I'm still not getting what I want. Let's pick up it up again on how exactly you got started in trading. You said that as a kid you got into gambling and then you bought some Philip Morris stock that somehow led to this particular niche.

I did sports memorabilia and then entered into the stock market. I started in stocks when I had $8,000, but once I had more money I couldn't put the money into tickets and sports memorabilia anymore so I went into stocks. It made sense to me. What I like about stocks is that once you put your money in then it doesn't cost you anything else.

But why did you get into dividend stocks specifically rather than growth stocks or any other philosophy of investing?

Because I wanted to retire. The object of work is so that you can retire. When you have enough money then you can retire. The reason you are working right now is probably because you need more money. I can't say that for sure because I don't know you, but 98% of the people are still working because they need more money and until you have enough money coming in from your investments you cannot retire.

Let's say you have a stock portfolio with a million dollars in it. You don't know what it is going to be worth tomorrow. Even if you have that money, a million dollars is not going to last you the rest of your life. Not if you're going to live thirty or forty more years it isn't, so you have to know what you've got to do with that money or you are going to tap it all out.

I started investing in dividend stocks for the reason that I wanted to retire. Most people invest for the wrong reason. They want to become rich. I'm all about cash flow. I want the cash to be coming in from my investments.

Now I will trade and I will buy stocks that don't pay dividends. I will do that now because I've got the dividend machine already in full gear, but for 99% of the people they should be investing and not trading. They don't know that.

I want our members to understand that you started out investing with only $8,000, but you retired at age forty-two because you were able to build up a dividend machine.

Yes. Once you start seeing the dividend checks come in you get motivated. When I saw the first check of $44 I was like, "Wow! Imagine if I can start putting more money into these stocks." What I would do is get an idea like cutting my lunch budget from $5 to $3 so that I could put the extra money aside and invest it. Then I'd say, "Okay, I'm going to get free samples at the mall" or "I'm going to shop for my car insurance." I was so much more aware of saving money to invest because I was very focused on building my income. And when my stock dropped, I didn't get mad like other people. I was happy because I could buy more of it.

You never worry about the dividend being cut?

Well no, because in a stock like Altria or a consumer goods company … let me state right here that that's the type of stock everybody should be starting with because they are simple. That's why consumer good companies are so expensive now. People are finally realizing that they are the right place to be. That's why utilities are doing good now. It's because people are realizing that, for instance, if you're a New York resident then you have got to go with Con Ed. You cannot go without it. If you're in a Coca-Cola or Pepsi Cola then it doesn't matter what the economy does.

There are some stocks that are risky, like if you buy energy or you buy banks or you buy things that are cyclical then that's a different story. You have to be able to buy some stocks at the right part of the cycle. You might have to wait years for your trade to work out whereas with the consumer goods stocks, as long as you are buying them right you are good and you should just keep adding to it.

I just kept seeing the quarterly dividend checks come out and they were bigger and bigger and bigger and bigger. I became addicted almost. And then I started using margin because I could borrow money at a certain percent. The first time I used margin was in 2000. I borrowed money at 7% and I was getting a 10½% dividend. I had an interest only loan. I didn't get it with a broker. I got it on my house. I got the 7% in the beginning when I started using margin and then I pledged my stocks off.

In other words, you looked at the whole thing as like a business where you were buying assets that were throwing off cash. You didn't really care that those asset values bobbed up and down in the marketplace as long as you knew you would be holding them for the long term and deemed that they would keep throwing off that cash flow into the future while retaining a good deal of their value. If that was your conclusion, you'd even borrow money to buy the stocks if the difference between the dividend yields and margin interest rate led to what you considered was a safe net rate of return.

Bingo. You nailed it.

Then you said, "What businesses are going to consistently do that?" That's why you focused on consumer goods stocks.

Right, because that was the easiest thing. Figuring out McDonald's or figuring out Coke or figuring out Pepsi ... they are not complicated businesses so I could understand them.

Now I invest in things like Herbalife and different things. For instance, I took a position in Herbalife because I was in network marketing. I know a bunch of attorneys and I don't think that network marketing is going to be deemed illegal by the FTC especially when the guy who was the Deputy Assistant to Obama, Alan Hoffman, appointed these people. He left Pepsi to go to Herbalife. A former FTC commissioner, Patricia Harvard Jones, left her lucrative law firm to go work for Herbalife. Obviously, these people know how the political winds blow. Plus, Eric Schneiderman and Kamala Harris are the attorney generals of New York and California and have been silent about the company as has been Elizabeth Warren.

To me, Bill Ackman is trying to scare a whole bunch of people into thinking that Herbalife is doomed. When people that look at charts just say, "Oh. The chart's broken," they aren't thinking. The minute the FTC rules then that stock is going to go up if they don't get closed down, and it will go down if they get closed down. No chart will tell you that. No financial report will tell you that. I have just done my own analysis. After doing this for thirty years I figured out the odds and I'm betting with Carl Icahn, William Stiritz, Soros, and Daniel Lowe who was in on it.

I listen to other people, too, but invariably I have to make the decision myself. But yes, to answer your question this is a business that I do. It's no different than owning a property except the beautiful thing is that it is easier. With a rental property you have to know how to fix things, you have taxes and you must do upkeep and maintenance. You also have to worry if somebody doesn't pay you. Not with stocks.

What's the chance that Apple is not going to pay their dividend or Altria? People will object and bring up to me, "Well what about Eastman Kodak, Bill?" Bill Gates pronounced Eastman Kodak dead in the '90s. The stock still ran up. It was a slow death for them. If I can see that Altria is losing share to Reynolds then I'll worry but until they start losing market share I've got a money machine that is just printing me money.

Let's consider somebody who also wants to start with investing rather than trading. Do you believe that dividend investing is the best initial road for general investors rather than growth stock investing, pure value investing without dividends, momentum investing and so on?

Absolutely. It's the only way for them. There are different ways of investing. You can momentum trade, you can try to buy high and sell higher, ... all these different things. The problem with them is that you are just starting.

My philosophy is that when you are starting out you don't know what you are doing so you should go with something basic. The most basic thing in investing is to buy a company and hold it, watch it and study it.

Do you have a pet? Let's say you have a dog. That dog knows you well. You know why? Because you feed it and it's dependent on you. If you watch one company in the beginning you should watch it and learn as much as you can about it. Then you can move to another one. After that you move to another one. It's just like weight lifting or like anything else. You should have a gradual progression of making progress.

The problem is everyone gets in it to get rich quick and there are a whole bunch of charlatans telling you that they are going to make you 2% or 1% a week. If they could do all that then why are they writing a book? What do they need to do a service for? They should be rich.

I think you should start out with that and work your way up. You have to start small and build yourself up. See, that's the thing with investing. My way is boring and you are not going to get rich fast but this is the way to get started. If you want to be a trader then you need to learn how to be an investor first so you can understand what the hell are you doing.

That's fantastic advice. Now let's move to your actual stock selection process. What criteria or methodology are you using to pick your stocks?

Dividend investing. For dividend investing, I have an eighteen point system. I cannot share all the details because some criteria are actual numbers and each sector is different.

Let's just take Altria, for instance, which is in the tobacco industry. Market share is my main thing with them. I don't care what the profits are because that moves back and forth. However, I want to make sure that they are the number one brand because when you are the number one brand you then control the price increases or the price drops in the marketplace.

Now, these companies don't consciously price fix. In the tobacco industry they keep the prices high. Some companies like Barnes and Noble and Amazon keep trying to underprice each other where nobody is going to make any money in the long run. That's a bad business. I try to see if the business is good. Like Buffett says, "Give me a hundred billion dollars and let me see if I can take the business share away from it."

In other words, the first question you ask about a potential stock is whether the business is good, but you have a different set of criteria for each market sector to determine if the business is good?

Correct. Each company, each thing has different parameters.

The first step is that you want to see if the business is good. For instance, Starbucks has a great business. The problem is that it's never cheap. You're always buying it at thirty and forty times earnings. I just don't know, I'm not savvy enough to know when Starbucks is going to stop being cool. It's out of my circle of expertise but I can ask other people to help tell me that.

The first question then is about the business. What's the second question?

The second question is your valuation. You have to see if you are getting a good deal. Let's say a company earns 12% a year and it can compound that. You are only going to earn about 12% a year if you buy the stock at a fair price. If you buy the stock at the wrong price it's trouble.

I'll give you a good example, which is Coca-Cola. Buffett told everyone to buy it in 1991 when it was at a certain price. In 1991, the price was just about 10x earnings. That stock was selling for 80x earnings in 1998. I told a client to sell it when it was 55 times earnings. I said, "This is crazy. Get rid of it." He kept it and it ran up to 80x earnings because that's what momentum things do. But then in a fifteen-year span, Coca-Cola now with the splits and everything is not much higher than it was back then because that would be the return if you bought it at the wrong time.

I don't like to pay more than fifteen times earnings for something. I just don't like to do it unless it's a special situation stock like Gilead. Gilead was a biotech stock that I bought. I gave it to my subscribers when it was $14 while they were working on a hepatitis C drug and if it was going to hit then it was going to be a *big hit*. Well, it did hit. I was willing to pay a little more for that potential because I understood things.

For the formula you basically have to find a good business that you understand and you have to find a fair valuation, which takes you time.

Some companies, like Ford, are in a very capital-intensive business. A P/E of 12 isn't good for Ford. It's too high because it costs too much money. Now take a consumer goods company like Altria. What do they have? They put tobacco into a machine with a conveyor belt and a product comes out. Technology helps their businesses every year. They cut costs all the time because machines don't cost what they used to cost to fix them.

You have to determine if you think that oil is going to fall, and if so then you buy the airlines, FedEx and you buy UPS. The trouble is that UPS dropped 10% yesterday not because the company stinks but because people just bid it up too high. Smart people then took their profits. So there is no set valuation system. The thing with investing is there is not a set valuation system. There are parameters that you use to eliminate things, but in the end it comes down to experience.

Those are the basic things and then after that it just depends on the particular sector. There are different things to look at and they are not the same for every stock. For every stock I look at different things. That's why I have to give an example because for one stock I think one way and for another stock I will look at other things. In the end, I have to see whether I know something that everyone else doesn't know.

You just have to have an edge. For instance, I understand network marketing. I understand certain businesses and it varies. Everybody wants a certain valuation system they can plug into. It doesn't work like that. It just totally doesn't. Investing is not like that. Like Buffett said, "The person with a high IQ doesn't beat the person with the low IQ." It doesn't work like that. A lot of it is just trial and error. It really is.

Why do you need to know something that the market doesn't know?

Well, because then you can distinguish between imaginary fear and real fear. Let me give you two examples. With Blackberry the stock dropped because Apple was eating its lunch. The iPhone was eating its lunch. If you talked to people then you could find that out. Same thing with J. C. Penney. You could find out that no one was shopping there anymore. You could find that fact out by asking people and get information that the market doesn't know.

What I do is this: before I pick a stock every month I have a play-off. I'll play stocks against each other. I'll pick the five stocks that I think are the best ideas and then I'll number them. I'll play number five against number four just like how the old bowlers tours used to be where you would bowl and whoever wins would get to play number three, then get to play number two and so on. And then what I do is I have a panel of people that I hire. I run the questions by saying, "Okay, you are going to be the bear. Tell me why J. C. Penney stinks."

I liked J. C. Penney at one point. It looked cheap. When I kept asking women about it they kept telling me, "I don't shop there anymore. I don't like it. They took away the coupon." I couldn't find anybody that liked it and I knew it was going to go down whereas like with Herbalife, I understand network marketing. I talked to a group of attorneys and when thirty-out-of-thirty attorneys tell you there is no way they are going to shut down with or without the people that got hired from the government then I feel I've got information that the average person doesn't have. I'm not afraid of what is going on. A lot of the stuff that appears in the media is BS or like what I told you about Prince Alwaleed. He doesn't know what he's doing. He is a contra-indicator.

Because you are not a customer of a particular company you then use other people to help evaluate how it is doing, and you are always looking for fear situations in the marketplace that will depress a stock's price, and then you …

Right. I'll give you a good example. I started buying Bank of America when it was like $10 or $11. Everyone said the bank would go broke. People kept saying that all the banks were going to go broke. The stock went from $10 to $5; I bought it all the way down and had a basis price of $7. When the stock got back to $10 I was up 30% from where I originally bought it. I was able to do this because I have the philosophy that the market is here to serve me, not guide me.

Our country doesn't work, in my opinion, without Bank of America. I thought all of the negative news was nonsense and it *was* nonsense. I was buying the stock under tangible book value, which means that if you liquidated the whole company they had more cash than the stock was selling for. To me, as long as you didn't believe that the banks were going to all go broke then the government had already proved it would step in and help the banks. That's just the way it is.

This sounds like the following story. A stock's price is depressed. Everybody is saying, "Oh, it's going to go bankrupt" or something similar so the bad news attracts your attention. You look at it and you value it. For this stock you said, "Well, let me look at the price versus book value." You then bought it after concluding it was safe and then you got a rebound in price for instant profits. But what about dividends in this story? Where did they factor into the picture? Were you buying it because of dividends?

Not Bank of America. Bank of America wasn't a dividend stock. For a dividend stock as long as I think that the dividend is good I keep buying the company and I'll even buy it down, like in 2008.

Here is a great example of a dividend stock. In 2008, Altria was selling for $21. The stock dropped in three weeks to $14. It dropped 30%. Now, the tobacco business didn't change. It's not like the company reported bad earnings and it dropped, which is real fear. It wasn't like a stock such as Radio Shack where nobody goes there anymore.

In Altria's case, it dropped because the liquidity dropped. People had to sell their flowers, not their weeds. They had to sell their good stocks in their portfolios. We had the Bernie Madoff crisis and all these people had to liquidate positions to raise cash so people just sold anything they could get their hands on. They dropped Altria from $21 to $15. In three weeks, it dropped and I knew that this was irrational so I bought it at $16. I bought it at $15. I bought it forty-seven times between $14.50 and $16.50 from October to March of 2009 and I borrowed the money to do it.

Because you knew the business wouldn't go bankrupt and you would still get dividend cash and ...

I was getting an 8½% dividend and my margin rate was 2½%. I thought, "Well geez, if I borrow $500,000 then I'm paying $12,500 to borrow the money and I'm collecting $42,000." I thought that was a good risk/reward proposition.

You never worried about your principal? You didn't worry that the stock price would go down?

No, because I'm not selling the stock so it didn't matter to me. I knew that the dividend and the earnings were not going to be messed up. People actually were going to smoke more during the crisis and that was exactly what ended up happening. People smoked and drank more because they were nervous, but the market does irrational things because nobody values it this way. They are only looking at their price charts. You know a chart person or trader is going to say, "It's dropping! It's dropping!" They don't want to know why. I want to know why. I'm looking for a bargain due to imaginary fear.

Are you then a dividend stock investor who's normally looking for "fear stocks" that you can buy?

Absolutely, because that is how you get a good price. This is where the horse racing analogy comes in. Let's say you were going to run a race against a person who is crippled. The odds are that you are going to win. Everybody knows that so they are going to make the odds accordingly. Nobody is going to bet on the cripple.

It's the same thing with investing. There are a lot of great companies. They are just overpriced and you can't afford them or you can buy them but you are not going to make any money with them going forward. The reason that Buffett, Icahn, Loeb and all the other investment stars are who they are is because they buy depressed assets and they make their money that way.

You have to be able to have the conviction to buy when prices drop. If you are worried about your principal then you're going to get scared to death. You can't worry about that. You have to focus on the dividend and the earnings because invariably the earnings are going to drive the companies forward.

You are basically saying, "Bill, here's what I do. I want a stock that I know is a good business. Warren Buffett has the same rule. I want it to keep making money and paying cash for as many years as possible into the future, which I can't fully predict, and I want to buy it at a depressed price if I can, so I look to buy it during fear situations."

Imaginary fear against real fear. Yes. That's it. You paraphrased it perfect. I buy imaginary fear.

Wonderful. You buy "imaginary fear." Do you have a list of stocks you are waiting to buy like this? Or do you just wait until a new stock, like Herbalife, is suddenly in the news so that it grabs your attention and then you analyze it to spot the imaginary fear and then pounce?

That's a great question. I have a list of stocks I want to buy. I have a shopping list. Obviously when they get into the news I start looking closer. I didn't like Herbalife at $65. At $35 I loved it.

Because that would double your yield, whatever it would be …

Exactly, exactly, exactly. See, Herbalife ended up cutting their dividend, which normally would make me nervous, but they did that to buy the stock back because Bill Ackman is short the stock big time and he has got to cover it at some point. The minute the FTC releases Herbalife from their investigation - if they release them and I'm betting they will - then the stock will shoot up. Right now, people won't put their money in it because they are afraid it's going to close. I believe that's nonsense.

You've got this Watch List and if something happens with the stock then you'll take a good look at it. Did you say that you actually hire a panel of people to help evaluate it?

Yes. I hire regular people, not investors. I know the numbers of the company. What I don't know, for instance, is whether housewives are going to J. C. Penney. Are people using Blackberrys? I don't know these things so I use a panel to tell me.

The biggest mistake that most investors make is they look at what *they like* or focus on what *they are thinking* and not what the consumer is thinking or what the world is thinking. Bill Ackman and George Soros, both famous investors, lost their shirts on J. C. Penney because they looked at the numbers. The numbers look great. The problem is nobody was going there anymore.

This idea of a panel is pretty unique and people would want to hear more on this because they might want to try this, especially when a large trade is at stake. This is one of the gems you have given me in this interview. Please explain the process of actually hiring people to help you evaluate stocks. What do you actually do?

I will tell a person that I will give him a $50 gift card for doing this. I don't pay them a lot of money and a lot of them will do it for free for me. Here is how it works. Let's say you are in the publishing business. Then I say, "Bill, I want to talk about Barnes and Noble. I want you to tell me about their future. What do you think about them?"

Okay, but how many people are you going to get for your panel to do this?

I get a panel of usually three or four. I get a person who is favorable and I get a person who is unfavorable. Sometimes I'll be the bull and they will be the bear and they will have to sell me or I sell them on the company.

Here's how I do it. I'll ask people, "Who shops at J. C. Penney?" First of all, I couldn't find anyone for this company. It took me thirty or forty people to find people who shop there. Most people never even shop there anymore. When I did find somebody they were lame like, "Well, I go there because it's traditional. My mom used to take me there" and I'll be like, "Well, do you like it?" "Well, yeah, kind of."

That told me everything I needed to know. I was trying to get them to tell me good things about J. C. Penney and while they didn't tell me bad things they just didn't tell me good things. I want to be with a company where they tell me something good. I try to find three people for each stock that will give me a bullish case, but I couldn't do it for J. C. Penney. I just couldn't. Women tell me that the company stunk and they used to shop there but they didn't anymore and that told me all I needed to know.

So for any stock you try to get several people to give you a bullish case and then what do you do?

And then I try to shoot holes in it, or I'll give a bullish case and they'll be bearish and they'll try to shoot holes into me, into my argument.

How did you find a bearish person if they are already a person who's shopping?

Well, I had people who already shopped at J. C. Penney and they didn't like it anymore. Well, they were telling me why they didn't like it and how Kohl's was beating their ass and this and that. Well, a Wall Street analyst hasn't shopped at J. C. Penney. This woman has.

This is interesting. Let's try to do this for McDonald's. What are you going to do?

I'll ask you, "Hey, you go to McDonald's, don't you?" You'll say, "Yeah, I do. I like it." I'll then say, "Good. Do you want to be part of a panel with me?" "Yeah, I'll be a part of it."

Then I'll say to someone else, "Hey, you go to McDonald's?" They'll say, "I used to, but I don't like it anymore." "What do you mean?" "I don't like it. They're not appealing to me anymore. They're concentrating on other things. I don't like it."

Then I'll put the two of them together. I'll listen to both sides of the story and I'll be in the middle. I don't need to ask them financial questions. I want to know why they like the company or why they don't like the company.

Do you get them on the phone? How does it work?

Yeah, I get them on the phone. Mostly, I get them on the phone. It'll be a three-way call or a conference call. I just try to get the information from them in order to try to find out things.

In other words, if you want to buy a stock then you find two or three people that use that company or its products or dropped them or use somebody else, you get them on the phone in a conference call and you start listening to a pro and con argument.

And then I decide it from there. Some people are adamant about the company. It doesn't mean that they are right or wrong. It just means that I need to hear their opinion. For instance, if you don't shop something then you don't know. It would be like a man trying to understand what it feels like to give childbirth. As men we don't know because we have never done it so we don't know. We need to ask a woman.

I find that this strategy works for me. It helps me find out things. It keeps me out of a lot of bad stocks that other people get involved in. Now it has kept me from some good ones, too, but in investing it's not about what you do right. It's about what you do wrong.

Do you do this for every stock, every big play?

Yes, yes. Every stock.

Wow! This costs you money every time you do this to just consider whether you want to buy a stock.

It's all relative to what I'm doing. A lot of people do this with me for free. I'll trade favors for others, like I'll say, "Hey, do you want to do me a favor?" Then in return they can call me and I'll do tax consulting for them or I will show them how to save money on their insurance. I don't always lay out money if I don't have to, but maybe I'll give them a copy of my book or my newsletter. I give them something of value, but some people don't want it. They just want to tell me if they are really bullish or bearish.

I don't want people that are lukewarm. When too many people are lukewarm about a company, that's a bad sign. They're not passionate about it.

I can evaluate the company's numbers. I don't need them for that. I need them for talking about the actual company and its products.

How long does that conversation last? You said you usually have two other people at the same time?

Well, it varies. If I can get two people arguing with each other that's what I'm trying to do. It just doesn't always happen that way. Sometimes somebody will sell somebody else and the other person will say, "Well, I kind of like the product, but I could see what you mean by, 'They are overpriced' and, 'They are this.'" Sometimes someone breaks down, generally speaking, like when you put two people in a ring and have them swinging at each other. At some point, someone is going to quit first or they are going to get knocked onto the canvass first.

This is a pretty ingenious thing that you do. Smart investors will love this because most just buy stocks after doing their own internet research or after just looking at charts. Who taught you to do this? Did you just discover this yourself?

I'll tell you where I learned this. When I was in college I had a group of guys where we would get together to watch and bet football. One morning we went to breakfast and we were arguing about a game. I really liked a certain team and I was going to bet on them and we had a discussion. This other guy said, "Look, they got three guys hurt, and every time they go from the East coast to the West, or the West coast to the East coast, they are messed up." I said, "What do you mean?" because I had never been to the West coast in my life. He said, "When you travel, like when they play a game, players get to the stadiums at seven o'clock in the morning. Well, that's four o'clock Pacific Time. Eastern people's body clocks are messed up."

He was explaining this to me because this guy had played college football, and so he explained the whole thing to me. Well, that made sense so I didn't bet on my team and of course they lost. Then I realized, "Let's get together next weekend." When we started doing this and we all agreed on a game, it hit! We didn't win all the time, but I realized that so many times I was going to bet a game and I was wrong. I learned that information, and learning and hearing things helps you make your decisions. Let's face it, if you're going to bet NFL football then everybody has the same information. They know who the quarterbacks are and they can run all the numbers in the computers all they want.

The question is, do you know something that someone else doesn't know? Or did someone bring up a point that you never considered for that stock? For instance, the other day on TV somebody brought up that last week was the first time that more hedge funds bought 30,000 long contracts for oil. It's the first time they have done this since oil was low like four or five years ago. When six smart people all see the same thing that tells me something. That helps me make decisions.

Most people move towards things. I move away from them meaning I want to avoid risks. I want to know where I'm going to die so that I don't go there. That's how you should be in investing. You want to avoid losers. That's the Buffett style. He doesn't try to hit home runs that triple in a week. He's looking for something that he knows is going to be good going forward that everyone else doesn't know is going to be good and that's how you get your edge. That's how I got the idea for doing this.

You have been doing this now for years?

Oh, yeah. I did it because I bet football until about twenty years ago. I bet football religiously. I could actually make a good amount of money betting. I even had a sports service for a while but it was pre-Internet days. It was too hard to get the money from people and stuff, but because I had an edge I was successful. In any case, from this experience I learned about getting information.

All right, you have this eighteen point system for evaluating stocks that pay dividends. You evaluate them by first asking if the business is good. If so, then you ask whether the stock is a good deal at this price. If so then you can buy it. If not because it's too expensive then you will look to buy it in any situation where the price drops as long as the future prospects are still good. You'll watch it and wait until the price drops because of some imaginary fear so that you can scoop it up at a bargain.

Right. You have to buy it on fear. That's how you get your bargain.

What are the other steps after that? You look at it as a good business …

I mean, you are looking for valuations. Again, you are just really looking for the right price. I've been watching the stock market for twenty-five years now. I know what the price of the stock should be. Just like if you go somewhere and you have been buying watches or you've been doing something else then you know what it should be. I just have a thing in my head that tells me what the price should be.

Most people who invest do not understand numbers. That's why they get turned on by charts. It's because they don't want to use numbers, but numbers are important. I look at this company's earnings, I look at certain figures, I value the company.

Buffett talks about intrinsic value all the time. Intrinsic value is how much a company is worth. Part of it is brand so you look at its brand. You look at its balance sheet. You look at its cash flow. Those three things will tell you intrinsic value.

Then you see if you have an advantage. Does this company have an advantage over the other companies? A company like Amazon is a great company as far as making a lot of sales. It makes a lot of sales, but I don't see how it makes any money and it doesn't so I don't want to own it. I can't because owning it is for a gambler and that's not for me. I'm not going to reveal all my systems, but I'm just saying that's enough for people to work with.

Buying the imaginary fear is the key. Without the fear you don't get the bargain.

Okay, so that's the catalyst. Your catalyst for buying an overpriced but solid company is when an imaginary fear situation pops up. That's when you can buy it at a great price.

Precisely.

This is for a good stock that has a good brand, balance sheet, cash flow, and/or other advantages.

Yeah. You also want it where people don't appreciate it, like Apple two years ago. If you read the news, back then people were talking about Apple like it was going to be Eastman Kodak. Some guy compared it to Eastman Kodak.

Herbalife made investment news headlines when Bill Ackman was shorting it, so everyone was alerted to the situation. How do you know when a stock that isn't in the headlines has popped up on the radars of enough people where we can then say that the public has truly succumbed to imaginary fear?

There are fifty stocks I watch. I use my Top 50 and then I put them on a screen and then I'll get a notification from my broker if any one of them has dropped 5% or 10%. I'll get a notification that will tell me the stock dropped 10%. That tells me to keep a watch on it.

See, a lot of it is news-driven. For instance, let's take oil. In the beginning of last year, if you look there was a whole bunch of people talking about $150 oil. Now you don't hear those people anymore. Everybody is now talking about how it's going to be worth $10. I just know from the past that oil has not traded at $10 since 1998. I don't think it's going to trade at that price. If you're selling $10 bills for $10 you are not going to get many takers. At $5 you are going to get a ton of takers.

Now in investing you just don't know what the price should be. The prices are sometimes nonsensical. That's why guys like Buffett and Icahn don't have to have jobs like other people. They can invest because they know when everything is wrong. They know. That's what they do.

It's hard to explain that to somebody, but I mean as regards buying bad news if you just bought bad news all the time you would outperform. Of course sometimes the bad news is warranted. You just have to know when that sometimes is and the numbers help you.

Remember people were comparing Apple to Eastman Kodak. I look at the numbers and I'm thinking that the business is not going to go broke. This company has got $160 billion of cash and their cash flow is one billion dollars a week. How is this company bad? Is it because they are not growing as fast as people think they are going to grow? That's nonsensical to me, but that stock drops 45% and the chart guys were all against it but I was buying it.

Do you ever use charts at all?

I look at them, but I look at the numbers more importantly. I really don't look at them. No.

I know you've got eighteen points for analyzing a situation. It starts out asking whether the business is good. Is it a strong business? Next, is the price giving you a good deal on the valuation? Does the brand have cash flow? As to the balance sheet, are there any numbers there that you are looking for that are particular investment criteria?

When you see a company with no debt then you know that the company hasn't needed to borrow money. Well, if you have any children and they have never borrowed any money from you and they are doing fine then chances are they know how to handle money.

So in a super recession those guys would be good.

Well, yeah. I'll give you an example. There is a company called Insperity. They are a help for small businesses or whatever. The point is that the company has a ton of cash and no debt.

Michael Kors is a retailer. I hate retailers because they have a ton of debt and you can't predict them. I mean, everybody lost their ass in Aeropostale and all these companies. However, with Michael Kors he's a designer but he went broke fifteen years ago so now he doesn't use any debt. Same way like Steve Jobs went broke, almost, and he got bailed out by Bill Gates. He didn't use any debt. A guy like that, he's not going to go broke because he doesn't have debt. Like Buffett says, if you are smart then you don't need debt and if you're dumb it will kill you.

A lot of times I bet on the jockeys and not the horse. I won't buy GE because I hate the CEO. I hate him. I think he is not smart. I won't buy his stock because I just don't think he knows what he's doing.

How about cash flow? What are you looking for?

Well, I just want to make sure that the cash flow is consistent. It depends on the business. For instance with cornflakes things don't really change affecting whether or not people buy them. But in a cyclical business, such as the auto industry, things are determined by the economy. If the economy is bad then people aren't going to buy cars. But like Intel, I bought that stock because everybody said the PC was dead. Well, the PC is not dead. If you have a company you don't want to write a letter on a laptop. You'll want to write it on a computer.

All right. First, let me ask you about dividends. When you are looking at stocks for creating a dividend-compounding machine you are going to make sure they have dividends. Are you looking for growing dividends or are you ignoring the dividend growth rate? How important is that to you?

Yeah, I want them to grow but if you are already seven feet tall you don't have to grow taller. Ideally, I want a stock that grows their dividends. Sure, I do. It doesn't always work like that but yes, I want dividend growth and the good companies will continue to grow their dividend because they are continuing to make money.

And the dividend itself is more important to you than the share price as long as you conclude that the business is going to hold up?

Well, yeah. I mean, think of it this way. If a business is spitting out a $2 dividend would you pay $10 for it? Sure you would. It's a 20% return. Would you pay $25 for it? Yeah, it's an 8% return. Would you pay $30 for it? Yeah, that's a 6½% return.

I mean if you are going to marry a woman then you are going to want a woman who's smart, funny, rich. There are different traits you want with an investment, too. There are main things and the other stuff is … well for instance sales and growth is bullshit. Amazon keeps growing but they don't make any money. In the end, if you sold $5 bills for $4 you can make a ton of sales. However, you just won't make any money. You'll get market share but you'll almost go broke. But see, Amazon makes their money because the stock has risen from $70 to $300 because everybody kisses Jeff Bezos' ass and they are all speculators and gamblers, but at some point that stock is going to be worth $50 again.

You're saying it's like the Japanese stocks in the '80s. The companies were going after market share but they weren't profitable.

Yeah, you got it. You just have to be able to see something. For some reason, people turn on other people the same way they turn on businesses. For me, I don't hear all that. All I focus on is the numbers. When the company is not paying the dividend that's like a person who is telling you something.

If you ask someone, "I want to see your police record" they might say, "Well, I'm not showing you." If they say, "I want to see your tax return" and they respond, "I'm not showing you," then they are not showing you for a reason.

Carl Icahn and Buffett have been doing it for forty-five or fifty years. They haven't scammed anybody. Nobody is calling them liars. People don't like Icahn because he's not like everybody else, but he's good at what he does. He's better than Buffett. He just doesn't kiss everybody's ass. He doesn't care if people don't like him.

Let me ask you a hypothetical question. There's a lot of talk in the marketplace now about the potential for a depression, deflation, or hyperinflation. Let's say that one of these scenarios develops in the future where everything crashes. What type of companies would you buy in each of those situations?

I would buy the same ones - mostly consumer goods companies.

Take a stock like Coca-Cola, which is a very easy stock to figure out. In deflationary times Coca-Cola is good because what do they do? They buy sugar, they buy syrup, they have trucks to drive the stuff everywhere. With lower gas prices the deflation helps them. Now conversely it hurts Coca-Cola when we have a strong dollar because they do a lot of sales outside of the United States so they have currency headwinds that they have to worry about. But invariably Coca-Cola is a company that is going to keep making money in good and bad times.

Now I don't own Coca-Cola anymore because I happen to believe it's overpriced, but I owned it previously. It was the first stock in my dividend machine. Actually, it was the second one. I loved it but I got out of it because there were other stocks that were growing faster. Also, I don't like the CEO of the company now and I don't like the direction they are going in. I just didn't feel comfortable as time went on so I got rid of it and replaced it with something better. Everyone has limited cash. It doesn't matter who you are when cash is limited and something is better than something else so then I switched from Coca-Cola to something better.

See, you are paying for the brand. Here, I'll give you a great analogy. If you are trying to run in a race and you are racing a world-class sprinter on a track then of course they are going to beat you. If I make it muddy they are still going beat you. Do you see what I'm saying? In a bad economic situation the best companies will still do well.

Many people want to use gold as a hedge for inflation. It's nonsensical. Gold is a fear trade. It's fear. It's the antithesis of what I talk about with dividends. If you bought gold in 2000 when it was $200 an ounce it's $1,300 an ounce now. But if you had bought Altria in 2000 then with the power of the reinvested dividends you earned about 15% more a year annually than with gold. That's because of the compounding, the power of the compounding.

Gold appreciated in that timeframe like 16% a year. If you took the price of it and you put 1.16 into a calculator for the last fourteen years you get like $1,300 for the price of gold. I believe Altria grew at 30+%.

Altria grew at a compounding rate that was double gold's growth rate?

Yes, yes, because of the compounding of the dividends. Part of the reason I got richer faster than I thought was when the stock … like in 2000 I got a 10½% dividend yield on Altria. I was like, "10½%? Wow this is crazy." But why did I get such a high dividend rate? It was because in 2000 nobody wanted dividend stocks. They wanted high flyers. They wanted to put $50 into a stock and turn it into $500 and like Buffett says, what wise people do in the beginning the fool does in the end. Just like with real estate or anything else. That's why bubbles are created.

Actually right now there is a bubble in dividend stocks. They are higher than they should be, but you'll still do better in the dividends stocks than you will in a treasury bond. That's why people continue to buy them. If you buy Altria at $54 it's higher than it was last year at $35 when you should have bought it, but it's still paying a 3½% to 4% dividend so the market price isn't as important. If you just want a return on your investment then if the dividend gets bigger the price of the stock will get bigger.

And over the long run the business isn't going to explode. It will just keep paying.

Well, unless you think somehow that somebody can knock them out of the box.

In a massive deflationary scenario, which many economists and central banks are worried about, you're saying that you would still buy consumer goods stocks?

Yes. You see, it's the same rules. At some price a stock or an investment is cheap. If I offered to work for you for free then what risk do you have? If you are not giving me your checkbook then you have no risk. I say to you, "I'm going to bring you new customers if you pay me a percentage of what I bring you." Well, there is no risk for you. The risk/reward is perfect. Well, that's the same thing with your investing. You are trying to find a company that everybody hates for some reason.

I couldn't understand why everybody hated Apple. Right now, everybody hates IBM. They hate them. IBM has been around a hundred years. This year they are going to earn $15 billion. Give me companies that are earning $15 billion of profit. There is not a hundred of them. There's probably not fifty of them but people are saying it's bad, it stinks, it's terrible. You know why? Because its stock price hasn't done anything. The company is doing okay, but see it's all perception for these people and if you are a speculator then you hate IBM because it dropped from $210 to $150. But if you are an investor like me you'll love it.

I think people now have a good bead on what you do. Like you said, you are partially a perception trader who waits. You're looking for good, solid businesses that will pay you dividends and then you just wait until the perception is bad so you can buy the company for cheap. You want that asset at a cheap price.

The reason I tell you all these stories is the light needs to go off in your head so you can see what I'm talking about.

Your strategy sounds familiar to what Buffett or some other famous investors have done, such as buying when there is "blood in the streets." That's when you get the greatest bargains of solid firms. We know that applying this principle consistently over the years has enabled you to compound your returns at about 20% annually and retire at age forty-two. Over time you have no doubt invested in a large number of companies. Do you look at dividend yield tables to find stocks paying the highest dividends and say, "These are the ones I'm going to buy when the price is right?"

No, no, no, because a lot of times a high dividend is evidence that there is a problem. I own a stock called Transocean. The dividend is going to get cut because the price of oil went to $48. I didn't see that coming. Now, at what price will the dividend get cut I don't know but the point is that I think the company may cut the dividend to buy the debt at 70¢ on the dollar, which is actually a better use of the money. When they announce that then the stock price will probably go up and not go down. I'm anticipating that this is going to happen, but I don't know.

Are you ever looking at a table of high dividend yielding stocks to spot possible purchase candidates?

No, no, no, no, no. I look at the companies.

So you have a list of roughly fifty good companies that you thought about over the years, which you know are good companies and which you want to own when the price is right. Those are the ones

you want to buy.

Yes. I'd like to own them. I'd love to own Panera Bread, but it's just never the right price for me.

You take a company like VISA, okay? It's a great, or MasterCard. They are both great businesses. People are spending money all around the world. They are not going to stop.

A company like eBay - they own PayPal and they are going to spin it off. I think Paypal is worth more than eBay and PayPal combined. I own eBay, that's one I own.

There are really good companies like Starbucks. It's a great company but everybody knows it. It's just never cheap. It's never been cheap for me.

I like companies where there is a lot of fear about it. Like IBM is the redheaded stepchild now. Everybody hates it and that gets me interested. When everybody hates something that is when I start liking it.

My Top 50 list is all the big companies like Apple, Google, Starbucks, Visa, MasterCard, Qualcomm. They are all good businesses. You can't try to replace them. Johnson & Johnson is another.

All the banks are good at certain prices so I watch them. You just have to buy them at the right time. The biggest banks - Citi, Wells Fargo, J.P. Morgan and Bank of America - control like 45% of the deposits in the United States. They are big.

I watch Kimberly Clark. They are in consumer goods. I look at Pepsi. I look at companies where I think you can't knock them out of the box.

This is a list of just good businesses. They will still be here in ten years but they might be too expensive to buy at any one particular moment in time. Therefore, you just buy these things when they are cheap and then compound your cash by reinvesting in any great opportunities when you get them.

You just let it roll. Just let it roll.

Is that pretty much it?

You summed it up. When you marry someone you are picking somebody that you hope over time is going to be somebody who can grow with you and learn with you. It's the same analogy as for picking a stock. You pick your stock like you pick your best friend. I pick a stock that I want to own for the next twenty or thirty years. I don't pick a stock that I want to jump in and jump out of.

If you ask half the people who buy stocks what the company's price earnings ratio is they don't know. You ask them, "Does it have any debt? Who is the CEO?" They don't know the answer to those questions either. When I pick stocks I try to know what I'm getting into.

Amazon is not on the list because …

No, it's a bad business to me.

What are some other good businesses people should keep watching besides the ones you mentioned?

Well, I told you about eight. I'll tell you some more. Exxon is a good business, not a great business. I shouldn't put Exxon in there because it's not a consumer goods company, but Kraft is a good business. I previously said Visa and MasterCard. Abbott Labs. AIG the insurance company … believe it or not is a good business. They just made a couple of mistakes a while back but it's a good business. IBM is a good business. Oracle is a good business. Microsoft is a good business. Intel. Cisco.

They are all powerful businesses. Think of the people you do business with. You readily do business with them. McDonald's is a good business. It's run poorly right now but it's a good business. GE is a good business that is run poorly now, but they are a good business. They have been around for a hundred years.

There is a stock called National Oilwell Varco. It's been around since 1862. It's been around a long time. It's been through all sorts of economic times.

You pick a stock like Johnson & Johnson or Altria. They have been around through depressions, they have seen 18% interest rates, they have seen 30% unemployment rates and they have survived through both good and bad. The dinosaur was the most powerful animal on earth at one time but it is gone now. The ant is still around. Survivors tend to be strong.

People think that I'm a gambler. The fact is that I'm betting with the house. I feel like I own a casino, I really do. I feel like I own the casino. I may have a bad day or week but I know that check is coming every three months.

Now we know exactly what you are doing and how you made your money. How would you compare yourself to Warren Buffett?

Buffett does the same things I do. When Buffett started out it was different for Buffett because when he started in the '50s and '60s nobody knew the game he was playing. It was like playing against blind people. It's like playing poker. How good you are at poker often depends on whom you are playing against. You could be a champion if you played against a bunch of bad people.

Investing is the same way. It's a game where you are competing against the smartest people on earth. You have to see something that they don't see. Buffett was like that. Buffett was an investor. He didn't try to jump in and jump out of stocks. He bought stocks and then he held them.

Once you get to a certain point you have to become a buy and hold investor because the tax ramifications of doing otherwise just don't make any sense. Buffett never sold a share of his Berkshire. Now Berkshire as a company paid tax but he never paid a dime of tax and then he gave everything away to Gates. Holding without selling is like having an interest-free loan from the government.

I have three stocks that I have enormous capital gains on. Obama is talking about raising the tax on capital gains. My friends asked, "What do you think of that?" I said, "I don't care. I'm not selling these stocks. He can make the capital gains tax 80% for all I care. I'm not selling them." All he is going to do is hurt the people he is trying to help.

You won't sell because you calculate that the business is going to last and the stock is still paying dividends. Even if the price of the stock went back to where you bought it you are still making good money.

I'd have to pay enormous capital gains so my wealth would go down. The alternative to that is when people say to me, "Okay, what happens if you need money?" If I need money I can go on margin. I can borrow money against my stocks.

I've been on margin straight for fourteen years because I'm borrowing money. You can borrow money at Interactive Brokers for 1.5% or 1.6%. If I can't make 1.6% on my money then I need to go somewhere else. I can just borrow from them and buy a stock that yields 5% or 6% and make the difference.

Now I do have to worry that the stock is going to crash, but a stock like Altria won't crash because their sales are going to be consistent. People are not just going to wake up and stop smoking. They're just not. They are not going to do that.

What websites are doing any hard work for you for your dividend investing?

I look at Yahoo Business. It's very good. You can see the cash and you can see the shares. Before I make an investment I spend fifty to one hundred hours studying a stock. Before I put a dime up I'm going to spend fifty to one hundred hours in study.

Someone says, "Fifty to one hundred hours? What do you do?" I look at the annual reports from the last twenty years. I talk to people about the company. I'll make a list of people who are friends of mine. I'll say, "Do you do business with this company or do you buy Johnson & Johnson bandages?" or "Do you do this?" I try to delve into things and try to get a feel on where the company is.

This is my life so I'm real serious about this. I say this to people all the time. If you were going to go up in a plane then you wouldn't want to find out in midair that the person who is flying the plane doesn't know what they are doing.

It is the same thing with investing. Most people are gamblers. I'm an investor.

When you get married you bet on your wife. When you buy a stock or you pick a friend then you are also betting. Before I know something, information is king. I can't study a universe of 60,000 stocks. I'm never going to know about Eaton Corporation even though it's based in Cleveland. I don't know about that. But if you tell me something about Altria, I know the CEOs. Nothing has happened in the last twenty-three years that I don't know about for that company.

A lot of people don't like the stock because it's not a Dividend Aristocrat since they didn't raise their dividend every year. Well, the one year they didn't raise their dividend was because they were being investigated by the government, which was trying to close them down, so what they did is they didn't raise their dividend. They didn't eliminate it. They just didn't raise it. They are not part of the Dividend Aristocrats because of that. Well, that's a stupid rule.

You have got some really wonderful gems here other than just the simple story of investing in good stocks that pay dividends when the price is right. The interesting thing is that you were a gambler, which is a similar history to that of many highly successful traders, and you then used those skills for investing. Many people would want to know about you and your techniques just because of this alone.

I did it because I'm the casino owner. The odds are in my favor in the sense that if you own a stock for a long time then go look at a chart, which is what I tell to chartists. Go look at a chart of any big company like Apple, Johnson & Johnson or whatever. You know where the chart is going? Higher. They are all going higher.

Now the trick is that if you knew Walmart thirty years ago then you had an advantage over someone else. I'm trying to get people to understand that if you just stick with what you know, not just in investing but in life, then you will be fine versus doing something you don't know. People just think they can jump in and jump out of things.

I have a friend of mine who is a trader. He showed me a system that he has. He's doing very good with it and obviously I can't share it. It works fine but he's not going to share it with anybody because if he shared it then it wouldn't work anymore.

Yes, he would lose his advantage. Everyone would copy it and then arbitrage its success away so that it wouldn't work anymore. That's what happens when something becomes too popular.

There is a book called *The Smart Money*. It's about this guy who bet with a professional gambler and they had this computer that picked the games. They were geniuses that put it together. The key to winning was that they had information that the average person just doesn't have.

If you have that information you have an edge like the people who knew oil prices were going to drop and bet accordingly. I didn't know that. I was short oil but then I got long some companies. I thought it would start to rebound in the $70s and it didn't. But long term, I know at some point the price of oil will be over $70 again. That will happen. I don't know when but I can just sit back and collect my dividend. If you own Exxon or Chevron … well, Chevron pays a 4% dividend. You can just sit back and collect your money and you'll be good. Oil companies aren't going to go out of business. They can't. You need oil to live. That's the difference between oil and gold.

You mentioned a couple of books. Are there any other books that have really impressed you that you think people should read to help them understand dividend investing?

Stocks for the Long Run, by Jeremy Siegel. It's the truth. It shows you how dividend investing can give better returns than growth stocks or index funds. That's a good book. That's a very good book so I recommend it to people. He shows you statistically why dividend stocks are better. He doesn't know how to pick them himself, mind you, but his numbers are correct and he shows you how to beat valuations.

I don't agree with some of the other things he says, for instance he thinks that you are going to have a hard time selling stocks in the future because of the baby boomers. I don't get into all the macroeconomic stuff. It's just about buying value. If you buy value you are going to be fine and if you don't you are going to have trouble. Otherwise, you are gambling.

I think that my own book, *The Great American Dividend Machine,* doesn't have all the numbers in it but my book will pay for itself because I have a chapter in it that has a ton of ways to save money that will more than pay for the book. I say my book is informational and inspirational as well. There is information like the basics that I gave you about investing but it's inspirational, too, because of the stories.

I'm not one that's big on books. Most books are full of hype. Someone is not going to tell you their secrets. Now, if you are a trader there is a book, there is a guy named Mark Fisher. For a trader,

Mark Fisher wrote *The Logical Trader* and it's a very good book. If you are going to trade then you should read this book. It's good. He makes total, total sense. He trades in and out of a position in ten or twenty minutes. I'm more of a swing trader. While I'll take a position I may take it off in a day or two days or I may hold it for six months. It depends. If I'm wrong with the trade I sit and hold it unlike most people who just cut and run. I don't do that.

I believe that people can now understand your basic method for dividend investing. In terms of the 80/20 rule applied to dividend investing, what are the fewest but also the very most important investment lessons you have learned over the years that people absolutely have to know, have to institute and have to master for success?

The first two things I talked about. You have to pick good businesses. That's the first thing you have to do right. Buying a good business at a bad price is not the mistake that people make, rather it's buying a bad business at a good price or they buy a bad business at a bad price.

You want to pick good businesses. Pick a company that you think thirty to forty years from now is going to be good. A company that you like and that you understand. You should try to understand the company. My biggest money is made on the easiest stocks. When I start trying to get complicated, it's hard.

Warren Buffett made his money on American Express, Coke, and Wells Fargo. He made his money backing up the truck and loading up with these issues. He wasn't trying to invent anything. Bill Gates made his money because he owned Microsoft that invented software. He's a terrible investor. Terrible. He's an intelligent guy but bad investor. Same thing with Jeremy Siegel.

As an investor, you have to be able to buy something. I would tell everyone what Buffett said, "Be greedy when others are fearful." That doesn't really tell you anything though. It's too general. Like I said, I think it's very important to find good businesses and then be able to spot bargains. You have to look at the numbers. You can't overpay for something. You have to buy it at the right price. The right business and the right price are crucial. Once you have that then you're good. You're good.

If you just bought a stock that had a P/E of under 15 and they raised their dividend every year and had a good predictable income then you'd do fine. The problem is that's like telling a person who golfs, "Make your eight foot puts and you're fine." It doesn't always work like that. And sometimes some stocks are on their way down. For a stock like Amazon, someone thinks it's a good business but they haven't looked at the numbers otherwise they would realize that the company doesn't make any money.

For your 80/20 rule of doing the fewest things with the biggest impact on success it would primarily come down to these two rules?

Yes, that's what I would say. I would say that those two rules are it because that's where you make your money.

When you see something you like then you have to be able to bet big and buy. Diversification is a bunch of baloney. For somebody who is brand new diversification is okay but if you are somebody who knows what they are doing then when you get an opportunity of a lifetime you have to be able to know that. You can't be scared of taking advantage of those situations. If you like a company you need to buy it.

But you have to check the numbers. If the numbers are good and it's a good business, chances are you'll do good. Obviously, you want something with some bad news. You want to buy some imaginary fear. That's going to give you the good price. Really, that is number two, which is getting the right price.

Is there any economic situation that you are hoping might happen to produce a fear situation for some of these stocks that you really want to buy on your Watch List?

I don't sweat things, I really don't. The people who are in charge of the country, contrary to what conspiracy people and other people will say, are watching matters. For instance, everybody worried that the banks would shut down. If the banks were going to shut down then the Chinese were going to come in and take them over. They wouldn't let it happen.

I'm not macroeconomic. There are two things that I can say that are kind of controversial but I'll say them. I don't ever believe interest rates are going to get high again. I also don't believe we are ever going to have hyperinflation. I just don't believe it's going to happen. Not because I'm pie in the sky but because inflation is caused by people chasing too few goods. There are plenty of goods today and there are plenty of people. I just don't see it. The real enemy is not inflation. It's deflation.

With deflation nobody wants to buy a house because they're saying, "Why should I buy something since it's going to be worth less?" That's why people are driving cars longer. I have a jeep that is twelve years old. Why should I buy a new one? It only has 40,000 miles on it so I don't need a new one. I can buy a Bentley if I lived in Florida, but I don't live in Florida. Why should I buy a nice car here in Cleveland? It doesn't make any sense. Do you follow me? I just don't think it will happen.

Try not to worry about the math. For me, how I look at macroeconomic things is that I'll look at the price of oil from a numbers point of view. Oil hasn't been this low since the world was in recession. Now why is the oil market this low? Well, there are a bunch of reasons. The Saudis are trying to hurt our fracking. They are trying to hurt Iran. They are trying to hurt Venezuela. They are trying to hurt Russia. But at some point the people that hold the debt on these people don't want things to crash. If the oil market crashes you are going to have a problem. The central banks around the world don't want that.

Right now countries are so much in debt. Everybody is borrowing money cheap. People say, "Well, how much lower can interest rates get?" Trust me, they can get lower. People can't afford to do things.

This has all been a big boon for me because I've been able to borrow money on margin. When I started using margin I was paying 7½%. I'm now paying less than 2%. That's crazy. That is why the rich get richer and the poor get poorer, but that's like saying that people who eat right and workout are getting in better shape than those who don't work out and don't eat right. That's common sense.

How could a regular person who doesn't invest any money in the stock market try to buy dividend stocks? How are they going to get ahead? You see what I'm saying? They are going take $10,000 and try to trade with it, or $50,000. That's like going to a casino with $50,000. The casino has more money than you do. You're going to lose that $50K before they lose their $40 million, trust me. Or billion. And that's the way things are today.

But with dividends it doesn't matter. You're in your own world. If you have a stock called Con Ed or Southern Company then you are just going to be waiting for your check to come in. You want to make those checks as big as possible so you could quit working. The object of work is so that you can make enough money so that you don't have to work, right? You like what you do, obviously, but you wouldn't do it for free.

That's the part you have to be thinking about. For macroeconomic stuff the real pros don't think like that. They don't. The real investor does. I can trade because I know the odds of things. I know when something is cheap. If I buy something that's cheap then at some point it is going to go up. Whether I use margin or options or whatever I'm going to make money. That's what I know.

Are there any other important things you want to tell people as advice that might correct some of the common mistakes you are always encountering?

First of all, the most important thing is that you save 10% of every dollar that comes in. At least 10% at the minimum. If you don't do that then anything else doesn't matter because you're not going to have any chips to play with. You have to save at least 10% of your money. That's the best financial advice you could ever give another human being.

Take that money and invest it in good paying dividend stocks. Just keep doing it. You can pass it on your children. I have a machine that I'm going to pass on to my daughter. My dividends at some point will be over a million dollars a year.

Your BillSpetrino.com website says, "A 25 year old who's portfolio is only $30,000 can buy a stock like with a dividend of about 8%. The $2,700 of annual dividends should double about every nine years at least. With no further investment this particular Dividend Machine should return over $86,000 annually at age seventy. Sound impressive? By reinvesting dividends the first fifteen years this amount should be well over $200,000 annually at age seventy. How many of your friends do you think will have done that? Not bad for a one time investment. See the importance of a dividend machine now?" Bill, do you have a rate of return on your portfolio I can report so they know how powerful this type of investing can be over the long run? I always want people to see many different styles of trading and investing, understand how they work and how to do them and understand the potential returns.

My newsletter has documented returns. The documented returns since I've started I believe are like 24% compounded. Now I'm not going to keep doing that because when I started the market was cheap. Going forward it wouldn't be that way. My goal is 12% a year.

That is for six years of *The Dividend Machine* newsletter.

If someone is going to buy an investment newsletter, they should check with *The Hulbert Financial Digest* to make sure the person is ranked because if they are not ranked by Mark Hulbert then you have to ask why not? Why wouldn't they want that accreditation?

How's your personal account?

For my personal investing returns, I can't document that number but on my personal account I've averaged 22% since I started.

That's as good as the best of the best value investors like Warren Buffett and Walter Schloss.

Well, it's easier for me because I'm managing less money. I'm not saying that I'm better than them. It gets harder when you are managing more money. The last three years I've done real well. I did 55%, 74%, and 44%, but that's not going to happen going forward. It can't. My personal goal this year is 20%. I use options, I use leverage, I use dividends. There are a bunch of things that I use to spike it but the trees don't grow to the sky. This low margin rate really helps me, though. I couldn't do that without margin.

Are you buying any high-yielding MLPs or Oil and Gas Trusts?

My next trade that comes out in my newsletter is going to be gas. I'm looking in that industry now. Anything that you buy in the energy industry that has a good balance sheet will do fine going forward. Those stocks are priced for $48 oil. I just don't believe that is going to be sustained. Things can happen for a short term but think of what it cost to produce a gallon of gasoline.

When you go to your pump and pay $1.75 there is a state and federal tax on that. The company only sees $1.20 or $1.30. Think about that. It doesn't make any sense. It just doesn't. It's out of whack right now. I just know that because I know how business works. At some point someone is going to bid the price of oil up. They are going to be buying it at $48. They are going to push it higher. It's just a matter of time.

If people want to really learn more about your investing style and stock picks, how can they find you?

I have three different things going on.

I have my book, *The Great American Dividend Machine*, which I recommend that everybody get. I have a chapter in there with a bunch of different tips for direct savings that will help the book pay for itself.

Then I have my Newsmax newsletter, *The Dividend Machine*. It's a $99 newsletter. You get a three-month trial. If you don't like it you get your money back. I've got around 65,000 subscribers to that and with people on trial it's probably around 80,000 subscribers.

And then if you want to trade or you want to learn how to be an investor I have an interactive school, BillSpetrino.com. The price on that is usually around a $600 deal. For your readers, however, I'll make it just $299 as a favor. If you just identify that you are one of Bill's readers you'll get it for $299. Again, if they don't like it I'll give them their money back. I don't need to take other people's money. That's not my thing.

I think with those three things they can understand how I do things. For $99 you can hire me through *The Dividend Machine*, or for $299 you can get on my interactive thing and ask me questions. I have an all-star team of people and this is another place where I get my group of people. I have BillSpetrino.com. I call it the "BIO" forum. It's <u>B</u>y <u>I</u>nvitation <u>O</u>nly because I don't want just any clown coming in there. I've got sixty people in it. It's like an all-star game.

I've got people from all over the world in it telling me things. That's like when people say Philip Morris stock isn't selling in Malaysia or the iPhone then I have people in Malaysia to give me the real deal. People will tell me, "It was selling great when I was standing in line." One guy told a story about how there was like a monsoon coming and the people wouldn't get out of the line. That's a pretty powerful product if people are willing to do that. "Get us tents." That's what they were telling the people from Apple. "Get us tents so we can stay out here."

That's a really valuable source of information when you are trying to figure out how strong the sales are for a company. That's pretty unique. It reminds me of Peter Lynch's fundamental analysis advice to get a feel for the actual product of a company and its marketplace sales before buying that stock.

My track record is good. With all my conservative stocks I have never had a loser. None. I had one loser on the aggressive side, but I tell everybody that 90% of your money should go into conservative stocks. Until you are rich you shouldn't be gambling.

If you have children you don't teach them the wrong things first. You teach them the right things first. They can learn how to drink and smoke and do other things once they get down the important lessons first.

The trick to investing is compounding. I do have good math skills and that helps me. There are a lot of guys with PhDs in statistics but they can't think. They have never gambled before. They don't understand. They just see a number, but they don't see what led to the number. They don't want to know. Because of their egos they don't want to ask some regular person. I don't mind asking a housewife for example. I think you should do this.

My greatest stock pick came from a nine-year-old when I took her shopping and she told me, "Daddy it's obvious. Everybody has the same case for Apple." That's how you learn. I'm constantly trying to learn. I read a lot and I study the companies. I still read for about three hours every day. I am on a constant quest to learn from the wisdom of others. From the very beginning that I entered this field I read every book I could find from some of the greatest investors of the world like Graham and Buffett.

People say it to me all the time, "Do you want to do this?" and I'll say, "No." They say, "Why not?" "Well, it has a 20% or 30% chance of losing." I'll also say, "Would you go up on a plane if you thought you had a 30% chance of it crashing?" They don't know the answer to that.

That's just it. If people save the money … you have got to save money or you won't have any chips to play with. That's the greatest thing you can teach your children. When $100 comes in then you take $10 and you don't ever spend it.

Beautiful. Bill, I want to thank you for this interview and revealing the principles involved with your investment technique. I sincerely hope that many people take your wisdom to heart to investigate this particular investment path because of the income, safety, and growth factors it has all bundled up into one.

Chapter 16
Charles Mizrahi
Beating The Market Through Ben Graham Investing

People try to master all sorts of trading methods and investment techniques to beat the stock market. Warren Buffett made his fortune by studying the techniques of Benjamin Graham, the father of security analysis. However, after years of developing a way to value stocks, near the end of his life Graham gave an interview, "Simplest Way to Select Bargain Stocks," where he explained a simplified technique that did away with complicated security analysis: "First, create as large a list as possible of common stocks currently selling at no more than seven times their latest (not projected) 12-month earnings. While Graham said to select shares with a P/E of less than 7, he explained that he arrived at this criteria because he wanted an earnings-to-price ratio (the inverted P/E ratio) that was at least twice the average current yield on top-quality (AAA) corporate bonds. Today we might use a P/E criteria of 10 or even 12. In any case, the low P/E requirement tends to be the first sieve that helps you select underpriced stocks selling at a discount.

"Once you have those initial candidates, you are looking to select a portfolio of at least 30 stocks (at a minimum) that not only meet the P/E requirements but also have strong balance sheets. You don't just want a low P/E but also want companies that are financially strong because they have a satisfactory financial position. His only screening criteria for this condition was that a company should own at least twice what it owes, so its debt should be less than half of its assets. How can you measure this? You can look at the shareholder equity/total assets ratio to get an idea of debt levels. If you look at the ratio of stockholders' equity to total assets and the ratio is at least 50 percent, the company's financial condition can be considered sound.

"Now for the selling rules. After you buy such a stock, you would sell it after it appreciated by 50% or after two years went by, whichever came first, and then simply repeat the process when funds became available and new stocks met the tests."

Fast forward to today where successful value investor Charles Mizrahi has updated these simple Ben Graham rules and proved that they work. The stocks within his Hidden Values Alert and Inevitable Wealth Portfolio are selected according to basic Graham value criteria, along with his own business judgement, and have readily beat the overall market over time just as Graham predicted. In this interview Charles explains how to apply this technique to value investing to soundly beat the market in a very simple manner.

Charles, I know you handle the stock picking for *Hidden Values Alert* and the *Inevitable Wealth Portfolio*, which are two value stock portfolio newsletters you publish, and you have also written books on value investing. What I want to know is how you initially got involved in trading and investing? What got you into this field so that it has become your career and life?

For that we have to go back to Elementary School. I was always interested in the stock market. I grew up in a middle class family where my father was a warehouse manager and we lived in a very middle class neighborhood. Taxi drivers were our neighbors as well as other blue-collar people.

From the time I was young I always loved the financial markets. They were always so fascinating to me. It was like a big puzzle trying to figure out where the pieces fall and who would profit from them and do well. When I was eleven or twelve years old I started reading about the stock market. I used to spend a lot of time at the library as a kid and in high school I used to spend a lot of the time in the back of the class reading annual reports. The teachers were pretty cool. They left me alone because I told them that if you leave me alone I'll share some of my stock picks with you and they enjoyed that. I wasn't too much of a good student in that sense, but I always knew that I wanted to be in the financial markets.

When I graduated from high school I went to college for one year and then I went down to Wall Street, which was only about a thirty minute train ride from my house. At the time the New York Stock Exchange had created an exchange called the New York Futures Exchange (NYFE), which was similar to the S&P 500 Index. They had the New York Stock Exchange Composite Index and they were looking for traders - floor traders - to buy and sell the Index. We were called "locals" in the trading pit, which used the open outcry system. I gathered up as much money as I could. I borrowed from my friends, my family and especially my grandmother and I became a local and traded on the floor of the New York Futures Exchange.

I was trading basically the Index on a very short-term basis using a lot of technical analysis because of lot of people down there used technical analysis and they taught me that that is what works. My longest time horizon was a one-hour (sixty minute) chart, so I really wasn't looking to buy and hold for hours. In fact, I was just looking to buy and hold, not even buy and hold, but just to continually buy and sell. That's called "scalping," and that's where I first got my taste of trading in the investment world.

By going on the floor you meet a lot of amazing people and you can watch the way human nature behaves. You can see what moves markets and you basically learn a lot. You learn a lot on the floor. Back then a friend of mine in Chicago said that six months trading soybeans is worth four years of business school. That really is true.

What type of things were you learning at that time that were mind shaking or still strike you today as quite valuable lessons for readers of today?

Temperament was the key. There were certain people there who regardless of which way the market was going always had an even keeled temperament. They didn't get overly excited when markets were going their way and they didn't get overly distressed when markets were going against them. If you make decisions based on emotion they are usually the wrong ones.

I watched and there weren't many of the floor traders like this. There were just a few who were very cool and steady customers. They would look at the market, do their analysis and then when they made a trade they wouldn't get excited or get depressed if things didn't go their way. They just looked at it in a non-emotional, intellectual way and I saw them make the most money.

You were impressed with their bearing alone and they actually were making more money than everybody else?

They weren't joining in the frenzy of things. They were standing apart from the crowd. When they were buying they didn't need to be buying in a rising market. They were just as happy buying in a falling market and selling into a bull market.

I noticed out of the corner of my eye, literally as well as figuratively, that these guys - and they were mostly guys although there were one or two women who traded on the floor - were the people who were making the most money. It didn't matter at the time when I was there that each one had a different philosophy and a different approach. One guy could have been a chartist and one guy could have been using algorithms or point and figure charts. It really didn't matter. They all were pretty successful and so it was really the temperament that really impressed me as to the key to success in investing and trading.

How did you go from trading the futures index to trading stocks?

I started trading the index and then as an extension of that people were asking me to manage their money. A floor trader is not set up to manage money. The only account you have is really your own. I left the floor in 1983. I was there for only about a year because it's a grueling business (it's from 9:30 every morning to 4:15 everyday) and it wears on you. You don't have many traders who were there for many years. Today that has all been replaced by computers, but in those days it wasn't.

I set up an investment advisory firm, but I couldn't do futures because that required the clients to put up more money and deal with margin, which nobody is interested in doing. What I did was mutual fund market timing. When my signals gave me a "buy" I bought a stock fund and when my signals gave me a "sell" I went into cash. We built a business on that which was a pretty successful money management business. It was rated one of the top among the asset allocators and tactical asset allocators over a ten-year, seven-year, and five-year period through the '80s and '90s.

I moved from trading the index into doing that and then after that we started to trade, but in a different division of our company, S&P 500 futures. Those were for more sophisticated investors, institutions and banks and we had some pretty sizeable accounts. We had several hundred million under management, which in those days was a lot of money, and we were trading indexes based on a technical approach.

How did that then progress to where you are now investing in undervalued stocks and publishing newsletters on how to do so? You started as a floor trader but went into mutual fund timing and then you went into S&P futures. I'm trying to trace how you finally got into individual stocks and value investing.

During this time period - from when I was on the floor to when I was trading futures - I was using technical analysis, which basically looked at price and volume and a whole bunch of other factors. I was not looking at the fundamentals at all, meaning the economy or individual stocks or anything of that extent. It was just one number and then we were using all sorts of mathematical models and computer algorithms on that. That's what we were doing for a good close to twenty years.

Then along came the 2000 dot-com bubble, and the relationships that had existed that my technical models were based on then no longer existed. For example, for the past seventy or eighty years when interest rates declined then stocks usually rose. Here it was the exact opposite, which is that interest rates were falling and stocks were declining. I looked at the model and the model didn't seem to be working. I saw this happen in 2000 and we stopped trading for our clients and gave everyone back their money and said, "I have to revamp this because this doesn't make sense." So even the best technical model will break and you basically start from new with a track record of one day, and you start a new model.

At the same time I had always followed Berkshire Hathaway and Warren Buffett. In those days before the internet I used to mail away for their annual reports to read, but I didn't see how it could apply to me. However in 2000 I realized that there was a sea change in the marketplace and I started reading. In fact, I read close to seventy to eighty books and everything on value investing. The reason was because I saw a research paper put out by Tweedy Browne called, "What Has Worked In Investing."

Yes, I've read it. It's great. You can find it on the internet at the Tweedy.com website.

I looked at that and I said, "Wow, this makes so much sense. Buying stocks or anything when they are selling at low valuations makes more money over time than buying things at high valuations." That just makes sense with everything in life.

For instance, when you go into a store you don't say, "Could you tell me what has increased in price and don't show me what you have on sale. I'm just going to buy things that keep going up." A suit that was $500 last week isn't a better suit this week because it's $700, but that's the way the market responded. People were buying things based on price and I was doing the same thing. The higher the price meant it was better while the lower the price meant get out.

Along came this notion of value investing. When I started reading this report, "What Has Worked In Investing," which was a study looking over fifty years of returns, the logic was so compelling. That's one thing that I pretty much pride myself in, which is that I'm an un-emotional person when it comes to making decisions. Even though I had twenty to thirty years invested in technical analysis I said there has to be a better way so I continued reading and researching and then I came upon *Security Analysis* by Benjamin Graham and David Dodd. All roads led to *Security Analysis* and *The Intelligent Investor* by Ben Graham, which was published in 1949.

You have read so many books on value investing. Would you still tell people looking to get into it that those are the two primary books to read or would you suggest different books?

Well the first one would definitely be *The Intelligent Investor*, especially chapters 8 and 20. If you don't get chapters 8 and 20, put the book down because this is not for you. Basically chapters 8 and 20 speak about Mr. Market, how to deal with the market and also how to deal with looking at a stock as a piece of a business and not as a wiggle or jiggle on a chart. If you can't capture that and that doesn't resonate with you then it will probably never resonate with you as an investor.

What Graham did is he brought together three main principles: stocks as pieces of businesses, how to deal with Mr. Market (a way of looking at price changes in the market and not panicking where he used the metaphor of a Mr. Market to represent stock market daily gyrations), and margin of safety (which is buying and selling only when you are buying something that is substantially less than the price that it is trading at). For example, if a business is worth a million dollars and the stock is trading at a price which values the business at five hundred thousand dollars then you would have a margin of safety. You would be buying a dollar worth of assets for fifty cents.

I would highly recommend *The Intelligent Investor* and especially Jason Zweig's commentary where he updates a lot of it, and also my own book, *Getting Started In Value Investing*, which was put out in 2007. This walks the investor through not knowing anything on investing and how to be a much more intelligent investor.

Great. Those are the books that would really help somebody who is interested in value investing?

Those would be the starting points and really it's quite simple, Bill. If you can't get through chapters 8 and 20 of *The Intelligent Investor* then you are never going to be a value investor.

Would you tell those people who don't click with those chapters to look someplace else? In other words, to use a different investing method if they fail that test?

I wouldn't have to tell them. They would tell themselves. There is an excellent speech that Warren Buffett gave. I'm sure you're familiar with "The Superinvestors of Graham-and-Doddsville"?

Yes. I used it to write my own book *Super Investing*. You can find it on the Columbia University website I believe.

That's really a seminal piece where Buffett makes the case for value investing over randomness or luck when picking the market. What he does is take nine investors and goes through their track record. He shows them all dealing in the stock market, all picking different stocks, all having different principles but all dealing with the same approach.

He uses the analogy that if monkeys and chimpanzees in a certain zoo were able to do something really unique then when that's the case we have to start looking at what the zookeeper is doing that's amazing. The zookeeper here was investor Ben Graham in what he was able to do with stock returns.

All of these investors follow that same approach and I think Buffett concludes in this speech that he gave in 1984 that there seems to be some perverse human characteristic that likes to make easy things difficult, and you can sit here and try to explain it to someone but if it doesn't resonate in just a few minutes then they are never going to get it. He said something to the effect that you either get it or you're never going to get it, and that's really true.

I've read that speech, which is a wonderful piece that helped shape my worldview. All the investors he mentioned in it had fabulous track records using some derivative of Ben Graham's basic value investing methodology. Since that time there are a lot of books out now like *Value Investors*, *Active Value Investing*, *Quantitative Value*, and so on. In your opinion do these new value investors use Graham's same ideas or something better? Also, when you go back to that speech that Buffett gave, who did you like the most that he mentioned? The big question is whether the new value investors today are doing the same thing or better, and what's successful and what isn't?

Okay, so that's a good question. Value investing is really a very large tent. There are so many people that claim to be value investors that are and there are also those who claim to be value investors that really aren't. There are many ways to apply this approach.

Some people apply it and just in this article, for example, Walter Schloss was mentioned. He had a tremendous career of fifty plus years of beating the market by three to four percentage points a year. He brought a portfolio of sometimes up to a hundred stocks and I think usually had maybe sixty or seventy stocks regularly in his portfolio. Some of these were companies that were on the verge of death, but he was getting more value than he was paying. On the other hand you have the Sequoia Fund run by Bill Ruane. He was doing something very similar to Warren Buffett. They both were taking very concentrated positions in just a few stocks.

There are many different ways of looking at it and it basically goes back to what skill set do you have? For example, I am not confident of holding 30% or 70% of my portfolio in one stock, but Buffett was and is. At one time in the 1960s he had close to 70% of his partners' funds in one stock, which is American Express. That takes an incredible amount of confidence, an incredible amount of knowledge and an incredible amount of confidence in your research. I'm not Buffett, I don't think I'll ever be Buffett and I don't fool myself to think that I am.

On the other hand you have other investors who have a wide portfolio of a whole bunch of value stocks that are a lot of dollar bills they bought for fifty cents. None are great companies but they figure that if they hold a good portfolio then some will do great and some won't, but the great will outdo the mediocre. Then you have another investor like Charlie Munger. When he met Buffett, Buffett was buying stocks like Graham, which was a whole basketful of cheap stocks regardless of the quality of business. Munger said that doesn't make sense. Munger wanted to buy quality companies.

Those were the giants who were the old guard. Today you have the new guard of guys like Seth Klarman of Baupost Group, for example, who has an unbelievable track record. I think even Buffett said at one point that if he was giving his money out to be managed then Klarman would be one. Klarman learned from Max Heine of the Mutual Shares fund, and that is also where Michael Price was. That was a very small shop where they learned how to analyze a company and buy a dollar bill for fifty cents. Klarman applies it not only to stocks but to bonds and to real estate.

Then you have guys like Bill Ackman, who are activist investors but also follow a value approach. They won't buy into something if they don't perceive that they are getting more value than what they are paying.

So it is an extremely wide tent of different approaches but they all follow the same principles of value investing, which is getting a dollar bill for fifty cents and that really is the key. For me to list which ones I like and which ones I don't they all have good points and they all have points that I don't feel comfortable with.

I mentioned that Buffett put a large percentage of his money into one stock, but I couldn't do that. Buying cigar butt stocks like Schloss or Graham were doing doesn't resonate with me either. I don't really know how to buy only quality companies like Munger. I'm not as confident as Munger in knowing what a quality company is, or rather I can figure out what a quality company is but I don't know if it will still be a quality company five or ten years from now. Therefore I try to take a little of everything such as buying quality companies when they are trading at discounted prices, staying away from cigar butts and diversifying my holdings among the portfolio.

Let's go to your approach. I know you have the *Inevitable Wealth Portfolio* and the *Hidden Values Alert* portfolios. Can you tell me what each of those are, what their track records are, the exact investing rules that you are using for picking those stocks and how that evolved?

Okay, so there are two newsletters. There is *Hidden Values Alert,* which started in 2006, and the *Inevitable Wealth Portfolio (IWP)* that started in 2009.

With *Hidden Values Alert* I looked around at the time because we used a lot of publishers and my partner said, "Well, why don't we publish a newsletter? You know a lot about value investing." We looked around and there really wasn't a good value investing newsletter. In fact there weren't any that we saw that had something that I would be comfortable using for investing. We started that newsletter in the beginning of '06 and the "hidden value" approach was simple. It was buying dollar bills for fifty cents.

We ask two questions before we buy a stock. The first question is, "Is the company financially sound?" If the answer was "yes" then we would ask, "Are we buying it at a bargain price?"

It had to pass those two filters - nothing more than that. By doing that we created three portfolios in that newsletter - a Prime Time portfolio that contained mid to larger cap stocks, Special Situation portfolio which was composed of slightly mid to smaller cap stocks, and a Bargain Basement portfolio which was what Buffett would have called "cigar butt" stocks. These are not quality companies by and large, but there were always twenty-five of them in the portfolio. The whole point was that they were small-caps that we were able to buy at discounted prices.

Fast forward to today. We send our numbers into the *Hulbert Financial Digest*, which is put out by Market Watch. We send them in each month and they keep our track record so it's much easier to relay what they are. What is really great is that all three portfolios at *Hidden Value Alert* (the Prime Time, the Special Situation, and the Bargain Basement) have outperformed the market since inception, which was rather interesting because each of them holds different stocks. There is very little overlap between the three portfolios. Each of the portfolios deals with different market caps and each portfolio deals with a different diversification.

For example, Bargain Basement always has twenty-five stocks, whereas Prime Time or Special Situation could come down to as few as five or six or as high as twenty stocks, so we really replicated over the past nine years or so what Buffett has found, which is that if you follow a value approach and you do it well then you could have different selections, different stocks, different market caps, different industries, a whole bunch of differences, but overall they should outperform the market, which all three of them have done.

But what is your general rule for telling whether a stock is financially sound? What is the exact rule and what is the exact rule for whether you are buying it at a discount? There has got to be some criteria that you are using that is a measurement we can follow.

Okay, before I give you the keys to the kingdom let me just explain what *IWP* was.

We started the *IWP*, the *Inevitable Wealth Portfolio*, when we saw the success of the Bargain Basement portfolio. Then we broke that out into being a portfolio of thirty stocks that are financially sound, trading at a discounted price, and the difference was that they were quality companies. It was really a blending of the Munger approach of getting good quality companies and getting them at a discounted price.

We started this in February 2009 or a little before that. I think we started in January 2009 when the bear market was already on its last leg, but when we started the market fell another 15-20% so we felt this was an excellent time because you could just run your finger down the newspaper and there were amazing companies like Disney, Microsoft, Carnival Cruises and Tiffany all selling at P/Es of 7 to 10, which was a joke. This was a price of seven to ten times earnings for world-class companies.

We put that portfolio together and that portfolio from then until now is also outperforming the S&P. All four of the portfolios all follow the same approach, yet we have different criteria for figuring out the price to pay and evaluating the balance sheet to see if the company is financially sound.

Now before I tell you more or less what some of the investing rules are, one must be aware that value investing is part science and part art. It is not physics. Investing is not physics where the formulas are predetermined and the results will always be the same no matter how many times you run the formula. It's not the same with investing. There is an art to it in knowing something about the business.

Take Blockbuster, for example. Prior to going out of business because of technological changes, Blockbuster had a great balance sheet and was trading at a discounted price, but if you didn't see the coming of what was going to happen to the company then you lost money. The same thing goes for the newspaper industry, so just giving a hard and fast rule could lead you down the path of disaster if you don't know something about the business.

So you can't just go by numbers. In other words, you really have to know something about trends?

Not trends. You have to know something about where the business is headed. For example, if you were investing in Blockbuster and didn't see what was happening to the DVD market or the VHS market then you were buying a buggy whip company. If you were buying newspaper companies five, six, or seven years ago because you thought they were cheap and you didn't see the power of what the internet was going to be then you would have lost money as well, so it is not so much trends in the stocks per se but seeing where the business is going.

That's the art part. You could find financially sound companies trading at discounted prices in a whole bunch of ways, but you have to always ask yourself, "Am I buying the next Blockbuster or am I buying the next Google?" and that really is going to be the key to your success. That's the art part.

You can't really quantify that. You can't really put a formula to it. You either have a good and extensive knowledge of business or you don't and you get lucky, so every time I think about buying a stock and adding it to one of our portfolios my job is that I must always ask myself, "Am I buying a Blockbuster or am I buying a Google?" If I can't answer that question then I pass. It should be quite evident that I'm not buying another Blockbuster.

Now do I make mistakes? Absolutely, absolutely, but the point is to limit your mistakes and don't make them so that it leads to a permanent loss of capital and you are out of the game. Does that answer the art and science part of the question for you?

Yes, it does but it brings up another question. Many people talk about Buffett and say he's really great because he has all these business models in his head and says, "I don't look at projections. I always look at history."

Right.

I'm wondering, out of all those value investors that you mentioned, who else impresses you with that sort of business knowledge?

Well, there is no one better than Buffett. No one is better than Buffett. He'll find new businesses that have enduring, competitive advantages or what he calls a "moat." His track record speaks to that - 20% annualized for fifty years - and if he didn't give away his money he would be the richest man in the world with over a hundred billion dollars so there is no one better. He is in a class by himself. For instance, you talk about Babe Ruth and then you talk about every one else so you put that aside. That's always a struggle.

He had losers as well, but the point is that the losers don't dominate. For example, he had *The Washington Post* for forty something years until they changed the company, Don Graham took it back and they did a swap or whatever. He also had *The Buffalo News*. These weren't great businesses the last seven to ten years so I don't think anyone can predict where industries are going 100% of the time. There has to be mistakes because no one has a crystal ball.

The thing about value investing in general and with me per se is that you don't want to pay for future growth. You don't want to pay for future growth because it's an unknown. No matter how good the projections look, no matter how great the next company's innovation is, I don't want to pay for that.

What do I mean by that? When we value a company we only value it based on trailing twelve-month earnings. For example, we are not looking for projected twelve-month earnings because they can be anything. I'd like to do my wealth based on a twelve-month projection but the projection is not real. Banks that lend based on projections usually end up losing money. Look at the real estate crisis. Every projection that every real estate developer gave to banks showed an upward growth but it didn't happen.

Projections are no more than that. They are trying to guess where the future is going to be and as human beings we have a terrible, terrible, terrible track record of predicting future events. There are so many books written on the subject of why humans are not geared up to make predictions and all the biases we have so therefore we try to stay away from that. We don't try to. We *do* stay away from that.

When we value a business or company, and let's just use a standard P/E (Price Earnings) ratio of 10, we are basically saying that last year's earnings times ten was more or less the price we want to pay for something. So if ABC company had a past twelve months earnings of $5 a share then I'd pay up to fifty $50 for the shares. If the shares are trading at $57 dollars then I'm not interested. If the shares are trading at $45 dollars then I'm definitely interested. If they are trading at $35 dollars then I'm even more interested.

When we look at earnings we are looking at *normalized* earnings, not if they had one great quarter or had a big judgment in their way or they had a big tremendous loss that was a one-time event. We try to normalize the earnings over a twelve-month period.

That's really it. We are not paying a nickel for future earnings and that's the key because when you pay for future earnings you run the risk of them not happening and then all your projections that you used based on those numbers that never happened throw your price out of kilter. In that case, what looked like a cheap price today based on projections can be an enormously expensive price tomorrow if those projections don't come true. The reason I don't have any confidence in predicting the future is that no one can do it. No one can do it consistently.

I've seen people use EBITDA instead of the P/E ratio for valuations. What do you think is the best measure for stock valuations?

Well, there are many screens that go through my head. For example, when you go to a doctor he doesn't base everything on your blood pressure. He'll take your blood pressure, he'll do an EKG, he might take an Echocardiogram, he might run your blood work and he's not going to rule you healthy or not healthy based on just one test.

You cannot say that you are healthy based on just the fact that your blood pressure is 110/70. If we took your blood work we could find out that you are dying of cancer. In stock picking it's the same thing in that trying to isolate and look at one number as the tell-all can run you into problems, and so we use the price-to-earnings (P/E) ratio based on a trailing twelve months period. I'm going to stress that we use twelve months of real trailing earnings, not projected earnings, and we normalize it. Most of the time we don't have to normalize any good companies but we look at that as our first screen. Then we go through a whole bunch of other different things.

For example, one thing we look at is free cash flow. We like to see a company generate a certain amount of free cash flow depending on the industry. Free cash flow is the money that is left in after paying out everything. That's the money that drops to the bottom line.

As an example, if we see a company that is worth a billion dollars it may generate a $100 million per year in free cash flow. Theoretically if I bought that whole company for a billion dollars then I'd have one hundred million dollars at the end of each year in cash that I can take out and do with whatever I want. That's a 10% return.

Now if I can then figure out if this company can continue doing what it's doing, ascertain whether it's a Blockbuster or Google, and whether there is some predictability to the company's stability and existence over the next five years then I just bought a bond with a 10% coupon. That's a great deal.

Where are you getting the numbers for this? Is there a website people can look at for getting these numbers and normalizing earnings?

No one does this. Normalizing earnings is basically what the investor has to do. If for example I had a business where I usually make $100,000 a month in earnings, but for the past twelve months I was in a lawsuit that required me to give my lawyer $10,000 a month as a retainer and that lawsuit is over, it doesn't take a genius to figure out that my normalized earnings now, without that lawsuit, will be much better by $10,000 a month because I don't have that expense anymore.

Odds are for anyone starting out that as a rule of thumb you should stick with the easy ones you know. As Buffett says, you don't make more money by finding more difficult situations. There are many ways to look and find companies that are trading for a P/E of less than 12, for example, and stop there. Once you find companies with the P/E of less than 12 then you can really basically say that they are trading at somewhat of a bargain price.

How do you tell what that benchmark should be for this year next year? This year you might be

using a P/E of 12. When would it be a P/E of 8?

Once again there are really no shortcuts. Think about it this way. What is P/E? A P/E is a price earnings ratio. Flip it around and it's really, "What percent, if I own the business, am I making through the earnings on the overall business?"

A P/E of 10 means the price I'm paying is ten times earnings. At the end of the year if a business worth one billion dollars is making a one hundred million dollars and I'm getting that hundred million dollars then I'm making a 10% return on the business. That's all that the P/E is telling us.

Now a P/E of 12 or 12½ is really an 8% return. For example, if I'm paying 12½ times earnings on that billion dollar business then just the reciprocal of the 12½ into 100 is 8, which means there will be an 8% return.

If I am paying 20 times earnings then I'm making a 5% return. If I'm paying 50 times earnings then I'm making a 2% return. That's the basic scale. The P/E is nothing more than that. If you flip it around and use an earnings yield then people would be much smarter when making investing decisions. You wouldn't pay 40 times earnings because it is really a 2½% return on a stock. That's what you are doing, right?

I understand you are using a normalized P/E and free cash flow figures. Do you ever look at whether the stock pays dividends so that you can reinvest that money? A company can make a lot of earnings, but it won't necessarily return to your pocket as cash unless it turns into dividends. Sometimes it is only reinvested in the company.

Well, it depends on the business. With certain businesses you never want them to pay dividends because the managers are so good at compounding money at great rates of return that why would you want it back so that you could put it in a bank yielding you only 1%? So dividends are not really a factor at all. When at the end of the day the earnings are there and the free cash flow is there and the balance sheet is strong then the payout is gravy because that's just above and beyond. That's returning shareholder cash. That will find its way somewhere so you wouldn't look at that.

You asked me the question of what was my P/E line. The P/E line for me is about 12. It's a P/E of 12 normalized. I have stocks in my portfolio where if you look straight on Google it will show you a P/E of 19, but Google is just taking the earnings and dividing it into the stock price. They are not really going through the whole earnings calculations because you could take earnings and make it into zero if you want by throwing everything against the income statement so that it just filters down to nothing. Just keeping it simple, if you look at companies with a P/E of 12 then what is that really saying? Demanding a P/E of 12 means that I'm not going to invest in a company unless I can get an 8% return if I get all the earnings back.

If you buy a stock for twenty times earnings you basically make a statement that says, "I'm willing to accept a 5% return on my money." If you buy stock at fifty times earnings, which is a P/E of 50 trailing, you're basically saying, "I'm willing to earn 2% on my money."

If people looked at it like that I don't think you would have had the bubble of 2000 where companies were trading at 1000 times earnings or had no earnings at all. Say you and I bought a pizza store tomorrow and I've put $100,000 in it as the absentee owner. The only question I will ask you at the end of the year is, "How much did we make?" If you say, "Hey Charles, on the $100,000 pizza business we made $50,000" then that is a 50% return on my investment. Now if you told me that we made only $1,000 or $2,000 then that is a 1% to 2% return, which is a P/E of 100 or 50. I don't need you for that. I can put my money in the bank and do better. It's a way of looking at stocks as businesses, the kind of yield they are throwing off and thinking about the sustainability of that earnings stream.

For example, look at a stable company like Wal-Mart, which is big. The GDP of this country grows at 2½%. Inflation is about 1% and if Wal-Mart does a good job they can earn another 1%, so over time their business is going to grow at around 4-5% a year. If I can buy Wal-Mart at a P/E of 10 (ten times earnings) then more or less my money will grow over time. Wal-Mart is not going to go out of business tomorrow and nothing is going to really change that would break that number down from growing at 5% to growing at 1%. Odds are it won't, so if I can buy that business at a P/E of 10 or better then the odds are that I'm going to make good money over time. I'm going to make a 10% return plus whatever growth there is, but if I buy that same company at a P/E of 20 then I'm only making a 5% return on my money. There's no room there.

For the risk I'm taking by buying a stock why don't I just buy a 10-year bond where I'm making 2½% and where I can sleep at night? In other words, if I'm willing to go and buy a stock then I need to be compensated for that risk of the unknown. It's not a T-bill. Therefore the minimum that I'm willing to accept is about a 12 to 13 P/E. That's the minimum, which comes out to about an 8% return on the earnings.

What are you looking for as free cash flow or any debt ratios?

The debt I will talk about in a second. As to the free cash flow, I don't want to pay more than 10 to 11 times free cash flow. If the free cash flow is $100 million then I don't want to spend more than $1 to $1.1 billion for the company. Usually that's my blood pressure test. That's my EKG test.

Usually both the P/E and the free cash flow are going to jive together and are going to show me more or less similar numbers. It's when I see that the P/E equates to a 10% yield and there is no free cash flow that my light bulb goes off and says something is wrong here. If a company is showing great earnings then where the heck is the money? Anyone can show a lot of paper earnings, but show me real money because you can't eat or spend inventory.

"Free cash flow" means the company is actually generating cash.

Cash. What the company does with that cash is a different story, but think about it this way. If we bought a business such as a pizza store where I put up all the capital as an absentee owner and you ran it and at the end of the year the accountant comes to you saying, "You made $20,000," then fantastic. You call me up and I shoot right over to the store. I'm waiting to take my share of that $20,000 cash return. We sit down with the accountant who says, "I'm sorry. You did make $20,000 on the books, but it's invested in the flour, it's invested in the cheese, it's invested in the sauce and invested in that cabinet you bought." We did make $20,000 on earnings but where is it? Where is it?

This is as opposed to having a business, like an accounting service, that at the end of the year made $10,000. There is no inventory involved. The $10,000 more or less falls to the bottom line. So you can make earnings, but if you can't turn your earnings into cash or anything close to cash then I don't want to be in a business where my money or the earnings would be sitting in inventory.

Are you looking at this primarily through just these two criteria?

Those two criteria really speak to the income statement and cash flow statement.

A lot goes into them but as a general rule for your readers if you are buying a business where the stocks have normalized P/Es of 12 or less and you stick with companies that sell for a free cash flow of 10, 11 or less then you are not really going to screw up big on the price side.

And when do you get out of them?

That's the $64,000 question. The other side of buying the business is not only the earnings and the cash flow. It's the balance sheet. What good is finding a business that generates tremendous earnings yet it can't pay the rent?

As we saw in the 2007 and the 2008 financial crisis there were companies that had great earnings and great free cash flow yet their balance sheets were so levered up that it didn't take much to put them out of business.

Remember that there are two factors we look for in every stock. Is it financially sound and is it trading at a bargain price. I already told you how to find the bargain price.

Now I'm going to tell you how we find financially sound companies. We use Graham's rule. He said, "When I want to buy a company, what I consider financially sound is a company that has (at least) 50% of the assets in equity."

In other words, if you have a house that is valued at a million dollars (that's your asset) and you have a mortgage on it of $800,000 then you are really levered up five times. Your only equity in the house is 20% or $200,000 and you have a million dollar asset. If market conditions aren't right it doesn't take much to wipe out your equity in a financial crisis.

This is as opposed to someone who has a $1 million house as an asset and they have a $100,000 mortgage, which means that they have $900,000 equity. This means that 90% of their asset is backed by equity, so for businesses and companies as a general rule if the equity-to-asset ratio is 50% or greater then you consider that a financially sound company. For example, if the assets of the company are $10 billion and they have $6 billion in shareholder equity (which is .6) we even consider that a financially sound company.

Isn't that a way of saying that if the company went bankrupt I'm going to get a certain amount of my money back?

Theoretically yes, but in reality never because management will find a way to spend that money. Nonetheless, what it is basically telling you is that there is enough equity there.

Think of this as an inverted pyramid. You don't want only 2% or 3% of your assets backed by equity because if those 2% or 3% get wiped out then your business is bankrupt. You want to have a higher shareholder equity ratio because it's more stability in the business. Think about what it's saying.

If you have a business like a semi-conductor company, which usually has high cash positions and a strong balance sheet, and the shareholder equity ratio is .75 (meaning they have seventy-five cents of equity for every dollar of assets), even if they go through a downturn they are still going to be able to pay their bills.

By the way, this answers your question about debt and so on and so forth. If you have too much debt then your shareholder equity will be decreased so those numbers won't jive. You won't be buying companies that are heavily debt-laden.

For example, if you look back at the financial crisis Lehman Brothers had around a 3% to 4% ratio of shareholder equity to assets. Bear Sterns had around a 4% shareholder equity-to-assets ratio, which means that a 3% or 4% decrease in their equity wiped out their whole business. That's how levered up they were. They were levered up thirty-three to thirty-five times. That's like me buying a million dollar house with maybe $50,000 down.

When you look at the market right now, which sectors are just catastrophes when you look at these types of general rules?

We take a bottom-up approach and not a top-down approach. At every party there is always going to be a couple of pretty ladies sitting on the sidelines for whatever reason. In terms of the industries we don't really look at the market that way because we look bottom-up, meaning we look at the individual stocks. However, I knew three months ago that energy companies were extremely undervalued. They were financially sound companies trading as if they were never going to sell another drop of oil or gas again. Over the last three months the technology companies keep populating my list along with a few pharmaceuticals.

You know Wall Street does its dance. It finds industries that it loves and then hates. We don't care about the ones that they love. We want the ones that they hate because that's where the money is. Over time we have been heavily invested in energy companies. Then the cycle changes to technology companies. Then the cycle changes to pharmaceutical companies. Wall Street falls in love and then falls out of love again.

When you run a screen to find these firms, and then maybe fifty pop up, what do you do next?

I wish fifty popped up. In a bull market we get a few dozen and in a bear market you get hundreds.

I previously looked at a screen of the same Graham criteria you mentioned. How do you finally decide that these stocks are the ones for the *Inevitable Wealth* Portfolio, *Hidden Assets Portfolio* and so on?

Great, you are right just to look at the screen and then pick them. I have a spot for three stocks while sixty make the cut according to the screen. The art comes into knowing which of the sixty makes the most sense.

For example, if the screen pops up with a company that is in a business which is very cyclical then I'll be more wary than if I had Microsoft pop up there. That really is where the art comes in. My son always asked me, "If I just follow this blindly then how would I do?" so we did a backtest from 1965.

If you just followed the two criteria and pick stocks with a P/E less than 10 and that are financially sound you would have outperformed the market. You didn't have to know anything about any company. You just picked whatever was available, you picked the top ten stocks.

The extra secret to the sauce is the art of me looking at twenty or thirty stocks that pass the screen where I can say, "Wow, this one is great. This other one is going to be a value trap."

And for that you are looking at quality factors or business models?

Both, both, both.

When a couple of stocks appear on the screen do you then use other criteria to pick between them or are you looking at business models like Warren Buffett would do in his mind?

For me it comes naturally because I've been doing this for so long and you keep building up a database in your mind from following companies.

When I have interns here and they show me a screen and pick three stocks I can look at it from five feet away and say, "I'd never pick those three and here is why because this or this is happening." How do you know that? Well you read *Value Line* and every day you learn something new about a company. If you think about two hundred and fifty businesses in a year then within four years you will learn something about a thousand companies. If you have a database in your mind and a name pops up then you will immediately know whether it is of interest to you or not.

I'll run a quick screen right now just to give you an example. The screen is a P/E less than 12 and the company is financially sound, which means an equity-to-asset ratio of at least .50% (.5). This is nothing fancy, so exactly what are we talking about?

I have right here a total of forty-two stocks. I will go down with you and immediately tell you what I'm interested in and what I'm not.

Sands China is a casino in China. I don't want anything to do with China. I don't trust their accounting. They're corrupt. That's the first one.

Next we have NewLink Genetics, which is a biotech company. They are small. I don't know what their pharmaceuticals are and what their new biotech interventions are. If I had some idea I'd know, but I didn't research it so I'm moving on.

Corning. Corning is interesting. I know a lot about Corning. I've researched the company for the past ten years. Corning makes the Gorilla Glass for Apple products. That's interesting. Why is it selling at a low price now? The balance sheet is fantastic. That definitely sparks my interest.

I'll keep going down the list. Here is a company called FutureFuel. They make ethanol. Why would I be interested in that at this point? Ethanol prices are going down and I'd rather buy Exxon.

In looking at the list you can go down it rather quickly. One name that just popped out to me is Michael Kors Holdings, which is an apparel manufacturer. The P/E is 11 and the balance sheet is pristine. The company just had a hit on their brand because they missed some earnings numbers and their stock got hammered. If you look at the company you are buying a great brand with a solid balance sheet. Nelson

Peltz said, "It's always easier to revive a solid brand that to start a brand from scratch," so when I see a brand name company with a strong balance sheet but selling at a discounted price that easily sparks my interest.

So just speaking with you and looking at Michael Kors Holdings I wish it would get a little cheaper. It's now selling at $48. I would really be interested if the company was selling at $40 or $42, which is ten times earnings or so. But that's the company that definitely jumps off the screen at me whereas with the other ones I'm just passing right through.

I see how you are buying them. You are running the screen and then your knowledge of businesses and companies is helping you say "yes" or "no." You are putting them in an A pile and a B pile, which is an acceptance and rejection pile, and sometimes you have another pile that needs some research.

Let me do an ABC pile. Right off the bat you have companies like Michael Kors Holdings, which is a no brainer. That is the A pile. The B pile is "let me do a little more research." The C pile, like the biotech company, is "I'm never figuring it out so I'm moving on."

Remember, they don't reward you and give you more money because you bought a difficult stock and you did a difficult analysis. I try to impress the interns here that you guys are not getting paid for writing up an extremely difficult and complex thesis. I don't care about that. If the company passes the criteria we use, if you can't tell me in thirty seconds or less why this is a buy from a business prospective then you don't really have a clear idea why this should go into any portfolio.

For example, say you are buying Coca Cola or Qualcomm or Corning. You don't need a five page thesis as to the extent of the business. I don't need that. I know what these businesses are. These are solid, big brand name companies.

Coca Cola is basically now transitioning into water and other products other than carbonated soft drinks. With Qualcomm everyone is concerned about the royalties decreasing now, but the company still has 79% of the chips market share and probably $7 billion of royalties coming from the handsets of every smartphone sold. If Mr. Market doesn't like it and puts it at another valuation that's ridiculous. I don't need much of a story to tell you why to buy it.

I like how you do this, but it only happens when you sell a stock from your portfolio or have some cash to buy more shares so the question arises as to when do you get out of a stock? For instance, I know that Ben Graham had a rule that he would hold a stock for either two years or a 50% return and then get out. After I discovered this two-year rule I also found that Mario Gabelli and several other great investors said they used it. I always wondered if it worked because it was half of the four-year cycle.

I can tell you that I did a lot of research on this. You're referring to an interview that Graham gave in 1976 to the *Financial Analyst Journal*. It was the last interview he did before he died. He also did another interview for *Medical Economics* in the summer of 1976 and he died in September.

The first interview in the *Financial Analyst Journal* was scathing. He basically dissed security analysts. He said, "I can't believe how this industry has grown to the point where these guys are spending their time trying to project future earnings." That's where he came out with the "I would buy an index fund" kind of thing. It was a throwback to the efficient market theory. It wasn't. He was basically saying that all this analysis is producing so little because now a security analyst has really strayed off the beaten path.

He did by hand a fifty-year stock picking backtest on the criteria of being low priced and financially sound which meant a shareholder equity ratio of .5 and the P/E of 10 or less. He saw it worked for fifty years by doing the backtest by hand. We went ahead and we hired a PhD to do the same test.

Wes Gray, author of *Quantitative Value*, is the guy we hired. He's a great guy. Wes is not only a great guy, he's a brilliant guy and he is a war hero. The guy has the full package. I've known him for five or six years and I had him backtest this from 1965 on because that's when the data becomes real. Without anything special - just the computer model picking stocks without any kind of subjectivity - the rules outperformed the S&P substantially.

So you are asking when to sell? In that article Graham said to hold two to three years. Two to three. He wasn't hard set on it. The point being that he wasn't so much looking for a cycle according to what I understand of it. He was basically saying, "I understand that when you buy a stock that is unloved and unwanted at a discounted price then it usually takes at least one plus years for Mr. Market to recognize that or for something to happen."

His concern was avoiding value traps. He didn't want money sitting in a value stock that kept getting cheaper over time with nothing happening since this took up capital in his portfolio of twenty-five to thirty stocks. Therefore he put a time limit on it. He lit a fuse when he bought it and if it didn't hit the 50% mark within two years then it was history regardless. We looked at that rule using two or three years and there really wasn't much of a difference.

Most people say to let your profits run. We also found out - because we have done this now for six years or so on one hundred and twenty closed out trades - how stocks did after we sold them. The bottom line is that on average a stock is about 20% higher after we sold it since we are in a bull market. Was it worth the risk to us to keep holding onto each of them instead of getting out at a 50% profit? The answer in my opinion is no because we are in a bear market and I try to let these things run so when would I have ever sold them? I probably would have captured less than the 50% return.

Are you subscribing to the idea that a stock is undervalued when you buy it and you sell it when it gets to fair value, or are you going to fair value plus a premium?

In *IWP* those two options are not even factored in. We basically say that if we buy a stock today then we give it two years or it goes up 50% and then sell, whichever comes first. Usually when a stock goes up 50% the P/E is no longer 10, and usually it goes into the 18 to 25 range really quickly because they become very popular.

I read somewhere that Joel Greenblatt also tested Graham's rules going back many years and confirmed that it worked. With what we discussed it seems like you are factoring the strength of the balance sheet and the cash flow statement into your selection process and by stipulating the P/E you are also taking into account the income statement because you are looking at earnings.

Yes, if you break that down into two things, which is where Graham's genius was, when he wrote *Security Analysis* he had fourteen criteria for stocks. When he wrote *The Intelligent Investor* he broke it down to seven. He was such a brilliant and intellectually honest guy that he was not concerned about changing his mind or changing the number of criteria. After fifteen years in the business he realized that there are only two main criteria for any successful company to go up in price. The company must be financially sound and be at bargain prices.

It is the same way as if a business broker dropped a list of companies on our desk and we could invest in any of them. What would we look for? The first thing we would want to find are companies that are financially sound. I don't want to go in and throw more capital at this business that we found. It could be low return or it could be a money pit so the first thing we look for is financially sound companies. That requirement will clear the water of a lot of them. Once we find the financially sound companies we then try to make the best deal possible and pay the least for them.

Some people would say, "Okay, I got that. However, what I use to determine what is financially sound for an oil company should be different from what I use for healthcare companies or consumer goods companies." Would you ever say you should use different criteria for different industries? For instance, you measure whether stocks are undervalued by using the P/E ratio, but maybe pharmaceutical firms should be evaluated by the price/sales ratio or you should use a P/E of 15 instead of 12. Have you ever played with those differences?

You bring up another good point, namely what about industry specifics for earnings and the balance sheet? Let's deal with the balance sheet first. There are certain industries where things are a bit different than in others. I'll give you one example.

Defense contractors have shareholder equity that is stated lower than it really is. The reason is because the pension liabilities for a defense contractor are paid by the U.S. Government so that when you look at the shareholder equity of defense contractors - such as Northrop Grumman, Raytheon or General Dynamics - the shareholder equity is really misstated. It's lower but it should be higher. It shows the liability there, but the company is really not paying for that liability.

Another example would concern what happened recently with some companies due to low interest rates. They took on debt that they never needed. The reason they took on the debt was they were able to sell bonds at 20-30 basis points above a five-year Treasury, or in the case I'm remembering Apple Computer was selling at a discount in 2010. They were getting less than the Treasury deal, so why not? Why not sell bonds and get $50-60 billion dollars of free money?

That goes on the balance sheet as a debt or loan, which will bring down the shareholder equity, so as a general rule you always look for the shareholder equity-to-assets ratio. But take the example of Apple. Apple's balance sheet is really understated according to that rule because they have long-term debt, which is nothing more than bonds that they got for free. They got free money by issuing bonds. They didn't have to issue debt but they did because they could.

As a general rule the shareholder equity ratio is 50%. That's what you look at. Here's another example. Let's say that I'm buying a house in your development or your cul-de-sac that is really a $3 million house because that's what every house on the block just went for. Let's also say that I'm able to get it for a million dollars because there was a fight in the family and the wife had to sell it quickly before they got divorced or for some other reason. If I go to the bank and I borrow a small amount of money, taking out a small mortgage, I might look overly leveraged based on the million dollars. However, if you look at the real valuation the house is worth two million dollars so it's not as leveraged as you might think looking at it from the outside.

Each business is different. However, if you start fooling around and buy businesses with lower shareholder equity-to-assets ratios then you are playing with fire because the bottom line is that businesses still have to pay their rent, they still have to pay expenses, they still have to have cash in the bank and they still have to have inventory. If those assets are supported by a small amount of equity then I don't care what business it is in. Eventually if that business is highly leveraged it will get hurt in a cash crunch as we saw earlier in the financial crisis of 2008.

Okay, so that's what you are doing for the balance sheet and then for bargain determination. You always use the P/E and never change any of your criteria for any industry.

Right.

You might have dealt with a number of variations of this in your mind or looked at it through research so I want to know whether you have indeed looked at other things and this is what you have finally settled on? That process of finally settling on this after trying other things, if you went through such a search, would be valuable to pass on to people.

You don't need to do that. It's not as complex as that. You don't need to start playing with price-to-sales and all those other ratios. That's all nonsense - the price-to-sales and price-to-eyeballs ratio and that kind of crap. Those are valuation metrics that come up when people can't justify a deal. Usually the private equity and investment banks come up with a new valuation matrix when earnings aren't there. For instance, you never see price-to-sales mentioned when there are big earnings. It's just a way of doing a deal.

I remember that back in 2000 the valuation criteria was eyeballs, in other words how many eyeballs were looking at something. These companies were never going to make money - the internet companies - so they came up with a new valuation. "Oh, it's not about the earnings. It's about eyeballs." Well you can't spend eyeballs so it didn't matter.

All these valuations are not that complex. Like I told my son, "If you just followed the rule of buying stocks with a P/E of less than 12 regardless of what industry they are in and used normalized earnings (for instance don't consider companies that had a legal settlement whereby earnings popped up 80% that year, which will never happen again), and you buy financially sound companies with a shareholder equity of greater than 50% then you are not going to screw up." You don't have to make these adjustments. You don't have to say, "What's a pharmaceutical?"

Eventually, which is interesting, these sectors will come back to earth. If you recall technology companies were the most hated, most villainous companies in 2000 yet by 2002 value investors couldn't get enough of them. They were trading many times for less than the cash in the bank. Think about that! You were able to buy tech companies back in 2002 for less than the amount per share they had in cash.

So you're saying just keep it simple, stay away from complexity, use very sound reasoning, forget the emotions and make sure you have a margin of safety, don't bet all your cash on just one thing and remember that eventually every sector bounces back after being out of favor (mean reversion).

What did Billy Beane do in *Moneyball*, which was so amazing?

He brought statistics to the game.

Yes, and what was the key statistic that wins baseball games?

Runs.

Okay, you can't get runs if you don't get on first base. Let me find players that have a good batting average, meaning they strike out at a much smaller percentage than they get walks. If a guy strikes out seven times out of ten then he is not going to get on base. If I have a guy who gets on base and walks seven out of ten times then I will try him because he's more valuable to me. It's called the "batting eye," which is the player's visual ability to judge balls thrown by the pitcher. He just started stacking his team players using this one criteria, which is players who got on base with a high percentage. That's the way you win baseball games.

With horse races, what wins horse races? The fastest horse wins so a guy came along, I think in the '70s, and he normalized horse racing times. That was Andy Beyer, who was a horse columnist for the *Washington Daily News*. Despite the fact that horses have all run in different races of different lengths at different tracks and are different calibers of horses, he came up with a formula called the "Beyer Speed Figure" that basically valued how fast a horse ran.

If you have all the horses in a race and one horse is a hundred, one horse is seventy, and one horse is ninety then the higher the speed value denotes the quickest horse in the race. That was it. Today if you open up any daily racing form Beyer's Speed Figure is listed prominently in there. That was a short cut. He took all the speed calculations, all of the different tracks, all the different things and isolated it into one number.

Billy Beane came up with one thing - runs. That's all he cared about.

Another example is Bill Walsh in football. Bill Walsh developed something called the "West Coast Offense." What was it? He asked himself, "How do you score touchdowns?" You score touchdowns by getting first downs. How do you get first downs? Well, you move the ball ten yards. How do you move the ball ten yards? Do you throw long passes or short passes?

He found out that if short passes were thrown then it took the players less time to run out. Therefore there was less possibility for the defense to sack the quarterback and the quarterback would have more completions. He therefore basically put more emphasis on passing than running.

Guess what? He won more Super Bowls. He took players who were average talents like Joe Montana and turned them into MVPs, and now his West Coast Offense is all over football.

Guys like Graham were able to take complexity, isolate the important factor or variable and figure out what that variable should be to have the highest degree of success. That's it.

Here's one more example. If you and I were picking a basketball team, what would be our first criteria for picking a basketball team?

Number of baskets.

No, we have to pick a team. You have a hundred players that came into our lobby now or into our backyard. How would we pick them? Give me one shortcut right off the bat.

Height.

That's it. Any guy over seven feet please move to the right. Everyone else, thank you and enjoy your trip home. When I have twenty guys over seven feet tall then I don't care how good the five-and-a-half foot tall guy can dribble. I know that if I have seven foot guys on my team I can win. For football, let me pick the offensive line up by giving me guys over three hundred pounds. I don't care how good the guy is at two hundred pounds.

That's it. That's really what it comes down to be. You find that one variable. You can sit here and try to work your ass off trying to find a hundred different things but at the end of the day it really comes down to one or two things. Baseball comes down to runs, horse racing comes down to speed, football comes down to touchdowns, basketball comes down to height, and in investing it comes down to cheap companies that are financially sound.

I hate to make it sound simple, but …

No, I like the simplicity because that is what I believe in. You have reduced it to Graham's simple formula and that is how you select stocks. So what I want to know now is what has made you successful at doing this where other people sometimes fail? Also, why are you better at this than others who also say they are buying undervalued stocks?

One word – temperament. Remember when we are buying these companies, when we are adding these companies to our portfolio there is a cloud storm, hurricane, tornado, ice storm, or hail storm over them because you can't have cheap stock prices with good news. You can't have good news with cheap stock prices. Remember, you are usually getting cheap stock prices when the perception out there is terrible, right? That is the only way it can happen, otherwise why would they be cheap?

The point is that it is extremely uncomfortable for people to buy things that are heading down but you have to make these stock buys when the companies have negative news or have headline risks. For instance, who the hell was buying oil companies back in December and November? Everyone knew they were going down. When my mother-in-law calls me up and says why the hell do we have oil companies dropping then I know it's a great buy because everyone knows that it's going down. Beautiful! That's when you get your best bargains.

It takes a lot of temperament in order not to be swayed emotionally and stick to the numbers for what they are. You have to understand that when you are buying these companies some people have to hold their nose when they do it. Some have to be forced to do it. It's not comfortable for most people to buy stocks that are going down and conversely to sell when things are going up.

Remember, we have a 50% sell rule at *IWP*. Many times subscribers will say, "Why the hell did you do that? It just went up another 20%." I don't care because if it goes up by 50% then the rule is to sell. When things are going well people just want to hold on but I'm saying the stock now is at a P/E of 28, we bought at a P/E of 10, so let's find something else with a P/E of 10. I don't hold overvalued stuff. Let's find undervalued stuff.

I remember that the value investor Walter Schloss had the same mindset. After he sold a stock he didn't care what happened to it afterwards, such as how high it continued to go. All he cared about was getting out at a profit and then finding another bargain so that he could reinvest his money and do that again.

That's right. Exactly. You hit the nail on the head.

Let me put it to you this way though. You are continually running a screen and then you evaluate the candidates that pop up.

Right.

Have you ever done it the other way around where you have your eye on some good companies that are always too expensive, so you put them on a watch list and just wait for some bad news so that they can pop down into a favorable price-parameter band where you can then buy them? For instance, do you have any lists such as fifty great franchises that you watch?

Yes, good point. The answer is yes, which is why I have *Hidden Values Alert* so I'm not stuck to such a strict criteria like I am at *IWP*. Remember that with *IWP* I'm not buying any stock with a P/E greater than 10.

I'm just thinking of some of the stocks we are holding at *Hidden Values Alert*. We are holding Apple. We have been holding Apple from December 2012. I always had my eye on Apple, no pun intended and they were selling for a P/E of 10 or 11 at the time we bought it. We still own it.

HCC Insurance is another one we own. I've watched this company and learnt as much as I can for about ten years. It's an insurance company … simple basic insurance, really well run management, and the company goes in and buys their stock anytime it is trading at or below book value so that's exactly what I did. We added HCC in September 2011 at $29 a share and just kept it. Yesterday they were taken out. They were acquired by Tokio Marine Insurance and we still have it but it's up 193%.

There were always companies that I had my eye on that are in my databank so that when I see or hear some earth shattering news about the company or breaking event I act. McDonald's, for example, was definitely on my radar list. It's not cheap enough yet, but I'm interested. I studied McDonald's for years and I'm just waiting for it to be a little cheaper than it is now.

What happens inevitably is that the more you learn about companies the more you start picking companies that you can really understand and resonate well with. It's not complicated. They are not hard to understand companies so you have these in your databank and when you see something out there - like fertilizer companies taking a hit because China stops buying fertilizer - they become bargains. Since you know something about fertilizer companies - that everyone needs fertilizer to increase the yield and that it's really a virtual monopoly business or oligopoly - then you know that if CF Industries is trading at a P/E of 10 you should buy it. It's up 140% because fertilizers aren't going away. Farmers still need it somewhere.

If I had to summarize your methodology I would say this. You run a stock screen with two criteria but then also you know of some great businesses and you wait to buy them when they get into trouble because that produces a favorable price.

Right.

And then when you are looking at all these potential stock buys you don't just go by the numbers. You have to know something about the actual businesses or companies to sift through them.

Right. Think about it this way and I want to be as simple as possible. Let's say you are serious and subscribe to *Morning Star,* which costs two hundred bucks a year. If you are serious about making money in stocks then you would do that. A problem is that most people want to get rich quick and want the fast thing, which is why they are always jumping from thing to thing, so those people will never be happy because there will always be another train that they are going to try to hop on. But if you took an eighteen-year old kid who is just starting out and asked what would I tell him then this is it.

It's very simple - spend a half-hour a day or twenty minutes a day or even fifteen minutes a day reading *Morning Star*. They have 1,700 companies they follow. Read about one stock a day and find out what it does. That's all, just so that when you walk away you have an understanding of what this business does, how the business makes money and what they sell. Business is pretty simple. It's about making things and selling things. That's really it so find out what this business does, how many segments does it have and what drives them. That's it.

At the end of the year you will know something more than the next guy over two hundred and fifty companies. Continue doing that for two years. You now have five hundred companies in your database, and of those five hundred companies in your mental database using the 80/20 rule (here it's going to be the 90/10 rule) there is going to be about fifty that you would love to own at the right price. When you know what they are and they pop up because you see them on the cover of the newspaper or in an article then it doesn't take much thinking, but most people don't want to put in that kind of work and time. It's that simple, it's that simple.

If you were twenty years old is that what you would want somebody to tell you as the road for investing success?

Read and learn. You don't have to do something everyday but you certainly can learn something everyday. Today you should try to learn just one more business. You just figure it out.

For example, let's take *Value Line*. I'm just using this as an example because I still have the current copy. I'm looking at *Value Line* Issue Four, June 12th, and in it there is the Aerospace Industry. There are about twenty-five companies in the Aerospace industry. You just flip through them. The first thing that should jump off the pages at you is, "Why are some of these defense aerospace companies going gangbusters and others are sucking wind?" You should be able to identify that.

Where are they going to learn the specific catalysts for an industry such as aerospace? That's difficult for beginners. They don't know what is the driving force for something or the meaning of

an important catalyst indicator such as the Baltic Freight Index for shipping.

Why are you going for difficult things? Let's be simple. What's the catalyst for the fast food business? If you just came out from being a monk in some monastery and you knew nothing and I wanted to turn you into an investor then eating is pretty simple. You don't have to figure out the Baltic Freight Index. Just go to McDonald's, go to Wendy's, go to Burger King and go to Jack In The Box and you'll know in thirty seconds what makes a restaurant great and what makes another restaurant not.

You don't have to be a genius or wait for some analyst to tell you that McDonald's has too many offerings and that when you stood in line in your car it took you fifteen minutes to place an order as opposed to Burger King that took you three minutes.

It's that simple. With the fifteen-minute time as opposed to three minutes you knew there had to be a screw up somewhere. I didn't need any catalyst to know this. What did I actually do? I got in my car and I went in line when they opened up their coffee business back in 2008/2009. My son and I drove around to three or four McDonald's in New Jersey and we saw how long it took them to complete an order. All of a sudden we said, "Wow, they got the franchise to do this because it only takes three minutes or two minutes to make a Frappuccino."

Then we went back a couple of years later. They had added so many things to their menu that we waited in line for fifteen minutes to get that same coffee. Two years later McDonald's says, "We have a problem," but if you went there you already knew so you don't need to be a genius.

You just have to read. Read the annual report of three or four companies in the same industry. Go visit them. Don't pick problems like the Baltic Freight Index. Not everyone is going to understand freight carriers or oil transport or what have you.

Do something simple. Go to Petco. Go to three or four pet companies and see why are they different. See what makes them work, why you liked going there and not going here.

I'll tell you what's easy. Go into Citibank and go into Wells Fargo and tell me who gave you better service. You would have to be from Mars if you can't figure out what the hell is going on in there. Go to apply for a loan at Citibank and do it at Wells Fargo and see what happens.

What else would you tell the people who are getting started or even the people who are near retirement and don't have money? What would you tell these guys to do?

Well if the old guy has no money now then I don't know what to tell you. It's really hard to make money when you have no money. To the old guy I would say don't get swindled. How could you make a fire if you don't have the wood?

In other words the priority is to stress to the young guy, "You better make sure that you don't become that type of old guy so here's what you need to do."

How did the old guy become the poor guy? It wasn't one bad decision or two bad decisions. It was a lifetime of bad decisions. If instead of putting two or three thousand dollars in an IRA every year he took it and went to Atlantic City or Vegas to gamble because that was of more value or a higher priority to him then don't be surprised when you wake up at seventy years old and you have zero in the bank.

Well let's back that out, okay? Let's say that you have a young guy in front of you. Would you tell him to become a successful investor? Without referencing your criteria, what's the general rule you would tell him for investing? Would you tell him to put his money into education and train himself if he wants a better future or start investing? If he is shooting for future prosperity down the road then what would you tell this guy?

As to education, if it's either eat bread or go to school then I can't make that decision. Assuming the guy has a job and is making money then I would tell him, "Just take your money every month, don't spend more than you make, and put 20% or 30% of your money into a S&P Index fund every month and eventually you will do well." You will be the market, which 90% of mutual funds and a majority of money management instruments cannot outperform, but you will so Buffett said that dumb money ceases to be dumb when it recognizes itself. It's that simple. If you put your money in the index then why do you have to beat anything? You have to beat zero.

Over time the U.S. economy continues to chug along. It continues to grow even at a 6-7% rate with a GDP of 3% or so and inflation rate of 1-2%. A good S&P company grows around 6% so just do the math. Over time it will do well. The S&P over one hundred years is 11% or so as opposed to the guy who has nothing today because he took that money and bought things that decreased in value like a nice gold watch or a fancy car instead of taking his money and putting it into a index fund. It's nothing more difficult than that. If you don't want to take the time or anything then do what John Bogle suggests, which is to just buy index funds and you're going to do great. In fact you will do better than most pension fund managers.

You previously mentioned that value investor Seth Klarman even looks at real estate using value investing. Would you suggest that people also put some money into real estate as diversification if they want to become wealthy?

Yes.

Okay, let's say that they are in their twenties or thirties. What as overall advice would you give them?

If they didn't want to put any work into it or they do? If you don't want to put any work into it then just buy an index fund, just buy an S&P Index fund. That's it. Finished, case closed, go home, I'll see you in thirty years, you'll be very happy.

For someone who does want to put some work into it then if you are willing to spend a little time you can beat the market. You can beat it by one to two percentage points a year, which compounds enormously over a thirty to forty year span. If you just follow my criteria or Graham's criteria and just buy financially sound companies when they are trading at discounted prices, and buy a portfolio of them - twenty or so - and sell them two to three years later at 50% or 60% profit or whatever it is then you cannot *not* make money.

You have seen and talked with so many investors and you have analyzed this industry and have

thoughts on the right and wrong ways to do things. If you had a magic wand and you could correct the biggest mistakes you see people making, or you could amplify what they are doing right, what would you wave your magic wand to accomplish if you really wanted to help people?

As to "doing right" I hardly ever see anyone doing the right things over the long term. If I could wave a wand I would basically shut off the emotional part of their brain and have them invest with their head instead of their heart. That means buying things that are on sale and selling things that are expensive. It's just that simple.

Do what you do when you go to the supermarket. You look for the specials. I have yet to see people who walk into the supermarket and say, "Could you please tell me where the most expensive stuff is that's not on sale because I just love to piss away my money?" What does every supermarket have? You walk in and they have the circular of price specials. Everyone grabs that to look for the discounts. Why the hell aren't you doing that when you are investing?

That's very good advice.

There's one thing you mentioned, which is real estate for example. I have a general rule on investing. If I don't understand it then I can't value it and if I can't value it then I can't invest in it. Keep those three points in check and you will save yourself a lot of money.

If I don't understand real estate - if I don't know where this building is going to be in five years or ten years in terms of the tenants – then I can't value it. If I can't value it then I have no reason to invest in it.

Why come to the game with such a disadvantage? If you don't know the valuation then you can't understand the business. Do you think that two out of three times you are going to make money? You are competing against me so what I'm selling you are buying and what I'm buying you are selling. Odds are that is the way it is going to be. Then you throw the Klarmans of the world in there and the Greenblatts and the Buffetts. What kind of chance do you have against them if you are coming to the game unprepared?

Would you even think of coming to a game, a chess match for instance, and try to beat the chess master? You're crazy, so there is no way you are going to beat guys that take this just as serious if not as serious or even more serious than chess masters do with their game, than bridge masters do with playing bridge, or that football players or baseball players do with their craft. You are walking into my craft without any background, just a couple of dollar bills attached to your hand, and you are saying, "I'm going to beat you." You don't have a shot in hell.

You already gave us a list of recommended books. Is there anything else you want to add in terms of useful advice? Are there any other life lessons you really want to give people for investing or for life in general? Is there anything that you want to use this chance to tell people?

Time is going to pass regardless. For what might seem like a trivial amount of money today if you just sock it away and invest it in something then you will wake up three, five, ten, fifteen years later and it's going to grow if it's invested in something. Time will pass regardless of what you do. If you say,

"I can't think ten years in advance, I can't think twenty years in advance," you don't have to. Just trust me. It will come with you or without you so you might as well go on for the ride and the best thing that can help you is time.

If you are young enough and you start out young enough then a small amount of money can become a huge amount of money. If you start too late in life then a sizeable amount of money cannot grow to a huge amount of money because you don't have the magic of compounding working for you since you don't have time. If you don't have time then in order to enhance your returns you will do stupid things which will increase your risk level and that's the last thing that you need to do.

Instead of playing catch up start at the beginning. Plant the seeds now. It takes a while for them to grow but trust me that the little oak tree, that little acorn that you fit in the palm of your hand will be a huge oak tree thirty years later that is so big that you couldn't even cut it down or climb it. It will not have grown so tall in one day. It will have happened over time so we start with the acorns now because eventually they are going to become oak trees, but if you start with the oak tree when you are seventy years old then there won't be enough wood to make your coffin.

And the big thing you are saying is to remove the emotions from that whole process?

Remove the emotions. Stick to a game plan, an approach that works, and stick to it. If it means investing in an index fund every month then stick to the process.

My son just got a job. He just graduated college and he got a job. Last night he was filling out a form from the HR Department to get his check, which was direct deposit. He goes, "Dad, should I put it in my Citibank account or my Charles Schwab account?" and I said, "Absolutely one hundred percent your Charles Schwab account. Have them put that money directly into your Charles Schwab account and then take 20% of it, move it to Citibank so that you can go out, go to bars, drink, take out girls, whatever you want, but if you leave the majority in there and you keep investing it then it's going to grow. It's going to grow. The beers that you drink are never going to give you any more satisfaction than they do for that moment, but the money that is there is going to give you freedom to do what you want in life." Really, if you ask me one life lesson it is that it's not what money can buy. It is the freedom it provides you.

Great advice. Charles, how can people follow you if they want to? Where can they find your websites and newsletters?

Okay, I tweet pretty often and my twitter feed is IWPeditor. Then there is *Hidden Values Alert* (HiddenValuesAlert.net) and there is the *Inevitable Wealth Portfolio* (InevitableWealthPortfolio.com).

Thanks Charles!

Chapter 17
Wesley Gray
Quantitative Value Investing

Wesley Gray, fund manager and author of Quantitative Value, joined me to discuss value investing ideas that really work so that anyone can approach value investing properly. Because Wes has evaluated hundreds of investing ideas by computer I asked about popular investing notions you should avoid because they are absolute failures despite all the hype. We also discussed his research on quantitative momentum strategies that you can compare with the momentum strategies of Geoff Bysshe and Marvin Appel.

Eventually our conversation got around to the topic of mega-wealthy individuals and family offices that manage their own investment funds. Along these lines Wes revealed his FACTS formula for wealth accumulation that the richest billionaires follow to maximize their investment returns over time. His book, DIY Financial Adviser: A Simple Solution to Build and Protect Your Wealth, summarizes these principles as well as how you can protect and grow your assets using simple tested models that readily beat the experts.

The whole gist of our conversation re-emphasizes the common theme found throughout these interviews time and again, namely that you should use tested models to trade or invest and avoid taxes and fees whenever possible. As a professional researcher Wes has tested countless systems to discover their pros and cons, advantages and flaws and you can keep abreast of many of his trading ideas and research findings at AlphaArchitect.com.

Wes, what we really want to do is start off from the beginning. How did you get involved in trading and investing? What got you into this field and what are you doing now that you are offering to the public? Basically what got you started, what did you go through, where are you now?

I'll go way back. I actually grew up on a cattle ranch around Eagle, Colorado, which is near Vail for people who need a landmark. When I was there I used to raise steers and a bunch of different animals for 4-H. When I was eleven or twelve years old I had this Hereford steer named Big Red. I sold it and I actually ended up with a couple grand, which when you're a kid is a lot of money. My dad said, "You know, I'm a rancher. I don't know what the heck to do with money. Call up your grandmother."

My grandmother from Southern California had been a real estate agent in Malibu in the '70s so obviously she had some money at the time. I called her up and I said, "Grandma Ginny, what do I do with this money? What do you recommend?" Literally she sent me a copy of Ben Graham's *The Intelligent Investor*. When I received it I actually read it.

I had always been into business and thinking economically even though I was just a kid. It just was always intuitive to me so I read Graham's book and I was like, "This makes so much sense. When you do investing it is just like buying businesses. You want to buy things that are cheap and not buy things that are expensive and you want to find things that are high quality, not junk."

I also was just enamored with the idea that you could have money and it could make more money for you. That's because my dad would pay me five cents to flip over each bail of hay when the wires weren't set right and when you work it basically just sucks, especially manual labor. I just thought it was really cool that you could have money and it could make more money for you. In any case, I initially got exposed to the whole Ben Graham value investment stuff super early on.

I went on through life and reached the age where I started getting actual money I could trade. When I was eighteen, instead of buying a mutual fund that my dad and my grandmother recommended or what have you I was like, "Okay, I can finally do this for myself." I literally started the minute they would allow me to open a brokerage account. I was trying to be Warren Buffett picking stocks.

Actually, my first stock ever was a stock called Swisher Sweets, which made cigars. I bought it when it was around six bucks. I bought it because it had a high return on assets, return on capital for like ten years. It was selling at a P/E of 5 or 6 and of course, just dumb luck, I buy this thing at $6 and literally three or four months later it gets bought out for $9.50. I was like, "Oh, wow, this whole value investing thing is so easy. Just buy cheap high quality firms and you'll make 50% every three months."

Now obviously later on in life I had to eat some humble pie, but that's what really got me triggered. I learned about value investing. I had great success right off the bat and I was like, "This is so easy that I'm going to be a millionaire."

Anyways, I got really enamored with business finance. I ended up going to the Wharton School at the University of Pennsylvania, which is like the Mecca of finance, and was in the weeds there learning all that I could. Then along that line I started working with a professor there, Chris Geczy, and I ended up basically becoming the department programming data monkey and was doing really well with that. All the professors wanted me to do all their dirty work.

When it was coming up to when I was about to graduate they were like, "Hey, did you ever think about being a professor and doing your PhD? Oh, by the way, you should go to University of Chicago because that's where we all went." I was like, "Well, I'm an undergrad. Don't you have to do a Masters degree or something like that?" They said, "No, no, we'll get you in. We know all the right people." So I applied for grad school and ended up getting into the PhD in Finance program there at the University of Chicago.

I started learning more finance and got more buried in the space trying just to read and learn as much as I possibly could about value investing and accounting, but also about quantitative techniques and how to think about financial markets. Fast-forward eight years because I took a sabbatical and actually joined the Marine Corps for four years, which is another story, but I graduated and ended up becoming a professor at Drexel University. I went on the job market, but since my wife was born and raised in Philadelphia she was like, "Guess where you're going?" and I was like, "Okay, I'm going to Drexel," which was in Philadelphia.

So we come out here and through this whole process I'm writing blogs about research I've been seeing or research that I've done personally and literally out of the blue I get a call from a billionaire because he read my blog. One thing led to another, I went up there and met him in New York, started doing consulting, then started doing more consulting and we basically became full-time consultants for him. We had been doing research on security selections specifically in value investment strategies.

Eventually I strong-armed him after some kicking and screaming. I said, "Hey, for you $20-30 million is like a basis point. For me, if I wanted to start an asset management business I could take my chump change and get some money from my dad but that's not going to be very credible." We then basically cut a seed deal in 2012 with his family and we launched a managed account on this quantitative value algorithm, which is what my book *Quantitative Value* is based on. We have been doing that for almost three years now. We launched an ETF equivalent about seven or eight months ago. We started with around $20 million and now we have around $260 million under management and I guess the rest is history. Now we are rocking and rolling in the business.

From inception until now isn't really enough time to show a clear differential or big track record difference between what you are doing and S&P 500 returns, but how is it doing so far?

We've been blessed. Since we started to manage accounts we are about 300 basis points a year over the index.

Is that for all three years?

No. Our CAGR (compound annual rate of return) is around 21% in change. The S&P value is what we use as our benchmark and is 18% in change so we have seen about 3% a year extra on average, but it's obviously been lumpy.

In the stub year 2012 we did really well, in 2013 we crushed it, in 2014 we got crushed, and then in 2015 so far we are basically in line with the index. The average CAGR spread is around 3%, but it has super high tracking error and is highly active value investing so it doesn't really track the S&P perfectly. Over that time period we have had a pretty lucky run, but it is long-term stuff that we are designed for.

Would you consider your method purely value investing without any momentum component?

It's pure value investing, but we do a lot of research in momentum investing as well. However, for this value system it is 100% a systematic way to exploit value investing as a pure play so there are no, at least directly, momentum elements involved in the quantitative value system.

We have another momentum specific system that just focuses on that aspect of the marketplace. With the two approaches we allow people to pick their poison as opposed to us mixing and mashing the two whereby no one then ever really knows what they are actually buying so this is a pure play value system.

How do those two differ and is the momentum or value system performing better? Also, traders and investors would be interested in knowing about your exact rules as well as what you evaluated that didn't work. I personally want people to know about that because there are a lot of crazy ideas out there and we need to tell people that some of these notions sound good but don't work in reality.

We have been doing value investing for a long time. Momentum investing is something we have been doing research on for a long time. We actually just launched live in a managed account here about four or five months ago on some qualified money and then we have ETFs coming out on it here around October. The reason we have never launched momentum on actual capital is because all the money we deal with is insanely tax sensitive. For value investing - because the turnover requirements are much lower - you can do a lot more tax management. That is one of the reasons, frankly, that we have an ETF. It's basically to deal with the tax problems.

We have only been able to implement value strategies. As to the momentum strategies we have been doing a live track for literally four months now, but it's in a qualified account that is not tax sensitive. And again, the reason for this is that momentum strategies - if you want them to actually work in expectation – need a lot of turnover and you have to do monthly rebalancing or rebalances every couple of months, but that's going to generate massive tax problems. All of the capital that we deal with hates taxes more than making money so we can't do that without an ETF wrapper.

We can talk in great detail about our momentum system if you like, but it sounds like we should probably focus on the value system for now. Does that seem reasonable?

Yes, let's focus on that first. What have you arrived at? Let's also hear about what didn't work, if possible, so we can we can pop some bubbles of wrong ideas.

The bottom line is what is value investing? It is trying to buy the cheapest, highest quality firms you can find, right? There is a great paper by the guys at AQR – it is called "Buffett's Alpha" - where they literally reverse engineer what Warren Buffett actually does. He can talk about what he says he does, but now with the benefit of hindsight we can reverse engineer all those trades and then quantify and identify what factors he's loading up on.

Basically, Buffett buys cheap, high quality firms and he uses some leverage.

So why would you ever do something different than buying cheap, high quality firms? You want it, right? That's the Ben Graham model. Even though Buffett doesn't necessarily say that explicitly, he'll say that you want to focus on quality and price simultaneously. The reality of what he actually does is that he buys firms that are cheap first, and then high quality meaning that quality is a secondary element after we have considered price. That's basically what our algorithm does and at a real high level we can go into the details on it.

Now, what are some things that don't work that may sound very similar to that approach?

As I mentioned, we buy the cheapest, highest quality firms. A lot of value investors listen to what Warren Buffett says, but don't know what he actually does. The classic anecdote is that Ben Graham was a guy who just bought cheap stocks, period. Then Warren Buffett apparently moved on beyond that and said, "Well, with Coca-Cola at 20 times earnings I'm willing to pay a little bit more because it's so high quality and that's still a value investment" whereas Graham might say, "Listen, I just buy cheap stuff, period."

Now Warren Buffett talks about that, but again, empirically, that's not what he actually does and there is a reason for that. The minute you move out of the cheapest stock bin then you basically shoot yourself in the foot no matter what the quality component. An example would be the Magic Formula framework where it's like 50% quality weighted simultaneously with 50% price. You mix those two things where you want to try to find this maximized quotient between quality and price. It's a very intuitive algorithm, but the problem is that empirically it just doesn't work.

Why? Because by accident sometimes - because you have 50% of weighting related to quality - you might buy a stock that is just not absolutely cheap in the bottom decile. And again, it's just the evidence that the minute you move out of the cheap stock bin with your investing dollars is the minute you start losing expected return. I'd say that is a nuanced rule that people should focus on.

All right. What I now want to know are your measurements for what's cheap and what's quality. What are your actual algorithms, measuring sticks or sets of criteria for determining these things? We know Graham used a P/E to find cheap stocks but did you come up anything different and more importantly, what have you tested that didn't work so that we can avoid those traps?

What I'll do is walk you through every step of our process. Some of this may not be traditional value investing but this is what we do. Standing at a real high level you have to figure out where is your playground, so first identify your universe. In our case it is typically mid to large, liquid, tradable stocks. Obviously, if you're doing this for a PA and you didn't care about taxes too much then you may want to move down the spectrum and do small or micro stocks, assuming you could get liquidity, but we are talking about big liquid securities.

Then the second step in our process - after we've identified the playground and before we even get into the whole game of what's cheap and what's not - is that we are trying to avoid the proverbial "falling knife." You don't want a situation where you buy a cheap stock at five times P/E but earnings get cut in half, it stays at five times P/E and we just lost half our capital, right? We want to avoid that type of value trap if at all possible so the second stage in our process is literally a bunch of forensic accounting screens where we are trying to identify things like aggressive accounting, manipulation, fraud or potential bankrupt firms.

For instance, you never want to buy a cheap firm that has a high probability of going bankrupt and you really need to worry about this because a stock is cheap for a reason. It is either going to go up 100% or you are going to lose all your capital and you are just buying risk.

How do you do this forensic screening to avoid risk? Do you run all the stocks past an Altman credit score or something like that?

There are a lot of things you do, but I'll speak specifically to the Altman Z-score because that's a traditional financial distress metric. The Altman Z-score was actually written in an article in the '60s or '70s and it is still programmed up in Bloomberg. People still use it even though there has been subsequent literature which basically said (1) in that original paper he had look-ahead bias so the result doesn't count, and (2) people have corrected for that and showed that it just doesn't work.

Yet everyone loves to use Altman Z-score even though there is no empirical evidence that it is actually a good idea. The literature has moved well beyond that and I would say the best technology in financial distress or bankruptcy prediction is a paper called "In Search of Distress Risk" by some guys at Harvard where they basically say, "Listen, Altman's Z-score was on the right path in the sense that clearly we want to look at some balance sheet type measures. This is because if you have a ton of debt or your current ratios are going terribly wrong then that could be an issue, but we also need to look at market indicators." For example, a really highly volatile stock price in the short run or huge excess returns that are way out of line with the market are a bad sign.

The bottom line is that when you use balance sheet financial statement information combined with market information and then build those into a statistical model then they are much better predicting out of sample bankruptcy so we just used that algorithm. I can send you the paper but if you just Google "In Search of Distress Risk" - I think Campbell and Harvey and another guy whose name I can't remember are the authors – that is the algorithm we use. It's like the Altman Z-score, but just actually one that in expectation works better.

In other words, you find large-caps or liquid stock issues and then you run them past a forensic accounting system to get rid of the potential losers. And then what do you do?

Now we are into the heart of value investing and this is, "How do you find the cheap stocks?" As you mentioned at the outset, finding cheap stocks can mean a lot of things to a lot of people. For example, we could do a P/E ratio. We could compute a book-to-market ratio. We could use free cash flow-to-enterprise value.

There are a hundred different ways in theory you could screen for "cheap" and you could also do CAPE (cyclically adjusted P/E) measures where you take an average of the past eight years of earnings for the P/E ratio. You can do composites where you average different metrics together like one-third price-to-sales, one-third price-to-book and one-third P/E. As you can imagine, there are just thousands of combinations.

Well, we are computer programmer guys so we just literally data mined that. We tested out every combination that you can ever imagine. In my book I think there are two chapters dedicated to just that. What we found was actually surprising because I was born on Graham and Dodd's *Security Analysis*. I was like, "Oh, doing a P/E ratio where the E (earnings) is an average of, say, the last seven to ten years (that's what Ben Graham said to use) is probably one of the better ideas. It makes intuitive sense." There is even a paper in the academic literature where they do that analysis in UK markets and they *show* that that's actually true.

We did all of this in the U.S. and we basically found that in the end the most robust, reliable and simplest way as well to identify "cheap stocks" that tend to have the best out-of-sample performance is enterprise multiple, so some form of either EBIT over total price value or EBIT over enterprise value works best. At least in-sample over the past forty to fifty years that simple metric seems to be the best.

Didn't James O'Shaughnessy find the same thing? I know you know his work. Did you find it confirming yours?

O'Shaughnessy and those guys are big fans of the composite a little bit more as opposed to single ratios. They do identify that enterprise value ratio or enterprise multiples are certainly good.

I think that is their best single number one rating metric rather than P/E.

Yes, that's right. And they do a combination, right, like composites?

Yes.

Which is fine. In research that we have not really ever published we wanted to understand and try to determine a great composite metric. I really like the composite idea intuitively because for example, take Google. For Google, why would you measure the company on price-to-book when the book value is the computers? Clearly, that is not the real book. The real book value is their human capital and everything so maybe you should use price-to-book, price-to-earnings, or price-to-sales and the composite is therefore going to tell you something better.

So what we did is say we are going to take a different track. We think business or investing is best when it's most business-like so who are the guys that buy businesses? Private equity guys. How do all my private equity buddies view business buying? They look at enterprise multiples because they have to buy the whole damn company. They have to buy the equity, the debt, and if there's any cash in the till they can throw it back in their pocket assuming they don't need it for working capital needs.

So what we did is we looked over time at the extreme cheapest securities based on price-to-earnings or cheap EBIT-to-total enterprise value or whatever, and then we compared amongst those names the propensity for buyout and take-over. Basically there is a much higher propensity for takeout amongst the cheapest enterprise value names as opposed to the cheapest, say, price-to-sales names or price-to-earnings names. This gave us a little more confidence that really what is driving the enterprise multiples edge is the fact that it is not just data mining, but rather it's probably due to the fact that a lot of times the names you buy in those buckets are names that private equity guys are also interested in buying because that is how they think about the world.

That's what I found out, too. You have to look at it as if you were sorting through companies and willing to buy the entire outfit. Whatever metric helps you do that works best. I also came to this conclusion exactly as you did figuring that this was what the private equity guys were looking at so therefore it made sense.

Yeah.

But have you found that the P/E ratio, just the simple P/E also works well? Graham used it and O'Shaughnessy found that it's pretty good just by itself. Since most people can't get the EBIT variations I'm wondering whether you feel the P/E is a good enough proxy for valuing stock prices?

Yes. Honestly, what we tell people is that if you are a do-it-yourself type then buy cheap stocks. However you measure it, on average if you have the guts to do the strategy then you will be better off than the market. At least that is what we have seen historically. You can do that any which way you want and maybe your own method is not perfect, but definitely they are all good.

All right, so now let me ask you this. Let's say you have an industry such as the oil industry comprised of Exxon and companies like that. Somebody wants to rate the stocks in this industry in terms of value. Instead of the entire universe of stocks, what would be your first best value metric for a specific industry, your second best, your third best, your fourth best and so on just off the top of your head?

We have done a lot of the industry data mining as well, and frankly we cannot get comfortable because we do a lot of robustness testing. You can always identify one thing or the other as important but you always want to look at first half, second half sampling and make small perturbations in your research design in order to actually believe in something. You want to see that it works on average all the time.

Basically, across all industries our favorite metric is definitely EBIT over total enterprise value or you can flip it. It doesn't really matter. That one is definitely my favorite.

I would say the second favorite is - and again we also do international stuff so this one is muddied - gross profits-to-enterprise value. Gross profits is another newer idea. A guy named Novy-Marx at Rochester has a lot of papers on it. I think DFA (Dimensional Fund Advisors), which is a huge value shop, is starting to incorporate some of that into their systems but I'd say that gross profits-to-total enterprise value would probably be number two.

Number three would probably be the good old-fashioned P/E.

Number four would be book-to-market or price-to-book as a lot of people call it. The reason that one is further down the chain is because DFA, which I think manages $450 billion, uses that metric so there is clearly a lot of competition on using it. Therefore I'm not sure you want to play on that one.

And then honestly one of the more surprising things we found - just because it's not in the tradition of how value investors think - is that free cash flow yields are actually the worst. They are still better than buying the market, but free cash flow yield metrics are probably my least favorite valuation metric out there.

That answers a lot of questions because people typically have pet theories on which valuation metrics are the best. From what you are saying investors just need to be consistent and if so they can use something simple like the P/E ratio, which is very simple.

Yes.

Now regardless of the metric you use, how do you find the cutoff line for what you consider cheap? Do you rate the entire universe of stocks or do a composite for an industry and say, "Well, for this industry this guy is at the bottom so this company is cheap." Do you put stocks in some type of deciles? What exactly do you do?

We have looked at all these things. The bottom line in investing is that the more you look and feel like an index the more you will have returns that look and feel like an index. Industry concentration is one of those things where if you do things that are sector neutral to make it look and feel like an index by having lower tracking error then all you are doing is diverting away from the core reason value works, which is buy with margin of safety, period. The logic is as follows. This is just an empirical standpoint, but I'll give you the story behind it.

The problem with doing that - constraining the investment system – is for example the following. If you say, "Hey, I've got to have 10% Tech because that's what the valuated S&P 500 index has" then you are going to get 10% Tech and you are going to buy the cheapest Tech stocks that are only fifty times earnings, not five thousand times earnings, but that's still a shitty investment because you are not buying with a margin of safety.

If you want to do a pure value system that actually exploits anomaly you have got to end up doing things that are painful. One of those painful things is buying and loading up in specific industries at a specific time. That's because industries are correlated cheap at the same time and so most of the value is just within an industry and you basically have to buy the cheap stocks, period.

If you don't, it's fine. You will still add marginal value but you are starting to decrease your marginal alpha and you are getting closer and closer to being a closet indexer, which is just going to lower your expected ability to beat the market.

But what exactly do you do? Do you take one thousand stocks and just find out what's cheap or do you do it by industry and say, "This industry is cheap so let's find the cheapest stock in this industry"?

It's top-down. You have 1,000 stocks. Let's say we boot out 100 of them because of the forensic screens. Now we are left with 900, so we go immediately down to the 10% cheapest stocks (bottom decile). Hence we would be looking at a bucket of 90 stocks irrespective of industry.

Obviously you are going to end up finding a lot of securities that are concentrated in one industry. For example, three or four months ago you were going to buy a lot of oil stocks. You were going to be 25% in oil and energy.

In other words when you are talking about industries you are not looking for a cheap industry group. It's just that after you go through your analysis to rid yourself of possible bankruptcies you were left with 900 stocks, but you then turn to the cheapest 10% of that filtered group and a lot of them are going to be in the same industry.

They are going to be whatever people hate. You will find the hated or undervalued industry naturally.

I just want to make sure people understand that. Now that's how you come up with what's "cheap," but how do you now determine what is "quality"?

For quality, we basically have a table that has two legs to it.

One of the legs is what we call a company's "economic moat." Your ability - at least historically - to generate returns on capital that are in excess of your "fair market return on capital" would be one element of quality. That is more of a historical vantage point in the assessment of, "Is this a good company at least historically?"

The second leg on that table is "current financial strength" and that is basically a snapshot or a pre-flight checklist of, "Can you sustain for the next few years?"

Why do we do it like that?

Well, in our context we are looking at cheap firms, the cheapest, and all of these firms have issues, right? They wouldn't be the cheapest unless they were having issues or some problem in the business at least in the short-term. Therefore we need to identity from all those cheap firms which ones have been historically good because we know on average that those are the ones that are going to mean revert back to their old ways. Therefore we need to look for an economic moat.

We also need to be certain that you have *current financial strength* because even if you are cheap and you have a historic economic moat if you can't pay your creditors tomorrow then the debt holders own the equity, not us. Therefore we need this two-legged table to have evidence that you are a good company, but also able to survive for the next few years so you can get through this rough patch that clearly the market thinks you are in and you actually probably are in, which is why you are so cheap. That's the framework.

I've got the philosophy down, so now what is your exact measurement or formula for current financial strength? What are the parameters for that and for the economic moat, or is that a subjective thing?

Again, everything we do is 100% systematic just so that we can maintain objectivity and not have obvious human bias problems. For the economic moat there are essentially three core indicators that go into that measurement.

The first one is long-term free cash flow generation. Literally the metric is that we sum up the past eight years of free cash flow divided by your current total assets and then we rank that relative to all the other companies in the universe. The idea is that a firm like Amazon, for example, always says they are just doing all this CAPEX (capital expenditure) because it's going to have huge returns on capital in the future. So okay, we are not going to look at your free cash flow this year because you say that this is going to be so great, but over an eight-year period we are going to get to call your punk card here because we are going to incorporate your CAPEX, and hopefully we have seen the return on that investment in the form of actual positive free cash flow. Then we rank that against everyone.

For example, a firm that will look really good here would be something like Microsoft. They just generate a ton of free cash flow over multiple year time stretches so at the margin that's a good thing. That's one angle on it, but we do a lot of different angles because we want to get the whole picture.

The other one is that we just look at long-term returns on capital and return on assets, and we are always talking about eight years here. The idea is that when we look at your eight-year geometric mean of the return on capital and you are Coca-Cola and it's been 15% for the past eight years and all the other guys out in the world are making 5% with volatility then clearly Coke has something special, right? This long-term return on capital measure over an extended period - ranked relative to everyone else in your universe - is a good way to sift out the good guys from the bad guys. That's the second angle on it.

The third angle on it is that you can dig deep into profit margin characteristics. For example, a firm like Procter & Gamble that has 50% profit margins almost every single year plus or minus a percent. We have metrics that measure that and you are going to score a firm like Procter & Gamble really high because everyone would love to have 50% gross margins every single year without fail. However the reason they are able to do that is probably due to some sort of special competitive advantage.

I'm not going into the details on that but basically on that one specifically we are looking at a Sharpe ratio. It's like a Sharpe ratio for profit margins. We are looking at the average of your eight-year gross margins divided by the standard deviation of your gross margins. The higher your average margin and the lower the standard deviation of that gross margin the better. We rank every firm on this and then rank that metric relative to everyone else.

Right. Is the final ranking score like one, two, three, four, five, etc. or do you turn the numbers into a normal distribution and thereby normalize them and rank them? Also, do you combine them

altogether into one number? What do you when you have these three?

What we do is the following. For the three core elements you first have your long-term free cash flow metric. We calculate that for every single firm and normalize it from zero to one hundred based on the distribution, so you are going to have a score of firms between one and a hundred. We do the same thing for the long-term return on capital metric, so everyone is going to get a score in the end between one and a hundred. Then we do the same thing for long-term margin characteristics by scoring all the stocks from one to one hundred.

Then just for simplicity's sake we just weight them one-third, one-third, one-third. In other words, we basically just take the average of these three metrics and then rank that number relative to everyone else in the universe. Therefore you are going to end up with basically a one to one hundred for your "economic moat" score.

Okay. You didn't try other things like squaring each of the numbers and adding them and taking a square root and then like …

Our base philosophy is to keep things as simple as possible and no simpler. One of the rules we like is what we call the "1 over N" (1/N) rule. This means that if you have three elements you just weight them one-third, one-third, one-third (N = 3 so 1/N = 1/3).

This sounds stupid but what we always do is start with that benchmark and then we'll do optimizations around that just to see what would happen. For example, later we'll try a 50% weighting on one factor and 25% and 25% on the others, and other various combinations. The idea is we want to make sure that it is kind of robust across all these metrics.

Then unless there is a really, really compelling reason to use the 1/N optimized version - and usually there is not - we just use what we call the Barney the Dinosaur style of 1/N. So we just do 1/N and weigh each of those elements as 1/3.

Clearly in-sample you can get one weighted combination that at the margin looks a little better due to optimizing, but it's probably due to the optimizing so you would expect that. So yes, you could definitely do that but we just choose not to do that approach.

So these three become the economic moat?

Yes. Next is the current financial strength. And for this are you by chance familiar with the Joseph Piotroski nine-point F-score?

Yes, I love it. I just haven't found a version that's updated because I read somewhere there are more accurate versions of his original formula, which is great. I think AAII computes it.

You might have heard about that from us because that's part of our book and I wrote some papers on that. In any case, the idea is great, right? It's super simple. It's a zero-one point scoring system where you can have up to nine points in total.

What we have done is we basically have taken that general concept and actually use a lot of his elements, but we came up with a ten-point score which we call the "current financial strength score." It's divided into current profitability, stability, and recent operational improvements. That's three different categories.

I guess the key difference that actually matters in a robust way of this checklist versus the F-score - which frankly is also a really good one if you don 't have Bloomberg or whatever to compute all this stuff – is that one of the things he uses is equity issuance. If you have equity issuance (which dilutes shares) that is obviously a bad thing, but if you don't it is a good thing.

The problem, as you are probably aware, is that it is not just about equity issuance because if I issue one share but I buy back ten million shares then that is actually a good signal, right? That's because on net the company is actively buying back stock so we replace that with net equity issuance, and that small change, which doesn't seem like a big deal, actually matters a lot.

This is because what you find as you look at the data is that a lot of firms issue equity because that's part of their option plans or whatever. There are also a lot of firms that buy back equity and we need to make sure we understand what the net element is there because that is what determines if the signal is good or bad. It is not just because you issued equity. So that's one element.

I'm trying to remember if there is another element that we changed in the system. I think it was on the operational improvements. I think we added one down there. The bottom line is that we use the F-score idea with our ten elements. I'll walk you through them here.

There are three in the current profitability segment. One is the return on assets. If it's positive, good and if not that's bad. With free cash flow, obviously if it's positive that is good and if not that's bad. With accrual you want basically your cash from operations to be greater than your net income with all else being equal so that you are not faking it. If you have higher cash from ops than income then good, otherwise bad. Those are the basic profitability metrics.

Then we move to the stability sector and there are three elements there. One of those is just your change in leverage. We want to make sure that your long-term debt-to-assets ratio year-over-year is decreasing rather than increasing. That's just a positive signal when you are buying cheap stocks that are having issues.

The other metric we use is the change in your current ratio. We want to have a positive year-over-year change in your current ratio which would highlight better liquidity whereas if you went in the opposite direction that might be a problem. And then the third one there in stability is your net equity issuance. In general we want you to be a net negative issuer because we want you to be buying back stock and not just issuing out stock and diluting us. If you are buying back stock on net that is positive, if you are issuing out stock on net that would be a negative. Those are your three baseline stability metrics.

Then we have four metrics that we consider in the category of basic recent operational improvements. The first one is the year-over-year change in the return on assets where ideally you want to have greater efficiency in getting a higher return on assets. The other one is your year-over-year change in free cash flow relative to the total assets. All else being equal, we want you to be generating more free cash flow this year than you did last year. The year-over-year change in margins is another. For this you only need to examine the gross margins, so again we would rather have you improving your gross margins and not decreasing your gross margins if possible. Then the other one is just the year-over-year asset turnover. We want your total sales turnover to be improving rather than decreasing year-over-year if at all possible.

That is basically the ten elements and we just assign a zero or one to all of those. That's like a pre-flight checklist or sanity check on these guys. Then when you add up the zero-one score for all these variables you basically get between zero and ten points on this scale. Ten would be great for the final score and zero would obviously be an issue. That's how our financial strength score works.

Okay. Let's summarize. You have 1,000 stocks and then you get rid of some of them using an algorithm that identifies distress risk. That weeds out 100 stocks that might go bankrupt.

There is a chance they could, yes.

Now, you have to rate the 900 stocks to see who is best within this group that is left. You have to rate them in terms of what is cheap and what represents quality.

Yup.

So in terms of what is cheap there are two things you are looking for - an economic moat score and a measure of the firm's current financial strength. For the current financial strength you use a ten-point modified Piotroski score?

Yup. Uh-hmm.

Okay. And then for the economic moat you have taken three variables or metrics and you combine them all into a single number that is between one and a hundred.

Yes, a composite moat score.

So now you have these two numbers for every stock that is left, which is 900 stocks out of the original 1000. What do you do now to pick the winners to invest in?

What we do is we are going to have this composite economic moat score scaled from zero to one hundred. We have also got this current financial strength score that basically runs from zero to ten. We scale it to a hundred so it's equivalent to the economic moat scale and then we 50-50 weight those.

Therefore you take an average of your zero to hundred economic moat score and your zero to one hundred financial strength score and that becomes the firm's quality score. Then those 900 securities are going to all have a quality score.

We'll do that in a program to build a database, but remember that this is all done after the forensics where we first get down to the cheapest 900 based on the enterprise multiples and then amongst those cheapest firms we then rank them on this quality score. We want to basically own the top 50% based on this composite economic moat plus current financial strength quality score.

And when do you sell a stock? For instance, in his final years Graham would sell a stock after a 50% increase in price or after two-years went by, whichever came first. What do you guys do?

There is always a tradeoff between taxes and frictions and expected benefits. In the context of value investing and specifically in the context of this algorithm here, we know that the higher the frequency of rebalancing then the higher the expected performance. If you do this every month, always reassess stocks using the model and always hold the cheapest highest quality stocks then the expected performance is much higher than if you did it every five years.

Every five years still works, but there is certainly a decay in the expected outperformance with a lower rebalancing frequency. The problem with a higher frequency - even though it has a higher expected benefit – is that it has higher tax burdens and frictional costs.

Therefore in managed account structures the best tradeoff that we found is the annual technique where you do it every year. You wait obviously for your winners so you get long-term capital gains and then your losers bomb out beforehand. Then throughout the year we also harvest so if there is a loser basically under 10% we'll blow it out, harvest the loss and then pop in a new name. That's obviously suboptimal but in the context of a managed account where you have tax sensitivity it's just the best you can do.

Now in the ETF structures - since we have a capital gains cleansing mechanism there where taxes are now a non-issue - we can just measure the benefit between expected excess returns and frictional costs (transaction costs) so we do that quarterly. We think if you did it monthly you would have so much friction and impact cost that it probably would bleed away any expected benefit. As to quarterly you'll lose a little bit, but because the frictional costs are so much lower that seems to be the sweet spot so that's how we do it and everything is automated.

Every quarter let's say we compute our forty-five cheapest, highest quality stocks. If you are a company that was in the portfolio before and you are in it now then you are still in the portfolio. If you were in the portfolio and now you are no longer in the portfolio then you're dead. We're popping in the new guy that actually is cheap - the cheapest and highest quality at that point in time. Therefore buy and sell rules are 100% fully integrated into the system.

If you're doing this though for somebody who had a retirement account and it's tax protected, like an IRA, you would rebalance it more often?

Yes, quarterly. Basically if you're either in a qualified context or in a non-qualified context and you leverage - like an ETF wrapper, which is basically what we do - then we think quarterly is the sweet spot for rebalancing.

Got you. I've seen several studies that show the same thing.

Yes.

All right. Now let's go into the things you tried that didn't work, but you thought should have worked. What surprising things have you guys found out that crushed some cherished notions out there in investment land? Also, what rules or principles have you proved that you really want to emphasize for investors and investment managers?

I'm going to make it really simple and put a little context on it.
All we do and did for a long time is research and I have literally backtested every scheme that

you can ever imagine at this point. I've already looked at every single academic paper that even smelled like a trading strategy. I probably looked at every thing you can ever even think about. In the end, when you really want to be intellectually honest about it and you throw as many grenades as you can at these different "alpha systems" then it really boils down to two strategies that I think have worked for the last hundred years and they're probably going to work for the next hundred years.

The first is value-based strategies where we are buying cheap stocks. That's good to go. The other one is momentum-based strategies - buying securities that have had strong relative strength relative to other securities in the market at a given point in time.

Those two systems, those core algorithms however expressed - because people can obviously complicate the hell out of them - as long as you are in those two veins I think you are probably good. Everything else I would say is questionable at best and data mining at worst.

Maybe a better way to summarize it is that everything else besides value and momentum doesn't work. I'll just keep it at that.

That's the very same conclusion I came to in *Super Investing*, which is to restrict yourself to just proven value and automated momentum strategies, but since you tested all these strategies what in particular doesn't work? Can you give me examples of several popular strategies that don't really work?

One class example might be merger arbitrage. That may be a little complicated but merger arbitrage is a trade where XYZ firm is going to get bought out by ABC and so the stock price moves up to say the $10 buyout price, but it only moves up to say $9.50. What a merger arbitrage trader would do is go and buy all these stocks at $9.50 and then wait for a few months to catch that little stub. They usually use a lot of leverage to try to magnify that 50¢ gain since it seems like a guarantee because someone is going to buy the company at $10.

Well, it's a great idea. A lot of people have tried it over time and in the past people were like, "Hey, this is what the fancy hedge fund guys are doing and there are movies about it." However, academic papers have come out that say, "Wait a second. This is just another scenario where basically you are picking up pennies in front of a steamroller."

That's because the merger arbitrage trade basically means you're capturing little pennies most of the time where it goes from $9.50 to $10, but a problem occurs when the market blows up and then all the IPO markets seize up, too. When the capital markets seize up then that $10 buyout vanishes and all of a sudden that stock which everyone thought was going to get bought out at $10 goes back to the original price of $5. However, you're levered up on a trade to capture 50¢ that now goes down $4 so you are bust.

Once people started thinking through the actual trade and its dynamics through thick and thin, it looks good on paper until you realize that you will go bankrupt every five or ten years. That might be an example of a trade that on paper looks and smells good and seems super sexy but in reality it's picking up pennies in front of a steamroller.

Great analysis. Are there any other big classes of investing where you want to say, "Don't do it, don't do it, don't do it"?

Okay, let me go to iShare's website real quick because there is always something there. Here is a great one: minimum volatility. Again, minimum volatility is another strategy where I don't think it works after controlling for what you are buying, which is essentially low-beta stocks. So, minimum volatility might be one.

Another obviously is growth. Growth is a terrible idea. Any time you pay a high price for anything, regardless of how good it sounds, it is just a sucker bet.

What about income as with dividend stocks?

Yeah, that's a dangerous one. Jack and I, one of my colleagues, have a paper published on this. High-yield, high dividend stocks historically have done very well because they tended to be value stocks. They were just cheap so that high dividend yield was a proxy for cheapness and we already know that buying cheap stocks works.

The problem with today's market is that every huckster out there is selling some yield product. Hence, now the high dividend yield stocks still have high yields with huge payout ratios, but they are not cheap relative to other stocks in the universe so you are no longer capturing the tailwind of value. I think that is going to be a total sucker bet because high yield by itself does not generate the excess returns. Buying the cheap out of favor or distress stuff that everyone hates generates excess returns. So high yield is bad idea unless you control for price.

Have you ever tried to create a portfolio or methodology that would buy dividend stocks of some form? It's like a Holy Grail for some people, but I've never found anybody who is really good at it.

The way you do it is you use shareholder yield, which is what our paper is about. There is actually an ETF based on our paper called SYLD or Shareholder Yield. I think O'Shaughnessy and those guys have managed account products on the same idea where you don't want to just look at dividends because a lot of firms don't pay money out via dividends anymore. They pay it in the form of open market repurchase so you have this composite shareholder payout. That certainly is a better metric than just straight up dividend yield. But again, the reason shareholder yield has worked historically is because it tended to be a great proxy and on average you just bought cheap stocks.

I think it still would be a great strategy to focus on high shareholder yield securities. You just want to make sure that those securities also have a cheap characteristic associated with them as well. Then I think you would be doing great, or on average you would have a good expected return versus shareholder yield stocks that are actually expensive on P/E or what have you.

Do you ever want to launch a portfolio like that?

No, we have QVAL and IVAL. QVAL essentially in many respects is capturing that same sort of risk profile. We thought about it, but launching these ETF products costs multiple hundred thousands of dollars. Would I like to maybe at some point? Sure. But from a business risk standpoint you want to focus and go slow and steady. I'm not sure if that is on the horizon but someone definitely should.

Okay, so what else do you want people to know that you have researched where you really want to

wake up everyone out there by saying don't get yourself into trouble along this route? What are the other rules or lessons you have learned that you want investors to know?

Another one I've seen recently - because we get pitched up all the time since we work for a family office - is the iBillionaire's Index. I think that is what it is called. The basic idea or the pitch is amazing. It goes like this: "Hey, you as an investor should invest money with firms where a billionaire founder still owns it and still has a lot of capital in his own name. If he is a billionaire then he must be smart and if he still has a lot of his money buried in the stock then he must really believe in it. What we are going to do is form an index where all we do is basically buy firms that have this characteristic."

The pitch is amazing. The problem is that the story doesn't match the evidence. The evidence is that it has no value added whatsoever. You can even argue that it may detract from value, but that is just another story I've heard recently. It's buying stocks that billionaire's own where the founders are still heavily invested in the company. I think it's called something like the iBillionaire's Strategy. It's a great pitch. Everyone is selling it. Empirically there is no evidence it actually does any better than just the S&P 500.

I want to turn to your big life lessons, but before that let's talk about momentum investing a bit, which is an active trader's favorite. What have you found that works for momentum investing and please touch on a comparison to value investing again and how these two work because as you said previously, and as I found out as well, these are the two methods that really work in the long run.

Value is fundamentally about over-reaction to bad news. To be successful at it you need to look at cheap stocks and have a five, ten-year horizon and don't care what the benchmark does. Period.

Momentum investing is all about under-reaction to fundamental good news. In those systems you basically want to own securities that have had strong performance over say the past twelve months. And again, to do that strategy it is unlike value investing where you can have slower turnover. In order to get momentum systems to work you have to trade them a lot so you have to rebalance the portfolio at least every quarter. If you rebalance the momentum system just once a year then you are better off buying the Vanguard S&P 500.

The other nuance with momentum, which is getting a little bit in the weeds, is that momentum systems can be magnified by looking at path dependency. How a stock got high momentum determines whether it is going to have a good momentum effect or a bad momentum effect.

What do I mean by that?

Well, consider stock A which is up 100%, but it did 200 days of 50 bips up every single day. And stock B, also up 100% but it's a biotech stock that was zero for 199 days and then one day it went up 100%. Comparing that slow grind momentum stock versus this crazy momentum stock you have to know that slow grind momentum tends to continue out in the future so you want to own those sorts of momentum securities that have that clean, smooth momentum. You don't want to own the ones that have jerky momentum on the path to get to 100%. If you use that trading rule within a momentum context and trade momentum with some degree of frequency then you are going to be in the ballpark of doing it right.

What type of rules did you finally end up with for momentum trading?

Basically, on momentum trading we are in the context of taxability within the ETF wrapper and then there are also frictional costs. We are not 100% there yet, but basically it's going to be between one month and two month rebalancing using a path dependency metric and we have some algorithm for all that. Basically we are looking for stocks that have slow grinding momentum versus whipsaw momentum.

The other element that we incorporate in our momentum systems is seasonality. Momentum has much larger premiums during, say for example, December when you've got window dressing effects working in your favor, i.e. all the mutual fund guys want to own the hot stocks before they post their December 31st books. They also have tax benefits going for them.

Therefore for all the stocks that have been doing well over the past eleven months in December people are not going to sell those until January, so December basically has a really, really nice momentum effect whereas January actually has a really, really terrible momentum effect. We just incorporate some of the seasonality into the system on top of the path dependency and then turn it over with high frequency.

When you look at your simulated track records, which does better over the long run? Is it the value investing or the momentum investing methods?

I hate to say this as a born and bred religious Bible thumbing Ben Graham fan, but I honestly have to give it to momentum. Momentum is just unbelievable if you can handle the volatility. If you have a long horizon and can deal with the tax problem then there just isn't really an argument. It's better on a horse race.

From my own research I found that value investing has about a 4% alpha over the market and given enough time momentum investing can have an alpha of 7% plus over the market returns. What have you found?

I think with plain vanilla value investing where you are just generic, use a cheap metric, rebalance annually and are tax managed … maybe you are going to get like 300 to 400 bips over the S&P but it's going to have a ton of tracking error.

As to momentum, let's say you rebalance at least quarterly and just use a generic cross sectional momentum system. In that case you are probably looking at 700 to 800 bips over the index *but* with the hell of a lot more standard deviations.

Let's say value investing gives you 300 to 400 over the index (3-4%) over a five, ten-year horizon versus 700 to 800 over the index (7-8%) through momentum investing over a five, ten-year horizon. It's pretty serious but it also comes with a lot more volatility.

If you had a twenty-year-old and he is starting to build his IRA would you put half in value and half in momentum? What would you advise him?

As to what I would advise him, first I want to understand what goal he's trying to achieve. If he just wants to whoop it on and does not care about volatility then I would say put it all in momentum.

If he was somewhat sensitive to the volatility of the system then clearly you'd want to say, "Hey, you should do 50% value investing and 50% momentum investing because those two systems tend to be not that correlated and you smooth out a lot of the up and downs that way."

I'd say that if you have a fifty-year horizon like a twenty-year old where you're not going to take it out until you're seventy and you just want to whoop it on, then go all-in with momentum investing. If you're a little bit more risk adverse, you probably want to 50-50 it.

Now here's an interesting question. On a fifty to seventy year horizon a lot of countries are going to have political unrest. They are going to have a depression, deflationary collapse, currency troubles, hyperinflation, see a banking system collapse, … you name it because all these things can happen. A lot of people right now are talking about the possibility of a deflationary collapse or hyperinflation because of all the excessive money printing and debt loads that can only be discharged either through default or the hyperinflationary route of excessive money printing. What type of stocks would you buy in each of these extreme crisis scenarios? Or, what type of model would you use to protect your money?

I know exactly what you are saying. Basically at the security selection level you have to be value, you have to be momentum, you probably want have some combination. The next question you had is, "Well, okay, so let's say you have the best momentum and value stocks in the U.S. but the U.S. becomes Zimbabwe. Well, you're screwed anyways, right? So how do we deal with that problem?" That's more about how do you deal with market timing and we do a ton of research on that.

Our opinion again goes back to momentum and trend following. Basically, follow the trend and follow the momentum. If the S&P starts blowing up and having a face rip then get out of that, go to cash and reallocate to markets or asset classes that have higher momentum. That seems to be a way to dynamically move across asset classes and protect yourself from riding it all the way to zero, which is not what people want to do.

What are the large asset classes you would follow and what market timing method would you use to be able to say, "We are measuring such and such that shows a signal so now we should switch to real estate (or whatever) …"

Again, our focus is on fees and tax management so you have to keep it somewhat simple, but the way we look at the world is that there are five core muscle movements here. You have domestic equity, international equity, real estate, bonds and commodities. It's like the Ivy Five, like in Mebane Faber's book called *The Ivy Portfolio* which outlines this.

Those five core muscle movement asset classes capture 90-95% of the returns of the biggest endowments out there. If you just stuck with those five asset classes then that's great.

Buy and hold is one thing. It is simple but even with 1/N on those five asset classes you are going to lose 45% during 2008 so what we like to do is apply long-term trend rules on these things. It doesn't matter what time period you use. You can use 10-month, 12-month, 15-month trends or something else because they are all about the same.

If an asset class busts through a long-term trend then go to cash and then once the thing gets back on trend then go back into the asset class. If you need to tax manage that then use futures to bring down your exposure. Don't sell out of the low basis asset. That is a complicated topic, but in general just risk manage via long-term trend rules across five big muscle movements and you are probably going to be okay.

Great. Let's have one quick question on momentum again to be perfectly clear as to what is best. Are you looking at each stock and checking the momentum of that company versus its industry or looking at the entire market universe of stocks and picking a stock that itself is better than all the other stocks in the universe?

On momentum it's the same philosophy as for value in our systems. Let's say you have 1,000 securities out there. You are going to calculate this momentum measure and you're going to buy, let's just say for easy math, the top 100 stocks or 10%, so you are going to own 100 of these best momentum stocks. You'd buy those and then you reassess or rebalance hopefully as frequently as you can, but you are probably doing it at least quarterly.

And you don't care if they are all in the same industry, such as the majority being all pharmaceutical stocks?

No. And again, if you do care that's fine. You are going to lower your tracking error, but if you have a long investment horizon then you are basically going to lower the expected return and actually lower your risk/reward characteristics. We just don't care about tracking error because that's not really our thing, but if you did care about that then obviously you would want to probably do a little bit of industry controls and what have you.

Let me use a single industry because some people are stuck with having to be in a certain sector. If you have to take the gold mining industry - because a lot of people think precious metals might pop up - and you really wanted to buy then what might be the best performing stocks in the gold and silver industry and what would you use for criteria to rate them?

Basically we don't buy them because they always pop up on all of those distress scores and they are also not quality. So even though they can be really cheap they are just crappy businesses in general. Frankly we just don't buy them because our system boots them out, but let's say I had to buy them and you had to specify what would be the selection criteria. Again it's value and momentum.

I would focus on buying the cheapest, most out of favor miners and we are talking about for maybe a tenth of them. Then for the other tenth I'd probably create a basket of those that had the highest relative strength within that sector and give it a whirl. That's what I would do if you put a gun to my head and said, "You have to buy gold miners. What technique would you use?" That's what I would do.

How about the oil industry? I want to see if you would come up with something different for each industry or if it would be the same thing?

It's basically the same thing and right now the most undervalued stocks are all in the Consumer Discretionary group. That's probably the most hated industry at the moment based on criteria of being cheap and historically high quality. Energy is also another one so Energy and Consumer Discretion are what we are in right now. We use the same systems across all industries just because we think the algorithms are designed to deal with a lot of the nuisances of all the different companies out there.

If somebody absolutely insisted on investing by industry groups or having stocks in certain buckets then what would you do?

If I wanted to insist on investing in certain industry groups and make it have a little bit less tracking error or have it deviate a little bit less from a standardized index (because I have to deal with career risk or what have you) what I would do is first figure out the weights in the S&P 500 for every single industry.

Let's say Tech has a 25% weighting and Energy is 75% just for example. What I would then do is rank all the securities within Tech, I would find the cheapest quantitative value stocks and do the same thing in Energy. Then once I got those ten or twenty names I would then weigh the Energy names as 75% of the portfolio and the Tech names as 25% of the portfolio so that way at least you are mirroring the industry components of the broader indexes.

Would you ever change the weighting of industries in the portfolio by some algorithm?

It depends on what my goal was. If I wanted to do some sort of relative strength industry system then we could do that, too. You could take the nine or ten SPDRs, rank them by relative strength and then within that group buy the top momentum or top value names. You could do that, too. That's not a bad system.

If all you want is performance then you just don't pay attention to industries. You just get your industry exposures from bottom-up security selection by either using a value or momentum investing system to choose stocks. Then whatever pops out as the stock and thus industry you are buying is the best way to do it if you just want to whoop it on.

If you have got constraints then you would do something different. A lot of asset manager investors have constraints because they can't do what we do since they would get fired due to having so much tracking error. You are taking a lot of career risk when you load up on an industry. So even though we know in expectation that that's the best approach over say a five, ten-year horizon, most people actually don't have that horizon. Then you have to do things that basically constrain the algorithms and you can evaluate the indexes or the sectors and what have you.

Overall the best solution is the one that we do. It's bottom-up security selection using value or momentum and you just use whatever pops out of the system.

Okay, Wes, I have your rules. Let's turn to wrapping it up. For these two types of investing what are the dos and don'ts for people? What are the dos and don'ts that you see they are violating and why are some people succeeding at this and others are failing?

Real simple. There are two rules. Rule #1 is that you have to be disciplined to the model. Too many people say they have a model, but they use it only half the time. They always override the model and then screw it all up so follow the model.

Rule #2 is that you have to have horizon. These systems by construction do not track everyday S&P 500 returns and it is guaranteed that they will underperform over short horizons at some point. But that is why they work. If they didn't underperform then every Arb Hedge Fund or Mutual Fund guy and the world would do them so you would be fighting against all the competition now. So follow the model and have long horizon and you will be successful in frankly any system, but value and momentum in particular.

Okay. Any books or other resources you recommend which can help people to become better traders and investors? Top books, top resources ... what do you recommend?

One of my favorites is not exactly exciting but is Kahneman's book, *Thinking Fast and Slow*. It walks through the psychology of how the human mind actually works, not how we think it works. I think that is critical.

I have to give a shout out for *The Intelligent Investor* and *Security Analysis* because those are my original Bibles.

Then another book that I just find really interesting made me think a lot about at least my political orientations was Richard Thaler's book *Nudge*, which is about designing choice architecture and understanding how people make decisions. I think that is also just a really cool book and made me think a lot about just how the world works and how the mind works. Those are three books I really like.

No other books that you recommend investors might want to read?

I like Gary Antonacci's book, *Dual Momentum Investing*. It's a more recent book. If you are into momentum investing and want to understand a baseline system that seems to work on a long haul and is digestible - it's not just math equations - then that is a really good book.

Ben Carson has a really cool book called *A Wealth of Common Sense*. I recommend it especially for beginners or people who just want to get an understanding of the industry and all of the conflicts of interest. It's for people trying to understand and navigate everything that we see out there. I think that's a great one for beginners.

Okay. Any advice you want to give people on positioning their assets for retirement if they are in their thirties, forties or in their fifties? For instance, do you recommend other asset classes like real estate or do you just want to keep the conversation focused on stocks?

Obviously you want to be diversified and we also have an investment framework. It's called the FACTS. You always want to follow the FACTS and the FACTS stand for the following:

(1) F - Fees. All else being equal you must minimize fees because you can't compound money that went to a manager.

(2) A - Access or liquidity. This is in the context of big family offices, but you always want to maintain liquidity. You want the ability to actually use your money when you want it because if it gets locked up then you are screwed. It is usually locked up when the most opportunities are out there because the hedge fund guy will say, "Hey, you can't take your money back," so access is important.

(3) C - Complexity. You want to try to minimize complexity because in general, complexity is usually a sales pitch to justify higher fees when the reality is that a simple system would work better.

(4) T is frankly the biggest one - Taxes. If you don't have a long-term tax deferral structure then

you are screwed because if you don't figure out how to avoid Uncle Sam's 50% carried interest every year then you are not taking advantage of compound interest and you are just wrong. You have to figure out how to make your investments tax efficient even if it's on non-qualified money. ETF wrappers are obviously one of the best things out there along these lines.

(5) S is just Search. That just stands for the fact that there is a lot of cost and a lot of brain damage associated with trying to figure out who the newest best manager is. If you keep it simple and you get a baseline framework like that one I had mentioned earlier with the five core muscle movement asset classes then that will minimize that search.

So focus on the FACTS to lower fees, maintain liquidity, keep it simple, never pay taxes or defer taxes, and don't put a lot of time and due diligence in trying to reinvent the wheel and invest in everything. Then I think you will probably do A-OK over the long haul.

Any life lessons or things you wish you had known earlier or you want to pass on to people? After you've done all this research I'm particularly interested in things you wish you had known earlier when you just got started in investing so that by using that knowledge you would have been much better off now, or anything we didn't discuss.

Really … taxes.

Honestly, almost every single person we work with is insanely rich. I always ask them, "Hey, how the hell did you do this?" and literally there is one overriding characteristic. They all made their money doing one thing or the other, but they all were very good at deferring their tax liabilities so that they could continue to compound. Warren Buffett is obviously the pinnacle example of that. So I would say find a way to defer your taxes would be the number one priority that I wish I knew fifteen years ago because I'd be a hell of a lot richer if I had followed that advice that no one told me about back in the day.

Then the other one is to just be disciplined to a system and don't over-think it because I'd also be a hell of a lot richer if I just followed a system and didn't think I was a superhero and bet on penny stocks that sound good but then go down 90%.

So follow a model and try to defer taxes. Those would be my two biggest things I wish I knew fifteen years ago that I know now.

Are there any other things you learned from dealing with so many mega-wealthy individuals? Any lessons that struck you that you want other people to know because you have learned something valuable from these guys?

I think that the FACTS framework is what I would pass on to people. Everyone thinks that the reason billionaires are so rich is because they get to see all the fancy hedge fund and private equity guys. That's entirely not true. They are rich because they don't pay fees, they maintain control of their capital, they keep it simple and they never pay taxes.

Access to cool, fancy Wall Street huckster or over-priced products is not how you get rich. That's how you get Wall Street people rich.

I think a re-occurring theme that we have identified is that really wealthy people are wealthy for a reason. They are smart and they realized that having someone else risk your money and get paid big fees on that is a great way to get them rich but not a great way to get you rich. That seems like common sense but common sense is not a common virtue when it comes to investing a lot of the times.

Wes, where can people learn more about you? You mentioned your book *Quantitative Value* that is available at amazon.com. Your website is AlphaArchitect.com. What else you can mention?

We are very transparent with education and research in everything we do. Our main outlet for information is to tell people to just head to www.alpharchitect.com and sign up for our newsletter and follow our blog. We pour out all our thoughts right there.

Any new books coming out in the future?

Yes, I have two new books coming out. One is called *DIY Financial Adviser* with Wiley's Publishing that should be coming out in November. Another book we are working on is basically the complement to *Quantitative Value*. It's called *Quantitative Momentum*. That one should be coming out in September or October.

For *Quantitative Value*, the mission there is that if we wanted to do value investing systemically then what is the best way we could come up with? And that's, "Here is the answer, here is the book."

Quantitative Momentum has the exact same thesis where we want to exploit momentum. What is the best idea we could come up with? Here is a book dedicated to the process. That book is going to be a little bit more highbrow like *Quantitative Value*.

Do It Yourself Financial Adviser is meant for much more mass appeal. What it literally does is walk through our lessons learned working with these big family offices and all of these rich people. It's about the basic lessons learned from the billionaires of the world such as how they make money and how they build their portfolios and how you can do that as a DIY "do it yourself" investor when you are just equipped with a few basic concepts and ideas. That's what that book is about. It's trying to help people out.

And the conclusion for that is to use the FACTS approach to investing?

Use the FACTS and we propose a simple asset allocation structure that infuses some value and/or momentum and some basic trend following risk management. It's not meant to be the end all, be all. It's just like, "Hey, this is an elegant but simple system that works and a lot of people could do it on their own if they just invested a little time and effort in the problem."

That's cool and it's exactly the type of message that I want for the public. Last chance … is there anything else you really want to say to people to help them out? If you had a magic wand and you could wave it so that investors out there would really get the message, what would you really want them to know?

Like I said you should follow the model, have horizon and avoid taxes and fees. From an investing standpoint that's pretty good life advice I would say.

Thanks, Wes.

It's been a pleasure, Bill.

Conclusion

There you have it. Each of seventeen remarkable traders and investors has shared the story of how he came to developing his successful trading or investing style. Each of their stories is unique. Several individuals have even become millionaires through their trading and/or investing prowess so I was sure to point this out. I have tried to record all their stories and transmit as much of their actual system rules as possible so that you might be able to duplicate their successful methods, or know what to investigate to develop something similar.

Some of these individuals have been traders, some investors, some researchers, some fund managers, and several are trading coaches or psychologists. The package of lessons they offer is a grand start for anyone who wishes to enter the field of trading and investing. Because of the nature of these interviews there are methods, rules, explanations and insights that will also be of use to veteran market participants. Seasoned professionals are always looking for powerful new insights and techniques and this book should help satisfy their needs.

I am also particularly pleased that these interviews achieved something rarely done, which is bring to you some of the actual trading rules and systems of experts that usually don't appear in print, including within sources like *Technical Analysis of Stocks & Commodities* or books like *Market Wizards*. From that aspect this material is unique and invaluable for pointing you in profitable directions. If you want to learn how to think like a trader or chart analyst, or learn the rules of value investing or momentum investing from individuals who have dealt with the issues for decades then the insights are here.

Perhaps most useful of all is the fact that each one has shared some final words of advice for others on errors people need to correct in order to become better at trading and investing. In addition, they have all been kind enough to talk about what they wished they had known when they had first gotten started in the trading field. Be extremely sensitive to taxes, use a trading coach, focus on the numbers rather than the chart, remember that the key to investing is compounding, learn to master your mind and emotions … these are some of the things that we all have trouble doing. If you were to incorporate the relevant insights you need into your trading life then you would surely be further ahead than others who are still trying to figure out the core principles to follow for trading and investing.

Having previously designed automated trading systems for Wall Street, worked with family offices and direct investments in businesses as well as being a trader and investor myself, people often ask me which of these various approaches I would follow if I was just starting out. Certainly I would pull a bit of wisdom from everyone and use it because everyone has something valuable to teach.

For instance, Dr. Gary Drayton's emphasis on mindfulness training will help anyone who wishes to become a trader, and having written books on meditation I can see where it would help people in other life areas as well. In general, however, you need to realize that there are many different ways to approach the markets. All of them have the aim of helping you earn you more money than a T-bill or bank account. Among these many alternatives, your own particular path would be different from mine because of different skills, appetites and interests. If a technique doesn't match with your personality and psyche then there is very little chance that you would do well with it no matter what it promises in terms of returns.

Nonetheless, let me note which individuals I would particularly study if I chose to follow a specific trading or investment style.

If I actually wanted to become a successful chart trader or swing trader I would focus on absorbing the lessons of Mike Ser and Andy Man, Raymond Barros, Eric Hadik, Tim Sykes and Gareth Solowoy. All of these traders study charts and interpret market movements through their own proprietary rules to come up with their winning trades. Experienced as they are, they have all made plenty of mistakes before becoming the profitable traders they are.

It is a great skill to take in lots of information, simplify it, and then come up with winning directional trades. In the "old days," each of these men might be put forth as the model of a great trader who calls his shots after an extensive analysis of the markets that welds together lots of diverse information. If you are truly interested in becoming an expert in subjective analysis – whether it includes chart patterns, cycles, Gann, Elliott Waves, technical indicators or others - these individuals talk about the techniques you must study and rules you should follow.

For help in mastering the human side of trading I would study the stories of Ramon Barros, the coaching lessons of Mike Ser and Andy Man and the techniques of Dr. Gary Drayton. One of the common lessons from this group is that get rich quick schemes simply don't work and that you should never try to make all your money in one trade. These individuals in particular stressed that you must play great defense and get out of losing positions quickly to protect your capital. As Warren Buffett said, the first rule of investing is not to lose money and the second rule is "see rule #1."

If I was primarily interested in day trading techniques then Dr. Adrian Manz's methods would demand my attention, and in particular the story of how they were developed from statistical analysis. Do they work? The proof of their effectiveness is the videos on his site and their outstanding real time track record. The whole idea is to use market tendencies to ride a bit of momentum and then get out of positions when you reach a high liquidity pool within the market. If I wished to become a day trader then this is where I would start.

If I wanted to slowly accumulate assets over time and also create a high-yield portfolio in a do-it-yourself manner then Fred Carach and Bill Spetrino have ideas I would like to combine. Bill has used the foundational framework of Warren Buffett to build his dividend portfolio (buying safe, quality stocks on the cheap when bad news depresses the price) while Fred has concentrated on the fundamental analysis of income shares to eventually win his financial freedom. Since Fred and Preston James both speak of the beauty of selling options to create extra income, those two approaches could also be combined within any portfolio to generate far more extra income. Marvin Appel mentioned some interesting ways to do this as well.

Despite the hundreds of investing methods touted out there, due to my own independent research I wholeheartedly agree with Wesley Gray that only two investing techniques have worked consistently over the past one hundred years and are also likely still to be working one hundred years into the future. This is the same conclusion I came to in my book *Super Investing*, which reveals the lessons I wish I had known when I first got started in the investments field and that I hope readers pass onto their children. *Super Investing* contains long-term investment strategies that can be used to create a legacy of great multigenerational wealth. As Wesley also concluded, the main techniques you should use for this are value investing and momentum investing.

For value investing, the methods of Bill Spetrino, Charles Mizrahi and Wesley Gray share similar techniques and common conclusions. Charles and Bill do stock selection on their own based on specific value criteria while Wesley has created a value stock ETF that automatically does everything for you. My personal preference is to just park money with others whose approach I like, and thus a portion of my funds would no doubt travel towards Wesley's ETF. In value investing for the long run, various studies have shown it can beat the market by 3-4% per year and so this would be one of the legs of my own diversified wealth accumulation portfolio.

For momentum investing, Wesley Gray's notes on quantitative momentum also match perfectly with the findings of Geoff Bysshe and Marvin Appel (as well as those put forth in *Super Investing*), namely that you need a tested technique to do this correctly and it requires lots of calculations, frequent rebalancings and also discipline to stay on track. There is a lot of management work required to make this work. Nevertheless, this is the approach that offers the greatest potential returns over time since it can achieve 7-8% more per year than the market over the long run. Geoff explains the methodology best and has a service if you want to trade signals like this on your own.

Because I have no special desire for excitement and don't want to have to monitor the markets every moment, I would definitely devote the largest portion of any wealth accumulation portfolio to automated momentum investing, but would outsource the process to professional managers who would do everything properly. One might devote a certain portion of their portfolio to momentum investing by outsourcing fractions of that allocation to different managers with different algorithms.

In short, I would put much of my money in several automated momentum stock trading systems since they perform better than market returns over the long-run. To buffer the volatility I might also put a smaller proportion of funds in value investing strategies, but here again I want someone to do all the work for me so I can forget about the markets and just let thing grow. If I wanted to watch the markets and do things myself then I would select different trader-investors to emulate, such as those within this book and in others like *Market Wizards*, but I am well past the stage where I need to feel like a hero to get high returns on my investments.

But enough of that. What I wanted to bring you in these interviews were the actual systems, models, rules and methods that various top traders and investors used to become wealthy, and you now have it. Not only that, but you have their words of wisdom as to what to do and mistakes to avoid if you want to be successful at trading the markets.

If you are more interested in income portfolios, hard assets or little discussed asset protection strategies (that might be of use during various types of financial crisis) then you might also check out *High-Yield Investments, Hard Assets and Asset Protection Strategies.* Active and passive investing are two sides of the investing arena, and I hope I have covered the bases, as well as the road to multigenerational wealth accumulation, within these books and *Super Investing*.

ABOUT THE AUTHOR

Bill Bodri is a Wall Street professional who has written several books in the investment and business fields that you might enjoy: *Super Investing: 5 Proven Methods for Beating the Market and Retiring Rich*, *High-Yield Investments and Asset Protection Strategies*, *Move Forward* and *Quick, Fast, Done*. For consulting, author interviews, or if you would like to be interviewed for any future publications, please contact the author via wbodri@gmail.com.

DO YOU WANT MORE FREE TRADER INTERVIEWS?

Do you want to receive more interviews like these? If so then please provide me with your email. Your first interview is with an investor who makes hassle-free money in real estate by trading properties back and forth like stocks. His rules are so good that he makes back his money for every deal in six to ten months! You will get his interview and other lessons including some of my special reports on high-yield investments, hard asset alternatives, the best foreign bank accounts, chart analysis, mindfulness practice for trading and other trading and investing matters. Just sign up at IncomeandAssets.com.

www.ingramcontent.com/pod-product-compliance
Lightning Source LLC
Chambersburg PA
CBHW080705220326
41598CB00033B/5316